History of the United States Civil Service

History of
THE UNITED STATES
CIVIL SERVICE

by

PAUL P. VAN RIPER

*Graduate School of Business and Public
Administration, Cornell University*

GREENWOOD PRESS, PUBLISHERS
WESTPORT, CONNECTICUT

Library of Congress Cataloging in Publication Data

Van Riper, Paul P
   History of the United States civil service.

   Reprint of the ed. published by Row, Peterson,
Evanston, Ill.
   Bibliography: p.
   Includes index.
   1. Civil service--United States--History.
I. Title.
[JK681.V3 1976]   353.006'09   76-2003
ISBN 0-8371-8755-9

353.006
V 274

Originally published in 1958 by Row, Peterson and Company,
Evanston

Reprinted with the permission of Harper & Row Publishers, Inc.

Reprinted in 1976 by Greenwood Press,
a division of Williamhouse-Regency Inc.

Library of Congress Catalog Card Number 76-2003

ISBN 0-8371-8755-9

Printed in the United States of America

to
Leonard D. White
(1891–1958)

Table of Contents

Preface

Over a quarter-century ago, H. G. Wells predicted that "a time may come when history, grown more penetrating, will have more to tell about clerks and less about conquerors." The increasing interest in administrative history is but a reflection of the fact that much of the work of the world is accomplished through vast administrative mecha· nisms in which the individual is usually anonymous.

The federal civil service has been such an institution almost from its inception in 1789. The history of the service does bring to light a few latter day conquerors. George Washington, Andrew Jackson, and Theodore Roosevelt, the presidents most directly involved in a personal way with the institutional setting of our national civil establishment, each turned it in new directions. Still, these directions were never more than a few degrees off course. The federal service as a basic political and administrative institution has possessed a power—some will say inertia—all its own. Presidents and Congresses may decree, but clerks carry out. This is not to suggest that the American national service has ever sabotaged our political system in the way this has occasionally been done in other countries. Indeed, the United States civil service has been unusually responsive and responsible. But administrative systems contain within themselves a life, force, and momentum all their own. The work of the government must be continuous and its administrative structure designed to handle routine as well as exceptions.

This volume is the story of one administrative system as it developed over time, as it responded to various political and social pressures, and as it functioned from day to day over more than a century and a half. In this story clerks are often more important than conquerors, though an inability to single out very precisely the role of individual civil servants, let alone to mention them all, inevitably leaves an administrative history such as this to some extent faceless.

The drama of this kind of history lies not in a panoply of dashing heroes and men on horseback, but in the cumulative impact of a vast quantity of earthy, day-by-day decisions and actions. The focus of interest in administration and organization is power rather than personality. This is not the temporary power evident for a few days or weeks in the aftermath of a battle, but power in a massive and continuous sense. The central administration of a nation which itself is a world power partakes of such might in the fullest measure. This study provides a view of the American ship of state less from the quarterdeck than from the engine room. The former may often suggest the illusion of motion and power, but the latter *is* power.

I have always been interested in administration and organization in one form or another, both as an active participant and as a passive observer. My concern with the civil service and public personnel administration dates, however, to my first work under Leonard D. White at the University of Chicago in 1938. Under Professor White's astute and friendly guidance the foundation for this study was laid even before World War II. 'Since then his own distinguished series of American administrative histories has provided an enviable model of excellence both in terms of the research underlying them and in their ability to bring administrative institutions to life. My own military experience in the United States and abroad during World War II introduced me in a very personal way to the vagaries of large scale public administration. As an Organization and Methods Examiner and Section Chief in the Office of the Comptroller of the Army during 1951–52, I found myself for the first time in the role of a civil servant and enmeshed in the myriad organizational and personnel problems of the Department of Defense. My teaching at Northwestern University, The George Washington University, and Cornell University has frequently enabled me to discuss and evaluate my concepts of public personnel administration not only with undergraduates but also with graduate students and many practicing civil servants. Finally, my close association with business administration as a member of the faculty of Cornell's Graduate School of Business and Public Administration has added the invaluable perspective of private personnel management.

In addition—but without divesting myself of responsibility for the facts and opinions in this book—I want to note my indebtedness to a number of friends and associates whose advice and assistance have been placed so generously at my disposal. Preeminent again is Leonard D .White, not only because of his own trail-blazing work in public personnel administration, upon which I have not hesitated to draw, but also for that inspiration and encouragement essential for the completion of a book which, of necessity, has been a long time in coming. Morton Grodzins of the University of Chicago was especially helpful at an early stage of the study, as was Charles S. Hyneman, now of Indiana University. The Social Science Research Council of Northwestern University provided travel grants which enabled me to expand my research and interviewing efforts considerably further than would have been possible otherwise. Louis Brownlow, Luther C. Steward, William H. McReynolds, Guy Moffett, Samuel H. Ordway, Jr., H. Eliot Kaplan, Harry B. Mitchell, James M. Mitchell, Frances Perkins, W. J. Voss, John W. Macy, Jr., and the late Kenneth C. Vipond have all permitted me to ply them with questions concerning events of which they had personal knowledge.

Joseph A. Connor and Walter E. Elder, when respectively Regional Director and Deputy Regional Director of the Seventh Civil Service Region, read much of an early draft of the manuscript, as did Jeremiah J. Donovan of the Public Personnel Association and John G. B. Hutchins, Professor of Business History and Transportation at Cornell. James R. Watson and Helen Drummond of the National Civil Service League, John W. Macy, Jr., and O. Glenn Stahl of the U.S. Civil Service Commission, Lionel V. Murphy of the Air Research and Development Command, and J. E. Edmonds of the Navy's Bureau of Aeronautics have read large segments of the final draft. John M. Blum of the Massachusetts Institute of Technology and Arthur S. Link of Northwestern University have reviewed the chapters dealing, respectively, with Theodore Roosevelt and Woodrow Wilson. Edward S. Flash, Jr., formerly associated with the Task Force on Personnel and Civil Service of the Second Hoover Commission and now a colleague at Cornell, has read the chapters concerned with events since World War II. Numerous present and former federal personnel officers and others concerned with public personnel management have been of assistance with respect to specific questions and data, especially Earl Brooks, Cecil E. Goode, Raymond L. Randall, Harold H. Leich, John E. Moore, Burton B. Moyer, Jr., Earl DeLong, Julius E. Eitington, Albert H. Aronson, and the late Michael E. Markwood. Flora M. Nicholson, Chief of the Employment Statistics Office, U.S. Civil Service Commission, has reviewed my statistics concerning federal employment and supplemented them at many points. Eleanor Linenthal has assisted me with respect to several legal problems. All of these persons have offered important suggestions.

To a number of graduate students I am also indebted. The special research contributions of Harry N. Scheiber, James H. Lare, Edward Novotny, and Dean F. Bock have been mentioned elsewhere in the book. Others who have helped me in my search for particular items of information or who have assisted in the tedious but important task of checking notes and references are Malcolm T. Shaw, Conrad P. Cotter, Thomas H. Patten, Jr., Kenneth E. Cook, L. Vaughn Blankenship, Bill and Peggy Ryan, Richard A. Peshkin, and James E. Torrey. The careful efforts of Willard H. Page and Harry N. Scheiber, who worked with me through the summer of 1956 as research assistants in connection with this study, deserve special mention. The crucial task of preparing the manuscript in its various drafts was undertaken with great care and accuracy by Gloria Baird, Frances K. Rea, Tazu Warner, Dorothy Finley, and Harriet Patterson.

In the realm of library and archival materials, I wish especially to acknowledge the advice and assistance of Mary Virginia Wenzel, formerly Librarian of the U.S. Civil Service Commission, and Elaine Woodruff, who succeeded her in this position. Edith M. Fox, Curator of Cornell's Collection of Regional History, has been most helpful with respect to the archives of the National Civil Service League. For the great mass of published material I have relied on the general libraries of the University of Chicago, Northwestern University, and Cornell University, along with the special libraries of Cornell's Graduate School of Business and Public Administration and the Public Administration Clearing House in Chicago.

Portions of the material in this volume first appeared as articles in the *Public Personnel Review, Personnel Administration, Public Administration,* and the *Virginia Law Weekly.* I appreciate the courtesy of the editors of these journals and their organizations in permitting me again to make use of these writings. I am also grateful to a number of authors and publishers for permission to quote from their works. These quotations are appropriately identified in the text, but a few should be accorded special mention. Material from Harry S. Truman, *Memoirs: Years of Trial and Hope* (New York: Doubleday and Company, 1956), p. 285, is reprinted with the permission of Time, Inc. That from *After Seven Years* (New York: Harper and Bros., 1939), p. 36, is reproduced with the permission of the author and copyright holder, Raymond Moley. Val and Francis D. Halloran have kindly authorized me to quote from the autobiography of their father, the late Matthew F. Halloran, *The Romance of the Merit System* (2nd ed.; Washington: Judd and Detweiler, Inc., 1929), pp. 118–19.

Dean C. Stewart Sheppard of Cornell's Graduate School of Business and Public Administration and former Dean Edward H. Litchfield, now Chancellor of the University of Pittsburgh, have been very helpful in terms of their sympathetic understanding of the problems inherent in a combination of educational administration, teaching, and research. To them, and to all others whose knowledge, understanding, inspiration, and skill contributed to this study, I am most grateful. It is only this combined effort which made it possible for me to complete this history of the United States civil service on the date below, the 75th anniversary of the Pendleton Act.

Paul P. Van Riper

January 16, 1958

CHAPTER 1

Introduction: The Pattern of Analysis

In the United States it has long been popular first to denounce "bureaucracy" and then to augment it. Our inability to live entirely happily either with or without a complex administrative arm of the national state is only a modern reaction to an ancient dilemma. The relation of citizen to public official, of governed to governor, has always posed a central problem of politics whatever the form or theory of government. When in a democracy the magistrate is declared to be at once both master and servant, the difficulties are only compounded.

The historical development of our American answer to the necessity of creating a great national bureaucracy [1] is the major concern of this study. Specifically, it is designed (1) to outline the general nature and effects of the social interaction which has produced a public service peculiarly in tune with our developing democracy, (2) to bring to light certain relatively neglected aspects of the growth of our expanding administrative mechanism, and (3) to suggest an approach to the development of a theory of administrative organization appropriate to a democratic, pluralistic state.

The continuous, and often bitter, political conflict over the control of public office in the United States provides the main theme for analysis. While the struggle of the merit system against the system of spoils and patronage will concern us most, the confines of the move-

---

[1] Unless the context clearly indicates otherwise, the word *bureaucracy* is used throughout this study in a neutral rather than derogatory or deterministic sense. The term refers simply to any sizable administrative mechanism as characterized more in detail by Max Weber and other analysts of large-scale public and private enterprise. For example, see Peter M. Blau, *Bureaucracy in Modern Society* (New York: Random House, 1956), p. 14.

ment known as civil service reform by no means form the absolute boundaries for discussion.

Nevertheless, some limits have had to be drawn. The reciprocal relationships of politics and economics manifested through our political spoils system and made clear by such students of American politics as Lincoln Steffens, Robert C. Brooks, V. O. Key, Harold F. Gosnell, and others cannot be more than suggested. Neither is this study intended as a detailed technical or legalistic analysis of the development of public personnel administration. Technical material is presented mainly in the form of generalizations or in the form of mildly detailed exposition when technical problems have been crucial to larger issues. Nor will we be much concerned with the experience of state and local governments. Their practices will be discussed only as they have influenced later developments on the national scene, or when the existence of a federal system of government has had a direct bearing upon public personnel management at the national level.

Finally, the discussion is limited almost entirely to the *civil* service of the *executive* branch of the federal government. The civil services of the legislative and judicial branches have been relatively small in size and unimportant during most of our historical development and require only the most incidental attention. The uniformed military service, the other major segment of the executive service, has been of more significance, especially in recent years, and is treated at somewhat greater length.

Major Assumptions

But boundary lines do not alone provide an adequate basis for the selection of certain facts and the omission of others which must characterize any investigation. Even more important are the assumptions most germane to the pattern of analysis.

The first assumption underlying this study, the simplest and yet the most crucial, is that *political, economic, and religious events and factors must be considered in a balanced analysis, if historical interpretations are to be most meaningful.*[2] The term "social" is used to

---

[2] Each of these three categories is used here in its broadest sense. Political and economic variables are identified with relative ease; but the meaning of the word "religious" needs amplification. The term is meant to refer not only to the doctrines—especially those relating to morals and ethics—and affairs of recognized denominations, but also to certain characteristics of the so-called secular religions, of which Marxism is a typical example. In the latter case, what is called "religious" is the combination of moral fervor, determined ritualism, rigid belief, and sense of exultation which often accompanies movements aimed at fundamental social renovation and which often produces many of the psychological and action effects associated with traditional religions. Unfortunately, there is no neutral term which conveys this state of mind and the events associated with it as well

refer to some more or less complex combination of these three variables.

By this first assumption the primacy of the economic in matters of historical interpretation is denied. The economic is crucial, but often no more so than the religious and the political, depending upon the flow of events during the period to be examined. Economic explanations of American history, though necessary counter-balances to earlier theological and political interpretations, have themselves been considerably overdone. The history of the public service in America cannot be studied without becoming heavily involved in the ethics and morality of the times, particularly as reflected through religious movements. Economics alone, even with politics, is simply not an adequate tool for analyzing the subject at hand. As William E. Hocking has said, "The 'economic factors' of modern life could not freely operate on men's minds until logical factors had prepared those minds and ethical factors released them." [3]

The second assumption concerns the interrelationships over a period of time among religious, political, and economic affairs. *There is always constant interaction among the political, the economic, and the religious.* These three great variables and all their components are in a constant state of tension, action, and reaction. Change one, and the others change too, with eventual repercussions back on the first—and so on, in a cause and effect relationship to which there is neither beginning nor end. This is the kind of interaction which is implicit in John Dewey's conclusion that "morality is a continuing process not a fixed achievement." [4] Civil service reform, like other social movements, has been subject to this type of dynamism.

Such changes do not, however, occur overnight. There is normally a considerable lag between what conceivably can or might be done and

---

as does the word "religious." Therefore the writer concurs with Crane Brinton, who under similar circumstances concluded, "No such term at present existing, we shall have to continue to use the word 'religion.'" *The Anatomy of Revolution* (rev. ed.; New York: Vintage Books, Inc., 1957), p. 193. The reader should further note that, while the terms "religious," "moral," and "ethical" are frequently used almost synonymously, this is by no means always the case. The context will make reasonably clear the frame of reference of each of these terms.

The three-cornered type of analysis underlying this study is new only in its application to the American public service. For well-known examples of the same type of analysis applied to other problems, see R. H. Tawney, *Religion and the Rise of Capitalism* (New York: Harcourt, Brace and Co., 1926); and Brinton, cited in this footnote, among others.

[3] *The Lasting Elements of Individualism* (New Haven: Yale University Press, 1937), p. 26.

[4] *Human Nature and Conduct* (Modern Library ed.; New York: Random House, 1930), p. 280. The second assumption, while partly supported by pragmatic theories of morality as typified by that of Dewey, rests fundamentally on the concept of dynamic social causation as outlined, for example, by Gunnar Myrdal in "A Methodological Note on the Principle of Cumulation," in his *An American Dilemma* (New York: Harper and Bros., 1944), pp. 1065–70.

what actually is done. For example, a society may hold to the moral views of a particular religion at some given point in time. At the same time the economic situation or the political mechanism may commence to press for change and reform may seem desirable. The tendency, however, is for the society first to act in terms of the old morality. But the old is seldom completely applicable to the situation at hand. The old will then be modified by the morally inventive until some new basis for action is discovered and a new solution reached. This concept, a variation on the well-known theme of cultural lag, applies to the reform of the American public service as well as to other movements for social change.

The third assumption is that *there is not now, nor has there been in the United States since the early days of the Constitution, any small privileged class which could block legislation in the manner in which it has frequently been estopped during periods of English history.* There have been fewer barriers between mass desire and governmental action in the United States than in most countries.

The type of class interpretation of civil service reform developed by J. Donald Kingsley with reference to the British civil service is appropriate—and then in a severely limited application only—to the analysis of but a few decades of American history since 1789.[5] For an individual to belong to a class in the European sense of the term, it is necessary for that individual not only economically to be a part of a class but for him to think as a member of that class. In the United States many people do not belong to the middle class in terms of their income, but the great mass of the people do belong to the middle class from a psychological standpoint. Class conflict demands the existence of at least two mutually incompatible classes, or two classes who think they are incompatible. Such have never existed on a significant scale in America during most of the period with which this study is concerned. Primarily for this reason, a class interpretation on a Continental model provides little insight into the development of the American civil service.

Some Preferences and Their Implications

Just as the student cannot avoid assumptions concerning factual matters and their inter-relationships in historical interpretation, he cannot avoid the problem of preferences and values.

Quickly discernible here will be a distinct preference for a prag-

---

[5] J. Donald Kingsley, *Representative Bureaucracy* (Yellow Springs, Ohio: The Antioch Press, 1944).

matic approach to decision making. This will be especially evident toward the conclusion of the study and occasionally in the evaluative segments of the summaries at the end of each chapter. Related to this preference is the value placed on the open and pluralistic society. By this is meant a society dedicated to Justice Holmes' free market place of ideas and to the methods of rational social action, as opposed to what Dahl and Lindblom have aptly described as the "tyranny of the 'isms,' " [6] whether from the Left or Right or any other point on the political spectrum. This is not exactly the doctrine of historical pluralism, which tends to discount the importance of the state. It is the doctrine of "live and let live," on the merits of which our constitutional system has been premised and the continuing value of which has been so cogently argued by Edward Shils in his *Torment of Secrecy*.[7] It is also important to remember that during America's only major retreat from a pluralistic conception of politics in favor of what is frequently described today as ideological politics we found ourselves relentlessly impelled toward civil conflict and the near destruction of our emerging nation. For these and related reasons, this study will reflect the judgment that the maintenance of a pluralistic society in the United States not only represents the conservation of the fundamental essence of the social concept on which this country has been built, but also the only firm foundation for the future.

These preferences have led in turn to an emphasis on a particular approach to bureaucracy. The literature on this subject has stimulated much comment and discussion among theorists, administrators, and the general public but has been quite unproductive of any solution to the problems of bureaucracy. Discussions of bureaucracy have generated considerably more heat than light from the point of view of the legislator or administrator who must deal with the more mundane and practical administrative mechanics of a great nation. This practical sterility of most analyses of bureaucracy has resulted from the polarization of two mutually exclusive concepts. On one side are found the more totalitarian-inclined followers (often implicitly rather than explicitly) of Max Weber, who view bureaucracy in a coldly rationalistic, deterministic, and often pessimistic frame of reference, and who frequently display a so-called "pure type" of bureaucracy as an ideal type for all governmental systems in a modern technological world. In many respects this is the form of bureaucracy which Alvin W. Gouldner has described as a "punishment-centered bureaucracy, . . . based on the imposition of rules, and on obedience

---

[6] Robert A. Dahl and Charles E. Lindblom, *Politics, Economics and Welfare* (New York: Harper and Bros., 1953), p. 5.

[7] Parts III and IV, (Glencoe, Ill.: The Free Press, 1956).

for its own sake." [8] Theoreticians of the extreme Right and extreme Left as well as many of those devoted to the concepts of efficiency engineering and social planning often embrace such a bureaucratic doctrine—a doctrine under which the administrator tends to conceive of any breakdown as the fault of obstreperous individuals being administered, rather than as a failure of the administrative mechanism he has designed.[9]

Diametrically opposed to this school of thinking are the devotees of free enterprise such as Ludwig von Mises and Friederich von Hayek,[10] vitriolic in their condemnation of societal rules of almost any type and highly suspicious of administrative efficiency in its Weberian sense. To von Mises the concept of rationalized administration leads only to "a gigantic post office" as the model of the future state,[11] with, presumably, a somewhat less than jovial Jim Farley as the dictatorial Postmaster General. To those who value pluralism but who also perceive the necessity for much large-scale, purposively directed organization, both public and private, in the solution of modern large-scale and technical problems, von Mises' world of almost unrestrained private endeavor seems little better than feudal anarchy and that of the Weberian-oriented group perilously close to an Orwellian *1984.*

Fortunately, America's pragmatism and pluralism have kept us from actually modelling our system of public administration in terms of either the mechanistic rationalization suggested by Weber or the corporate anarchy of von Mises. Despite considerable pulling and hauling, we have made no irrevocable commitment to either extreme.

Yet the polarization of bureaucratic concepts has left our pluralistic democratic society without a theory of administrative organization, as Dwight Waldo has so well demonstrated in *The Administrative State.*[12] At least, no one has done much about such a theory as yet. What is needed, as Lincoln Steffens indirectly suggested in his *Autobiography,* is a governmental administrative system which will combine Justice and Mercy, a system without the complete but coldly impersonal efficiency of the former or the personalized chaos of the latter.[13]

---

[8] Alvin W. Gouldner, *Patterns of Industrial Bureaucracy* (Glencoe, Ill.: The Free Press, 1954), p. 24.

[9] See Blau, as cited in footnote 1, pp. 21–22 and 27–36; and John Jewkes, *Ordeal by Planning* (New York: The Macmillan Co., 1948), ch. x and elsewhere.

[10] Ludwig von Mises, *Bureaucracy* (New Haven: Yale University Press, 1944); Friederich von Hayek, *The Road to Serfdom* (Chicago: University of Chicago Press, 1944).

[11] Von Mises, as cited in footnote 10, p. 125.

[12] Pp. 206–12, (New York: The Ronald Press, 1948).

[13] P. 847, (New York: Harcourt, Brace and Co., 1931).

This suggests in turn that there is a middle position. In point of fact the development of the American public service represents not just a compromise of two disparate and theoretical approaches to governmental administration but a real integration. This is the true meaning of the American experiment in bureaucracy; and it is from this point of view that many of the judgments in this study have been made.

To denote this middle position, the phrase *representative bureaucracy* has been chosen. It refers to a bureaucracy characterized by a minimal distinction between the bureaucrats as a group and their administrative behavior and practices on the one hand, and the community or societal membership and its behavior, practices, and expectations of government on the other. Put in another way, it is a bureaucracy broadly representative of the society in which it functions, both in terms of its personnel and in terms of its behavior pattern and practices. This does not mean that a bureaucracy need be a carbon copy of business for it to be termed representative. But it is intended to suggest a governmental administrative system which is as close to the grass roots of the public ethos as possible.[14]

If this approach to bureaucracy stimulates further concern with the crucial problem of the development of a theory of administration for the democratic state, its main purpose will have been served.[15]

Some Generalizations

The development of certain fundamental generalizations about the American public service is now possible. These may be introduced by referring to the suggestion of Graham Wallas that the greatest political contrivance of nineteenth century England was the invention of the nonpolitical civil service.[16]

Individuals receiving positions in a nonpolitical civil service are

[14] The writer has appropriated for this analysis a terminology probably developed first by J. Donald Kingsley. See Kingsley, as cited in footnote 5; also Gouldner, as cited in footnote 8, p. 24 and elsewhere; and Norton E. Long, "Bureaucracy and Constitutionalism," *American Political Science Review*, XLVI (September, 1952), 808. While the meaning here attached to "representative bureaucracy" is not precisely that of Kingsley, Gouldner, and Long, it appears to be reasonably consistent with their points of view.

[15] As implied above, the writer is using the term "representative bureaucracy" in two senses at various points in this study, both of which should be clear from the context. From a factual and descriptive point of view, the term is used to denote in a general way the most significant of the historic developmental trends of the American public service. From a preferential standpoint, the term represents to some extent another formulation of an "ideal type" of bureaucracy, designed in this case for the purposes of a pluralistic, democratic society. As such, this formulation of bureaucracy will provide a fundamental standard for judgment of the development of the American public service and its prospects for the future.

[16] *Human Nature in Politics* (3rd ed.; New York: Alfred A. Knopf, 1921), p. 263.

normally selected by competitive examination procedures. They are exempt from political selection and pressure and are forbidden to take part in many types of political activity, particularly those of the partisan variety. In return for political neutrality they receive relatively secure tenure and compensation together with—much more in some countries than in others—status and prestige. In the United States we denote such an arrangement as a civil service *merit system*. The personnel selected and functioning under a merit system may be denoted as the permanent or competitive civil service.

An entire civil service may be either nonpolitical or political or some combination thereof. Public employees selected through an examination system open widely to public competition have been a novelty, except in the Orient, until relatively recent times. Before the nineteenth century most civil servants were chosen upon what have been called, not always too appropriately, political grounds. That is, most public appointments were made on the basis of partisanship, influence, wealth, family, personal loyalty, blackmail, or charity, rather than intelligence or competence to do the work. This is the system of patronage as opposed to the merit system. It should not be inferred, however, that the latter, because of the implications of the word "merit," is necessarily more efficient than the former. As the next chapter makes clear, a patronage system, though it usually tends in that direction, is not necessarily a spoils system, a term reserved for the more personal and partisan varieties of patronage politics. Conversely, as evidenced in nineteenth century China, the merits recognized by a merit system may not be geared to the needs of the state.

The pressures resulting from the centralization of power and resources in the modern state forced the first changes in the nature of the public service of the great European nations.[17] By the middle of the nineteenth century the governments of the Western world were faced with ever increasing demands for the political control of economic affairs. If these governments were to police and even occasionally to operate economic organizations of a vast and complicated nature, they had to be competently staffed and organized. Nevertheless, the liberal (used in its historical sense), capitalistic elements in much of western Europe often feared the growth and cost of a great bureaucracy of public officials; and they usually had no desire to see governmental power extended more than immediately necessary. In

17 See especially Sir Ernest Barker, *The Development of Public Services in Western Europe, 1660-1930* (New York: Oxford University Press, 1945), almost the only comparative analysis available. Unfortunately few social scientists have concerned themselves with the historical development of modern administrative institutions.

an effort to keep expanding governmental bureaucracies from getting out of hand, the concept of the nonpolitical civil service was evolved as a solution. A politically neutral public service was often the European answer, especially the British answer, of a liberal, capitalistic society confronted with the necessity to control itself.

America's liberal democracy followed the general pattern of Europe. However, the development of the civil service reform movement in the United States differed from that of Europe in three major respects: (1) the reform was formally adopted several decades later; (2) for many years it assumed a less thoroughgoing and less completely nonpolitical form; and (3) it developed certain distinctive characteristics.

The basic reasons for the differences are simple. In Europe the necessities forcing a noncompetitive, collectivistic approach to problems were much more pressing than in this country. National boundaries were close. Wars were imminent. The economic system was less bountiful in its outpourings. The ethics of capitalistic individualism and Protestantism had a less firm hold. Government never retreated as far from economic control as in the United States, and a return to the supervision of economic development by the state was simpler than in this country.

In the United States, enormous areas of free land and three thousand miles of ocean between this country and its potential enemies provided a unique foundation for decentralized governmental authority. The economic system faltered later than in Europe, and ethical controls were more individualistic. It is no wonder that movements for governmental administrative reform in the United States followed rather than led the nineteenth century world, and gave this country the opportunity to profit from prior examples, good and bad.

Coupled with a constitution prescribing both a separation of powers and federalism, these uniquely American conditions made for a more politically oriented civil service and for one with characteristics all its own. We did not import indiscriminately. Our own politicians, correctly representing the views of their constituents, saw to that. We borrowed, but we also invented.

The result has been a civil service more completely democratic than any yet devised. Unlike that of England and most of the rest of the world, it has been based upon the idea of a classless society. It has borne an intimate relationship to the political parties of the day and has assumed a special significance in the struggles between the President and Congress. It has made its own contributions to personnel practices within the private sector of the society and has in turn been influenced by them. As the European intellectual heritage received by America was modified by time and circumstance, so also has been the European doctrine of civil service reform. Indelibly stamped upon it are the imprints of institutions and cultural habits singularly American.

The Future

The future will undoubtedly reflect the historical development of the federal civil service traced in this study. But older methods must be adapted to new conditions to make bureaucracy both workable and satisfying in terms of our modern, complex American culture. The basic outlines of such a change, unfortunately, are as yet largely undefined, much less agreed upon. Nevertheless, it is hoped that the suggestion of a framework for the further molding of our representative bureaucracy, a suggestion which underlies this interpretation of the American public service, will provide a foundation upon which to build.[18]

18 See the section on Representative Bureaucracy in ch. xvii.

CHAPTER 2

Bureaucratic Beginnings: 1789–1829

During the formative years of the American national government, its public service was one of the most competent in the world. Certainly it was one of the freest from corruption. Repeated attempts by the most bitter opponents of the Federalists, in political control until 1800, failed to uncover significant evidence of deliberate malfeasance in office. Nor were the Jacksonian critics of the Jeffersonian Republicans, who largely directed the affairs of the nation between 1800 and 1829, much more successful in their efforts to discredit their predecessors on grounds relating directly to efficiency and economy.

Even more impressive is the obvious envy of American administrative methods publicly displayed during the Napoleonic period by the British Radicals—among them Bentham, Cobbett, and Sydney Smith—in their biting criticism of their own public service.[1] Can we account for this unusual state of affairs?

In part the answer lies in the generally recognized political and administrative skills collectively represented in the Founding Fathers, who, reacting against those aspects of British administration which had annoyed and harassed them most during the colonial period, sought deliberately to improve upon the original British administrative design which they knew so well. Just as important, however,

---

[1] Eulogy of the British civil service, at the expense of our own, has been endemic among American political analysts for more than a century. That American administration should have been a similar object of praise among British governmental reformers at an earlier date is almost unknown on this side of the water. See S. E. Finer's comparative analysis of American and British central administration in his "Patronage and the Public Service: Jeffersonian Bureaucracy and the British Tradition," *Public Administration*, XXX (Winter, 1952), 329.

were the implications of the new Constitution of 1789 for the future of American public administration at the national level.

The Centralization of Administration

That the Articles of Confederation provided a decentralized administrative system is an understatement. Reflecting our passionate and historic desire to confine government within minimum bounds, the power of administration was from 1781 to 1789 as fragmented as the general political power from which it stemmed. The developing discontent with the political system of the Articles, especially with the economic trends which it fostered, stimulated the move toward administrative as well as political centralization that characterized the Constitution of 1789.

Division of powers. While the fundamental law of 1789 represented centralization, it did not by any means provide for a unitary state. The new constitutional system, unlike British government, was based on a dual division of powers embodying both federalism and separation of powers. This precluded the parallel development of the American and British public services.

The effects of federalism upon the national public service were not immediately apparent except in terms of a reduced pressure upon the central government for the performance of additional functions. This helped to keep the federal service smaller in size than would have otherwise been the case. The longer-run implications of this vertical division of power will be discussed later.

The horizontal division of power, especially the separation of powers between the executive and legislative branches, produced results almost immediately observable. Of fundamental importance was the creation of a President whose method of selection largely bypassed Congress. This new office and the executive establishment it was designed to head were separated from the legislative branch. Moreover, a special provision of the Constitution, which has received little attention from analysts of American government, was inserted to insure that there would be none of that intermixture of legislative and executive personnel characterizing many European governments. Paragraph 2 in Section 6 of Article I, which evidently stems from a similar paragraph in the Articles of Confederation, reads:

No Senator or Representative shall, during the Time for which he was elected, be appointed to any civil Office under the Authority of the United States, which shall have been created, or the Emoluments whereof shall have

12

been encreased during such time; and no Person holding any Office under the United States, shall be a Member of either House during his Continuance in Office.

From the very beginning, the intent of this paragraph has been clear and its rule accepted. More than any other constitutional provision or group of provisions it has prevented the development in this country of a British type of administrative system in which legislators are also the chief administrators. To Americans steeped in the separation of powers doctrine, the desirability of forbidding dual office-holding in two branches of the government has seemed so self-evident that we have tried to export this concept to a number of foreign countries —for example, Germany during the occupation after World War II. That it should fail to be accepted there is not surprising, for, as the British example shows, there is little evidence that simultaneous membership in both the legislative and executive establishments is incompatible either with the development of a civil service of high caliber or with democracy.

The administrative power. Much more controversial in the early days of the Constitution was the extent of the administrative authority of the President, especially in matters of appointment and removal of department heads, officers, and employees—as the levels of public employment have been legally designated under the terms of the Constitution.

Typically, the Articles of Confederation had provided for the appointment of "civil officers" by the "United States in Congress assembled." [2] The new document drastically revised this procedure and placed the power of appointment primarily in the hands of the new executive branch, and especially those of the President. That this was done with some misgiving is quite clear from the records relating to the Constitutional Convention. The often scandalous and punitive exercise of the executive appointing power by colonial governors and the British Crown was well known to the Founding Fathers.[3]

As protection against an unscrupulous executive, the delegates agreed to limit his appointing authority for the more important offices by the advice and consent of the Senate. The Constitution finally provided that the President

---

[2] Art. IX.

[3] Charles E. Morganston, *The Appointing and Removal Power of the President of the United States,* U.S. Congress, Senate, 70th Cong., 2d Sess., Senate Doc. 172 (Washington: Government Printing Office, 1929), pp. 1–14 and elsewhere, contains a brief summary of the Convention's concern. For typical royal and proprietary patronage practices, see Donnell M. Owings, *His Lordship's Patronage: Offices of Profit in Colonial Maryland* (Baltimore: Maryland Historical Society, 1953).

. . . shall nominate, and by and with the Advice and Consent of the Senate, shall appoint Ambassadors, other public Ministers and Consuls, Judges of the supreme Court, and all other Officers of the United States, whose Appointments are not herein otherwise provided for, and which shall be established by Law; but the Congress may by Law vest the Appointment of such inferior Officers, as they think proper, in the President alone, in the Courts of Law, or in the Heads of Departments.[4]

Further, in emergencies

The President shall have Power to fill up all Vacancies that may happen during the Recess of the Senate, by granting Commissions which shall expire at the End of their next Session.[5]

These provisions endowed the new executive branch with a real, though not unlimited, power over appointments to public office.

No reference at all was made to the power of removal except as it might operate through impeachment proceedings—a long and tedious process. This failure to provide specifically for the location of the removal power was the cause of the first major constitutional controversy within the newly-formed government.

The "decision of 1789." The quarrel arose in connection with the creation of the first of the executive departments, the Department of Foreign Affairs. Following some preliminary parliamentary skirmishing, James Madison introduced into the House of Representatives on May 19, 1789, a proposal providing, among other things, for the removal of the head of this department by the President alone. This precipitated an extended and involved debate upon the proper seat and use of the removal power. In general, the argument lay in a straggling continuum of several differing positions, none of them held by a majority of either house. At one extreme were the few who would have limited the power of removal to impeachment; at the other extreme was the minority who would have upheld an almost unlimited right of removal as incidental to the general executive power. Extending periodically over two months, the debate was detailed and occasionally bitter. All the old arguments of the Constitutional Convention were dredged up to support the varying positions. The Federalist concept of a strong executive, which had narrowly survived the debates of 1787–88, again ran headlong into the fears of the antimonarchists and the supporters of the legislative branch as the true representative of the people.

Though the direct evidence is scanty, the great debate on the removal power may have turned more on confidence in President

4 Art. II, Sec. 2, Par. 2.
5 Art. II, Sec. 2, Par. 3.

Washington than the constitutional theories and fine-spun arguments of our early legislative leaders. In any event, the final bill—the passage of which was assured only by the favorable vote of Vice-President John Adams in the Senate on July 18, 1789—implied congressional endorsement of an almost unrestricted power of removal as a prerogative of the President.[6] Nevertheless, it is clear that Congress never fully accepted anything approximating such a sweeping interpretation until long after the attempted impeachment of President Andrew Johnson in 1868, an event which revolved around the same constitutional problem. The difficulty of determining the precise division of authority over appointments and removals as between the President and Congress was to provide a continuing basis of contention.

This much is clear, however. At stake in 1789 was no less than the power and authority of the entire executive branch of the new government, for the power to appoint without the concurrent power to remove severely limits executive control. Whatever the reasoning behind the legislation passed at this time, the end result—at the very least a recognition of the practical administrative difficulties involved in a congressional attempt at too detailed a control of the executive— is most important for the purposes of this discussion. The so-called "decision of 1789" gradually became a precedent for executive power over both appointments and removals, which, in all our history, has been effectively challenged only once and then only briefly in the tempestuous days of President Johnson. Its administrative effect, as Leonard D. White has pointed out in *The Federalists*,[7] was to provide a far firmer base for executive authority and control of the developing federal service under the Constitution than had been found in either law or practice under the Articles of Confederation.

In the light of future events, it must again be emphasized that the participants in the discussion—on both sides—recognized the possible

[6] It was so interpreted by Chief Justice William Howard Taft in 1926 in the Myers case in which a postmaster who had been appointed with the advice and consent of the Senate was removed by the President alone before the conclusion of the subordinate official's statutory term of office. *Myers* v. *United States*, 272 U.S. 52 (1926). For the full documentation of this well-known case, much of which is historical in nature, see U.S. Congress, Senate, *Power of the President to Remove Federal Officers*, 69th Cong., 2d Sess., Senate Doc. 174 (Washington: Government Printing Office, 1926). However, the Supreme Court found it desirable in 1935 to retreat somewhat from Taft's determined position in the Myers case, decided a scant nine years earlier. See *Humphrey* v. *United States*, 295 U.S. 602, also known as *Rathbun, Executor* v. *United States*. This involved the removal of a member of the Federal Trade Commission by President Franklin D. Roosevelt on grounds other than those authorized by Congress. In brief, the Supreme Court concluded that such an official held a "quasi-judicial" status which Congress was constitutionally entitled to protect.

[7] Leonard D. White, *The Federalists* (New York: The Macmillan Co., 1948), pp. 20–25.

uses to which the executive control over public office could be put, should a strong-minded president be so inclined. During the Federalist period the ideas of spoils politics and rotation in office were only temporarily dormant in terms of effective political action. Even congressional reconsideration of its decision of 1789 was never too far from the minds of men in public life.

A Clean Slate

But, if practical as well as theoretical and legal bases for the exploitation of public office existed in 1789, why did that manipulation not immediately come about in the form popularly associated with Andrew Jackson? Part of the answer lies in the fact that political parties were not yet well-developed on a national scale. Early political allegiances were primarily state allegiances, often of a personal rather than party character. It took some years for these diverse loyalties and interests to coalesce along regional and national party lines. Such political unity as there was during the first years of the new government lay under the amorphous aegis of the Federalists, who, in turn, were dominated by the personal prestige of General Washington. During his term of office, the country was governed by an essentially one-party system, a state of affairs which, with brief intermissions—of which that at the turn of the century was the most important—continued until the late eighteen twenties. Tenure of office tends to be taken for granted in a one-party system, and the characteristics of civil servants are likely to reflect the political and moral ideals of those in power.

Federalist democracy. The government of the Federalists was not the democratic government we know today. Rather, it was a semi-aristocracy based upon a universally restrictive suffrage and extensive property qualifications for elective office-holding. There was no free manhood suffrage in 1789, and even Thomas Jefferson was reluctant to carry his interest in the common man to its logical political conclusion. Not only was the suffrage limited but there was no secret ballot. In the states especially, influence could be and was used as freely as its possessor might feel appropriate.[8] While revisionist historians have been able to demonstrate that the suffrage laws were in

---

[8] Dixon Ryan Fox, *The Decline of Aristocracy in the Politics of New York* (New York: Columbia University Press, 1919), is most illuminating on this point. For an analysis of political practices in a state where influence was less blatantly exercised but equally real, see Charles S. Sydnor, *Gentlemen Freeholders: Political Practices in Washington's Virginia* (Chapel Hill: University of North Carolina Press, 1952).

fact less restrictive than equivalent legislation would be today and have thrown considerable doubt upon the accuracy of voting statistics as compiled, for example, by Charles Beard in his *Economic Interpretation of the Constitution of the United States*,[9] they have not been able to dispute or explain away the fact of Federalist control during the last years of the eighteenth century, a control which was hardly fully democratic in a modern sense, even though it was well to the left of contemporary English developments.[10]

Federalist power reflected the essential conservatism of the times, a general social tendency which Henry Adams noted in 1889,[11] and which Clinton Rossiter reemphasized more than sixty years later. If, as Rossiter concludes, the political theory of the Revolution was "remarkable" for its "deep-seated conservatism," [12] in 1800, according to Adams, "as yet this trait was most marked, at least in the older societies of New England, Pennsylvania, and Virginia." [13] Despite the reality of considerable electoral and political democracy in colonial and revolutionary America, the conceptual and societal framework in which most political and economic decisions were cast until the time of Jackson was conservative.

Within such a social climate the Federalists came into office and remained for more than a decade, relinquishing their power only to the "gentlemen freeholders" [14] of the Virginia dynasty, who differed with their predecessors on little but the tactics of conservatism. There were no former wage-earners or artisans among the fathers of the Constitution. There were few indeed to be found in any positions of political prominence—either elective or appointive—in the early history of our country. Faithfully reflecting the voters they represented, the Federalists as well as, to a considerable extent, their Jeffersonian Republican successors, supported the interests of the commercial, landowning, shipbuilding, merchandising, clerical (used in its religious sense) , and professional groups. The government of our early days was a government led by the well-educated, the well-born,

9 (New York: The Macmillan Co., 1913).

10 Two careful analyses of colonial suffrage practices are Richard P. McCormick, *The History of Voting in New Jersey* (New Brunswick, N.J.: Rutgers University Press, 1953); and Robert E. Brown, *Middle-Class Democracy and the Revolution in Massachusetts, 1691–1780* (Ithaca, N.Y.: Cornell University Press, 1955). Brown is especially critical of previous suffrage analyses. See pp. v–viii and 1–77, and especially footnote 55, p. 52.

11 See his *The United States in 1800* (Ithaca, N.Y.: Cornell University Press, 1955), which reprints the first six chapters of Vol. I of Henry Adams' *History of the United States during the First Administration of Thomas Jefferson* (New York: Charles Scribner's Sons, 1889).

12 *Seedtime of the Republic* (New York: Harcourt, Brace and Co., 1953), p. 448.

13 As cited in footnote 11, p. 42.

14 Sydnor, as cited in footnote 8.

the prosperous, and their adherents. In short, it was a government by the upper classes.[15]

As might be expected, such men turned more to the executive in 1789 than to the legislature; and in designing the institution of the Electoral College they attempted to remove the selection of the new executive from what they considered to be the contaminating influences of popular passion. In the cry of Alexander Hamilton— "Your people, sir,—your people is a great *beast!*" [16]—one senses the Federalist view of the implications of a more complete democracy. To the Federalists, instability, inflation, and incompetence were the products of decentralization as typified by the Articles of Confederation. Washington, Hamilton, and their followers desired sound money, uniform regulation of commerce, and a stable government in the hands of their friends. They hoped for a strengthened executive which might provide the leadership which had seemed so lacking during the previous period so "critical" to them. Only under such circumstances, they felt, could there be an intelligent development of policies which might form the basis for an enduring republic.

That many of these men supported the power of the President in removals as in other things was to be expected, despite the fact that the Revolution had been directed against an overbearing executive in the form of the British crown. They wanted a responsible executive, to be sure, but not an impotent one. They concurred with Hamilton ". . . that all men of sense will agree in the necessity of an energetic Executive." [17]

The Federalist civil service. An essential arm of an "energetic Executive" was, of course, a relatively stable and efficient administrative service. President Washington himself led the way toward the establishment of such an institution. His principal requirements for office-holding were character, competence, and loyalty to the Constitution. But Washington was politically astute as well as personally incorruptible, and he well understood the slender threads of support on which hung the life of the new nation. That he paid deference to a desirable geographical distribution of appointments as well as to the opinions of senators, congressmen, and governors did not mean that his appointees failed to meet his standards. The calls of need, even of

---

15 The upper class economic and social position of federal office-holders in the state of New York during this period is described in detail by Arthur Jay Alexander, "Federal Patronage in New York State: 1789–1805" (unpublished Ph.D. dissertation, Department of History, University of Pennsylvania, 1945). See also Anson E. Morse, *The Federalist Party in Massachusetts to the Year 1800* (Princeton: The University Library, 1909); and Sydnor, as cited in footnote 8.

16 Adams, as cited in footnote 11, p. 60.

17 From No. 70 of *The Federalist* (Modern Library ed.; New York: Random House, [1937]), p. 455.

his beloved veterans, were courteously deferred and those of nepotism firmly denied. While the standards of the other leading administrative officials were not always as high or as rigidly held to, they were sufficiently similar to promote the development of a public service for which the new nation needed to make few apologies.

The total problem of recruitment and management of the federal public service was immensely simplified by the small size of the service of Washington's day, as well as by the fact that there were few holdover officials from the administrative regime of the Articles of Confederation. Washington and his cabinet together made only a few hundred appointments.[18] By 1801 the entire executive civil service comprised only about 3,000 persons,[19] of whom no more than 10 per cent resided in the capital.[20] To keep perspective, however, one must remember that there were then few other organizations even approaching this size, the state services being the principal competitors.[21] It is no wonder that British observers remarked on the relative economy of the American mechanism, for their own central establishment contained during this period twice the number of civil servants per capita and cost annually at least three times as much to maintain, excluding the upkeep of the Royal Family, the charges for which more than equalled those for the rest of the civil service.[22]

Removals were fewer still. President Washington evidently effected only seventeen, all for reasons of character or efficiency.[23] Nor were department heads any more active in this respect. That the selection was on the whole successful, at least for the more important positions, is borne out partly by the few removals and partly by the relatively small number of defalcations. That, however, the public service of our early days reached a plane of efficiency unequalled in our history is to stretch the truth considerably. While there is evidence that federal office-holders compared favorably to their counterparts in private life, standards of commercial and administrative responsibility, as well as the requirements of what would today be called "good

18 *American State Papers, Miscellaneous*, I, pp. 57–68.

19 Same, pp. 260–319. This figure includes at least 1,000 part-time employees, especially deputy postmasters. For reasons to be explained later, early federal employment statistics are at best approximate.

20 This percentage has remained almost constant to the present day.

21 There is evidence that the civil service of the state of New York was as large as that of the federal government in 1801. Howard Lee McBain, *De Witt Clinton and the Origin of the Spoils System in New York* (New York: Columbia University Press, 1907), p. 79. Business firms employing over a hundred people were rare in 1800.

22 Finer, as cited in footnote 1, pp. 332 and 346. These estimates are, of course, only approximate. Finer also estimates that British salaries were three times those of American civil servants. Same, p. 332. It should be remembered, however, that the British civil service performed many activities which in this country fell to the states.

23 Carl R. Fish, *The Civil Service and the Patronage* (New York: Longmans, Green and Co., 1905), p. 13.

19

administration," were distinctly in their infancy the world over. It is only in comparison to what was then considered good practice in the administrative world that Federalist standards were high.

That the early efforts to develop an effective and responsible civil service in the United States were currently appreciated is evident from the gradually rising prestige of office-holders as a group. Memories of British nepotism and corruption still lingered, and politics often seemed more attractive than administration. But the integrity of General Washington, the relative care in the choice of public officers, and the general success of the new administration combined to create an atmosphere in which a civil servant, unlike his Continental counterpart, might not feel superior to those about him, but in which he might be inspired to maintain his honor and respectability. White concludes in his study of the Federalists, "The first precedents of office-holding in high place were honorable ones." [24]

Transition: 1797–1801

The Federalists were neither administrative nor political angels, however, and their opponents fully realized the ultimate political and economic ends to which the Federalist civil service of relative competence was dedicated. To say that Federalist office-holders were generally honest and competent is one thing. To infer that Federalist appointments—among them Washington's—were nonpolitical or were the results of an almost modern conception of a merit system is completely to distort the reality.

To begin with, Washington's political beliefs were decidedly "Federalist," despite his sincere attempt to mitigate partisan strife, and his appointments to the public service clearly reflected these beliefs. Above all, the first President required prospective federal office-holders to have been supporters of the new Constitution, acceptance of which was a highly "political" question from 1787 to 1789 and even later. That Washington in particular and, to some extent, his successor, John Adams, made no requirement of prior service in politics for appointment to public office is true, but they both, especially Adams, often required the proper political opinion. In the important state of New York, for example, Howard L. McBain concludes that, while there was not too much "littleness" in the Federalist patronage policy, there was a kind of "exclusiveness" which prepared the way for future objections.[25] All this is a far cry from the later concept of

24 As cited in footnote 7, p. 320.
25 As cited in footnote 21, ch. ii.

political neutrality as the proper role of a civil servant under a modern merit system.

At the same time the general character of American society was changing. The continued pressure of the social forces generated by the Revolution and the gradual translation of political and economic ideals into practice were beginning to make themselves felt by the last years of the eighteenth century. Nor was the Constitution any permanent barrier to change. Many property qualifications for state and local offices were abolished, and most of those remaining were considerably lowered. At the federal level, the Electoral College quickly developed into little more than a rubber stamp of popular opinion. In the minds of many, the Presidency, even more than the legislative branch, commenced to represent the people as a whole. The bulwarks of Federalism were gradually crumbling.

Such changes did not come about without determined efforts by those in power to forestall them. Not only did the Federalists object to the extension of the suffrage and even propose the closing off of the frontier to further settlement, but they also began to manipulate the public offices more and more obviously to maintain their partisan position. In so doing, they set a dangerous precedent from which they, in turn, were soon to suffer.

Even so, the first Adams administration represented only a transitional movement toward full partisan use of the offices. John Adams' New England conscience and his personal ideals of honesty and probity in public affairs were sufficiently strong to prevent his pressing the use of the patronage to its logical end. He and many of the leading Federalists simply could not move far beyond the limits of their own ethics. Adams normally tried to be above partisanship, but, caught in the dilemma of conflicting policies, his actions did not always match his ideals. Carl Russell Fish concludes that

. . . On the whole, Adams seems to have developed no such systematic policy of appointments as Washington, but to have yielded more to influence, time, and circumstance; he was more moderate than some of his advisers, but more proscriptive than the first president; the line of division that he drew was not exactly between the Federalists and Republican parties, but rather between those with whom he agreed, as Gerry and Marshall, and those with whom he differed, as Pickering, Hamilton, and Jefferson.[26]

But the trend was fairly clear. Appointments were more factional than under Washington. The Alien and Sedition Acts, energetically used to intimidate opponents of the Federalists, developed into our

[26] As cited in footnote 23, p. 21.

first punitive political exploitation of "loyalty." Finally, the nonpartisanship of the chief executive evaporated in the last days of Adams' regime when the Federalists engineered some questionable additions to the lower federal judiciary and over-hastily tried to fill these lifetime offices with their own adherents.

Jefferson Finds That "Few Die and None Resign"

With the ink hardly dry on the notorious "midnight appointments" of his predecessor, Thomas Jefferson assumed control in 1801 of an administrative system almost entirely manned by Federalists. Contemplating this politically desolate scene, he was moved to observe, "If a due participation of office is a matter of right, how are vacancies to be obtained? Those by death are few; by resignation, none. Can any other mode than that of removal be proposed?" [27]

As a partisan but also as a practical administrator and political conciliator, Jefferson then devised the useful doctrine that there should be something of an *equal division of the offices* between the parties. This was his principal contribution towards a theory of public office-holding, and he soon began to experiment in this direction.[28] In other respects, Jefferson generally followed the appointing practices of Washington, emphasizing such things as character, fitness, and geography.

The Federalists were somewhat prepared for administrative reverses, but hoped that partisan removals by Jefferson would bring strong popular protests. Precisely the opposite was true. Jefferson's mild opening maneuvers were hailed as only right and proper by most of his adherents, and the general public, then as now, found little of interest in the plight of a displaced civil servant, especially if he had been active in partisan politics. Therefore, after a year of caution, Jefferson grew bolder and eventually removed several times the number of officers of the presidential class [29] displaced by both his predecessors.

[27] Letter to Elias Shipman and others, a Committee of the Merchants of New Haven, in Saul K. Padover, *The Complete Jefferson* (New York: The Tudor Publishing Co., 1943), p. 518.

[28] McBain indicates that a similar kind of evolution toward a division of the patronage among the parties, and finally to a complete monopoly of the offices by the party in power, developed in the civil service of the state of New York. De Witt Clinton, during his first period of political influence, seems to have pursued a policy similar to Jefferson's. In New York, however, the full-scale development of the spoils system out of these early (1800) tendencies came much more rapidly than in the national government. As cited in footnote 21, pp. 103, 116, 156–58.

[29] Offices of the presidential class in the federal government consist of those whose incumbents are appointed directly by the President. Most of these offices are also subject to senatorial confirmation. Unfortunately, reasonably accurate statistics on presidential as op-

By the summer of 1803 removals declined, Jefferson evidently considering that a proper balance had been obtained. But he still consistently favored Republicans for future vacancies, as his opponents had favored themselves on earlier occasions. Jefferson made nothing like a clean sweep of the patronage. However, he proscribed enough public employees so that he, certainly as much as Andrew Jackson, is entitled to be considered the founder of the spoils system in American national politics. From this point on, notes Fish, "party service was recognized as a reason for appointment to office, and party dissent as a cause for removal." [30]

The Jeffersonian Republicans were not content merely to set one precedent for the public service. To them also must be given much of the credit for the first "economy" movement. The Republicans of 1800, like their modern namesakes—but not for entirely the same reasons—feared both the expense and the encroachments of a centralized national government. The increasing appropriations of the Federalists for military expenses and for civil expansion were momentarily curtailed. Some positions were abolished or consolidated and temporary reductions in personnel were enforced. But the acquisition of Louisiana and the demands of a continually expanding economy eventually provided Jefferson with more jobs to fill than ever before. Nevertheless, the concept of limited government, first associated in this country with the name of Jefferson, has been a powerful force in our political development; and periodically it has had its repercussions on the public service. If government is to be looked on with suspicion, so also are its immediate agents.

Despite economy measures and an extensive political turnover and despite the association of Jefferson with a developing American democracy, there is little evidence that he or his main associates made any real indentation on the essentially upper-class nature of the federal civil service. Fish's conclusion that "the majority of the appointees came from the same class of the population as those under the Fed-

---

posed to non-presidential appointments have seldom been published. Excluding presidential commissions in the uniformed military services, the proportion of presidential offices has been estimated by the writer as about one in ten federal positions for the years 1800 to 1810. For the number of presidential offices at Jefferson's disposal, see Fish, as cited in footnote 23, p. 42. The proportion declined to about one in twenty under Lincoln and to slightly less than one in thirty by 1923. U.S. Civil Service Commission, *Fortieth Annual Report* (Washington: Government Printing Office, 1923), p. 100. It has since declined to much less than that. Most of the remaining public employees are appointed by other officers in the executive branch, as designated by Congress under the terms of the Constitution. In general, the most important offices are among those found in the presidential class. In the early eighteen hundreds offices held by cabinet members, postmasters, collectors of customs and internal revenue, territorial and foreign officers, district attorneys, marshals, naval officers (civil), surveyors, and a few other types of personnel fell in this class.

[30] As cited in footnote 23, p. 51.

eralists" [31] is borne out by more recent research.[32] To be sure, agriculture as well as commerce received its political awards under Jefferson. But it was the affluent freeholder, not the laborer, who was
recognized. American government in the early years of the nineteenth
century was still the prerogative of those with considerable means.
While Jefferson liberalized the requirements to a limited extent,
even appointing a few "wild Irishmen," [33] it remained for another
generation to break the monopoly and reconcile Jeffersonian theory
with practice.

Marking Time

Fortunately for Madison and Monroe, they inherited a civil service
already well adjusted to the demands of Jeffersonian-Republican
politics. With the continuing increase in the size of the federal
establishment, there were ample opportunities for these chief executives and their department heads to make appointments satisfying to
their more importunate partisans without displacing men already in
office. The number of civil offices to be filled more than doubled from
1800 to 1816, increasing to over 6,000. This was stepped up to more
than 8,000 in 1821 and the figure rose steeply to nearly 20,000 in
1831.[34] These increases reflected the needs of a nation rapidly expanding both in population and geographical area.

As the period from 1809 to 1825 was one in which the problem of
federal civil patronage was less pressing, neither discussion nor practice was violent. Only two developments aroused comment worth
mention here. One concerned the increasing tendency, deplored even
in its day, of appointing congressmen and senators to executive office
following their support of one or another presidential candidate in
the Congressional Caucus, the single most important presidential
nominating body during our early history. This tendency of legislators to seek refuge in the administrative branch seems to have been
aggravated both by the importance of the Caucus and also by the
relatively low salaries of legislators compared to the higher adminis-

31 Same, p. 49.
32 Alexander, as cited in footnote 15, ch. x. Leonard D. White has also concluded,
"Standards of appointment from 1789 to 1829 conformed to a single pattern." *The Jeffersonians* (New York: The Macmillan Co., 1951), p. 368. These analyses, especially that of
Alexander, tend to throw additional doubt upon the Beardian theories relating to the support of the Constitution and should be pursued further.
33 Fish, as cited in footnote 23, p. 50.
34 U.S. Bureau of the Census, *Historical Statistics of the United States, 1789–1945* (Washington: Government Printing Office, 1949), p. 294. This publication will hereafter be cited
as *Historical Statistics*. These totals are conservative, as they evidently do not include contract postal workers or the growing number of blue collar workers.

trative officers—though the pay of the latter, as befitted a country of republican principles, was none too high. These difficulties, however, were rapidly resolved as the party convention took over the functions of the Caucus and as legislative salaries improved.

More controversial over a far longer period was the Four Years Law of 1820, credit for which is generally laid at the door of then-Secretary of the Treasury William H. Crawford. Whether this act was passed to tighten up fiscal controls on a wide range of public officers by requiring more regular presentation of their accounts or whether it represented a deliberate attempt by Crawford to improve his patronage position with a view to his presidential candidacy in the forthcoming election is not too clear. Whatever the purpose, the effective result, by setting a four-year term of office, was to throw a large number of major offices open to new appointments every four years,[35] something which had not been customary up to that time and which in a sense amended the legislative decision of 1789. Madison considered the law a usurpation of presidential prerogative and Monroe is said to have regretted that he signed the bill. But it remained on the books for several decades and served as the precedent for many similar types of legislation which, while not requiring removals, certainly facilitated rotation in office.

The patronage policies and practices of Madison and Monroe, while patterned to some extent after those of Washington and Jefferson, were not as clearcut. To a considerable extent this reflected the political confusion of the period during and after the War of 1812. The Federalist party was dying and new political alignments were taking place, though slowly and with considerable partisan backing and filling. Madison attempted to make the War of 1812 more a national than a party concern, and his appointments reflected this policy. Monroe seems to have let well enough alone during the Era of Good Feeling which followed. There was seldom any great need for them to be more precise, even if their concepts of the Presidency had been more dynamic. They inherited a regime in which the more important political and administrative changes sought by the Republicans had already been initiated by Jefferson. Moreover, along with Washington and Jefferson, Madison and Monroe found it difficult to conceive of a public service built on foundations of other than relative tenure, honesty, and reasonable competence. They still

---

[35] Four year terms were established at this time for district attorneys, collectors and surveyors of customs, naval officers, money agents and receivers, registers of land offices, army paymasters, the apothecary-general and his assistant, and the commissary-general of purchases. For more details concerning the Four Years Law see Fish, as cited in footnote 23, pp. 65–70.

represented the first generation of national political leadership. A new generation with new concepts of administration and office-holding would be needed to break conclusively the strength of the Federalist tradition.

The Twilight of an Era: 1825–1829

Under the second Adams the problem of the public service and its disposition once again became a major political issue. The focus of attention was the famous "Corrupt Bargain" charge of the defeated Jacksonians, that Clay had in 1825 swung his support to Adams in return for the position of Secretary of State. That Adams actually appointed Clay to the office made the accusation doubly damning. But this imbroglio was only the cover for more fundamental difficulties.

John Quincy Adams faced the accumulated dissatisfactions of a democracy which was rapidly becoming more of a political reality than most of the Founding Fathers had dared to imagine. That he was essentially a minority president from 1825 to 1829, having received fewer electoral votes even than Jackson, left his position politically hopeless. Nevertheless, an unbending integrity and conscience did not permit the President to adopt the political maneuvers of a spoils politician. Washington's main tests for eligibility to public office were also the requirements of John Quincy Adams. Some of his political friends were not so particular and constantly urged Adams to follow their advice and example, but on the whole the public service remained much as it had been for forty years.

Possessing the power of removal as well as of appointment, a strong-willed president alone could briefly maintain the tradition of relative tenure inaugurated by his predecessors. But the dam was ready to break. When the new democracy of the Jacksonians could capture the Presidency, it would capture the bureaucracy as well. Only four years of a Puritan, and basically Federalist, conscience stood between one era and another.

The Upper Classes and the Offices

While the "gentlemanly" control of federal public office in the United States was for a short time almost as effective as that which J. Donald Kingsley records as typical of late eighteenth century England, the results were almost the reverse. The civil service of the opening years of the Constitution was relatively competent and honest, while that of George III has been described by Kingsley as the "Old Corruption." [36]

The mere fact of semi-aristocracy did not alone determine the traditions of the public service in our early national government. The nature of the morality and conscience of many of these men of substance, as reflected in public affairs, must be considered in accounting for the difference between eighteenth century America and eighteenth century England. The political and moral ideals of a British "fleshly aristocracy" [37] contrasted strikingly with those of Washington and his immediate successors. Their ideals were fundamentally influenced, in turn, by what they felt were the adverse economic consequences of the incipient disintegration under the Articles of Confederation as compared to the political possibilities of the new Constitution. Moreover, these ideals of a public service of character, competence, and relative tenure persisted for some time after reaching their peak of political acceptability in the closing years of the eighteenth century.

To assume, however, that the first four decades of American politics were entirely quietly competent would be utterly false. Our early politicians were realists and the relevance of office to action and to political power was well understood. The patronage had been exploited for all it was worth in England and in the colonies. Most of those prominent in party affairs, both in state and nation, were only too well aware of the power of spoils adroitly maneuvered. While it is fair to conclude with White, "that no President before 1829 undertook to buy leadership or legislation with patronage," [38] it is also clear that both Washington and Jefferson, and those who immediately followed them, based much of their political power on a careful distribution of the offices to those of a similar political persuasion. Federalist "exclusiveness" and Republican retaliation were not accidental.

That the personal and partisan interests of political realists of the caliber of most of the Founding Fathers and their associates should be accompanied by administrative expertise, intelligence, and a high sense of responsibility to the country at large was indeed fortunate. Not only was a new nation placed on firm political foundations, but also its early civil service was established with a reputation for integrity and capacity that is remembered to this day.

[36] *Representative Bureaucracy* (Yellow Springs, Ohio: The Antioch Press, 1944), p. 19.
[37] Finer, as cited in footnote 1, p. 333. He continues, "It is a far cry from the *Memoirs of Harriet Wilson* to the stern and unbending front of George Washington."
[38] White, as cited in footnote 32, p. 43.

SUPPLEMENTARY NOTES

The sources of information for a study such as this are so many and varied that it is not possible to analyze them in any detail without writing another book. However, these supplementary notes, which amplify the running notes, will give a more complete bibliographical picture of selected aspects of civil service problems.

For American administrative experience under the Articles of Confederation see Merrill Jensen, *The New Nation: A History of the United States During the Confederation, 1781–1789* (New York: Alfred A. Knopf, 1950), especially pp. 360–74, which summarize the administrative system under the Articles; and Jennings B. Sanders, *Evolution of Executive Departments of the Continental Congress, 1774–1789* (Chapel Hill: University of North Carolina Press, 1935).

The major secondary works bearing directly on the history of the U.S. civil service since 1789 can be counted on the fingers of one hand. The first century of American civil service experience is most thoroughly treated in Carl Russell Fish, *The Civil Service and the Patronage,* as cited in footnote 23, which, however, is far more adequate on patronage practices than on internal personnel management. Though published more than fifty years ago, Fish's research can be challenged in only a few respects, most of which are dealt with in the succeeding chapters of this study. While Fish covers the period from 1789 to 1900, he is most satisfactory for the years up through the controversy over the Tenure of Office Act of 1867. His analysis of the events leading up to the Pendleton Act of 1883 is still useful on many matters, but his treatment of the second administration of Cleveland and that of McKinley is most cursory. Fortunately, A. Bower Sageser, in *The First Two Decades of the Pendleton Act* (Lincoln: University of Nebraska, 1935), picks up where Fish becomes less adequate and brings both detail and focus to the history of the civil service between the Civil War and 1903. His bibliography for this period is outstanding. For the twentieth century there is only the monograph by Darrell H. Smith, *The United States Civil Service Commission* (Baltimore: Johns Hopkins Press, 1928), which is Service Monograph 49 of the Institute of Government Research. While it contains a useful bibliography, this is a very limited work emphasizing primarily the legislation and other official measures affecting the organization and powers of the Commission between 1883 and 1927. Supplementing all of these to some extent is the well-written popular treatment issued for some years (it is now out of print) as an information pamphlet by the U.S. Civil Service Commission, *History of the Federal Civil Service,* Form 2499, prepared in the Information and Recruiting Division, text by M. Barris Taylor (Washington: Government Printing Office, 1941).

More broadly oriented but in many ways more helpful are the incisive, ground-breaking administrative histories of Leonard D. White, *The Federalists,* as cited in footnote 7; *The Jeffersonians,* as cited in footnote 32; *The Jacksonians* (New York: The Macmillan Co., 1954); and *The Republican Era* (New York: The Macmillan Co., 1958). This series fills an immense gap in our understanding of early American administrative practices and institutions. White is especially useful for his analysis of internal personnel management in the federal service before the Civil War. It was the publication of *The Federalists* and *The Jeffersonians* which stimulated S. E. Finer to make the comparison of early nineteenth century British and American central administration cited at the beginning of this chapter.

Supplementing these works are certain important analyses of special aspects of the federal civil service which cover not only the period dealt with in this chapter but the full span of American public administrative development. On legal distinctions and precedents involving the federal civil service see Edward S. Corwin, *The President: Office and Powers, 1787–1948* (3rd rev. ed.; New York: New York University Press, 1948). Joseph P. Harris, *The Advice and Consent of the Senate* (Berkeley and Los Angeles: University of California Press, 1953), is the definitive study of senatorial-presidential relationships over appointments.

For the most complete analyses of opinion as to the precise intent of the crucial appointment and removal legislation of 1789, both on the part of those who participated in the debate and those who were dealing with the problem later, see the briefs and opinions in the Myers case, and the detailed studies by Edward S. Corwin, *The President's Removal Power* (New York: National Municipal League, 1927); Charles E. Morganston, *The Appointing and Removal Power of the President of the United States,* as cited in footnote 3; and James Hart, *The American Presidency in Action, 1789* (New York: The Macmillan Co., 1948), pp. 152–248. Morganston concludes that the intent of Congress, particularly the House, was clearly in support of the theory "that the power to remove officers appointed by the President and the Senate vested in the President alone." P. 27. Corwin is highly critical of this interpretation as applied by Chief Justice Taft in the Myers case. Hart's position is somewhere in between, emphasizing the practical rather than the legal effects of the controversy in these terms: "The legislative decision of 1789, in its bearing upon the *crucial* relation of the President to the *department heads,* has thus, in any view, had profound effects upon the constitutional development of the Presidency. It is the considered opinion of the present writer that the net result has been to help save that great office from the dangerous disintegration which every *administrative* position taken in 1789 other than that of the House majority would have invited." P. 248.

CHAPTER 3

The Victors: 1829–1865

In many minds the spoils system is equated with Andrew Jackson. This is not entirely accurate. Jackson did not even come close to overturning the federal civil service during his eight years in office after 1829. He made few more removals, percentage-wise, than had Jefferson nearly thirty years before. Nor can we give him credit for originating the celebrated formula, "To the victor belong the spoils!," for history has declared this to be the political epitaph of Senator William L. Marcy of New York.

Nevertheless, credit for formulating the ancient practices of spoils politics into a widely accepted and systematic political doctrine, applicable to the national as well as to the local scene, must be given primarily to Jackson. Moreover, the Jacksonian accession to power in 1829 marked a distinct shift in the form and direction of American politics, with the spoils system in many ways the hallmark of the change. From this time on, the spoils system, with all its implications for total political power as well as its suggestion of personal political gain, was rapidly to acquire recognition as one of the more distinctive features of American political life. That this rising institution should be so intimately connected with public office was to have a profound impact upon the federal civil service.

The "Task of Reform"

There was no question but that the political multitude was hungry for office in 1829. Had Jackson had any doubt about it, the circumstances of his inauguration should have convinced him. The capital was the scene of an office-seeking mob such as it had never before witnessed. If Chief Justice John Marshall feared for the state of the nation, most of the extraordinary crowd of March 4, 1829, were more optimistic. A kind of exultation marked the comings and goings of the throng and even Daniel Webster noted a sense of millennial deliverance in the air.

The inaugural. The people were coming to claim the government. General Jackson did not disappoint them, though few present at his first inaugural could actually have heard his spoken words. Two paragraphs of his short address were devoted to the patronage—in words which his supporters could not fail to understand, cautiously though they were phrased:

> The recent demonstration of public sentiment inscribes on the list of Executive duties, in characters too legible to be overlooked, the task of *reform,* which will require particularly the correction of those abuses that have brought the patronage of the Federal Government into conflict with the freedom of elections, and the counteraction of those causes which have disturbed the rightful course of appointment and have placed or continued power in unfaithful or incompetent hands.
>
> In the performance of a task thus generally delineated I shall endeavor to select men whose diligence and talents will insure in their respective stations able and faithful cooperation, depending for the advancement of the public service more on the integrity and zeal of the public officers than on their numbers.[1]

As Jackson suggested, the "task of reform" was conceived by the Democrats as having a double-barrelled objective: (1) the reorientation of the civil service toward more democratic ends, and (2) the reduction of the service in size. Lineal descendants of what may be called the left wing of the Jeffersonian Republican party, the Jacksonians in a general way resembled their predecessors in their attitudes toward the public service. Jackson differed greatly, however, with Jefferson on the completeness with which he sought these dual ends of democracy and limited government. With regard to the former he was to be much more successful than Jefferson. With regard to the limiting of the personnel and functions of the federal bureaucracy, he was, in the face of an expanding economy and expanding demands for new governmental services, to be as frustrated as most presidents elected on a platform emphasizing the curtailment of public expenditure.

---

[1] James D. Richardson (ed.), *Messages and Papers of the Presidents* (New York: Bureau of National Literature and Art, 1905), II, 438. The italics are evidently Jackson's. Hereafter, the placing of the word *reform* in quotes indicates a reference to the Jacksonian variety. The unadorned word refers to a more modern conception.

The mandate of 1829. By 1829 the mandate of the voting public was clear. The Revolutionary ideals of freedom, equality, and political democracy were finally to be brought to full fruition. All through the first quarter of the nineteenth century the social bases of an upper class government had been declining. By the end of this period white manhood suffrage was almost a complete reality. Acquisitive economics, based on free contractual arrangements and buttressed by an expanding frontier and a rapidly developing urban industrial revolution, was forcing "gentlemen" in both the North and South to the defensive. The churches had been disestablished and there was little in the prevailing ethical system to slow the movement. The conservative temper of 1800 was rapidly becoming a thing of the past except in the South and in a few enclaves in the Northeast, where a Federalist type of conservatism was able to maintain itself for many decades. Dixon Ryan Fox has traced for New York this decline of "the fortunes of a class, accustomed by training and tradition to the conduct of affairs, but forced to yield before what seemed to them the great disaster of democracy." [2]

But the new democracy did not come without a fight, under the strain of which the budding political parties of 1800 regrouped and coalesced on a more well-organized and national basis. Of this complicated story, only one facet deserves mention here; namely, the political function of the public offices, particularly in the states. We find that the political leaders in the states and smaller jurisdictions, in their grass roots attacks on aristocracy and on each other, had begun to manipulate the state and local civil establishments for partisan purposes long before the spoilsmen were able to capture the federal citadel. Carl Fish quite properly relates the origin of the spoils system, as both a political means and end, to the practices of state and local politicians during the period from 1800 to 1829. Those of the North and West, particularly in New York and Pennsylvania, had led the way. [3]

On the surface the primary function of patronage politics lay in its financial and organizational support of the budding partisan machinery. Democratic politics is expensive politics when considered in terms of the vast superstructure of American parties, though democratic partisans then undoubtedly considered the cost negligible in comparison to their deprivations, real and fancied, under the Federalist regime. Fish is probably justified in concluding that in "America,

---

[2] *The Decline of Aristocracy in the Politics of New York* (New York: Columbia University Press, 1919), p. vi.

[3] Carl R. Fish, *The Civil Service and the Patronage* (New York: Longmans, Green and Co., 1905), pp. 79–104.

the spoils system paid for the party organization which enabled the democracy of Pennsylvania to rule after 1800 and which established 'a government of the people' in the United States in 1829." [4]

More submerged, with its effects not fully understood for more than half a century, was a growing alliance between politics and private enterprise, which accounted in part for the rapid development of the new nation but also for the more sordid aspects of the acquisitive society of the Gilded Age to come. As commercial and business activity came more and more to characterize American economic efforts, business methods of decision-making as well as business concepts of organization were increasingly translated onto the political scene. Bargaining by individuals and corporations was becoming as accepted a method for arriving at decisions in American politics as it had long been in business; and campaign managers such as Martin Van Buren were organizing politics much in the manner of a private entrepreneur dealing with commerce. This new trend in public affairs was to reach its apex after the Civil War, but it was clearly evident by the Age of Jackson. Behind the widespread desire for turnover in public office lay not only democratic theory as espoused by Jackson but also a twilight zone of political machination of all descriptions. We may even use the word "corruption" if we do not push it too far. Desire for a federal office by no means always stemmed simply and solely from a desire for the salary. In some cases, yes, but in many there were more far-reaching gains in the mind of the recipient and his associates. The control of public office often meant control of the political and economic destiny of, if not the nation, a great portion thereof. Then as now, public personnel administration could be equated with power as well as a livelihood.

By 1829 the balance of power had shifted on the national scene, as it had already shifted on much of the state and local scene. The old regime and all it represented was under attack everywhere. In the public service, after forty years, the bureaucracy of the Founding Fathers was troubled with superannuation and with a developing concept of at least a moral property right in federal office. In a number of cases families had maintained themselves from father to son in the civil service, the Nourse family being preeminent in this respect. These developments, coupled with widespread resentment at the monopolizing of public office by representatives of the upper classes, provided a real basis for a rising crescendo of democratic complaint. Though the general competence and personal integrity of office-holders were relatively unassailable, passionately partisan eyes began to

4 Same, p. 157.

magnify even the most minor peculations. When John Quincy Adams stubbornly attempted to maintain the status quo, he only succeeded in further raising the blood pressure of his opponents. Jackson and his friends, not insensitive to the demands of their supporters, bent themselves to the task of "reform." Or, as Jackson's contemporary, the fiery New Hampshire editor, Isaac Hill, less elegantly put it, "The barnacles shall be scraped clean from the ship of state." [5]

Loaves and Fishes

Thus the new President was impelled to mention "reform" of the public service in his first inaugural address. Nevertheless, he went about it most circumspectly and with what may seem a surprising awareness of the sensibilities of the Senate. It is not widely remembered that Jackson had himself twice briefly served in the Senate and once in the House. The popular stereotype of Andrew Jackson pictures him as an impulsive, untutored, and politically inexperienced military man striding rough-shod over the polished floors of the White House as well as over the bodies of his opponents. In fact, as modern historians such as Arthur Schlesinger, Jr., make clear, he was urbane and courteous in hearing out those who presented reasonable arguments for or against public policy, though firm and unbending in decision. He was also a lawyer and a successful merchant and planter, as well as a man of considerable experience in the legislative, judicial, and executive branches of government prior to his accession to the Presidency. Jackson well understood the nature of the political problems and institutions with which he dealt.

The proscription. His first nominations were for the usual high offices where turnover had always been assumed. Truly punitive removals did not commence until the Senate had adjourned, and only on a limited scale. Recess appointments were then offered to such important yet controversial supporters of the President as Isaac Hill and Amos Kendall. Not until almost a year had passed did these interim appointments come before the Senate for formal consideration. Commencing on January 4, 1830, and continuing through the following weeks, Jackson began to present a growing list of nominees for vacancies created by outright removal of the incumbents. But Erik M. Eriksson, in his careful study of Jackson's appointing and removal policies, concludes, "Only 121 of the nominations made to the Senate

---

5 As quoted in Marquis James, *The Life of Andrew Jackson* (Indianapolis: Bobbs-Merrill Co., 1938), p. 498.

at this session of Congress were to take the places of office-holders who had been removed!" [6] Certainly this was not a complete turnover, even among the presidential offices at the top of the executive pyramid!

To be sure, some of Jackson's subordinates were not so careful, especially in the extensive field services of the Post Office and the Treasury. But Eriksson's thorough investigation of the Jacksonian proscription clearly indicates that during the General's entire eight years of office it is highly unlikely that more than one-fifth of the federal public service was removed for partisan reasons, and perhaps nearer a tenth. [7] There was no clean sweep. Both Jackson and Jefferson found themselves obligated to cleanse the political stables and to readjust the civil service in accord with the election returns, but the efforts of Jackson were at most only a fraction more strenuous than those of his predecessor.

Moreover, there is no evidence that General Jackson intended his proscription to be more extensive than it was. Jackson's concepts of office-holding were in many respects quite as high as those of his predecessors, even if circumstances were not as favorable. It is clear that he conceived of "reform" as reform, and not as revolution, even though many of his friends and supporters, in high as well as low places, were not so restrained. On March 31, 1829, the President wrote to his new friend and advisor, Martin Van Buren, "The people expect reform—they shall not be disappointed." But, he added, "It must be *Judiciously* done, and upon *principle*." [8]

What is principle to some may, however, be partisanship to others. Hardly had the President been elected before his opponents commenced to exaggerate their "terror" of events to come. Rumor followed rumor, and the psychological impact must have been great. The actual removals, though less than expected by some or hoped for by others, lent substance to the charges of wholesale partisan retribution. Regardless of the justice of their attacks, Jackson's opponents wielded every resource at their command in an attempt to discredit the new administration and its policy of "reform." The spoils system was still novel enough in American national politics that its introduction and encouragement sparked violent controversy—controversy further fanned by executive-legislative as well as personal

6 Erik M. Eriksson, "The Federal Civil Service Under President Jackson," *Mississippi Valley Historical Review*, XIII (March, 1927), 524.

7 Eriksson's conclusion is confirmed by Leonard D. White, *The Jacksonians* (New York: The Macmillan Co., 1954), pp. 308–9.

8 John Spencer Bassett (ed.), *Correspondence of Andrew Jackson* (Washington: Carnegie Institution, 1929), IV, 19. The italics are evidently Jackson's.

antagonisms. Magnified by word of mouth, blared forth in the press, and exaggerated in the heat of political conflict, the Jacksonian readjustment of the public service soon became the American symbol of political partisanship, while the famous phrase of Senator Marcy became its slogan.

As modern evidence demonstrates, the hullabaloo over the patronage represented more fiction than fact. The opposition to the doctrine of spoils was sufficiently strong to compel the Jacksonian partisans to move with considerable care. Not only did the President delay as long as possible before introducing to the Senate his nominations for replacement of politically proscribed officials, but also he again felt compelled publicly to justify his actions. In his opening message to Congress on December 8, 1829, President Jackson amplified the brief references of his first inaugural into the classic American doctrine of spoils.

The theory of spoils. When the President reached the problem of "reform" of the public service, he first condemned what has often since been popularly labeled the "tendency of bureaucracy." Many of his phrases might well have come from some of the campaign literature for the election of 1952, so modern is the ring:

> There are, perhaps, few men who can for any great length of time enjoy office and power without being more or less under the influence of feelings unfavorable to the faithful discharge of their public duties. Their integrity may be proof against improper considerations immediately addressed to themselves, but they are apt to acquire a habit of looking with indifference upon the public interests and of tolerating conduct from which an unpracticed man would revolt. Office is considered as a species of property, and government rather as a means of promoting individual interests than as an instrument created solely for the service of the people. Corruption in some and in others a perversion of correct feelings and principles divert government from its legitimate ends and make it an engine for the support of the few at the expense of the many.[9]

Less persuasive now are Jackson's next observations, though in 1829 they were undoubtedly not only appealing but also closer to fact. Nevertheless, these few sentences constitute a theory of the nature of public office, which even yet is reluctantly relinquished:

> The duties of all public officers are, or at least admit of being made, so plain and simple that men of intelligence may readily qualify themselves for their performance; and I can not but believe that more is lost by the long continuance of men in office than is generally to be gained by their experience.

9 This and the quotations immediately following are from Richardson, as cited in footnote 1, pp. 448–49.

Finally, the President proposed a specific remedy and buttressed it with additional theory and argument. In essence, these words represent the logic of American democratic theory as applied to public office—a logic still compelling:

I submit, therefore, to your consideration whether the efficiency of the Government would not be promoted and official industry and integrity better secured by a general extension of the law which limits appointments to four years.[10]

In a country where offices are created solely for the benefit of the people no one man has any more intrinsic right to official station than another. Offices were not established to give support to particular men at the public expense. No individual wrong is, therefore, done by removal, since neither appointment to nor continuance in office is a matter of right. The incumbent became an officer with a view to public benefits, and when these require his removal they are not to be sacrificed to private interests. It is the people, and they alone, who have a right to complain when a bad officer is substituted for a good one. He who is removed has the same means of obtaining a living that are enjoyed by the millions who never held office. The proposed limitation would destroy the idea of property now so generally connected with official station, and although individual distress may be sometimes produced, it would, by promoting that rotation which constitutes a leading principle in the republican creed, give healthful action to the system.

Through such simple phrases the doctrine of spoils was endowed with the dignity of a political theory most appealing to American democratic sensibilities. Not only did the spoils system meet the earthy needs of practical politics but also to many of its advocates, including Jackson himself, there was a certain "justice" and "principle" to the doctrine, which reached far beyond the passing events of the day. It somehow touched a responsive chord among the yearnings and aspirations of that impetuous democracy which had for the first time bestowed upon a westerner the highest office within its jurisdiction.

Counterattack

If the Jacksonians accepted the President's pronouncements with enthusiasm, others, as indicated earlier, did not. From the beginning a jealous Senate sniped at the presidential program, particularly as it related to his patronage policies. The Senate was the stronghold of the partisan opposition since the Jacksonians were in control there by only a narrow margin. It was also the institutional center around which rallied those who feared the Jacksonian conception of the

10 A reference to the Four Years Law of 1820.

President as a popular leader. At first the retaliation took the form of resistance to nominations for presidential offices. Despite Jackson's political triumph, several of his appointments were turned down by a unanimous or nearly unanimous Senate. Daniel Webster remarked, "Were it not for the fear of the out-door popularity of General Jackson, the Senate would have negatived more than half his nominations." [11]

The intensity of the continuing quarrel is best illustrated by the Senate's refusal in 1832 to confirm the appointment of Martin Van Buren, earlier approved as Secretary of State, as ambassador to Great Britain, after Van Buren had already arrived in Europe. Incredibly enough, the vote was arranged so that Vice-President John C. Calhoun, who by now had broken with Jackson, might cast the deciding ballot against his former ally. On the whole, however, most of the presidential appointees survived the ordeal untouched except by the often vicious harangues over their personal and political characteristics. Congressional controversy over the manners and morals of public officials was even more violent in 1829 than now.

The next ammunition furnished to Jackson's enemies lay in the form of mutual recriminations within the official family itself, of which Calhoun's treatment of Van Buren was by no means the only example. There is also considerable evidence that Justice John McLean, Postmaster General before President Jackson appointed him to the Supreme Court, looked with regret on the introduction of spoils into the organization which he had previously built up and greatly strengthened.[12] But from 1829 on, the office of Postmaster General developed into a reward for successful political generalship.

The removal of Duane. More spectacular by far, however, was the President's search for a Secretary of the Treasury who would carry out presidential orders concerning the removal of federal funds from the United States Bank, so hated by the Jacksonians as the symbol of opposition. Kicking Secretary Louis McLane upstairs to the Department of State and removing Secretary William J. Duane outright, Jackson accomplished his purpose. At the same time, he ended an ambiguous relationship between the Treasury and Congress, dating back to 1789. Considering its power over the purse strings as a major bulwark against despotism, Congress had long encouraged— and the President and the Treasury had generally accepted—a con-

---

11 Webster to Mr. Dutton, May 9, 1830, in *The Writings and Speeches of Daniel Webster* (National ed.; Boston: Little, Brown and Co., 1903), XVII, 501.

12 See Wesley Everett Rich, *The History of the United States Post Office to the Year 1829* (Cambridge: Harvard University Press, 1924); and Dorothy G. Fowler, *The Cabinet Politician* (New York: Columbia University Press, 1943), for the political history of the Post Office in the nineteenth century.

cept of the Treasury as a semi-independent agency responsible as much to Congress as to the President. In 1833 Secretary Duane maintained that before he could remove the funds he would have to consult Congress. Despite tradition, Jackson exercised his right of removal and stated bluntly that support of the executive in matters of public policy was as much the duty of the Secretary of the Treasury as of any other administrative officer. This doctrine has since remained unquestioned. A Supreme Court decision shortly thereafter made it clear that Congress was not devoid of authority to place responsibility for many types of decisions on department heads and sub- ·ordinate officers. But the Court has seldom interfered with the exercise of presidential power through the removal of officers and employees in the executive branch. Thus the controversy over the independence of the Secretary of the Treasury formed another episode in the continuing struggle of the President and Congress for the control of the personnel of the national government within a constitutional system emphasizing a division of powers.[13]

The debate of 1835. The removal of Duane also did much to spark the second extended and prolonged legislative debate on the nature of executive-legislative relations concerning appointments and removals. Carrying on intermittently throughout the sessions of the Twenty-third Congress, the arguments resulted in the creation of a special Senate committee, headed by John C. Calhoun (still in violent opposition to Jackson), to report on proposals for the control of the executive patronage. Calhoun's committee reported its findings on February 9, 1835, and this report, together with an earlier one made in 1826 under the direction of Senator Thomas H. Benton of Missouri, was immediately ordered printed for public as well as legislative distribution. The findings were directed at two matters which were then interrelated as a result of the Treasury episode—namely, the President's removal powers and his authority over the disposition of public funds. The committee recommended that the Four Years Law of 1820 be repealed and that the President be forced to report to the Senate the reasons for a removal at the time of nomination of a successor.[14]

---

[13] Whether the peculiar relationship of the Treasury to Congress in the first decades of the Republic reflected, naturally enough, a British concept of the Treasury as the agent of the British Parliament in support of its recognized power over finance, is not clear. For the beginnings of this interesting, and for a while important, legislative-Treasury relationship, see Leonard D. White, *The Federalists* (New York: The Macmillan Co., 1948), pp. 116–27. For its demise, see White, as cited in footnote 7, pp. 34–40.

[14] For the Calhoun report see U.S. Congress, Senate, Committee on Executive Patronage, *Inquiry into the extent of Executive Patronage; the expediency and practicability of reducing the same; and the means of such reduction*, 23d Cong., 2d Sess., Senate Report 108, February 9, 1835 (Washington: Duff Green, 1835). The Benton report, which was ordered

A large proportion of the Senate took part in the debate precipitated by this report which was so obviously directed at President Jackson by the opposition. On several occasions the famous triumvirate of Clay, Calhoun, and Webster displayed the eloquence and oratory so often associated with the pre-Civil War Congress. The finality of the "decision of 1789" was attacked by Daniel Webster and others. Henry Clay would have gone so far as to reduce Jackson to the position in which President Johnson later found himself.[15] Calhoun deplored the extension of executive power and its influence as exerted through the patronage. Again, the whole balance of executive-legislative relations was at stake.

Skillfully worded though they were, the remarks of these statesmen added little to what had gone before. The argument was old and most of the pertinent theories had long since been phrased and rephrased. Nor were the solutions proposed more original. Clay, Calhoun, and Webster were not especially interested in the promotion of efficiency in public business. Their desperate desire was to limit the power of the President!

Therefore, their remedies for the evils of patronage were fundamentally negative remedies—remedies which forbade rather than proposed, as far as the appointing power of the executive branch was concerned. At most, the effect of their measures would have been to transfer control of the patronage from the hands of the President to those of Congress—a highly dubious transaction if these men were really serious in their declared intent to destroy the power of patronage. On their proposals for reform of the public service it is no wonder that Fish sarcastically comments, "If these men, after ten years of discussion of the civil service, could not propose measures better calculated to improve it, their ability has been overrated." [16] Their proposals were, however, well designed for the undermining of the power of the executive branch—their ultimate goal.

In the end, of course, the redoubtable old General won out. While certain of Calhoun's proposals to curtail presidential power were accepted by the Senate, they died in the House. The House, naturally,

---

reprinted in 1835 as Senate Report No. 109 of the same committee and date, originally appeared as U.S. Congress, Senate, Committee on Executive Patronage, *Inquiry into the expediency of reducing the Patronage of the Executive Government of the United States,* 19th Cong., 1st Sess., Senate Report 88, May 4, 1826 (Washington: Duff Green, 1826). For further analysis of what White calls "Whig views on the removal power," see White, as cited in footnote 7, pp. 40–44; and Fish, as cited in footnote 3, pp. 140–43.

15 The Tenure of Office Act of 1867 was passed in a congressional attempt to prevent President Johnson from removing civil officers, including cabinet members, without the Senate's consent. As a result of his refusal to abide by this legislation, Johnson shortly thereafter was impeached.

16 Fish, as cited in footnote 3, p. 142.

has seldom been as interested as the Senate in increasing the latter's power of confirmation. Moreover, at this time the House, which was popularly elected in contrast to a Senate still selected indirectly through the state legislatures, was the center of Jacksonian strength in Congress. Not until after the Civil War would the problem of reform of the civil service again require so much of the time and talent of our legislative branch.

The Ins and the Outs

While the spoils system did not again become a major target of criticism before the Civil War, it was not because of any decline in the manipulation of public office. Rather, we find a crescendo of partisan revenge.

Had the Jacksonians been able to maintain themselves in uninterrupted power as long as had the inheritors of the mantle of Jefferson, it is quite possible that the turnover of the public service from 1830 to 1860 might have resembled that of the period from 1800 to 1830. But the Panic of 1837 cut short the hopes of Martin Van Buren and initiated a period of party instability which was to continue to 1860. That the civil service would reflect that same instability was almost a foregone conclusion.

The first proof of the firmness with which the Whigs believed in the high-minded patronage principles which their leaders, Clay and Webster, had expressed so eloquently in the 1835 debate on the removal power came in 1841. As might be expected, retaliation had bred only retaliation. Though the Whigs had castigated the Jacksonian practices concerning the patronage, they nevertheless felt compelled by practical considerations to follow precedent and so agreed in a decision of the Cabinet in March, 1841.

At this time the usual throng of office-seekers again descended on Washington and plagued the waking hours of the leading politicians. Their importunate demands may have contributed to the untimely death of the first President Harrison. The precipitate change to Tyler brought with it no lessening of the pressure, especially as Tyler gradually moved back to his original Democratic allegiance and became engaged in a bitter quarrel with his Whig associates. Removal followed removal. The process repeated itself upon the full return to power of the Democrats under Polk. When the Whigs acceded to power again in 1849 under President Taylor, removals and resignations increased. Approximately 30 per cent of the civil offices were redistributed during the first year of his executive tenure. When Taylor died in July, 1850, and Fillmore acceded to the Presidency, he, too, did not hesitate to reward his political friends. But since Fillmore was much less at odds with his associates than Tyler had been under similar circumstances, the rate of turnover was slowed somewhat for the first time. Nevertheless, the doctrine of rotation had obtained such a hold in twenty years that, when Pierce succeeded to the White House on behalf of the Democrats, extensive removals of federal office-holders for purely partisan reasons no longer excited more than passing comment.

It was left to James Buchanan in 1852 to carry the device to its logical conclusions. Buchanan, a Democrat, succeeded Pierce, another Democrat, this time following a regular election, not just the unexpected death of the current incumbent. Still, Buchanan followed the established trend, though not without some doubts within his official family as to the wisdom of this policy. Even that old New York partisan and then-Secretary of State, William L. Marcy, is reported to have protested, "I certainly should never recommend the policy of pillaging my own camp." [17] Nevertheless, realities overcame scruples again and the offices were delivered up to the victors in an accelerating tempo from 1856 to 1860. The growing and bitter internecine warfare over the slavery issue within the Democratic party unquestionably contributed greatly to the increasing turnover. By 1860 the doctrine of spoils had obtained so adhesive a grip upon the political machinery of the United States that it has yet to be completely broken—if indeed it can or should be broken.

In only one area of the country did the spoils system fail to triumph—the South, particularly in the states bordering on the Atlantic. This region did not take to the politics of patronage as did the North and West. Even Buchanan recognized this fact and adjusted his policies accordingly. The best explanation for Southern restraint seems to have lain in the preservation of an upper-class white political control up to the time of the Civil War. Essentially agricultural, the South was also less rent by economic—hence, political—quarrels than most of the rest of the country, though the controversy over the union somewhat fragmented even Southern politics for several years after 1850. These characteristics supported the maintenance of an upper-class and Federalist attitude toward public office long past its political obsolescence elsewhere.[18]

17 Quoted in White, as cited in footnote 7, p. 314.
18 On Southern reluctance to endorse the doctrine of spoils see, for example, Fish, as cited in footnote 3, pp. 42–43, 98–99, 157 and 166; and Jesse T. Carpenter, *The South as a Conscious Minority* (New York: New York University Press, 1930), pp. 254–57. This reluctance is especially noteworthy in light of the reversal of Southern behavior since the Civil War. It is also interesting to note that the constitution of the Confederacy reflected Federalist rather than Jacksonian concepts of the public service.

The Spoils of War

In all probability, the American Civil War has the distinction of being the most extensive modern conflict won with the aid of a public service built up primarily by means of the spoils system. In fact, there is good reason for maintaining that the war could not have been won by the North without a highly partisan exploitation of the patronage. The value of the spoils system must therefore be judged in terms of ends as well as means.

Under Abraham Lincoln the spoils system reached new heights. The most complete sweep of the offices thus far was made. For instance, 1,457 out of a total of 1,639 presidential officers were replaced.[19] Subordinate employees suffered in proportion. In all fairness, it must be admitted that Lincoln had more factions to conciliate than his predecessors. The Republican party was a conglomerate of disunities, a civil war was in the offing, and loyalty, political and national, was paramount.

From 1861 to 1865 the policy of Washington, selection according to relative capacity and fitness, was almost entirely forgotten. Until the opening of hostilities Lincoln's appointive policies were devoted essentially to maintenance of the Union. After the beginning of the conflict the problem became one of maintaining Northern unity. Normally taking a direct hand only in the filling of the most important offices, Lincoln left the bulk of the nominations for presidential as well as for subordinate offices to his political friends and advisors. The military forces as well as the civilian establishment were exploited freely, and political generals were notoriously numerous. With more offices at his disposal than any president up to that time, and faced with the urgency of the imminent disintegration of the Union, Lincoln appears to have used—or permitted the use of—the appointing powers at his command as deliberately as they could have been used for practical, and usually partisan, political purposes. The only thread of consistency in the executive appointing policy during the years from 1861 to 1865 seems to have been the practical one of preservation of the Union via preservation of the Republican party.

That the Union was preserved lends considerable merit to the judgment that the process was not ineffectual. As Fish has pointed out, "If Lincoln had made appointments for merit only, the war might have been shortened; on the other hand, he might not have preserved a united North to carry on the war." [20] Lincoln was, however, far

19 Fish, as cited in footnote 3, p. 170.
20 Same, p. 172.

from insensitive to the problems posed by the methods of appointment used by his administration. On one occasion, contemplating the throng of office-seekers and Congressmen in his outer office, he was moved to observe that the spoils system might in the course of time become far more dangerous to the Republic than the rebellion itself.[21] When pressed to sweep the offices anew after his reelection in 1865, the President flatly refused. For the first time since 1829 the principle of rotation in office received a forthright setback. The decline of the spoils system may well be dated from this decision by President Lincoln.

The "System" of Spoils

Thus far we have considered the political rise of the spoils system and its meaning in terms of broad theoretical and practical ends. But what were the mechanics of patronage politics? What was sought and received? How was the patronage managed? What was the meaning of the spoils system as an administrative device?

From an administrative point of view, the spoils system was primarily designed to man, finance, and control the political machines of the new democracy. However, the spoils system performed another important managerial function for which it has seldom been given due credit. It also provided a much-needed channel for the recruitment of personnel for the rapidly expanding national government. While with respect to either of these functions we cannot precisely plot the spoils system with straight lines and boxes in the manner of modern organization charts, it is, nevertheless, entitled to be called a "system." By the eighteen fifties its general form, structure, and methods of operation were plainly observable and well understood.

The sinews of politics. In understanding the spoils system we must first remember that before the Civil War politics and administration were inextricably intermixed in the American public service at all levels. There were few politically neutral, professional managers in the modern sense of the term. From the first days of the Constitution there had always been a certain mutuality of political interest among politicians, administrators, and employees. This the Jacksonians had sought, with signal success, to turn to patently partisan ends. While

---

21 Frederick Bancroft (ed.), *Speeches, Correspondence and Political Papers of Carl Schurz* (6 vols.; New York: G. P. Putnam's Sons, 1913), II, 155–56; III, 295. This story seems to have been a favorite with Schurz, for he repeated it many times. For a detailed analysis of the patronage policies of the Lincoln administration, see Harry J. Carman and Reinhard H. Luthin, *Lincoln and the Patronage* (New York: Columbia University Press, 1943).

OFFICE-SEEKERS AT WASHINGTON DURING THE INAUGURATION.

These Gentlemen, who are ready, like good Patriots, to serve their Country, are all ORIGINAL LINCOLN MEN. 'Tis true, they voted for Pierce and Buchanan; but this was a deep game to insure the Election of Lincoln in 1860.

From *Harper's Weekly*, March 16, 1861.

Federalist and Jeffersonian Republican executives had often required only the proper political opinion, the Jacksonians and those who came into power after them usually required—indeed, took for granted—positive partisanship. The civil servant received not only a livelihood and an opportunity to serve but often also an opportunity for personal gain. He might even expect to rise into a position of political power and prominence, with potentially immense pecuniary and psychological rewards. That politics was often a touchstone to success in private enterprise via land grants, franchises, and government contracts only heightened interest in public office. In return, however, public servants were expected to contribute their votes and a portion, often substantial, of their time, energy, and income to the political party to which they were indebted for their employment. All this was not a matter of contract, though such might be implied. Rather, it was usually a recognition of a sort of partnership, often entered into with considerable enthusiasm by all concerned. Loyalty to one's political party was as appropriate, and just about as frequently assumed, as loyalty to the nation, a church, or an individual state. Most frequently the penalty for both administrative and political failure was removal. In addition, however, one might be cut off from any access to other types of political favors, both those directly at the command of the party, such as nominations, and those available only through governmental channels, such as contracts. On the whole the motivations and methods of private enterprise were those of the spoils system.

From an organizational point of view, the President was at the top of the system, acting both as party chief and chief executive. Underneath were the members of the Cabinet, the most important of whom, from a party organization point of view, were the Postmaster General and the Secretary of the Treasury. Their key position stemmed not only from their duties but also from the fact that the agencies under their control were by far the largest in the civil establishment and the closest to the grass roots of the nation. At first the Treasury predominated in influence as a result both of its early close relationship to Congress and of the Four Years Law of 1820, which especially affected Treasury employees. The rise of the Post Office to partisan prominence came with Jackson. The terms of postmasters were limited to four years for the first time in 1836, and, in addition, senatorial confirmation was then first required for postmasters receiving over $1,000 a year. Then, too, the Post Office had by this time become by far the largest of the executive departments. For more than a century the Post Office continued to be at the center of the administrative workings of the spoils system, an arrangement which Congress and party leaders are still loath to disturb.[22]

Especially were employees in the field offices outside Washington, then as now comprising about 90 per cent of the federal civil service, impelled to contribute their energies to the rapidly consolidating political party system. District attorneys, postmasters, collectors of customs, and a host of other officials were frequently representatives of both the public service and the party. More often than not the greater portion of their efforts was devoted to partisan rather than administrative purposes.

Energy, however, was not all that was required. Financial contributions, historically known as "political assessments," were also expected. The practice of assessment of office-holders for political purposes was well developed by 1840. Even Lincoln is reported to have written to remonstrate with an office-holder who refused to pay up.[23] Demands were usually whatever the traffic would bear, and by 1860 assessments were wrested from office-holders almost in the name of civic duty. Especially prevalent in the states but still far from unknown in federal circles, this practice continued on into the twentieth century. "Two per cent clubs" are still to be found among state employees, and candidates for public office are still expected to contribute substantially toward party campaign expenses.

Considering the traditionally close relationship of the press to politics, it is not surprising that from 1830 to 1860 many editors were appointed to office. The awarding of printing contracts to friendly printers and publishers was an old political custom which the creation of the Government Printing Office in 1860 helped to counteract.[24] But the appointment of large numbers of newspapermen to positions of administrative responsibility in the federal government dates primarily to the time of President Jackson. Two of the General's principal advisers, Amos Kendall and Isaac Hill, were editors of note, and Kendall was appointed Postmaster General in 1835. The editors of the *Cincinnati Advertiser,* the *Ohio People's Press,* and the *New York Courier and Enquirer* were among those receiving awards for their

---

[22] Fowler, as cited in footnote 12, contains one of the best analyses of the "system" in the spoils system, with special reference to the key position of the Post Office in the control of federal patronage. See also Fish, as cited in footnote 3, ch. viii, "Machinery of the Spoils Systems," pp. 173–85.

[23] Fish, as cited in footnote 3, p. 180. For a brief history of political assessments during the middle of the nineteenth century see Frederick W. Whitridge, "Political Assessments," *Cyclopedia of Political Science,* John J. Lalor (ed.), I (1882), 152–55. For the earlier developments of this and related practices discussed in this section, see White, as cited in footnote 7, pp. 325–46 and elsewhere.

[24] See especially White, as cited in footnote 7, pp. 284–99, on this then serious problem.

orthodoxy after the election of 1828. Over fifty representatives of the press were so honored by Jackson and nearly the same number by Lincoln.[25] The fact that for many years postmasters possessed the personal privilege of "franking," frequently worth a substantial sum, explains in part why some seemingly negligible rewards for party orthodoxy proved so attractive. The press has always been close to partisan politics, but in the period before 1865 the relationship was perhaps more blatantly on a *quid pro quo* basis than in any other period of our history. Appointments of newspapermen to office contributed in no little measure to the affinity. Fortunately for a democratic society concerned with the freedom of the press, this practice has gradually declined, partly as a result of the increasing circulation and financial stability of newspapers since the Civil War. However, the relationship of the parties and the press, especially with respect to printing contracts, is often still quite close in state and local governments.

Finally, we come to a species of political middlemen who served as patronage brokers. In return for partisan support, segments of the patronage were frequently delivered up by the President and cabinet members to governors, other state officials, national and local party committeemen, and political bosses. However, for constitutional as well as practical reasons, the bulk of the most attractive patronage posts gravitated into the hands of the legislative members of the party in power. The Senate has always possessed the legal power of confirmation of appointments. As the Constitution fails to draw a clear line between offices which are subject to confirmation and those which are not, it quickly became accepted practice for the Senate to draw its own liberal rules. The practice of confirmation was gradually applied to a wide variety of the middle and upper level offices and even to some of the lesser ones, such as the smaller postmasterships. From the beginning President Washington consulted closely with many members of the House of Representatives as well as the Senate on appointment matters before nominations, and all presidents have followed this example. But within three months of the beginning of the first session of Congress, the Senate had pressed even further. At this point Benjamin Fishbourn, a well-qualified nominee for the post of naval officer for the port of Savannah, was rejected by the Senate as a whole because the two senators from Georgia desired to press their own candidate in opposition to the declared choice of the President. Here the Senate was clearly endeavoring to extend its authority to the actual nomination process and to substitute its

---

25 Eriksson, as cited in footnote 6, pp. 525–32; and Carman and Luthin, as cited in footnote 21, pp. 118–29.

judgment for that of the President, something clearly not contemplated by the Constitution. By the time of the Jacksonians this sort of practice, in which the whole Senate bows to the personal desires of a majority party senator from the home state of a nominee, was by no means unusual. Eventually dubbed "Senatorial Courtesy," the procedure has continued on into mid-twentieth century. Thus, one way or another, much of the nominally presidential and cabinet patronage fell to senators of the party in power; and some of it, such as postmasterships, gradually came to be considered the perquisite of representatives.

Even legislators themselves often sought office during this period. For the higher offices, especially those comprising the Cabinet, this has always been considered proper; but pressure by senators and representatives for even the lower administrative offices was pronounced in the period before the Civil War. The information is most complete for Jackson's administration, though the tendency antedated his term. One list shows fifteen ex-senators and twenty-six ex-representatives as recipients of presidential appointments between 1829 and 1834.[26] Nor did all of these appointments represent "lame ducks." Long continuation of this practice for other than top positions might have undermined the cherished American principle of separation of powers. However, as legislative salaries and alternative occupational opportunities in private enterprise improved, the practice declined, except with respect to senators and congressmen who have been retired to private life by defeat at the polls.

Underlying all this was the meaning of the patronage to the President in terms of political control and direction of the government. In a political system rent by federalism and the separation of powers, some means had to be found to bridge at least some of the gaps in this dual division of authority. Otherwise nothing might be accomplished. It is not too much to say that one of the few major forces which lay at the command of a nineteenth century president who wished to think and act in terms of national rather than local interests was the power of the patronage. From 1829 on, public offices became recognized pawns in this as well as other political bargaining processes.

Such was the anatomy of the spoils system as a support for partisan politics. As political parties assumed a more modern form, characterized by national conventions, central committees, and large scale requirements for funds, the civil service became more and more intricately tied in with the party organization at all levels. By 1860

26 Eriksson, as cited in footnote 6, p. 333.

the two were almost inextricably entangled. That the administrative efficiency of the civil service should to some extent suffer was to be expected, though the decline was considerably less precipitous than is commonly supposed. The Jacksonian genius lay in politics rather than administration. Spoils politics was played according to the fluid rules of personal and political loyalty and expediency, a fascinating sort of game which the politicians and most of the public thoroughly understood, supported, and appeared to enjoy.

The spoils system as a recruiting device. Probably Washington has been the only president in our history to know personally a large proportion of the federal public servants. Between 1792 and 1861 the federal civil service increased fiftyfold—from roughly 1,000 employees to 50,000 or more. During the same period the population increased only eight times. The prediction of James Madison in 1788, that "the numbers of individuals employed under the Constitution of the United States will be much smaller than the number employed under the particular states," proved hopelessly wrong.[27] The growth of the country was demanding constant expansion of the public service, regardless of the Jeffersonian conception—accepted by many of the Jacksonians as well—of government as a necessary evil.

Finding interested and qualified applicants and making appointments soon became more than a one-man job, if it had ever been that. Even Washington had found it continually necessary to consult his friends on personnel matters. As the years went by, it became increasingly urgent for the President to obtain help and counsel, not just because it was politic to do so, but because in the United States no effective system had yet been devised to nominate large numbers of competent men for public office. The Constitution provided no answer, and the senatorial proposal of the eighteen thirties, for devolution of the selection of personnel almost entirely upon individual members of Congress to the exclusion of the President, would have been, if anything, a step backward.

In a real sense, the development of the "courtesy" system, senatorial and otherwise, was an answer to internal executive as well as external partisan problems. That it was not the only answer is clear from both the experience of the Federalists and the Jeffersonian Republicans, and from the later lessons of modern civil service reform. But, for the time being, the system sufficed.

Even so, the chief executive's appointment and removal burden often reached intolerable proportions. The diary of President Polk reveals especially well the anguish and torture to which American

---

[27] *The Federalist* (Modern Library ed.; New York: Random House, [1937]), p. 301.

chief executives have often been subjected under the spoils system. The deaths of Presidents Harrison and Taylor have been related in part to the unrelenting pressure brought by seekers of public office. Even Lincoln said that he felt like "a man so busy in letting rooms in one end of his house that he cannot stop to put out the fire that is burning the other." [28] It is no wonder that much of the initiative for reform of the spoils system was later to come from the White House.

Jacksonian Personnel Administration

Though the spoils system was triumphant by 1865, continuity with the past was never completely lost. One of the important contributions of Leonard D. White's analysis of the Jacksonian bureaucracy has been to point out a certain persistence of the Federalist and Jeffersonian Republican tradition of tenure in office throughout the period immediately prior to the Civil War.[29] We have already noted that Jackson dismissed no more federal officers than did Jefferson. Despite the rising tide of spoils, there constantly remained a stratum of the civil service which helped to maintain continuity and competence in administration. Even the most partisan of executives could comprehend the need to maintain a basic level of administrative efficiency by retaining a few key officials. Hence the comptrollers, auditors, and chief clerks of the departmental service in Washington frequently kept their positions through several administrations. So did a portion of the minor clerks, a number of the small group of scientific and technical personnel, and the officer corps of the army and navy. In the field agencies politics reigned, though not always to the exclusion of integrity and competence. In a sense the federal service was manned and managed through two personnel systems, though at this time that governed by the principle of spoils was by far the most dominant. Ever since the time of Jackson the proper relationship between these two systems has been a matter of considerable concern and argument.

The chief clerks. The details of personnel administration were largely under the jurisdiction of the chief clerks in each of the major establishments both in Washington and in the field. They maintained the employment rolls and records, exercised general supervision of employee activities, assigned work, oriented new employees, and maintained other relevant records. Training was unknown in a modern

---

[28] Ward Hill Lamon, *Recollections of Abraham Lincoln* (Chicago: A. C. McClurg and Co., 1895), p. 212.

[29] As cited in footnote 7, pp. 347–62. Fish also supports this view.

51

sense; promotions were relatively few, efficiency ratings in an embryonic state, and retirement policies nonexistent. There was, of course, no more legal protection against removals in the public service than in business. The government labor policy toward both blue collar workers and unions resembled that of the private administrative world. There was as yet no concept of the government as a model employer. The major difference between public and private employment lay in the hours of work. While the government offices in Washington were open from eight to ten hours a day in the eighteen thirties, for example, most clerical employees actually were on duty only six hours a day,[30] as compared to the ten to twelve hour day then common in the commercial world. Short hours, coupled with the frequent fees and other income supplements of public office, may partially account for the great interest displayed throughout the nineteenth century in all levels of public employment.

Examinations. Only in a few aspects did the public service of the pre-Civil War era presage that of the twentieth century. Following several congressional discussions of governmental efficiency in the later eighteen forties and early fifties, the Senate on March 7, 1851, requested the cabinet officers to submit their recommendations on the examination, promotion, classification, and pay of clerks in the federal establishment. The entire cabinet, except for Daniel Webster of the State Department, recommended the use of a simple, qualifying test, then described as a "pass-examination," for the initial appointment of clerks. However, in light of the constitutional appointment prerogatives of the executive, there was hesitation to make examinations compulsory. Nevertheless, in 1853 Congress made pass-examinations a requirement for entrance into a large proportion of the clerical offices in Washington. Since the testing procedure was at the mercy of department heads, its administration lacked uniformity. Pass-examinations were taken seriously mainly in connection with the appointment of fiscal employees, though the statute requiring them remained in effect until the Pendleton Act of 1883 established the present Civil Service Commission.

Where the idea of examinations for entrance into the public service originated is hard to say now. Certainly formal examinations were no part of business personnel practices at this time; and the British experience with civil service examinations, then barely under way, had as yet made no impact on America. Entrance examinations for the military academies dated from 1818 and 1819, and examinations for army surgeons were given as early as 1814. Also, before 1853 the

30 White, as cited in footnote 7, p. 400.

Treasury had for a while conducted examinations for entrance into some of its accounting positions. These examinations seem to have stemmed from the practical necessities of Treasury administration, which, more than in many departments, made knowledge of certain elementary commercial techniques essential. In a report by the Secretary of the Treasury in 1854 we find the modest requirements then current:

This course of examination has required that the applicant shall—1st, be able to write an ordinary business letter, in a fair and legible hand; 2d, that he shall show himself to be acquainted with the first four rules of arithmetic, and capable of ordinary celerity in the use of them, and 3d, that he shall evince some knowledge of the generally received principles of accounting.[31]

The pre-Civil War applicants for Treasury posts were evidently not overtaxed. In all likelihood, however, these requirements were comparable to those—applied more informally, no doubt—of the typical commercial houses of the day.[32]

Shortly after the approval of pass-examinations for clerical employees, Congress provided for similar examinations for a limited number of consular "pupils." But this first attempt at deliberate development of a career foreign service died a quick death a year after its initiation. It was revived in an emasculated form in 1864. Senator John P. Hale of New Hampshire, in a typical contemporary objection to this form of recruitment, is reported as saying, "I am opposed to it, not because I think our consuls are educated too highly as a general fact, but I dislike this way of doing it. If we begin here where is it to stop? We shall have then to appoint pupils as ambassadors, and, when you begin that, there is no ending!" General John A. Quitman, a representative from Mississippi, put it even more bluntly, saying in effect, "that consuls were diplomats and that the best diplomacy was the diplomacy of the backwoods, the honest diplomacy of republican freemen." The controversy, in the opinion of Henry Adams, reflected a continuation of long-standing legislative-executive antagonism. Congress seemed to be afraid its patronage would be cut and the President's increased.[33]

Salary scales. A far more lasting contribution to public personnel administration was initiated by the "classification" law of 1853. For

---

[31] U.S. Treasury Department, *Report of the Secretary of the Treasury on the State of the Finances for the Year Ending June 30, 1854*, 33d Cong., 2d Sess., House Exec. Doc. 3 (Washington: A. O. P. Nicholson, 1854), p. 98.

[32] Unfortunately there is no history of private personnel practices in this country.

[33] Hale and Quitman are quoted in Henry Brooks Adams, "Civil Service Reform," *North American Review*, CIX (October, 1869), 462–63 and elsewhere.

some years departmental clerks had been complaining about the insufficiency and inequality of pay in relation to duties and responsibilities, but little had been done about it. The pay for departmental employees was still based on legislation dating from 1818.[34] Intervening enactments, which, in the continuing congressional attempt to control the executive, were becoming more and more detailed, had left the problem of regularization of pay and duties pretty much up in the air. The result was a hodge-podge of administrative and legislative regulation. A cabinet report in 1852 had recommended that some system of classes for clerical employees be devised and that pass-examinations then be required for applicants to these positions. Congress finally agreed that something should be done. By an act of March 3, 1853, it directed the heads of all the departments except the Department of State, which was included two years later, to group their Washington clerical employees under four classes, keeping in mind their actual duties. In 1854, the classes and their pay scale were as follows: Class I at $1,250, Class II at $1,400, Class III at $1,600, and Class IV at $1,800. Chief Clerks of Bureaus and Chief Clerks of Departments were to receive $2,000 and $2,200 respectively. These salaries represented, however, no great improvement over those of 1818. On the average, the increases meant perhaps a raise of $200 or so at the bottom and $100 or less at the top of the clerical grades.

Department heads were given a great deal of leeway in the required adjustment and were supposed to organize their employment force so that there was equal pay for equal work. But there was no central agency to see that this was done. Moreover, the new legislation provided systematic pay scales for less than a tenth of the federal positions. The more important officials, the employees in the field services outside Washington, and the sub-clerical and blue collar workers were excluded. In present-day terms, the laws were really nothing but salary standardization acts, providing only incidentally for a minimal duties-classification. Certainly they are most unimpressive to the modern classification expert. But they seem to have been the best that anyone then either could invent or considered desirable to invent. Moreover, it is important to note that the laws of 1853, 1854, and 1855 [35] remained major bases for the classification and pay of the federal government's clerical employees for nearly seventy years. No major change occurred until the Classification Act of 1923 radically revised the legal and administrative bases for the description and pay of government jobs. Compensation and classification remained for the

---

34 Salaries were temporarily increased in the eighteen thirties by a bonus system. The bonus system was also employed from 1864 to 1867.

35 The State Department and Census Office were included at this time.

most part a matter of day-by-day legislative whim, typically applied to individual positions or small groups of positions, until the resulting unwieldy edifice threatened to collapse during World War I.[36]

In general, we can say that before the Civil War no one devised a practical program for administrative reform of the civil service. If anyone deserves credit for prophetic insight in this period, it is not Clay, Calhoun, or Webster but Senator Robert M. T. Hunter of Virginia. It was largely at the inspiration of this southerner that the pass-examination statutes of the eighteen fifties were enacted. Unfortunately, Hunter joined the Confederacy as its first Secretary of State and was thereafter lost to the federal scene.[37]

Whether the difficulty lay in the paucity of ideas or in the unfavorable political climate is difficult to determine. Undoubtedly the fact that modern standards of private business management were still in an embryonic stage had much to do with the failure to develop more systematic procedures in the public service. Certainly, almost the entire weight of contemporary political theory and practice militated against any attempt at more modern methods. A civil war and recurrent political and economic crises would be necessary to convince the average voter and the average legislator of any need for reform. There is little evidence to contradict the view that most people were quite satisfied with the organization, if not the immediate personnel, of the federal bureaucracy of pre-Civil War days.

A Radical Institution

In conclusion, let us briefly review the spoils system as a dynamic social institution. With the rise of the new democracy of the Jacksonian era, the public service established by the Founding Fathers became a major focal point of attack by the political leaders of the newly-enfranchised electorate of the nineteenth century. To the voters of 1829 the holdover bureaucracy with its roots in the discredited Federalist regime seemed the final bastion of aristocracy—hardly an object of pity in a democratic revolution.

The selection of Andrew Jackson as President personalized the power and aspirations of the new electorate. It also placed at his mercy the administrative services of the federal government. Jackson sought to adapt these services to the newly vitalized ideals of equality

---

36 The major study of the development of classification and pay standards in the American public service is Ismar Baruch, *History of Position-Classification and Salary Standardization in the Federal Service, 1789–1941* (2d ed., P.C.D. Manual No. A-2; Washington: U.S. Civil Service Commission, 1941). See also White, as cited in footnote 7, pp. 376–93.

37 See Leonard D. White, "Centennial Anniversary," *Public Personnel Review*, XIV (January, 1953), 3, for the story of Hunter's endeavors.

of opportunity, social mobility, individual freedom, and popular government. Equality was reflected in attempts to limit the tenure of office and to pass the offices around. Any suggestion that a man of average intelligence was not fit for any and all public offices was indignantly rejected as a denial of the power and wisdom of "the people." The validity of class and institutional barriers to the free rise of individual talent was vehemently attacked. Above all, the new democracy felt, if it did not always logically perceive, that exploitation of the patronage by and for the grass roots was vital to the control of a government which for so long had represented position and property.

The development of the spoils system into so pervasive an institution was undoubtedly intensified by the various constitutional, sectional, and administrative problems of the period. Spoils politics was related to the democratic ideals of an expanding nation as well as to the political and economic framework within which these ideals functioned. After 1829 the federal offices, like state and local offices before them, were used openly and explicitly as fuel for partisan purposes. In the eyes of the common man of Jacksonian persuasion, unquestionably the spoils system represented a "reform" which tightened the bond between the people and their government.

In the days of its youth the spoils system was a *radical institution* which, to the fastidious and apprehensive, did not appeal any more than the tumultous democracy it represented. Even President Jackson and many of the more responsible exponents of "reform" in 1829 would have been astonished at the "pillaging" which later developed. Still, those who would reform all things too often forget that the American federal service was politically recast to keep it responsive to the will of the people.

For many years events were such that no other system seemed possible or desirable. But, as all social institutions may carry within themselves the impetus for their own destruction, so with the spoils system. Some of the very forces behind the development of this democratic device began, even before the Civil War, to lay the groundwork for its eventual decline, if not for its complete downfall.

SUPPLEMENTARY NOTES

Federal Civil Employment Statistics

The writer, with the assistance of James H. Lare, has made a detailed though not exhaustive study of federal civil employment statistics, particularly those for the executive branch. This study reveals that currently available statistics are, in general, open to question. Those for the eighteenth and nineteenth centuries are especially uncertain.

Statistics prior to 1816. The best source for figures prior to the publication of the first *Official Register of the United States* in 1816 appears to be the estimates for the years 1792 and 1801 made from *American State Papers, Miscellaneous,* I, pp. 57–68 and 260–319, by Leonard D. White in *The Federalists,* p. 255. Yet an analysis of the data in *American State Papers* strongly suggests that they fail to include all of the clerks and laborers employed by the federal government in those years. Moreover, the 1801 data include deputy postmasters, while those for 1792 exclude them. A compilation prepared between these dates, *The United States Register for the Year 1795* (Philadelphia: Mathew Carey, 1794), lists approximately 425 employees in the executive civil service. This figure includes customs collectors and lighthouse superintendents and keepers, for example, but does not include any deputy postmasters or laborers. Moreover, all three sets of figures make little distinction among part-time, full-time, and contract employees. All in all, the writer has gone far enough into these data to suggest that the executive civil employment totals commonly used for the period before 1816 are too low, perhaps by as much as 50 per cent, depending upon what offices are included and how the calculations are made.

1816 to the Civil War. The most comprehensive compilation of figures on federal employment in the executive civil service appears in the Census Bureau's *Historical Statistics,* cited in footnote 34 in the previous chapter. In this publication see the table entitled "Series P 62–68.—Government Employment—Federal Government Employment: 1816 to 1945," p. 294, and the explanatory notes on p. 284. These notes refer in turn primarily to the *Statistical Abstract* for 1946 and to U.S. Civil Service Commission records. However, when one pushes further, it is clear that the common source for nearly all civil employment totals in the executive branch before 1900 is the *Official Register of the United States,* sometimes known as the "Blue Book." The *Register* was first published in 1816, and has appeared either annually or biennially ever since under the successive auspices of the Department of State, Department of the Interior, the Bureau of the Census, and, since 1933, the Civil Service Commission. The date of each issue of this series refers to the year for which data are included, rather than the year of publication.

However, this publication, too, is subject to serious question. Let us take the issue for 1816, *A Register of Officers and Agents, Civil, Military, and Naval, in the Service of the United States* (Washington: Jonathan Elliott, 1816), as a fairly typical example. By counting the number of names in a column and multiplying by the number of columns, one can only conclude that the figure of 6,327, the one reported for 1816 in *Historical Statistics,* must include almost all the personnel indicated by the title of this issue of the *Register.* By this much the figure is an over-estimate. However, this and most other issues of the *Register* fail to include the laborers who were employed in the mint, navy yards, and other establishments requiring skilled and unskilled labor. Moreover, the lists of clerks and clerical help also appear to be incomplete. By this much, the figure of 6,327 is an under-estimate.

Where does this leave us? Considered as a whole for the period between 1816 and 1860, the writer feels that the figures presented in *Historical Statistics* and based on the *Official Register* are too low, by perhaps as much as 25 per cent. In other words, the numbers of clerks and laborers omitted exceeds considerably the military and legislative personnel erroneously included. For example, it is known that the navy yards employed over 7,000

57

workmen in 1857. White, *The Jacksonians,* as cited in footnote 7, p. 406. This number alone is more than 20 per cent of the *Historical Statistics'* executive civil service total of 33,300 for 1851, and about 15 per cent of the 49,-200 reported for 1861.

The Civil War period. Accurate totals for the Civil War period are even more elusive. First of all, there is the figure reported immediately above for 1861, the accuracy of which is suspect to begin with. The next year for which *Historical Statistics* reports a total is 1871. This time the figure, also based on the *Official Register,* is 53,900. For the years in between there is only the Civil Service Commission's estimate of "over 60,000" for 1867, contained in the Commission's ninth annual report for 1892, p. 238, also based on the *Register.* These latter two totals are even more questionable because of the known tendency of the federal service to expand greatly during a full-scale war and then to fail to contract to anything like its original level of employment. Carl Fish notes, for example, that the patronage "was enormously increased by the war." *The Civil Service and the Patronage,* as cited in footnote 3, p. 171. Only Lionel Murphy essays an estimate of northern civil employment during the war. He suggests that the total number of civilians on the federal payroll in 1865 actually ran as high as 100,000. See "The First Federal Civil Service Commission: 1871–75 (Part I)," *Public Personnel Review,* III (January, 1942), p. 31. With this estimate the writer concurs, though it may be off by as much as plus or minus 20 per cent.

As for the Confederacy, the writer has been unable to find any published figures or estimates of civil employment, even after a diligent search of the most promising secondary materials. However, with the assistance of Harry N. Scheiber, it has been possible to piece together a good deal of primary and secondary data and to estimate the Confederate civil service at close to 70,000 at the height of the war. This startlingly high figure, which appears to be reasonably accurate, is explained in part by the large numbers of employees in the Niter and Mining Bureau and the Engineer Bureau of the Confederate War Department, where many civilians worked in government operated enterprises of a logistical nature. The 70,000 figure also includes many Negroes, most of whom were paid regular wages, along with a considerable number of women and some children. As the North must have employed as many or more civilians in its central governmental establishment than the South, the estimate of 70,000 for the Confederacy tends to confirm Murphy's estimate of 100,000 for the North.

Altogether, civil public employment at the national levels must be considered as well over 150,000 by the beginning of 1865, and 175,000 might not be too high.

1865 to 1883. For this period we must come back again almost exclusively to the *Official Register.* Again, the *Register* is still suspect, for approximately the same reasons as outlined above for the period before the Civil War. In turn, it is likely that the totals recorded in *Historical Statistics* are too low by up to 25 per cent.

Since 1883. Apparently the *Official Register* remained the principal source for civil employment statistics in the executive branch until the early nineteen hundreds. The problem of inclusions and exclusions now becomes even more complicated. The *Historical Statistics'* figure of 166,000 for 1891, for example, is supposedly based on Civil Service Commission records. But the Commission does not report this figure until 1910, having previously reported the figure for 1891 as 183,488 in its ninth annual report for fiscal year 1892 (p. 238). In this same report the Commission states that this total for 1891 is especially accurate (p. 237); but, even so, the agency also states (p. 238) that "A portion of the force of the civil service, consisting of laborers and others temporarily engaged, of agents in the secret service, and of others paid out of 'lump' or contingent appropriations, is not borne upon the Department rolls."

Such inconsistencies are apparent for almost every year between 1883 and World War I. There are also similar inconsistencies, though less frequent, for the years between World War I and 1933. For example, *Historical Statistics* shows a great jump in executive employment between 1912 and 1913, from 395,460 to 469,879. However, the Employment Statistics Office of the Civil Service Commission has confirmed to the writer that this jump is probably merely the result of the inclusion, for the first time, of clerks in fourth-class post offices and substitute railway mail clerks in the total for 1913. In other words, this large increase stems largely from a revised statistical base rather than any splurge in creating offices.

When one begins to compare the more recent series of statistics on federal civil employment put out by the Civil Service Commission, the Bureau of Labor Statistics, and the Department of Commerce, the picture is even more confusing as a result of differing statistical approaches. However, the three agencies prepared a revised series in 1955 and now use the same figures. For purposes of this study, the Commission's regularly published data on federal civil employment seem to be reasonably inclusive since 1933, and quite so since World War II. For other periods both the Commission's regularly published data and those contained in *Historical Statistics* and most other sources are suspect.

For the years up to 1908 the writer has relied mainly on Civil Service Commission estimates as modified by his own research and has reported what appear to be the most accurate rounded figures available, along with brief notations here and there as to the difficulties involved. For the years since 1908, the federal civil employment totals reported here are rounded versions of a "revised series for the executive branch" provided the writer through the courtesy of Flora M. Nicholson, Chief of the Employment Statistics Office, U.S. Civil Service Commission. However, even for some of these years, the writer has indicated in appropriate notes elsewhere in this study that there are interpretative problems involved in their use.

Other sources. There are several other compilations of federal civil employment data, among which that by Solomon Fabricant, *The Trend of Government Activity in the United States since 1900* (New York: National Bureau of Economic Research, 1952), is the most inclusive and important. However, this type of study has aimed at translating employment into full-time equivalents in order to arrive at some sort of estimate of the distribution of the national labor force. Such full-time equivalents are not of much assistance in a study such as this, where one is more interested in the influence of the government upon the nation through the individuals employed directly by it, whether full-time or not. It should be noted that Fabricant's sources are essentially a combination of all those reported above.

CHAPTER 4

"Snivel Service" to Civil Service: 1865–1883

When Artemus Ward thought of blaming the Union's pell-mell retreat at Bull Run on a rumor of three vacancies in the New York custom house, the popular Civil War satirist was not merely joking at the army's expense. He was also symbolizing the tenacious grip of the spoils system on American life and politics in the eighteen sixties. Ward was correct in implying that for many Americans the offices had become almost ends in themselves, overshadowing in importance even the question of the fate of the nation. A few years later this same point of view would be expressed more forthrightly in the classic remark of a certain Mr. Flanagan of Texas, who has been widely quoted as blurting out at the Republican National Convention of 1880, "What are we here for if not for the offices?" [1]

A Conservative Institution

Though the spoils system was in many ways a *radical* innovation in 1829, it had in less than forty years undergone that metamorphosis

---

[1] As quoted in James Parton, "The Power of Public Plunder," *North American Review*, CXXXIII (July, 1881), 43. Parton incorrectly refers to the gentleman as Mr. "O'Flanagan." Most contemporary quotations of Flanagan's remarks resemble that of Parton. Parton is not precisely accurate, however, though he does convey Flanagan's meaning quite well. Webster Flanagan was a delegate-at-large from Henderson, Texas, and he rose to protest civil service reform in these words: "*Mr. President:* Texas has had quite enough of the civil service. During the last four years, sir, out of 1,400 officers appointed by the President of the United States, 140 represented the Republican party. We are not here, sir, for the purpose of providing offices for the Democracy. There is one plank in the Democratic party that I have ever admired, and that is, 'To the victors belong the spoils.' After we have won the race, as we will, we will give those who are entitled to positions office. *What are we up here for?* [italics added] I mean that members of the Republican party are entitled to office, and if we are victorious we will have office. I, therefore, move to lay the amendment on the table." *Official Proceedings of the National Republican Conventions of 1868, 1872, 1876, and 1880* (Minneapolis: Charles W. Johnson, 1903), p. 536.

which is common to most successful reform measures. By 1865 it had become a *conservative* institution.

The vitality of spoils. The times were robust. Economics was predatory and politics was manipulated to support economics while the spoils system helped maintain both. The blatant as well as discreet use of position, power, and political plunder made it relatively easy to silence many critics who might otherwise have joined the ranks of the more militant crusaders against the acquisitive society of President Grant. With the advent of a new type of politico-business man such as the astute Thurlow Weed of New York—the political ancestor of Mark Hanna—the organizational genius of American entrepreneurs was turned to politics, and the spoils system grew more pervasive than ever. Manipulated by the Jacksonians to destroy the status quo of 1829, patronage politics now became a mainstay of the new established order. However, to consider the gradual refinement of spoils politics as a kind of deliberate conservative conspiracy is to stretch the point considerably.

By 1865, contrary to the hopes of the Founding Fathers, political parties were considered a positive good. A new theory of government had developed. The historian, Charles R. Lingley, has well described it:

In the field of actual politics, parties are a necessity and organization is essential. It is the duty of the citizen, therefore, to support the party that stands for right policies and to adhere closely to its official organization. Loyalty should be rewarded by appointment to positions within the gift of the party; and disloyalty should be looked upon as political treason. One who votes for anybody except the organization candidates feels himself superior to his party, is faithless to the great ideal and is only a little less despicable than he who, having been elected to an office through the energy and devotion of the party workers, is then so ungrateful as to refuse to appoint the workers to positions within his gift. Positions constitute the cohesive force that holds the organization intact.[2]

There is little question but that the general public of 1865 accepted the spoils system as right and proper. The Jacksonian idea of the simplicity of the duties of public office still held sway in the sixties and seventies. Most Americans saw no reason why rotation in office was either inefficient or otherwise undesirable. In the early sixties even such a well-informed person as Henry Adams spoke to E. L. Godkin, editor of the *Nation,* about civil service reform as "something Prussian."[3] And Godkin, himself a reformer of note, admitted that "in the inner political circles, between 1868 and 1878 it was known as

2 *Since the Civil War* (New York: The Century Co., 1924), p. 118.
3 Allan Nevins, *The Evening Post* (New York: Boni and Liveright, 1922), p. 436.

'snivel service reform,' and was a source of much mingled disgust and amusement." [4]

In fact the spoils system and its mate, machine politics, developed a sort of massive inertia, detectable to this day. It was this dead weight of custom, practice, machine maneuver, tacit alliance of politics and economics, personal political selfishness, and sheer practical partisan advantage which any post-Civil War reform movement had to counteract. Even if it had been the only object of public concern in the eighteen sixties, reform of the public service would have been a considerable task.

Forces for change. A great deal has been written about the philosophy, ethics, and practices of that period in American history between 1865 and 1900, known variously as the "Gilded Age," the "Great Barbecue," or the "Era of Expansion"; and there is no need here to more than touch on certain highlights of the times. It is enough to say that the social gears began to clash again not long after 1865. The Civil War had really settled only two problems—slavery and the nature of the Union—and it had intensified many more.

Most obvious was the widespread agrarian unrest under deflationary policies, supplemented by the protests of those who felt that life was not completely heavenly in the new industrial communities. The great economic depressions of the post-Civil War years, the rash of political scandals during the Grant administration, the Granger movement, the Farmers' Alliances, the Knights of Labor, the great railroad strike of 1877, Henry George, the Ku Klux Klan, and the Populists all testified to the changing times. In the eighteen sixties, seventies, and much of the eighties, many Americans were by no means pleased with their proportion of the rewards of progress and were busily engaged in inventing ways of improving their condition. Political democracy via universal suffrage was about to be used to renew the economic democracy which had been largely taken for granted under the Jacksonians.

Underneath all this strife lay the fact that a fundamentally agrarian social order was being required to adjust to something new and different. The bitter quarrel between the Radical Republicans and President Johnson over control of the new Republican party only dramatized further the forces at work. Moreover, the hangover of agrarian ideals tended to impede any realistic appraisal of either the decline of agriculture or the rapid expansion of American industrialism.

The early formulas for solution of the problems of the decades im-

---

[4] E. L. Godkin, "The Civil Service Reform Controversy," *North American Review*, CXXXIV (April, 1882), 383.

mediately after the Civil War, including civil service reform, often seemed confused and lost amid a morass of conflicting emotions, events, and interpretations. Economic expansion continued so rapidly that it was difficult to keep abreast of it, let alone consider it in a prophetic or philosophic fashion. Words, ideas, and reality became so inextricably scrambled that it is a wonder that anyone bothered to try and untangle anything. The nation improvised temporarily and partisanly as it grew, amid controversy often bitter and occasionally violent.

That America was ripe for consideration of some sort of governmental reform in the decades after the Civil War now seems clear. That any successful reform had to conform to the concept of Jacksonian political democracy as well as to the predispositions of a rising industrialism was undoubtedly true also. But reform movements do not just happen: someone must produce an acceptable and salable product. Among those who endeavored to do so was the little eddy of civil service reformers.

Protests against the so-called vices of patronage were nothing new as has been shown in previous chapters. Clay, Calhoun, and Webster had all lamented the effects of the spoils system. Lincoln, too, had feared its impact on the Republic. There had also appeared before 1865 some few glimmerings of modern civil service reform such as the elementary examination and classification techniques of the eighteen fifties. Unfortunately, their lessons tended to be lost in the great emergency and emotionalism of the Civil War. Not until the late eighteen sixties did reform of the public service become more than a dream. Then the powerful energies and ideals of the Anti-Slavery Society and similar organizations of the forties and fifties took up the cudgels. As the sixties moved into the seventies, civil service reform and its new generation of champions, along with other reform movements involving such things as money and the tariff, slowly but surely came to occupy a prominent place among the current political issues.

Foreign Inspiration

The basic idea for our post-Civil War version of civil service reform, involving the modern conception of a "merit system," [5] came to the United States primarily from England after 1865. There is practically no indication that foreign experience with a nonpolitical merit system made any impression upon American political and social thought before 1860.

It was not that Americans knew nothing of other foreign experience.

[5] See definitions on pp. 8 and 100.

William H. Seward, as Secretary of State, had in 1862 commissioned John Bigelow, consul-general at Paris, to study French tax collection procedures, and Bigelow recommended that the French method of selecting tax collectors by examination be adopted in the United States. The important report on the civil service sponsored by Congressman Thomas A. Jenckes in 1868 contains some eighty-two pages of information about Chinese, Prussian, French, and English civil service procedures.[6] But most of the American reformers looked to the British example as more relevant to American institutions than Continental or other foreign experience. For example, George William Curtis, pre-eminent among the early civil service reform group in this country, went to considerable trouble to correspond with Sir Charles Trevelyan, Sir Stafford Northcote, John Stuart Mill, and others at the center of the still consolidating British reform movement. A letter by Trevelyan to a Mr. C. Brace of New York, dated February 8, 1869, opens:

Mr. John Stuart Mill has requested me to furnish you and Mr. Jenckes of Rhode Island, and others who are labouring with you to engraft into the political system of the United States a modern improvement which has already borne excellent fruit in the 'old country' and its dependencies, with such information as may be likely to assist you in this good work.

Trevelyan concludes his six page summary of British practice and philosophy with the observation:

This is *our* experience. It is for you, and those who are acting with you, to judge how far it is applicable to the circumstances of the United States. It will be an unexpected happiness if, while we are working for the Mother Country, we also benefit her mighty Transatlantic Daughter by the example of just principles properly applied.[7]

---

6 U.S. Congress, House, Joint Select Committee on Retrenchment, *Report: Civil Service of the United States*, 40th Cong., 2d Sess., House Report 47, May 25, 1868 (Washington: Government Printing Office, 1868), pp. 110–202. For a reprint of the Bigelow report see pp. 176–82. This document reprints much of a similar but briefer report issued by the same committee in 1867, also under Jenckes' sponsorship. U.S. Congress, House, Joint Select Committee on Retrenchment, *Civil Service of the United States*, 39th Cong., 2d Sess., House Report 8, January 31, 1867 (Washington: Government Printing Office, 1867). Moreover, the 1868 report also contains extensive extracts from a most comprehensive survey of the conditions of public employment. It was conducted by means of a thirty-seven point questionnaire (reprinted on pp. 17–18) directed to several hundred major federal officials. The extracts from the replies occupy more than eighty pages of the report and are a unique mine of systematic information about the nineteenth century American public service.

7 C. Brace was almost certainly Charles Loring Brace, a man with some interests in civil service reform though best known for his children's welfare efforts. Brace was independently wealthy and, during his extensive travels abroad, had become acquainted with Mill. This apparently unknown letter was discovered by Lionel V. Murphy in the files of the library of the U.S. Civil Service Commission while preparing his important study of the almost equally unknown Civil Service Commission of the Grant administration. For this and other reference to British experience, see his "The First Federal Civil Service Commission: 1871–1875," *Public Personnel Review*, III (January, July, and October, 1942), 219 and elsewhere.

In the initial consultations of the short-lived Civil Service Commission appointed by President Grant in 1871 there was constant reference to English documents and English experiences. Later on, a study of the British civil service made by Dorman B. Eaton, another prominent reformer, at the request of President Hayes, was reprinted by Harper and Brothers in a twenty-five cent paperback edition and widely read for a work of its kind.[8] Indeed, most of the many references to foreign experience with civil service reform found in congressional speeches, documents, and reports after 1870 are to the British example. In view of the close cultural connections between the two countries, the relationship concerning civil service reform is not surprising.

Early Legislative Efforts

In 1864 Senator Charles Sumner, a Republican from Massachusetts, introduced the first of a twenty-year series of civil service reform bills aimed at the eventual extinction of the power of patronage through the application of modern merit system techniques. Despite the political prominence of its author, the proposal was lost in the legislative confusion attending the close of the Civil War, and Sumner did not pursue the matter further. A second attempt to introduce the new idea was made in late 1865 by Congressman Thomas A. Jenckes, a Republican from Rhode Island. Jenckes seems to have been interested in the idea of civil service reform for several years before the introduction of his bill. A wealthy patent lawyer, Jenckes had the time and inclination to go into the matter in some detail. His membership on the congressional Joint Select Committee on Retrenchment, formed as a result of the usual concern with economy after a major war, provided an added incentive for inquiry into governmental administrative matters. He was also familiar with European experience, having been in correspondence with both Trevelyan and Northcote. While Sumner must receive credit for the first modern civil service reform proposal to be introduced in Congress, Jenckes may be considered the first American to approach civil service reform with the single minded attention such a matter deserved.

The pre-Civil War attempts at control of the patronage had generally assumed the form of a limitation on the presidential power of removal. Both Sumner and Jenckes—the latter in considerably more detail—proposed to attack the problem in the manner of the English

---

8 Dorman B. Eaton, *Civil Service in Great Britain* (New York: Harper and Bros., 1880). The publishers, in a recent letter to the writer, say, "The regular edition sold for $2.50, the paper for 25 cents. It appears in our catalogues as late as 1896."

reformers, through a refined limitation on the power of appointment. In more modern terms we can say that Clay, Calhoun, and Webster approached reform through closing the "back door," while the later reformers preferred screening the "front door."

For this purpose we find both Sumner and Jenckes proposing a commission, on the English model, to sift applicants for appointment to the executive branch. Still a relatively novel idea in these days, the proposal failed to stir legislative enthusiasm. However, Jenckes' bills of 1865 and 1867 and his elaborate report of 1868 furnished considerable ammunition for such men as Curtis and Carl Schurz, who made civil service reform an integral part of their program for a new morality in public affairs. Newspapers such as the *Chicago Tribune,* the *Boston Post,* and the *New York Evening Post* all commented at some length—and generally favorably—on the proposals of Jenckes. The *Nation* and the *North American Review* joined the chorus. From this time on, the press and periodical literature on civil service reform increased noticeably.[9]

Darkness Before the Dawn

Hardly had Sumner and Jenckes introduced their civil service proposals when the President and Congress became engaged in the most bitter internecine warfare ever waged under our separation-of-powers Constitution. Much has been written of the famous conflict between President Johnson and the Radical Republicans and there is no need to repeat the entire story here. However, it is important to note that the main vehicle through which the contending forces waged their quarrel was the federal public service.

Underneath the quarrel lay, of course, the antagonistic reconstruction policies of the President and the Radical Republicans who controlled Congress. To further his own ends President Johnson had not hesitated to exploit his appointing power to influence the congressional elections of 1866. The Radicals, fearing the formation of a presidential political machine, determined to curb the chief executive's power over the offices through the famous Tenure of Office Act

---

9 For one list of press and periodical articles concerning the Jenckes proposals see "Appendix F" of the report of the Joint Select Committee on Retrenchment as cited in footnote 6, pp. 90–110. Here a large number of the better-known newspapers and periodicals are quoted in considerable detail.

For another gauge of public concern see appropriate headings in *Poole's Index.* The number of items listed under "civil service reform" noticeably increased in the late eighteen sixties. Also indicative of the trend in public opinion is the following remark concerning the Jenckes bill, taken from the contemporary periodical press. A. G. Sedgwick concluded in an article on "Objections to the Civil Service Reform," *Nation,* VIII (April 29, 1869), 329, that "Almost all the prominent journals of the country have declared themselves in its favor."

of 1867, passed over the President's veto on March 2 of that year. This legislation required Senate approval for the *removal* of any officer first confirmed by that body—including cabinet members. Together with threats of impeachment for disobeying the law, it was their answer to the presidential challenge. Not by any means the first of its type of legislative proposal,[10] the Tenure of Office Act was a traditional though somewhat extreme attempt to wrest control of the patronage from the executive branch and give it to Congress. The Radicals were merely following in the footsteps of Clay, Calhoun, and Webster. When Johnson defied Congress by summarily removing Secretary of War Edwin M. Stanton, a Radical supporter, the House quickly voted impeachment and the conflict was on.

Once again the failure of the Constitution clearly to allocate the removal and appointing powers led to violent political altercations. Not by any means was the "decision of 1789" considered the final word on the matter in the eighteen sixties. The whole constitutional question of the executive power of the President in relation to the power of Congress was re-opened. The failure of the impeachment trial in the Senate by one vote upheld the "decision of 1789," but by the most tenuous of threads. For the time being, Johnson was ruined on the national political scene, though, ironically, he later became the first and only ex-president to return to the Senate. The end effect of the Radicals' attempt to submerge the Presidency was to give Congress for many years a political supremacy which it had not possessed since the days of Madison and Monroe. The Tenure of Office Act was, for example, not repealed until 1887. The custom of Senatorial Courtesy[11] became even more firmly entrenched, and the exploitation of the spoils of office, including the public service, became more and more blatant.

A Flash of Light

While the triumph of the legislative branch over the executive appeared to bode ill for the federal service, the unsavory wrestling between Congress and the President over the patronage gave the civil

---

[10] For legislation of a similar nature in the early eighteen sixties see A. Bower Sageser, *The First Two Decades of the Pendleton Act* (Lincoln: University of Nebraska, 1935), p. 13–14.

[11] In its consultative sense, this custom might well be titled "Congressional Courtesy," since from at least 1840 it has been customary to consult members of the House of Representatives of the party in power, rather than Senators, concerning the appointment of postmasters in their districts. This custom still continues, despite the use of what Harris, with considerable justification, calls "pseudo-civil-service examination" in the selection of postmasters. Joseph P. Harris, *The Advice and Consent of the Senate* (Berkeley and Los Angeles: University of California Press, 1953), pp. 342–43.

service reformers much fuel for active and effective propaganda. Moreover, the threatened defection of the more progressive wing of the Republican party and the rehabilitation of the Democratic party forced the Republicans carefully to consider their position in the election of 1868.

The Act of 1871. Civil service reform, while no major issue at this time, was championed by persons as prominent as Carl Schurz and George William Curtis, both influential in Republican circles; and the more liberal elements of the party were finding the doctrine attractive. The general issue of reform aroused enough attention in the debates and literature of the day that Grant declared for civil service reform shortly before his first inauguration. He followed this up, surprisingly, with a formal request for civil service legislation in his second message to Congress in December, 1870.

Congress then made motions toward a consideration of the subject. Several proposals, one by Senator Carl Schurz, were drafted and referred to the proper committees. None of them, however, seemed destined to come anywhere near an actual vote until Senator Lyman Trumbull of Illinois, in desperation, succeeded on the last day of the short session of 1870–71 in attaching a reform proposal as a rider to the sundry civil appropriation bill. Even then the measure was passed with difficulty, and more credit must probably be given to the fact that the Republicans had suffered the usual mid-term reverses in 1870 and were seeking to bolster their position than to the fact that Grant had given the measure his blessing. In this undistinguished and not entirely legitimate fashion, the first modern civil service legislation in American history came into being.

What did the new law provide? At first glance it seems innocuous enough—certainly nothing revolutionary. The rider of March 3, 1871, is all of one sentence in length and, in its entirety, reads:

Sec. 9. That the President of the United States be, and he is hereby, authorized to prescribe such rules and regulations for the admission of persons into the civil service of the United States as will best promote the efficiency thereof, and ascertain the fitness of each candidate in respect to age, health, character, knowledge, and ability for the branch of service into which he seeks to enter; and for this purpose the President is authorized to employ suitable persons to conduct said inquiries, to prescribe their duties, and to establish regulations for the conduct of persons who may receive appointments in the civil service.[12]

[12] 16 U.S. Statutes 514 (1871); see also Section 1753, Revised Statutes.

Clearly under the act of 1871 it was not mandatory that the President accomplish anything. Had it been otherwise, the act would probably not have passed. Undoubtedly many of the Republican leaders assumed that President Grant would let the matter die. But to the surprise of almost everyone the President appointed a commission of seven persons, later known as the Civil Service Commission, and gave them directions to draw up suitable rules and regulations for initiating a real reform. Moreover, Grant selected George William Curtis, the leading reformer of the day, to be the chairman of the group and gave him considerable support for more than two years.[13]

Part of Grant's surprising personal interest in civil service reform stemmed from the fact that he, too, was feeling the pressure of patronage. However, as the President soon found himself at odds with the more liberal wing of his party and more dependent upon the patronage minded conservatives, he did not pursue the matter far. When Congress finally balked at renewing the small appropriation which had been granted the Commission, the President let the whole matter drop. In any event, it is interesting to note that the first executive leadership for reform came under the guidance of the President most associated with its debauchery.

The role of the Grant Commission. Though the operations of the first Civil Service Commission slowed to a kind of suspended animation some three years after its initial formation, it deserves to be considered as something more than just a historical curiosity. As Lionel Murphy, the principal student of the activities of this agency, has clearly shown, the experience of this first attempt at reform of the public service helped prepare the ground for much that was later accomplished on a far firmer basis under the authority of the Pendleton Act of 1883.

By April, 1872, Curtis and the other commissioners, three of whom were also full-time federal employees, succeeded in drawing up a group of civil service rules acceptable to the President. These rules were comprehensive and detailed. Patterned roughly after the British experience, they laid down procedures and devised terminology in use to this day. One must look to the law of 1871 and to the Commission which first interpreted it, rather than to the Pendleton Act of 1883, for the precedents for much that is today considered fundamental to modern governmental personnel administration. Far more credit is due Curtis and his fellow-commissioners than they have usually been given. As Murphy says:

[13] For the only thorough study of the Act of 1871 and the Civil Service Commission resulting from it, see Murphy, as cited in footnote 7.

Much of the terminology and many of the concepts employed in the proceedings, reports, and other recorded activities of the Commission still prevail. Among these are: "Civil Service Commission rules," "application," "test," "grade," "eligible," "ineligible," "register," "military preference," "position," "vacancy," "apportionment," "probation," "promotion," "classification," "superannuation," "political assessments," "pernicious political activity," "boards of examiners," "ratings of 70 per cent," "three highest eligibles," "policy-deciding officials," "certificate," and many others.

Most significant of all is the fact that the principle of competitive examination was adopted in a form the nature of which was very closely analogous to the British application and administration. Also of considerable significance is the fact that the examinations developed and used from 1872 to 1875 served as a basis for those used in 1883.

The first Civil Service Commission attempted to solve other personnel problems which were not recognized in the Act of 1883, such as position-classification, efficiency ratings, and superannuation. It undertook to administer competitive promotions, to determine positions for inclusion in, or exclusion from, the competitive system based upon their duties and responsibilities, and to decide such other exemptions from the operations of the rules as were deemed practicable or necessary.

Thus a small group of men, without a popular following but skillful in speech and phrase in behalf of a new political morality, forced a trial in administrative reform upon a hostile Congress and an unenthusiastic President. Although the Civil Service Commission through which these advocates put their views into operation was itself short-lived, its legacy was the design for subsequent civil service machinery. Its procedures for civil service administration were not fabricated from a pattern of revolt, but were drawn up after a study of British civil service practices and a consideration of the experiences in administration of the government-members of the Commission.

In their efforts these civil service reformers sought to place the responsibility for administration upon the President and the heads of departments. In the evolution of administrative management their work becomes most significant as marking the beginning of the President's rise to the actual leadership of administration in the federal government.[14]

Thus, while the rider of 1871 was exceedingly brief and general, and was not then pressed far in terms of implementation, it gave the President powers over the personnel of the executive branch which he had never possessed unchallenged before. *This early legislation is still in force* and is yet considered a primary source of presidential authority in federal personnel management.

The creation of the Grant Commission was a landmark in two other respects. For the first time the federal government was provided with a central personnel agency. More important, however, this was the first major attempt to provide the President with the advice and assistance which is considered so necessary under modern theories of line

14 Same, pp. 322–23.

and staff relationships.[15] Murphy is quite right when he dates modern governmental administrative reform in the United States from the civil service rider of 1871. That the reform was proposed and supported at this time largely for other reasons makes it no less significant.

The demise of the Grant Commission. Nevertheless, when considered for its immediate practical impact on the federal service, the Grant Civil Service Commission was at best modestly effective. Under the new civil service rules, the Commission slowly introduced competitive examinations into the Washington departments, the New York custom house, and the New York post office. The latter two agencies had been perennial centers of gross fraud and corruption. As might have been expected, the new regulations and the new agency did not meet with the approval of the spoilsmen in Grant's administration; and Grant, characteristically, could not resist the appeals of his political friends. At the appointment of a prominent spoilsman as surveyor of customs for the port of New York, Curtis resigned from the Commission and Dorman B. Eaton took his place. Finally, in 1873, Congress failed to renew the Commission's modest appropriation, which had never exceeded $25,000. Grant then announced that if Congress again failed to provide funds for the Commission, he would abandon the system. Such an equivocal stand only encouraged the Commission's opponents, and no funds were forthcoming in 1874. While the President did not formally abolish the Commission itself in 1875, he revoked the rules and closed down the examining boards in Washington and in the field. Eaton and the other commissioners were left with their rider and a questionable title to office, but with no salaries, no duties, no funds.

The Fight Continues

Meanwhile, the relationship of the little group of active civil service reformers to the Grant administration had become, after the brief and tentative truce from 1871 to 1873, something less than cordial. Even as early as June 15, 1871, the well-known journalist-reformer, E. L. Godkin, who had recently transferred his allegiance from England to the United States, flayed the reform efforts of the Grant administration from his vantage point of the *Nation* and concluded:

---

[15] The President's "official household," in the White House had been formalized to some extent by legislation in 1857. This permitted a private secretary, a steward, a messenger, and a small contingency allowance of $750—a far cry from the present White House establishment. Leonard D. White, *The Jacksonians* (New York: The Macmillan Co., 1954), p. 83.

EXCERPTS FROM A COMPETITIVE EXAMINATION

Given by the Grant Civil Service Commission in the U.S. Circa 1873 for Federal Government Clerkships in Washington, D.C.

LETTER AND BRIEF

Upon completing each paper, the candidate should note on it the exact time he has been engaged upon it, and sign it. Upon completing the first five papers he should return them to the examiner.

Write a letter, of about one page . . . to the head of the Department in which you seek an appointment, giving the date and place of your birth . . . a statement of your education and of your occupations to the present time, especially such as, in your opinion, have tended to fit you for a clerkship under Government . . . . indorse upon it a summary or brief of its contents.

This exercise is designed to show your skill in simple English composition.

ARITHMETIC

Notation and numeration. Write in figures the following numbers: Nineteen thousand and seventeen . . . decimal one million, one hundred and three thousand and six ten millionths.

Write at length the numbers expressed by the following figures: 98,705,001 . . . 1,000,000.000001.

Addition. Add the following columns of figures and write the footings underneath the proper columns: (Here follow two long columns of nine to ten-digit numbers.)

Common and decimal fractions. Give the operation at length in each case: (Problems of addition, subtraction, multiplication, division and conversion of common and decimal fractions follow.)

Miscellaneous examples. (Give the operations at length in each case.) A government officer collected $24,728, on which he was entitled to a commission of ⅜ of one per cent. What was the amount of the commission?

An army fought two battles. In the first it lost 16 per cent of the original number, and in the second 12½ per cent of the remaining number, after which it mustered 36,750 men. What was its original strength? (Four other examples follow.)

BOOK-KEEPING

What are the principal points of difference between double-entry and single-entry book-keeping? Name the principal books required in book-keeping. Give the journal entry on the books of James Smith of the following transaction: October 9, 1873, James Smith bought of Thomas Brown merchandise to the amount of $2,350, of which he paid $1,000 in cash, the remainder being charged to him on Brown's books.

ACCOUNTS

John Thompson, postmaster . . . on the 1st of July, 1873, owed the United States $98.54; July 9, 1873, he received from the Post-Office Department stamps of the value of $893, with which he was charged; July 16 he collected for the Department a draft for $890 on the postmaster at Brownsville; August 3 he paid a contractor the amount due him for a quarter's services, less a fine of $28.75 for neglect of duty, on a route the compensation of which was $900 per annum; August 7 he paid a draft drawn on him by the Department for $489.53 . . . (Other transactions follow.) State his account with the United States in the form below.

ORTHOGRAPHY

Copy *all* of the following words, and correct the spelling of such of them as are incorrectly spelled: Separate, privelege, eligible, offerred, preferred, receit, neccessary, trafficking . . .

SYNTAX

Copy *all* of the following sentences, and correct such as contain errors in syntax: Him who the money was received by should be held accountable. The difference between him and I is not great. Neither the President or Secretary were present. Which of the two courses is preferable? He done his work very well. (Seven sentences and a draft letter follow.)

HISTORY, GEOGRAPHY, AND GOVERNMENT

History. When, by whom, and for what causes was the Declaration of Independence adopted? Name the thirteen original States. Name at least six of the principal battles of the Revolutionary War. Name the Presidents who were elected for two terms of office. At about what dates were steamboats, railroads, and telegraphs first used in the United States?

Geography. Name the States which border on the Atlantic Ocean and those which border on the Pacific. Name the States by or through which the Mississippi River flows. Name the three principal mountain ranges and the five largest rivers of the United States. What is the difference between latitude and longitude? Give the proper definition of a peninsula and of a cape, and an example of each in the United States.

Government. What do you mean by the Constitution of the United States? How can it be amended? What is the difference between the method of selecting Senators of the United States and the method of selecting United States judges, and how do the tenures of these two classes of offices differ? By whom are laws made in this country, and which is of the higher authority, a law or a constitution? What is meant by trial by jury? What instrument defines the powers of Congress, and what instrument the powers of a State legislature?

"The political world, while approving of civil-service reform in the abstract, already begins to express strong doubts whether 'this particular measure' is just what is needed, or can do any good." [16] On the other side of the ledger there was considerable praise for Curtis' administration of the Civil Service Commission. Even the opposition expressed occasional grudging approval. One editorialist, writing in support of the reform, noted that old General Benjamin Butler, a violent partisan, could not seem to conceive of honest service in such a responsible place as Curtis' position, and asked to see a copy of the examinations. It is reported that he was finally satisfied that all was legitimate.[17]

Reform as a major political issue. In the early seventies, civil service reform for the first time rose to the status of a real political issue. Behind this development was a continuing concern for administrative retrenchment after the Civil War as well as a beginning understanding of the administrative requirements of the modern state. But much more important at this time was the reaction in many quarters to the endemic political scandal characterizing the Grant administration. These were the days when Jim Fisk and Jay Gould, profiting from their association with the President, almost cornered the nation's gold supply. The Crédit Mobilier scandal brought to light the placing of shares of Union Pacific stock in the hands of government officials in order to influence legislation, and resulted in the discrediting of Vice-President Schuyler Colfax. In the "Salary Grab" of 1873 Congress voted itself a 50 per cent increase in pay, retroactive to December, 1871. A little later Secretary of the Treasury W. A. Richardson resigned after it was discovered that he had permitted the payment of exorbitant commissions to friends of prominent politicians for collecting overdue internal revenue taxes. While it was well known that the Governor of the District of Columbia had been involved in contract frauds, Grant rewarded him with another high-level appointment in the District. The American Minister to Brazil defrauded that country of $100,000 and fled, while the Minister to England lent his name to a mine swindle. The new Secretary of the Treasury B. H. Bristow then uncovered the existence of a "Whiskey Ring" which had, with the connivance of Grant's private secretary and a number of Treasury officials, defrauded the government of millions in taxes on distilled whiskey. The series of scandals culminated in March, 1876, with the hasty resignation of Secretary of War W. W. Belknap, who was proved to have sold Indian post-

16 "Chapter in the History of Civil Service," *Nation*, XII (June 15, 1871), 412–13.
17 "A Promising Reform," *Scribner's Monthly*, VI (May, 1873), 97.

traderships. Though Grant accepted his resignation "with great regret," the House instituted impeachment proceedings which were only thwarted by a technical ruling that the Senate had no jurisdiction over a man out of office. When one considers that corruption was just as rife in state and local government—these were also the days of the notorious Tweed Ring in New York City—it is no wonder that many were exercised over the state of the nation. Never had public morals fallen so low.

As part of their answer to the corruption of the times, the Liberal Republicans picked up civil service reform as an issue in the campaign of 1872. Through their platform of May of that year, this group became the first political party to commit themselves in writing to the idea of governmental reform through a modern merit system. Significantly, the regular Republicans adopted a similar plank a little later in the same year. Four years later both Republicans and Democrats officially advocated the new reform. At this time Curtis himself helped write the Republican plank; and the Republican candidate, Rutherford B. Hayes, who called reform a "paramount necessity," became the momentary idol of the reformers. The Democrats were less enthusiastic and called for reform in more general terms.

Tentative steps forward under Hayes. After the Hayes election imbroglio, there was considerable doubt as to the good intentions of the leaders of the Republican party of 1876. Nevertheless, because of the new President's previous stand on civil service reform, there was still some hope that he might be able to force some improvements in the executive establishment. Certainly the general public at the time of the election was more receptive than ever before to some kind of reform action. As John Jay somewhat over-optimistically concluded not long after Hayes' election, "Every honest and patriotic citizen is ready to cry 'God speed!' to the President in his efforts to restore the purity of the national service." [18]

For a time the Hayes administration came up to the reformers' expectations. In June, 1877, the President issued an executive order stating that federal officers should be neither required nor permitted to take part in active politics and that a mild law of 1876, the first against political assessments, would be enforced.[19] In Hayes' first annual message he advocated security of tenure and more impersonal appointment procedures. His selection of Carl Schurz as Secretary of the Interior pleased many people besides the reformers, and Schurz

---

[18] "Civil Service Reform," *North American Review*, CXXVII (September, 1878), 287.

[19] While this statute contained penalties for infractions, it forbade only officers not confirmed by the Senate to give or to receive assessments as among each other. It had been passed during the campaign more as a sop to reform than anything else.

quickly set up and enforced a model merit system in his department. Hayes then set out to perform the Herculean task of reforming the New York custom house by a frontal attack. Following the report of a special commission appointed by the President to investigate that government agency, General Chester A. Arthur, the incumbent Collector of Customs, was finally removed in 1878 after he had refused to resign. The course of these and other Hayes' reform maneuvers seems to have provoked Senator Roscoe Conkling, Arthur's political sponsor and a spoilsman of note, to a bitter indictment of George William Curtis at the New York State Republican Convention of 1877.[20]

Despite stiff opposition from within the Republican party, Hayes persisted in his efforts to reform the custom house; and in 1880 he turned his hand to the New York post office. There he strongly supported Postmaster Thomas L. James in applying the examination system devised by the now-defunct Civil Service Commission of 1871. In addition, the President commissioned Dorman B. Eaton to study and report on the English civil service system. Eaton's report was printed in 1880 and met with a good response. All in all, Hayes' outspoken attitude certainly aided the progress of the reform.

It is a little too much, however, to consider the Hayes administration a *reform* administration, in the sense that any great or lasting penetration of the spoils system was made. The politicians, and some segments of the public, had yet to be convinced. While Hayes removed the federal troops from the South, fought Conkling to a standstill over the New York patronage, and supported Schurz and James, he nevertheless failed to carry through with his early pronouncements against political activity and assessments. Moreover, his appointment policies, considered as a whole, were distinctly uneven from the point of view of the reformers. Except for Schurz, no member of Hayes' cabinet made even a pretense of civil service reform. Still more disturbing was the scandalous generosity with which the President rewarded each member of the special commission who had helped him gain the Presidency in the disputed election of 1876.

While both the reformers and the politicians seem to have been disgruntled over the efforts of the Hayes administration in the field of civil service reform, not all was lost by any means. The well-known social scientist, William Graham Sumner, summed up the situation accurately in an issue of the *Princeton Review* for 1881 when he wrote, "It is said Mr. Hayes has done very little. In fact, when we consider the nature and difficulty of the task, he has done a great

---

[20] See Alfred R. Conkling. *Life and Letters of Roscoe Conkling* (New York: Charles L. Webster and Co., 1889), p. 541.

From *Puck*, April 13, 1881.

This is not the New York Stock Exchange, it is the patronage exchange, called U.S. Senate

deal." [21] The lag was not so much with the people as with the leaders of both political parties, who had yet to be shown that public opinion was such that they could no longer safely oppose the reform.

Organized Reform

Outside governmental and party circles the general agitation for reform continued to grow, despite the death of its two earliest champions, Charles Sumner in 1874 and Thomas A. Jenckes in 1875. More important, the movement began to organize. The New York Civil Service Reform Association was formed in May, 1877, and by 1880 claimed 583 members in thirty-three states and territories. The National Civil Service Reform League was organized in August, 1881, with George William Curtis as president.[22] While the membership of these organizations was not large, their propaganda effort was considerable for its day. For example, from the time of their formation both societies fostered the publication of numerous monographs and pamphlets for popular distribution. Available in quantity lots at low prices, they were useful propaganda devices. In the years 1880, 1881, and 1882 the New York group alone circulated more than half a million papers, pamphlets, and documents on reform. Articles were written, essay contests held, addresses made, and petitions sent to Congress. The magazine of the Massachusetts affiliate, the *Civil Service Record,* reported on the month by month progress of the reform.

Personalities. The reformers themselves were, in many ways, an impressive group. Movements for reform usually first find their expression in a few articulate individuals with a tenacious singleness of purpose. Through them an issue becomes verbalized and either accepted or rejected by those to whom it is presented—depending upon the skill with which the presentation is made and upon the predispositions of the public involved. Civil service reform has been no exception, and to understand the success of the movement one must first understand these early reformers of the late eighteen seventies.

The leading advocates of civil service reform after the Civil War nearly all came from the northeastern portion of the United States. The early membership of the National Civil Service Reform League and its affiliated societies was heavily eastern and its headquarters was, and still is, in New York City. If the spoils system symbolized

---

21 "Presidential Elections and Civil Service Reform," VII, n. s. (January, 1881), 143.

22 For the history of the National Civil Service Reform League see Frank M. Stewart, *The National Civil Service Reform League* (Austin: University of Texas Press, 1929). The association is now known as the National Civil Service League and is still quite active, with its headquarters in New York City.

the power of the West, civil service reform in its earlier stages was strictly an eastern device.

The central figure from 1865 to 1890 was that stately gentleman and orator, George William Curtis. A New Englander of Puritan stock, he early turned his energies to literary work, becoming political editor of *Harper's Weekly* in 1863. An anti-slavery partisan, he soon associated himself with the Republican party and was long influential in its organization. Though he never held elective office, he was on at least one occasion a potential candidate for the Presidency. After the Civil War he became greatly interested in the promotion of civil service reform, being named by President Grant to head the Civil Service Commission of 1871–1875. One of the founders of the National Civil Service Reform League, he was president of both it and the New York Civil Service Reform Association until his death in 1892. All told, his varied civic activities were staggering. An accomplished speaker, he was much sought after for all kinds of civic, educational, and commemorative occasions. Toward the end of his career he served for several years as Chancellor of New York University.

Of the other outstanding leaders, one more achieved nation-wide prominence—Carl Schurz, whose extraordinary career included emigration from Germany, followed by service as American Minister to Spain at age 32, Civil War General, United States Senator from Missouri, Secretary of the Interior under President Hayes, editor of the *New York Evening Post,* and for nearly a decade president, following Curtis, of the National Civil Service Reform League. Somewhat less widely known was the prominent New York lawyer and expert in municipal affairs, Dorman B. Eaton. Eaton followed Curtis as chairman of the Civil Service Commission of 1871–1875 and became the first chairman of the more permanent commission formed as a result of the Pendleton Act of 1883. Thomas Allen Jenckes, whose greatest service to the movement was already behind him at this time, had been, until his death in 1875, continually consulted by the other leading reformers.

Among the secondary group were such men as Moorfield Storey, E. L. Godkin, General Jacob D. Cox, Everett P. Wheeler, John Jay, General William A. Aiken, Horace White, Edward Carey, Sherman S. Rogers, Edward M. Shepard, Frederic Cromwell, Silas W. Burt, Richard Henry Dana and a considerable number of like personalities, all of whom would probably have appeared in a *Who's Who* of their day.[23] Before the turn of the century this early group was comple-

---

[23] Storey was a Boston lawyer of independent means and international reputation; Godkin, an influential political essayist and long-time editor of the *Nation;* Cox, a general in

mented by such outstanding personalities as Charles J. Bonaparte, William D. Foulke, Daniel C. Gilman, Theodore Roosevelt, and Woodrow Wilson.[24]

Beyond these men were the other members of the various civil service reform societies affiliated with the National Civil Service Reform League, as well as those—less well identified or identifiable— who helped by speeches, an article or two, or the simple addition of their voices and votes to further the movement.

But, for the most part, the reform was initiated and carried through by a comparatively few individuals representing the top strata of politics, law, business, journalism, and education. These few used their unusually large personal influence, their avenues of publicity, their writing ability, and their oratory to bear down heavily upon the evils of the spoils system. Thus a small group of predominantly wealthy and politically conscious easterners with a philanthropic turn of mind, aided by an aroused public opinion, laid the basis for the Pendleton Act of 1883.

Why should such men be "reformers," with all the stigma sometimes attached to the word? Civil service reform added nothing to their income and little to their individual or collective prominence. There were many other available "issues." Theirs was no clamor of an impetuous Jacksonian democracy, no rising of the underprivileged. They had long since "arrived." Yet they all chose to spend an inordinate amount of time and energy in attempting a reformation of the American public service. What kind of a point of view did they represent? What did they seek?

Ends and means. These men were above all deeply concerned with

---

the Civil War, governor of Ohio, and Secretary of the Interior under Grant; Wheeler, a prominent New York lawyer, candidate for governor in 1894, and member of a host of civic and social committees; John Jay, a grandson of the Chief Justice of the same name, New York lawyer of means, one-time president of the American Historical Association, and Minister to Austria from 1869 to 1874; Aiken, president of the Norwich, Conn., Nickel and Brass Co.; White, for many years associate editor and editor of the *New York Evening Post*; Carey, well-known *New York Times* editorial writer for forty-six years; Rogers, wealthy New York lawyer prominent in Republican circles, but also a personal friend of Grover Cleveland; Shepard, long a power in New York Democratic politics and counsel for the Pennsylvania Railroad; Cromwell, treasurer of the Mutual Life Insurance Co. and director of several other enterprises; Burt, a civil engineer, first civil service examiner in the U.S., and member of the New York Civil Service Commission for several years; and Dana, a proper Bostonian who helped draft the Massachusetts civil service law of 1884, author of the first Australian ballot law passed in the U.S. in 1888, and later president of the National Civil Service Reform League. For others, many of whom were of equal stature, see Stewart, as cited in footnote 22.

24 Bonaparte was a grandson of a brother of the French Emperor, a well-known Baltimore lawyer, and Secretary of the Navy and Attorney General under Theodore Roosevelt; Foulke, a prominent Indiana lawyer, historian, and author, and later a member of the U.S. Civil Service Commission; and Gilman, a distinguished president of The Johns Hopkins University. The others need no mention.

the maintenance of liberty.[25] Though they possessed a type of social consciousness, they held strongly to that individualistic orientation which characterized the political and economic elite of their day. They were certainly not interested in ameliorating life through any form of welfare state. Rather, they fought in the eighteen seventies and eighties, as they had fought in the fifties and sixties, to free the individual from disastrous and demoralizing restraints. Lionel Murphy concludes in his study of the early Grant Commission that "these reformers regarded this demand [for civil service reform] as a second emancipation." [26]

Most of the reformers, and the great bulk of their adherents, had sided with the abolitionists in the slavery controversy. Their abiding devotion to freedom, absorbed for years in lifting the Negro from his position of degradation, was easily transferred to an attack upon the kind of gross corruption which, under the Grant administration, for example, seemed to be debauching the nation. To them, the emergence of the spoils system represented only the insidious development of another kind of slavery, this time of the body politic instead of the Negro. The spoilsman, often characterized by the reformers as representing a new aristocracy of plunder and patronage, replaced the slaveowner as the jinni of evil. Neither, they said, had any moral right to his superior position or to his ill-gotten gains. The proper attack on both was an appeal for elemental justice in the name of an ultimate freedom.

Their discussions, their publications, and their public pronouncements literally "preached" this doctrine. Even the sophisticated Curtis, perhaps the most popular after-dinner speaker of his day, saw fit to turn the first report of the abortive Civil Service Commission of 1871 into a sermon. Indeed, it is a report, as Murphy says, "unique among those that have been made to a president." [27] Prepared largely by Curtis, this fifty-page document begins soberly enough, but after a few pages of introduction quickly develops a distinctly Old Testament eschatological flavor, declaring, "The moral tone of the country is debased. The national character deteriorates." As if this and forty more pages like it were not enough, the report resoundingly con-

25 This is the fundamental thesis of Ruth M. Berens in her excellent comparative study of the civil service reform views of George William Curtis, Dorman B. Eaton, and Carl Schurz, the early leaders of the movement. See her "Blueprint for Reform: Curtis, Eaton and Schurz" (unpublished Master's thesis, Department of Political Science, University of Chicago, 1943). All the additional available evidence, especially that provided by Stewart, as cited in footnote 22, and Murphy, as cited in footnote 7, supports Miss Berens' general interpretation of the motives of the first generation of reformers, which is also the interpretation presented here.
26 As cited in footnote 7, p. 319.
27 Same, p. 226.

cludes: "The improvement of the Civil Service is emphatically the people's cause, the people's reform, and the administration which vigorously begins it will acquire a glory only less than that of the salvation of a free Union." [28]

The 1874 and last official report of the same Commission, this time penned principally by Eaton, successor to Curtis as head of the agency, again introduced the new reform with a peroration on the immorality of the system of spoils and plunder. Though somewhat less preachy than Curtis' effort, the document contains page after page of moralistic analysis and is typical both of the approach and literary form of the great bulk of the reformers' appeals. Following an introduction, there appears a listing of "The Evils to be Remedied," the first of which is described in these terms:

1. There had been developed, mainly within a single generation, and was existing with fearful powers of expansion and reproduction an aggressive and unscrupulous spirit of mercenary partisanship, which, promoting and dominating the pursuit of politics as a trade, and seeking public office and party and caucus leadership principally for the spoils of money and patronage they could command, was degrading all party action in popular estimation and impairing alike official integrity, political honor, and private morality. This spirit developed and animated all over the country large numbers of little and great partisan combinations, faithful to no party principles, inspired by no patriotic sentiments, conducting no useful debates, contributing nothing to public intelligence or public virtue, but meddlesome and insatiable, everywhere, whenever any official selection was to be made, or any official authority was to be exercised.

The report then continues in much the same vein, punctuated frequently by such phrases as "The chief object of such bad men . . . the mass of honest, intelligent citizens . . . a few able bad men . . . have defied the mass of the people." [29] One can hardly imagine an official governmental agency's report of today couched in such terms. But nearly all the early civil service reform literature was composed in this moral phraseology. Curtis and Eaton, Carl Schurz and the rest wished, above all, to purify politics. They wished to apply private, middle-class morality, as they understood it, to public affairs.

28 A reprint of the report is found in Charles E. Norton (ed.), *Orations and Addresses of George William Curtis* (3 vols.; New York: Harper and Bros., 1894), II, 29–80. The quotations are from pp. 37 and 80, respectively. Curtis is considered the author of the document, though all seven members of the Commission undoubtedly contributed in one way or another to the final product. Certainly they all signed and approved it. Among the seven was Joseph Medill, then editor of the *Chicago Tribune* and soon to be Mayor of Chicago, one of the few westerners interested in civil service reform at this early stage.
29 U.S. Civil Service Commission, *Report of the Civil Service Commission to the President*, 43d Cong., 1st Sess., Senate Exec. Doc. 43, April 15, 1874 (Washington: Government Printing Office, 1874). This is a ninety-one page report, supplemented by an appendix of nearly equal size. These and the above quotations are all from page 10.

The paramount reform. The civil service reformers' position stands out in even greater relief when one realizes that for more than thirty years they held the introduction of the merit system to be the most essential governmental reform. Despite their frequent association with other movements with reform overtones, involving such diverse ends as child welfare and the Australian ballot, civil service reform was to them always the paramount reform. As early as 1872 Carl Schurz wrote to a friend:

I have long considered the reform of the civil service, the destruction of the corrupting and demoralizing influence of the patronage, the elevation of the moral tone of our political life, as one of the most important problems, second, perhaps to none among those we have to solve for the success and perpetuation of our republican institutions.[30]

In 1879 George William Curtis stated, "There is no political reform which would tend so much to the relief of so many evils as a rigorous diminution of the patronage." [31] In 1880 Dorman B. Eaton concluded his study of the civil service of Great Britain with the observation that "To secure the best men for officers and leaders is, next to the creation of government itself, the most difficult problem of statesmanship—the greatest achievement which political wisdom can make." [32] Charles J. Bonaparte declared before the annual meeting of the National Civil Service Reform League in 1890, "It is the function of Civil Service Reform to provide for all other reforms, whether legislative or administrative, in our polity, the necessary plant for their work." At the same meeting Lucius B. Swift titled his address, "All Other Reforms Should Be Subordinated To Civil-Service Reform." [33] As late as 1897, Charles Stuart Smith, a well-known New York business man, philanthropist, and municipal leader, wrote to Carl Schurz, "Civil service is the keynote and the one remedy for all our political ills, and you are now the high-priest of this religion." [34] These are only a few of the many similar expressions of faith.

Strange as these fervent conclusions may seem today, *in a way the reformers were right!* The economic reforms considered so essential by others would not have been possible except for civil service reform. A relatively stable and effective civil service is indispensable for the

---

30 Quoted in Berens, as cited in footnote 25, p. 209.
31 Same, p. 33.
32 Eaton, as cited in footnote 8, p. 419.
33 National Civil Service Reform League, *Proceedings at the Annual Meeting, 1890* (New York: The League, 1890), pp. 45 and 52. The Reform League will hereafter be cited as "NCSRL" and its annual proceedings as *"Proceedings."*
34 Frederick Bancroft (ed.), *Speeches, Correspondence and Political Papers of Carl Schurz* (New York: G. P. Putnam's Sons, 1913), V, 411.

functioning of the modern state. The civil service reformers diagnosed better than they knew or than others have usually given them credit. They did put first things first. But in so far as they thought that the moral regeneration which they associated with the merit system was *alone* sufficient to remedy most of the evils they saw—this was essentially the position of Curtis, for example—they were politically and economically naive.

Typifying the moralistic approach of nineteenth century Protestantism to the remedy of social evil, the attitudes and actions of the civil service reformers possessed all the defects of that approach. Substantive economic and social matters were seldom mentioned by the reformers. Abhorring socialism and disavowing Henry George (it is questionable if they really understood either point of view), they had no interest in any redistribution of economic goods through governmental intervention. They were deeply disturbed about *people,* not things. Wealth, to them, was the proper product of individual endeavor, and, as such, was not a subject for legislative disposal. Economically, they represented the Gilded Age in which they as a group had been able to function with such signal success.

The "political man." Basic to their reform was the assumption of the existence of a sort of "political man" with a sense of obligation toward his fellow men, especially the unfortunate and downtrodden. His constant foe was the politically "bad man" of the spoils system, who perverted the body politic by his "evil" ways. *The "economic man" of the classical economists at last had his political counterpart!* As Ruth M. Berens has concluded in her penetrating analysis of Curtis, Eaton and Schurz, this political man of the civil service reformers

. . . was a good citizen, loving liberty but preferring the public welfare to his private well-being. He put policy above party, and where virtue was at stake, maintained his independence. The economic man who was to become the future civil servant held the government service in great esteem, and was anxious to take upon himself the mantle of public stewardship. He prepared himself carefully for the examination and strove to the utmost in the competition. Once appointed, he was attentive to duty and anxious to secure promotion. He loved his country, desired security, and was content with a modest salary, since merit brought advancement. The political and economic man, who moves like a beneficent robot through the pages of reform literature, is not held up as an ideal—a procedure which would neither have taxed the credulity of the reader nor biased the assumptions of the reformers —but with a surprising superficiality assumed as a foundation upon which to base reform.[35]

The civil service reformers urged that, once the political man had

[35] As cited in footnote 25, p. 271.

arrived at his official post in the public service, he be free to prove his merit. Should he not prove competent, he was then to be removable at pleasure. The modern idea of the "closed back door" for civil service appointees held little attraction for these men. With the political man ensconced in office during good behavior, a new political morality would be generated which would be the salvation of the country.

Economy and efficiency as motives for reform. But what of economy and efficiency as well springs of civil service reform? In an analysis of the British reform movement of 1850 to 1870, H. R. G. Greaves concluded that the English reformers were only partially attacking privilege. "More important was their aim of achieving economy and efficiency. They represented a tempering of the romantic ideas of 1789, of justice and equality, by the rational utilitarianism of the middle classes." [36] In searching for the reason for the success of civil service reform in the United States, Carl Russell Fish has likewise concluded—though more tentatively—that the mainspring of reform lay in its attempt to apply the rapidly improving business methods to government.[37] Whatever the correctness of this type of analysis for British experience, it is not a full and satisfactory explanation of our American experience.

It is quite clear that only secondarily—and not a very close second at that—were the reformers interested in efficiency and economy, the dollars and cents value of the merit system. They mentioned these things, but they almost invariably referred to the "greater" moral issues. Eaton, especially, understood the problems of what we today would call "good administration," meaning efficient administration. But even to this able New York lawyer, accustomed to corporate endeavor, efficiency in administration was but a corollary to his major purpose: the achievement of a new morality in public affairs.

Schurz, Curtis, Godkin of the *Nation,* and the lesser lights as well, all took essentially the same position. The pages of the *Proceedings* of the National Civil Service Reform League, the pamphlets published by the same organization, and its monthly publication, *Good Government,* were littered for years far more with ethical and moral arguments than with appeals to any sense of "economy and efficiency." These watchwords of the era of President Taft were still around the corner.[38]

---

[36] *The Civil Service in the Changing State* (London: George G. Harrap and Co., Ltd., 1947), p. 13.

[37] *The Civil Service and the Patronage* (New York: Longmans, Green and Co., 1905), p. 245.

[38] After an extensive analysis of the efficiency and economy views of George William Curtis, Ruth Berens notes, "Now with all due respect to Professor Fish, the weight of

Nor was this moral approach tongue-in-cheek propaganda, put out solely for effect. To be sure, it may be called propaganda; but it unquestionably represented the real beliefs and considered thoughts of those who put it forth. Though the reformers may be accused of failing to analyze through to fundamentals, they cannot be accused of insincerity despite their wealthy and upper level background. Any suspicion of hypocrisy was dissipated by the fact that leaders of the type of Schurz and Curtis had always been well known as champions of freedom, justice, and the underprivileged. It was men such as these who presented civil service reform, expressed in heavily moral terms, as their solution to the problems of the day as they saw them.

The Climate of Opinion

For propaganda to be effective it must be tuned to its audience. Against the backdrop of the reputed materialism and acquisitive economics of the Gilded Age, we may well ask whether the reformers knew their body politic. On the whole, they did. This does not mean, however, that their task was easy.

Fundamental concepts. Whatever their ways of making a living, most Americans still spoke, and frequently thought and acted, in highly moralistic terms. After all, this was also the Victorian Age and the heyday of the McGuffey readers. With religion and religious symbolism so important in American, especially nineteenth century American, life and action, it is no wonder that civil service reformers couched their appeals in such moral terms. Not only did the reformers believe in their own propaganda and design it to their own tastes, but they also spoke the language of the bulk of the citizenry of their day. The reformers were also fortunate in that a wrapping of morality was more becoming to the merit system than to most competing nostrums. After all, "merit" is, by definition, "good." Nevertheless, other reforms often assumed a similar Victorian garb. The reformers

the evidence to be found in the work of Curtis suggests that at least one of the leading reformers of 1883 agreed with his colleagues of 1836 [Clay, Calhoun, and Webster] in placing primary emphasis upon the purification of politics." As cited in footnote 25, p. 113. For similar conclusions respecting Eaton and Schurz and the reformers as a whole, see same, pp. 199–200, 254, and 260–73. With Berens' view, this writer concurs on additional grounds. Several years ago the writer became interested in attempting a "symbol-analysis" of civil service reform literature to see if it might be feasible to differentiate in any quantitative way between symbols of "efficiency" and symbols of "morality" in the literature put out by the National Civil Service Reform League, the center of the movement. Such symbols proved fairly easy to identify, and an analysis of a considerable sample of articles and speeches contained in the *Proceedings* of the League over the ten-year period from 1882 to 1892 revealed a more than two to one ratio in favor of symbols of "morality." The writer is also convinced, after perusing two dozen or so volumes of entrepreneurial history, that the business methods of the Gilded Age were not nearly as advanced as Fish implies. The business man of 1880 may have understood accounting but his personnel practices were nothing to excite emulation.

had no monopoly on morality, and as late as 1896 William Jennings Bryan, while arguing for bimetallism, would electrify the nation with his "crown of thorns" and "cross of gold."

With liberty, too, the reformers were on solid ground. Liberty had been a guiding concept for American democracy from the very beginning. The Civil War had been fought in its name. From the standpoint of the historic doctrines of natural rights the reformers' analysis was comprehensible. But it would take considerable selling to convince the voting public and the politicians that the spoils system, which had also been sold in the name of libertarian reform, was in fact now a repressive institution.

Most important for the reform, however, was its individualistic base. The society of the Gilded Age believed in such fundamentally individualistic doctrines as laissez faire economics, Protestantism, and political liberty. The civil service reformers' version of the application of business methods to government, their assumption of the need for and the possibility of a political man—a morally upright economic man in political office—to rescue other economic men in a time of distress sounded quite logical to their contemporaries. This was a political individualism to match an economic individualism, a proposal completely in tune with the times. That such a proposal was abstract was a hindrance in reaching those who thought concretely, but it had the advantage of being difficult to refute because of its vagueness.

While the reformers on the whole sought morality much more than efficiency, the trends of the day were in their favor with respect to both. The modern rationalization of business methods had started, particularly in the fields of accounting and cost control which lay at the basis of profit. The costs of government were being increasingly scrutinized after the Civil War, and Jenckes' report on the civil service in the late sixties was in part aimed at retrenchment. In so far as civil service reform could be sold as economy, it would meet a rising tide of acceptance. It would, however, need to face the persuasive, though usually implicit, argument of the spoilsmen that businessmen had more to gain than to lose from the tacit alliance of politics and economics in the period after the Civil War.

In several other respects the reform movement was at greater disadvantage. The foreign, and especially the British, origin of the concept of modern civil service reform was an asset only in as much as it demonstrated its practical feasibility. Nor was the system of examinations well understood or appreciated. While this method for the selection of personnel was well known in the military and academic worlds, it was certainly anything but accepted in any formal way in the economic and political worlds. The remaining supports of the merit system, political neutrality and tenure in office, were even more suspect. The former had never been an object of reverence in this country, and the latter had received a positive repudiation fifty years before. Even if they had not been naturally so inclined, the reformers did well to sell their proposal more in terms of morality than anything else.

Timing. By 1880, the voting public was recovering from its post-Civil War acquisitive orgy and beginning to reassess its position. Workaday Christianity was becoming a bit fearful for its own salvation. Some "economic men" were even prepared to trumpet their distress. The smell of reform was in the air, and by 1880 both major and several minor parties were testing the atmosphere. But, when the time came—and this, too, was uncertain—on whom would the accolade fall? While there was a distinct predisposition for change throughout the nation, civil service reform was by no means the only reform being pressed upon public attention in either moral or other garb. Moreover, the active opposition to civil service reform included most segments of the formidable political and economic mechanism of the day.

Certainly the party professionals had to be convinced. While there was already considerable popular sympathy for civil service reform, the groundswell of public opinion was not yet strong enough to force these partisan leaders to accept a proposal which so greatly threatened their immediate interests. It would take more than pamphlets and oratory to make a substantial and permanent dent in the encrustation of fifty years. Even the shocking array of scandals during the Grant administration had failed to unseat the party in power. Moreover, civil service reform was then, and is frequently yet, tedious and lacking in drama, especially when compared to the economic and political glamor of the acquisitive doctrine of spoils. By 1880 civil service reform still possessed no slogan even remotely to compare with Marcy's ringing phrase, "To the victor belong the spoils!" As the Beards have noted, "Agitation over the spoils system went on, making ripples here and there on the smooth surface of orthodox custom without alarming the politicians." [39]

"An Office or Your Life!"

By the end of the Hayes administration it would probably have seemed to anyone cursorily surveying the situation that the spoils

39 Charles A. and Mary R. Beard, *The Rise of American Civilization* (rev. ed.; New York: The Macmillan Co., 1936), II, 551.

system was about as firmly entrenched as ever. Congress had tried civil service reform under Grant and politicians of the legislative branch showed little disposition to renew the experiment. After Hayes, the reformers were quick to support James A. Garfield, who espoused their cause. But with Garfield's sudden and violent death causing the Presidency to fall into the hands of Chester A. Arthur, the deposed spoilsman Collector of the port of New York, reform hopes plummeted. Civil service reform might again have received the treatment which befell the earlier efforts of Sumner, Jenckes, and Schurz had there not occurred a series of dramatic incidents which impressed upon both the public and the politicians the realities of the spoils system.

By far the most dramatic was the assassination of President Garfield in 1881. Garfield's assassin, Guiteau, was found to be a disappointed office-seeker. This was blared throughout the nation by literally thousands of headlines and editorials, and the reformers were quick to seize and enlarge upon the fact for their purposes. Shortly after the President's death, Dorman B. Eaton typically declared:

. . . With marvelous promptness and unanimity, hardly less in foreign countries than among ourselves, the source and significance of Guiteau's acts have been found in our spoils system of administration. . . . From a thousand pulpits the great fact, with solemn admonitions, has been proclaimed. On the myriad pages of our journals, of every section and class, the truth has been daily uttered in words of mingled anxiety, shame, and detestation.[40]

Orlando Potter, a member of the New York Reform Association's executive committee, immediately gave two thousand dollars for the wide distribution of literature on President Garfield's favorable views toward reform. A striking and popular cartoon in *Puck* pictured Guiteau pointing a pistol and demanding, "An office or your life!"[41]

All this stirred the popular mind and the reform cause leaped forward. The spoils system could at long last be equated with an evil which was easily understood by the voting population. Spoils equalled murder. Both the morality and the logic were elemental and compelling. They were even more powerful when coupled with the disturbing memories of other events. The Crédit Mobilier, the Whiskey Ring, the threatened impeachment of Secretary of War Belknap for malfeasance in office, and the manipulations in the New

---

40 "Assassination and the Spoils System," *Princeton Review*, VIII, n.s. (September, 1881), 148. For extensive excerpts from the current press, see the special edition of *Harper's Weekly* for July 8, 1881, XXV, 478–79.

41 From the color lithograph cartoon by "W.A.T.," titled "A Model Office-Seeker," in *Puck*, IX (July 13, 1881), 317. Also of great influence were the frequent cartoons on the subject of spoils by Thomas Nast in *Harper's Weekly* throughout the eighties.

York custom house were all quickly recalled. The denunciations uttered by the reform prophets took on a reality they had never quite assumed before. Early in 1882, Andrew D. White, the well-known first president of Cornell University, observed:

. . . The people seem to be thinking effectively. The circumstances of the death of the late President have stirred men's minds deeply in all parts of the country. . . . Newspapers which were formerly luke-warm are now recognizing, on the one hand, the necessity of a change, and on the other, the pressure of public opinion.[42]

While this weight of public opinion was being demonstrated, certain other dramatic events further strengthened the force of the reform movement. One group of incidents concerned the levying of political assessments. Despite Hayes' threat to enforce the law of 1876, which forbade assessments by a limited group of federal officeholders upon each other, the statute had never been taken very seriously. Until 1882 no successful prosecution had ever been made under the terms of this act. However, when game was finally caught, it was no small fry but General Newton M. Curtis, an employee of the Treasury Department as well as treasurer of the Republican State Committee of New York. General Curtis publicly collected considerable sums, and a complaint was brought by the newly organized Civil Service Reform Association of New York. Curtis was convicted and fined $1,000. Upon appeal to the United States Supreme Court, the conviction was upheld with but one member dissenting. The court not only agreed that the law against political assessment was valid, but implied that civil service reform legislation in general was constitutional.[43]

This decision was a double blow to the politicians. General Curtis was prominent in the Republican political hierarchy, and assessments were a prime source of political revenue. Moreover, the case strengthened the hand of the reformers by attaching the stigma of illegality to an important component of the spoils system. On December 20, 1882, the *New York Tribune* stated that "they [the spoilsmen] will do well to regard the decision and the outspoken popular disapproval of the past assessments." Typical of the periodical press was the declaration that the "intelligence of the conviction of Curtis . . . gave great strength to the Reformers in the estimation of the public, a public often too apathetic to read their articles in the magazines

---

[42] "Do the Spoils Belong to the Victor?" *North American Review*, CXXXIV (February, 1882), 131.
[43] *Ex parte Curtis*, 106 U.S. 371 (1882).

90

A MODEL OFFICE-SEEKER

"I am a Lawyer, A Theologian and a Politician!"
Charles J. Guiteau.

and papers." [44] The effective decline in political assessments may be directly related to this court decision concerning the law of 1876, the forerunner of the Hatch Act of Franklin Roosevelt's administration sixty years later.

A second controversy over assessments arose when a complaint was also made against Representative J. A. Hubbell of Michigan, chairman of the Republican Congressional Committee. Hubbell maintained that the contributions he had been collecting were voluntary and that the law did not apply. When the issue came to a head, the Attorney General ruled that Hubbell was immune from prosecution because the law of 1876 was not meant to include congressmen. Hubbell publicly continued his previous policy, but amid a storm of controversy and criticism. Even President Arthur found it necessary to make a public statement disapproving assessments, and Hubbell eventually failed of renomination.

The final turning point came with the election of 1882, in which civil service reform developed as the principal issue in many states. A great proportion of the press came to the aid of the movement. For example, the *New York Times, Herald, Evening Post,* and *Tribune* along with *Harper's Weekly* all joined to back the merit system. In 1884 the editorialist E. F. Hall diagnosed that

. . . It was such an engine as this that the Reformers had to help them in the canvass of 1882, and it swept every thing before it. Day after day and week after week it discharged its volleys, "hot and heavy," of solid argument and of telling facts, of scathing invective and of poignant wit, against the abuses and scandals of the spoils system, against the supercilious indifference towards reform of the dominant party in Congress and the deliberate violation of the promises and pledges of conventions and platforms, and against the organized system of robbery and blackmail involved in the levying of political assessments as practiced by Honorable Jay A. Hubbell, "of Bedouin ancestry," chairman and treasurer of the Republican Congressional Executive Committee.[45]

Sageser, in his detailed study of the early years of the Pendleton Act, has concluded:

. . . The material [on civil service reform] written from 1881 to the spring of 1883 is more voluminous than in any ten-year period in the history of the movement. The year of 1882 was even more prolific because of the fall elections and the attempts of the reformers to stop political assessments.[46]

44 E. F. Hall, "Civil Service Reform," *New Englander,* XLIII (July, 1884), 461.

45 As cited in footnote 44, p. 461. See Allan Nevins, as cited in footnote 3, p. 451, for the attitude of the *Evening Post.*

46 Sageser, as cited in footnote 10, p. 45. This is also borne out by the writer's analysis of the entries under "civil service reform" in *Poole's Index* for various years.

From *Puck*, July 13, 1881.

THE AMERICAN MAELSTROM

Our Manifest Destiny Unless there is Real Reform in the Civil Service

Meanwhile, Senator George H. Pendleton, a distinguished Ohio Democrat and former vice-presidential candidate, had on December 15, 1880, introduced a new measure to reform the civil service. At first his proposal, based on Jenckes' earlier efforts, received scant attention. Then, in 1881, Dorman B. Eaton went to see Pendleton and proposed that a bill drawn up by the New York Civil Service Reform Association be substituted ᵥfor the Senator's measure. Pendleton agreed and the new measure was placed before the Senate in January, 1881. No action was taken during the session; the politicians had yet to be convinced. It remained for the assassination and the other events described above and below to bring the movement to its legislative climax.

Reform at Last

The mid-term election of 1882 proved one of the worst Republican defeats since the Civil War. Many predicted that the next president might be a Democrat. Republican consternation was great, because a Democratic administration was expected to have no mercy for Republican office-holders. "The effect" of the election reverses, said George William Curtis before the Civil Service Reform League in August, 1883, "was amazing." [47] The *New York Tribune* remarked that "now it is delightful to see the zeal of these new converts preaching the blessed truth that those who are in ought not to be put out." [48]

The Senate debated Pendleton's bill, brought up before it again in December, 1882, and made a number of changes, which, if anything, improved the bill. "The House," as Curtis noted, "which was so eager to make the bill a law that it would not tolerate debate and loudly cheered the proposal of an immediate vote, was the same house that five months before had derisively and angrily refused to give a paltry sum and to aid a single experiment of reform." [49] Shortly thereafter the President signed the well-known Pendleton Act, which became law on January 16, 1883.[50]

Thus, within less than three years of Hayes' departure from the White House, a new statute, creating a new Civil Service Commission on a far firmer basis, was passed by overwhelming legislative majorities. Civil service reform had profited as never before from the political tragedies of the spoils system. As a later observer cynically put it in 1888, "The devil was sick, and the devil a monk would be." [51]

---

47 Hall, as cited in footnote 44, p. 462.
48 December 14, 1882.
49 Hall, as cited in footnote 44, p. 462.
50 22 U.S. Statutes 403 (1883).
51 Frederick Powers, "The Reform of the Federal Service," *Political Science Quarterly*, III (June, 1888), 259.

SUPPLEMENTARY NOTES

For the most complete study of the development of civil service reform between the Civil War and the Pendleton Act, see Ari Arthur Hoogenboom, "Outlawing the Spoils: A History of the Civil Service Reform Movement: 1865–1883" (unpublished Ph.D. dissertation, Department of History, Columbia University, 1958). From this period on, the National Civil Service Reform League played a major role in the movement for civil service reform. Frank M. Stewart, *The National Civil Service Reform League*, as cited in footnote 22, covers the history of the League until March, 1928. The political theories of the early leaders of the League are, however, most completely laid bare in Ruth M. Berens' excellent "Blueprint for Reform: Curtis, Eaton and Schurz," as cited in footnote 25. The various writings of William D. Foulke, especially his *Fighting the Spoilsmen* (New York: G. P. Putnam's Sons, 1919), are both vivid and helpful for the activities of the second generation of reformers. The League's own records for the period from 1880 to 1941 are now located in the Cornell University Library's Collection of Regional History, along with those of the New York Civil Service Reform Association for the same period. These records have been of considerable assistance to the writer and will hereafter be cited as "NCSRL Papers," with further notations referring to "boxes" and "files." For a useful catalog of many of the League publications, see Stewart, as cited in footnote 22, pp. 278–85.

The Grant administration has been generally ignored as a source of administrative innovation. The biographers of Grant pay no attention to his connection with civil service reform, nor does Grant himself in his autobiography. There is need for an adequate treatment of Grant as an administrator. However, we are much indebted to Lionel V. Murphy for his definitive study of "The First Federal Civil Service Commission: 1871–1875," as cited in footnote 7; this is administrative history at its very best. That Murphy was (he still is) a practicing public personnel administrator when he wrote these articles is a notable fact in itself, for American civil servants have produced few of the provocative analyses of American administrative institutions so characteristic of the relatively prolific writings by British civil servants over decades.

CHAPTER 5

Americanizing a Foreign Invention:
The Pendleton Act of 1883

There seems to be a general impression both at home and abroad that the civil service in the United States has, as Americans sometimes put it, "just growed" without much conscious direction. To a limited extent this is true. Certainly civil service reform was not adopted as fully in as short a period of time as was the case in Great Britain.

However, a fairly complete and firm legislative foundation for the development of a civil service based on examinations and merit in the English manner has existed in the United States since the passage of the Pendleton Act of 1883.[1] It is important, therefore, that we consider this fundamental piece of legislation in some detail, not only because it was the first legislation of its kind in this country, but also because it today enjoys the unusual distinction of remaining on the statute books without fundamental change since its passage three-quarters of a century ago. Essentially a modification of a British political invention in terms of the constitutional and administrative inclinations of this country, the Pendleton Act becomes even more intriguing as a case study in cross-cultural adaptation, a topic of increasing interest and concern in the modern political world.

What kind of law, then, was this new civil service reform act of 1883, passed so precipitately by a Republican Congress hitherto apathetic at best toward governmental reform of any sort?

---

[1] We may even push this back to 1871, in terms of precedent though not of effective action, if we consider the short-lived Grant Commission.

96

The Legislative Debate

The legislative debate which preceded the passage of the Pendleton Act was limited almost exclusively to the Senate. When the bill came before the House nearly all attempts to discuss it were literally shouted down, and it was overwhelmingly approved. The most likely explanation for the difference in legislative attitude lies in the fact that the members of the House knew they would be affected by the next election far more than the members of the Senate. The House was taking no chances. Reform was too important an issue at this time.

Fortunately for any analysis of congressional intent, the Senate debate was detailed and exhaustive.[2] Nearly all the major problems involved in the legislation were discussed at length. A sizable number of amendments—with only a few deliberately obstructionist—were considered and many adopted. The likely effects of the proposed legislation upon the constitutional position of the President and Congress, upon the party system, upon the civil service, and upon the public in general were thoroughly explored. Political assessments, the corruption of the previous twenty years, and the history of the reform before 1883 both in the United States and Great Britain were presented in detail. All in all the debate fills nearly 200 pages in the *Congressional Record*. That the argument frequently revolved around a strictly partisan quarrel over responsibility for the system which was to be reformed is quite true. But the major portion of the debate, occupying by far the greater part of the Senate's time for two weeks, was to the point.

This debate, plus the reports of two Senate committees, together with a consideration of the implications of certain events of the preceding twenty years or so, make possible a fairly clear analysis of the thinking involved in the new legislation.[3] An analysis of the

[2] Carl Fish describes the debate as "entirely unworthy of the occasion, hardly touching any of the serious considerations involved." *The Civil Service and the Patronage* (New York: Longmans, Green and Co., 1905), p. 218. The writer does not accept this judgment for the reasons indicated in the text.

[3] For the debate see the *Congressional Record*, which records almost daily discussion in the Senate from December 12, 1882, through December 27, 1882, the date of the passage of the bill by the Senate. For the only important hearings on the legislation see U.S. Congress, Senate, *The Regulation and Improvement of the Civil Service*, 46th Cong., 3d Sess., Senate Report 872, 1881 (Washington: Government Printing Office, 1881); and U.S. Congress, Senate, *Report of the Committee on Civil Service and Retrenchment*, 47th Cong., 1st Sess., Senate Report 576, 1882 (Washington: Government Printing Office, 1882). In the House there were no committee reports of even minor importance. The House approved the bill on January 4, 1883, and President Arthur signed it on January 16. For a more detailed chronology, see USCSC, *Civil Service Act: Legislative History*, a currently updated copy of which is maintained in the Commission's library. For another type of analysis of the Act of 1883, done more in terms of a chronological consideration of amendments and counter-amendments, see A. Bower Sageser's important study of *The First Two Decades of the Pendleton Act* (Lincoln: University of Nebraska, 1935), ch. ii.

voting shows that the later claims of both parties for credit for passage of the act are not entirely justified.[4] The Democrats by no means fully supported Senator Pendleton. If anything, the law must be considered primarily a Republican measure, spurred somewhat by the assassination of Garfield. However, this event has been overrated as an immediate cause of the enactment of the Pendleton Act. After all, Garfield had been shot a year and a half before its passage. More important as a motivating force for Republican action in late 1883 were the Republican reverses in the election of 1882. The Republicans were apprehensive about the 1884 election, while the Democrats were hopeful. Nevertheless, the sponsor of the new law was a prominent Democrat and the legislation profited from the careful attention of representatives of both parties.

Fundamentals of the Act

The Pendleton bill as reported to the Senate provided, basically, for the adoption of the British civil service system in the United States. A commission was to administer competitive examinations; entrance into the public service would be possible only at the bottom; a full-scale career service was implied; and the offices were not to be used for political purposes. Throughout the Senate debate, reference was constantly made to European experience, and especially that of the British. However, the act as finally approved followed the British reform pattern only in a very general way.

In America, as in England, the central concept was that of *competitive examinations* for entrance into the public service. The Senate Committee on Civil Service and Retrenchment, in reporting the Pendleton measure, said:

The single, simple, fundamental, pivotal idea of the whole bill is, that whenever, hereafter, a new appointment or a promotion shall be made in the subordinate civil service in the departments or larger offices, such appointment or promotion shall be given to the man who is best fitted to discharge the duties of the position, and that such fitness shall be ascertained by open, fair, honest, impartial, competitive examination.[5]

---

[4] As tabulated by Sageser, as cited in footnote 3, pp. 57 and 59, the final votes in the two houses were as follows: In the Senate the bill was passed by 38 to 5, with 33 absent. The affirmative vote included 23 Republicans, 14 Democrats and 1 Independent; the negative vote, 5 Democrats; and those absent, 14 Republicans, 18 Democrats, and 1 Readjuster (Independent). In the House the bill was approved by a vote of 155 to 47, with 87 not voting. The affirmative vote was cast by 102 Republicans, 49 Democrats, and 4 Nationals (Independents); the negative vote, by 7 Republicans, 39 Democrats, and 1 National, with those not voting, 39 Republicans, 41 Democrats, and 7 Nationals. In its partial crisscross of party lines, the vote was fairly typical of our national legislative practice.

[5] U.S. Congress, Senate Report 576, as cited in footnote 3, pp. IX–X.

Though the old idea of pass-examinations was occasionally referred to in the Senate committee reports and the debate to follow, Congress showed no inclination to challenge the fundamental idea of entrance into the public service via a really serious competition.

Congress also accepted the idea of relative *security of tenure* for employees entering the service through the examination system. The whole idea of entrance by examination meant, in itself, a considerable guarantee of tenure, because it tended to eliminate the incentive for removals. Beyond this, under the new law appointing officers could not discharge classified employees [6] for refusal to be politically active. To be sure, this prohibition was not reenforced by any criminal penalty and its execution was entirely up to the pleasure of the executive branch of the government. There was little the Civil Service Commission could do by itself about political removals, other than investigate and publicize the facts. But as long as Congress favored the elimination of politics from the competitive service, President Arthur's support was assured.[7]

The final concept for which any debt is owed to the British is that of the *neutrality* of the civil service. Congress forbade any employees covered by the new act "to coerce the political action of any person," and the new Commission was directed to prepare rules to implement this prohibition as well as that directed against political removals of competitive employees. Further, the Senate amended the act to provide substantial penalties for political assessments of or by competitive employees, or by any other federal officials.[8] However, only in the case of assessments was any criminal penalty attached to the provisions designed to insure neutrality. Again, the constitutional authority as well as the inclination of the chief executive was to be relied upon. It would take a President Cleveland and a President Theodore Roosevelt to turn this possibility of developing a nonpartisan civil service into something approaching reality. In effect, the Pendleton Act *demanded* nonpartisanship in initial selection procedures (for

[6] The term "classified service" has always been interpreted to cover positions where political removal is forbidden. Until about 1895 the terms "classified service," "classified employees," "competitive employees," "positions under the merit system," and "permanent service," while not exactly synonymous, were reasonably interchangeable; and they have been so used through this chapter and the next two to follow. However, after this date, the term "classified service" became sufficiently ambiguous, for reasons explained in the supplementary notes to ch. viii, that it has been used with much more care in the chapters covering the period from McKinley's administration to the present.

[7] See President Arthur's messages to Congress on December 6, 1881, and December 4, 1882. Moreover, everyone understood that the trouble was with the legislative rather than the executive branch. The former, not the latter, had forced the dissolution of the competitive system as first established under President Grant.

[8] The inclusion of other federal officials was designed to preclude a repetition of the Hubbell case, mentioned in the previous chapter. The law of 1876 against assessments was substantially reinforced.

a limited number of positions) but only *encouraged* nonpartisanship in other matters.

We can conclude, then, that the American legislation of 1883 stimulated the development in the United States of a *merit system* founded on British precedents: that is, a system of civil service recruitment and organization based on (1) competitive examinations, (2) relative security of tenure, and (3) political neutrality. On the other hand, the new act also reflected peculiarly American patterns of thought and action. If we appropriated the main outlines of the foreign device, we were anything but abject copyists. We thoroughly adapted it to the American political and social climate.

As early as December 6, 1881, President Arthur had referred to the Pendleton bill, even then before the Senate, in his first message to Congress and had noted its "conformity with the existing civil-service system of Great Britain." But he had also noted with prophetic insight that "there are certain features of the English system which have not generally been received with favor in this country, even among the foremost advocates of civil-service reform." [9] The problem was to reconcile British ideas with American experience and inclination.

The Power to Hire

First of all, the American conception of a proper competitive examination for public office differed radically from that of the British. Even the relatively down-to-earth examinations used by the Grant Commission had been criticized as too theoretical. Therefore, the Senate, by an amendment to the original legislation, instructed the new commission to make its tests "practical in character" and related to the duties that would be performed. The Senate and the public were averse to the academic essay-type of civil service testing then—and frequently still—current in Great Britain. Ever since 1883 testing development in this country has consistently reflected this basic American idea of the desirability of the "practical."

Many senators were especially incensed over the proposal of the Pendleton bill to permit entrance into the public service *only* "at the lowest grade." Finally, Senator Pendleton himself proposed an amendment to strike out the offending provision. It was overwhelmingly accepted without even the formality of a roll call. Another

9 James D. Richardson (ed.), *Messages and Papers of the Presidents* (New York: Bureau of National Literature and Art, 1905), VIII, 60.

amendment opened up promotional examinations to more general competition than had been originally envisioned. We had no desire to develop an entirely ingrown civil establishment.

While the British civil service was normally closed to outsiders except at the bottom, the American federal service was to continue to be infiltrated by new talents at all levels. From 1883 to this day, one may enter the American public service at almost any level and at almost any age. Indeed, the adoption of age and other restrictions tending to prevent this mobility have been on many occasions, and often still are, bitterly attacked as "undemocratic."

Throughout the entire history of the public service the federal offices have never been permitted to form any kind of closed bureaucratic system on the European pattern. Such a mobile system, approaching the mobility of private employment, is unique among modern national public services. Its foundation was firmly embedded in the legislation of 1883. It has been responsible for the continuance of the representative type of bureaucracy which the Jacksonian Democrats had first declared to be a fundamental requisite of the democratic state.

In details of recruitment procedure the act also paid its respects to the Jacksonian theories of democracy in public office, and especially to the idea of rotation in office. No more than two members of the same family were declared to be eligible for public office. The majority of the clerical offices in the city of Washington were to be filled according to an "apportionment" of offices among the states, based upon population. Later in 1883, this last provision was interpreted to mean "as nearly as may be practicable." Its inclusion in the act undoubtedly secured much political support for the reform which otherwise might have been withheld. The authors of the legislation of 1883 and their political supporters, knowingly or unknowingly, were taking as few chances as possible that the American civil service might not be representative of the nation as a whole, in terms of geography, mobility, ideals, and outlook.

The Power to Fire

Americans also refused to accept the almost absolute security of tenure that has often been guaranteed to European civil servants, and which reflects the veneration by Europeans of the mechanism of the state. Both the original civil service reformers and many subsequent American legislators have consistently fought against an overly absolute tenure as undesirable and unnecessary for civil service re-

101

form. Life tenure in office had been repudiated in 1829 and there was no desire to revive the idea in 1883. Besides, the removal power was a potent political tool which could not be lightly discarded.

Since 1829, the principal American controversy about tenure had been over whether the power to remove should be left primarily in the hands of the President or in the hands of Congress. That the removal power of the President was left largely untouched was the outstanding difference between pre-Civil War attempts at reform and the Act of 1883. Under the new legislation there was no bar to opening the so-called "back-door" to the classified service, as long as removals were not for partisan reasons. Undoubtedly the failure of the principal effort to limit the executive removal power, the attempted impeachment of President Johnson, helped force political minds to think in other terms. Senator George F. Hoar, a Massachusetts Republican, represented a fairly typical opinion when, during the course of the Senate debate on the Pendleton Act, he said:

> The measure commends itself to me also because. . . . It does not assert any disputed legislative control over the tenure of office. The great debate as to the President's power of removal, . . . which began in the first Congress, . . . does not in the least become important under the skillful and admirable provisions of this bill.
>
> It does not even . . . deal directly with the question of removals, but it takes away every possible temptation to improper removals.[10]

Nonetheless, a portion of the credit for this innovation must be given to the reformers, who consistently emphasized that, if the *front-door* were properly tended, the *back-door* would take care of itself. The supervision of the one would remove the incentive for the abuse of the other. George William Curtis, for instance, felt in 1876 that any system of "removal by lawsuit" would completely demoralize the service:

> Having annulled all reason for the improper exercise of the power of dismissal, we hold that it is better to take the risk of occasional injustice from passion and prejudice, which no law or regulation can control, than to seal up incompetency, negligence, insubordination, insolence, and every other mischief in the service, by requiring a virtual trial at law before an unfit or incapable clerk can be removed.[11]

---

10 *Congressional Record*, 47th Cong., 2nd Sess., 1882, XIV, Part I, 274.

11 As quoted in Ruth M. Berens, "Blueprint for Reform: Curtis, Eaton, and Schurz" (unpublished Master's thesis, Department of Political Science, University of Chicago, 1943), p. 50. As we have become more security minded with respect to employment, both public and private, recent legislation and custom have tended to close the back door; but, compared to European practice, it is still ajar.

Senator Pendleton accepted the reformers' view of the proper way to regulate dismissals, and it was not successfully challenged in the debates that followed. The Act of 1883 left the President in control of his own household as far as the power to fire was concerned. Once more the "decision of 1789" was reaffirmed.

Administrative Details

From an administrative point of view, the act was based firmly upon the experience gained from the ill-fated Grant Commission of 1871–75. In fact, the new law provided that the President should have all the powers of the 1871 legislation not inconsistent with the Pendleton Act. Similarly, the simple clerical classification acts of the eighteen fifties and an already existing military preference statute of a mild, exhortatory character were specifically integrated into the bill. Senator Pendleton, in answering the first question put to him after concluding his initial speech in favor of the bill, replied:

. . . this system is not entirely new, but . . . to a very large extent in certain offices in New York, in Philadelphia, and in Boston it has been put into practical operation under the heads of the offices there, and . . . they have devised, with the assistance of the commission originally appointed by General Grant, but largely upon their own motion, a system which I suppose would, to some extent, be followed under this bill.[12]

The careful statement of a careful legislator, his remarks indicate where indebtedness was due.

The agent of the executive branch in the establishment of the new personnel system was to be a bipartisan Civil Service Commission of three full-time members appointed for indefinite terms by the President with the advice and consent of the Senate.[13] The administration of the system was to be directed by a chief examiner.[14] He was to

---

[12] *Congressional Record*, 47th Cong., 2nd Sess., 1882, XIV, Part I, 207. The New York, Philadelphia, and Boston references were to experimental postal and custom house competitive examination systems established in these cities under the authority of the rider of 1871 and continued, with some success, until they were incorporated in the larger program fostered by the Pendleton Act.

[13] In 1883 it was anticipated that the commissioners would serve perhaps indefinitely. However, within a decade or so it became customary for the commissioners to offer their resignations on the occasion of a change in administration. To provide more continuity, Congress directed in 1956 that the commissioners serve for six-year, staggered terms. They may be reappointed. Most commissioners have served for less than six years, and this new legislation could in fact provide more continuity than that of 1883. However, the 1956 law did not place any barrier in the way of removal by the President other than that suggested by the six-year term; and the resignation custom may, of course, still continue.

[14] In the nineteen thirties the "Chief Examiner" was retitled "Executive Director and Chief Examiner," and in the late nineteen forties "Executive Director." Under Reorganization Plan No. 5 of 1949, effective in August of that year, the administrative direction

coordinate the work of the local examination boards, composed of government employees in local areas. The members of these local boards remained attached to their departments and were only to be loaned to the Commission for examination purposes. Just a very few permanent employees were expected to work full-time for the Commission itself. As the work became more and more complex and less a part-time operation, the dependence upon other departments for "details" of working personnel, full-time as well as part-time, caused the Commission many headaches. Full-time details ended in the nineteen twenties, but the "local board system" still remains very much alive today. However, it now supplements the activity of a greatly expanded body of full-time Commission employees numbering more than 4,000 since 1950.

The new agency was required to keep the necessary records, conduct investigations, and make reports to Congress through the President. As soon as possible, it was to publish its rules implementing the act, subject of course to the approval of the President. For housekeeping purposes the Secretary of the Interior was designated to provide quarters and essential supplies for the new organization. He had, however, no other jurisdiction over the Commission. This arrangement was not entirely satisfactory and was completely terminated by 1925.

Turning to minor details, the act provided for a probationary period of six months. Applicants were forbidden to present recommendations from senators and representatives which referred to matters other than character and residence. Drunkards were made ineligible for governmental positions. Appointments were to be made from "among those graded highest." This latter phrase was then used for constitutional rather than administrative reasons as a result of an important opinion of the Attorney General, discussed in detail shortly. In effect, this provided that the regulations must offer some discretion for the appointing officer. That the "rule of three" (a rule of "four" was adopted from 1883 to 1888), followed still today, was originally based upon constitutional necessity, rather than upon administrative desirability or upon any occult power of the word "three," is often forgotten. The act also provided that any commissioner or other public employee who might be found guilty of any collusion or corruption in the administration of the examinations should be open to punishment by a fine of up to $1,000 or imprisonment up to a year or both.

---

of the work of the Commission was placed officially under the authority of the Chairman (formerly known as the "President") of the Commission. There is, however, still an Executive Director who is in fact the day-by-day chief administrative officer.

Constitutional Questions

In yet another important respect the Pendleton Act reflected the peculiarities of the American Constitution .as well as those of the political tendencies of the times. The new legislation, for the most part, was *permissive* rather than mandatory. The act itself placed only slightly over 10 per cent of the positions in the federal public service—mainly clerical positions in Washington and in post offices and custom houses employing fifty or more persons—under the merit system to form the *classified civil service*. The remainder of the civil service was left *unclassified,* to be brought under the new regulations by Executive Order when and if the President saw fit. The only public officials exempted from the authority of the President under the act were laborers and those whose appointments were subject to the advice and consent of the Senate. These exemptions accounted for roughly 20 to 30 per cent of the federal civil service, which in the eighteen eighties averaged over 140,000.

The permissive nature of the act—a relatively unusual characteristic in American legislation—stemmed from two somewhat different but temporarily compatible sets of circumstances. It was both politically and administratively impossible in 1883 to apply the merit system to the entire federal civil service. Administratively, the Civil Service Commission simply was not ready to do a complete job as yet. It takes time to develop examinations, to organize boards to administer the examinations, and to obtain the cooperation of the departmental agencies and the general public.[15] Permissiveness also had its political advantages. The politicians were able to announce that they had accomplished the desired reform—the rest being up to the President— knowing full well that they would not be hurt through a too sudden or drastic curtailing of their patronage. If the act permitted an orderly retreat of parties from their prerogatives of plunder, it made possible as well the gradual administrative development of the merit system.[16] Had the merit system been forced to wait for precise formulation and expansion by successive Congresses, no one knows what the

---

[15] In testifying before the Senate Select Committee to Examine the various Branches of the Civil Service on January 13, 1881, concerning the Pendleton proposal, Dorman B. Eaton said, "Another observation I want to make is, that I think no law should be passed which would require the application of this system of examinations to the whole civil service of the government at once, or even to all that part to which it is legitimately applicable, as I have defined it. It would be too large altogether. . . . We have got to create the machinery. . . . In bringing new men together and entering for the first time upon a new system, you would be utterly overslaughed and broken down if you were to be required to carry it all on at once." U.S. Congress, Senate Report 872, as cited in footnote 3, pp. 19–20.

[16] In his study of civil service law, Oliver P. Field regards this permissiveness as a defect in the federal personnel legislation. *Civil Service Law* (Minneapolis: University of Minnesota Press, 1939), p. 4.

result might have been. Under the law of 1883, the President was free to move as fast or as slowly as political circumstances might permit, under the broad, general rules laid down by Congress. The permissive feature was thus a recognition of practical political as well as administrative realities.

It probably was also necessary from a constitutional point of view. From the very beginning of the civil service reform movement, a large number of congressmen and politicians questioned the constitutionality of the new political device. Lionel Murphy, in his history of the first Civil Service Commission appointed by President Grant, has described how the new plan for centralized control of public personnel administration in the hands of a commission was attacked as an unconstitutional invasion of the powers both of Congress and of the President over personnel matters. The members of this Commission felt they had to defer any plans for a merit system until they first received an opinion by Attorney General Akerman on the constitutionality of the proposed arrangement.[17]

Akerman's opinion, however, did not fully resolve the conflict. One cannot join what is deliberately put asunder. He insisted that it was not constitutional for Congress by law to give to the Commission power which the Constitution places in the President, the department heads, and the courts of law. Congress "has no power to vest appointments elsewhere, directly or indirectly." However, in support of the Commission, Akerman went about as far as he could go. He concluded that "the test of a competitive examination may be resorted to in order to inform the conscience of the appointing power, but cannot be made legally conclusive upon that power against its own judgment and will." And further:

> . . . Though the appointing power alone can designate an individual for an office, either Congress, by direct legislation, or the President, by authority derived from Congress, can prescribe qualifications, and require that the designation shall be made out of a class of persons ascertained by proper tests to have those qualifications.[18]

The ultimate constitutional dilemma involved in the regulation of the powers of appointment and removal within the American framework of government is well put in the unusually forthright conclusion to Akerman's opinion:

---

[17] 13 Op. Att. Gen. 516 (31 Aug. 1871). This was well before the Curtis case of 1882, discussed in the previous chapter, in which the Supreme Court implied the constitutionality of civil service reform.

[18] For this and the quotations above, see same, pp. 521 and 524.

The act under which the present civil-service commission has been organized gives the President authority "to prescribe such rules and regulations for the admission of persons into the civil service of the United States as will best promote the efficiency thereof," and this very ample authority will certainly embrace the right to require that the persons admitted into the service shall have been found qualified by competent examiners.

It has been argued that a right in Congress to limit in the least the field of selection, implies a right to carry on the contracting process to the designation of a particular individual. But I do not think this a fair conclusion. Congress could require that officers shall be of American citizenship of a certain age, that judges should be of the legal profession and of a certain standing in the profession, and still leave room to the appointing power for the exercise of its own judgment and will; and I am not prepared to affirm that to go further, and require that the selection shall be made from persons found by an examining board to be qualified in such particulars as diligence, scholarship, integrity, good manners, and attachment to the Government, would impose an unconstitutional limitation on the appointing power. It would still have a reasonable scope for its own judgment and will. But it may be asked, at what point must the contracting process stop? I confess my inability to answer. But the difficulty of drawing a line between such limitations as are, and such as are not, allowed by the Constitution, is no proof that both classes do not exist. In constitutional and legal inquiries, right or wrong is often a question of degree. Yet it is impossible to tell precisely where in the scale right ceases and wrong begins. Questions of excessive bail, cruel punishments, excessive damages, and reasonable doubts are familiar instances. In the matter now in question, it is not supposable that Congress or the President would require of candidates for office qualifications unattainable by a sufficient number to afford ample room for choice.

Very respectfully, your obedient servant,

A. T. AKERMAN [19]

There was little else that Akerman could say under our existing constitutional arrangement, and the principles of his opinion still govern today. No wonder Oliver Field, nearly seventy years later, considered the legal basis of our federal merit system to be somewhat uncertain and concluded that in the states, all of which also operate under the separation-of-powers doctrine, as well as in the federal government:

The theory upon which civil service laws have been upheld as constitutional, in so far as they affect the appointing power itself, is that the officer to whom the appointing power is given retains that discretion which it was intended he should exercise in making appointments, but that as an aid to his exercise of the power, another body may be given the power to determine the qualifications necessary for the position under consideration.[20]

After Akerman's opinion and much discussion of the problem,

[19] Same, pp. 524–25.
[20] As cited in footnote 16, p. 13.

Congress did not feel that it should—it is questionable if it legally could—go too far in making the provisions of the Pendleton Act mandatory upon the President. Indicative of current thinking on the subject was the testimony of George William Curtis before the Senate Committee on Civil Service and Retrenchment on February 26, 1882. Curtis was speaking here of two bills then before the Committee—that of Pendleton and another temporarily proposed by Senator Henry L. Dawes of Massachusetts—and in reply to questions by two senators concerning the effect of the bills upon the relationship of the President to the proposed Commission:

. . . Of course the bills in no sense change the President's constitutional power. The Pendleton bill simply recognizes that the President appoints, and substantially they both provide for the same exercise of power, so far as that is concerned, although the exercise is different in its details. If the President chose to disregard it, he would take no action, and there would be no remedy except in public opinion. *The whole thing presupposes a friendly President.*[21]

During the entire legislative debate and in the two major committee reports there was no attempt to change the presidential relationship described by Curtis.

There were, however, those like Senator Charles H. Van Wyck of Nebraska and Senator Wilkinson Call of Florida, who felt that the Pendleton bill—because it affected the power of the President so little—was unnecessary in light of the legislation of 1871. If the bill only outlined what the President already had authority to do, then why bother? But in 1882 the Senate accepted the proposition that, without congressional approval and encouragement, it was impossible for the executive branch to carry out the reform alone. Moreover, the portions of the bill which provided for criminal sanctions for several types of offenses were clearly beyond the power of the executive branch acting alone.

As a result, this act—and others like it, such as the more recent Ramspeck Act of 1940—for the most part merely authorizes, but does not require, the President to place offices in the classified civil service and under the merit system. This means that the great bulk of the federal employees under the merit system are there by Executive Order. Thus it would probably be legal for the President today to return to the processes of spoils politics a great many of the public offices now under the merit system. All the President needs do to

21 U.S. Congress, Senate Report 576, as cited in footnote 3, p. 178. The italics are added.

accomplish this is to issue another executive order. Actually several presidents have returned positions to the unclassified service, McKinley, for instance, returning several thousand during his first term in office.

To put the whole problem another way: the constitutional realities of a separation of powers made it impossible for the American Congress to make the competitive system mandatory in the way that it had been made mandatory in Great Britain. From a superficial examination it might seem as if both countries had faced a similar problem, one to be solved in a similar fashion. British constitutional opinion, like American, agreed that the executive branch could be advised, but not directed, in its selection of personnel.

But the similarity ends there. The British Crown is not, nor was it in mid-nineteenth century, an executive comparable to the American Presidency. The one is shadow; the other is real. There has never been any great conflict in modern England arising from the separation of powers. That the British competitive system was the result of a series of Orders in Council is well known, but those Orders in Council actually represented the Cabinet which in turn represented the legislative branch of the government. British reform was therefore the result of legislative requirement and legislative mandate.

In the United States the legislative branch had attempted to coerce the executive branch in a similar fashion in the eighteen sixties and failed. The Pendleton Act recognized that failure and attempted to avoid another such impasse. American constitutional realities simply are not British constitutional realities and the American version of British civil service reform has reflected, and will continue to reflect, such fundamental differences in governmental systems.

Safeguards

Since the Pendleton Act left the President's power to hire and fire relatively unimpeded, what safeguards were planned by a Congress which had not long before threatened a president with impeachment in an effort to control his relationship to public office-holders?

In the first place, the development of the merit system was considered as effective a check against the President as against Congress. Further, no more than two members of the agency administering the new law were to represent the same political party. Finally, the Civil Service Commission was to be outside the traditional administrative hierarchy. The new agency was to be as nonpolitical as possible and as free from interference from either the executive or the legislative branches as feasible under the American Constitution.[22] The Civil Service Commission thus became the first of the separate commissions, devised to remove controversial issues from the hands of the usual administrative and political channels and thus to avoid some of the most acrimonious of the presidential-congressional conflicts. The emergence of a new [23] administrative pattern on the federal scene was undoubtedly related to a perception by Congress—whether consciously verbalized or merely sensed does not matter—that the relatively novel idea of political neutrality in civil service selection methods deserved a relatively novel administrative solution if it was to survive.

Nevertheless, the Civil Service Commission differs in several important respects from later regulatory boards such as the Interstate Commerce Commission. The members of the Civil Service Commission may be removed by the President without restriction. While it is their duty to advise the President on matters of policy affecting the public service, the Pendleton Act specifies that the regulations made by them derive their authority from and will be promulgated by the President. Hence, the Commission cannot properly be classed as an *independent* commission, though it represents a political innovation of some importance.

The End of Two Eras

Just as 1829 marked the end of the bureaucracy of the Founding Fathers, 1883 marked the first great inroad into the spoils system of the mid-nineteenth century. Twice within a hundred years the American public service had been "reformed." What fundamental contrasts can be drawn between the two movements?

The Jacksonian movement can best be described as a class bursting of bonds. As the new democracy received the ballot—its ticket of admission to participation in government—it insisted on a show to its pleasure. And the cast of characters was adjusted accordingly. American democracy moved by the logic implicit in its premises to a

---

22 The Senate Committee on Civil Service and Retrenchment, on reporting the Pendleton bill in 1882, said: "Such a board is necessary to secure the coherence, the authority, the uniformity, the assurance of freedom from partiality or influence which are vital to the system." U.S. Congress, Senate Report 576, as cited in footnote 3, p. X. Earlier, in reporting the same bill to a previous Congress, the Senate Select Committee on the Civil Service also concluded, "The commission needs a firm tenure, and should be as far as practicable removed from partisan influences. It needs to have knowledge of the practical methods of the departments, without falling under mere official control." U.S. Congress, Senate Report 872, as cited in footnote 3, p. 12.

23 The word "new" is justified in so far as the Civil Service Commission was the first federal agency of considerable importance and permanence to be organized as a semi-independent, bipartisan agency for what, in the days of its formation, was considered a kind of policing function.

recognition—practical this time, not theoretical—of the implications of both liberty and equality. Public office was to become almost a perquisite of citizenship and "rotation" the watchword. The spoils system provided a system of recruitment for public office very little at odds with the individualism of the day. May the best man win! The whole mechanism reflected the ideals and attitudes of American nineteenth century agrarian democracy.

In the decades immediately after the Civil War, however, individualism seemed to be producing inequality. The "best" men were winning by more of a margin than many people liked to see. And not a few questioned whether those who were winning were actually the "best." What had once been intended as an opening up of public office to the mass of citizens had all the earmarks of becoming the opening up of office to plundering by the politically privileged.

In 1883, contrasted to 1829, there was no new class to turn to, nor any particular desire to turn the clock back to 1829. If democracy was not satisfied with its own product, then it would have to reform itself. There was no one else to do it.

The invention of the merit system of recruitment for public office by examination made possible a new reformation of a different sort. Essentially a foreign idea, imported from a Europe which had faced similar problems earlier, civil service reform, suitably modified to conform to American ideas of a mobile, classless society, was a scheme brilliantly devised to meet the needs of our version of the modern democratic state.

First, the Civil Service Commission could distribute offices more systematically and rationally than the spoils system had ever been able to do. While the new scheme did not guarantee a partisan apportionment of offices to the party in power, it certainly did not guarantee offices to the opposition. If a compromise had to be reached, political neutrality in the distribution of public office was reasonably acceptable to all concerned.

Second, the merit system provided a remedy for those who objected to the obvious corruption and the oligarchical tendencies of the combination of business and politics into which the spoils system had developed. Civil service reform did again open up many of the public offices to all on a new kind of equal basis; [24] and it provided through a new measure of merit, the examination system, the rewards for individual effort so prized in American life.

Finally, the new reform laid the foundation for the development of

---

[24] As Dorman B. Eaton said in testifying before the Senate Committee considering the Pendleton bill, "This bill assumes that every citizen has an equal claim to be appointed if he has equal capacity." U.S. Congress, Senate Report 576, as cited in footnote 3, p. 6.

111

that technical expertise crucial to the operation of the modern state. And it reached this goal without offending the democratic sensibilities of the great mass of American citizens. Posing no overt threat to the overpowering individualism of the day, it nevertheless gave implicit promise of other reforms to come. Once again a form of latent antagonism between liberty and equality—potentially so explosive in a democracy—was temporarily pacified.

CHAPTER 6

Morality in Office: 1883–1897

When the Pendleton Act is placed in full historical perspective, one further fact of significant import is clear. The first positive reform legislation with long-range implications, upon which the American electorate and its representatives could agree after the issue of slavery was settled, was the civil service reform statute of 1883, the basis of federal personnel management to this day.

In competition with the civil service reformers for the mind of the public were the advocates of a tariff-for-revenue-only, those who would cheapen the currency and regulate the railroads, the importers of European proletarian remedies, as well as the supporters of the more homespun doctrines of men like Henry George. Yet the "man-milliners," the "carpet-knights of politics," and the "grasshoppers in the corner of a fence" with their "rancid, canting self-righteousness" —as Senator Roscoe Conkling of New York had scathingly dubbed the civil service reformers in the eighteen seventies [1]—were the first to break through the defenses of the Gilded Age. Even the spectacular fall of Conkling himself can in part be laid at their door. No rebels against the established order, no one-sided partisans in the heyday of such partisanship, the little group of civil service reformers gloried in their hour of triumph significantly before their competitors.

While their organization was sound, their propaganda well tuned, their proposal modestly practical, and many events lay in their favor, the same could be said of many of their rivals. Moreover, the total

---

[1] See especially Conkling's well-known speech before the New York State Republican Convention at Rochester, N.Y., on September 26, 1877, as reproduced in Alfred R. Conkling, *Life and Letters of Roscoe Conkling* (New York: Charles L. Webster and Co., 1889), pp. 538–49.

effort of the civil service reformers, as expressed in money and man-power, never compared to that of the Knights of Labor, the Grange, the Northern and Southern Alliances, the Greenbackers, the Anti-Monopolists, or even the Prohibitionists. The secret of the reformers' success lay elsewhere.

Can we account for this reversal of fortune, this Cinderella-like emergence, in spite of more glamorous and well-heeled rivals, of civil service reform as a major political issue on the national scene? [2] If we can, we may also be able to explain the curiously mingled success and failure of the Cleveland era which, for civil service reform, was a period of administrative implementation as well as political decline.

Moral Reform

Any reformer must declare that something is wrong and that something else is right, in a moral and ethical sense. Whether his views are accepted will depend in considerable part upon the predispositions of his audience with respect to such things. To put the matter in terms of our frame of analysis: Economics may provide the ammunition but ethics controls the trigger of the political pistol. We have already discussed to some extent the economic and political unrest characterizing the Gilded Age, as well as the fundamental moral basis of civil service reform. We have not, however, yet considered the implications of the prevailing attitude toward the proper function of government. After all, it was in the civil service reformers' attempt to turn the government to their own limited ends that they collided most obviously with the efforts of their competitors.

The pervasiveness of the historic American preference for limited government is a matter of record and needs little amplification. This preference was still overwhelming in the period after the Civil War. Americans were quite prepared to have their government protect civil rights, but any broad governmental regulation of economic affairs other than that implicit in the protection of private property was out of the question. Moreover, there was no concept of a right to a living. As more than an imperfect vision, the modern version of social security was still well beyond the political horizon. Charity was the best the Protestant Ethic could then prescribe for those in economic distress. Yet such distress was becoming more and more obvious among large segments of American society. The question became:

2 The same happened on the state and local scene. New York and Massachusetts became early rivals of the federal government in the realm of public personnel administration, with fairly comprehensive statutes as early as 1883 in the case of New York and 1885 in Massachusetts. On the whole, however, state and local government have lagged behind the federal government in civil service reform.

Who would take care of the economic man who fell into bankruptcy, when he had no right to a competence and charity was much
less than enough? What part would a voluntaristic, cooperative
society, possessing an ingrained fear of coercive control of individual
and corporate effort, permit its government to play in any reaction
to economic stresses and strains? Such was the moral dilemma which
faced most Americans as they approached any renovation of their
political mechanism during the Gilded Age.

In all likelihood the keystone in the reformers' arch of triumph
lay in their ability to hit on a formula which seemed in its day to
provide a sword for this Gordian Knot. Whether either the reformers
or the general public quite realized what was involved is irrelevant.
The answer was deceptively simple and therein lay much of its
strength. All the reformers really proposed was a *political man,* a
model of virtue and the personification of justice and duty, to rescue
the economic man from the headaches of overindulgence. Unfortunately, their resolution of the public dilemma was, like an aspirin,
no resolution at all. It was merely a reaffirmation of the individualistic
ethics of the ancient commandments of the biblical prophets. Moral
reform—for which civil service reform was both the symbol and
prime political end—was a sort of recognition that the economic
man would have to return to first principles in both business and
government as the price of survival.

The diagnosis and cure offered by the political reformers disagreed
fundamentally with that advocated by the economic reformers. Of
the distinguished E. L. Godkin, for example, it has been noted that
he:

. . . while condemning the spoils basis of conservative politics . . . was utterly amazed to learn that the western agrarians, who agreed with him
when he lashed corrupters and corruption, were in fact primarily interested
in cutting down railway rates by legislation, on principles which seemed to
the sapient editor to involve sheer confiscation.[3]

While the Knights and the Grange fought for economic equality
through a frontal assault on the bulwarks of liberal capitalism, the
civil service reformers proposed a sort of fifth column infiltration of
the spoils system, an important political base for the sustenance of
the acquisitive creed. To Curtis, Eaton, and Schurz, and to a growing
number of voters, the power of public plunder was gradually linked
with the increasing gravity of economic disorder. The Grant scandals,
the postal frauds, Garfield's assassination, and the other many trage-

---

[3] Charles A. and Mary R. Beard, *The Rise of American Civilization* (rev. ed.; New York:
The Macmillan Co., 1936), II, 566.

dies directly attributable to the doctrine of spoils were painfully obvious to the man in the street.

Once a majority of the electorate became aware of the practicality of civil service reform and the need for a change, they began to press through their elected representatives for the renovation of a surface evil which for the moment appeared at the root of it all. Everyone could unite to *throw the rascals out!* It was only a short step to the concept of morality and honesty in public office. Under new leadership, that individual effort which was thought to be the central fact of economics and that sense of individual responsibility which lay at the core of the Protestant Ethic would be applied with new energy to government and politics as well. A society which had always cherished cooperative effort in times of trial could now unite to solve its difficulties. But at this time it was still too much to expect the general public to accept the radical regulatory doctrines of the economic reformers on a national scale. The ethical trigger was not yet fully set for a strike at the fundamentals of the social system.

In this political vacuum civil service reform temporarily triumphed, along with Grover Cleveland, who in many ways and for many years personified public morality on the American national scene. What did this first wave of post-Civil War governmental reform actually mean in terms of its own central concern, the federal civil bureaucracy?

Under Way

For the first two or three years after the passage of the Pendleton Act, until civil service reform was, in part at least, a reality, public interest in the movement remained at a consistently high level. Certainly civil service reform was one of the major issues in the campaign of 1880 and more especially in that of 1884.

First reactions. The Act of 1883, with its permissive and limited application, was received with varying reactions. Many politicians were hostile. Most of the reformers were frankly pleased because the result was considerably beyond their expectations of only a few months before. The more realistic felt that there was much yet to be accomplished but held with the *New York Tribune* that "today half a loaf is better than no bread." [4] Everyone understood that another crisis might well arise with the next election. In preparation, the National Civil Service Reform League tightened its organization. Meanwhile, the administration of the new act was in the hands of

---

4 December 29, 1882.

President Chester A. Arthur. He could make or break it, and he had only the precedent of General Grant on which to rely.

Fortunately for reform, the presidents since Grant, while attempting to retrieve for their office something of the power and prestige lost during Johnson's administration, had become engaged in a running battle with Congress over the control of appointments. During the course of this struggle both Hayes and Garfield supported civil service reform as much for its recognition of presidential authority in this matter as for other reasons. Following in their footsteps, Arthur, the former spoilsman Collector of the port of New York who had been ousted by Hayes, proved anything but the spoilsman chief executive that many had feared. He appointed an excellent Civil Service Commission with Dorman B. Eaton at its head. A set of rules was drawn up, based upon those of the Grant Commission, and in February, 1885, the President reported that the experiment was generally a success.[5]

Election of 1884. The election of 1884 represents the height of civil service reform as a political issue, with the conflict between the spoils system and moral reform brightly illuminated by the contrast between Grover Cleveland and James G. Blaine, the Republican candidate. To the reformers and the Liberal Republicans,[6] and to many others, Blaine, of Mulligan Letters fame,[7] represented the essence of the system which they were trying to undermine. Cleveland, if not the acme of perfection from a reformer's point of view, nevertheless symbolized honesty and integrity in public office. With the issues clearer than usual after the Civil War, Blaine was defeated by a narrow margin, as forecast in part by the Republican congressional election setback of 1882.

For the first time in twenty-four years Democracy would reign, and Republican consternation was great. Therefore, under considerable pressure from harassed Republican leaders stampeded by the thought of a Democrat in the White House, President Arthur made the first *post*-election additions to the classified service. This set a precedent by which civil service reform was to profit immensely in the next

---

5 James D. Richardson (ed.), *Messages and Papers of the Presidents* (New York: Bureau of National Literature and Art, 1905), VIII, 276.

6 They were often known as Mugwumps or Independents. A number of the civil service reformers belonged to this group. Basically Republican in allegiance, they nevertheless occasionally bolted to the Democrats when they could not stomach Republican leadership or activities.

7 These were letters which allegedly contained statements by Blaine indicating that he had used his congressional position to favor tariff and railway legislation in return for monetary favors. The fact that Blaine seized the letters and quoted from them to his advantage, while at the same time he refused to let anyone else look at them, did little to quiet suspicion.

twelve years. Arthur and the Republican leaders hoped, of course, to keep a portion of the public service from falling into the hands of the opposition, who, after being out of power for a quarter of a century, would have no mercy with Republican office-holders. Arthur opposed too great a coverage because he feared the reaction of the Democrats. From November, 1884, through February, 1885, approximately 1,200 positions were classified and saved for the incumbents, presumably Republicans.[8] At the end of Arthur's term, the Republicans had left approximately 15,000 offices in the classified service. The remainder— some 125,000 offices—were available for such uses as the incoming administration might find for them.

The First Cleveland Administration

The friends of the merit system well understood that its real trial would come with this first change from a Republican to a Democratic administration.

Stresses and strains. Grover Cleveland entered the White House as a reformer, but not necessarily as a civil service reformer. Though from New York, he had no formal connections with the National Civil Service Reform League, whose headquarters was in that state. Long before his inauguration he was pursued and besieged from all sides in efforts to discover his stand on the offices. Avoiding commitment at first, the President-elect finally in December, 1884, essayed a cautious public reply to a letter from the Reform League:

> That a practical reform in the Civil Service is demanded, is abundantly established. . . . I regard myself pledged to this, ... But many now holding . . . positions have forfeited all just claim to retention, ... while Democrats may expect all proper consideration, selections for office not embraced within the Civil Service rules will be based upon sufficient inquiry as to fitness.[9]

During his first term, Cleveland generally lived up to the ambiguity of his initial statement. At first proceeding carefully and slowly with appointments, he found himself by the fall of 1885 faced with something close to a party revolt. Thereafter, he modified his stern initial policy until there were sharp protests from many directions, including

8 U.S. Civil Service Commission, *History of the Federal Civil Service*, Form 2449, prepared in the Information and Recruiting Division, text by M. Barris Taylor (Washington: Government Printing Office, 1941), p. 63.
9 As quoted from the Cleveland papers in A. Bower Sageser, *The First Two Decades of the Pendleton Act* (Lincoln: University of Nebraska, 1935), pp. 79–80.

the civil service reformers. That the President did not and could not in his first term fulfill all the hopes of men such as Carl Schurz lay in the desperate fact that Cleveland was subjected to as much partisan political pressure of all kinds and varieties as any of the presidents except perhaps Lincoln. The Democratic party had been starved for a quarter of a century and was not to be denied. The spoils system was still very much alive in the minds of the politicians, not to mention a considerable portion of the general public.

From *Harper's Weekly*, February 28, 1885.

HAVE THE DEMOCRATS AN ELEPHANT ON HAND?

Cleveland's major appointments were generally considered as favorable to reform. However, the Civil Service Commission, subjected to its first turnover in top personnel, fared only passably well. One appointee, A. P. Edgerton, proved so ill-suited that Cleveland was forced to remove him. Of the others, and there were several, only Charles Lyman, a former civil servant who was the Republican successor to Eaton, could be called outstanding. He served continuously until 1895. Cleveland left the classified service untouched. Through a nearly equal mixture of normal growth and modest additions, it

119

almost doubled in size, approximating 27,000 positions at the end of Cleveland's first term.[10]

Outside the classified service matters did not fare so well for incumbents. Cleveland was becoming sufficiently sophisticated as a politician to realize that he was obliged to satisfy the major demands of his party leaders if he hoped to put through any program at all. Therefore the traditional political turnover continued in many segments of the government. In the unclassified service the new appointments made during the first eighteen months of the new regime probably involved 50 per cent of the positions available.[11]

The Presidency gains. Not only did President Cleveland have to face the demands of his own political supporters for the usual spoils of office, but also he found himself confronted with as formidable a challenge to executive authority over appointments and removals as Congress had seen fit to issue in nearly two decades.

The imbroglio commenced as an effort of the Republican dominated Senate to embarrass the new administration by insisting on the right of Congress to know the reasons for removals before the Senate would agree to confirm new appointees for the positions thus left vacant. Congress hoped to use the power of confirmation to force the Cleveland administration into admitting to removals for partisan purposes. Such an admission would rebound to Republican benefit, as the Democrats would be made to appear as something other than wholehearted advocates of reform.

The details of Cleveland's fight with Congress over the removal power, a kind of miniature replica of President Johnson's quarrels with the legislative branch, have been thoroughly outlined by Cleveland's biographers.[12] What is important here is that again the President won out. Cleveland bluntly stated that the Tenure of Office Act of 1867, still on the books, was unconstitutional, and he stood upon the constitutional right of the President to make removals as he saw fit. Nevertheless, he scrupulously kept the Senate well-informed concerning new appointments requiring Senate ratification. Public opinion supported the forthright stand of the President, and Congress

---

[10] For the period before 1900 data on the classified positions are much more accurate than those relating to the executive civil service as a whole. See the annual reports of the Civil Service Commission and, especially, the Commission's *The Classified Executive Civil Service of the United States Government*, Form 2909 (Washington: Government Printing Office, 1933), which summarizes the development of the classified service in detail.

[11] From a special report of the National Civil Service Reform League in March, 1887, as quoted in Frank M. Stewart, *The National Civil Service Reform League* (Austin: The University of Texas Press, 1929), p. 50. See also Allan Nevins, *Grover Cleveland* (New York: Dodd, Mead and Co., 1932), pp. 248–52.

[12] See, for instance, Nevins, as cited in footnote 11, ch. xv.

From *Puck*, March 4, 1885.

THEIR LITTLE FUNERAL

finally backed down. In 1887 the Tenure of Office Act, by then a dead letter, was quietly repealed.

Thus ended the last major constitutional quarrel in American history over the authority of the President and Congress with respect to the removal power. The decision of the First Congress as to the proper place of the removal power was reaffirmed and, essentially, it has not been questioned since. Cleveland's victory placed him in the limelight as a successful and forceful president and greatly increased the stature of the Presidency as an institution. In addition, Cleveland reenforced his position with the civil service reformers, for the repeal of the Tenure of Office Act had long been one of their objectives. The legislative about-face represents the demise of the once powerful school of thought which would have "reformed" the patronage by transferring the power over the public service from the President to Congress. No longer would anyone try to reform the civil service by the methods of Clay, Calhoun, and Webster.

Post-election reform. After his failure at reelection, Cleveland followed the example of Arthur and, for the same reasons, made by far his greatest single first-term extension of the classified service, classifying more than 5,000 positions. That his post-election classification was no greater was not the fault of the Democratic leaders, who begged from all sides that he save more Democrats by placing their positions under the merit system. The President, like his predecessor, felt that if he went too far he would jeopardize the entire system. That he would not do, for he was never a spoilsman by theory or personal inclination.

In a painstaking report on the accomplishments of the first administration of Cleveland, a special committee of the National Civil Service Reform League concluded:

Tried by the standard of absolute fidelity to the reform as it is understood by this League, it is not to be denied that this administration has left much to be desired. But upon the showing of this report which has neither concealed nor extenuated the most injurious facts, if our estimate of the situation be just, the administration under enormous disadvantages and perplexities has accomplished much for the reform of the civil service. Whatever just disappointment may have been felt, it is undeniable that the old "spoils system" has been seriously shaken.[13]

The Decline of an Issue

This grudging admission of accomplishment from the chief organization behind the civil service reform movement was typical of the

13 Quoted in Stewart, as cited in footnote 11, p. 50.

misunderstandings which occasionally plagued Cleveland and many of his successors in their relations with reform leaders. It is also symptomatic of the problem faced by any reform group which has grown up to consider its own issue as paramount.

To men brought up to believe that civil service reform was the primary reform, it seemed almost heresy to believe, as Cleveland and his successors did, that other matters might occasionally be of greater importance. The reformers could not sympathize with Cleveland's opinion that

. . . To me the importance of general administrative reform has appeared to be superior to the incidental matter of civil service reform. Good government is the main thing to be aimed at. Civil service reform is but a means to that end.[14]

Election of 1888. While most of the reformers still appreciated that Cleveland offered more to their cause than any other political figure of his day, they nevertheless were partially split as between Cleveland and Benjamin Harrison in the election of 1888. Though Harrison made few campaign remarks on the subject, he was considered as favorable to civil service reform. Before his nomination, he had criticized the Cleveland regime for failing to adhere to the principles of the reform. Many of the so-called Mugwump Independents, among whom civil service reformers were prominent, chose to remain with Cleveland, but some felt that Harrison offered the most to the cause. The division of the Independents, together with the general failure of the administration satisfactorily to settle other burning issues of the day—notably, the tariff and money issues—favored the return of the Republicans by a small margin.

From this time on may be dated the decline of civil service reform, along with moral reform in general, as a major political issue in its own right. To begin with, the success of the Pendleton Act made the problem seem less crucial. Moreover, the movement had never favored an overt resolution of the substantive economic problems confronting the nation. Even when the civil service reform group understood the basic economic issues involved in the strikes, depressions, agricultural unrest, and agitation of the day, they widely differed among themselves about the main causes and, especially, the best remedies for the ills of the body politic. Like so many liberals today, the reformers could agree on "good government" but found that they disagreed on what the government was good *for*. Seldom after the eighteen eighties were the Independents able to rally their forces around a

14 Quoted in Nevins, as cited in footnote 11, p. 215.

single man or within a single party. Thus the reformers gradually tended to scatter their once unified efforts as they themselves became more and more entangled with the other problems which were gradually forcing themselves to the front of the political scene.

Benjamin Harrison

President Harrison quickly proved a disappointment to the civil service supporters and to the other reformers who had endorsed him. First, the effective date for the operation of Cleveland's last classification order was delayed until May 1, 1889. This was done in part at the request of the Civil Service Commission, which had been unable to complete the paperwork required for the change. But Harrison did nothing to prevent wholesale removals in the railway mail service, where most of the offices classified by Cleveland lay, before the effective date of the order.

Several unfortunate initial appointments by the new chief executive did little to mend matters, especially those of John Wanamaker of Philadelphia as Postmaster General and James S. Clarkson as First Assistant Postmaster General. Neither was even remotely interested in civil service reform. Under their guidance the Republicans immediately and obviously put the removal machinery into full gear in the unclassified offices. While they were not much more thorough than Cleveland had been, they proceeded somewhat more rapidly and with much less caution in the matter. Of the political orientation of the Post Office Department at this time, Dorothy Fowler has graphically noted:

> First Assistant Postmaster General Clarkson was also even more efficient than Mr. Stevenson (the first Adlai Stevenson, who had held a similar post under Cleveland and was soon to be Vice-President) in removing the fourth-class postmasters. It was estimated that his average was one removal in every three minutes while the Democratic Assistant Postmaster General had averaged only one every fifteen minutes.[15]

T. R. onto the stage. From the point of view of the future of the merit system, the most fortunate executive action turned out to be the appointment of the rising young politician, Theodore Roosevelt, as a Civil Service Commissioner. First appointed by Harrison in May, 1889, he was reappointed later by Cleveland and served until May, 1895. However, it is quite clear that Roosevelt, under Harrison, did

---

15 Dorothy Fowler, *The Cabinet Politician* (New York: Columbia University Press, 1943), p. 214. The First Assistant Postmaster General has often been the administrative official most directly in charge of Post Office patronage.

not by any means direct all of the affairs of the Commission,[16] notwithstanding the later inferences of some of his more enthusiastic admirers.[17] He was able to use his political connections and undoubted ability to help maintain the integrity of the Commission during the worst of the patronage pressure. But his well-known methods of direct action did not altogether commend him then, as later, to the Republican politicians. In 1889 the other commissioners were considered equally efficient, and it is partly in retrospect that Roosevelt has been singled out for especially high praise as an effective commissioner.[18]

It was not until Cleveland's second administration that Roosevelt assumed his most important role in the affairs of the Commission. Cleveland then repeated his earlier practice, a practice notably followed later by Woodrow Wilson and Franklin D. Roosevelt, under which the Commission member representing the party *out of* power was, for all practical purposes, treated as the chief commissioner. Under such an arrangement it was possible for a president publicly to favor the extension of the merit system without appearing to be too partisan. In addition, it tended to solve the administrative problem of efficient operation of a multi-headed agency. For the chief executive could freely appoint whomever he chose as the minority party representative—he has usually chosen a well-known supporter of the merit system—while his choices from his own party were limited by partisan considerations not always conducive to much knowledge of or concern about the merit system.[19]

Election of 1892. By 1892 the machinations of the Republican spoilsmen had thoroughly alienated most of the reform faction. Partisan removals had been so frequent and appointments so indiscriminate that the National Civil Service Reform League resolved:

. . . the solemn promises of the Republican platform of 1888 have been broken, the voluntary pledges of the President are unfulfilled, and the claim of the Republican party, however strong may be the desire of individual Republicans, to be distinctively the party of civil service reform, is not sustained

---

[16] See Sageser's analysis of Roosevelt as a civil service commissioner, as cited in footnote 9, pp. 141–42.

[17] William Dudley Foulke, *Roosevelt and the Spoilsmen* (New York: National Civil Service Reform League, 1925), pp. 11–41.

[18] For a compilation of some of the typical official correspondence of an early Civil Service Commissioner, see U.S. Civil Service Commission, *Theodore Roosevelt, United States Civil Service Commissioner* (Washington: Civil Service Commission, 1940).

[19] For a comment on President Franklin D. Roosevelt's use of this device, see Don K. Price, "Staffing the Presidency," *American Political Science Review*, XL (December, 1946), 1158–59. The likelihood of further effective use of this device has diminished since 1949, when the administrative control of the Commission was specifically placed in the hands of the Chairman, almost inevitably a member of the party in power.

by the course of the administration, and against this gross breach of plighted faith with the people of the United States the National Civil Service Reform League earnestly protests.[20]

The Civil Service Commission was excepted from this condemnation for its generally excellent standards in the administration of the classified service under Harrison. Secretary of the Navy Benjamin F. Tracy was also widely commended for the institution of a much needed reform in the Navy Yards, where he installed a registration employment system for laborers. This system was eventually adopted by President Theodore Roosevelt for all such positions. Tracy also refused to continue the practice of employing a great number of extra laborers during election months.[21] Nevertheless, Harrison's manipulation of the 1892 Republican convention through federal office-holders, a now well-developed political practice, did nothing to improve either the reformers' view of his administration or his relations with powerful elements in his own party.[22]

Cleveland easily captured the Democratic nomination, and the majority of the more influential Independent and reform elements again supported him. Because of public reaction to the patronage and other spoils practices of the Harrison administration, civil service reform was in 1892 an issue somewhat more important than it had been in 1888, but it was at best a very poor third to the tariff and silver questions.[23]

Following precedent, Harrison proposed his greatest extension of the merit system immediately after his defeat. Uniquely, and typically, President-elect Cleveland encouraged the civil service reformers to support the Harrison classification, a type of classification which many of the reformers had criticized. The former President had had enough trouble with spoilsmen in his previous administration and welcomed the proposal to simplify his patronage problems before he came into office. No incoming president of any opposition party has, however, since emulated this astonishing self-denial.

That these post-election classifications were not exactly based on a zeal for merit was fully understood both by the reformers and by the politicians. The latter had always welcomed these actions as fortunate opportunities for the politically distressed. They were now reluctantly condoned by the reformers as a necessary evil in accomplishing the extension of the merit system. In 1892 an Indiana politician of

20 NCSRL, *Proceedings*, 1892, p. 43.
21 Stewart, as cited in footnote 11, p. 57.
22 Fowler, as cited in footnote 15, pp. 220–21.
23 See Sageser, as cited in footnote 9, p. 173, for several contemporary rankings of important issues in the campaign of 1892.

Republican persuasion, named L. T. Michener, wrote to Harrison's private secretary, E. W. Halford, and observed that, while there was "much hypocrisy" in such classification without examination, it was "fashionable hypocrisy" and he, as a Republican, was all for it.[24] In his last months of office, Harrison extended the classified service to in-

FALSE WEIGHTS AND MEASURES IN THE NEW YORK CUSTOM-HOUSE.

From *Puck*, September 23, 1885.

clude over 7,000 more offices, his total additions to the merit system approximating 8,500 positions.[25]

Cleveland Again

If Cleveland's position was difficult in 1885, it was doubly so in 1893. The tariff, the silver question, foreign relations, labor disturb-

---

[24] Quoted in same, p. 161.

[25] U.S. Civil Service Commission, *Fourteenth Annual Report* (Washington: Government Printing Office, 1897), pp. 138–39. Hereafter the United States Civil Service Commission will be cited as "USCSC" and its annual reports as, for example, "*Fourteenth Report*, 1897."

ances, and a panic commanded the attention of the President, while in his antechambers the pressure for public office continued unabated. Shortly before his inauguration the President-elect paced up and down the floor while confiding to a friend:

I suppose at times you will not approve many things I do, but I want you to know that I am trying to do what is right. I have a hungry party behind me, and they say I am not grateful. Sometimes the pressure is almost overwhelming, and a President cannot always get at the exact truth, but I want you to know, and all my friends to know, that I am trying to do what is right—I am trying to do what is right.[26]

Patronage policies. Cleveland's initial appointments were received well enough though with no great enthusiasm. The Civil Service Commission was an early object of interest and speculation, especially in light of the extensive Republican post-election additions to the merit system. Despite the key position of the Commission in relation to the patronage, Cleveland retained intact the Harrison Commission, consisting of two Republicans, Lyman and Roosevelt, with only one Democrat, George D. Johnston. Following disagreements among the commissioners, especially between Roosevelt and Johnston over the propriety of the Harrison post-election classification, Cleveland accomplished the second and last outright removal ever made from the Commission when he displaced Johnston, a Louisiana Democrat generally conceded to be unsympathetic to reform.[27] The reformers hailed both Johnston's removal and the appointment of John R. Proctor of Kentucky as his successor. Proctor had become State Geologist in 1880, and in this position had set up a small merit system of his own, a distinct rarity in state government at this time. After these appointments, the affairs of the Commission seemed to run considerably more smoothly.

Not so, however, the affairs of the President. Caught between the dilemma of his desire for reform balanced against the necessity to obtain congressional support for his program, the President was unable to placate both. Though no nonpartisan chief executive, he

26 Cleveland to Dr. Milton Merle Smith, pastor of the New York church which Cleveland often attended. Robert McElroy, *Grover Cleveland* (2 vols.; New York: Harper and Bros., 1923), II, 8.

27 In the Commission's *Ninth Report*, 1892, Johnston formally disagreed with the recommendations of his colleagues over the extension of the classified service. The *Tenth Report*, 1893, was signed only by Lyman and Roosevelt although Johnston was not yet removed when the report was made. For Roosevelt's side of the story see Foulke, as cited in footnote 17, pp. 38–40. For Johnston's side of the argument see Josephus Daniels, *Editor in Politics* (Chapel Hill: University of North Carolina Press, 1941), pp. 24–26. Only on one other occasion, during World War I, has the Commission been involved in such an obvious and public internecine quarrel.

applied the standards of honesty and integrity in office to Democrats as well as to Republicans. As a result, the President proceeded somewhat more slowly in the distribution of the patronage than had been his custom on previous occasions. Nevertheless, in adjusting to the demands of local Democratic politicians the concessions continued to mount, despite a conscious presidential effort to maintain high standards of appointment. That he did not entirely succeed was due more to the magnitude of the job than to his intentions.

Several of Cleveland's department heads, particularly the Secretary of State and the Secretary of the Treasury, were not as scrupulous as their chief. Moreover, the Civil Service Commission itself was behind in its work. By March 4, 1893, not more than half of the newly classified offices were supplied with eligible lists and the delay gave the Democrats time to fill a number of the offices before the final deadlines could be set. But with presidential backing as well as the support of the Postmaster General, head of the department most affected, the classification was completed with less machination and maneuver than had been the case four years previously.

The most spectacular manipulation of public office during the Cleveland regime must, however, be laid directly at the door of the President himself. Cleveland desired the repeal of the Sherman Silver Purchase Act and called a special session of Congress for this purpose in 1893. To placate influential Senator Daniel W. Voorhees of Indiana, once an anti-Cleveland inflationist and in 1893 the Chairman of the Senate Finance Committee, the President deliberately permitted him virtually to control the federal offices in Indiana. In return, instead of fighting the President, the Senator reversed his longstanding position and became the leader of the forces for repeal. With others, particularly reluctant members of Congress, Cleveland strategically withheld offices, pending their consent to the legislation he proposed. In the end the President prevailed and the Sherman Silver Purchase Act was written off the statute books by a narrow margin.[28]

The roll of presidents deliberately manipulating public office for the furtherance of their political programs now included Cleveland without question. Careful control of the patronage has often been the only means available to a chief executive who wishes—for high as well as low purposes—to bridge the constitutional gaps between President, party, and Congress. Cleveland, by 1893 as experienced in party affairs as any American alive, well understood this fundamental principle of American politics.

[28] For this story in detail see Nevins, as cited in footnote 11, pp. 541–48; and Sageser, as cited in footnote 9, pp. 184–86.

129

Happy ending. While the President created something of a furor by his patronage policies in relation to the silver question, he must also be given credit for the most extensive classification of federal jobs made during the first half century after the passage of the Pendleton Act. Percentage-wise, though not in absolute numbers, it was the greatest ever made in the history of the federal service. In his second term of office Cleveland extended the merit system almost to the limits which even the reformers then conceived to be the ultimate goal. In a series of orders—all *pre*-election this time, for Cleveland did not expect or wish a third term—the President included more than 37,000 positions under the merit system. The final action alone, one of the largest single classifications ever made, "covered-in" nearly 30,000 positions on May 6, 1896.[29] Normal growth of the service accounted for more than 6,000 further additions to the classified service.[30]

By the end of Cleveland's second term, close to 50 per cent of some 190,000 federal civil employees were under the merit system. Still outside were about 75,000 postal workers, a number of employees in miscellaneous or "confidential" positions, several thousand laborers, and appointees confirmed by the Senate. Laborers and those subject to senatorial confirmation were specifically excluded by the provisions of the Pendleton Act. Many of the miscellaneous positions were posts for which political appointment was proper or for which it was impractical to recruit through examination. Much part-time and seasonal employment came under the latter category. It had always been contemplated that "confidential" employees such as private secretaries would be excluded. While three-fourths of the postal offices were in fourth class postal establishments and subject to classification, the postal service was still generally considered a legitimate realm for spoils. To tamper much with it at this time might well have sparked a partisan reaction sufficient to undo some of the important classifications made in other departments. Even so, Cleveland had attempted to control the worst patronage abuses in the Post Office, and fewer complaints were made of postal patronage manipulations than had been heard in years.

By 1896, the bulk of the offices which it was then either legal or politically and administratively practical to place under the merit system were included, and in many of the rest the spoils system was on the defensive. There were those who felt that the President had gone too far and too fast, and this criticism was to play an important

29 For a summary of the positions covered by the Order of May 6, 1896, and of the extensions of the classified service made during the Cleveland era, see USCSC, *Fourteenth Report*, 1897, pp. 136–40.
30 See Table 4 in Sageser, as cited in footnote 9, p. 190.

role in the years immediately to follow. But the general public seemed to approve, and the civil service reformers rejoiced.

In a very different tone from that which it had taken in 1888 the National Civil Service Reform League resolved in 1896:

The League heartily congratulates the country on the truly remarkable progress of the reform under the second administration of President Cleveland, and especially during the past year, ... For this great achievement, advancing as it does the fundamental principles of free government, President Cleveland deserves the sincere and heartfelt thanks of all good citizens.[31]

The final crisis. In the campaign of 1896 the Democratic nomination went to William Jennings Bryan, an avowed spoilsman whose platform, as far as the offices were concerned, resembled that of his political ancestor, General Jackson. During his last months in office Cleveland, as is often the case with outgoing presidents, was left almost without a party. With public attention largely focused elsewhere and with the nomination of William B. McKinley as the Republican candidate, it seemed for a while as if the merit system might end up in similar circumstances.

On the brighter side, while McKinley had never been outspoken on reform, he had voted for the original Pendleton measure and had always supported the Commission's appropriation requests. These facts, opposed to Bryan's outspoken attitude on the patronage, prompted the National Civil Service Reform League, for the first time, officially to support the candidate of one party—and this despite knowledge of the spoilsman tendencies of many of McKinley's political cohorts.

But the principal issues lay elsewhere, and even the reformers were not entirely united. Bryan's blunt threats of a return to 1829 were obscured in the emotionalism of "16 to 1." As the great forces of our agrarian past met and were vanquished by those of the industrial future, economic rather than moral reform held the center of the stage. In its repudiation of Bryan, the election of 1896 assured the effective continuance of the Civil Service Commission, but it also presaged the end of civil service reform as a political issue.

"A Public Office Is a Public Trust!"

By the end of Cleveland's second administration civil service reform was a reality and the merit system was here to stay. From a legal point of view the extension of the classified service to a majority of the federal public offices was primarily a presidential accomplishment.

31 *Proceedings*, 1896, pp. 39–40.

131

That is, the extensions were made in the name of the chief executive. The forces involved, however, were complex and cannot be explained by simple reference to executive orders.

Underneath the progress of the reform was, first of all, the pressure of public opinion. Sufficient to help force the initial adoption of the Pendleton Act, public opinion was still powerful enough in the decade and a half after 1883 to frustrate any major attacks upon the developing movement. The phrase, "civil service reform," as Allan Nevins has remarked, "does not possess either a mellifluous or an exciting sound." [32] But to a generation brought up on the Mulligan Letters, the Star-Route frauds, the resignation of a Secretary of War under threat of impeachment, the Whiskey Ring, and the assassination of a president by a disappointed office-seeker, civil service reform was full of meaning—a meaning which Schurz, Godkin, Curtis, and the rest lost no time in driving home. Moral reform was in the air and civil service reform was inseparable from the general movement. Politicians might gnash their teeth and Conkling might resign from the Senate in protest, but the merit system maintained its essential integrity. Many times during this period one or the other house of Congress took what the Columbus, Ohio, *Dispatch* once referred to as Congress' "annual fling at the merit system," [33] when it voted out the Civil Service Commission's appropriation on one day and voted it back again the next. On no occasion, however, did both houses support an emasculation at the same time. No president would have dared to other than veto such an action had it been taken. The public had had its fill of the more vicious aspects of patronage politics.

Beyond popular interest, however, lay other forces at work. The presidents themselves, and particularly Cleveland, appreciated the merit system for the relief it gave them from the perpetual importunities of office-seekers. This toll on presidential time and energy was a major factor, for instance, in Cleveland's public encouragement of the post-election classification of President Harrison. Nor were the presidents alone in feeling the pressure for public office. Requests for expansions of the classified service often came from harassed department heads as well.[34] In cases of extreme political desperation, especially after adverse elections, the extension of the merit system was the result of the influence of the spoilsmen themselves. In other cases, especially those involving the growing number of scientific and tech-

---

32 As cited in footnote 11, p. 234.
33 February 19, 1900.
34 The Secretary of Agriculture was one of these. Warner W. Stockberger and Virginia B. Smith, *Personnel Administration Development in the United States Department of Agriculture: The First Fifty Years* (Washington: Department of Agriculture, 1947), pp. 54 and 98–100.

nical positions, the spoils system was simply inadequate as a recruitment device.

The influence of the thousands of public employees themselves on reform is extremely difficult to assay. Those who were about to become unemployed through a change of administration were among the most vociferous for reform. Others brought pressure to bear through the embryonic employee unions, just commencing to be of influence in the eighties and nineties. The postal unions, for example, participated fully in the agitation which brought about the passage in 1888 of a so-called "eight hour law" for government employees.

Finally, as agriculture, labor, commerce, and industry came more and more under the regulation of the federal government, these great pressure groups became increasingly insistent upon regulation by competent personnel divorced from the worst ravages of partisan politics. As early as 1887 Woodrow Wilson stressed this point of view in his famous essay on public administration: "A body of thoroughly trained officials serving during good behavior we must have in any case: that is a plain business necessity." [35] The device of the merit system, with its emphasis on expertise and its connotations of political neutrality, was eminently suited to some of the newer tasks of government.

All these forces conspired to promote the development of civil service reform and to cement it in as a permanent part of our governmental heritage by the end of the century. Considering our history from the Civil War to the Spanish-American War, it is probably not too much to say that civil service reform was one of the extremely few permanent and lasting reforms made during this entire period. As the Beards have said:

. . . All in all, between 1865 and 1897, there were put upon the federal law books not more than two or three acts which need long detain the citizen concerned only with those manifestations of political power that produce essential readjustments in human relations.[36]

That the Pendleton Act was among these select measures is not only to the credit of such men as Curtis and Schurz, but even more to the credit of Grover Cleveland who may be considered the one man most responsible for the initial support of the new reform in the all-important political arena.

If anyone typified the moral *political man* of the civil service reformers, Cleveland did. Though he was sophisticated in the methods

[35] The "Study of Administration," *Political Science Quarterly*, II (June, 1887), 216.
[36] Beard and Beard, as cited in footnote 3, II, 341.

of politics and could offer the patronage to Senator Voorhees in return for support, this was only the exception which proves the rule. But even then, Cleveland's ultimate ends were obscure. After all, he merely sought the repeal of the Silver Purchase Act, and not the passage of new legislation. For the most part the personification of Marxist "bourgeois morality," he and the reformers, along with most of the voters, felt that somehow *good government,* amorphously defined more in moral than efficiency terms, was the end of all ends. Neither Cleveland nor Congress nor the general public could agree on much else, as is evident from the fact that between 1884 and 1900 no party succeeded itself. The old ethical dilemma arising from a willingness to act but an inability to conceive of action through government was still controlling.

Nevertheless, even if good government was not the answer to all the ills of the nation, all was not lost. Cleveland and his supporters not only provided a new administrative base for the support of the state but they also forced people to think of office-holding in somewhat more moral terms. Out of his regime came the new slogan: "A public office is a public trust!" The modern concept of a nonpolitical civil service received one of its greatest inspirations from a man who sometimes gave evidence of attempting to be a nonpolitical president.

To espouse the cause of civil service reform was to be expected of a man deeply concerned with morality in politics, and he pushed the merit system about as far as it could have been forced under existing legislative and administrative machinery. That he was relatively so successful in this one matter is directly related to the fact that he symbolized the widespread reaction against the dishonesty and misrepresentation so prevalent in the Gilded Age. As John Chamberlain has so well summarized in his *Farewell to Reform:*

The Cleveland era in American history, which followed the darker days of Republican supremacy, was little more than a plateau on which social forces canceled each other. Cleveland himself championed no ism; he had no theory of government beyond a diurnal conception of duty and common sense learned in a preacher's household. He made the last stand for an idealism that was chained to no definite social philosophy, but merely to the abstract and tricky doctrine of Righteousness. But he symbolized an urge towards honesty in a society that had looked too long upon economic debauch, and that was shortly to look upon the rising sun of Progressivism.[37]

Cleveland's foremost biographer, Allan Nevins, agrees that one of his "striking achievements" lies in the fact that "he restored honesty and

37 (2d ed.; New York: The John Day Co., 1933), pp. 7–8.

134

impartiality to government at a time when the service had become indispensable to the health of the republic." [38] By Grover Cleveland's own personal qualities and by his insistence on the same qualities in others, he left his personal imprint upon the American public service as have few other men.

SUPPLEMENTARY NOTES

As indicated briefly in this chapter, the merit system also began to be accepted at this time as a basis for the reorganization of public personnel administration at state and local levels. Unfortunately, there is no general study of personnel developments at these levels except that by Oliver P. Field, which is a detailed analysis of civil service law in state and local government for the period immediately prior to its publication. *Civil Service Law* (Minneapolis: University of Minnesota Press, 1939). A bird's-eye view of the progress of the merit system in the states, cities, counties, and special districts may be obtained from the Civil Service Assembly (since January 1, 1957, renamed the Public Personnel Association), *Civil Service Agencies in the United States: A 1940 Census* (Chicago: The Assembly, 1940), and its 1943 supplement. More specifically for the period before 1900, see the early annual reports of the U.S. Civil Service Commission, which periodically summarize personnel developments outside the national government and which contain useful bibliographies. For the period between 1900 and 1925, see Sarah Greer, *A Bibliography of Public Administration* (New York: National Institute of Public Administration, 1926), especially ch. iii. Leonard D. White, in his *Trends in Public Administration* (New York: McGraw-Hill Book Co., 1933), summarizes many state and local administrative trends from 1900 to 1930, including those in personnel administration. See also for this and more recent periods the various editions of Leonard D. White, *Introduction to the Study of Public Administration* (New York: The Macmillan Co., 1926, 1939, 1949, and 1955); and O. Glenn Stahl, *Public Personnel Administration* (New York: Harper and Bros., 1936, 1941, 1950 and 1956); as well as the *Proceedings* of the annual meetings of the Public Personnel Association, organized in 1906 as the National Assembly of Civil Service Commissions and known as the Civil Service Assembly of the United States and Canada after 1928, and the Association's journal, *Public Personnel Review*, which commenced publication in 1940. The Golden Anniversary issue of this journal, titled "Perspective in Public Personnel Administration," XVII (October, 1956), is especially important for its historical content. There are, of course, a host of further articles and specialized studies concerning state and local personnel administration, access to which is best obtained through the usual reference sources.

[38] As cited in footnote 11, pp. 765–66.

CHAPTER 7

Public Personnel Administration
in the Gilded Age: 1865–1900

Thus far modern civil service reform has been considered largely in terms of its impact upon the national political scene. Between the Civil War and the turn of the century the fundamental problem facing the new reform was that of gaining political acceptance. The decisive defeats of William Jennings Bryan in 1896 and again in 1900 were, among other things, to signify such acceptance. For the Great Commoner was the last presidential candidate publicly to espouse Jacksonian patronage policies as a fundamental plank in his platform. Patronage was by no means dead, but by the end of the nineteenth century it was clearly on the defensive and the merit system was flourishing.

However, the acceptance of a controversial proposal almost inevitably means its demise as a major political issue, and such was to be the case with civil service reform for many years to come. During the next decade and a half especially, the development of federal personnel management and the merit system must be chronicled more in terms of day-by-day administrative skirmishes than broad partisan battles on a nationwide front. Therefore, both as a backdrop for events to come and as a summary of such personnel precedents and practices as had emerged during the last decades of the nineteenth century, it is appropriate to outline briefly certain developments in the more prosaic regions of that civil establishment which was soon to support our emergence into the spotlight of world affairs.

Let us now consider (1) the early development of the Civil Service Commission as a central personnel agency, (2) the concurrent evolu-

136

tion of departmental personnel policies and administration, (3) significant changes in the social composition of the federal civil service by 1900, and (4) the prestige and power of the national bureaucracy in the Gilded Age. The terms "personnel agency" and "personnel administration" do not properly belong to the nineteenth century. Nevertheless, it is important to understand what they might have meant in the days of Grover Cleveland.

The Central Personnel Agency

The Pendleton Act never formed the basis for anything like a mid-twentieth century positive personnel system, nor was it intended that it should. The Civil Service Commission of 1883 was created to neutralize the effects of the spoils system upon our federal service and, it was hoped, upon our entire political and social system. In its annual report for 1891 the Commission flatly stated:

> While one of the main purposes of the [Pendleton] law is to improve the public service, yet this can hardly be considered its prime object. Its prime object is to remove from American politics the degrading influence of the patronage system.[1]

Certainly any ideas of amelioration of working conditions or of careful utilization of manpower were strictly incidental to what the reformers, and most other Americans, considered to be the fundamental purpose of the new organization—namely, policing the patronage.

In general, the new agency followed the initial blueprint laid down by the Grant Commission of 1871–75. The Commission advised the President and with the latter's approval laid down the general regulations governing the operation of the merit system. Beyond the supervision of these regulations, known officially as "Rules," the Commission undertook two principal types of activity: (1) administration of the civil service examination system for entrance to the classified service, and (2) investigation of violations of the political activity regulations of the President and of the Pendleton Act.

Examinations. As the Commission acknowledged in its first report to the President:

> The most important and exacting duties of the Commission are connected with the examinations and other tests of character and capacity for which the act provides, and which, subject to the rules, it places in charge of the Commission.[2]

1 USCSC, *Eighth Report*, 1891, p. 131.
2 USCSC, *First Report*, 1884, p. 11.

The Commission's principal administrative officer, the "chief examiner," supervised the operation of the competitive system. The examinations themselves were given by local boards of civil service employees, organized under the direction of the chief examiner with the consent of the department head involved. The principal duty of the chief examiner was "to secure accuracy, uniformity, and justice on the part of all the examiners." [3] He therefore travelled a great deal, setting up and supervising the local boards under his jurisdiction.

At the beginning, a local board of three members was formed in each post office coming under the rules, and boards of from three to five members in each customs district. For the executive departments in Washington a central board of ten members was selected, which supervised the examinations for the departmental service and marked and graded all papers. Then as now, papers were graded in terms of a maximum score of 100, with 70 as passing. Besides these regular boards there were special boards for testing unusual knowledge or skills and special *ad hoc* boards for the territories or other areas where examinations were the exception rather than the custom. Altogether, there were by 1897 about 850 boards throughout the country and the chief examiner was forced to ask for increased appropriations to enable him properly to manage their activities. Much of his supervision was reduced by that time to supervision by mail only, not too satisfactory at best.

The examination procedures resembled those current today. There were application, character reference, apportionment, and similar problems of detail to be met. Registers were formed of those who passed and, beginning with those who made the highest grades, individuals were then certified to appointing officers in need of personnel. The appointing officers could ask in turn for special examinations for particular positions or for such exceptions as might seem appropriate. In addition the Commission could on its own responsibility set up noncompetitive examinations where appropriate and make such exceptions to the rules as necessary, though it was required regularly to list such actions in its annual reports. During the early years there was little criticism of the policies of the Commission on these matters. The examination problem was, however, often complicated by the lack of any systematic duties-classification [4] or job de-

3 Same, p. 17.
4 Several meanings may be attached to the word "classification." The phrase position-classification" or "duties-classification" refers to the arranging of positions in a systematic fashion so that there is equal pay for equal work and so that similar jobs are called by similar names. The military services, during World War I, began to use the word "classification" to refer not to positions at all but to a system set up to determine differential individual abilities. During the first decade or so of the Pendleton Act, the

138

scription scheme in the federal government, and there was unquestionably unnecessary duplication and confusion in the examining process. This difficulty became more marked as the classified service rapidly increased in size.

All examinations were prepared by the Commission in Washington and forwarded to the local boards. Numbering systems were used to keep the grading anonymous. Sample copies of the examinations of this period appear from time to time in the annual report of the chief examiner, which was usually appended to the annual report of the Commission and printed for the information of the President and Congress. These examinations were normally quite "practical" and of the achievement type which has always been associated with American civil service testing.[5] They were largely graded in Washington.

By the eighteen nineties the Commission had begun to develop examinations

. . . to test the qualifications for positions where a greater or less amount of intelligence is necessary as a measure of ability, but where there are no special duties to be performed which require a special character of qualifications, as for ordinary clerks, messengers, etc.[6]

In other words, the Commission was constructing, to the best of its ability, a forerunner of tests of "general intelligence" at least a decade before 1900. These tests were put in the form and terminology of general educational level tests and were, in the eighteen nineties, known as "first-grade," "second-grade" and "third-grade" examinations. They were considered equal to various levels of the ordinary common or grade school educational requirements. Not modern "short-answer" or "objective" tests, such as have characterized both public and private employment procedures since World War I, they nevertheless tended in that direction and represented a transition from essay testing to more current practice.

Besides achievement and general education tests, the Commission used a third general class of formal examinations to cover positions which involved some peculiar experience or skill, especially of a

phrase "classified service" was roughly equivalent to "competitive service," "permanent service," and the words "under the merit system;" and the term is so used up through this chapter. However, by 1900 the technical meaning of "classified service" had become so broadened that the term soon lost much of its significance as a means of clearly distinguishing the merit system from the patronage. Therefore, for reasons outlined in the "supplementary notes" to ch. viii of this study, the writer, when discussing twentieth century matters, has used the term "classified service" only in contexts where its meaning cannot easily be misunderstood.

5 For early specimen sets of questions see, for instance, USCSC, *Second Report*, 1885, pp. 94-130.

6 USCSC, *Fourteenth Report*, 1897, p. 75.

mechanical character. These were usually known as "fourth-grade" or "trades" examinations and many of them resembled modern demonstration type testing systems in which the person being examined exhibits his skill before the examiner.[7] In addition, the Commission introduced in 1896 and 1897 what have since become known as "nonassembled examination" techniques: that is, a rating of training and experience was substituted for a written examination. This kind of testing is now almost routine for many types of more advanced positions. In the beginning, however, it was applied primarily to scientific and technical positions such as Supervising Architect of the Treasury and Chief of the Anthropological Division of the Smithsonian Institution. Oral tests, other than those which might be given informally by employment officers to candidates coming from the registers, were not a part of the Commission's examining system in the nineteenth century.[8] Promotion examinations, authorized by the Pendleton Act, were tried on several occasions, but proved difficult to administer and were abandoned for many years. It was not until the 1950's that much more was done.

All this is not to say that the Commission was using fully modern testing techniques in the nineteenth century. For instance, there is apparently no record of the employment of a professional psychologist in the federal government prior to World War I. There were not, of course, many employed anywhere before that time.[9] In the use of new examination methods the Commission was, in many ways, well ahead of industry, the colleges and universities, and most of the few professional psychologists of that time, and was to continue in the lead for many years.

The chief examiner of the Commission was in occasional consultation with leaders of business and industry during this period. In 1897 he reported:

. . . During the past year perhaps one hundred of the prominent business men in Washington and elsewhere have been consulted in reference to the different varieties of practical tests, and their advice has been found of the greatest value.[10]

[7] Same, p. 76. For examples of application forms and for descriptions of the principal types of tests given by the Commission in 1897 see same, pp. 83–99.

[8] Their systematic use by the Commission itself apparently dates from about 1910. USCSC, *Twenty-seventh Report*, 1910, p. 47.

[9] For private industrial and educational experience at this time see Walter D. Scott, Robert C. Clothier, and William R. Spriegel, *Personnel Management* (5th ed.; New York: McGraw-Hill Book Co., 1954), ch. xv, "The First Fifty Years of Applied Psychology."

[10] USCSC, *Fourteenth Report*, 1897, p. 80.

He then invited further suggestions. Even so, this seems to have been primarily a one-way street. There is practically no evidence that the Commission's work made any impression upon commercial and industrial practice at this time. If anything, the governmental examination system was, rightly or wrongly, considered "impractical" and a bit too "academic" for serious consideration elsewhere.

Moreover, it is interesting to note that the Commission was for many years apologetic for its examinations. In the same report quoted above, the chief examiner made this curious explanation of his concern with private testing practices:

It is the aim of these examinations to apply the same general rules and tests in the selection of employees for the Government service as are now employed with the best results in the management of the most successful business concerns. . . . In the present state of commercial development and intense business rivalry it is preposterous to imagine for a moment that the employees of a business firm of any importance are selected for any other reason than their demonstrated superiority for the special line of work at which they are to be employed. The recommendations of each applicant for employment by any of the great banking, insurance, manufacturing, or railroad corporations of the country are most carefully scanned and the record of each man thoroughly investigated before it is possible for him to secure employment in their service.[11]

However, other evidence from the many entrepreneurial histories for the nineteenth century does not at all support this optimistic view of private industrial practice before 1900.[12] Nor does the chief examiner anywhere in the lengthy report from which the above excerpt is taken reinforce his conclusion with any examples of especially exemplary examining practices in the world of private enterprise. One can only suspect that the chief examiner, in an endeavor to bolster his case by analogy, was guilty of exaggeration here for the benefit of Congress, for whom his report was prepared. Indeed, there is a good deal of evidence that the introduction of modern testing techniques into widespread use in the private industrial world was stimulated by the de-

[11] Same, p. 75.
[12] For typical examples of contemporary commercial employment practices, see Boris Emmet and John E. Jeuck, Catalogues and Counters (Chicago: The University of Chicago Press, 1950), ch. ix, particularly p. 138; Evelyn H. Knowlton, Pepperell's Progress (Cambridge, Mass.: Harvard University Press, 1948), ch. viii; and Ralph W. and Muriel E. Hidy, Pioneering in Big Business (New York: Harper and Bros., 1955), ch. xx, especially pp. 597–99. These three studies concern Sears, Roebuck and Co., the Pepperell Manufacturing Co., and the Standard Oil Co. of New Jersey, respectively. For the rudimentary nature of private personnel administration in nearly all respects at this time, see also Oscar W. Nestor, "A History of Personnel Administration, 1890 to 1910" (unpublished Ph.D. dissertation in Economics, Graduate School of the University of Pennsylvania, 1954).

141

velopments within civil and military governmental administration, rather than the reverse.

Investigations. While the primary administrative emphasis of the Commission was upon its examining function, it was hardly less concerned about subversion of the merit system through (1) fraud or collusion in examinations, (2) illegal appointments, (3) political coercion and removals, and (4) political assessments. The Commission's authority in some of these matters—assessments, for example—extended into the unclassified as well as the classified service.

In these investigative functions, the commissioners were hampered considerably by limited funds, the lack of authority to subpoena, and their limited power of enforcement. Their main weapons were publicity and such departmental and presidential support as might be forthcoming. Fortunately, support of the presidents was reasonably constant during this period, if not so much could be said for all department heads.[13] President Theodore Roosevelt finally required all government employees to give the Commission information it requested. Eventually Congress authorized the Commission "to administer oaths to witnesses in any matter pending before the Civil Service Commission." But a few prosecutions were under way by 1890.

While the Commission was faced with innumerable difficulties in fulfilling completely its investigative functions, there is good evidence that its work produced results. Frauds in examinations were negligible by 1900, illegal appointments were declining, and assessments and political removals were being curbed. Considerable further progress would be made in the next decade with the wholehearted support of Presidents Theodore Roosevelt and Taft.

The Commission was required by law to report regularly on its investigations; its annual reports for many years document case after case. A brief example is the case of the post office in Norwalk, Ohio, which well illustrates the nature of the work as well as some of the difficulties involved:

NORWALK, OHIO, POST-OFFICE

It was alleged that the postmaster, Frank M. Roth, had made removals for political reasons. Mr. Bunn, of the Commission's force, made a full report which, in the opinion of the Commission, showed that Mr. Roth had been guilty of discriminating against some of his subordinates for political reasons, as charged. In one case in particular, the Commission deemed the evidence conclusive, and wrote to the Post-Office Department on May 1, 1894, as follows:

13 See A. Bower Sageser, *The First Two Decades of the Pendleton Act* (Lincoln, Neb.: University of Nebraska, 1935), p. 150, for examples of difficulties arising from handicaps to the Commission's investigating power.

The Commission has the honor to forward herewith the report of Examiner Bunn's recent investigation of civil-service matters at Norwalk, Ohio, post-office, and to recommend that Thomas Briggs be reinstated as letter carrier, it appearing that he has been removed really for political reasons. The further recommendation is respectfully made that John O'Brien be removed at once for mendacity in striving to mislead an officer of the Commission, engaged in conducting an examination under the direction of the Commission, and for having striven to procure the removal, for his own benefit, of a person in the classified postal service.

In response the Department sent a number of statements made by the postmaster and others who had been instrumental in having the man removed, and a supplemental investigation was made by Mr. Bunn. Upon this the Commission wrote to the Department on May 19, as follows:

These papers justify the statements and conclusions of Mr. Bunn's first report, and discredit the criticisms that have been made upon it. It is still the opinion of the Commission that the carrier, Briggs, should be reinstated forthwith. If any carrier had acted as Postmaster Roth has in this matter the Commission would have expected his removal, and would have said nothing against his being removed, and the Commission thinks that the postmaster should at least be reprimanded for what he has done.

The carrier, Briggs, was not reinstated, nor was the postmaster punished in any way, as far as the Commission knows; but the carrier, O'Brien, was removed.[14]

Other personnel matters. The Commission was also concerned with the recruitment of personnel for federal positions. However, in this as in many other matters, the dual personnel system established under the Jacksonians still prevailed. Outside the classified service, the locating of talent for administrative posts was primarily a departmental and political matter. Within the classified service minimal standards were developing about as rapidly as the examination system became perfected. By 1900 the Commission, with departmental concurrence, had been able to develop entrance criteria for the great bulk of the positions within the classified service. This meant, in turn, something of an improvement in the caliber of personnel coming into the service.

However, there was still nothing like a concept of "positive recruitment" and would not be until World Wars I and II. For most posts, except in the rapidly developing technical and scientific realms, there were more than enough prospective applicants. Examinations were announced and applicants appeared. It was as simple as that.

The Commission's administrative burdens relating both to examination and recruitment were largely a function of the extension of the classified service. This was essentially a simple process, involving merely the publishing of an executive order declaring that the personnel occupying particular positions as of a given date were to be

14 USCSC, *Eleventh Report*, 1894, p. 302.

considered in the classified service. To be sure, there was frequently a quick rise in turnover among such employees as patronage minded supervisors took care of their political friends before the effective date of the presidential order. Not until the nineteen twenties was any important group of federal civil employees required to pass examinations before they could be sure of remaining in positions covered into the classified service. Until then both employees and positions were simultaneously brought under the provisions of the Pendleton Act, a process which quickly became popularly known as "blanketing-in."

The civil service rules were themselves constantly undergoing changes and revisions, and they were recodified in both 1888 and 1896. However, the basic character of the rules remained relatively unchanged throughout this period. The most important change came as a result of President McKinley's Executive Order of July 27, 1897, as amended and strengthened on May 29, 1899. Thereafter, it was required that

No removal shall be made from the competitive classified service except for just cause and for reasons given in writing; and the person sought to be removed shall have notice and be furnished a copy of such reasons, and be allowed a reasonable time for personally answering the same in writing.[15]

This regulation provided an important new control over the removal authority of appointing officers. However, it was some time before this change in procedure was fully effective, as its enforcement depended entirely upon the attitude of the President and his determination to hold his cabinet members and chief administrative officers to account.

Equally significant for the future was the developing pattern of veteran preference. The basic statute, one of March 3, 1865, was reenacted by reference in the Pendleton Act and gave preference almost exclusively to disabled veterans. However, the cases involved never amounted in this period to more than a few hundred a year. Nevertheless, the precedents of "5-point" preference in examinations, of disabled veterans at the top of the registers, of exemption from apportionment regulations, of reinstatement without time limit, and of preference in reductions-in-force were all recognized by 1889 even though their enforcement, also dependent at this time on executive attitude, was sometimes desultory.[16]

Nearly all other aspects of personnel administration came within

15 USCSC, *Fifteenth Report*, 1898, p. 51; see also the discussion on pp. 19–20.
16 For a catalog of veteran preference statutes and regulations since 1865 see USCSC, *History of Veteran Preference in Federal Employment* (Washington: Government Printing Office, 1955).

the province of the department heads, though the Civil Service Commission did not hesitate to recommend improvements in such matters as position-classification and the correction of such abuses as the assignment of laborers to clerical work. Only President Cleveland paid much attention to these recommendations and in 1888 several minor changes which could be accomplished by executive order were made. More fundamental actions required congressional approval, and none was forthcoming during this period except for the Pendleton Act itself.

Internal management. In its own establishment the Civil Service Commission was not entirely the master of its household, being dependent, though decreasingly so, upon the Secretary of the Interior for accommodations and supplies until after World War I. During the period under discussion here, the Commission moved from one place to another every few years as space problems became more pressing.[17] In 1883 the total full-time force available to the Commission was six persons, including the three commissioners, a chief examiner, a secretary, and a stenographer. The Commission's own employees were classified in 1888. By 1890 they had increased to seventeen, principally by the addition of ten clerks and a laborer. In 1895 the Commission was successful in its request for much-needed help and the total permanent force, excluding "details" of clerks from various departments, was upped from twenty-two to sixty-two and remained at that figure until the time of the Spanish-American War. The appropriations available for the administration of the merit system largely reflected salaries and varied from $12,814.80 for 1883 to $98,340 for 1898.[18] The entire travel budget of the Commission never exceeded $6,000 a year until 1897. One can readily see that the new agency was not overwhelmed with funds for supervising examinations and policing the federal service.

The work-load of the agency can be roughly estimated from the fact that during the fiscal year ending June 30, 1897, the application division received and disposed of 237,000 pieces of mail in reference to information about examinations. This correspondence resulted in

---

[17] The early family and housing problems of the Commission itself are recounted in some detail in the autobiography of one of the Commission's first employees. See Matthew F. Halloran, *The Romance of the Merit System* (2d ed.; Washington: Judd and Detweiler, Inc., 1929). See also USCSC, *First Report*, 1884, p. 7; and the Commission's collection of correspondence entitled *Theodore Roosevelt—United States Civil Service Commissioner* (Washington: USCSC, 1940), Letter 10 and elsewhere.

[18] USCSC, *Thirteenth Report*, 1896, pp. 102–104 and 117–18. These pages contain an analysis of the Commission's financial and personnel position for each year from 1883 through 1898. These figures do not, however, include monies for supplies and housing provided by the Interior Department, nor do they include numbers of "detailed" employees.

52,108 applications, followed by the appropriate notices to appear for examinations. A total of 2,591 examinations were arranged through some 850 local boards. Over 33,000 sets of examination papers were graded, though the Commission was then running several months behind in its examining work as a result of the Cleveland classifications. Finally, more than eighty investigations were undertaken, varying in location from the Fort Peck, Montana, Indian Agency to the Parkersburg, West Virginia, Internal Revenue District.[19] Beyond these routine tasks the Commission set up in 1896 a service records division, contemplating a central personnel records system for the entire classified service. The continual complaint of the new agency, not an unusual one, was the lack of personnel to carry out its assigned tasks.

Achievements. In general a study of the initial efforts of the Civil Service Commission gives an impression of relative orderliness and efficiency. The burden was great but the new agency apparently handled it well. Operating without particular fanfare the Commission, for the most part, carried on quietly and effectively.

Occasionally, however, there were quarrels within the official family. Theodore Roosevelt was especially susceptible. On at least two occasions, the commissioners themselves publicly disagreed, and Cleveland found it expedient to remove both Commissioners Edgerton and Johnston. But on the whole the agency functioned as well as any other agency and better than many. At least there was never through its early history, nor in more recent years, any hint of that kind of political corruption and chicanery which has been associated from time to time with most of the other segments of the executive branch of the government. Even a thorough investigation by the incoming Republican administration of President McKinley failed to turn up anything derogatory and the Civil Service Commission was reluctantly given a clean bill of health.[20]

By 1900 the initial precedents of the Grant Commission were quite fully implemented, and the general framework of merit system procedures was, on the whole, well established in a form easily recognizable today. Clearly the work of the Civil Service Commission was slowly having an effect on the federal service. Yet this effect was manifested almost entirely in terms of the enforcement of standards

---

19 USCSC, Fourteenth Report, 1897, pp. 281–407. The eighty-odd cases contained in this report include only the most important and do not include cases started but either dropped or not completed.

20 U.S. Congress, Senate, Report of the Committee on Civil Service and Retrenchment, 55th Cong., 2d Sess., Senate Report 659 (Washington: Government Printing Office, 1898). The result of a Senate resolution of March 23, 1897, passed from the desire of the new Republican Congress to look into the operation of the civil service under Cleveland, the report is a mine of miscellaneous information about the nature of the civil service at the turn of the century.

of employment and political activity and was at best only tenuously related to the development of public personnel administration in any broader sense. The personnel problems of the federal service were to be solved at this time primarily by controlling the entrance into the public service. If the "front door" could be regulated, the "back door" would take care of itself. Little thought was yet given by the central personnel agency—or anyone else—to the government employee *after* he once became a member of the civil establishment.

Moreover, the influence of the Civil Service Commission never extended to more than half of the personnel of the executive branch before 1900. The dual type of personnel management which had characterized the period before the Civil War was only emphasized by the creation of the Commission and the formal division of federal civil employees into the classified and unclassified services. To get the full flavor of public personnel management at this time one must examine the operations of the great executive departments. Here the patronage and merit systems both held sway, sometimes in almost complete isolation from each other but more often in a curious intermixture of the old and the new.

Departmental Personnel Administration

Throughout most of the nineteenth century the federal executive civil service was divided among seven major agencies, each headed by a cabinet member reporting directly to the President. These were the Departments of State, Treasury, War, Navy, Interior, Post Office, and Justice. In one form or another, all of these antedated 1800 except Interior, which was organized in 1849. In 1862 agricultural activities were brought together to form an eighth separate executive establishment under a Commissioner. Though always known as the Department of Agriculture, this agency did not gain full cabinet status and its head the title of Secretary until 1889. The Department of Labor became an independent agency without cabinet status in 1888 and was merged into the Department of Commerce and Labor in 1903. Outside the departments the only organizations of any long-run importance before the passage of the Pendleton Act were the Smithsonian Institution and the Government Printing Office, both created before the Civil War. No separate commissions of any significance were created within the executive branch until the eighteen eighties. The structure of federal administration during the Gilded Age was still relatively simple. Nevertheless, public administration at the national level was becoming increasingly complicated after the Civil War. The establishment of the Civil Service Commission in 1883 and the Interstate Commerce Commission in 1887 presaged the break up of the neatly hierarchical executive organization first set up by the Federalists.

From the contemporary reports of the executive departments themselves together with those of the Civil Service Commission and such investigating bodies as the Cockrell Committee and the Dockery-Cockrell Commission—the Hoover Commissions of their day—one obtains the impression that the same sort of loose and free-wheeling administrative activity which was typical of, say, 1850 was still widely prevalent in the eighties and nineties. Most of the worst post-Civil War abuses had been cleaned up by the eighties and many administrative procedures, especially those involving financial accounts, had been tightened up; but to be more complimentary on the subject of general administration would be to exaggerate the state of the administrative art, both public and private, before 1900. Cleveland undoubtedly raised the moral sights for public office-holders at both the higher and lower levels, but neither he nor those who preceded him were much more administratively minded than were the Jacksonians. The period of the Gilded Age, like that which came before it, was primarily one of intense political activity rather than of administrative innovation.

In the departments the merit system ran headlong into the traditional intermixture of politics and administration which had characterized American public management since 1829. While the Civil Service Commission, as a relatively new and independent agency, was free to concentrate on personnel administration via the merit system, the other agencies of the executive branch were not. In them personnel management inevitably found itself intermingled with and affected by partisan politics, substantive program requirements, and administration in general. Viewed from the more isolated vantage point of the Civil Service Commission, progress in personnel management elsewhere must have seemed halting and uneven. Between 1883 and 1900 it is clear that less than a majority of cabinet members were reasonably consistent supporters of the merit system, and some of these implemented the new reform in their agencies more as a result of executive or other pressures than from any deep sense of conviction. Nevertheless, some progress was made in departmental personnel management during these years. With the experiences of the Department of Agriculture, the one executive agency whose personnel practices are a matter of extensive and systematic record,[21] providing the major

---

21 For this section the unique study by Warner W. Stockberger and Virginia B. Smith, *Personnel Administration Development in the United States Department of Agriculture: The First Fifty Years* (Washington: Department of Agriculture, 1947), is invaluable, especially since Dr. Stockberger took part in many of the events he describes. In 1925

backdrop of illustrations, let us consider the main facets of public personnel management as they most closely affected the day by day work of civil servants in the final decades of the nineteenth century. **The chief clerks and appointment practices.** In the departmental headquarters, bureaus, and larger field establishments, the chief clerks still reigned, though in some cases they were now assisted by "appointment clerks." They continued to direct both the budding personnel system and the administrative supervision of agency activities. There were no full-time federal personnel offices designated as such in the nineteenth century. Not until after the First World War was personnel administration at the departmental or bureau level considered much more than a special sort of record keeping.

The Appointment Clerk of the Department of Agriculture listed for the year 1897 an outline of his duties and responsibilities, which have been summarized as follows:

. . . According to this statement it was the duty of the Appointment Clerk to prepare for the signature of the Secretary the documents effecting all appointments, promotions, reductions, transfers, furloughs, and resignations for the entire Department; to maintain a biographical record of each employee; to conduct the business of the Department with the Civil Service Commission; and to advise the Secretary on the application of the civil-service Law, rules, and regulations; to keep records of all transactions of his office, and to brief and file all documents relating to the work thereof. It was also his duty as a member of the Board of Promotion Review to examine the efficiency reports, recommendations for promotion, and applications for promotion, and to recommend appropriate action thereon to the Secretary. The Appointment Clerk also compiled the data for the Official Register or Blue Book, which at the time included information concerning each employee in the entire Department. In addition, he prepared reports in response to resolutions of Congress, requests of the Secretary and of the Civil Service Commission. The Appointment Clerk, whose salary was $2,000 per annum, and two clerks at $1,200 each, comprised the entire staff of the Central Personnel Office.[22]

The Department of Agriculture was by this time the first of the great executive departments to come almost entirely [23] within the classified

he became the first full-time director of personnel in the federal government and, until his death in May, 1944, he was considered the dean of federal personnel men. See Eldon L. Johnson, "The Administrative Career of Dr. W. W. Stockberger," *Public Administration Review*, I (Autumn, 1940), 50. See also, especially for contemporary scientific and technical personnel problems in the Department of Agriculture, Charles W. Dabney, Jr., *Civil Service in the Department of Agriculture*, U.S. Department of Agriculture, Office of Experiment Stations, Circular 33, January 26, 1897 (Washington: Government Printing Office, 1897). Dabney was then Assistant Secretary of Agriculture. At this time the department contained about 2,500 civil employees.

22 Stockberger and Smith, as cited in footnote 21, pp. 83–84. The term "Central Personnel Office" is the authors' designation and not that of the Department.

23 An executive order of June 10, 1896, excluded only the Secretary, his own private secretary, and manual laborers. Same, p. 55.

149

service, and the above summary may be taken as representing departmental personnel practices at their most enlightened and systematic level before 1900.

Within the unclassified service political influence was yet the sesame to public office, except for a growing number of scientific and technical positions where the need for expertise was recognized. Occasionally however, an appointing officer, goaded beyond endurance, would refuse to give in. William G. LeDuc, Commissioner of Agriculture from 1877 to 1881, is reported as telling off an overly persistent senator: "Senator you may go to the Senate or go to Hell so far as this case is concerned; the offending clerk will not be restored to the rolls while I am Commissioner of Agriculture." [24]

Despite such not too infrequent rectitude, most of the subterfuges that we still today associate with the spoils system were in full sway. Temporary employees could be employed without going through standard merit system procedures, and they were frequently hired, especially in election months. Extra laborers were apt to be employed in the navy yards, for example, at politically strategic intervals.[25] One congressman desired the Commissioner of Agriculture to place a man at his disposal to do some writing for the legislator. When rebuffed, he retaliated by instigating a congressional investigation of the agency.[26] "Made" work might be resorted to where appropriations allowed.

The exploitation of the decennial census staff for patronage purposes was especially flagrant, with spectacular statistical inaccuracies occasionally stemming from the efforts, or lack of them, of ill-trained enumerators. The census of 1890 has been reliably estimated as understating the population of New York City by as much as 200,000.[27] A few years later, William D. Foulke had the opportunity to examine in detail the books of the then-Superintendent of the Census, Robert P. Porter. Foulke's report on what he found provides one of our best and most graphic analyses of patronage practices within the unclassified service:

I found that, like the Secretary of Patronage in England in former days, he kept regular books of account with Congressmen informing each, whether Senator or Representative to whom patronage was given (and these were mostly Republicans), how many positions were at his disposal. I ex-

24 Same, p. 13.
25 This was largely stopped, however, by Secretary Tracy under Harrison. Sageser, as cited in footnote 13, p. 162.
26 Stockberger and Smith, as cited in footnote 21, p. 12.
27 For a discussion of this situation see William D. Foulke, *Fighting the Spoilsmen* (New York: G. P. Putnam's Sons, 1919), pp. 64–72.

amined two of these books of account. In one of them the appointments were classified according to States and in the other they were charged to the particular Congressman on whose recommendation they were made. The latter book was a ledger of over four hundred pages. At the head of each page appeared the name of the Congressman charged with the appointments. In the left-hand column were the numbers of the files containing the recommendations and credentials, then followed the names of the appointees and the grades and salaries. By means of this book the relative rights of members of Congress could be adjusted and it could be seen at a glance whether any particular member had overdrawn his account. A peculiar feature of this book was that after a Congressman retired the clerks appointed by him were transferred to another account where the appointees of ex-Congressmen were all thrown together, perhaps as the subjects of early decapitation.

I was informed there were other books of the same character as this ledger in the Census Office covering other periods of time. I could not help thinking of the similarity of this catalogue to a live stock register.[28]

The maintenance of registers of this type is still not entirely unknown. To make the distinctions between the classified and unclassified offices even more clear to those who were interested in the available patronage, it became the custom during this period, after a change of administration from one party to another, for Congress to order the publication of lists of public offices in the form of what have since become known as "Plum Books." A ready index to the available jobs, their salaries, and tenure, these compilations were in great demand.[29]

Classification and pay. Position-classification and salary administration presented at this time, as formerly, a peculiar combination of administrative discretion and congressional whim. Such matters were outside the jurisdiction of the Civil Service Commission, except as it was occasionally involved in decisions as to whether a given position was inside or outside the classified service, a decision which sometimes depended on the pay and duties assigned. However, the Commission recommended and President Cleveland approved on June 29, 1888,

---

28 Same, pp. 73-74.
29 One of the first of these manuals, which are among our most important sources of data concerning the composition of the public service of their day, is U.S. Congress, Senate, Civil List: Method of Appointment and Term and Tenure of Office, 52d Cong., 2d Sess., Senate Misc. Doc. 61 (Washington: Government Printing Office, 1893). The next, somewhat more detailed, and provided for the convenience of the Republicans in 1897, is U.S. Congress, House, Tables Showing the Number of Positions in the Executive Civil Service of the United States, Classified and Unclassified on June 30, 1896, 54th Cong., 2d Sess., House Doc. 202, a report by the USCSC, edited by Theodore L. DeLand (Washington: Government Printing Office, 1897). The most recent example is U.S. Congress, Positions Not Under the Civil Service, 83d Cong., 1st Sess., Senate Doc. 18, Parts I and II, prepared by the USCSC (Washington: Government Printing Office, 1953). As the agency normally requested to prepare these documents, the Civil Service Commission has found itself functioning as a reluctant broker in what might be called the patronage "exchange."

a revision of the position-classification structure for the departmental services. But, this was easier said than done, and department heads, in the absence of any special enforcing authority or agency, did very little. In any event, all Cleveland was attempting to accomplish was a mild salary standardization rather than full position-classification. The Commission was well aware that the fundamental problem of insuring equal pay for equal work was still unsolved.[30]

Further complicating this matter were certain statutes. Congress had authorized many executive agencies to employ their workers only on a "statutory roll" basis, whereby each specific job was listed in the appropriation act. Others could use the "lump sum" method. In some departments both were used simultaneously for many years, effectively destroying any possibility of equal pay for equal work. The statutory roll system controlled some abuses but was of no help to agencies with seasonal work-loads. Moreover the statutory roll salaries were not always the same for similar positions. Where lump sums were available for salaries the pressures were often to create more jobs at less pay, especially when the jobs might then be available for political purposes. The Commission summarized in its report for 1887 just how this particular abuse had typically worked:

. . . So great was the importunity for place under the old system of appointments that when $1,600 and $1,800 places became vacant the salaries thereof would be allowed to lapse, to accumulate, so that these accumulations might be divided among the applicants for place on whose behalf patronage-mongers were incessant in importunity. In place of one $1,800 clerk three would be employed at $600 each; would be employed, according to the peculiarly expressive language of the patronage-purveyors, "on the lapse." "In one case," said a person of reliability and of accurate information testifying before the Senate committee on civil-service reform and retrenchment, "thirty-five persons were put on the 'lapse fund' of the treasurer's office for eight days at the end of a fiscal year to sop up some money which was in danger of being saved and returned to the treasury." Unnecessary employés abounded in every department, in every customs office, and in almost every postoffice.[31]

This sort of example could be multiplied many times, though increasingly less so after 1883. Salaries and duties basically reflected political and social rather than administrative theories. Moreover, the pay scales themselves were but very little higher than those outlined

---

[30] For criticism of the existing classification system, still based fundamentally on the legislation of 1853, see almost any of the annual reports of the Commission through World War I—for example, *Fourth Report*, 1887, p. 116. See also Ismar Baruch, *History of Position-Classification and Salary Standardization in the Federal Service, 1789–1941* (2d ed., P.C.D. Manual A-2; Washington: USCSC, 1941), pp. 15–23.

[31] *Fourth Report*, 1887, p. 122.

in pre-Civil War legislation. The typical departmental and field office clerk still received from $800 to $1,200 a year.[32]

Efficiency ratings. The more modern types of efficiency ratings may be dated from 1887, though there had been desultory efforts at merit rating as far back as the eighteen fifties.[33] Considered desirable as an adjunct to the system of promotion examinations with which the Commission was experimenting, President Harrison supported them with his authority in 1887. In his first annual message on December 3, 1889, he stated that he had directed the departments to consider the problem of efficiency and

. . . whether a record might not be kept in each bureau of all those elements that are covered by the terms 'faithfulness' and 'efficiency,' and a rating made showing the relative merits of the clerks of each class, this rating to be regarded as a test of merit in making promotions.[34]

The Secretary of Agriculture then, for example, on December 8, 1891, directed that the President's request be implemented by the chiefs of each bureau, division, and office. Each such establishment was to keep a *daily* record of attendance, punctuality, efficiency, and deportment for all employees. Each heading was to be scored on a scale of ten. In at least one section of the department, records were compiled and analyzed monthly,[35] with the result that enormous amounts of mathematical calculation seem to have been involved, with, we may assume, the same objections to the results that one finds in more modern times—for approximately the same reasons. After continuing attempts to develop the system in various departments, it gradually foundered on the rock of inadequate duties-classification, the same hazard which largely foiled promotion examinations and which was threatening the entire examination system.

Efficiency ratings were never tied in much with probation, which appears to have been used somewhat more extensively in connection with dismissals than during recent years. For a decade before 1900 the Commission records an attrition rate of about 2 per cent as a result of dismissals during the six months probationary period then customary. This compares to estimates of considerably less than 1 per

32 Baruch, as cited in footnote 30, pp. 17–18.

33 For the history of efficiency ratings since the Civil War, see W. Brooke Graves, "Efficiency Rating Systems: Their History, Organization and Functioning," U.S. Congress, Senate, Subcommittee of the Committee on Post Office and Civil Service, *Hearings, Efficiency Rating System for Federal Employees,* 80th Cong., 2d Sess. (Washington: Government Printing Office, 1948), pp. 185–251. For earlier years, see Leonard D. White, *The Jacksonians* (New York: The Macmillan Co., 1954), pp. 403–404.

34 James D. Richardson (ed.), *Messages and Papers of the Presidents* (New York: National Bureau of Literature and Art, 1905), IX, 54.

35 Stockberger and Smith, as cited in footnote 21, p. 44.

cent in recent years.[36] While the early Commission frequently pointed to its 2 per cent figure with pride, there is no good evidence that the probationary period has ever been used as it could and probably should be in the federal establishment.

Nor was the removal power in general always wielded to aid efficiency. The "back door" was open wide until 1897, when President McKinley required written charges to be filed, with a copy to the employee and a chance to be heard. As there was no enforcement agency for these regulations, discipline all through this period depended upon the desires of the appointing officer and the political connections of the employee. The Civil Service Commission did, however, police removals for political reasons within the classified service and the civil service rules forbade discrimination on account of religion. But enforcement of the latter regulation was primarily dependent on the whims of the individual administrator, for the Commission had no real authority in this matter and seldom attempted to intervene.

Employment conditions. From the standpoint of health and safety, working conditions in the public service were probably as good as anywhere else. There were cases of overcrowding, and there were cases where health hazards undoubtedly existed. Stockberger and Smith have described one such situation existing in the Department of Agriculture in 1888:

> The chemical laboratory installed in the basement of the main building had become a source of annoyance and of apprehension. Obnoxious fumes permeated the office of the Commissioner which was directly over the Laboratory and menaced the health of employees in other parts of the building. Sometimes the fumes were so bad the Commissioner had to go outside for fresh air. One day there was a chemical explosion directly under the Commissioner's office but fortunately no damage resulted.[37]

Safety regulations were few in number and seldom uniform in application. There were medical examinations prior to appointment in some cases, but this was by no means regular practice. Workmen's compensation and employee pension plans were, of course, nonexistent at this time, and there was very little pressure for them before 1900. Lunch rooms and facilities were occasionally provided.

Leave regulations, for both annual and sick leave, were before 1883 largely up to administrative discretion. After this date Congress provided that thirty days leave with pay might be granted, with, for many, up to thirty days more for sickness. There was no requirement

---

[36] William E. Mosher, J. Donald Kingsley, and O. Glenn Stahl, *Public Personnel Administration* (3d ed.; Harper and Bros., 1950), p. 155.

[37] As cited in footnote 21, p. 32.

of uniformity, however, and there were a good many variations in practice.

Hours of work were also still somewhat haphazard, though they were gradually being standardized. In the nineties the offices in Washington and the various custom houses kept hours from 9 until 4. The post offices generally conformed to local business practice. In 1883 Congress set working hours for many clerical employees at not less than seven. However, department heads could and did modify these hours and uniformity was still the exception. For skilled and unskilled workmen President Van Buren had set a ten hour day in 1840, thus providing the only federal action before the Civil War which may be interpreted as supporting the concept of the government as a model employer. Agitation for the eight hour day for these "blue collar" workers continued after the Civil War and by 1892 the eight hour day had been extended by law to most government employees.[38] Nevertheless, despite these statements of principle, the hours of work still varied widely. About 1903 Harry G. Richey, a distinguished federal engineer then working in Joplin, Missouri, wrote his superior, the Supervising Architect of the Treasury Department, to ask whether the eight hour legislation applied to himself in the field. In a terse note the Supervising Architect advised him, "You are employed by the year and your services are continuous." [39] Other employees with lenient supervisors or political influence were often more fortunate. It was yet not too unusual for civil servants in some establishments to be absent from work and to arrange for their friends, wives, or relatives to report for them.[40] A few managed to work at

---

[38] For a brief summary of the history of legislation on hours of labor in the federal government, see Committee on Department Methods—better known as the Keep Committee—*Annual Leave, Sick Leave, and Hours of Labor* (Washington: The Committee, 1906). For specific information for the year 1892, see USCSC, *Tenth Report*, 1893, pp. 29–31. See Sterling Spero, *Government as Employer* (New York: Remsen Press, 1948), ch. v, "Government 'Workmen, Laborers and Mechanics' and the Shorter Work Day," for nineteenth century policies with respect to blue collar workers.

[39] Harry G. Richey, *Government Service as a Career* (New York: Vantage Press, 1956), p. 19. This is one of the very few autobiographies by an American permanent civil servant. For others covering periods in part relevant to this chapter, see Halloran, as cited in footnote 17; Harvey W. Wiley (chief chemist, Department of Agriculture), *An Autobiography* (Indianapolis: Bobbs-Merrill, 1930); William Alanson White (medical administrator, St. Elizabeth's Hospital, Washington, D.C.), *Autobiography of a Purpose* (New York: Doubleday, Doran, 1938); and Isaac M. Cline (principal meteorologist, Weather Bureau), *Storms, Floods and Sunshine* (New Orleans: Pelican Publishing Co., 1945). Compared to their British counterparts, American permanent civil servants have produced almost no reflective personal accounts of public administration in operation.

[40] For references to these practices, see Lucille Foster McMillin, *Women in the Federal Service*, Form 3321, USCSC (Washington: Government Printing Office, 1941), pp. 3–5. Clara Barton, later founder of the Red Cross, held a position of clerk-copyist in the Patent Office for a number of years and, during the Civil War, paid a substitute to perform her duties while she served as a nurse at the front. Though it has never been substantiated by federal records, Miss Barton herself claimed to have been the first

home and avoid any supervision at all. But the general tendency by the turn of the century was to standardize on the eight hour day, which was shorter than the working day of many persons in business, industry, and agriculture where toil from sun-up to sun-down was still frequent. In his 1909 vocational guide for persons considering public service, one of the first of its kind, El Bie K. Foltz describes the enticements of federal working conditions:

Not only is tenure of office and income secure under the Government during good behavior, but the services performed are surrounded with a dignity not seen in private life. The Government employee has the added advantages of earning a comfortable living, congenial work, short hours, long vacation, ample provision against sickness, a chance to educate himself and his family and, most important of all, time to live. The worries and haste to succeed, common in commercial life, are entirely absent.[41]

There is a good deal to be said for Foltz' description of federal working conditions as compared to those in much of private industry in the Gilded Age. It is quite possible that these conditions had something to do with the continuing press of applicants for public positions even at the lower levels.

However, by 1900 federal wages and working conditions for white collar employees were either remaining the same or were becoming less favorable, while those in private industry were rapidly improving. This suggests that the introduction of the merit system may have had some unanticipated consequences. Sterling D. Spero, one of our principal authorities on public employee unionism, notes that the placing of a number of postal positions under the merit system was followed by a decline of congressional interest in these positions which were no longer of value for the purposes of party spoils. In the long run, he contends this was responsible for the lack of improvement in working conditions, to which, in turn, he attributes the development of the influential postal employee unions, the first unions of importance to be formed among government white collar employees.[42]

General personnel policies. One can only conclude that departmental personnel policies were highly "personal" and often "political." The following analysis of the personnel policy of Jeremiah M. Rusk, Secre-

woman appointed to a full clerical position on the same basis as men and at the $1,400 level. It is certain, however, that her employment dated at least as far back as 1854. Same, pp. 4–5.

41 El Bie K. Foltz, The Federal Civil Service as a Career (New York: G. P. Putnam's Sons, 1909), p. 229. This is one of the first of a long line of similar popular manuals by private authors designed to familiarize prospective applicants with the details of the federal government and civil service procedure.

42 Sterling D. Spero, The Labor Movement in a Government Industry (New York: George H. Doran Co., 1924), pp. 26 and 61.

tary of the Department of Agriculture from 1889 to 1893, is probably applicable to most executive agencies shortly before 1900:

> Secretary Rusk's personnel policy was never formally stated, but its general outlines are revealed in numerous instances in which his decisions— or directions affected the interests or welfare of various employees. Each case was individually settled by the Secretary, subject to the current pressures. Consistency of standards in personnel practices was lacking. Usually considerate and forbearing, on occasion he was firm and decisive. He could lend so attentive an ear to Members of Congress seeking a promotion for a constituent that he would grant the increase requested although "we have scarcely enough money in her division to last the year through," and just as readily refuse to promote admittedly efficient and deserving employees in order "to make a good showing as to the economical expenditure of money." [43]

Certainly, if one were looking anywhere in the federal government for a particularly objective administration of personnel matters before 1900, it was not to be found except perhaps in the operations of the Civil Service Commission itself.

In general, about all we can conclude is that personnel administration in the Gilded Age, at the departmental and field service levels, had risen modestly at best above that typical of the Jacksonian era. Only gradually were either the Civil Service Commission or the executive departments to take on those additional functions necessary to convert the public personnel system of the Gilded Age into its modern counterpart. The movement for economy and efficiency, the doctrines of scientific management, and the pressures of two great wars were yet to make their mark on the framework set up by the Pendleton Act.

The Changing Bureaucracy

The only class-oriented change in the social composition of the federal bureaucracy came after 1829. But even the Jacksonian movement was not as precipitate as proclaimed. In the eighteen seventies and eighties moral reform, aimed at the ethical elevation of public life, was neither revolutionary nor the exclusive property of any one political party.

Even the rapid turnover of political parties in power, which characterized the later Jacksonian period as well as that of Cleveland, did not alter the character of the federal civil service in any startling way. The social composition of both of the major political parties, from

43 Stockberger and Smith, as cited in footnote 21, p. 40.

which candidates for the patronage were drawn, was during this period essentially similar despite the claims of their more vociferous adherents. This is especially obvious in comparison to parties abroad. Many of the critics of the merit system in 1883 feared that it would lead to the return of an aristocracy of office-holders. Is there any evidence that such began to emerge during the Gilded Age? On the whole, it would appear not. The early reports of the Civil Service Commission and the National Civil Service Reform League, as well as the periodical literature,[44] are full of discussions of this possibility, but, by 1900 the matter was largely dropped. If anything, the argument lay the other way round. A principal charge against the spoils system had been its tendency to foster the development of another sort of aristocracy, the aristocracy of "plunder and patronage." But by 1900 this debate over aristocratic tendencies was largely dead from both points of view as far as the federal civil service was concerned.

Social origins. Where did federal employees come from at this time? This is most difficult to answer in detail but there is some generalized evidence, of both a positive and negative sort. Above all, the personnel recruited through both the patronage and merit systems continued, as before the Pendleton Act, to enter the public service at all ages and with all kinds of backgrounds. The act of 1883 did not provide for a closed personnel system on the British model, nor did the Civil Service Commission try to evade the manifest intent of Congress. Age, health, and formal educational requirements were held to a minimum; examinations were normally open to applicants from all walks of life and most age groups; and there were no noticeable barriers to final appointment in terms of birth, religion, social position, wealth, or education—provided one could pass the examinations. The apportionment provision of the Pendleton Act together with the custom of Senatorial Courtesy insured a widespread geographical distribution in the origins of public employees, especially those at the capital.

Therefore, only one conclusion seems reasonable here: that the recruitment and appointment system for the classified service and for much of the unclassified service, did not significantly favor or unduly discriminate against any particular social group at the expense of other groups, with the exception of women and Negroes. The former were somewhat discriminated against under terms of law, and the latter more by a disinclination on the part of appointment officers to favor them. But both of these groups were entering the service in greater and greater numbers after 1883 and certainly found it as easy

44 See, for example, E. L. Godkin, "The Danger of an Office-Holding Aristocracy," *Century,* II, N.S. (June, 1882), 287.

to enter the public service as any other comparable employment. Of other possible bases of discrimination, only the formal barrier of the requirement of citizenship, which was not always rigidly enforced, excluded any considerable group of persons at this time. However, this requirement was no major hurdle because citizenship was much more easily obtainable then than now. As Dorman B. Eaton had prophesied in 1882, the Pendleton Act did open up the offices again on a kind of equal basis.[45]

"Female clerks." The most spectacular change in the social composition of the public service since the Civil War has stemmed from the introduction of women into the service. They entered especially rapidly after the invention of the typewriter, which was coming into use about the time of the approval of the Pendleton Act. The employment of women in the public service paralleled in general their increasing entry into private industry,[46] and thus maintained the representative character of the government service.

The widespread employment of women in the federal service, as other than postmistresses in small towns, appears to have commenced in the Treasury. The Jenckes Report of 1868 gives evidence of considerable numbers of women in nearly all the Treasury operations. The answers to Jenckes' questionnaires, as excerpted in this report, indicate also that several other agencies were considering their employment. Indicative both of this and of the custom of paying women less than men for equivalent work is the answer given by the Librarian of Congress, A. R. Spofford:

36. No females as yet employed. Under competitive tests, I think half the number here employed might usefully be women, and that the resulting economy to the government would be great. For example, I know of educated and practically industrious women, who could do all that assistant librarians receiving $1,200 to $1,800 now do, and who would think themselves well paid at $1,000 per year.[47]

The first federal legislation concerning "female clerks"—the quaintly deprecating phrase then current—was passed in 1864. This set their pay at $600 a year, about half that of men for similar work.[48] Though

45 Ch. v, above, note 24.

46 For the best survey of the early employment of women in the federal civil service see McMillin, as cited in footnote 40. See also Avice Marion Saint, "Women in the Public Service," *Public Personnel Studies*, IX (January–February, 1931).

47 U.S. Congress, House, Joint Select Committee on Retrenchment, *Report: Civil Service of the United States*, 40th Cong., 2d Sess., House Report 47, May 14, 1868 (Washington: Government Printing Office, 1868), p. 47.

48 USCSC, *History of the Federal Civil Service*, Form 2449, prepared in the Information and Recruiting Division, text by M. Barris Taylor (Washington: Government Printing Office, 1941), p. 27.

there was no question of women's rights to public employment after 1870, forcing appointing officers to accept women was another matter. The Pendleton Act said nothing on the subject and the Commission accepted an appointing officer's request for the certification of men or women or both without question until after World War I. There was a tendency in the nineteenth century to consider the employment of women as subversive of morals, religion, and public policy; and appointment policies frequently reflected such views.

Nevertheless, their employment increased. The Civil Service Commission estimated in 1893 that there were nearly 6,000 postmistresses, mostly in small towns and scattered among a total of about 70,000 postal offices. In other positions the Commission concluded:

. . . In the customs service they are only employed as inspectresses, with here and there a clerk. Of all those employed in whatever capacity in Washington less than one-third are women; and in the classified service at Washington about one in seven of those appointed is a woman. They are employed as typewriters, money counters and assorters, and in various subordinate capacities. In the Indian school service women are employed as matrons, teachers, and nurses. They are never employed in the railway mail service. Their pay is the same as for men for the same work, but their employment as a rule is confined to the lower grade.[49]

Despite a statute of 1870 authorizing but not requiring equal pay for equal work, women did not always receive such consideration until the passage of the Classification Act of 1923, which finally assured their equal treatment. The top salary paid a woman as of July 1, 1891, was $1,800.[50] Not until 1912 was a woman appointed as a bureau chief.[51]

By 1904 women in the national civil service constituted 7.5 per cent of the total service. Until recent years, far fewer women in proportion to men were employed in the field than in Washington; and during depressions they tended to be dropped before men.[52] Nevertheless, their employment steadily increased until World War I, when the public employment of women—in terms of percentage of the total government service—reached unheard of heights from which the female sex has yet to retire.

[49] Tenth Report, 1893, pp. 31–32.
[50] USCSC, Ninth Report, 1892, p. 234. Table 10 lists "Salaries of Females in Government Service." Only seven women received $1,800 and only 63 women received salaries greater than $1,400, out of a total female employment of over 8,000. These figures do not include the Post Office, but do include the remainder of the federal public service. It is doubtful, though, if any postmistress exceeded these amounts.
[51] Julia Lathrop of the Children's Bureau, appointed by President Taft, received a salary of $5,000.
[52] See the chart in McMillin, as cited in footnote 40, p. 13.

Scientific and technical personnel. Less obvious, but more important for its indication of the changing functions of the public service, was the steadily increasing percentage of professional and scientific workers after the Civil War. By 1896, the first year for which adequate data are available, the figure had climbed to 2 per cent,[53] primarily representing medicine, engineering and the mechanical arts, and the physical and biological sciences.

The growing recognition of the need for skilled public employees also had direct repercussions on the extension of the classified service, for many of the first bureaus to be placed completely under the merit system were those with heavily scientific and technical duties. The early Secretaries of Agriculture felt especially strongly that the only way they could obtain and hold competent employees for their somewhat specialized agency was through the merit system, and the department was classified as far as the laws would permit by 1897. Undoubtedly, the sometimes spectacular work of these men advertised the public service in a way which presented a decided contrast to the patronage scandals of the eighteen sixties and seventies. The entry of such men continued apace and in 1900 they provided approximately 3.43 per cent of the total intake.[54] The trend was clear, with a reciprocal affinity between the merit system and scientific and technical work fairly well established by 1900. At the same time these men were clearly having an impact upon federal policies, something that subordinate employees had not often been able to accomplish in earlier years. The problem of the "expert on tap or on top" was beginning to arise, as is clear from the *Autobiography* of Harvey W. Wiley, a distinguished Chief Chemist in the Department of Agriculture and advocate of pure food and drug legislation.[55]

Negroes. The merit system was especially important as a vehicle for bringing increasing numbers of Negroes into the public service. According to the only study available, the federal public service in 1881 contained only 0.57 per cent Negro employees. However, this rose to about 5.86 per cent under Taft in 1910.[56] Though the civil service rules did not explicitly forbid racial discrimination, few photographs, for example, were required of any applicants until the administration of President Wilson. Indeed, the generally impersonal nature of the

---

53 Leonard D. White, *Trends in Public Administration* (New York: McGraw-Hill Book Co., 1933), p. 271. See also A. Hunter Dupree, *Science in the Federal Government: A History of Activities to 1940* (Cambridge, Mass.: Harvard University Press, 1957).
54 Same, p. 276.
55 As cited in footnote 39.
56 Lawrence J. W. Hayes, *The Negro Federal Government Worker* (Washington: Howard University, 1941), p. 153. The figures quoted here are at best, as their author warns, only careful estimates.

examination system encouraged Negro employment, particularly in the city of Washington, and the effective entry of the Negro into the federal public service must be dated from 1883. Especially noteworthy was the entry of numbers of graduates of the new Negro colleges and universities by 1890. At this time the Negro employees included four consuls in the State Department, a division chief in the Treasury, the recorder of Interior's General Land Office, at least three collectors of customs, and, at the top, the Hon. Blanche K. Bruce, a former senator from Mississippi and the Recorder of Deeds for the District of Columbia, who was paid in fees at an estimated $18,000 a year.[57] The opening opportunities for the Negro in public employment certainly functioned to aid his social rise in general.

Veterans. The preference granted to disabled veterans in 1865 never involved more than a few thousand persons over a fifty year period. The Pendleton Act reaffirmed this preference as well as that concerning reductions-in-force laid down by a statute of 1876. Between 1883 and 1919 there was no further significant preference legislation for veterans, despite the continuous prodding of Congress by the Grand Army of the Republic.[58] Several executive orders defined the manner in which these preference statutes would be implemented, but nothing else was enacted. The facts that failure to conform to these statutes carried no penalties and that there was, until 1883, no central agency to administer and enforce the preference regulations, meant that they were not always rigidly applied.

There are no figures showing the precise extent to which veterans came into the public service before 1900. We know that 45 disabled veterans were appointed under the preference rules during the fiscal year of 1901. In 1904, there were 2,175 Civil War veterans and 388 veterans' widows employed in the Washington departments, a figure equal to approximately 10 per cent of the civil servants in the capital.[59] Most of these did not enter the service through the operation of

---

[57] USCSC, *Eighth Report*, 1891, p. 6; and *Ninth Report*, 1892, pp. 236–37. The latter contains the only report by the Commission before 1900 on Negro federal employment totals, and shows 2,393 Negro employees in the agencies in the city of Washington. The same report also lists the principal positions held by Negroes in Washington at this time.

[58] For the failures of the G.A.R. see Paul Joseph Woods, "The G.A.R. and Civil Service" (unpublished Ph.D. dissertation, Dept. of History, University of Illinois, 1941). The G.A.R. evidently started its agitation too late and the interests of northern and southern veterans were never combined. There is no study of the Spanish-American War veterans' failure to obtain preference. The available evidence points to the conclusion that in 1900 the Civil War veterans were still too important a pressure group and felt too strongly that the War of 1898 was more a vacation than a fight to permit the veterans of the latter conflict to obtain special privileges which Civil War veterans had not been able to obtain.

[59] USCSC, *Eighteenth Report*, 1901, pp. 10–11; and *Twenty-first Report*, 1904, pp. 186–88. See also U.S. Bureau of the Census, *Statistics of Employees*, Bulletin 94 (Washington: Government Printing Office, 1908), pp. 56–58.

the veteran preference regulations. Nor did any of the other forms of preference granted under varied circumstances to such groups as Filipinos, railroad employees, and Indians radically affect the functioning of the merit system.

The principal significance of these developments lay less in the past than in what they presaged for the future. Most of the precedents were set for a more full scale preference system, and the Civil Service Commission now provided a central agency for the policing of the system. It is reasonable to conclude that, without the Commission and the merit system, veteran preference as a widespread and effective practice would not have been possible. Somewhat less important was the fact that the veterans were a little older than the rest of the service. The developing superannuation problem undoubtedly stemmed in part from the long continuance in service of many Civil War veterans. Appointing officers were especially reluctant to remove such veterans. Otherwise, the entrance of numbers of veterans along with women and Negroes only tended further to insure the representative character of the service.

Blue collar workers. By 1900 the increasing requirements of the service for skilled and unskilled workmen and mechanics, together with those for scientific and technical personnel, made the term "clerical" insufficient to describe the nature of federal employment. Of a grand total of about 300,000 executive civil servants in 1903, approximately 53,000 could be considered as blue collar workers, though that term was not then used.[60] While this was not a great increase since the Civil War in terms of percentage, again it showed a growing diversity in federal functions.

Unions. More important perhaps was the union tradition which many of the federal workmen brought with them. Public employee unions, except among skilled workmen and employees of the Post Office, were relatively rare before 1900. But the union movement was gradually growing within the federal service, though efforts to unionize clerical workers in general were no more successful in government than in private enterprise.

Following in the steps of the larger labor groups, and particularly because of their relationship to the government, the federal unions were non-partisan and interested primarily in the amelioration of working conditions. The passage of the "eight-hours law" for postal workers in 1888 represents one of the first successful union efforts in

---

[60] These figures are derived from a recalculation of data in U.S. Bureau of the Census, *The Executive Civil Service of the United States,* Bulletin 12 (Washington: Government Printing Office, 1904), pp. 9 and 52. The 53,000 figure, which is probably conservative, includes navy yard employees, a few "miscellaneous," and all of those listed as "mechanical" or "subclerical and laborer" in this report.

this respect, as well as one of the few official attempts during the nineteenth century to implement the concept of the government as a model employer. In its passage the postal unions had the full backing of the American Federation of Labor and other union groups. While there was no anti-strike legislation in effect at this time, tradition as well as the anti-political provisions of the Pendleton Act discouraged strikes, boycotts, and the like. Even so, there were a few widely scattered and small scale strikes in the government service at intervals. But the embryonic government employee unions formed no real threat either to other employees or to the government at this time.

Prestige and Power

If the offices were available to anyone who sought them, what was the caliber of the applicants? Here we get into the difficult question of what constitutes the "best people" as well as the matter of prestige.

Occupational mobility. First, let us consider the average age of entrance and its implications. There were relatively few public employees below the age of twenty-five.[61] This would tend to indicate that relatively few individuals chose the public service for their initial career attempt; rather, in typical American fashion, they chose it as one of several career efforts. The average age at entrance, between 25 and 30 for both men and women during this period, would tend to confirm this conclusion.[62] Further, it is interesting to note that the Commission frequently pointed out with pride that its examination system was bringing "mature" men and women, rather than "school boys," into the service.[63]

Standing alone, facts of this sort have encouraged many to conclude that the public service was a last desperate choice for second-rate talent. Unfortunately, there are no comparable data on age of entrance into private firms at this time. Our mobility being high, it is likely that the age of entrance into many such firms could not then have been much under 25. Perhaps the public service has been depreciated just because no other data have been available. There is, as we have seen, ample evidence that the conditions of public employment were in some ways more favorable throughout the nineteenth century than those in private industry, except at the top. It may be argued,

---

61 U.S. Bureau of the Census, as cited in footnote 59, p. 12. There is a good deal of additional information concerning age groups but this particular figure seems most useful here.

62 For the ages of competitors in 1887 and 1888, see USCSC, *Fifth Report*, 1888, pp. 24–25. The average age of entrance in the nineteen twenties was 28. USCSC, *Forty-seventh Report*, 1930, p. 15. This appears to have remained fairly stationary over decades.

63 See USCSC, *Fifth Report*, 1888, p. 25, for example.

therefore, that a good many of the more observant workers, especially at the middle and lower levels, became aware of these facts and eventually sought public employment. Certainly, the turnover rates in the classified service were never as high as in many private industries before World War I. All in all, age and turnover data seem quite inconclusive, one way or another, as to the caliber of public employees coming into the service before—or after—1900.

Education. Unlike information on occupational mobility, evidence concerning the educational levels of federal employees before 1900 is comprehensive for part of the service. The annual reports of the Civil Service Commission present an unbroken series of comparable yearly tabulations of the educational levels *claimed* by *all competitors in examinations* for *all branches* of the federal service from January 16, 1884, through June 30, 1896. Recalculations from these tables show that during this period between 10 and 13 per cent of those examined had had *some college training,* varying from very little to a full degree.[64] During the fiscal year of 1897, of 666 persons *appointed* through examinations to the departmental service in Washington, 159, or 23.8 per cent, had "attended college." [65]

Even though we may not be absolutely sure of the definition of the word "college" as here used, and even though there may have been some boosting of educational claims by applicants, these are still startlingly high percentages for the eighties and nineties. This is especially true when one considers the fact that as late as 1940, only 10.1 per cent of the adult population twenty-five years and older had completed at least one year of college. By 1950 this percentage had risen to only 13.2.[66] The implications are even more suggestive when one considers that the federal service took on the average only from the upper 65 per cent of its college trained applicants during the period in question. Unfortunately, we evidently have no similar sta-

[64] See the annual reports of the Commission for this period. For three years of data presented together, see USCSC, *Fifth Report,* 1888, p. 26. The original tables break down the educational backgrounds of prospective employees into "common school," "academy," "high school," "business college," and "college." In the percentages above only the "college" figures have been used. If the additional "business college" percentage is included with the "college" percentage, the combined percentage varies yearly from about 15 to nearly 20 per cent.

[65] USCSC, *Fourteenth Report,* 1897, p. 19. With these data is the notation, "It will be seen that 75 per cent of those appointed had no collegiate education, while most of the college men were appointed to places requiring technical qualifications, in which a collegiate education is essential, as Patent Office examiners, meat inspectors, specialists in the Department of Agriculture, etc."

[66] U.S. Department of Health, Education, and Welfare, Office of Education, "Statistics of Higher Education: Faculty, Students, and Degrees, 1951–52," ch. iv, sec. 1, *Biennial Survey of Education in the United States, 1950–52* (Washington: Government Printing Office, 1955), p. 42. The year 1940 is the earliest year for which data are available on the educational attainment of the adult population.

tistics on educational levels of applicants for positions in any segment of private industry for the same period, though it is doubtful that they would show equally high percentages of college trained applicants. If we equate education and the "best people," then a very strong case can be made that the federal service was anything but scraping the bottom of the manpower barrel before 1900.

Prestige. Opposing these data is the well-known lack of prestige of the federal service of this period. A quotation from Foltz' 1909 manual for applicants, presumably those who might be considering adding themselves to the above statistics, is revealing:

. . . Yet there is one field of activity, embracing hundreds of thousands, broad in scope, high in ideals, and honorable in duties, that is seldom thought of as presenting opportunities for a career. *Who ever heard of a father counselling his son to adopt Government service as a career?* Sometimes the sordid attraction of politics appeals to the family's head; but he looks at the Government through the eyes of the gamester, and when it comes to the question of adopting public service as a career the idea becomes a remote one. It is well enough to play at politics or to spend a few years in Federal employ, thinks he; but, outside the officers of the army and navy, no branch of the Federal service occupies his serious attention as presenting opportunities for a son's career.[67]

Typical of the views of the times, opinion was certainly no more favorable in the last years of the nineteenth century.

Nevertheless, the number of applicants for federal examinations remained consistently high, even through periods of relative prosperity. The growing recognition of the selective effect of the examinations is attested to by a brief note in the chief examiner's report to the Commission for 1899. "During the past year my attention has been called to many cases where persons whose names were on the Commission's registers of eligibles have obtained desirable positions with private employers as a result."[68] Pirating from the public service was no novelty fifty years ago.

To what extent does the prestige of an occupation determine the competence of the people who enter it? Little attention has been given to this question. The educational data presented above indicate that many quite competent people were entering the service *despite* its low prestige. Perhaps one explanation lies in differential motivations as between business and government, motivations which have little to do with comparative talent and intelligence. After all, the period just before the turn of the century was noted for its "social

67 As cited in footnote 41, p. 228. Italics are added.
68 USCSC, *Sixteenth Report,* 1899, pp. 34–35.

Gospel" and for the rapid development of charitable and similar institutions. The concept of "service" is heavily underlined in such few reminiscences as we have of civil servants of the time.[69] The public service and private enterprise may have been drawing from quite different strata of motivation.

What was the federal government doing with the talent it had? The evidence here is also inconclusive and impressionistic. In-service training was infrequent outside the military. Transfers of employees from one agency to another were accomplished more often during this period than in earlier periods but were not standard practice. Most employees made their careers within one agency. The higher reaches of the civil service were still heavily political, though in the Department of Agriculture even bureau chiefs came under the competitive system and a career service was clearly developing by 1900. Even so, Secretary J. Sterling Morton wrote a young man considering scientific work in one of the experiment stations in 1894, "Take my advice and keep out of the public service." He recommended private enterprise, "over which political changes can have no control," as affording much greater chance for advancement.[70]

Yet the Civil Service Commission reported in 1897 that "of the number appointed through examination since 1883, about 70 per cent remain in the service, or about 37,000." [71] Evidently many were not as pessimistic as Secretary Morton, though we know nothing about the length of service of this 70 per cent. We do know, however, that, of the classified service within the District of Columbia in 1903, 62.5 per cent had been in the service for five years or more and 43.4 per cent for ten years or more. In the field service the corresponding percentages were 45.2 and 26.5 respectively. As might be expected, the periods of service for unclassified employees were substantially less.[72] These data, too, are subject to various interpretations and there are few comparable data for private industry. Comparative turnover statistics for later years would suggest, however, that, on the average, employees in private enterprise stayed with an individual concern certainly no longer than public employees chose to remain with the government.

Power. Analyzing from the point of view of the currently popular concept of "power," one can only conclude that the civil establishment of the federal government was not at the center of power in the Gilded Age. J. P. Morgan, Mark Hanna, and the Senate were the

[69] This is true in the case of all the works cited in note 39 above.
[70] Stockberger and Smith, as cited in footnote 21, p. 68.
[71] USCSC, *Fourteenth Report*, 1897, p. 538.
[72] U.S. Bureau of the Census, as cited in footnote 60, p. 19.

symbols of power at the turn of the century. If anything, the civil service of 1900 shows up as somewhat less influential in a Lasswellian sense [73] than it had been during the first two decades after the Civil War. Politics and economics were still tied together at the upper levels of the service, but less so on the whole than previously. After all, it was this liaison at which the moral reform movement was aimed. Cleveland and the civil service reformers were to some extent successful in their ultimate aim of destroying the aristocracy of "plunder and patronage."

On the other hand, the public service was developing into a positive arm of the state. The end of the century can, from the standpoint of the power position of the civil service, be characterized as something of a lull between two storms—that of the Grant administration and that of the New Deal to come. The decline of the attacks on the civil service as "aristocratic" meant simply that none feared it much at this time in the way that they had once and would again nearly a half century later.

SUPPLEMENTARY NOTES

Unfortunately, there are almost no studies of the changing social composition of the federal bureaucracy during the nineteenth and early twentieth centuries. Such as have been made are summarized in three principal sources: Leonard D. White, *Trends in Public Administration,* as cited in footnote 53, pp. 239–308; Reinhard Bendix, *Higher Civil Servants in American Society* (Boulder, Colo.: University of Colorado Press, 1949) ; and C. Wright Mills, *The Power Elite* (New York: Oxford University Press, 1956) . Most of the studies, moreover, are aimed at analysis of the top levels of the bureaucracy and not at the structure as a whole.

However, data for more inclusive work appear to exist. They have been tapped lightly before, especially by White, and some of them have been drawn on by the writer. Especially important are the "Plum Books," cited earlier, and two monumental studies published by the U.S. Bureau of the Census and covering the years 1903 and 1907, *The Executive Civil Service of the United States,* cited in footnote 60, and *Statistics of Employees,* cited in footnote 59. These two bulletins contain unique breakdowns of the federal service in terms of age, sex, marital status, veteran status, and a number of other significant variables. When combined with residence and other data in the long line of *Official Registers,* the extensive data in the annual reports of the Civil Service Commission, and other miscellaneous sources, these should furnish a reasonably adequate base for a complete book-length study, which is badly needed. This writer can only highlight the more significant developments.

[73] Harold D. Lasswell describes the study of politics as "the study of influence and the influential. . . . The influential are those who get the most of what there is to get. Available values may be classified as *deference, income, safety.* Those who get the most are *elite;* the rest are *mass.*" From the well-known opening paragraphs of his *Politics: Who Gets What, When, How* (New York: McGraw-Hill Book Co., 1936).

CHAPTER 8

The Dividing Line: 1897–1909

The clear-cut Republican victory of 1896 was something quite different from the bare electoral majorities of the Cleveland era. The events of the next decade were to show that not only a temporal but also a political and social dividing line had been reached. As a main instrument of the changes to come, the federal civil service, too, was to feel the impact of the twentieth century from many directions.

In 1896, however, the prospect of the accession of William McKinley to the Presidency did not suggest any great break with the Gilded Age. To the contrary, a major question at this time was whether or not another relatively uninterrupted period of Republican office-holding might mean a repetition of the more unsavory events of the eighteen seventies and a reversal in fortune for civil service reform. After all, the new reform had received its greatest gains under the preceding Democratic administration of Grover Cleveland, and the mandate of 1896 could be interpreted in either one of two ways. From one point of view William Jennings Bryan and his Jacksonian patronage policies had been repudiated; but one could also say that, by implication, so had Grover Cleveland and his policy of moral reform and support for the merit system. Indeed, the first tendency of the new administration was to incline toward the latter viewpoint.

The Critical Period [1]

Though considered not unfriendly to civil service reform at the time of his nomination, William McKinley proved a disappointment

---

[1] Charles J. Bonaparte, Theodore Roosevelt's friend and cabinet member, wrote in 1902: "A historian of Civil Service Reform will perhaps one day head his book or chapter describing McKinley's first term: 'The Critical Period of the Merit System in the Federal Service.'" *Good Government,* XIX (August, 1902), 118.

169

to the supporters of the theory and practice of the Pendleton Act. However, he and his cohorts, dubious as a few of them may have been from a reform point of view, were always more acceptable than Bryan and the Democratic politicians who, denouncing Cleveland, bargained the offices right and left during the campaign of 1896. Then and for the remainder of his political life, William Jennings Bryan remained the foremost spoilsman of American politics. Not a representative of the business-in-politics school, typified by Thurlow Weed and Mark Hanna, he was a Jacksonian throwback who believed in deliberate exploitation of the offices for purposes of political loyalty and party unity. To him, as to the Jacksonians, tenure in office was the badge of aristocracy and injustice. To the reformers the motivations behind spoils politics mattered little. Manipulation of the offices was undesirable for any reason, be it social and economic reform or the need to force a legislative program through Congress. They took McKinley at his word concerning the offices, without paying too much attention to his political friends, and his word was from their strict standards better than Bryan's.

Appointment policies. But McKinley was no Grover Cleveland. Though he insisted there were things a man should not do even to be President, he was not the man to sacrifice party to personal ideals. The election appeared to be a mandate for Republican conservatism. There were nearly forty thousand fewer offices for disposal in 1897 than there had been in 1889. The pressure commenced. It was only a question of how far McKinley would permit the relaxation of the rules of his predecessor. Willian Allen White has described McKinley as

. . . deeply, essentially, a politician; honest enough, brave enough, intelligent enough for politics—and no more so. He knew the rules of the game, and played the game like a gentleman when gentlemen in politics were scarce. . . . In politics the first maxim is to take care of your crowd. Politicians of the better grade often put the second maxim first. McKinley did. He was never too selfish for his own ultimate good.[2]

As far as the public service was concerned, McKinley "took care of" his party, but he avoided wrecking it through an overdose of spoils. He steered a careful path through the reform issue as through most other issues.

The Cabinet was well received. Initially, all but Secretary of War Russell A. Alger and Postmaster General James A. Gary were considered to be sympathetic to the merit system. As a group, however,

2 William Allen White, *Masks in a Pageant* (New York: The Macmillan Co., 1928), pp. 154–55.

THE CIVIL SERVICE BUBBLE.

A Beautiful Outside and a Very Hollow Inside.

From Columbus, Ohio, *Dispatch*, September 7, 1900.

they did not live up to expectations. They generally operated their agencies as they pleased and, with the exception of Secretary of the Navy John D. Long and his Assistant Secretary Theodore Roosevelt, resisted cooperation with the Civil Service Commission.

Though many of the secondary appointments were considered as evidence of the President's interest in the merit system, objections were quickly leveled at the influence of the powerful political bosses of the day, whom McKinley consulted and through whom the bulk of the minor patronage was distributed quite thoroughly if not always wisely. The *New York Times* spoke in 1897 of McKinley's "farming-out" of the jobs to state bosses where "disgraceful" selections were made, but compared this favorably to the "Barmecide feast" under Harrison.[3] The most important of these bosses was Senator Marcus Alonzo ("Mark") Hanna, wealthy Ohio businessman and Chairman of the Republican National Committee, who controlled an immense amount of the patronage and has been given credit for handling his share most astutely. As in most previous administrations, the spoils system immediately swung into full play as far as existing regulations would permit.

Congress, still not content, went even further and began an ambitious attack upon the Pendleton Act itself. Fortunately for the government service, the House and the Senate could not agree on the action to be taken. At the same time, in McKinley's annual message to Congress on December 6, 1897, his reference to the civil service ended with the warning that "The system has the approval of the people and it will be my endeavor to uphold and extend it."[4] The *New York Evening Post* concluded that this was as near a challenge to Congress as one "of McKinley's temperament" could give.[5] As Congress kept up its legislative threats, McKinley did find some support, at least from the press. The *Cleveland Plain Dealer,* for instance, remarked on January 13, 1899, "It is interesting to note the manner in which the efforts of certain members of Congress to strike down the civil service barriers were denounced by the newspapers of all parties."

The order of 1899. Still the pressure from within the Republican party relentlessly continued. McKinley began to weaken. It had long been argued, with some justice, that the last great classification order by Cleveland, covering-in some 30,000 positions, had been too sweeping and that it had included positions to which examinations were not easily applicable or political neutrality appropriate. Just before

---

3 December 27, 1897.
4 James D. Richardson (ed.), *Messages and Papers of the Presidents* (New York: Bureau of National Literature and Art, 1905), X, 50.
5 December 24, 1897.

the fall election of 1898 it was rumored that the President had "quietly given out" information that about 6,000 offices would be taken out of the classified civil service. The party leaders were encouraged, but a momentary storm of public indignation at the suggestion may have taken McKinley somewhat by surprise.

There was solid fact behind the rumor, whether it was given out by McKinley or not. Earlier in June, 1898, the Civil Service Commission had itself proposed that certain positions then in the classified service be exempted from examination, and had publicly agreed with portions of a report by the Senate Committee on Civil Service and Retrenchment, which recommended similar changes.[6] The Commission referred its proposal to the President following consultation with the department heads. McKinley then simply held the matter on his desk for several months.[7]

Meanwhile the President notified the National Civil Service Reform League of his purpose to make certain exemptions from the classified service as Cleveland had set it up in 1896. In late 1898 the League issued a public appeal that the action should not be taken. But at its annual meeting in December it was reported that both the Interior and Treasury Departments were operating as if exemptions had already been made.[8] Still McKinley took no formal action. Finally, on May 29, 1899, the long-expected ax fell through an executive order affecting approximately 10,000 positions. Nearly 6,000 positions formerly under full merit system protection were excluded from it, while some 4,000 positions were allowed to remain in the classified service but were excepted from examination.[9] With the opening of the "front door" to the latter group of positions, their incumbents were left protected only by the mild anti-political removal provision of the Pendleton Act and many of them were removed forthwith.

If the Commission itself did not draft the final executive order, it was in sympathy with it; and one of the Republican Commissioners, John B. Harlow, publicly defended the action in a letter to the *St. Louis Globe-Democrat* in which he said:

I desire also to inform you that the rules as amended on May 29 have this in their favor, that for the first time they are the result of the united

6 U.S. Congress, Senate, *Report of the Committee on Civil Service and Retrenchment*, 55th Cong., 2d Sess., Senate Report 659 (Washington: Government Printing Office, 1898), pp. 2–3.

7 USCSC, *Sixteenth Report*, 1899, pp. 21–22 and 72–83. This report gives the Commission's view on the transaction.

8 NCSRL, *Proceedings*, 1898, pp. 8–11.

9 USCSC, *Seventeenth Report*, 1900, pp. 203–206. See also the "supplementary notes" to this chapter for the meaning of certain developing refinements in the use of the term "classified service."

173

discussion of the President and his entire Cabinet, and are an innovation to that extent.[10]

Cornelius Bliss, who had resigned as Secretary of the Interior early in 1899, stated to the press that the Commission was consulted on all matters except perhaps the time of issue.[11]

The result was a furor of comment, for the Civil Service Commission was put in the unprecedented position of seeming to lend official sanction to a deliberate spoils raid by Republican politicians. But not all of the comment was adverse. The *Commercial Advertiser, Sun,* and *Mail and Express* of New York, the *Record* and *Inter-Ocean* of Chicago, and the *St. Louis Globe-Democrat* all were favorably inclined to McKinley's move upon the theory that Cleveland's last executive order had gone too far too fast. Mark Hanna was quoted as feeling that the order was a "sensible remedy for a bad condition of things created by President Cleveland." Yet the National Civil Service Reform League, in a review of public reaction to the move, concluded that "It is the very evident judgment of the country that the action taken has been most unfortunate." [12]

That the opposition to the order was not stronger and more effective was a tribute to McKinley's astuteness in political maneuver, as well as to the solid political position of the Republican party. For fifteen years no president had dared to undo the classifications of his successor for fear, in part at least, of upsetting the precarious political balance of the times. This time the reformers and considerable segments of the press raged, but to little avail. Hanna's view was sold sufficiently well to take the edge from the criticism, and the only large scale trimming of the classified service in American history was deliberately consummated. The local politicians applauded and many appetites were only whetted for further concessions.

Therefore, the act providing for the census of 1900 was permitted to exclude 3,500 new positions from the merit system. The War Emergency Acts called for close to 2,000 temporary appointments to be made outside the civil service rules. The rural free delivery service was, from 1897 to 1902, kept from the merit system by designating it as "experimental." The Attorney General, the Secretary of the Interior, and the Secretary of the Treasury all took the opportunity publicly to ignore the opinions and recommendations of the Civil Service Commission.[13]

The Spanish-American War. Out of the Spanish-American War arose

---

10 July 7, 1899. See also USCSC, *Seventeenth Report,* 1900, pp. 13–14, for a more formal concurrence.
11 *New York Mail and Express,* June 10, 1899.
12 From an editorial in *Good Government,* XVII (July 15, 1899), 1.
13 USCSC, *Seventeenth Report,* 1900, pp. 207–209.

the only events during the first term of McKinley that came even close to upsetting the grip of the Republican party upon the country. The War Department, under the ineffective guidance of Alger, had been granted permission by Congress to employ several thousand temporary workers through sources other than the Civil Service Commission, despite the fact that the Commission had formally stated that "never in the history of the Commission were there so many names upon the eligible registers." [14] The War Department patronage was largely in charge of Assistant Secretary George D. Meiklejohn, who eventually became involved in a minor scandal concerning the promotion of business activities in the Philippines under the guise of official duties. As the turnover rates later indicated, the group thus hired through the spoils system was anything but select. Moreover, Alger was not a competent administrator. The whole military operation was, from an administrative point of view, a fiasco and McKinley was finally forced to replace Alger with Elihu Root. Only the quick success of the war and the reforms initiated by Root forestalled a major Republican political disaster. [15]

The question of governing the new territories arose next. From the spectacular administrative failures of the War Department McKinley had learned to make his major appointments carefully. He selected William Howard Taft and Leonard Wood to head the principal territorial governing commissions. The merit system was from the beginning employed in the Philippines and, in a modified form, in Puerto Rico. The United States Civil Service Commission immediately established cooperative relations, which were maintained for many years, with the Philippine and later the Puerto Rican Civil Service Boards. That the United States avoided many of the worst aspects of exploitative colonialism was due, in part certainly, to McKinley's foresight in nipping in the bud many of the bases for such exploitation. McKinley also gave firm and continued support to Secretary of War Root and Commissioners Wood and Taft in their efforts to give the new dependencies a competent administration. There were few scandals in the American management of the Philippines, Puerto Rico, and Cuba. [16]

---

[14] Same, pp. 23–24.

[15] As in the Civil War, patronage politics invaded the military as well as the civil services. See Walter Millis, *The Martial Spirit* (Boston: Houghton Mifflin Co., 1931), pp. 153–59; and Francis Butler Simkins, *Pitchfork Ben Tillman* (Baton Rouge: Louisiana State University Press, 1944), p. 363. For example, Senator Tillman of South Carolina, an inveterate place hunter, proposed a list of military appointments to McKinley and reported that he was satisfied with what he got.

[16] On this subject see William Dudley Foulke, *Fighting the Spoilsmen* (New York: G. P. Putnam's Sons, 1919), p. 123; USCSC, *Seventeenth Report*, 1900, pp. 28–30 and 327; USCSC, *Eighteenth Report*, 1901, scattered; and Philip Jessup, *Elihu Root* (2 vols.; New York: Dodd, Mead and Co., 1938), I, chs. xvi, xvii, and xviii.

Election of 1900. Despite their predominantly Republican sympathies and McKinley's tardy conversion to the merit system via the territories, the reformers were seriously divided in the campaign of 1900. With neither candidate offering much for civil service reform, the imperialistic policies of the Republican party alienated men such as E. L. Godkin and Carl Schurz, whose humanitarian sympathies and sense of morality were deeply outraged by the implications of the new American colonialism for native peoples. Schurz even resigned at this time as President of the National Civil Service Reform League rather than embarrass the League by his support of William Jennings Bryan, who, though an avowed spoilsman, vigorously supported anti-imperialism. Others such as William Dudley Foulke stayed with the Republicans. Many of this group were much less disturbed by the issue of imperialism and felt that McKinley's more recent actions, as well as Theodore Roosevelt's vice-presidential candidacy, presaged well for the future of the merit system. Moreover, the Republican platform at least commended "the policy of the Republican party in maintaining the efficiency of the civil service," a plank, however, which deserved the comment of the Worcester, Massachusetts, *Evening Post,* that "The civil-service plank in the republican platform is worthy of Hanna. It took a good deal of nerve to draft it, and a good deal of self-possession to read it to an intelligent assembly without a smile." [17]

Nevertheless, Roosevelt carried the reform banner high for the Republicans and fired salvos in his usual manner, declaiming that "the spoils-monger and spoils-seeker invariably breed the bribe-taker and bribe-giver, the embezzler of public funds and the corrupter of voters." [18] The *Washington Star* argued the unusual, though probably valid, point that the spoils view of Bryan threatened prosperity in the capital, since before civil service reform "credits were hazardous. Bad debts were the rule. Failure stared the merchant in the face unless he possessed a large capital." [19] There was some public interest in the merit system as a political issue and might have been more had the Democrats concerned themselves with the matter, but the major issues were the war, imperialism, money, the trusts, and, above all, prosperity.

The Republicans won out easily only to have their expectations turned into dismay with the assassination of McKinley six months after he again took office. The stock exchanges were uneasy and Mark Hanna almost refused to have supper on the funeral train with "that damned cowboy." But a few hours later T. R. and Senator

17 June 22, 1900.
18 *New York Journal,* July 1, 1900.
19 October 26, 1900.

Hanna allegedly sealed a political bargain with clasped hands.[20] The Republican party thus remained for the time being united, and the merit system unexpectedly found itself under the watchful eye of a powerful patron.

Trends in Governmental Reform

While William McKinley had represented the conservative wing of the Republican party, Theodore Roosevelt certainly did not. Old Guard Republicanism was greatly disturbed upon his sudden accession to the highest office in the land. As to Roosevelt's exact place in American politics, opinions vary sharply. In a very real sense T. R. was the culmination and supreme representation of most of the conflicting and confusing views of his day. A picturesque and powerful personality, it was to be the sign of his political genius that he could straddle the gap between Uncle Joe Cannon and William Jennings Bryan.

Powerfully entrenched on one side was Republican conservatism, typified most clearly by the Republican Old Guard, its legislative representatives—Speaker Cannon and Senators Aldrich, Spooner, Platt, Quay, and Hanna—and those dependent on them. That the prosperity of business made for the prosperity of all was their firm belief. That some business successes might seem to others to be something besides the logical results of simple efficiency in individual effort was difficult for them to understand.

T. R. and Progressivism. Opposed to Mark Hanna and much that the Old Guard stood for was the rising tide of Progressivism, demanding not only doses of the moral reform of the eighties and nineties but considerably more. Like the Populists in their distrust of the large aggregates of industrial capitalism, the Progressives represented less an agrarian concern over railroad rates and deflation than the growing middle class fear of monopoly power in both the economic and political worlds. Richard Hofstadter has well characterized the heart of the Progressive—as opposed to the Populist—doctrines as "the struggle over organization." [21]

The problems of organization were conceived as of three primary types: (1) the organization of monopoly for which anti-trust legislation, control of banks and finance, and the independent regulatory commissions were the proper restraints; (2) the highly organized po-

---

[20] Herman H. Kohlsaat, *From McKinley to Harding* (New York: Charles Scribner's Sons, 1923), pp. 102–103.

[21] *The Age of Reform* (New York: Alfred A. Knopf, 1955), ch. vi. See also Kenneth E. Boulding, *The Organizational Revolution* (New York: Harper and Bros., 1953).

litical machines for which the remedy was the refurbishing of electoral democracy through such devices as the short ballot, the primary, the direct election of senators, and the initiative, referendum, and recall; and (3) the reorganization and rationalization of administration and management, within industry for obvious reasons and within government for the more effective control of corporate capitalism.

We need not concern ourselves here with the first two of these problems, except to note that only the first of the Progressive organizational aims represented anything like a frontal assault on the prime sources of economic and political power. As such, the controversies over the tariff, the trusts, railroad rates, and commercial finance sparked the most spectacular fireworks of the first decade of the twentieth century and were, from the standpoint of the Progressives, the least satisfactorily settled. Somewhat more successful was the move for the organizational overhauling of our machinery for recording the voice of democracy. The cities and states energetically addressed themselves to this problem, and the Seventeenth Amendment, providing for the direct election of senators, represented the culmination of the movement at the federal level.

Most important for our purposes here was the third of the Progressive organizational concerns. Least suggestive of radical political or social change, though carrying within them the seeds of modern bureaucracy and the power of the positive state, the movement for the reorganization of state and local government and the concepts of economy and efficiency, scientific management, the general staff, cost accounting and budgeting, and modern personnel administration were espoused by liberals and conservatives alike. This type of reform was easy to take. From the industrial and commercial viewpoint this seemed more like hard common sense than reform. From the political realm there were a few reservations of a Jeffersonian sort, but who could much quarrel when the issue was put in terms of the application of business methods to the antique red tape characterizing the amorphous public administration of the Gilded Age, so well illuminated by the reports of the Cockrell Committee and the Dockery-Cockrell Commission. After all, administrative reform—referring to administration in its modern sense—did not directly challenge the right to own and manage, without restraint, any given piece of property, large or small. If concessions had to be made to the clamorous public, it was possible for the representatives of economic and political power to make these first.

Perceptive as always to the public will, Theodore Roosevelt was quick to recognize the relative saleability of the various segments of the Progressive trilogy. Skirting the first, which he found difficult to

178

formulate or accept, and with lip service to the second as a threat to his own political power, T. R. came out openly and effectively for only two things: administrative and moral reform.

Toward the end he could write in his autobiography that "by the time that I was ending my career as Civil Service Commissioner I was already growing to understand that mere improvement in political conditions by itself was not enough." [22] But it is probably correct to say that he never understood economics. Instead he saw everything through the moral lenses of the Cleveland era in which he had been brought up. Steffens wrote to his father in 1904 that "Roosevelt was so much of a Democrat and Cleveland is so much of a Republican that they meet in the middle. They are very good friends, too." [23] The specific ground on which these two controversial individuals met was morality. Roosevelt himself argued by letter with Steffens in 1908, "Curiously enough, events have forced me to make my chief fights in public life against privilege, but I know from actual experience . . . that what is needed is the *fundamental fight for morality*." [24] In his conception of righteousness as the prime political solvent he represented the past, the still resplendent mantle of moral reform.

In terms of the future, Theodore Roosevelt deserves to be considered as the first president since James K. Polk and possibly General Washington who either understood or much cared about administration as we think of it today. T. R.'s seeming preoccupation with politics has obscured this aspect of his undoubtedly great contributions to public life. Of T. R.'s biographers only John M. Blum in his incisive portrait of the "Republican Roosevelt" has tried to do him much justice on this score. [25]

Through his backing of Elihu Root and the revolutionary concept of the general staff, the development of an organization to complete the colossal task of the Panama Canal, the reform of the consular service, his work with Taft in the development of civil government in

---

[22] Theodore Roosevelt, *An Autobiography* (New York: Charles Scribner's Sons, 1921), p. 158.

[23] Letter to Joseph Steffens, March 5, 1904. Ella Winter and Granville Hicks (eds.), *The Letters of Lincoln Steffens* (2 vols.; New York: Harcourt, Brace and Co., 1938), I, 167. Despite Steffens' statement, the relationship of T. R. and Cleveland can only be described as a guarded friendship.

[24] Roosevelt to Steffens, June 12, 1908. Same, p. 199. Roosevelt's italics.

[25] John M. Blum, *The Republican Roosevelt* (Cambridge, Mass.: Harvard University Press, 1954), pp. 14–21. Illuminating also are Alfred D. Chandler, Jr., "Theodore Roosevelt and the Panama Canal: A Study in Administration," *The Letters of Theodore Roosevelt*, Elting E. Morison, editor (8 vols.; Cambridge, Mass.: Harvard University Press, 1951–54), VI, 1547–57; and Leonard D. White's commentary on the administrative accomplishments of T. R. as revealed in *The Letters of Theodore Roosevelt*, in "The Public Life of 'T. R.,'" *Public Administration Review*, XIV (Autumn, 1954), 278.

the Philippines, his constant support of the Civil Service Commission, the reorganization of the Forest Service, the creation of the meat inspection service, his reorientation of the Navy toward modern warfare, his Keep Committee's concern with departmental methods and procedures, and the establishment of the Department of Commerce and Labor with cabinet status, T. R. did much to reorganize the executive branch and prepare it for a new role in both foreign and domestic affairs. By his concern for lines of authority, his awareness of the need for delegation of power, his clear and steady support of his subordinate staff, his emphasis on research and committee work as a basis for modern decision-making, his evident attempt to attract the intelligence and energy of youth into the public service, and, above all, by his own example, he provided that great energizing force without which mere reorganization is no more than an arid sort of reshuffling. In his comprehension of administration in action Theodore Roosevelt was a far cry from the presidents of the era of congressional government. Sometimes President Hoover has been considered the outstanding administrator among the presidents. But, in a recognition that effective public administration is, after all, fundamentally based on effective political power, T. R. far outshone the great engineer. In his understanding that modern positive government is equally fundamentally based on effective administration he clearly outranks his distant cousin, Franklin D. Roosevelt.

That he could recognize the existence of social and economic injustice endeared him to many. That his method of attack was still primarily that of the essentially conservative political man—*now an administrator as well as a moralist*—made him acceptable to nearly everyone else. In addition, he had what Cleveland never had, an extraordinary ability to advertise and sell his product and an extreme sensitivity to the realities of political power, without which morality and administration can be little more than platitudes.

Those who felt Roosevelt's wrath or sensed the frequent legislative futility of his boundless energy perceived a certain elusiveness in his argument. If to the world of modern economics he seems confused, T. R. had nothing on the voters of 1900. But those who accepted Roosevelt's approach—and a large proportion of the voting population welcomed it—considered him to be the epitome of statesmen. If vitality and power can be equated with accomplishment he was a very great man. Whatever else may be said, he bridged a certain gap between the Right and the Left and between the past and the future. By his final political intransigence in 1912 he even made possible the fruition of much of the Progressives' more substantive economic program in the Wilsonian legislation of 1913 and 1914.

180

T. R. and civil service reform. What does all this have to do with civil service reform? Just this: compounded with the catalytic effect of his own ambitions, the analysis above goes far to explain why on the one hand T. R. frequently compromised with Hanna, Platt, and Quay in the cause of political power, and why on the other he was a leader in civil service reform. No LaFollette with a social program of his own, he was enough of a realist to know that he must come to terms with his Old Guard if he was to remain at the Republican helm. He also perceived with "his hips," not his brain, so Lincoln Steffens told him,[26] that the political necessities demanded some kind of action. Civil service reform was one of the few reforms which directly menaced no great private interests. T. R. could vehemently and publicly stand for morality, honesty, and efficiency in office and be unchallenged. Even more, he could administratively implement these doctrines, as he could few others, without treading on too many toes.

Roosevelt's support of civil service reform was but a further reflection of his recognition of the administrative phase of the Progressive movement. From this time on, civil service reform was to be identified with the movement for more effective political machinery and organization as well as with the pressure for moral political men. The merit system began to merge with a larger whole: general administrative reform, sometimes aimed at economy and efficiency in terms of dollars and cents and sometimes at bolstering the power of the positive state. The transmutation of the concepts of the Pendleton Act into the more inclusive idea of public personnel administration as a tool of management must be dated from the first years of the twentieth century.

Appointment and Removal Policies

As a whole, Roosevelt probably made as satisfactory appointments as any president since 1829. He insisted on at least honest, if not always efficient, men even from Senators Platt and Quay, who controlled much of the Republican political machinery in New York and Pennsylvania respectively. William Allen White has characterized the difference between McKinley and T. R. on appointments:

. . . Certainly McKinley had stood for clean men in high places. Many of McKinley's appointees had been men of the highest type. It is only fair to say that McKinley, on the whole, found better men for high places than

---

[26] *Autobiography of Lincoln Steffens* (New York: Harcourt, Brace and Co., 1931), p. 579.

Roosevelt chose. It was in choosing high-grade men for the minor appointments and fighting for these men that Roosevelt made his mark.[27]

However, in all fairness to his predecessors, it must be remembered that Theodore Roosevelt was able to foster the development of the public service under more favorable conditions than McKinley, for example. Roosevelt succeeded a Republican president who had already accomplished most of the desired political readjustment of the service. Moreover, T. R. had been a Civil Service Commissioner himself and thoroughly understood the technical as well as political problems involved in any matters relating to the federal service.

Practical politics. Nevertheless, Roosevelt faced one immediate and pressing problem. While he had suddenly been catapulted into the Presidency, he by no means controlled the Republican party. Indeed, there were many of the Old Guard who, like Hanna, found it difficult to reconcile themselves to the fact of a progressively-inclined resident of the White House. How was it that he was able to unite, on the surface at least, such diverse elements within his own party as La-Follette and Aldrich, Borah and Penrose? Not that he made them his friends, but he did prevent the open break that later occurred under Taft.

Much of the answer lay in the power of Roosevelt's personality. It was difficult to say "No" to T. R. when he was his most ingratiating, and many equally feared his wrath. But one of his most important undercover weapons, permitting him to maintain and even heavily to reinforce his position, was the patronage.

His first remark, when warned that a break between him and Hanna would wreck the Republican party, was "What can I do about it? Give him complete control of the patronage!" That he did not have to do, but he reaffirmed to Hanna that he would carry out McKinley's policies as he had publicly promised.[28] He kept McKinley's cabinet almost intact. Significantly, his first change was the appointment of Henry C. Payne, a veteran Old Guard politician and vice chairman of the Republican National Committee, as Postmaster General. However, he made few other immediate changes of any kind in the more important offices. With respect to the minor offices, T. R.'s removal policy remained that which he bluntly stated early in October, 1901, in answer to an Illinois representative's "pressing claims" on the patronage. "As long as a man proves himself fit and efficient

27 As cited in footnote 2, p. 309. See also Blum, as cited in footnote 25, pp. 49–50.
28 Kohlsaat, as cited in footnote 20, p. 103.

his position is safe. When he shows himself unfit and inefficient he will be removed." [29]

From the very beginning it was possible for the leaders of the party to sense a determined hand beneath the compromises of a politician. To be sure, Roosevelt made several appointments only because he thought McKinley would have made them or wanted them made. But as for other new appointments, he early began to exercise his presidential prerogatives and set his own standards. On the 11th of October, 1901, Roosevelt wrote to his close friend, Senator Henry Cabot Lodge of Massachusetts:

. . . In the appointments I shall go on exactly as I did while I was Governor of New York. The Senators and Congressmen shall ordinarily name the men, but I shall name the standard, and the men have got to come up to it.[30]

T. R. recognized the fundamental constitutional problem underlying the power of appointment. He said in his autobiography: "In consequence the Constitution itself forced the President and the Senators from each State to come to a working agreement on the appointments in and from that State." But as usual, he made his own interpretation of the Constitution and went on to say:

. . . My course was to insist on absolute fitness . . . as a prerequisite . . . and to remove only for good cause. . . . Subject to these considerations, I normally accepted each Senator's recommendations for offices of a routine kind, . . . but insisted on myself choosing the men for the most important positions.[31]

Moreover, if an appointee originally proposed by a legislator stirred up public indignation or if congressmen did not come through with reasonable legislative support, the President did not hesitate either to request another name or to reject the legislative advice entirely.

From the beginning Roosevelt gave considerable thought to the relationship between appointments and control of the Republican party. At first the party machinery lay under the firm hand of Senator Hanna. A close associate of McKinley and chairman of the Republican National Committee, Hanna was at this time perhaps the nearest to a national political boss the United States has ever had. While

[29] Joseph Bucklin Bishop, *Theodore Roosevelt and His Time* (2 vols.; New York: Charles Scribner's Sons, 1920), I, 155.
[30] Same, pp. 157–58.
[31] Roosevelt, as cited in footnote 22, pp. 358–59.

183

T. R. and Hanna never formally broke, the President quickly undertook to reduce Hanna's formidable political power through undermining his control in states outside Ohio. Even in Ohio, Roosevelt soon frequently and frankly dealt on many patronage matters with Hanna's rival, Senator Joseph B. Foraker. The President's policy was essentially one of divide and conquer, with the patronage as a principal weapon of separation. There is no need to go into this intricate story here.[32] The measure of Roosevelt's ability as a practical politician lay in the fact that, within a year after he had taken office, he had reduced Hanna almost to a figurehead and had captured the Republican party organization completely. Before the next election, the President had dictated the choice of a new national chairman against the wishes of most of the Republican National Committee and had manipulated the progress of the Republican national convention of 1904 so smoothly toward his own renomination that the gathering found it difficult to spread out its business over the three days that had been planned.

The idea of encouraging the Republican party in the South seems to have intrigued both Presidents Roosevelt and Taft. T. R., on his first day of receiving visitors as President, said to three southern congressmen, "If I cannot find Republicans I am going to appoint Democrats. I intend to make such appointments as will induce every Southern man to respect the Republican party." [33] Nevertheless, no matter how hard he tried, he ran up against southern sentiment which simply would not be reconciled with another of his views, expressed in a letter of 1903, "I certainly cannot treat mere color as a permanent bar to holding office." [34] The incompatibility of his desires with reality was first most pointedly demonstrated in the violent southern reaction to a White House dinner with Booker T. Washington. It was made even more evident when bitter protests were raised over the appointment of a prominent and hitherto respected southern Negro as collector of the port of Charleston. Roosevelt was manifestly at a loss as to what action to take and he wrote his friend Lyman Abbott, in 1903:

. . . In South Carolina, at Florence, I have just reappointed a negro postmaster with the approval of the entire community. Why South Carolina should go crazy over the appointment of an equally good negro as Collector of the Port of Charleston, I do not know. Why the southerners should be glad to visit the White House in company with a colored arch-

32 For the most succinct account of T. R.'s systematic undermining and replacement of Hanna as boss of the Republican party, see Blum, as cited in footnote 25, pp. 37–54.
33 Bishop, as cited in footnote 29, I, 154.
34 Same, p. 169.

deacon, and yet feel furious because I received in only slightly more intimate fashion a great colored educator, I am again at a loss to understand.[35]

But with his customary tenacity he would not give up, and he continued throughout his administration his attempt to reconcile what refused to be reconciled.[36] In reality his only successes lay in capturing complete control of the southern Republican party organization and in encouraging the entry of Negroes into the service.

His control of his party also served the President's legislative purposes, with, again, the patronage always in the background as a legislative incentive. In her study of Post Office politics, Dorothy Fowler lists instance after instance in which Roosevelt was a most practical politician in his exploitation of the offices for this and other purposes.[37] When Steffens asked what were Roosevelt's plans for meeting the patronage demands of the legislative leaders, T. R. snapped back with:

. . . Deal with them. If they'll vote for my measures I'll appoint their nominees to Federal jobs. And I'm going to tell them so. They think I won't, you know. I'm going to call in a couple of machine senators and a few key congressmen and tell them I'll trade.

Steffens protested that he might obtain better results with a "few reluctant concessions." " 'No, No,' he came back with his whole body. 'I'm going at it my own way. I want service out of the men I appoint, too.' "[38] The extent to which T. R. was willing to "deal" is illustrated in his admission to Steffens that his "worst appointment" was the selection of the brother of a senator's mistress for a legal position. He justified this action on the basis that he had to "get" that senator, who hated him "personally and politically," so that the senator would support his program.[39] Nevertheless, with his usual openness and directness of approach, T. R. even managed to make his shadier deals somehow seem right. William Allen White later remarked, "Such bald candor as Roosevelt's had not been seen in the White House since Jackson's time."[40]

35 Morison, as cited in footnote 25, III, 639. Booker T. Washington was a frequent adviser to T. R. on southern, and especially Negro, appointments. Blum, as cited in footnote 25, p. 44.
36 See Simkins, as cited in footnote 15, pp. 415–18, for details of T. R.'s fight with Congress over the incredible case of Dr. William D. Crum, the collector at Charleston mentioned above. The fight lasted more than six years.
37 Dorothy Fowler, *The Cabinet Politician* (New York: Columbia University Press, 1943), pp. 262–303.
38 As cited in footnote 26, p. 577.
39 Same, p. 505.
40 As cited in footnote 2, p. 314.

Maintaining standards. Nor was the President reluctant to enforce his standards of public office-holding. He could eventually boast, with considerable justice, that he had been instrumental in the conviction of two senators for fraud and corruption.[41] He relentlessly pursued the timber and land frauds in Oregon, and early in his first term he forced a reluctant Postmaster General to investigate and prosecute to the full extent of the law a series of postal violations uncovered by one of his assistants. By T. R.'s very energy in the prosecution of dishonesty in high office he erased these scandals from the debit side of the Republican political ledger. If possible, they made him more popular.

This same energy in law enforcement was also displayed within the framework of the merit system. William Dudley Foulke has related that in an interview on behalf of the National Civil Service Reform League early in October, 1901, Roosevelt

. . . told me he intended to remove all officers who had violated it [the civil service law]; to restore the old rule limiting reinstatements; to restrict temporary appointments; to bring Porto Ricans into the classified system; to require employees to furnish testimony to the Commission under penalty of dismissal and to forbid auditing and disbursing officers to pay salaries to those illegally appointed. These declarations were highly satisfactory to the League.[42]

A large number of the investigations made by the Civil Service Commission stemmed from violations of the provisions against political removals, political assessments, and illegal political activity. Political removals caused no great problem. Each case had to be investigated on its own merits, but there was usually a fairly solid basis of fact from which to derive judgments.

Political assessments, however, still caused considerable difficulty. Direct personal approach of one federal office-holder by another had long been considered forbidden by the Pendleton Act. However, solicitation by letter was another thing. Attorney General Richard Olney, under Cleveland, had held that it was permissible under the law to request contributions through the mail. The Commission felt itself hampered by this and a similar ruling by Attorney General Judson Harmon. Roosevelt's Attorney General obligingly reversed these former opinions, and, in one of October 17, 1902, ruled that federal office-holders could not request contributions from each other by

---

41 Roosevelt, as cited in footnote 22, pp. 372–74.
42 William Dudley Foulke, *Roosevelt and the Spoilsmen* (New York: National Civil Service Reform League, 1925), p. 52.

186

mail.[43] Another loophole in the law was thus plugged. By 1906 Civil Service Commissioner Henry F. Greene optimistically reported that, "on the whole, it may be safely said that the political assessment is as to the Federal service in the main a thing of the past."[44] That there were still some problems Greene did not deny. Prompted by an assessment scandal involving Senator Quay, Roosevelt, in 1907, strengthened the Commission's hand by formally revising its rules condemning assessments. This gave the Commission an official backing in its investigations, which it had not possessed before.[45]

Even more perplexing had been the problem of enforcing the regulations against general political activity by office-holders. President Cleveland had made the first real attempt to enforce the provisions against political activity through an Executive Order of July 14, 1888. However, he had not distinguished between the classified and the unclassified services in laying out the bounds within which public officials might exercise their political rights. This Roosevelt felt was unrealistic. It had certainly proved unenforceable. Therefore on June 13, 1902, the President stated in a letter to the Civil Service Commission that he had studied President Cleveland's regulations against "pernicious" activities and had come to the conclusion that a distinction must be drawn between the classified and unclassified services. He felt that outside the classified service it was impossible to go beyond the statement, "Office-holders must not *use their offices to control political movements,* must not neglect their public duties, must not cause public scandal by their activity." Within the merit system, however, it was a different matter, and he felt politics of all kinds should be rigorously excluded.[46] This dual interpretation of the limits of political activity lasted with practically no variation until the passage of the Hatch Acts under Franklin D. Roosevelt.

Roosevelt's desire to bring to account those who refused to obey these laws and rules was quickly implemented. In the second report of the Civil Service Commission issued after Roosevelt became President, it is recorded that he removed, for cause, the collector of customs at El Paso and the appraiser of the port of New York. The collectors of internal revenue at Louisville and Nashville were permitted to resign. The postmaster of Philadelphia and the surveyor-general of

---

[43] 24 Op. Att. Gen. 133 (1902). Shortly after this ruling, the civil service rules were modified to conform.

[44] "The Enforcement of the Provisions of the Civil Service Laws in Regard to Political Assessments," *Good Government,* XXIII (December, 1906), 154.

[45] Executive Order of June 3, 1907. For a discussion of the situation at that time see William Dudley Foulke, "Restriction of the Political Activity of Officeholders," *Good Government,* XXIV (December, 1907), 109.

[46] USCSC, *Nineteenth Report,* 1902, pp. 145–47; Commission's italics.

Idaho were not reappointed when their term expired. All of these men had been investigated to their discredit by the Commission under McKinley,[47] who nevertheless had refused to take action. Nor were these officials small fry. They were Republican leaders in their areas, and the repercussions were so widely felt that in its next report, for 1902–03, the Commission stated that there had been a "marked decrease" in complaints concerning violations of the civil service laws. In its summary for the fiscal year of 1904 the Commission noted "very marked progress in the observance of not merely the letter, but the spirit of the act and rules." [48] By 1905, it remarked that the number of cases to investigate was "very small." In the one case considered important for that year, the President summarily removed the offender, an assistant treasurer at Philadelphia, for nepotism and fraud in examinations.[49] There was no increase in reported violations during the remainder of Roosevelt's administration.

The open shop issue. One of Roosevelt's more spectacular administrative decisions resulted from what became known in 1903 as the Miller Case. A. W. Miller, an assistant foreman in the Government Printing Office, was removed from his position by the Public Printer because he was expelled from the craft union to which he belonged. Miller appealed to the Civil Service Commission on the grounds that his removal was unlawful. The Commission investigated and upheld Miller and requested that he be reassigned. On July 13, 1903, Roosevelt wrote the Secretary of Commerce and Labor that Miller would be reinstated and flatly ruled:

. . . There is no objection to the employees of the Government Printing Office constituting themselves into a union if they so desire; but no rules or resolutions of that union can be permitted to override the laws of the United States, which it is my sworn duty to enforce.[50]

The case created so much publicity revolving around the question of the open or closed shop in the government service that Samuel Gompers and other labor leaders requested an interview with the President. He received them late in September and politely but firmly and publicly reaffirmed his decision. The storm raged but it seems not materially to have affected the President. As a result of Roosevelt's decision the federal service has retained an open shop policy ever since.[51]

---

47 Action against the collector at Nashville had been pressed since 1897. See "The Removal of Collector Nunn," *Good Government*, XIX (January, 1902), 2.

48 *Twenty-first Report*, 1904, p. 19.

49 *Twenty-second Report*, 1905, p. 20.

50 For this and related communications see USCSC, *Twentieth Report*, 1903, pp. 147–50.

51 For more than forty years, however, there has been a sort of *de facto* closed shop in both the Government Printing Office and the navy yards. Neither the government nor the unions have dared force a showdown on the issue since T. R.'s time.

The problem of exceptions. The one aspect of Roosevelt's appointment policies for which he was criticized by the Reform League concerned the matter of individual personal exceptions to the merit system rules. His answer was that it was better to make a few individual exceptions than to follow the McKinley policy of excepting large groups of positions. At least Roosevelt must be given credit for unusual care in observing the boundary line between the classified and unclassified services. He required the classified service to be as nonpolitical as the proponents of the Pendleton Act intended it eventually to be.

Americans have never carried the idea of a nonpolitical civil service to the same lengths as the British, for our Jacksonian heritage is still with us. But the idea has gradually been applied to that part of the public service selected through competitive examinations. As that part of the service became more and more inclusive the idea of neutrality seemed more appropriate and acceptable. By the end of T. R.'s term in office it was considered almost on equal terms with the ideas of examination and relative security of tenure as a fundamental aspect of the American version of the merit system.

Support for the Civil Service Commission

The President was not so absorbed in his own role as a protector of the merit system that he neglected the Civil Service Commission. Indeed, he moved quickly to reinforce the powers of the Commission as an agent of the chief executive.

New policing powers. Under McKinley, the Comptroller of the Treasury had ruled that he would not go behind the certificate of an appointing officer to see whether an employee had been hired according to the civil service rules.[52] As a result, the Commission was seriously hampered in the enforcement of its examination requirements for entrance into the classified service. Roosevelt quickly gave directions in 1901 that payments would not be made if the Commission found any violation of the law. At the same time the President required that all employees must testify before the Commission under penalty of dismissal. Thus it was possible for William D. Foulke, although a bit too strongly, to conclude in 1920 that Roosevelt "was the only President who from the beginning to the end of his career could be relied on to enforce the civil service act by taking by the scruff of the neck and kicking out of office anyone who violated it."[53]

Personal relationship of the President and the commissioners. In his handling of the top personnel of the Commission itself the President

---

[52] See USCSC, *Twentieth Report,* 1903, p. 120.
[53] As cited in footnote 42, p. 100.

gave further expression to his belief in the merit system. Early in his administration he selected as commissioners three men of widely recognized ability who were to work together for the better part of two years. Roosevelt retained in office his old Democratic friend, John R. Proctor, with whom the President had served on the Commission under Cleveland. As the new Republican members he selected, first, the prominent civil service reformer, William D. Foulke, a distinguished Indiana lawyer and personal friend, and, second, James R. Garfield, son of the martyred President and later Secretary of Commerce and Labor. All three were personally congenial as well as administratively competent. They were able to cooperate in a most effective fashion and were responsible for many of the technical improvements made in the federal personnel system under Theodore Roosevelt.

Of course, these men were actively supported by a man who was not only their chief executive, but who also counted them as among his more intimate circle of friends. Foulke has said of their relationship with Roosevelt:

. . . It was indeed an unalloyed delight to serve as Civil Service Commissioner under such a President and with such colleagues as Proctor and Garfield, who were close personal friends. We used to make our New Year's calls together on the President and were always at the frequent hospitalities at the White House.[54]

Naturally, this relationship with the President smoothed many paths for the commissioners. Consequently, it was officially stated in 1902, apparently for the first time, that "The Commission desires to express its gratification at the spirit of friendly cooperation which exists in all the departments of the Government in the enforcement both of the letter and the spirit of the civil-service act." [55]

In 1905 the rapport was still sufficiently strong that the Commission, though composed of different men, again felt justified in a lengthy pat on the back of the higher officials in the government and stated:

. . . It is also most gratifying to report that the work of the Commission is greatly facilitated by the hearty spirit of cooperation shown by the members of the Cabinet and by the bureau chiefs in Washington. While the merit system is not so well understood outside the District of Columbia, very few complaints have been received in regard to the enforcement of the rules in the outside services. It is also believed that even those officials who for various reasons are opposed to the principles of the civil service law appreciate that they are expected to enforce it vigorously, and viola-

54 Same, p. 67.
55 *Nineteenth Report*, 1902, p. 20.

190

tions of the rules either in letter or in spirit are constantly decreasing in number.[56]

Seldom, before or since, has the Commission praised in such eulogistic terms the cooperation it has received from the remainder of the executive branch of the government.

Toward Positive Personnel Management

Albert de Roode, a New York lawyer and long time member of the National Civil Service Reform League, told that body in 1904: "The matter of labor regulations is one of detail in the administration of the civil service, but it is in the *details* that the progress of civil service reform must now be made." [57]

President Cleveland had by 1896 placed half of the government service under the merit system. By 1901 it was not only possible but necessary to consider the technical administrative problems of the rapidly growing governmental service. Anyone can understand the necessity of enforcing a law, but it sometimes takes considerable ingenuity to implement a law so that its full intent and potential may be realized. That the President himself and most of his civil service commissioners and department heads comprehended the latter problem is to the credit of the Roosevelt administration. The most important new regulations relating to law enforcement in terms of evasion of presidential appointment and removal policies have already been discussed. What of those duller but equally important instructions which merely insure that John Doe gets his pay on time rather than two weeks late, or which enable the government to secure the best workers rather than merely the better?

The Keep Committee. In the first decade of the century administrative reform was in high gear in the cities, where "muckraking" was both fashionable and effective. Governor Charles Evans Hughes had commenced to pry the lid off corruption in the state of New York. Business itself realized with somewhat of a shock that the first billion dollar Congress was only the first. Dollars and cents became matters of greater concern as economic competition grew more intense and as taxation increased. Technical competence became more valued. The movement was toward concentration and centralization and the watchword was becoming "economy and efficiency."

Roosevelt's most deliberately organized reply to this trend was his

---

[56] *Twenty-second Report*, 1905, p. 9.
[57] NCSRL, *Proceedings*, 1904, p. 107. Italics added.

appointment in 1905 of the Keep Committee, officially known as the Committee on Department Methods, whose task he described as to "find out what changes are needed to place the conduct of the executive business of the Government in all its branches on the most economical and effective basis in the light of the best modern business practice." [58] The Committee concentrated on departmental methods and organization, but also raised some questions about the condition of the public service. The most important of these went to the heart of the major inadequacies of the Pendleton Act in regard to the pay plan of the national government and the related problem of superannuation. In one report the Committee called attention to the fact that the last general salary legislation dated back more than fifty years, and recommended a thorough revision of the duties-classification system for employees in Washington along with increased pay for all employees. Elsewhere, a pension plan was suggested, the costs largely to be borne by contributions of the employees. A report on hours of work and sick and annual leave recommended more uniform practices. Nothing of any immediate importance came of these proposals, despite a specially prepared bill to implement the recommendations on duties and pay and despite two messages to Congress from the President containing estimates for the cost of the proposed new salary scales.[59] Congress was not yet ready for the major overturning of precedent which such legislation would require, although by now it was at least willing to consider these types of problems.

Pay and position-classification. In a less public way Roosevelt's energetic Civil Service Commission, with the willing support of the President, also endeavored to straighten out some of the kinks in the pay and position-classification policies of the federal government. Lack of a systematic position-classification scheme was still a constant and severe handicap to the Commission, for there was inevitably much needless duplication in examinations as well as inefficiency in certification and placement of those examined. As far as possible the Commission combined registers, and requested departments to be more specific in their requisitions for personnel.

In the absence of a coordinated pay plan, equal pay for equal work

[58] As cited in footnote 22, p. 366.
[59] The Keep Committee's reports were never published in any systematic form and copies are rare. Those on personnel are in the Library of the Civil Service Commission. They are: Committee on Department Methods, *Annual Leave, Sick Leave, and Hours of Labor* (Washington: 1906), *Classification of Positions and Gradation of Salaries for Employees of the Executive Departments and Independent Establishments in Washington* (Washington, 1907), and *Superannuation of Civil-Service Employees of the Government* (Washington, 1908). For a summary of the work of the Committee and a catalog of its publications, see Gustavus A. Weber, *Organized Efforts for the Improvement of Methods of Administration in the United States* (New York: D. Appleton and Co., 1919), pp. 74–83.

was impossible to achieve. The laws of 1871 and 1883 gave the President broad powers to regulate the civil service, but they did not give him much authority over salaries. Any new system of position-classification which might be devised would seriously affect the pay plan of the government. Therefore, action on both matters had to wait for congressional implementation. The Commission could only mend and patch and recommend, but that it did. In its reports for the fiscal years of 1902 and 1903 the Commission made clear the need for legislative action, and in 1908 it remarked that it was pleased to see that the Committee on Department Methods was advocating a new position-classification system with grades of pay for each classification.[60] But with Congress the Commission was no more effective than the President on these matters.

Promotion and transfer. Position-classification was related to still other problems of the day. The Commission found that promotion regulations were impossible to enforce until proper lines of promotion could be determined and the relationships of positions to each other clarified. In 1902 the Commission concluded after twenty years of frustration:

. . . Until . . . reclassification is made the Commission does not feel justified in promulgating and attempting to enforce any uniform system of promotion regulations, but urges that each department and bureau adopt, in cooperation with the Commission, a system of promotions, including examinations where feasible, which will best meet the conditions within the department or bureau.[61]

Service-wide regulations for transfers and reinstatements likewise depended upon service-wide agreement as to the nature of classes of positions. The Commission was powerless to prevent the increasing shifting of employees from one department to the other in a search for higher pay and the bidding of agencies against each other except by extremely rigid transfer regulations. In 1901 the Commission ruled that employees who had not served at least six months in their positions were ineligible for transfer,[62] and in 1903 it limited transfers to those cases where the positions could not be filled by promotion.[63] Nevertheless, the Quartermaster General protested to the Secretary of War in 1904 that he was losing his skilled stenographers and typists to other departments where they received more pay.[64] In desperation

60 *Twenty-fourth Report*, 1907, p. 16.
61 *Nineteenth Report*, 1902, p. 24.
62 *Eighteenth Report*, 1901, p. 300.
63 *Twenty-first Report*, 1904, p. 15.
64 Same, pp. 15–16.

at its inability to meet the more basic issues involved, Congress in 1906 forbade transfers from department to department unless an employee had served three years in one department.[65] At best only a stopgap measure, this legislation remained in force until the First World War.

Examinations and recruitment. In 1904, the Commission reported for the first time that it felt that it could examine successfully for almost anything. The Chief Examiner noted that he continually was striving to make examinations as practical as possible, even at the scientific and technical levels.[66] For some time the Commission had been publishing specimen copies of its examinations for public information.

The apportionment clause of the Pendleton Act was meant to secure adequate representation in the public service for all sections of the country. However, its application is limited to the departments in Washington and it need be applied to them only when practicable. It has always been difficult to devise an adequate basis for the apportionment, and the system has been changed several times.[67] In 1904 and 1905 it was discovered by the Commission that the South was consistently underrepresented in the federal service despite the apportionment. Therefore, with President Roosevelt's encouragement, the Commission made a concerted effort to publicize the opportunities available and the fairness of the merit system. Letters were sent to all southern senators, interviews were printed in many southern papers, and special examinations were held for states behind in the apportionment. In the spring of 1907 Commissioner John A. McIlhenny, himself a southerner, made a tour of the South to develop interest in the government service. The efforts were successful, for the apportionment shortly thereafter showed that the southern states were receiving their appropriate share of the federal offices. Since that time there has been little sectional variation in the apportioned service, except that stemming from the fact that those states nearest to Washington have, for obvious reasons, tended to find it easier to receive their share than those farther away.

The career concept appears. Even at this early date the Civil Service Commission was not oblivious to the problem of developing a career system in the public service. In 1905 it deplored the "lack of opportunity in the service" and what it considered to be an excessive turnover. It should be noted, however, that the Commission's judgment concerning "excessive turnover" was not developed from any direct

65 *Twenty-third Report*, 1906, pp. 45–46.
66 *Twenty-first Report*, 1904, pp. 11–12.
67 USCSC, *Twenty-eighth Report*, 1911, pp. 16–17 and 135–38, outlines the early history of this problem.

comparison with private industry at the time. In all likelihood, even during the height of the spoils system, turnover rates in the federal government have never equalled those of, for example, heavy industry in this country. There is, however, very little conclusive evidence on this point for the period before World War I.

In the Roosevelt Commission's opinion, "The great defect in the Federal service today is the lack of opportunity for ambitious, well-educated young men." A contributing cause, it felt, was the failure to place many of the higher positions under the merit system.[68] Nevertheless, the Commission still reflected the typical American fear of the development of an established bureaucracy. "It is necessary," it said in 1903, "to guard against the tendency toward making a privileged class of those already in the service and defeating the just claims of persons of superior qualifications seeking original entrance." [69]

Reorganization within the Commission. In 1903 the Civil Service Commission applied for as usual, and finally received, a large increase in its appropriation.[70] The National Civil Service Reform League remarked that this was the first time that Congress had "passed the appropriation asked for by the Commission without any opposition whatever." [71] The additional income permitted the Commission to enlarge its activities as well as to dispense with a major proportion of the employees who had been detailed to it from the departments under the authority of previous legislation. For the first time it had a really adequate working force which it could call its own.

At the same time the Commission completed a careful study of the formal procedures under which it operated and requested President Roosevelt to approve a new set of regulations governing the merit system. He did so, and the new Rules of 1903, the first since 1896, proved to be so well designed that they were not rescinded and fully replaced until 1938.[72]

A significant change was represented by the revised definition of those whom, in the opinion of the President, the Act of 1883 permitted to be brought under the merit system. The problem of laborers had long agitated the minds of those interested in the merit system. Roosevelt made it clear that he considered the Pendleton Act to exclude only "mere laborers" and not skilled workmen. Issuing executive orders to implement his definitions with systems of registration

---

[68] *Twenty-second Report,* 1905, p. 23.
[69] *Twentieth Report,* 1903, p. 77.
[70] See USCSC, *Twenty-first Report,* 1904, pp. 32–36, for an analysis of the Commission's financial position. This increase was about 70 per cent.
[71] "The Fifty-seventh Congress," *Good Government,* XX (March, 1903), 39.
[72] For further analysis of the Rules of 1903 see USCSC, *Twentieth Report,* 1903, pp. 8–11.

and, where appropriate, examination, he, in effect, extended the merit system to many of the lower categories of positions.[73]

Other provisions of the new regulations gave the Commission more discretion and more real authority than it had before enjoyed. For example, age limits were made more flexible, subject to agreement among the Commission and the departments. In order to open examinations to Puerto Ricans and Filipinos, following the decisions in the Insular Cases, it was agreed to permit applications by all persons who owed allegiance to the United States. The control of temporary employees was tightened by requiring that such appointees must come from existing registers if at all practical, with the Commission as the main judge of practicality. Reinstatements were systematized. The removal regulations were clarified. The new provisions described earlier, concerning the payment of persons illegally employed and the requiring of testimony from all government employees, were included. The long list of positions technically within the classified service but "excepted" from examination, known then and for a half century more as *Schedule A*, was revised with a view to placing as many as possible of these positions fully within the merit system. Appointing officers were authorized to require, even for those positions remaining on the "excepted" list, an examination by the Commission.

At the same time the Commission coordinated certain rules changes to implement a revised organization for examination management, which was designed especially to permit more efficient service in the field. Approximately 90 per cent of the federal civil service has always worked outside the District of Columbia. After experimenting since 1897, the Commission came to the conclusion that its system of examination through a thousand or so relatively unsupervised local boards had resulted in a grave lack of administrative control and was conducive to evasion and fraud. By the Rules of 1903 the local boards, though not reduced much in number, were organized into thirteen districts under district secretaries responsible to the Commission alone. The authority of the secretaries was explicitly set forth in regulations. Periodic reports to the central office of the Commission were required. All examinations were still prepared and rated in Washington, but the registers and the graded examination papers were returned to the districts where they were available at a central headquarters for the information of the local appointing officers. The secretaries supervised the local boards in their areas and aided in maintaining and training the personnel of the local examining groups, who were subject to considerable turnover because they were

[73] USCSC, *Twenty-second Report*, 1905, pp. 11–13, and *Twenty-sixth Report*, 1909, p. 163.

merely detailed employees of the postal, customs or other agencies. This system, with minor variations, principally in the form of additional delegations of power to the district representatives, has been maintained to this day.[74] Altogether, a thorough-going job of organizational and procedural revamping and streamlining was done as far as existing legislation permitted.

The trend of accomplishment. Certainly never between 1883 and 1938 was the public personnel system so thoroughly analyzed and overhauled in a detail sense. What was most needed now was legislation to remedy the inequalities that had arisen through more than a century and a quarter of miscellaneous wage and salary legislation. In the first part of the twentieth century relatively few persons thoroughly understood these problems. Many Americans still considered the public service a refuge for the unemployed. The snowballing effect of military pensions made the question of civil pensions politically impossible. Not until more than another decade had passed would public opinion be sufficiently aroused to support the fundamental legislation already needed in 1900. However, the efforts of the commissioners and the President between 1901 and 1909 allayed many of the worst of the evils and made it possible for the Commission to function reasonably satisfactorily during the unprecedented demands of the First World War. In fact, it is to a Roosevelt-appointed President of the Commission and a Roosevelt-appointed Chief Examiner that a large share of the credit must be given for the wartime accomplishments of the government's chief personnel agency.

Departmental Personnel Management

It was evidently during the Presidency of Theodore Roosevelt that the word "personnel" first came into use in the federal government in its modern sense. The word occurs for the first time as a key index term in the annual report of the Civil Service Commission for the fiscal year of 1909. A report made by the Secretary of Commerce and Labor in 1910 may well be the first departmental report to contain the term "personnel" in its heading. This report, reprinted in the annual report of the Commission for 1910, is titled simply "Personnel."

---

[74] For the best description of the reasons for and the development of this "boards of examiners" system see Frank M. Kiggins, "The Establishment of Civil Service Districts—An Administrative Reform," *Good Government*, XXI (December, 1904), 96–106. Kiggins was then Chief Examiner of the Commission. For a recent account of the system see James P. Googe and John J. Brennan, "What Happened to Boards of U.S. Civil Service Examiners?" *Personnel Administration*, XII (July, 1950), 16.

All this is evidence of the growing development of personnel administration as we know it today. While departmental management was still not modern by any means, there was considerable progress in systematizing procedures within departments as well as within the Civil Service Commission. The Keep Committee and the later Commission on Economy and Efficiency under President Taft, along with the developing commercial practices, were having their effect. While the chief clerks and the appointment clerks still supervised such personnel management as there was, career patterns of a modern sort had already emerged in the Department of Agriculture, the Department of State, the Treasury and elsewhere.

Moreover, in the Department of Agriculture, for example, a sort of personnel committee was created as early as 1905. This committee, composed of the Assistant Secretary, the Chief Clerk, and the Solicitor was directed "to consider, and if necessary to investigate, all charges of dereliction of duty and actions prejudicial to the interests of the Department by employees thereof and to recommend appropriate action to the Secretary." It is reported that "the investigations of this committee not only had a salutary effect upon the deportment and efficiency of employees of the Department, but also relieved the Secretary from time-consuming details." [75] Times were changing in the departments, though clearly in a conservative and evolutionary manner.

The Legislative, Judicial, and Military Services

Congressional patronage. Still legally outside the merit system proper were all uniformed military personnel as well as all civil employees other than those of the *executive* civil service. Legislative civil employees attached directly to Congress numbered under a thousand in 1901.[76] They were chosen completely through the spoils system, and a committee appointed to investigate House employees and employment procedures reported an amazing state of affairs in early 1901. William D. Foulke has well summarized some of the more lurid revelations of this political backwater of the spoils system:

. . . Persons appointed to perform certain work were assigned to occupations entirely different. Thus the House telegrapher worked in the station-

---

[75] This and the preceding quotation are from Warner W. Stockberger and Virginia B. Smith, *Personnel Administration Development in the United States Department of Agriculture* (Washington: Department of Agriculture, 1947), p. 135.

[76] USCSC, *Eighteenth Report*, 1901, p. 15. This figure—779 to be exact—evidently refers to those employed directly in connection with Congress and probably does not include, for example, the Library of Congress. Legislative employees of all categories numbered 1,758 in 1904. USCSC, *Twenty-first Report*, 1904, p. 188.

ery room, while the man who actually performed the work of telegrapher was paid from an appropriation of $900 for the "hire of horses and wagons and cartage for use of clerk's office." Meanwhile the man who received $1200 as telegrapher spent his time in the library compiling biographies of the members of Congress, a "leisurely place" where "you didn't have to perspire a great deal," though $400 additional appropriation was recommended by the clerk in evident appreciation of the statesmanship recorded in these biographies. One of the pages "who could not read and write" was put to driving a team and the man employed as driver cleaned the floors and scrubbed the spittoons. The locksmith served as a messenger and though he was absent from April until after the Christmas holidays, he received $1440 a year.

The librarian and his subordinates were also absent for long periods and the library, consisting of some 300,000 volumes was scattered from dome to basement with piles of books in unused rooms until the librarian himself testified that it would be all right for a barnyard but for books it was terrible.

One Smith, who was pretty fond of "old barleycorn" got an appropriation of $600 for "loafing about." He had a good run of the books which were in the rubbish pile and knew to what part of the pile to go for certain volumes. The business of keeping this rubbish pile was farmed out by other employees to this man.

The folders were absent a great deal and others were employed and paid to do their work.

The door-keeper testified, "I do not like to criticize members, but that is the situation. They go and say, 'I have got to have my man home' and he must go home."

The door-keeper was further asked: "Have there been any other cases of absenteeism except among the folders?" To which he replied, "No, except those who naturally go." Of this our committee observed: "It would appear that these two classes, those who naturally go and those who go through the artificial assistance of Congressmen form a pretty large aggregate."

There were dozens who were paid when they were not there at all. One of the employees in the cloakroom was there on and off for only three or four months during a period of three years and he was spared from going to Washington even to receive his salary. The vouchers were sent to him and he filed receipts in the disbursing clerk's office "just as all the other gentlemen who go home do."

The disbursing officer testified: "It is no question for me to find out whether they are there or not."

The office which kept such admirable check upon expenditures itself cost about $14,000 a year.[77]

Though relatively few employees were concerned, the investigation made something of a splash. It illuminated once again the tend-

---

[77] William Dudley Foulke, *Fighting the Spoilsmen* (New York: G. P. Putnam's Sons, 1919), pp. 137–39. For the original report see U.S. Congress, House, *Report of the Special Committee to Investigate the Appointment and Payment of Employees of the House,* 56th Cong., 2d Sess., House Report 2978, February 23, 1901 (Washington: Government Printing Office, 1901).

199

encies of the spoils system when allowed to flourish without control. The Civil Service Commission called attention in its annual report to the conclusion that the "results [were] extremely unsatisfactory" but "likely to continue under the administration of any political party as long as such a system is maintained." [78]

The judicial service. As with the legislative service, the judicial civil service of approximately 3,000 employees [79] was selected through other than merit procedures. Though never subjected to such a study as that made of congressional employees in 1901, the judicial service has only infrequently produced major scandals of the type recorded above. It is true that nine out of the twelve impeachments recorded through our political history have been of judges,[80] but this disproportionate judicial share of such actions has reflected mainly our constitutional restriction against the removal of judges by any other means. Corruption in the federal judiciary, when it has occurred, has usually involved such matters as receiverships, from which staggering sums have sometimes been derived, threats of prosecution or deliberate failures to prosecute, and the like.

The military services. The Spanish-American War clearly showed up many inadequacies in the organization of the Army. A major result was the introduction of the concept of the general staff by Elihu Root with the support of President Roosevelt. From the standpoint of personnel procedures the most important result of the new general staff legislation was to provide for a systematic rotation of military officers between Washington and the field. No longer would it be possible for an individual officer to remain in a staff or command position in Washington for more than, in most cases, four years. This reform was accomplished in part to strengthen civilian control of the military and in part to insure adequate field and command training for the officer corps.

For many years a main route of entrance into the lower ranks of the military officer corps had been through examinations. President Roosevelt attempted at an early date to end the traditional influence of partisan politics in high military appointments. When Senator Jo-

---

[78] *Seventeenth Report*, 1900, p. 24.
[79] USCSC, *Eighteenth Report*, 1901, p. 15. The judicial service numbered 2,880 by 1904. USCSC *Twenty-first Report*, 1904, p. 188.
[80] The other cases have involved a senator, a cabinet member, and President Andrew Johnson. Only four of the twelve were convicted, all of them judges. The others were either acquitted or for various reasons, such as resignation, held to be not subject to any final action via the impeachment process. The essential difficulty in removing federal officers through the impeachment process is that it is cumbersome and time-consuming. Moreover, most actions warranting impeachment can be adequately dealt with through other remedies. This is especially the case with civil officers of the executive branch. Military officers are not subject to impeachment proceedings, but to courts-martial.

seph W. Bailey of Texas wanted a promotion to brigadier general for a political friend, a promotion which Bailey indicated the Legislature of Texas also favored, Roosevelt replied, "It is opposed by all the man's superior officers."

"I don't give a damn for his superior officers," Bailey countered.

"Well, Senator, I don't give a damn for the Legislature of Texas," replied the President." [81]

Roosevelt was generally successful in his effort to keep politics out of the military. However, all permanent officer appointments and the higher temporary officer appointments still are a matter for senatorial confirmation. Except for the highest positions, this is now usually a formality causing little difficulty. Roosevelt also brought about a renewed emphasis on physical fitness for military personnel, and he was able to some extent to reorient military training toward more modern concepts of warfare. He was less successful in making any indentation on the customary military promotion policies, which were based almost entirely upon seniority. Not until during and after World War I were major inroads made on this system.

Growth of the National Service

The contribution of Theodore Roosevelt to the extension of the merit system was (1) so to improve the machinery that the administrative work resulting from further extensions could be handled, and (2) to make many of the extensions which were yet possible but which his predecessors had left undone.

Expansion of the merit system under T. R. Within his first few months of office, Roosevelt restored to the merit system a large portion of those offices removed under McKinley. T. R. and the Civil Service Commission then commenced to include portions of the Post Office Department under the merit system. An opening wedge was driven in the rural free delivery service by an order of November 27, 1901. This "covered in" approximately 9,000 employees.[82] The administration of this extension was made doubly troublesome by the fact that the patrons of any route had to be consulted before an appointment could be made final. Nevertheless this difficulty was overcome and the system was reported to be working satisfactorily by 1905.[83] T. R. concluded his operations on the Post Office Department late in his second term by a final extension, approved beforehand by Taft, involving

81 Bishop, as cited in footnote 29, I, pp. 156–57.
82 USCSC, *Nineteenth Report*, 1902, pp. 9–12.
83 USCSC, *Twenty-second Report*, 1905, pp. 18 and 126–27.

201

fourth-class postmasters north of the Ohio River and east of the Mississippi.

The census force had also long been a center of political spoils, and the Commission had periodically recommended its full classification. The matter came to a head over the creation of a permanent census bureau not long after Roosevelt became President. For the first time since 1883 Congress then itself attempted to prescribe whether or not particular groups of employees would be placed under the merit system. The legislators did not wish to place the *permanent* bureau outside the merit system, but they wished to provide that many of the *temporary* political appointees hired by the head of the bureau for the census of 1900 be transferred to the permanent agency and, hence, automatically into the classified service. Congress was afraid, with good reason, that the President would fire the temporary workers and hire a new staff through the Civil Service Commission. After an amusing session in which all kinds of proposals to forbid the President from influencing the disposition of the temporary employees were considered, Congress gave up the attempt as constitutionally impossible. Roosevelt then, as Congress had feared, did not permit the bulk of the temporary spoils appointees to be transferred into the merit system. Most of them were released after a few were selected to augment the staff of the permanent bureau.[84] The patronage problem again arose with the legislation providing for the census of 1910, when Congress provided that the entire force be selected outside the competitive examination system. This the President vetoed in 1909 shortly before going out of office. Under President Taft a compromise proposal was accepted.

Other important extensions were the full classification of the bulk of the personnel of the Isthmian Canal Commission in 1904, of several miscellaneous types of so-called confidential and fiduciary employees in 1905, and of the hitherto politically important deputy collectors of internal revenue in 1906. Important changes leading to a more careful selection of State Department consular personnel were made by law and by executive order in 1906. The career system in this department may be dated primarily from these actions. The year 1907 was the first year in which Roosevelt made no extensions at all, but neither did he make any withdrawals. At the end of his incumbency approximately 60 per cent of the service was fully under the merit system. If laborers employed under various types of registration systems are included, about 67 per cent of the civil service was operat-

---

[84] For details of this controversy see Foulke, as cited in footnote 42, pp. 59–62; and Foulke, as cited in footnote 16, pp. 80–82.

ing under some form of controlled selection system.[85] The same percentage was under the merit system in 1939, thirty years later, though a high of 80 per cent had been reached in 1927.

The extent of public employment. In 1905 the Civil Service Commission made one of the rare contemporary estimates of total public employment. Including all branches of the government, civil and military, there were an estimated 406,714 "persons in the public service of the United States during the fiscal year ended June 30, 1904" who received compensation from the federal government totalling more than 250 million dollars. These figures included 275,698 executive civil employees. Later evidence indicates that the civil employees at this time probably exceeded 300,000. Therefore the Commission's grand total of government employees must be considered conservative.[86]

Under Theodore Roosevelt, as might be expected, the civil service underwent considerable expansion, increasing in size from perhaps 275,000 in 1901 to 365,000 or so in 1909. Some of this increase is accounted for by the Spanish-American War, but the growth was caused primarily by the expanded activities and functions of the national government during the first decade of the twentieth century.

Roosevelt's Election Campaigns

The effects of patronage manipulation in presidential campaigns have long been recognized though the facts have been difficult to ascertain. Because of Roosevelt's unusually firm stand on the use of offices for political purposes, his actions during two presidential elections aroused an extraordinary amount of speculation and comment.

The election of 1904. By 1902 Roosevelt had captured the Republican party in a most thorough fashion. Any possible threat from his chief rival, Mark Hanna, was ended by the latter's death early in 1904, and the President was unopposed for reelection later that year. There is no question but that in his "practical politics" with Senators Quay, Crane, Lodge, Spooner, Allison and others lay the main support of his by now almost impregnable party position. Firmly in the saddle,

---

[85] The annual proceedings of the National Civil Service Reform League give the best summaries of the yearly activities of the President along miscellaneous lines not always covered by the annual reports of the Commission itself.

[86] For the Commission's contemporary report on public employment see its *Twenty-first Report,* 1904, p. 188. However, the *Thirty-ninth Report,* 1922, p. vii, shows the "approximate number of employees in civil service classified and unclassified" for 1903 as 301,000. This figure represents a revision by the Commission of its earlier figure for 1903. The figure of 301,000 is apparently accepted by the Bureau of the Census. *Historical Statistics,* p. 294. For the period before World War I, as for the earlier decades, federal employment statistics are at best approximate and can be safely used only to show a general trend. Total salary data also are only approximate and are probably more conservative than the total employment figures.

he could afford to break precedent with respect to the Republican National Convention of 1904. The *New York Evening Post* of February 6, 1904, quoted the President as saying:

. . . No person in the classified service will be permitted to take part in the convention . . . no non-classified civil servant, even, shall take part in the convention, where anyone else can be sent who will be equally loyal and intelligent.

Though substantially carried out, this renunciation meant little with respect to the course of political power. There was no other candidate in the field.

Of course, during the campaign proper the Republican organization made use of all the unclassified employees it could press into service, and Congressman Charles W. F. Dick of Ohio and some others gained considerable notoriety in connection with political assessments.[87] On the Democratic side William Jennings Bryan again put forth the curious old Populist suggestion that postmasters ought to be elected to prevent their partisan activity.[88] But Judge Alton B. Parker, the Democratic candidate, did not support such views, and the election of 1904 was relatively uneventful in terms of the public service. Civil service reform was itself not an issue, for Roosevelt could not be attacked on that score. Even the Democratic platform once again cautiously embraced the merit system.

Turning over the reins in 1908. In the election of 1908 Roosevelt received far more criticism, but this time for his activities on behalf of Taft. The question was whether—and, if so, how—Roosevelt manipulated the patronage to secure Taft's nomination. A great deal of research has been done on this question and there is only one possible conclusion. Of course Roosevelt used the patronage.[89] In accounting for his actions he ingeniously explained, "I have appointed no man *for the purpose* of creating Taft sentiment, but . . . I have appointed men *in recognition* of the Taft sentiment already in existence." [90] But at the same time he wrote to Taft and volunteered to "cut off their [certain federal officials'] necks with the utmost cheerfulness if you say the word!" [91] Curiously, the National Civil Service Reform League

87 Fowler, as cited in footnote 37, p. 285.
88 As quoted in "The Federal Service," *Good Government*, XXI (September, 1904), 131–32.
89 For example, see Fowler, as cited in footnote 37, pp. 290–97, for the most thorough analysis.
90 Henry F. Pringle, *Theodore Roosevelt* (New York: Harcourt, Brace and Co., 1931), p. 497. Evidently the italics are Roosevelt's.
91 Roosevelt to Taft, January 6, 1908. Henry F. Pringle, *The Life and Times of William Howard Taft* (2 vols.; New York: Farrar and Rinehart, Inc., 1939), I, 322.

found little evidence of machination in its investigation of the situation. But it did not have access to all the data, and Roosevelt had given out "the word." That was sufficient for the Republican party of 1908.

The fall campaign was full of charges and countercharges over the method of Taft's nomination. Little, however, could then be proved, and Taft's own popularity took the edge off the argument. Bryan, once more the Democratic candidate, at one point took the novel but probably realistic point of view that he "would rather risk the influence which a President can bring to bear upon civil-service employees than to risk the influence which railroad owners can bring to bear upon railroad employees." [92] On another occasion he was quoted as advocating a Jeffersonian division of the offices between the two parties.[93] The reform group, as in 1904, was generally behind the Republican candidate, a confirmed advocate of the merit system, rather than Bryan, whose spoils views were equally well-known. However, civil service reform remained far in the background as an issue, and the overwhelming election of William Howard Taft turned on other considerations.

Nevertheless, with the elevation of Taft to the Presidency, the future of the federal service seemed likely to be tranquil. If anything, the prospects were positively brilliant compared to what they had been during and after the election of 1896.

T. R. and the Public Service

In any summary of Roosevelt's contributions to the various phases of the development of the merit system the importance of the administrative and technical reforms made during the years 1901 to 1909 must be emphasized. The ability of the Civil Service Commission to survive during the First World War can be traced directly to the refinement of the civil service system during the first decade of the century, for few other significant improvements were made from 1909 to 1917. Under Roosevelt's administration the merit system was pushed almost to the limits of the Pendleton Act, and technical progress was such that it kept pace with the extension. That more was not done on the fundamental matters of pay and position-classification was probably because neither the public nor Congress fully understood or appreciated the underlying problems involved.

But Roosevelt was much more than a mere technician in his impact

[92] As quoted in USCSC, *Twenty-fourth Report*, 1907, p. 10.
[93] *New York Times*, October 16, 1908.

on the federal service. By his energetic enforcement of the law in general Roosevelt, like Cleveland, left a legacy of openness and honesty from which the service undoubtedly benefited. Whether or not he always *was* open is a questionable matter, but he usually gave that impression. Roosevelt's journalist friend, Lawrence F. Abbott of the *Outlook,* commented:

. . . At the close of his administration the public began to feel as it ought always to feel, that the badge of public office is a badge of respect; it began to regard Federal officials as well as Federal clerks as it regards the officers and enlisted men in the Army and the Navy. Certainly this was what Mr. Roosevelt wanted to accomplish.[94]

Civil service reform was a field in which Roosevelt's concept of "applied idealism" could be given full rein and he took full advantage of the opportunity. By the time he left office the merit system was firmly enough established that his former Civil Service Commissioner, William D. Foulke, could write in 1925:

The career of Theodore Roosevelt has been so picturesque and inspiring in other fields that what he did for the reform of the Civil Service has been largely overlooked and yet nowhere else was his official work more permanently useful to his country.[95]

Foulke is correct. As the years have passed, one of the most real and lasting influences of Theodore Roosevelt has lain in his emphasis on the necessity for honesty and efficiency in public administration.

Even in T. R.'s own day there was a unity in action and a cooperativeness in effort among those who worked with him that have not often occurred in the history of the American public service. Whether this can be attributed entirely to the influence of the President is an arguable question, but of the administration of Theodore Roosevelt no less an authority than Lord Bryce has remarked that he had

. . . never in any country seen a more eager, high-minded and efficient set of public servants, men more useful and creditable to their country, than the men doing the work of the American Government in Washington and in the field.[96]

---

[94] Lawrence F. Abbott, *Impressions of Theodore Roosevelt* (New York: Doubleday, Page and Co., 1923), p. 118.

[95] Foulke, as cited in footnote 42, p. 5.

[96] As quoted in William D. Lewis, *The Life of Theodore Roosevelt* (New York: The United Publishers, 1919), p. 258. See also Lewis' discussion of the public service, pp. 249–58, leading to this quotation of Lord Bryce. Lord Charnwood also refers to this opinion by Bryce. *Theodore Roosevelt* (London: Constable and Co., Ltd., 1923), pp. 114–15.

That the President was introducing new blood into politics and the public service in the form of young men such as James Garfield, Gifford Pinchot, and Felix Frankfurter has been noted by both William Allen White and Henry L. Stimson, who were themselves among those young men.[97] With his energy, dash, and liberal pose, Roosevelt could not have helped but impart a sense of manifest destiny to those sitting behind even the most dismal desks in Washington. Morale is a difficult thing to assay and objective evidence is scanty, but Bryce was surely correct in his estimate of the American public service in the early days of the twentieth century.

SUPPLEMENTARY NOTES

Refinements in the concept of the "classified service." Soon after 1883 it became the custom to divide the classified service into "competitive," "noncompetitive," and "excepted" categories. Positions were exempted from competitive examinations for a variety of reasons: inapplicability of examinations, temporary nature of positions, need for merely minimal standards, political pressure, etc. It was also occasionally useful from a political point of view to gain credit for placing offices within the classified service, without in fact changing their status very much. By 1903, for example, there were nearly 80,000 offices, about 70,000 of them in the Post Office Department, which were technically in the classified service, but which were in the noncompetitive or excepted categories. USCSC, *Twenty-first Report,* 1903, p. 170. Until 1910 the noncompetitive and excepted positions were lumped together and regularly listed in the annual reports of the Civil Service Commission under *Schedule A.* That year the noncompetitive positions (subject only to noncompetitive examination) were broken off into a *Schedule B.* This categorizing mechanism lasted until 1953, when *Schedule A* was again divided, with most policy-making posts listed in a new *Schedule C.*

Schedule A, listing positions exempt from examinations, was in 1900, and continued to be, the most important of these schedules in terms of the number of offices involved. "Classification" of these positions merely signified their inclusion under the political removal protection of the Pendleton Act and various executive orders, often frail shields at best. T. R. and Taft brought many but by no means all of the offices previously under *Schedule A* under full merit system procedures. Therefore, from this point on, the writer has used the term "classified service" more cautiously, turning more and more to the phrases "under the merit system," "competitive service," and "permanent service" to signify positions where competitive examinations and full merit system procedures were applicable. The technical distinctions outlined above have always made it difficult to portray the extent of the Civil Service Commission's jurisdiction and to delineate precisely the boundaries between the spoils system and the merit system. All statistics with respect to either are of necessity approximate.

[97] White, as cited in footnote 2, p. 306; and Henry L. Stimson and McGeorge Bundy, *On Active Service* (New York: Harper and Bros., 1947), pp. 3–7.

The judicial service. For information concerning the appointment and tenure of judicial officers and employees, especially judges, who represent a segment of the federal civil service only touched upon in this study, see Carl McFarland and Homer Cummings, *Federal Justice* (New York: The Macmillan Co., 1937); Evan Haynes, *The Selection and Tenure of Judges* (Newark, N.J.: National Conference of Judicial Councils, 1944); Arthur T. Vanderbilt (ed.), *Minimum Standards of Judicial Administration* (New York: National Conference of Judicial Councils, 1949), ch. i; James Willard Hurst, *The Growth of American Law: The Law Makers* (Boston: Little, Brown and Co., 1950), ch. vii; and Joseph P. Harris, *The Advice and Consent of the Senate* (Berkeley and Los Angeles: University of California Press, 1953), ch. xvii.

CHAPTER 9

Economy and Efficiency: 1909–1913

Though reluctantly and without enthusiasm, William Howard Taft was for four years to find himself almost as fully dedicated to the "strenuous life" as his predecessor in the White House. President Taft's honesty, integrity, and intelligence have never been questioned, but his political inadequacies, in comparison to T. R., were as staggering as some of the problems with which he was compelled to deal.

A moral political man in the Cleveland sense, Taft found it equally difficult to decide what the government should be good for. Unable to find or devise a legislative program on which he himself could wholeheartedly embark, he left his party distraught and divided. Even when he succeeded in discovering a single issue, such as Canadian tariff reciprocity, for which he was prepared to do battle, he found it difficult to organize the necessary legislative support. He continually found himself, therefore, at a political dead end.

If Taft was uncertain in his politics, he was on firmer ground with respect to the merit system. Here he had both experience and conviction, from which the federal service was to derive considerable benefit. Nevertheless, effective personnel management is no substitute for firm policy guidance. Under a series of shocks the unity of politics and administration which had characterized the executive branch under Theodore Roosevelt was to evaporate quickly under President Taft.

Political Trends and the Offices

Top-level appointments. The first of these shocks stemmed from Taft's cabinet selections. Evidently Taft had given some sort of promise to retain certain of Roosevelt's appointees. Nevertheless, he soon made

209

an almost complete change of department heads, resulting in his well-known "Lawyer's Cabinet." These executives were not particularly antagonistic to the merit system, but they represented a turn away from the moderate Progressivism which had done so much to give the federal service a new sense of mission under Theodore Roosevelt. Almost immediately, for example, Gifford Pinchot, Chief Forester in the Department of the Interior, found himself at odds with his new chief, Richard A. Ballinger, whom Pinchot accused of giving away public lands and mineral resources in violation of Roosevelt's conservation policy. After some vacillation, Taft removed Pinchot, who quickly appealed to Roosevelt's friends in opposition to Taft. The President, who was by no means against conservation, found himself caught in the middle. To placate an aroused public opinion he finally permitted Ballinger to resign in 1911.

Taft, who was a good deal more reserved than Roosevelt, also sent into eclipse most of the coterie of personal friends who had surrounded T. R. and become known as the "Tennis Cabinet." All in all, Taft's preliminary appointment policies seemed to suggest a certain amount of suspicion on the part of the President of those who had been close to his predecessor. Matthew Josephson has suggested that it was this new and not altogether happy relationship between Taft and his top-level appointees on the one hand and the rest of the service on the other which effectively ended the *esprit de corps* of the Roosevelt administration.[1] Certainly, there occurred noticeably fewer indications of spontaneous departmental cooperation with the Civil Service Commission in the Commission's annual reports for 1909 to 1913, compared with the number of friendly sentiments, expressed almost yearly, under Theodore Roosevelt. However, Josephson's explanation is too simple, and one must look as much to Taft's relationships with his party and with Congress as to his top-level appointments in any analysis of the morale of the federal service at this time.

Insurgency. President Taft's difficulties with his party began with his decision to support a downward revision of the tariff. This was a move which the Progressive, or "Insurgent," wing of the Republican party applauded. However, the Old Guard did not; and when the Payne-Aldrich bill reached the Senate it was quickly turned into a mockery of the original presidential intentions. At this point, Vice-President James S. Sherman, an experienced ex-senator from New York, advised the President "to begin to hit. I would send for Hitchcock [Postmaster General] and shut off the appointments of postmasters until the

1 *The President Makers* (New York: Harcourt, Brace and Co., 1940), p. 288.

bill is passed." [2] Though dissatisfied with developments, Taft did not follow this advice and remained aloof.[3] In effect, he allied himself with the Old Guard, and when he described the Payne-Aldrich bill as "the best tariff bill the Republican party ever passed," the indignation of the Progressives knew almost no bounds. It now appeared that with respect to both appointments and policy-making the President had gone to the Right.

Taft's inability to control his party became even more apparent with the fight over "Cannonism." During this struggle to break the almost dictatorial power of the Speaker of the House,[4] Taft first used the patronage as a political club. As nearly as a date can be established, this was in late January or early February of 1910, less than a year after Taft had assumed office.[5] Just a few weeks earlier the President had replied to a letter from Representative George W. Norris of Nebraska, asking Taft's intentions concerning the use of the patronage, by saying:

If I conclude to withhold the patronage from any person . . . it will not be for the purpose of compelling him to vote for the legislation . . . but it will be for the purpose of preventing his use of the patronage in the district which he represents to create opposition to the Republican administration and its policies, with the probable result of sending a Democrat back to Congress.[6]

This answer was obviously specious. Within a very short time the withholding of patronage from the Insurgents fighting Cannon became a reality. From early 1910 until the fall of the same year the distribution of offices was handled through special representatives of the party known as "referees" or through congressional or other members of the conservative wing of the party. After the Insurgents for the most part survived and even consolidated their positions in the primaries of the summer, Taft made overtures for peace by declaring that the distribution of the patronage was now back on its normal basis.[7] But the quarrel was not over and groundwork for the Republican split of 1912 was laid. By the time of the opening of Congress in

[2] Archie Butt, *Taft and Roosevelt: The Intimate Letters of Archie Butt* (2 vols.; New York: Doubleday, Doran and Co., 1930), I, 41.

[3] Henry F. Pringle, *The Life and Times of William Howard Taft* (2 vols.; New York: Farrar and Rinehart, Inc., 1939), I, 428.

[4] For the fullest account of this story, as well as of the Insurgent movement as a whole, see Kenneth W. Hechler, *Insurgency* (New York: Columbia University Press, 1940).

[5] Pringle, as cited in footnote 3, II, 613.

[6] Taft to Norris, January 11, 1910, same.

[7] George Mowry, *Theodore Roosevelt and the Progressive Movement* (Madison: University of Wisconsin Press, 1946), pp. 152–53.

December, 1910, there was even talk of the Insurgents opposing Taft's renomination.

The patronage may be used to bridge gaps in the constitutional framework, but it is only effective if it is astutely managed and if the breach is not too wide. Moreover, the Insurgents as a group were unusually difficult to coerce, for they were secure in their own political power in their own local areas. William Allen White wrote to Taft in 1910, "When you discipline [through patronage] a man like Bristow [Joseph L., Senator from Kansas] who has the people behind him, you are merely disciplining the people." [8] As Franklin D. Roosevelt was also to learn to his discomfort, presidential purges must be subtle to be effective.

Why Taft at first refused to use the patronage to force the conservatives to accept his tariff legislation but reconsidered and used it against the Insurgents has been discussed by Henry F. Pringle, his biographer, who concludes that the President hesitated to use the patronage because of his views of the Presidency as an office of limited powers.[9] George Mowry, in his later study of the Progressive movement, criticizes this point of view and suggests that the most likely answer lay in Taft's own inherent conservatism. As Mowry correctly notes, "He never used the patronage against a conservative." [10]

The final break. The impact of the patronage on the Republican party split of 1912 also traces back to a decision by Taft which at first had little connection with his decision to fight Theodore Roosevelt for the nomination. Typically, however, this decision involved a partial reversal of Roosevelt's appointment policies. Early in his administration, Taft adopted the policy of refusing to appoint Negroes to offices in the South. Instead, he struggled to build up a "lily-white" Republican organization. He was no more successful in reaching his goal than Roosevelt. However, as a by-product of this effort, he, again like Roosevelt, gained control of the southern Republican delegations to the nominating convention.[11]

The story of Taft's break with Theodore Roosevelt is well known and no one has questioned the view that Taft's renomination stemmed in large part from a deliberate manipulation of the southern delegations to the Republican national convention, which were largely composed of federal office-holders. Perhaps Taft had as little directly

---

8 Letter of February 3, 1910. Walter Johnson (ed.), *Selected Letters of William Allen White, 1899–1943* (New York: Henry Holt and Co., 1947), p. 106.

9 As cited in footnote 3, I, 425.

10 As cited in footnote 7, p. 55.

11 For aspects of the story, see Pringle, as cited in footnote 3, I, 390; and Butt, as cited in footnote 2, II, 511.

to do with it all as Pringle concludes.[12] Nevertheless manipulation occurred, and he knowingly benefited thereby. It is ironic that the same process which Roosevelt had manipulated to secure Taft's nomination in 1908 was used so successfully by Taft against T. R. in 1912.

The influence in Republican nominating conventions of southern delegations consisting largely of federal office-holders has long been a source of factional quarrels and considerable scandal. In some southern areas almost the sole reason for the existence of a Republican party organization has lain in the control of the federal patronage, and in turn the control of delegations to the national convention. During most of the twenties, for example, southern federal patronage was worth a good many millions of dollars and was on occasions the cause of bitter political recrimination. After the disaster of 1912, the Republican party gradually reduced the proportion of southern delegates to its national conventions. By 1932 the southern delegations were still important, though their proportionate strength was little more than half that of 1912.[13]

Developments in Personnel Management

At the very time that Taft was unsuccessfully manipulating the patronage against the Insurgents, he also pleaded strongly for the extension of the merit system. This made the presidential position even more ambiguous. Pringle has concluded that the President's desire for economy and efficiency combined with his unfortunate experiences with the patronage were the important reasons behind his pro-civil service reform views.[14] However, this analysis does not do Taft full justice, for he had supported civil service reform in the Philippines long before he became President. In fact, he never opposed the merit system. More than this, he frequently supported and strengthened it.

The higher offices. Throughout Taft's administration, and particularly after his quarrel with the Insurgents, he advocated the extension of the classified service to include the higher offices, most of which were subject to senatorial confirmation and beyond presidential jurisdiction as defined in the Pendleton Act. Congress took no action, however, as presidential-congressional relations continued to deterio-

12 As cited in footnote 3, II, 611.

13 For a still useful summary of the problem, see Richard Boeckel, *Patronage Influence in Nominating Conventions* (Washington: Editorial Research Reports [1927]).

14 See Pringle, as cited in footnote 3, I, 425; and Butt, as cited in footnote 2, II, 522–25, for the details of what is known as the Norton (referring to Taft's personal secretary) letter of September 15, 1910, involving the use of the patronage against the Insurgents. Taft later said to Butt "that Norton's letter on patronage was the most serious mistake which had been made during the Administration."

rate. In light of present-day recommendations to the same end, it is interesting to note that Taft's Attorney General recommended in 1912 that all attorneys and assistant-attorneys be placed under the merit system. Having tried a nonassembled test for the selection of lawyers for his agencies, he was satisfied that this procedure could and should be followed. The other cabinet members did not all agree, however, and the Civil Service Commission did not recommend action to Taft.[15]

Holding the line. When there was danger that a census bill would in effect merely divide the spoils of the census bureau between the two parties, Taft, even before he assumed office, threatened to veto it. The result was a law requiring the selection of a large proportion of the census employees by a mild variation of the merit system. Not long afterward Taft endeavored to improve the consular regulations issued earlier by Roosevelt and applied them to as much of the diplomatic service as possible. In 1912 the positions of a large number of skilled workmen in the navy yards, who had already been placed under special employment regulations by Roosevelt, were formally placed within the classified service and under political removal protection.[16] Taft's principal attempt to extend the classified service came with the inclusion, late in 1912, of the remainder of the fourth-class postmasters within the merit framework. This order affected about 35,000 persons, most of whom received less than $1,000 a year. Unfortunately, the new Democratic administration of 1913 was largely able to circumvent the intent of Taft's classification through a series of procedural manipulations. Only briefly during Wilson's second term, and then not again until the middle thirties, were these offices to find themselves under reasonably firm merit system protection.

The President's most decisive act, from the standpoint of preserving the service from the inroads of partisan politics, was his veto of the legislative, executive, and judicial appropriation bill of August, 1912, because it provided for a seven year tenure of office for all classified employees. Congress was allegedly attempting to solve the growing superannuation problem by any means other than a costly pension plan.

By 1911 the Civil Service Commission reported an estimated total number of federal employees, civil and military, of 513,854. This was an increase of over 25 per cent since 1904. Much of this increase had taken place in the civil branches of the government during the Roose-

---

[15] See USCSC, *Twenty-ninth Report*, 1912, pp. 201–202; and *Thirtieth Report*, 1913, p. 10.

[16] This action was based in part on the rider of 1871 and in part on an opinion by Roosevelt's Attorney General to the effect that the Pendleton Act excluded only "mere" laborers.

velt administration. Of this total, approximately 385,000 were in the executive civil service, with about 70 per cent of these under some version of the merit system. The military service, officers and enlisted men, totalled over 120,000. The legislative civil service approximated 2,600, while the judicial service neared 4,500.[17]

Refining the selection system. The most important innovations made by the Civil Service Commission itself were in the field of examinations. By 1910 the newly decentralized district system was so perfected that it was possible to give local examinations in almost any required specialty. A revised register system with an ultimate audit by the Commission in Washington further facilitated the problem of appointments in the field services. Also in 1910, *Schedule A,* listing classified positions excepted from competitive examination, was divided into *Schedule A* and *Schedule B.* This formalized a distinction developed several years earlier between classified jobs for which no examination was necessary and those for which a non-competitive examination only was required. The Commission regretted, however, that the officials of different departments could not yet agree on the qualifications necessary for positions even as uncomplicated as that of elevator operator. Such disagreements seriously affected the Commission's examining program.[18]

The Commission felt that its examinations were more practical than ever, but it inclined to the belief that for an increasing number of positions it would be advisable to test more for general intelligence than for specific miscellaneous knowledge. For a good many years the Commission had been developing what it considered to be tests of general ability for clerical employees. In 1910 it concluded:

. . . These tests of the general intelligence of applicants for clerical and minor clerical positions are increasingly favored by Government officials on the ground that they find it easier to train in clerical duties a new appointee who has attained eligibility in such tests than one whose eligibility is secured as the result of a high mark in some examination which would require special knowledge rather than general intelligence.

At the same time the Commission indicated that it had been experimenting with oral tests. It concluded that such tests "will be found a beneficial addition to the examination," and "especially for positions in which personality is an important factor." These views are most

---

[17] *Twenty-seventh Report,* 1910, pp. 154–55. This estimate also contains a breakdown of employees in the judicial service, the only such listing the author has discovered for any year before the First World War.

[18] For details of these developments, see same, pp. 19 and 41–42. See also the supplementary notes to ch. viii, above.

illuminating in that they again indicate the precocious concern of the Commission with modern testing concepts.[19]

By 1911 the Commission reported that it had now fully developed the nonassembled examination technique for the more important scientific and technical positions, many applicants having objected to the use of ordinary written examinations. At the same time the Commission was studying the problem of the kind of scientific and professional knowledge for which it ought to test—specific factual knowledge or general scientific background. In 1911 it concluded, as it had with the clerks, that it favored the test of general background and ability wherever possible.[20]

In 1913 the Chief Examiner reported that as a result of additional appropriations he was able more thoroughly to inquire into personal fitness for many of the higher positions, and that examination techniques generally were improving. However, he felt that the examination announcement system of the Commission was inadequate for the higher offices.[21]

Removal procedures. Under Taft the question of the proper method of removals under the merit system came to a head. President McKinley had been the first chief executive to limit in any way the removal power of his appointing officers, by requiring that reasons be given for removals and that the employees be allowed a chance to reply. No trial or pseudo-court procedure was demanded. Roosevelt had returned to almost the original system of unlimited discretion in removals. In the winter of 1911–12 Taft finally reinstated the McKinley rule, but not until Congress threatened legislation.[22]

Unions. At the same time, Taft ran into the first serious problems which any president experienced with unions of public employees. The unions objected to the so-called "Gag Orders" of Theodore Roosevelt, which Taft had reaffirmed,[23] and which were designed to prevent government employees from pressing personal and political claims on Congress except through the heads of departments. These rules, combined with the anti-political activity provisions of the Pendleton Act, effectively barred union activities in legislative matters. The anti-union actions of Post Office Department officials and other heads of executive agencies did little to improve an already explosive situation. Moreover, government employees wanted legislation clearly

19 For the quotations above and a general summary of the Commission's attitude toward examinations in 1910, see same, pp. 46–47.

20 Twenty-eighth Report, 1911, pp. 31 and 36–38.

21 Thirtieth Report, 1913, pp. 25–31.

22 Executive Orders of July 27, 1897, May 29, 1902, October 17, 1905, December 9, 1911, and February 8, 1912.

23 Executive Orders of January 31, 1902, January 25, 1906, and November 26, 1909.

specifying their right to affiliate with recognized unions of organized labor.

Finally, in late 1909, the American Federation of Labor actively entered the political arena on behalf of the rights of federal employees. Senator Robert M. LaFollette of Wisconsin introduced a series of Anti-Gag measures. At first, Taft publicly expressed his opposition. But, when it became apparent that Congress favored the legislation, Taft modified the Gag Orders, hoping to forestall congressional action.[24] The final outcome, however, was the important Lloyd-LaFollette Act of August 24, 1912.[25] This basic legislation not only permitted employees to petition Congress and recognized their right to affiliate with national labor unions, but also included the protection of the original McKinley executive order concerning removals.[26] Altogether the legislation gave a considerable impetus to the movement for public employee unionization. It is still the basic authority for much of their present organization and activity.

The growing power of labor unions in general was brought to bear upon the government in still another way at this time. Largely at their request Congress held extended hearings during the last part of Taft's administration on the practices associated with the Taylor school of "scientific management." Fearing the "speed-up," many labor leaders testified against the use of stop-watch management techniques, and especially those just being introduced into government arsenals. Congress acquiesced and in 1914 commenced a legislative ban on time studies in the military agencies of the government, which was not substantially lifted for nearly forty years. While such techniques have seldom been forbidden in other than the Departments of the Army and Navy, these indications of legislative disapproval made public administrative officials reluctant for many years to accept and apply to the public service many of the managerial refinements often associated with Taylorism. Only during the Korean conflict were most of these restrictions finally lifted, thus permitting the development of engineered standards as part of the present extensive work measurement program of the federal government.[27]

24 Executive Order of April 8, 1912.

25 37 U.S. Statutes 555. For details of the struggle see Sterling Spero, *Government As Employer* (New York: Remsen Press, 1948), pp. 151–80.

26 Such congressional limits on the removal powers of the lesser appointing officers are probably constitutional. Whether they are proof against the presidential removal power is doubtful. Nevertheless, except as modified by certain statutes authorizing summary removal in security cases, the provisions of the Lloyd-LaFollette Act have been and still are generally accepted in practice. See Edward S. Corwin's discussion of the removal power in *The President: Office and Powers* (3d rev. ed.; New York: New York University Press, 1948), ch. iii.

27 See U.S. Bureau of the Budget, *Legislative Restrictions on Time Studies in the Federal Government* (Washington: The Bureau, 1945), with *Addendum* (1948); and Spero,

Enforcement of the merit system. In most matters Taft was a firm friend of the merit system. But in some aspects of enforcement of the rules, he was lax. It was this laxity which William D. Foulke had in mind when he once wrote that "in Mr. Taft's administration of the civil service law there appeared just a little of the same quality which led to disaster in regard to other public questions." [28]

Shortly after his inaugural the President requested the resignation of Commissioner Henry F. Greene, originally appointed by Roosevelt. Greene possessed a reputation for honesty and efficiency in his activities on behalf of the Commission, but as a result he had made political enemies. Apparently Taft was willing to sacrifice Greene to the exigencies of politics, and in his place he designated James T. Williams, Jr., a young newspaperman with little experience in personnel management, who remained with the Commission only twenty days. Williams' successor, William S. Washburn was highly regarded, but the whole transaction did not strengthen the Commission.

The principal criticism, however, was directed against Taft's evident unwillingness to hold his principal appointing officers to as strict account as had been the custom of Theodore Roosevelt. Thus, in 1911, the Commission complained about the increase from 15,445 to 18,557 temporary appointments during the preceding year, despite fewer total appointments and little natural increase in the service.[29] In the enforcement of the political activity and political assessment rules, the Commission gave most of the departments credit for "willing cooperation," but added:

. . . But in some cases there has been long and, in the commission's view, unnecessary delay in taking action. Allowing a year or two to pass before action is taken upon a distinct offense is manifestly inimical to good administration. . . .[30]

In one prominent case the President himself procrastinated for nearly three years in moving against a recognized offender whose activities clearly warranted suspension at least, and then permitted the man to

---

as cited in footnote 25, ch. xix, "The Stop Watch and Mechanization." The unions were able to delay the introduction of new machinery to some extent in establishments such as the Bureau of Engraving and Printing. It is also interesting to note that since 1898 Congress has forbidden the use of time-clocks in the departmental agencies in Washington. What the long run meaning of engineered standards will be is not yet clear, though they may encourage types of incentive pay systems which are most difficult to apply without such standards and which the government has not in the past been able to utilize.

28 William D. Foulke, *Fighting the Spoilsmen* (New York: G. P. Putnam's Sons, 1919), p. 214.

29 *Twenty-eighth Report*, 1911, pp. 14–16.

30 Same, p. 19.

remain in office with the mildest of reprimands.[31] The National Civil Service Reform League frequently complained during this period of Taft's reluctance to proceed against merit system violations with the same energy and directness which had characterized the efforts of Theodore Roosevelt to maintain standards.[32]

On the other hand, there were few scandals of major importance in the federal service during this period. Certainly the merit system received reasonable support in comparison to that provided by any president up to this time except Theodore Roosevelt. But, by contrast with T. R., the efforts of Taft were perceptibly less forthright and prompt.

The Commission on Economy and Efficiency

Taft deserves much of the credit, however, for initiating the first full-scale and systematic inquiry into the administrative mechanism of the federal government. This was conducted during his administration by the well-known Commission on Economy and Efficiency, whose recommendations were eventually, if not at this time, to have considerable impact upon both public administration in general and personnel management in particular.

Background. By the end of the first decade of the twentieth century the nation-wide movement for administrative reform was reaching its initial crest. The cumulative effects of rapid increases in taxation and governmental expenditure, the example of managerial reform in private industry, and the desire to improve the effectiveness of the national administrative system for its new and increasing functions all conspired to interest both Congress and the President in the wearying task of inquiring into the details of public management.

Civil service reform easily fitted into the broader outlines of general administrative reform. For the latter was clearly impossible except as the governmental personnel system brought into the public service individuals capable of applying the newer managerial techniques to public affairs. The business value of the merit system was now quite apparent, even to conservatives. The older group of civil service reformers and the National Civil Service Reform League still emphasized the moral, rather than the efficiency, benefits of the reform; hence their influence in this period of economy and efficiency was far less great than it had been in the eighties and nineties. The Reform

---

[31] For details of the "Neal Case" involving assessments, see Foulke, as cited in footnote 28, pp. 215–18.

[32] For example, see "Political Activity of Rochester Federal Officeholders," *Good Government*, XXVII (November, 1910), 81.

League first clearly recognized the rising importance of the efficiency side of its argument around 1909, but not until the beginning of the First World War did it decisively change the emphasis of its propaganda.[33]

Nevertheless, by 1910 more than just a few specialists were beginning to realize that there were fundamental personnel matters with respect to which the Pendleton Act was sadly deficient. Under Theodore Roosevelt the Keep Committee had already pointed out some of the existing difficulties. Nearly all of them stemmed from the lack of a comprehensive position-classification and pay plan. Superannuation was a secondary question which was being agitated by the employees themselves, and which depended in part for solution upon the answer to the first problem. Some of the hesitancy of Congress to tackle the problem lay in the fact that it had no well-devised position-classification and pay plan before it. More of its reluctance may be traced to a belief that public employees were paid too much anyway. Efficiency tangled with economy in the discussion of position-classification and pay. Yet there was only one way for government wages to move. That was *up*. Amazing as it may seem, there had been no general adjustment of federal wages since the eighteen fifties. According to the Civil Service Commission, the typical government clerk in six departments in Washington was receiving in 1903—and there was no basic change before World War I—on the average $2.70 *less* a year than he received in 1853.[34]

In 1908 the reform government of the city of Chicago announced that it was beginning to attack the problem of position-classification realistically. A modern plan based on the systematic study and comparison of the duties of actual positions was put into effect during the next few years and became the subject of widespread comment.[35] Much of the impetus for a similar plan in the federal government came from the successful experience of Chicago. This is one of the few cases in which local public personnel reform activities have preceded and directly influenced the federal government.

President Taft, himself a man of considerable administrative expe-

[33] Frank M. Stewart, *The National Civil Service Reform League* (Austin: The University of Texas Press, 1929), pp. 185–89.

[34] USCSC, *Twenty-second Report*, 1905, pp. 148–49. The rates for subclerical positions dated to 1866 and 1870.

[35] For the early history of the Chicago movement by one who was instrumental in the development of the new position-classification system, see Edwin O. Griffenhagen, "The Origin of the Modern Occupational Classification of Positions in Personnel Administration," *Public Personnel Studies*, II (September, 1924), 184. This was also a period in which interest in the merit system was rapidly growing in many cities. Between 1905 and 1915 the number of municipalities with merit systems tripled from 105 to 315. Civil Service Assembly, *Civil Service Agencies in the United States: A 1940 Census* (Chicago: Civil Service Assembly, 1940), p. 22.

rience and deeply concerned with problems of organization and methods, made his special contribution to the administrative reform movement in his successful effort to obtain congressional support for a Commission on Economy and Efficiency. Directed to undertake a thorough investigation of the administrative and business practices of the national government, the Commission entered relatively uncharted territory. No full study of this kind had ever been made before. Congress appropriated $100,000 in 1910 and the Commission went to work early in 1911.

ASHINGTON: SUNDAY, SEPTEMBER 8, 1912.

CLERKS' PLEA FOR PENSIONS DOESN'T APPEAL TO HIM

"Western Man" Writes The Post That Federal Employes Are Better Paid Than Any in Private Business—Lives Easy Compared to Agriculturists—Cites Cases of Men He Knows to Illustrate His Argument—But There's Another Side.

He must start milking cows at 4 a. m., while United States clerks, "silk clad," report at 9 and have a "cinch."

From somewhere out of the great West there came into the National capital a visitor who spent a few weeks among ...

From *Washington Post,* September 8, 1912.

Recommendations. The essential contribution of the Commission's report was to point out with innumerable illustrations the lack of uniformity and business method in the operation of the agencies of the executive branch of the government. In the personnel realm the Commission investigated with considerable thoroughness such matters as hours of labor, annual and sick leave, superannuation of civil service employees, the system of efficiency records kept in one branch of the

221

Treasury, electric lighting in federal buildings, as well as the problem of equal pay for equal work.[36]

Early in 1913 the Commission recommended:

The amendment of the civil-service law so as to broaden its functions and give to the Executive a bureau of personnel which will not only have charge of the examination of applicants and the certification of their qualifications for appointment, but also will be responsible for developing individual efficiency records throughout the service; for submitting recommendations with respect to the classification of positions according to work done, and the establishment of salary grades within each classification; for promulgating general rules governing discipline; for making inspections to determine the welfare conditions under which employees are required to work; for arbitrating disputes between officials and subordinates, in so far as in the opinion of the executive these may involve questions affecting the service as a whole; for giving attention to and representing the interests of individuals in the service as distinct from questions of economy of management and the interest of the manager.[37]

This was revolutionary doctrine for the federal service. The idea of a central personnel agency of a positive character was thereafter never to be forgotten, though the bulk of the necessary enabling legislation was not forthcoming for many years. Some of it is still not fully outlined in the statute books.

Reactions. The only congressional reaction to the personnel work of the Commission cannot be traced to its final reports. But the creation in 1912 of a Division of Efficiency within the Civil Service Commission was a reflection of the public concern with economy and efficiency, a concern generated in part by the publicity attending the efforts of the Commission. In some respects an early predecessor of the General Accounting Office, the Division was designed essentially as an investigative arm of Congress and placed under the Civil Service Commission more for housekeeping than any other purpose. Very quickly the two agencies, one representing the legislative and the other the executive branch, found themselves at odds with each other. Shortly thereafter, the Division of Efficiency became the Bureau of Efficiency, which was to exist as a separate agency for nearly two more decades. The creation of this bureau was indicative of a legislative desire to concern itself with the more abstruse administrative workings of the federal

---

36 For a complete list of the Commission's publications see Gustavus A. Weber, *Organized Efforts for the Improvement of Methods of Administration in the United States* (New York: D. Appleton and Co., 1919), pp. 94–103.

37 U.S. Congress, Senate, *Message of the President of the United States Submitting for the Consideration of the Congress a Budget, With Supporting Memoranda and Reports,* 63d Cong., 3d Sess., Senate Doc. 1113, February 26, 1913 (Washington: Government Printing Office, 1913), p. 117.

service. But it was hardly a step toward a more positive type of personnel management. Rather, its creation was a reflection of the historic distrust of the chief executive by the legislative branch of the government, under a constitutional separation of powers. Congress was not yet ready to admit the necessity for the unreserved delegations of power to the executive branch which the Commission on Economy and Efficiency so earnestly recommended.

Though the Commission's proposals failed to result in much immediate legislation, they certainly stimulated vast amounts of publicity and public discussion which prepared the way for later action. The essential argument of Theodore Roosevelt's Keep Committee, that the public service suffered from certain fundamental troubles which could be relieved only by congressional action, became more and more obvious. Above all, the fact was established that inequalities in pay and status among the employees of the various departments and agencies were not only causing widespread dissatisfaction but also were the basis of budgetary difficulties, innumerable unnecessary transfers from agencies which paid less to those which paid more, and considerable confusion in the workings of the examination and recruitment system.

There is no basis, however, for the charge that the personnel system of the American public service was at this time far behind that of American private industry. In its recruitment system of selection through examination the government service was still far ahead of all but the most advanced industrial organizations. As to pay, hours, leaves, and working conditions the public service had little for which to apologize. Any troubles involving these matters stemmed more from inequalities than from inadequacies. But a few industries were commencing to out-distance the government in the development of a positive personnel system well-integrated with the other aspects of management. Moreover, in its treatment of the problems of position-classification and in its unwillingness to face the reality of superannuation the personnel mechanism of the American civil establishment was lagging in comparison with a number of the more advanced private organizations, though not in comparison with private industry as a whole.[38]

The State of the Service in 1913

Whatever the condition of the morale of public employees under Theodore Roosevelt, it must be considered as worse under President

[38] For private personnel practices at this time, see the May, 1916, issue of *The Annals,* LXV, entitled "Personnel and Employment Problems in Industrial Management."

Taft. Under Taft the dynamic executive leadership of T. R. faded away, as did many of T. R.'s appointees. Certainly the attempt to coerce the Insurgents by means of the patronage and the eventual disruption of the Republican party did not improve the already uncertain political future of many public employees. The political planlessness of the party in power promoted administrative inactivity, indecision, and insecurity.

In addition, in the face of a rising cost of living, the bulk of the federal service had received no substantial wage increases since the middle of the nineteenth century. The political forces in control of legislative affairs, instead of supporting federal civil employee salary and superannuation legislation, appear to have ignored these problems almost completely in favor of an efficiency interpreted almost entirely in terms of dollars and cents. To make the neglect more obvious, during the period from 1900 to 1912 increasing pensions were granted to the exceedingly vocal veterans. The hostile attitude of the Post Office Department to postal unions and the removal of a number of the union officers behind the façade of the Gag Orders made discontent rife in the largest federal agency.[39]

Taft's administration, however, was responsible for a certain number of improvements. At least his Commission on Economy and Efficiency widely publicized the conditions of the public service. The Civil Service Commission fostered several refinements in examination techniques which were to have considerable bearing upon future practices. The Lloyd-LaFollette Act, if it can not be ascribed to Taft, who fought it, must be credited to the Congress of his term in office, prodded by the powerful figure of Samuel Gompers. Taft made two of the largest single extensions of the merit system by placing certain skilled workmen and fourth-class postmasters within the classified service. However, the inclusion of skilled workmen under the merit system merely formalized employment regulations already in effect; and the new appointment procedures for postmasters contained a number of political loopholes.

Therefore, considering the general state of the service by 1913, Pringle's conclusion that the civil service benefited far more from the ministrations of Taft than from those of Theodore Roosevelt seems most unwarranted.[40] The period from 1909 to 1913 was a period in which employee discontent was steadily rising, to burst forth momen-

---

39 Sterling Spero, *The Labor Movement in a Government Industry* (New York: George H. Doran Co., 1924), scattered.

40 Pringle says, "As presidents go, Taft was an honest and fairly effective friend of civil service. It may at least be said that he was a better one than Theodore Roosevelt." As cited in footnote 3, II, 608.

224

tarily under Taft in the form of the Lloyd-LaFollette Act and decisively under Wilson in the birth of the National Federation of Federal Employees.

Though more important than it is sometimes given credit for being, civil service reform was at best a partial answer to the problems engendered by the Gilded Age. As the distinguished political scientist, Henry Jones Ford, trenchantly put it in 1903:

. . . we have had a great deal of civil service reform with so little improvement that the sessions of civil service reformers are consumed by lamentations over the evil tendencies of the times. As is the habit of reformers, although they admit the evil sequences, they are unwilling to regard those sequences as results, and the only remedy they have to offer is stronger and bigger doses of reform. Nevertheless the fact is incontestable that the period following the imposition of civil service reform upon American politics by executive fiat exhibits an exacerbation of all the maladies for which civil service reform was prescribed. Even the most hardy civil service reformer will not contend that following the act of 1883 and its rapid development by executive orders, there was any increase of moderation, order, judgment and control in the management of public affairs. On the contrary there was a marked increase of passion and recklessness in our politics.[41]

A bitter and not entirely persuasive indictment, there is nevertheless something to be said for his point of view. Honesty and efficiency in the administration of existing legislation are of little consolation to someone who seeks, above all, a change in the status quo. Moreover, by obscuring the need for a resolution of more fundamental conflicts, they may eventually even promote serious disorder.

If the answer to the amorphous yearnings of the times was not to be found in the *moral political man* then perhaps *the political and administrative machinery at his command was the source of political evil.* Such was the implicit thesis of much of the Progressive doctrine of the early twentieth century.

In the period up to 1912 it was still too soon for the substantive economic proposals of the Populists, though refined by time and oratory, to be widely accepted before all other alternatives had been tried and tested. Between 1890 and 1910 the Australian ballot, the initiative, referendum, and recall, the direct election of senators, the commission form of local government, and the rest, all took their turn in the political pageant. Civil service reform too, after McKinley's initial gesture to the traditional policies of patronage, was refined and refurbished by Theodore Roosevelt and Taft more nearly in accord with

[41] Henry Jones Ford, "The Results of Reform," *The Annals*, XXI (March, 1903), 77.

the newer standards of administrative acceptability. In the fact that it lent itself to the more modern concept of efficiency as well as to the older morality lay the reason for the relevance of civil service reform to the political programs of interest to the chief executives of twentieth century America and to the voting citizenry they represented.

But now civil service reform no longer occupied the center of the stage. Relevant to the larger issue—yes—and easily associated with it, the merit system found itself relegated to the role of merely one of a numerous cast of characters and was forced to give up its place as the hero of the political drama. The new contribution of civil service reform was to lie in its relationship to economy and efficiency, to democratic machinery-tinkering, and to political and administrative reorganization, the bases of our second phase of effective political renovation after the Civil War.

Trend and Tendency

By the time of the First World War the American public service was approaching in form and spirit the model set by the modern European democracies, especially that of the British. The competitive examination system was firmly installed, though modified to accord with the social mobility more typical of America than Europe. Tenure in office, while still not encouraged to the extent often encountered abroad, was becoming more and more secure, with superannuation fast developing into more of a reality than had been the case for nearly a century. And, despite our Jacksonian heritage, we had begun to accept and apply the European idea of the political neutrality of the public service, though we have never accepted the full anonymous political objectivity of the British civil service and we have been reluctant to extend the merit system to the higher offices.

As our American society has been more heavily weighted with individualism and social mobility, less imbued with a veneration of the state and its representatives, and under fewer economic or military compulsions to systematize and rationalize its governmental administrative system in, for instance, the German manner, we have followed rather than led much of the Western World in the development of a civil establishment on the European model. This does not necessarily mean, however, that we have been administratively any less efficient, for efficiency can only be judged in terms of the effectuation of ultimate social desires. That the American public service in the early years of the twentieth century reflected—from almost any point of view—a reasonably effective instrumentalization of the general desires of the American voting public seems fairly clear.

While some groups of American citizens have always deplored the necessity for any public service at all beyond a minimum policing establishment, there were in the days of Theodore Roosevelt and Taft few attempts to curtail the service. Rather, the effect of the Progressive period was to increase both its influence and size. A few other Americans, mostly academicians, now and then bewailed our reluctance to accept the British administrative pattern and tradition in their entirety, but Congress and the bulk of the voting public expressed no regrets.

CHAPTER 10

"Deserving Democrats:"[1] 1913–1917

Under the protective aegis of Theodore Roosevelt and William Howard Taft the appointment practices of the federal government tended to follow the principles of civil service reform more completely than ever before. The term "civil service" was rapidly becoming so nearly synonymous with the "merit system" in the public mind as to give rise to a semantic confusion which has plagued us forever afterwards.

At the end of the first decade of the twentieth century, the merit system was sufficiently taken for granted, despite the vigorous and vocal protests of William Jennings Bryan and other advocates of the spoils system, that the Civil Service Commission felt impelled to remark in its annual report for 1910:

Two-thirds of all the positions under the National Government and a lesser proportion of State, county, and city positions are filled through the competitive-examination system. The progress made during the past year gives promise of the early application of the system to all positions in national, State, and city governments, other than elective positions and those of officers responsible for administrative policies and their immediate personal assistants or deputies.[2]

Who can blame the Commission for a certain amount of over-exuberance during the friendly regimes of T. R. and Taft? The spoilsman days of Harrison, Cleveland, and even McKinley must have seemed like a bad dream.

---

[1] This phrase is taken from a controversial letter by William Jennings Bryan, mentioned on p. 231.
[2] *Twenty-seventh Report*, 1910, p. 33.

228

Purity or Partisanship

But with the election of 1912 Republican rule was ended. No wonder Mrs. J. Borden Harriman noted with amusement early in 1913 that "the Republicans were funny, so frankly astonished at being ousted, and all sitting around waiting for the heavens to fall." [3] Indeed, the realization that it was within the power of one man, Woodrow Wilson, to dismiss large segments of the public service must have come as a shock to many public employees used to tenure in office, and especially to those with known Republican leanings.

THERE WILL BE A LOT OF MOVING IN AND OUT AT WASHINGTON NEXT MARCH

From *Chicago Tribune*, November 11, 1912 (Copyright: John T. McCutcheon).

[3] From *Pinafores to Politics* (New York: Henry Holt and Co., 1923), p. 186.

229

President Wilson had been a vice-president of the National Civil Service Reform League.[4] As Governor of New Jersey he had used the patronage, to be sure, but he had no record of partisan interference with the state's embryonic merit system, established in 1908. From his previous declarations, both as a Democratic candidate for President and as a private citizen, his friends in the League assumed that, in office, Wilson would hold back his hungry associates with a reasonably tight rein.[5] Nevertheless, Wilson's first term must be considered a period of some regression as far as the development of the classified civil service was concerned.

The initial pressure. The first and most obvious of the influences conspiring against the merit system was the Democratic party, which had been without the sustenance of federal patronage since 1897. Colonel Edward M. House, Wilson's confidant and adviser, wrote to Walter Hines Page on September 7, 1912, just before the election:

. . . The wise man will not envy Governor Wilson even in success, for, as you say, the office-seekers will sorely beset him. They are cheerfully dividing up the honors now, and the numbers engaged in this pleasant pastime will increase as the campaign grows older.[6]

As predicted, the pressure rapidly mounted. Requests poured in and, after the election, Wilson's campaign manager, William F. McCombs, over-hastily presented the President-elect with a "list of the faithful" and proposed a cabinet. Repelling these suggestions, Wilson left the politicians high and dry and went to Bermuda for a month's reflection. Meanwhile, Colonel House, too, found that his mail was "heavy with applications." [7]

Speculation was rife as to the cabinet selections and the presidential

---

4 Wilson was elected a vice-president of the League on December 15, 1910, and served until the annual meeting held December 5, 1912. Shortly before this meeting the President-elect requested that his name be omitted from the list of officers on the grounds that he did not believe it wise to have his name associated with any organization during his term as president, although his "interest in and sympathy with the work of the Civil Service Reform League had not been and cannot be abated." From information supplied the writer by James R. Watson, Executive Director of the League, in a letter of September 27, 1957. Interestingly, Wilson's policy with respect to membership in such organizations was the reverse of Theodore Roosevelt's. T. R., though not a vice-president of the National Civil Service Reform League until 1916, was made a vice-president of the New York Civil Service Reform Association in 1894 and remained in this office all through his years in the White House. On T. R.'s relationship to these organizations, see "Diamond Anniversary of Civil Service," *Good Government*, LXXIV (July–August, 1957), 40.

5 William Dudley Foulke, *Fighting the Spoilsmen* (New York: G. P. Putnam's Sons, 1919), p. 226. For Wilson's views as a candidate see "The Candidates and the Diplomatic Service," *Good Government*, XXIX (November, 1912), 106.

6 Charles Seymour (ed.), *The Intimate Papers of Colonel House* (4 vols.; Boston: Houghton Mifflin Co., 1926–28), I, 84.

7 Same, p. 85.

intentions concerning the offices. Still no definite word came from Wilson. While the President-elect was making up his mind, those who could not reach him pursued those who were more available with innumerable claims for consideration. Senators especially were immediately hounded. "I was fearful that we might not find Democrats to fill the offices, but I am being rapidly disillusioned," Senator Thomas P. Gore of Oklahoma was reported as saying "with a sigh, as he laid down telegrams from two of his best friends making application for the same place." The senator also remarked on the large numbers of " 'Original' Wilson Men." [8] Champ Clark told reporters that he was keeping four stenographers busy with replies to office-seekers.[9] In December, McCombs said to House that office-seekers were "driving him crazy." [10]

The Cabinet. Finally, however, Wilson returned, announced his cabinet, and prepared to take over the administration of the government. On the merit system, as on other matters, the cabinet members held widely divergent views. On one side was Secretary of State William Jennings Bryan, shortly to obtain considerable notoriety for his letter to Walker W. Vick, Receiver General of Customs of the Dominican Republic, on August 20, 1913, which read in part:

Now that you have arrived and are acquainting yourself with the situation, can you let me know what positions you have at your disposal with which to reward *deserving Democrats?* Whenever you desire a suggestion from me in regard to a man for any place there call on me.[11]

Opposing Bryan's well-known spoilsman views were those, for instance, of Secretary of the Interior Franklin K. Lane, a man keenly interested in the morale and welfare of his employees, who was pleased that he had relatively little patronage to dispense. Oswald G. Villard has justly described Lane as

. . . perhaps the first Cabinet officer to concern himself intimately with the employees in the big building of his Department. He knew that they were human beings and not automata; that their nerves of energy and initiative were likely to be atrophied in a few years.[12]

---

8 *Washington Post*, November 13, 1912.
9 *Washington Star*, November 22, 1912.
10 Conversation of December 6, 1912. Seymour, as cited in footnote 6, I, 96.
11 Author's italics. Ray Stannard Baker, *Woodrow Wilson* (8 vols.; New York: Doubleday, Doran and Co., 1931–39), IV, 40. See same, pp. 36–43, for additional material on "Bryan and Deserving Democrats."
12 *Prophets True and False* (New York: Alfred A. Knopf, 1928), p. 217.

He soon became noted for his organization of the Home Club, consisting of more than 1,700 members of the Department of the Interior and designed, as Lane put it, for solution of the problem of "teamwork" in a "disjointed Department." [13] The other members of the Cabinet were of varying, if not so extreme, views. As a whole they may be considered somewhat more inclined to spoils than their immediate predecessors, if for no other reason than because the Democrats had been out of office so long. Nevertheless, as a group they supported the merit system better than had been the case with McKinley's departmental heads.

Wilson decides. The announcement of the cabinet appointments failed to answer the question as to what Wilson's personal policy toward the offices would be. Despite his pre-election pronouncements in favor of merit and his post-election silence,[14] the place-hunters did not despair. On the eve of his inauguration Wilson was besieged in his hotel and elsewhere by the office-seeking acquaintances of his personal and political friends. Evidently tiring of the constant pressure, the new President announced a "shocking innovation" [15] on March 5, the day after his inauguration:

> The President regrets that he is obliged to announce that he deems it his duty to decline to see applicants for office in person, except when he himself invites the interview. It is his purpose and desire to devote his attention very earnestly and very constantly to the business of the government. . . . It is his intention to deal with appointments through the heads of the several executive departments.[16]

This intention he reaffirmed personally to his cabinet at its initial meeting.[17] At the same time he remarked to Postmaster General Albert S. Burleson, "It makes no difference whether a man stood for me or not. All I want is a man who is fit for the place, a man who stands for clean government and progressive policies." To Bryan, a dyed-in-the-wool party man, this was startling, almost subversive, doctrine.[18]

The wily Burleson merely bided his time and a few days later arrived at the presidential offices with the first list of prospective postmasters. The President refused to accept Burleson's list and demanded

13 Letter to Albert Shaw, April 8, 1914. Anne W. Lane and Louise H. Wall (eds.), *The Letters of Franklin K. Lane* (Boston: Houghton Mifflin Co., 1922), pp. 148–50.

14 House is quoted as saying that few congressional leaders or other politicians, including Wilson's campaign manager, were consulted before March 4. Seymour, as cited in footnote 6, I, 101–102.

15 Baker, as cited in footnote 11, IV, 26.

16 Same, p. 14.

17 David F. Houston, *Eight Years With Wilson's Cabinet* (2 vols.; New York: Doubleday, Page and Co., 1926), I, 40.

18 Paxton Hibben, *The Peerless Leader* (New York: Farrar and Rinehart, Inc., 1929), p. 322.

to see the papers so that he could personally select the proper men for the offices. Burleson did not argue but sent over an entire desk full of dossiers by two messengers and promised more to come. At this Wilson capitulated, but not until he had pondered the matter for a full week and thoroughly explored the situation with Burleson, who at one point reported that he was "paralyzed" by some of Wilson's views. Nevertheless, the Postmaster General steadfastly maintained his position that the entire success of Wilson's program depended upon his ability to manage the party and that, if Wilson did not distribute the patronage to the satisfaction of the party, he might as well give up before he started. Stressing the dependability of the party regulars, Burleson emphasized his hope that the President would understand their willingness to go along with him if they could find the chief executive at all cooperative. In the end Wilson was convinced. Requesting "no more papers to be sent to the White House," he eventually only queried, "Where do I sign?" [19] Thus ended Wilson's first major political lesson as president.

From this point on, Wilson consulted actively with senators and representatives on patronage as well as other matters. After all, this did not conflict with his elevated conception of presidential leadership. From having at first implied that even senators might have to deal through cabinet members,[20] the President had by the middle of March so modified his approach that Senator William J. Stone and Speaker Champ Clark of Missouri were said to have gone away from the White House satisfied.[21] A little later the *Kansas City Star* noted that jobs were being held up until the passage of the tariff legislation, and reported:

. . . Senator [William Howard] Thompson of Kansas got five postmasters through yesterday. It is generally understood that the Garden City senator, who was in conference with the President yesterday, will stay with his party on the Underwood Bill.[22]

By the sixth of May, 1913, Wilson was sufficiently convinced of the political value of the patronage to write, "I shall hope in every possible instance to comply with the recommendations and wishes of my colleagues in the House." [23] He thereafter constantly consulted with

[19] For a fuller account of Wilson's conversion see Baker, as cited in footnote 11, IV, 43–54. See also Arthur S. Link, *Wilson: The New Freedom* (Princeton, N.J.: Princeton University Press, 1956), pp. 158–75. Link describes Wilson's decision to operate through the party as "one of the early decisive turning points in Wilson's presidential career." Same, p. 159.

[20] *New York Times*, March 6, 1913.

[21] *Baltimore News*, March 11, 1913.

[22] May 5, 1913.

[23] Baker, as cited in footnote 11, IV, 48–49.

Burleson, and eventually concurred with his view that the old party standpatters would be more constant in their support than many of the so-called "progressives." [24] Wilson not only rewarded those who supported him but deprived those who thwarted him, as House Majority Leader Claude Kitchin discovered to his sorrow when he struggled with Wilson over America's entry into the First World War.[25]

But despite his early "decision" on the patronage, or perhaps more because of it and his innate dislike of the bargaining process it involved, Wilson always considered that the problem of appointments was one of his greatest burdens. On September 10, 1913, he said, "The matter of patronage is a thorny path which daily makes me wish I had never been born." [26] On March 20, 1914, he told the National Press Club in Washington, "There are Post Offices to which I wouldn't think of mailing a letter, which I can't think of without trembling with the knowledge of all the heart-burnings of the struggle there was in getting somebody installed as Postmaster." [27] To an ex-scholar primarily concerned at first with the concepts of a broad social program and after 1916 with the complex problems of a war-torn world, the necessity to umpire quarrels over such administrative minutiae must have seemed almost unbearable.[28] Nevertheless, he accepted, with as much grace as he could muster, the necessities of practical politics and governed himself accordingly.

Once Wilson saw the political light, he followed it consistently. He still made many appointments independently, but he worked primarily within the party rather than against it. He never entirely gave up his support of the merit system, yet he nevertheless bowed to the pressure sufficiently to obtain the legislation he desired. Arriving thus at a politically pragmatic conception of the proper use of the patronage, Wilson gradually assumed an attitude not unlike that of Theodore Roosevelt toward the bestowal of public office. Wilson, however, pursued his policy without Roosevelt's intimate knowledge of the administrative details of personnel procedures. As a result of this and other factors to be considered later, Wilson, like Taft, followed a somewhat uncertain course in his relationship to the civil service.

That the President had a definite economic program which he wished to see enacted and that at the same time he had a hungry party also differentiated him from his two immediate predecessors. As

24 Same, p. 49.
25 Alex Mathews Arnett, *Claude Kitchin and the Wilson War Policies* (Boston: Little, Brown and Co., 1937), p. 201.
26 Baker, as cited in footnote 11, IV, p. 53.
27 Same, p. 54.
28 See also William G. McAdoo, *Crowded Years* (Boston: Houghton Mifflin Co., 1931), pp. 523–24.

far as manipulations of the public offices might further his legislative aspirations, Wilson did not hesitate to make them. He refused, however, to permit spoils politics to develop to such an extent as to jeopardize the success of his administration. At that point he apparently endeavored to draw a line.

It was the fate of Woodrow Wilson, unquestionably a civil service reformer of some considerable conviction, to be lifted to the Presidency at a time when a majority of the voting public in this country, for the first time since the Civil War, favored the enactment of a program of substantive economic reform on a national scale. Stability and tenure in public office are compatible with moral and administrative reform but, as was clearly illustrated in the days of Andrew Jackson, a program of economic reform involving a frontal attack on the status quo is likely to result in the disruption of many time-honored institutions, among them the public service. That the public service did not in 1913 suffer more from Democratic manipulations was probably a result of the fact that the Wilsonian program was, after all, only modestly revolutionary. While there may have been fighting in the political streets, there were few pitched battles; and the antagonists armed themselves accordingly.

The Victors: 1913–1917

The legislative position. The first congressional patronage stone to be thrown at the merit system came in the form of a section of the Underwood Act of October 3, 1913, providing for an income tax force which for two years could be selected as Secretary of the Treasury William G. McAdoo might desire. Beyond this, on October 22, 1913, a deficiency appropriation act provided that collectors of internal revenue and United States marshals could appoint bonded deputies without complying with the civil service regulations. More than 3,500 positions were involved. Wilson himself supported this legislation with a public statement that in his opinion there had never been any intention to include these offices under the merit system. He further explained:

. . . The control of the whole method and spirit of the administration of the proviso in this bill which concerns the appointment of these officers is no less entirely in my hands now than it was before the bill became law; my warm advocacy and support both of the principle and of the bona fide practice of civil-service reform is known to the whole country, and there is no danger that the spoils principle will creep in with my approval or connivance.[29]

29 USCSC, *Thirty-first Report*, 1914, p. 138.

Less forthright than those of Theodore Roosevelt and as ingenuous as some of the Taft pronouncements, the Wilsonian spoils apologetics were at best a tribute to the strength of the merit system in the public estimation.

Nevertheless, congressional exceptions to the merit system continued with tacit presidential approval. The Federal Reserve Act of December 23, 1913, provided that the Federal Reserve Board might employ its personnel without regard to the civil service rules. This legislation did, however, authorize the President eventually to include the Board's positions within the classified service. In July, 1914, the Secretary of Commerce was authorized to appoint commercial attachés after such an examination as he, rather than the Civil Service Commission, might determine. Limited exceptions to competition were made in the legislation providing for the Federal Trade Commission, and similar provisions were applied not long after to the Federal Farm Loan Board, the Shipping Board, and the Tariff Commission.

The postal controversy. Meanwhile, the President himself encouraged the manipulation of the postal service by holding up, through an executive order of May 7, 1913, the classification of fourth-class postmasters as originally ordered by Taft. Wilson's order further stated that these postmasters might not obtain the classified status which Taft had planned for them to acquire automatically until they had passed examinations open not only to incumbents but also to other interested persons. At the same time Wilson retained Taft's provision for selection from the three highest on the register. While on the surface these actions seemed hardly in conflict with merit principles, in actuality they did much to undermine them. Under Roosevelt and Taft there had been examinations, but only when there was need to replace an incumbent. Now new examinations were to be held and a separate register established for each and every post-office involved in the order. There were seldom a great number of candidates for any one postmastership. Therefore permission to select from the first three names on the register, as opposed to the Roosevelt policy of automatic appointment of the one at the top, normally allowed an appointing officer to choose a candidate of the proper political persuasion. In effect, most of the fourth-class postmasterships were again open to patronage. Postmaster General Burleson admitted in November, 1913, that he was not hesitating to consult congressmen concerning the "character and fitness" of candidates for the fourth-class postmasterships.

The National Civil Service Reform League protested that such consultation violated the Pendleton Act and asked for an opinion from the Attorney General. Nothing came of the request. The League then asked permission to investigate the Civil Service Commission's files to determine the status of the enforcement of the merit system in the Post Office Department. The Commission had for years been most helpful in supporting the efforts of the League to further the merit system. But at this point the Commission, to the League's great indignation, refused to cooperate.[30] Burleson had his own way.

In 1916 Congress approved the motorization of the rural free delivery service. The legislation was then made an excuse for a political reorganization of this service. The Reform League again applied for permission to inspect the records, but Commission president John A. McIlhenny again refused on the grounds that such an inspection might embarrass the administration. Commissioner Hermon W. Craven supported him. The League then went to the President and a lengthy three-way correspondence among the President, the members of the Commission, and the League became the subject of much public comment. Finally, the President said that he owed it to the League to look into the matter, but no action was ever taken.

That all was not harmonious in the official family is indicated by the fact that the Civil Service Commission itself disagreed in its annual report for 1916 as to the real condition of the postal service. Commissioners McIlhenny and Charles M. Galloway felt that the available statistics supported Burleson's view that the merit system was being upheld as much as could be expected. Commissioner Craven took the same statistics and argued that the situation was far from what it ought to be.[31] In this disagreement lay the seeds of further dissension, which, however, was not to break forth into public view until after the end of the First World War.

The Foreign Service. Under policies dating back to McKinley's Secretary of State, John Hay, the Foreign Service had begun to be professionalized. Theodore Roosevelt and Taft had furthered this development, and by 1913 both ministerial and consular posts were largely staffed by career men. To William Jennings Bryan, Wilson's new Secretary of State, this was an intolerable state of affairs for a new administration. Moreover, as a perennial candidate for the Presidency, Bryan found himself with political obligations of vast proportions. Consistently a spoilsman, Bryan maintained that diplomatic posts were properly political appointments, a point of view with which Wilson apparently agreed as far as major posts were concerned. Certainly

---

30 See Foulke, as cited in footnote 5, pp. 233–54, for the most critical and detailed account of patronage politics in the Post Office Department under Wilson. See also Daniel C. Roper, *Fifty Years of Public Life* (Durham: Duke University Press, 1941), p. 129, for another view.
31 USCSC, *Thirty-third Report*, 1916, pp. xi–xx and xxv–xxvi.

the President did nothing to deter Bryan from making a clean sweep of the top levels of the Foreign Service. Within a few months, a decade and a half of tenure was shattered and an extraordinary group of political hacks and friends of Bryan were installed all over the world.[32]

Wilson kept control of key diplomatic assignments, such as those to Britain and France; and he kept Bryan from overturning the lower level career consular service which had been established under Roosevelt. But, in what Wilson's biographer, Arthur S. Link, has described as "the greatest debauchery of the Foreign Service in the twentieth century," Bryan quickly ran roughshod over the rest of the service.[33] After Bryan left the Cabinet, Secretary of State Robert Lansing was able somewhat to restore the previous policies, but it was to be more than thirty years before the Foreign Service was again on a career basis comparable to that prior to 1913.

A political issue. By the end of 1913 the press frequently was criticizing the Wilson administration for its political spoilsmanship.[34] In fact civil service reform became a campaign issue in 1916. Charles Evans Hughes, the Republican candidate, attacked Wilson for his appointment policies.[35] During the campaign the Reform League's controversy with the Civil Service Commission over the latter's refusal to grant access to its records was publicly aired.[36] Vice-President Thomas R. Marshall's frank remark, "If there is any office under the government which a Democrat can't fill I believe that office should be abolished," [37] was widely condemned. Both Wilson and Hughes stated that they were in favor of extending the merit system, but Hughes, especially, raised the issue again and again.[38] A poor third to preparedness and the Adamson Act,[39] civil service reform was nevertheless an issue of sorts, and there was little the Democrats could say on their own behalf. While Hughes lost the election, Burleson, ironically, was bitterly attacked at the opening of Congress by, among others, Champ Clark for endangering the Democratic victory through an undue con-

---

32 See Link, as cited in footnote 19, pp. 103–10; and Baker, as cited in footnote 11, IV, 36–43, for details of this story. George Harvey, "The Diplomats of Democracy," *North American Review*, CXCIX (February, 1914), 171, is a biting summary of Bryan's decimation of the ministries in Latin America, an area in which Roosevelt and Taft had been especially eager to appoint competent career personnel.

33 Link, as cited in footnote 19, p. 106.

34 For example, see the *Philadelphia Press*, December 22, 1913, the *Boston Evening Post*, December 24, 1913, and the *New Orleans Picayune*, August 14, 1914.

35 See, for instance, the *New York Times*, August 12, 1916.

36 *New York Tribune*, August 16, 1916.

37 "The Civil Service Issue in the Presidential Campaign," *Good Government*, XXXIII (October–November, 1916), 94.

38 Same, pp. 93–95.

39 This act established an eight-hour day for employees of common carriers engaged in interstate commerce and, according to many, set a dangerous precedent.

cern for merit in his management of the fourth-class postal appointments.[40]

Aftermath. Wilson's greatest and almost his sole contribution to the extension of merit principles came after his reelection. Then he provided that, under certain limited circumstances, first, second, and third-class postmasters—those of the more important cities—would be selected through a version of the merit system, in which he would appoint, subject to the usual senatorial confirmation, the top man on the register rather than follow the "rule of three." Received with public acclaim, if not that of his party, Wilson's action laid a foundation for the more complete provisions made for these offices later.[41]

The Civil Service Commission

Throughout most of Wilson's administration John A. McIlhenny of Louisiana, a Democratic member appointed by Roosevelt in 1906, remained as president of the Commission. After accepting the resignations of the other two incumbent commissioners, the President had appointed, as the second Democratic commissioner, Charles M. Galloway, a South Carolina newspaperman, former secretary to Senator E. D. Smith of that state, and clerk of the Senate Committee on Immigration. The Republican place had gone to Hermon W. Craven of Seattle, Washington, a lawyer and former deputy county prosecutor. The Chief Examiner was George R. Wales of Vermont, generally considered an able man, and himself appointed commissioner in 1919.

Family squabbles. Neither Galloway nor Craven possessed experience in civil service procedures or personnel administration, and it appears that from a fairly early date the three commissioners did not always get along. When Wilson eventually accepted McIlhenny's resignation in 1919, after the three commissioners had served together without change since 1913, he at the same time requested the resignations of Galloway and Craven. This was the only case in which the entire Commission has, in effect, been removed all at once. The reasons behind this action will be discussed in the next chapter, but it was alleged in 1919 that the commissioners were engaged in a quarrel of at least two years' standing and that they then were at the point of throwing paper weights at each other.[42] Part of their difficulty—failure to agree on postal matters—has already been mentioned.

40 *Washington Post,* March 9, 1917.
41 George T. Keyes, "The Competitive Classification of Presidential Postmasters," *The Annals,* LXIV (March, 1916), 147.
42 *Boston Evening Transcript,* March 14, 1919.

The Division of Efficiency. The first technical problem inherited by the Commission from President Taft's administration was the organization of the new Division of Efficiency. This organization was especially designed to administer efficiency ratings for public employees, required for the first time by the same act which created the division. Before the Commission could go far, legislation passed in 1916 made the division a separate agency named the Bureau of Efficiency. The new bureau was given exceedingly broad powers of investigation. A year later Congress formally requested the Bureau to study the "methods of transacting the public business in the Civil Service Commission and report to Congress through the President at the next regular session of Congress." [43] This report was not actually completed and delivered until the time of Harding's administration.

The success of the Bureau in carrying out its efficiency rating function is still a subject of considerable argument, for service ratings have always been desirable but most difficult to administer. A numerical rating scheme was developed and gradually put into operation throughout the federal government. Efficiency ratings had been used in the public service before. But this was the first occasion when a single agency was given authority to standardize their use throughout a large segment of the federal government. However, the lodging of the efficiency rating function, an executive matter, in an agency which became in 1916 almost solely an adjunct of Congress caused many difficulties. In the long run the development of a true central personnel agency was retarded. The National Civil Service Reform League remarked as early as 1918 that "the Bureau of Efficiency, that curious anomaly," ought to be restored to "its former status as an adjunct of the Civil Service Commission." [44]

Employees' compensation. Another important innovation on the federal personnel scene lay in the creation of the Employees' Compensation Commission in 1916, also designed to function as a separate agency. The same act which organized this new commission provided workmen's compensation for all civil employees and a few other categories of workers. Legislation covering specific hazardous occupations dates as early as 1882, but this was the first comprehensive act applying to the entire civil service.[45] The administration of this act, now performed by the Department of Labor, has never been transferred

---

43 USCSC, *Thirty-fifth Report*, 1918, p. 40.
44 *Good Government*, XXXV (October, 1918), 145.
45 See Gustavus A. Weber, *The Employees' Compensation Commission* (New York: D. Appleton and Co., 1922); and Carroll H. Wooddy, *The Growth of the Federal Government* (New York: McGraw-Hill Book Co., 1934), pp. 379–82.

to the Civil Service Commission, though the shift has been proposed many times.

Housekeeping. The Civil Service Commission itself did not suffer at the hands of Congress to any extent during the Wilson administration, except for the aforementioned legislative exceptions from the merit system and the amputation of the Division of Efficiency. The Commission did not receive all the money it wanted, but its appropriations gradually increased until in 1915 it spent $434,200, compared to about half that in 1904.[46] It almost doubled its full-time employees between 1903 and 1915, while the local boards which used temporarily detailed employees grew from nearly 1,000 to 2,800 in number.[47]

The major problem with which the Commission had to contend was the increasing load of examinations. In 1915 it reported an arrearage of 50,000 papers at the beginning of the year, but it had reduced the figure to 30,000 by the end of the year.[48] By the time of the First World War it was operating relatively currently. This increase in workload, funds, and personnel was primarily a reflection of the gradually increasing size and functions of the federal service. During Wilson's first term, the civil service expanded from a figure of about 425,000 in 1912 to about 480,000 in 1916.

Rules changes. A precedent-shattering pre-war change in the rules permitted government employees to participate in the women's suffrage movement. Wilson himself suggested to McIlhenny that such agitation was not incompatible with the merit system since it was not a partisan political movement in the ordinary sense.[49]

A less publicized but much more important change in the rules occurred when the Commission on May 27, 1914, ordered photographs to accompany all applications. This had been required for territorial positions for some time but never before for jobs within the United States. Whether or not this change was directed solely at Negro applicants for public office is not absolutely certain. However, the Wilson regime was the subject of bitter attack by Negro organizations for its discriminatory policies toward Negroes. The President replaced the few Negro diplomats with whites and, as had Taft, refused to appoint Negroes in the South. At the same time, Burleson and Secretary Wil-

---

46 See Woody, as cited in footnote 45, pp. 47–48, for comparative statistics on the number of employees and the expenditures of the Commission for the years 1915, 1920, 1925, 1930, 1931, and 1932.

47 USCSC, *Thirty-second Report*, 1915, p. 24.

48 Same, p. 20.

49 See Lane and Wall, as cited in footnote 13, pp. 145–46; and Josephus Daniels, *The Wilson Era: Years of Peace* (Chapel Hill: University of North Carolina Press, 1944), pp. 458–59.

241

liam G. McAdoo commenced a policy of segregation in the postal and Treasury offices, respectively.[50]

The southern orientation of the Wilson administration is well known. Certainly the patronage went heavily to the southern members of Congress, and southern opposition to Negro appointments, both within Congress and the Cabinet, seems to have been instrumental in the decline of Negro federal employment from nearly 6 per cent of the total civil service in 1910 to about 4.9 per cent in 1918.[51] Moreover, there is conclusive evidence that the President, despite public protests and the efforts of many Progressives, fully approved of the segregation measures taken in various departments and agencies.[52] The period from 1913 to 1921 deserves to be considered the most critical period in the recent history of Negro federal civil employment. Historically, the Negroes have received their greatest inducements to enter the public service under Republican administrations. Under Franklin D. Roosevelt, however, the relationship of Negroes to the Democratic party was considerably improved and the percentage of Negroes in the federal civil service rose slightly from an estimated 9.59 per cent under Hoover in 1928 to 9.85 per cent in 1938.[53]

Organizational effectiveness. The relations of the Civil Service Commission and the executive departments seem to have been relatively peaceful, with the exception of the Post Office and occasionally the Department of State. With the backing of Roosevelt and Taft, the auditing powers of the Commission had been increased and its influence over the details of recruitment and appointment procedure, particularly within the classified service, was more powerful than ever.

Nevertheless, from a review of the Civil Service Commission's annual reports between 1913 and 1916 one cannot help but receive an impression of a relatively static administrative situation within the Commission. The Commission was performing its duties as well as ever, but it is doubtful that much progress was being made. Of course, the general attitude of the Democratic administration was seldom encouraging to the further refinement of the merit system.

The reports of the National Civil Service Reform League are extremely critical of the Commission. But a majority of the Reform

50 See Laurence J. W. Hayes, *The Negro Federal Government Worker* (Washington: Howard University, 1941), pp. 37–58; and Link, as cited in footnote 19, pp. 243–54, for a summary of the policies of the Wilson administration toward the Negro.

51 John M. Blum, *Joe Tumulty and the Wilson Era* (Boston: Houghton Mifflin Co., 1951), pp. 158–59; and Hayes, as cited in footnote 50, p. 153.

52 On September 8, 1913, Wilson wrote to the editor of the *Congregationalist and Christian World,* "I would say that I do approve of the segregation that is being attempted in several of the departments." Quoted in Link, as cited in footnote 19, p. 251. Public controversy over the Wilsonian segregation policy did, however, check its spread.

53 Hayes, as cited in footnote 50, p. 153.

League was Republican, and its reports were always a fraction more critical of Democratic than Republican patronage policies. Moreover, with the Commission refusing to open its books on the postmasters, the opinions of the League may not have been entirely unbiased on other matters. The most reasonable conclusion is that the Commission was functioning in an acceptable if not creative or courageous fashion.

Pay and Perquisites

By 1916 the interrelated problems of wages and salaries, position-classification, and employment conditions had become especially pressing. In these as in other matters, the affairs of the public service were approaching a climax.

Pay. In practically every report of the Civil Service Commission from 1900 through the First World War the Commission expressed difficulty in obtaining workers of one type or another, primarily because of inadequate pay. As might be expected, the pressure was first felt in scientific and technical fields. In his annual report for 1900 the Secretary of Agriculture lamented that he was losing his professional workers because of low salaries. He concluded that only the access to large-scale research facilities kept some of them in his employ. Thirteen years later the Secretary was still reporting:

The securing of men of the requisite training and experience in the various fields of agricultural science has been one of the serious problems which for some time has confronted the department. Two causes have tended to bring about this situation. One has been the low maximum salary which the department is permitted to pay to its scientific investigators as compared with the salaries paid by outside institutions and commercial concerns. The other has been the comparatively small number of strong, virile men who have been trained in scientific agriculture.[54]

Not only do the annual reports of the Civil Service Commission reveal that the problem facing the Secretary of Agriculture was not unique, but a special study by the National Civil Service Reform League further documented the basic underlying problems. The effects of low salaries were by now being reflected in an increasing number of declinations of appointments and withdrawals from the civil service registers.[55] As the inequalities continued to mount, employees either resigned and sought positions in private industry or they attempted to transfer to more lucrative posts elsewhere in the govern-

---

[54] From the annual report of the Secretary of Agriculture for 1913, p. 12, as quoted in USCSC, *Thirty-first Report*, 1914, p. 141. For the Secretary's problem in 1900 see USCSC, *Seventeenth Report*, 1900, pp. 324–25.

[55] "Withdrawals from the Civil Service," *Good Government*, XXIV (April, 1907), 31.

ment service. The turnover figures for the federal civil service, though their precise accuracy may be questioned, nevertheless indicate a trend. The separations from the service more than tripled from 1903 to 1917, with voluntary separations accounting for most of the increase.[56] Congressional legislation severely limited transfer privileges but did not attack the root of the problem. The entire federal pay and position-classification structure was creaking at the joints.

While comparative income statistics are not too reliable, one may fairly conclude from available figures that government wages were static, while both private industrial wages and the cost of living were rising. Thus, two forces were at work to the disadvantage of the federal service. Moreover, there was little in the form of other types of compensation or fringe benefits to make up for the declining real wages. The situation was well documented even during Wilson's first term, as evidenced by the annual report of the Department of Commerce for 1916:

> For 60 years the rates of compensation to clerks have remained stationary, and for about 46 years to the subclerical grades. The available figures on file in the bureau of Labor Statistics, based upon wages in selected industries, all of which, however, were not uniform for the entire period covered, but which can be accepted as typical, show an increase in daily average wage of 137.4 per cent from 1854 to 1915. In other words, daily wages in 1915 were $2\frac{1}{3}$ times as much as in 1854.

The department continued to explain that the cost of living from 1854 to 1915 had increased 14.1 per cent, with most of the increase coming after 1900, while from 1915 to 1916 alone it had jumped 16 per cent. The conclusion was

> . . . that wages in all branches of industries have more than kept pace with the increased cost of living, but that no increase has been made in the wage scale of Government employees, notwithstanding the fact that since 1854 the daily task of all wage earners has been steadily decreasing, while the Government employee has received increased hours, with no consequent increase in compensation to offset, in a measure, the increased living cost.[57]

56 Mary Conyngton, "Separations from the Government Service," *Monthly Labor Review*, XI (December, 1920), 11.

57 U.S. Department of Commerce, *Annual Report for 1916* (Washington: Government Printing Office, 1916), pp. 33–39. Paul H. Douglas, in testimony before the congressional committee considering the Welch Bill in March, 1928, outlined the situation even more precisely. His and the department's conclusions are in fundamental agreement. According to Douglas, the average income of the government's clerical employees in the District of Columbia in 1892 was $1,096. This figure was slightly lower in the field services. By 1900 the average income of departmental clerical employees had actually decreased, and by 1916, the last pre-war year in which no bonus or other type of salary increase was given, it had increased only to $1,174. At the same time, the average annual earnings of em-

Forces at work. Nevertheless, the prevailing public opinion before World War I was that government employees were overpaid. Typical of this point of view is the following item from the *New York Evening Post* of April 6, 1899, which was presented in argument against employee requests for civil pensions on a noncontributory basis: "The government certainly ought not to give it to them in addition to their salaries, when they average to receive twice as much, on a conservative estimate, as persons similarly employed in the outside world." This argument has a familiar ring and unquestionably overstates the case. Still, there was solid basis in fact for this type of conclusion throughout most of the nineteenth century. When one considers that the hours of work of government employees were frequently much shorter and the vacations and sick leave much more liberal than in private industry, the *Post's* position appears much more rational. But 1913 was, except for the period of the Great Depression, the last year in which an office-seeking throng crowded Washington in the way we associate with the nineteenth century. By the end of Wilson's first term federal posts offered almost no comparative economic advantages.

Can we account for the narrowing gap between wages for public and private employment? The answer can best be given in terms of "democracy." Much of the country unquestionably believed that the civil service was paid too much. With Congress tuned to the public and highly conscious of democratic concepts of equality, it is no wonder that nothing was done about federal salaries until it became depressingly obvious that some action had to be taken or the service would perish. This point was soon to come, and, in accordance with democratic theory, wages were maintained for the lower and middle positions at levels about equal to those in private industry, and for the higher positions about equal to those of Congress itself. This was clearly democracy at work, especially a democracy which refused to equate the state with anything higher than private endeavor.

It has been suggested that Congress grew less attentive to the needs of civil servants as the merit system made the offices increasingly useless for political purposes. At most, however, this is true only to a very

ployed workers, other than government employees, increased from $494 in 1892 to $767 in 1916. In addition, the length of the industrial work week had decreased, while that of federal workers remained stationary at best. Douglas concludes that, considering the rising cost of living alone and ignoring the decreasing differential with private industry, government workers, in effect, received salary reductions of 9 per cent by 1914, rising to 30 per cent by 1926. U.S. Congress, House, Committee on Civil Service, *Salary Increase for Certain Civil Service Employees—Welch Increase Salary Bill*, 70th Cong., 1st Sess., Hearings on H.R. 6518, March 19, 20, 21, 22, and 29, 1928 (Washington: Government Printing Office, 1928), pp. 15–35. Douglas' figures are for calendar rather than fiscal years.

limited extent. Postal employees, who have been most closely tied in with Congress, have on occasion received pay increases before the rest of the service. But, on the whole, they have had about as much difficulty as other workers in obtaining legislation which would relieve their many grievances relating to working conditions. Moreover, the evidence in state government would also tend to suggest that the merit system has at best only very mildly militated against public employee wages. For example, the state of New York, which has had a merit system as long as the federal government, is well ahead in terms of wages of the states around it, and especially of those states whose public employment is still largely subject to spoils. In some types of employment, wage scales in New York have been even more liberal than those of the federal government.

Pensions. Not only were employees worried about living expenses before the First World War, but they were also concerned with other problems relating to the conditions of their employment. The quarrels over removal procedures, already discussed, were allayed somewhat by the Lloyd-LaFollette Act in 1912. The problem of civil pensions, however, was as yet unresolved.

From 1886 to 1914 more than seventy pension bills were introduced into Congress.[58] The essential problem was two-fold. Would Congress permit pensions at all, and, if so, who would pay for them? The example of the great financial load caused by military pensions was instrumental in influencing Congress to turn down all suggested civil pension legislation for many years. It did not wish to set up another great class of public pensioners. Even a contributory plan was suspect, for it was always argued that, if the plan were started and proved insolvent, the government would have to make up the deficit.

Most individuals and groups favoring civil pensions during the first years of the twentieth century advocated contributory plans, as the only plans Congress was likely to consider. However, as the salary situation became more acute, the advocates of direct civil pensions, paid in full by the government, greatly increased in number. The United States Civil Service Retirement Association, formed at the turn of the century by interested public employees, split over the issue in 1910.[59] With the civil servants themselves unable to agree, Congress, of course, felt under no great compulsion to act, and the whole matter lay unresolved for another ten years.

---

[58] For a summary of civil pension legislation prior to 1914, see U.S. War Department, *Annual Report of the Secretary of War for 1913* (Washington: Government Printing Office, 1913), pp. 57–60.

[59] Sterling D. Spero, *The Labor Movement in a Government Industry* (New York: George H. Doran Co., 1924), pp. 281–82.

Other employment conditions. Promotion systems based on service ratings were considered desirable, but they were almost impossible to administer on any equitable basis since there was no standard pay and position-classification scheme. This does not mean that they were not tried, but the results continued to be unsatisfactory.

Welfare activities were practically nonexistent except in occasional agencies such as the Department of the Interior under Secretary Lane. Even there, these activities were almost solely dependent upon Lane, for there was little or no legal backing for them. Systematic health precautions or programs were largely limited to the Army, Navy, and Treasury departments. Even after the War it was reported that "seven departments have not a single hospital or emergency room, only one of them has a rest room and a doctor in attendance, and none of them has a nurse, even though the total force involved aggregates almost 20,000 employees." [60] In the field of safety there was little or no positive activity toward accident prevention, but workmen's compensation was granted to all in 1916.

Training for the public service, on any organized and carefully planned basis, was likewise almost nonexistent outside the Army and Navy and a few specialized agencies such as the Forest Service. In 1905 President Roosevelt ordered that no government employee, under penalty of removal, could help anyone else pass a civil service examination. The order was aimed at fraud and collusion, but its long-range effect was to block any attempts at training through employee organizations. As far as colleges and universities were concerned, there was a limited recognition of their responsibilities at the National Conference on Universities and Public Service. This was called in 1914 by Mayor John P. Mitchel of New York City after a preliminary report in 1913 by the Committee on Practical Training for Public Service of the American Political Science Association. The immediate results of these discussions were negligible, but they laid the foundation for a more thorough integration of the educational system with the needs of the public service. [61]

Before the Storm

The personnel problems of the public service immediately prior to the First World War were basically those which any large and rapidly-expanding organization might expect in a period of growing infla-

---

[60] William E. Mosher, "A Federal Personnel Policy," *Monthly Labor Review*, XI (July, 1920), 19.

[61] Leonard D. White, *Trends in Public Administration* (New York: McGraw-Hill Book Co., 1933), pp. 259–62; and National Conference on Universities and Public Service, *Proceedings* (Madison: Cantwell Printing Co. [1915]).

tion.[62] But no effective legislative action could be taken until these problems had been fully comprehended by both Congress and the executive branch, not to mention the voting public. What was needed was some catalytic event to make the situation so obvious that Congress would be obliged to assist in developing the legislation so badly needed for the full rationalization of the federal public service. That a world war was necessary to provide the final stimulus is questionable.

Occasionally the executive departments themselves took some kind of action to improve their employment procedures. Yet no agency possessed any modern central departmental personnel section. In the main, the departmental chief clerks or their assistants were still the personnel officers—often in their spare time—and remained so until the end of the next decade. Sometimes the departments seriously damaged a morale already none too high. The activities of the Post Office Department in the name of economy were certainly instrumental in provoking the postal unions to bitter attacks against Taft's Postmaster General Hitchcock. The unionization authority granted by the Lloyd-LaFollette Act, passed partly as a result of this conflict, did not prevent Wilson's Postmaster General Burleson from doing everything in his power to lengthen hours and reduce wages in order to operate the postal service at a profit.

Outside the government, there were now two agencies primarily interested in the state of the public service. The National Civil Service Reform League, which had served since 1883 as a valuable publicity agent for the Civil Service Commission, was still more concerned with the protection of the merit system than with the details of modern personnel management. In 1906, the National Assembly of Civil Service Commissions [63] was formed as a professional association of civil service commissioners and personnel officers from the principal merit systems throughout all levels of government. Though its objectives were not always clearly defined before the First World War, this organization served as a valuable clearing house for ideas and information.

In addition, the movement for economy and efficiency in governmental affairs was still continuing, though the war was seriously to reduce its momentum. Methods of governmental administration were, despite the change of the party in power, gradually being tightened up. This rationalization of the federal civil establishment reflected,

---

62 See Henry Moskowitz, "Old and New Problems of Civil Service," *The Annals*, LXIV (March, 1916), 153.

63 In 1928 the organization was renamed the Civil Service Assembly of the United States and Canada. In 1957 it was again redesignated, and it is now known as the Public Personnel Association. See J. J. Donovan, "The Civil Service Assembly: 1906–1956," *Public Personnel Review*, XVII (October, 1956), 312.

248

of course, a fundamental trend within the whole of American industrial organization, where the concepts of "scientific management" were receiving wide recognition and trial. From 1900 to the First World War, and with an accelerating momentum, administrative methods of all kinds were being refined throughout all phases of American organizational activity, public as well as private. As went management in general, so went public personnel administration, albeit lethargically, during the years of the Wilson administration.

CHAPTER 11

The Bureaucratic War Front: 1917–1921

The civil service was almost as immediately involved in the events of the First World War as the military service. This is best illustrated by the rise in public employment that started in 1916. Then the number of civil employees of the federal government totalled more than 480,000. By June of the following year the figure had jumped to approximately 520,000, while by November, 1918, the Civil Service Commission recorded a high point of civil employment at an estimated 917,760 persons. After the end of hostilities, the number of employees rapidly dropped to about 840,000 in 1919, to 700,000 in 1920, to 600,000 in 1921, and to what proved to be a post-war normal of about 560,000 in 1922.[1]

Preparedness

The first emergency problems involving the employment of civilians stemmed from the Mexican border campaign. The head of the Tenth Civil Service District, including Texas and Louisiana, reported to the Commission in 1916:

The problems arising from the temporary employment of hundreds of civilians in all lines of endeavor—mechanical, clerical, and technical—in connection with the Army mobilization on the Mexican border, are yet to be solved when this is written. Not the least of these problems now

[1] For a summary of most of the statistical data available concerning civil employment during the First World War, see Stella Stewart, *The Federal Service in World War I and in the Post-War Period* (Washington: Bureau of Labor Statistics, 1943). The figures quoted here exclude employees of the nationalized railroads and telephone, telegraph, and cable systems as well as the thousands of civilian volunteers associated with the draft boards, the food and fuel programs, etc.

250

engrossing attention is that of satisfactorily keeping records so that none of these temporary employees may be lost sight of and their identity as temporary employees disappear. This will be no small task when it is considered that persons have been appointed in all sections of the country, and sent to the border for temporary service and are being transferred indiscriminately, whereas temporary employment under ordinary conditions is purely local and comparatively easy of supervision.[2]

From the spring of 1916 on, the recruitment problems of the Civil Service Commission rapidly increased in both magnitude and complexity. The number of initial appointments to the civil service for the fiscal year of 1917 was double that of 1916, and that for 1918 was two and one-half times that of 1917.[3] This placed a heavy burden on the Commission, but one which, up to the declaration of war with Germany, it carried with little difficulty. The Mexican campaign merely provided a small-scale dress rehearsal for greater things to come.

The increased employment burden of the Commission was not only a result of demands for a greater absolute number of public employees. It was also a result of the growing need to replace civil personnel inducted into the armed forces, a need first felt during the Mexican border clash. In the summer of 1916 Congress enacted legislation similar to that now in effect, which authorized public employees called into the armed services to return to their former jobs. This was soon implemented by executive orders which set up reemployment registers and which outlined more precisely the procedures by which former civil servants might be reinstated at the end of their military service. For the first time in our history an attempt was made to systematize the return to their original positions of public employees called away during wartime emergencies.[4]

Up to the actual declaration of war against Germany in the spring of 1917 there was no greatly expanded demand for civil employees from any segment of the executive branch except the War Department. Despite frequent suggestions that the War Department might expedite employment procedures by hiring outside the framework of the merit system, this agency consistently refused to consider such an alternative. Secretary of War Newton D. Baker was especially adamant on this point, and throughout the wartime period his department maintained close relations with the Civil Service Commission. Late in 1917, however, the Ordnance Department created its own extensive

---

[2] USCSC, *Thirty-third Report*, 1916, p. 139.
[3] USCSC, *Fifty-seventh Report*, 1940, p. 131.
[4] See USCSC, *Thirty-fourth Report*, 1917, pp. xi and 18, for some of these laws and regulations. During the Civil War one might himself hire a substitute to hold down a position pending return.

machinery for independent recruiting, especially of civilian employees for the arsenals. The Quartermaster General and the Adjutant General soon followed suit, though on a smaller scale.[5]

From the standpoint of the future of personnel administration, the most important development lay within the military itself. Early in the war the Army introduced a "personnel-classification" scheme into its established procedures. This was the first time any really large organization, either public or private, attempted, on a systematic basis, to determine the capabilities of all its individual members and to assign them accordingly. Not perfect by any means, the new system was an innovation of first rank.[6] The experience gained with this device was utilized by the entire military establishment during World War II.

The Navy Department, too, was gradually stepping up its operations in accord with a "big navy" policy. Here Secretary of the Navy Josephus Daniels had in the early years of the Wilson administration introduced a major change into the Navy's officer personnel system when he established merit and sea duty, rather than seniority, as requisites for officer promotion.[7] Later the Army also emphasized matters other than time in grade as indexes of military efficiency. Modern military personnel procedures date largely from these innovations of World War I. There were also considerable repercussions on private industry.

Not until early 1917 was any real planning for wartime emergencies possible for the Civil Service Commission or other governmental agencies. In his effort to keep the United States at peace, President Wilson firmly discouraged any overt preparations for war. Civil Service Commission representatives were not officially warned to prepare for war until March 26, 1917, just ten days before the declaration of hostilities.[8] The War and Navy Departments then endeavored to develop estimates of their future civilian employment needs for the guidance of the Commission.

5 From a copy of a letter to President Wilson from Richard Henry Dana as President of the National Civil Service Reform League, January 5, 1918. NCSRL Papers, IV, Jb5.

6 For the development of this classification system see Committee on Classification of Personnel in the Army. *The Personnel System of the United States Army* (2 vols.; Washington: [War Department], 1919). As compared to civilian "position-classification," military "personnel-classification" refers to an arrangement of people separated according to abilities rather than of jobs separated according to duties.

7 Josephus Daniels, *The Wilson Era: Years of Peace* (Chapel Hill: University of North Carolina Press, 1944), pp. 279–87.

8 Date supplied by the late Kenneth C. Vipond, a wartime employee of the Commission and one-time Assistant Chief Examiner, in an interview on September 2, 1948. See also Josephus Daniels, *The Wilson Era: Years of War and After* (Chapel Hill: University of North Carolina Press, 1946), pp. 22–30.

Civilian Recruitment [9]

With the formal beginning of hostilities on April 6 of 1917 the demands for civilian employees began to rocket. Direct phone lines were established between the Commission and the major war agencies, and twenty-four-hour service was frequently provided. The effect of the first request for immediate action from the War Department has been related by Matthew Halloran, a long-time employee of the Commission:

The first call from the War Department came to me by telephone late one afternoon for one hundred and twenty-five stenographers and typists to report the next morning at ten o'clock. The Department said that it did not care for a list of names and examination papers, but wanted people immediately for assignment duty. If it could not get them at the time mentioned it would go on the outside and make the appointments, it was stated. On my desk were now three 'phones, one direct with the War Department. I at once reported this request to Mr. McIlhenny [President of the Commission]. He said, "How can we get them on such short notice?" I replied, "With the Commission's permission one hundred and fifty telegrams will be at once sent to the eligibles living nearby to report next morning to this office at nine o'clock for immediate appointment. Those found willing to accept will be sent to the War Department." He said, "Telegraph them. In all matters of appointment you are now the Commission. Call upon help whenever needed in any part of the office. If any question is raised, come to me. Report to me daily." The fullest cooperation existed at all times. I never had occasion to ask him to back me up. My force was kept busy sending telegrams till after six o'clock. The next morning promptly at nine o'clock one hundred and forty-five persons responded and one hundred and thirty-five said they would accept and report at once for duty. These I sent to the War Department. At nine forty-five the War Department clerk, William D. Searle, called me up and said, "Do not send any more. The corridors are lined with people. There are not enough desks to place them." The first call was met and filled on the dot. Mr. McIlhenny was delighted. The same expeditiousness was used throughout whenever the occasion required.[10]

Early successes. Still another wartime innovation developed from the Commission's dealings with the Navy. A little more than a month after the war started, Franklin Roosevelt, then in charge of the naval shore establishments as Assistant Secretary of the Navy, requested through Louis M. Howe, even then his secretary, that the Civil Service Commission immediately furnish 1,400 men for the Philadelphia

[9] For the problems involved in the use of source materials for this section, see the "supplementary notes" to this chapter.
[10] Matthew F. Halloran, *The Romance of the Merit System* (2d ed.; Washington: Judd and Detweiler, Inc., 1929), pp. 118–19.

navy yard, including some hard-to-get specialists. The Commission replied that it could recruit them in other parts of the country, but that many of the men had no money for travelling expenses. Would the Navy advance them the money? Howe replied that it would, and a new system of recruitment was started, which the War Department later followed.[11] Through the entire war much of the greatly expanding recruiting for arsenals and navy yards was handled through the Commission's local boards, aided in publicity matters and staff work by the military departments and frequently by the Department of Labor, the American Federation of Labor, and private industry.

At the beginning of the war the Commission reported that there were approximately 100,000 names on its eligible registers, which it began to augment as rapidly as possible. During the fiscal year of 1917 the number of examinations increased 37 per cent and the number of appointments doubled. By November, 1917, the Commission had been asked to supply approximately 100,000 additional workers to the federal service over and above the normal complement of peacetime employees and replacements.[12] Evidently, the Commission was able to meet major personnel needs during the first months of the war. In May, 1917, the National Civil Service Reform League stated, "In spite of niggardly appropriations and other mechanical difficulties the United States Civil Service Commission is not only keeping its head above water, but it is swimming vigorously and is keeping well in advance of the severe schedule that has been imposed on it." [13] However, the League warned that the Commission needed additional funds as well as the cooperation of other agencies in the accurate estimation of wartime personnel needs. It further suggested that a personnel officer be appointed within the Council for National Defense, to coordinate the Council's and the departments' requests to the Commission. Later it proposed the creation of a special advisory board to assist the Commission in its emerging employment problems.[14] Neither of these last two proposals was ever adopted. The Commission itself was apparently pleased with the public support it received. It reported in 1917:

. . . Without the active support of public opinion and the unwavering cooperation of the President and heads of departments, the maintenance of the civil-service rules in their entirety would not have been possible. The

---

11 As recalled by Guy Moffett, wartime employee of the Civil Service Commission and one-time Assistant Chief Examiner, in an interview on April 23, 1947.

12 USCSC, *Thirty-fourth Report*, 1917, pp. vii and xix.

13 "The Initial Victory," *Good Government*, XXXIV (May, 1917), 34.

14 See same; "The League and the National Defense," *Good Government*, XXXIV (June, 1917), 37–38; and "The Civil Service Throughout the Country," *Good Government*, XXXIV (August, 1917), 57.

effective coordination of the civil and military branches of the Government was possible only by the enforcement of the merit system.[15]

Criticism in mid-stream. By the fall of 1917 the National Civil Service Reform League began to be increasingly critical of the efforts of the Civil Service Commission. The League was especially disturbed by the growing number of exceptions to and exclusions from the merit system which were being permitted.

Personnel hired under the War Risk Insurance Act of 1914 were, before its amendment, outside the merit system. By an executive order of November 21, 1917, President Wilson authorized Herbert Hoover to choose his staff for the Food Administration without complying with the civil service rules. The Fuel Administration was then accorded the same authority. In its annual report the Civil Service Commission maintained that the Food Administration order was made on its advice, because part of the money with which the employees were paid came from other than federal sources. Nevertheless, in January, 1918, the Bureau of Printing and Engraving, hardly an emergency agency, was for the duration of the war permitted to employ without regard to the civil service rules. This exemption was followed in March, 1918, by the extension of the same privilege to the United States Employment Service and to the ordnance plants of the War Department. In July, 1918, skilled laborers of the Government Printing Office and employees of the War Labor Administration Service were also excepted from examination.

These exceptions were attacked by the Reform League as evidences of the inability of the Commission to supply adequate lists of eligibles. Taking a further tack, the League charged that appointing officers were finding fault with clerical registers which contained eligibles with too academic a background and no experience.[16] The Commission defended itself in its annual report for the fiscal year of 1918 by saying that in its opinion the merit system had been preserved, and that all exceptions had been carefully considered and were as the law intended.[17]

Whether the Commission simply could not fulfill all its obligations or whether it was encouraging legitimate exceptions is difficult now to determine. It is the opinion of some that McIlhenny and Chief Examiner George R. Wales, through their willingness to compromise on a few exceptions, prevented the wholesale suspension of the merit system. Certainly many of the new wartime organizations, manned by

---

[15] *Thirty-fourth Report,* 1917, pp. v–vi.

[16] For example, see *Good Government,* XXXV (February, 1918), pp. 17–18.

[17] *Thirty-fifth Report,* 1918, p. vii; see pp. 88–89 for a list of the exceptions made by executive order during the fiscal year of 1918.

persons not always familiar with merit system rules and regulations, often found them irksome and wished to get out from under the Commission's rather strict employment controls. Fiorello H. La-Guardia, then a congressman, has blamed this tendency together with the temptations of patronage:

The number of civilian jobs we were creating by our acts of Congress was enormous. I made every effort I could to have as many of these jobs as possible subject to our Civil Service regulations, whenever that could be done without any hindrance to the war effort. There was great danger that our whole system of appointment by Civil Service examination . . . would be broken down if we allowed the excuse of war emergency to be used for that purpose by greedy politicians. There were plenty of cases where the excuse that we could not wait for such a thing as a Civil Service examination was being used to get political henchmen jobs whether or not they were qualified for the work. A big food survey was ordered by act of Congress. I succeeded in getting an amendment passed providing that the jobs created under that survey should come under Civil Service, after I had read a letter from J. A. McIlhenny, President of the Civil Service Commission, assuring us that his organization could handle the job without any delay. But I failed in a similar effort to prevent exemption from Civil Service regulations for the large increase in the personnel of the Bureau of Mines to handle our greatly expanded explosives production. Democratic Congressmen then in the majority wanted as many "deserving Democrats" as possible to get those jobs, no matter what their abilities or qualifications.[18]

In fairness to the Wilson administration, it must be admitted that the exceptions allowed were not sweeping and that nearly all of them were for the duration of the emergency only. Moreover, such agencies as the Food and Fuel Administrations had permission to use the Commission's registers as they saw fit, a privilege of which they frequently took advantage. Nevertheless, there were many exceptions made and some of them are hard to justify.

But the League had more than the fact of exceptions to point to as evidence of Commission inadequacy as the war got under way. All through the summer of 1917 the League kept prodding the Commission to request more adequate appropriations for its expanded workload. Apparently funds were available for the asking, but it was not until late September that the Commission was granted an allotment of $250,000—a sum equal to about two-thirds of the Commission's annual appropriation—from the President's special funds for national security and defense. At the same time the League was objecting to the Commission's seeming failure to adjust its procedures to wartime

18 *The Making of an Insurgent* (Philadelphia: J. B. Lippincott Co., 1948), pp. 154–55.

requirements. In November, 1917, both the Commission and the Ordnance Department requested the League to assist them in several types of recruitment. In so doing, the League discovered that the Commission was still conducting five-and-one-half-hour typist examinations. The League quickly recommended that these be cut to one hour, a proposal to which the Commission agreed. In February, 1918, the League noted that the Commission was still grading most of its field service examinations in Washington. All through the winter of 1917–18 the League kept pressing for more positive recruiting methods and more streamlined examination procedures, citing at various times a number of complaints from wartime agencies. That the Commission did not entirely appreciate the gadfly attitude of the League at this time is clear from a series of letters between League and Commission representatives. Nevertheless, the League's criticisms apparently had some effect. The spring of 1918 seems to have marked both the low point of the Commission's prestige in the eyes of the Reform League as well as a significant revision of Commission procedures.[19]

Full stream again. From March, 1918, the evidence points to a greater realization by the Commission of the necessity of new and streamlined methods. In its report for the fiscal year of 1918 the Commission indicated that it had decentralized many more operations to its field districts. It spoke of "making" eligibles through contacts with universities and training schools. It urged stenographic pools in the departments. It revised its methods of recruiting publicity so far as to send out traveling recruiters, who advertised through local newspapers and organizations, and then rated and put the successful applicants on the train. It was successful in supplying laborers to build temporary housing needed in Washington. The bulk of the personnel used to build the Muscle Shoals dam was hired through the Commission, and it supplied workers for many of the Army cantonments being constructed throughout the nation. Both the War and Navy departments gave the Commission authority to employ labor directly without consulting the departments, and over 80,000 persons were thus furnished in 1917 and 1918. All told, in nineteen months the Civil Service Commission examined slightly less than a million individuals and placed approximately 400,000 of them in the public service.

The Commission as a wartime recruiting agency. Aside from its initial successes, the effectiveness of the Civil Service Commission during World War I is difficult to evaluate. Almost all of the public criticism of the Commission's efforts came from the Reform League, which, in

[19] For details of this controversy, see the Reform League's monthly periodical, *Good Government*, Vols. XXIV and XXV, 1917–18; and the NCSRL Papers for the winter of 1917–18.

light of its earlier controversies with the Commission over the postal service, cannot be considered an entirely unprejudiced source. Moreover, during the period of greatest League criticism, the winter of 1917–18, the disastrous influenza epidemic was impeding all administrative matters, private as well as public. Finally, while there was little public praise of the Commission, the only important tribute to its efforts, made by Secretary of War Baker in late 1919, is an impressive one:

. . . I desire to express my appreciation of the untiring and efficient efforts of the Civil Service Commission.

During the entire war the department and the commission have worked in helpful cooperation. The commission through its various representatives scattered throughout the country recruited many thousands of civilian employees, examined into their qualifications, and also into the qualifications of other thousands recruited by various bureaus of the department in cooperation with the commission and otherwise. It is doubtful whether this important work could have been performed satisfactorily by the department without the aid of the commission; certainly not except at great inconvenience and probably vastly greater expense. The results have justified and strengthened the department's confidence in the efficiency of the civil-service system. . . .[20]

In final analysis, the question of whether the Commission faltered somewhat in midstream or whether it steadfastly preserved the merit system in the face of great obstacles is largely a matter of opinion which will probably never be settled. The only reasonable conclusion in terms of the information now available is that the Commission did quite acceptable work under unprecedented conditions. As pointed out by the National Civil Service Reform League, its major difficulties seem to have lain in an initial inability to foresee the need to alter its examination procedures and to decentralize its operations.

Any deeper probe of the Commission's wartime activities must evaluate the impact of personal differences among the commissioners. They had been at odds before the declaration of war and apparently the breach widened as time passed. At least twice during 1917 Commissioners Craven and Galloway together obtained interviews with President Wilson, and of one of the two interviews Ray Stannard Baker has indicated that "unsatisfactory conditions" within the Commission formed the subject of discussion.[21] What these "conditions" were is hard to state precisely. Presumably they had to do with Com-

---

20 U.S. War Department, *Annual Report of the Secretary of War for 1919* (Washington: Government Printing Office, 1919), p. 87.
21 *Woodrow Wilson* (8 vols.; New York: Doubleday, Doran and Co., 1931–39), VII, 148 and 153.

missioner McIlhenny, President of the Commission, for he was conspicuously absent from these two conferences. An original appointee and personal friend of Theodore Roosevelt, a long-time and well-informed commissioner, and a man of extensive political and social connections who fully knew his way around official Washington, McIlhenny seems to have "run" the Commission sometimes in a dictatorial manner not always fully appreciated by his colleagues.[22]

But even the Reform League recognized that the defects which it criticized had been largely remedied by the spring of 1918, and at no point was the Civil Service Commission in serious trouble. How much the commissioners own disagreements added to the confusion and temporary delay in the mobilization of their agency's full potential is pure speculation. All we now know is that after the Armistice it was only a few months before all three of the commissioners retired amidst a barrage of publicity.

Improvisation

Relaxing the rules. A number of civil service rules changes were, of course, necessary to meet the emergency. Age limits were either modified or eliminated. The residence and apportionment requirements were waived for emergency agencies. Reinstatement privileges were lengthened. The old rigid transfer regulations were modified. The President authorized the Commission to give noncompetitive examinations whenever it felt they were appropriate. It was even permitted to utilize state, county, and municipal civil service registers should they be available and meet federal requirements. Scientific, technical, and professional employees were allowed to resign and take important state, county, municipal, or foreign positions with the understanding they might be reinstated within three years without loss of status.[23]

Housing. A major public employee problem during the entire emergency was housing, especially in Washington. In the fall of 1917 the Commission reported to President Wilson that a lack of housing was seriously affecting the civilian employee recruiting program in the capital. However, it was a full year before any large-scale construction commenced. During that time the number of governmental employees in the District of Columbia increased from 40,000 to 120,000. By August, 1918, the resignations were equal to 50 per cent of the ap-

---

[22] This is also the conclusion expressed in an interview on April 27, 1947, by H. Eliot Kaplan, an employee of the National Civil Service Reform League during the First World War and later the Secretary of the League.

[23] See executive orders of March 26, April 17, and May 22, 1917.

259

pointments, with inadequate housing a major factor in many separations. By September, 1918, the situation became so critical that further appointments in the capital were almost completely suspended. The problem was never satisfactorily solved.[24]

Military service of federal employees. The effects of military enlistments and the draft upon federal employment during World War I are difficult to measure. Moreover, the data are scanty. About all we know as to the number of federal employees who went into uniform, is that in the Department of Commerce alone, a relatively small agency, over 1,800 people were involved.[25] If other federal departments lost employees to the military in proportion, perhaps as much as 20 per cent of the federal service was lost in this manner. Meanwhile, the government faced the touchy question of deferments for civil servants. After considerable vacillation, it was decided that men eligible for military service might be held in their civil positions only on the specific request of department heads. Some 5,000 of those stationed in Washington, comprising about 4 per cent of the departmental service, had been thus deferred by October, 1918.[26] In the field service, where there were fewer key positions, the percentage deferred was unquestionably much less.

Women. Under the necessities of wartime, women finally came into their own in the public service. During the war, women received 75 per cent of the Washington appointments and 50 per cent of those in the field.[27] Ultimately more than 20 per cent of the civil service employees were female, compared to between 5 and 10 per cent before the war. After the First World War and up to 1940 there continued to be about one woman in the service for every four to five men, with about 40 per cent of the service in the District of Columbia consisting of women.[28]

At this time appointing officers were not required to select women

24 See USCSC, *Thirty-fifth Report*, 1918, pp. xiv–xv, for a summary of the efforts made.
25 William C. Redfield, *With Congress and Cabinet* (New York: Doubleday, Page and Co., 1924), p. 220.
26 "Civil Servants and the Draft," *Good Government*, XXXV (October, 1918), 147–50.
27 USCSC, *Thirty-sixth Report*, 1919, pp. xx–xxi.
28 U.S. Department of Labor, Women's Bureau, *Women in the Federal Service, Part I: Trends in Employment*, Bulletin 230–I (Washington: Government Printing Office, 1949), pp. 18–19. This document, together with *Part II: Occupational Information*, Bulletin 230–II, comprise the most complete study of the role of women in the federal service for the years from 1923 to 1947. For additional data, especially for earlier periods, see Lucille Foster McMillin, *Women in the Federal Service*, Form 3321, USCSC (Washington: Government Printing Office, 1941); and Avis Marion Saint, "Women in the Public Service," *Public Personnel Studies*, IX (January–February, 1931), 15. For their status in a particular year, see U.S. Department of Labor, Women's Bureau, *The Status of Women in the Government Service in 1925*, Bulletin 53, by Bertha M. Nienburg (Washington: Government Printing Office, 1926).

or even to consider them for vacancies. A 1910 amendment to the civil service rules permitted the Commission to certify women unless the appointing officer specifically said he did not wish them. This helped them some, and up to the First World War the percentage of women in the public service had been slowly rising. During and after the First World War the rights of women in public employment became associated with the general suffrage struggle. After a survey by the Women's Bureau of the Department of Labor had revealed that women were still excluded from 60 per cent of the examinations, the Civil Service Commission opened all tests to both sexes on November 15, 1919. This was a major victory for women's rights. But final discretion remained with the appointing officer. This is still true today. Women have yet to occupy major positions in proportion to their numbers.

The development of the merit system has aided rather than impeded the placement of women in the government service. One effect, however, of the inclusion of women within the public service, especially in the earlier days, has been to depress wages. Used primarily in the lower-paying positions, women also frequently accepted, especially before 1900, reduced wages compared to men in similar positions. In the government service as elsewhere this increased the proportion of low-paid, relatively unskilled positions and depressed the general wage level. This tendency was almost completely eliminated by World War I. The Classification Act of 1923 finally required that women be paid the same as men for equal work.

Temporary employees and turnover. Temporary employees were required in great numbers. The rapid accessions and separations of these employees, together with the movement of personnel resulting from military inductions and from the inducements of higher wages and better working conditions within private industry, tremendously accelerated the turnover in the federal service. Commissioner Wales stated in 1919 that, while the normal turnover rate before the war was 13 per cent annually, it rose to an average of 41 per cent during the war. However, he compared this favorably to the rates in private industry during the same period and referred to several large Detroit industrial plants where the turnover rate averaged 225 per cent during 1916.[29] The government has always been more successful than most industrial employers in retaining its employees. Nevertheless, the turnover rates were often two and one-half times those of the pre-war period and were proving tremendously expensive. For example, about

29 NCSRL, *Proceedings*, 1919, pp. 12–20.

a third of the government's professional and technical employees were replaced each year during the emergency, and declinations of appointments increased from 30 to 50 per cent.[30]

On the Periphery

Government ownership. Representing a distinctive chapter in federal public administration was the brief governmental control and operation of most American communications facilities during World War I. The telephone, telegraph, and cable companies came under the Postmaster General in 1918. While Burleson did not upset most personnel procedures, he opposed needed wage raises. When the unions objected and sought relief through strikes, the Postmaster General maintained the same aggressive anti-union position with respect to the wire services that he had shown in his own department. Taking the position that all wire service employees were now public servants and forbidden to strike, he fired a number of employees and union officials and supported his actions with the argument that the Lloyd-LaFollette Act did not specifically authorize the right to strike. In this he was technically correct, but neither did the act forbid strikes. All this brought Burleson considerable notoriety as well as the enmity of most organized labor. In addition, Burleson was firmly of the belief that great savings could be made by the permanent ownership of the wire services by the government, especially in combination with the already existing postal stations and personnel. He had in mind the combination of these services with the post offices, which had been typical of France for many years. However, no savings materialized during the war, and the very considerable criticism of the Postmaster General's operation of the wire services undoubtedly influenced President Wilson to recommend their return to their original owners shortly after the end of the war. Congress quickly concurred, with the result that these services remained under governmental control for barely a year.[31]

More important to the success of the war was the centralized control of the railroads, which had seemed incapable of the unified effort

---

30 For an analysis of the available figures see Mary Conyngton, "Separations from the Government Service," Monthly Labor Review, XI (December, 1920); and USCSC, Thirty-sixth Report, 1919, pp. viii–xi.

31 On these matters see the annual reports of the Post Office Department for 1917 through 1920; Albert S. Burleson, "Why We Should Keep the Wires," Forum, LXI (January, 1919), 152; William Hard, "Mr. Burleson, Back From Boston," New Republic, XIX (May 3, 1919), 15; William F. Willoughby, Government Organization in Wartime and After (New York: D. Appleton and Co., 1919), pp. 195–98; and U.S. Post Office Department, Government Control and Operation of Telegraph, Telephone, and Marine Cable Systems (Washington: Government Printing Office, 1921).

necessary to handle the vast logistical support required for the military operations in Europe. Under the direction of Secretary of the Treasury McAdoo, a precarious situation was straightened out and permanent ownership of the railroads was briefly considered. Nevertheless, they were returned to their owners not long after the return of the wire services, though the Transportation Act of 1920, which accomplished the transfer, greatly strengthened the government's hand with respect to future regulation.

We know a good deal about the personnel decisions involved in McAdoo's direction of this sizable segment of American enterprise.[32] The Attorney General early ruled that railroad employees were not subject to the Pendleton Act. On August 31, 1918, however, Secretary McAdoo issued a directive that no railroad employees should take part in partisan political activity. The major immediate problem was that of wages and salaries. As Director General of the Railroads, the Secretary was authorized to regulate these matters with considerable discretion. Amazingly, he set top salaries at $25,000 to $50,000, while he himself received but $12,000. In marked contrast to Burleson's policies, McAdoo's wage raise authorizations for the lower levels were generally in accord with the cost of living. They were also considerably more generous than those granted to the bulk of public employees by Congress. In carrying out these financial policies he received little criticism. It is an interesting commentary on American psychology as concerns governmental and business matters that such differentials could have been permitted without much protest or even any great comment at the time.

Volunteers. Important in its implications for the future was the great influx of dollar-a-year men into the governmental mechanism at all levels. This type of employment stemmed from a desire to circumvent a federal statute of 1905, which forbade the employment of personnel by the federal government without compensation. Congress, jealous of any infringement of its investigative powers, had aimed at controlling Theodore Roosevelt's practice of using unpaid commissions for presidential advice. While the statute failed in this respect, it was more successful in reducing potential claims upon the government and in preventing undesirable assumptions of governmental authority by persons improperly appointed. A decision by the Attorney General in 1913 distinguished between "gratuitous" serv-

---

[32] See William G. McAdoo, *Crowded Years* (Boston: Houghton Mifflin Co., 1931), pp. 473–74; USCSC, *Thirty-fifth Report*, 1918, p. xvii; Walker D. Hines, *War History of American Railroads* (New Haven, Conn.: Yale University Press, 1929), especially pp. 26–27 and ch. xiv, "Labor"; and W. M. W. Splawn, *Government Ownership and Operation of the Railroads* (New York: The Macmillan Co., 1928), ch. xvii.

ices and voluntary services which had, in essence, been contracted for. Nevertheless, there was still some ambiguity in the 1905 legislation, and the dollar-a-year device was invented to overcome any objections. In addition, the Defense Act of 1916 authorized the use of experts from industry "without compensation." [33] Large numbers of persons entered the public service during World War I under these two devices, particularly the first. The Council of National Defense, the War Industries Board, and allied agencies used especially large numbers of volunteers. Nearly all regular departments and agencies employed them too, including the War Department and the Navy, though the former much more than the latter. The Civil Service Commission itself used over one hundred dollar-a-year employees, mostly in army camps at the end of the war to explain opportunities in the public service to returning veterans.[34] Many more persons, for patriotic or other reasons, besieged the civil and military agencies for appointments. Mrs. J. Borden Harriman has described some of the difficulties involved for all concerned:

. . . Even before war was declared and ever since, people have been swarming to Washington with all sorts of propositions. Being New York business men, most of them, they are terribly impatient of the delay. They will have to learn how slowly the wheels of government grind. People seem to think that because you live in Washington you can go out and pick commissions and appointments off trees. Like everyone else, I am having the most unique requests. I have worn out my boot leather running between here and the War Department.[35]

While some of these volunteers were accused of using their public position to promote private interests, such was far from the general case. On the whole the use of such persons worked well for emergency purposes. The alternatives were to raise government salaries to astronomical heights, draft labor and management, or put the experts in uniform. The first two alternatives were not even considered, but the

33 Apparently this term, from which the now-common designation of "WOC" has come, was first officially used in this statute.
34 For a general study of the problem, with a brief historical introduction, see U.S. Congress, House, Antitrust Subcommittee of the Committee on the Judiciary, *Interim Report on WOC's and Government Advisory Groups*, 84th Cong., 2d Sess., April 24, 1956 (Washington: Government Printing Office, 1956). See also USCSC, *Thirty-sixth Report*, 1919, p. 111; and Josephus Daniels, *The Wilson Era: Years of War and After* (Chapel Hill: University of North Carolina Press, 1946), pp. 237–39.
35 Mrs. J. Borden Harriman, *From Pinafores to Politics* (New York: Henry Holt and Co., 1923), p. 222. The National Civil Service Reform League records contain considerable correspondence with persons who offered their services and who did not receive replies from the departments or the Civil Service Commission. The League officers were most critical of the Civil Service Commission in the handling of such offers. NCSRL Papers, IV.

last was frequently done, as in the case of General Charles G. Dawes and many others.

Beyond the volunteers who participated directly in the administrative process, civil or military, there were the myriads of others manning the draft boards, serving on industry committees, assisting in food and fuel conservation, and the like. There are no firm estimates of the total personnel involved, but the Four Minute Men assisting the Committee on Public Information numbered at least 75,000, and the membership of the American Protective League, an officially recognized adjunct of the Department of Justice, probably reached 250,000.[36]

The Civil Service Commission's estimates of full-time civil employment become grossly inadequate when we add to them the employees of the nationalized railroads and wire services, the men and women in the armed services, and the hordes of volunteers of all types and varieties. Direct public participation in the affairs of the national government at the height of World War I probably topped eight million by a considerable margin. This participation in large-scale governmental action in time of crisis was not soon to be forgotten, with delayed results in years to come.

Loyalty

After the repeal of the Alien and Sedition Acts, our next major effort to wrestle with the tricky problem of loyalty investigations had occurred, as might be expected, during the Civil War, when the loyalty oath became the symbol of fidelity.[37] Civil War experience was neither satisfactory nor applicable to World War I conditions. While little can be said for the "Red Scare" which followed the war, the Wilson administration must be given credit for proceeding with a minimum of fuss and feathers in its public employee loyalty program during the war. Actually, the very existence of President Wilson's loyalty program, initiated the day after the congressional resolution proclaimed a state of war, was largely forgotten until well after World War II.

The first step was taken by the Civil Service Commission on April 5, 1917, when it wrote President Wilson as follows:

---

[36] James R. Mock and Cedric Larson, *Words That Won the War* (Princeton, N.J.: Princeton University Press, 1939), p. 118; and Carl McFarland and Homer Cummings, *Federal Justice* (New York: The Macmillan Co., 1937), p. 421.

[37] The principal study of loyalty procedures during the Civil War is Harold M. Hyman, *Era of the Oath* (Philadelphia: University of Pennsylvania Press, 1954).

The Commission considers it to be its duty to suggest the desirability of an order intended to safeguard the public interest in the present National crisis by excluding from the government any person of whose loyalty to the government there is reasonable doubt.[38]

Wilson replied on April 7 with the following directive:[39]

CONFIDENTIAL

EXECUTIVE ORDER

In the exercise of the power vested in the President by the Constitution and the resolution of Congress of April 6, 1917, the following order is issued:

The head of a department or independent office may forthwith remove any employee when he has ground for believing that the retention of such employee would be inimical to the public welfare by reason of his conduct, sympathies, or utterances, or because of other reasons growing out of the war. Such removal may be made without other formality than that the reasons shall be made a matter of confidential record, subject, however, to inspection by the Civil Service Commission.

This order is issued solely because of the present international situation, and will be withdrawn when the emergency is passed.

WOODROW WILSON

The White House
7 April, 1917

Issued directly to the Commission, the order was shortly relayed to the other departments and agencies, along with a request "that in each case of removal under this order you advise it [the Commission] under confidential cover of the name of the person removed and of the fact that the removal is made under this order."[40] Under the terms of this brief but sweeping authorization, seemingly at odds with the intent of both the Pendleton and the Lloyd-LaFollette acts, action commenced in the departments. At the same time, another executive order authorized the Commission to refuse to examine or certify an applicant for a position in the civil service if there were reason to suspect that his appointment would be against the public interest on the grounds of suspected loyalty.[41] A little more than a year later Con-

---

38 As quoted in Harry B. Mitchell, "The President's Loyalty Plan," *Personnel Information Bulletin* of the Veterans Administration, V (November, 1950), 2–3.

39 Same, p. 3.

40 For a copy of Commission President McIlhenny's letter to the Attorney General and the latter's acknowledgment, see Edward S. Corwin, *The President: Office and Powers* (3d rev. ed.; New York: New York University Press, 1948), pp. 433–34.

41 Mitchell, as cited in footnote 38, p. 3. This and the above orders were never promulgated as is the case with most executive orders and evidently were so little known as to excite no comment or challenge during World War I. Issued primarily under the general authority of the President, these directives are suggestive of the constitutional power of the President and the constitutional limits of congressional action with respect to removals when the President cares to contest the issue.

gress passed the Sedition Act of 1918, which contained the following provision:

> . . . That any employee or official of the United States Government who commits any disloyal act or utters any unpatriotic or disloyal language, or who, in an abusive and violent manner criticizes the Army or Navy or the flag of the United States shall be at once dismissed from the service. Any such employee shall be dismissed by the head of the department in which the employee may be engaged, and any such official shall be dismissed by the authority having power to appoint a successor to the dismissed official.[42]

This sweeping legislation was repealed in the spring of 1921, but there is as yet no evidence that Wilson's original order was ever withdrawn as the President evidently contemplated when he issued it.

There seems to be no record of the cumulative actions taken by the departments under the authority of either Wilson's order or the Sedition Act, despite the request that the departments and agencies report to the Commission.[43] But there is information concerning the Commission's loyalty operations under its own special authorization. Commencing almost immediately to screen applicants, the Commission formally noted in its annual reports that from 1917 to 1921 it investigated and "debarred from future examinations" a total of 868 persons for reasons relating to "disloyalty." Over 800 of these cases probably arose during the wartime period, but at least 51 of them were reported as being decided during the two years *following* the cessation of hostilities.[44] Apparently the Commission's loyalty program terminated with the formal termination of the war in 1921. Exactly what was the basis for determining the nature of "disloyalty" is not clear. All we can be sure of at this time is that loyalty was investigated in some fashion both during the war itself and for a period after it as well. But these activities quickly faded from public memory and failed to form any effective precedent for the future.

Reconversion of the Civil Service

The orderly reduction in size of the governmental establishment and the reassimilation into the service of those who had left for the armed forces were immediate and pressing necessities at the end of the

---

[42] 40 U.S. Statutes 555.

[43] From correspondence with Professor Hyman, author of the study of Civil War loyalty procedures, cited in footnote 37, the writer understands that a study of World War I procedures may be forthcoming.

[44] These figures are calculated from data provided in the Commission's annual reports for 1918, p. xxiv; 1919, p. xxix; 1920, p. xxxii; and 1921, p. xlvi.

First World War.[45] Unlike in World War II, no category of temporary "war service employees," subject to immediate release from the civil service at the end of the conflict, had been established. Nevertheless, the reduction of the service throughout 1919 and 1920 was accomplished without too much difficulty, assisted more by the natural course of events than by any deliberate efforts of the government.

While most agencies were rapidly decreasing in size, a few were increasing their working forces. The Bureau of War Risk Insurance, the Federal Board for Vocational Education, the Internal Revenue Service, and certain branches of the Treasury, War, and Navy departments were among those hiring additional personnel after the war. The Commission immediately recommended the establishment of a more complete system of reappointment registers, and this was authorized by President Wilson on November 29, 1918. It was soon discovered that these registers would not fully meet the demand. The greatest requirement was for technical employees, who were then the ones most rapidly leaving the service and returning to private enterprise. In the War Department, for instance, of a group of seventy-seven employees to be released only seven desired reappointment and not all of these were of the categories most sought for by other agencies. Nevertheless, these registers furnished three-fourths of the eligibles needed within the District of Columbia for about a year and a half.[46] That they did not furnish the entire number was principally because poor housing conditions and inadequate pay kept many from remaining in the government service. Others who had come to the capital or elsewhere only for temporary wartime reasons left to resume their normal occupations. Thus, while the service was quickly reduced in numbers, it was extremely difficult to maintain a desirable occupational balance.

At the same time, the reemployment of military personnel was undertaken. An executive order of July 18, 1918, guaranteed to civil employees serving in the military reinstatement in their original departments within one year of discharge and in any other agency within five years. The Secretaries of War and the Navy also permitted the Commission to place representatives in discharge stations to explain the new provisions as well as to advertise for new personnel of the required skills.

---

45 For contemporary accounts of some of these reconversion problems see Herbert E. Morgan, "The Civil Service in Post-War Readjustment," *The Annals*, LXXXII (March, 1919), 100–10; USCSC, *Thirty-seventh Report*, 1920, pp. i–xl; and Halloran, as cited in footnote 10, p. 140. See also Stella Stewart, *Demobilization of Manpower, 1918–1919*, Bulletin 784, U.S. Bureau of Labor Statistics (Washington: Government Printing Office, 1944).

46 USCSC, *Thirty-seventh Report*, 1920, pp. xi–xii.

The most specific congressional assistance to civil demobilization was an authorization for the payment of transportation expenses to those who would return to their homes within a given period. But by greatly reducing the funds of the United States Employment Service and by cutting the appropriations of the Civil Service Commission, Congress was otherwise more of a hindrance than a help. The Commission found that it again had to resort to details of employees from other departments in order to accomplish its work. In addition, the Commission found itself subject to the same rapid turnover of personnel which was afflicting other governmental agencies.

By 1922 the volunteers and dollar-a-year men had almost entirely departed and the civil service had returned to a figure of about 560,000.[47] This was to represent the post-war level of the service for the next ten years.

Veteran Preference

Out of the First World War came the first full scale, enforced veteran preference regulations.[48] This time the veterans did not make the mistake of Civil War veterans who waited until memories were dim. They organized quickly and secured the swift enactment of several sweeping preferential provisions by Congress. The first was contained in a section of the census act of March 3, 1919, which granted preference in the Washington departments only. The second was a part of the deficiency act of July 11, 1919, and provided for preference generally throughout the classified service. Not only were honorably discharged veterans themselves included but also their widows and the wives of those too disabled to obtain government employment. Finally, by congressional act and executive order, age limits were waived; veterans were permitted to go to the top of the registers for which they received passing marks; their passing mark was made five points lower than that for nonveterans; many physical requirements were waived; and reinstatement privileges were liberalized. The Civil Service Commission analyzed the situation in its report for 1919 and concluded that, while the preference laws might not then react to the detriment of the service, they might in the future when there

---

[47] Herbert Hoover has noted the rapidity of the demobilization of a large segment of the Food Administration. Within sixty days Edgar Rickard "had reduced our other staff from some 3,000 then in the Washington office to about 400. Equally rapidly were the State and local organizations liquidated." *The Memoirs of Herbert Hoover: Years of Adventure* (New York: The Macmillan Co., 1951), p. 280. He suggests also that the term "administrator" was probably first used with respect to his position as the head of the Food Administration. Same, p. 242.

[48] The principal reference work on veteran preference is USCSC, *History of Veteran Preference in Federal Employment* (Washington: Government Printing Office, 1955).

were fewer veterans and only the more inefficient were searching for employment.[49]

From March, 1919, to November, 1920, the Commission received 80,000 claims for preference. Of these 75,000 were allowed, and 60,-000 claimants succeeded in passing the examinations. A total of 15,750 of these were appointed. About 1,500 veterans were reinstated in the same period.[50] The result was that for the year 1920 veterans comprised 13.6 per cent of the total number appointed. This figure rose to 28.91 per cent the following year and to the highest figure that it ever reached before World War II, 34.12 per cent, in 1923. During only one year from 1921 to 1940 were veterans less than 20 per cent of the total number of appointees.[51]

At its second national convention the American Legion indicated that it had established satisfactory liaison with the Civil Service Commission and that veterans were actually receiving the preference to which they were legally entitled.[52] Of course, from time to time there developed questions of interpretation and policy as to the relative preference of various classes of appointees as well as the total amount and form of the preference. President Harding made a major adjustment in these factors in 1923 when he distinguished between nondisabled and disabled veterans and established our present form of 5 and 10-point preference for nondisabled and disabled veterans, respectively. Both types of veterans lost their privilege of going to the top of the registers, but retained their below-normal passing marks of 65 and 60. After complaints that disabled veterans were not receiving adequate appointments, President Coolidge again placed disabled veterans, along with the wives of those too disabled to obtain employment and the widows of all kinds of veterans, at the top of the registers. At the same time all veterans were accorded preference over nonveterans of equal efficiency in case of reductions-in-force. During the twenties and thirties no other special preference was granted veterans with respect to removals.[53]

By 1934 veterans occupied approximately one-fourth of the total positions in the federal civil service. This was a large proportion of the service to come from a group which then composed less than 10 per cent of the total adult population.[54] A few studies have been made

49 *Thirty-sixth Report*, 1919, pp. xvi–xix.
50 USCSC, *Thirty-seventh Report*, 1920, pp. xiv–xvi.
51 USCSC, *Fifty-seventh Report*, 1940, p. 134.
52 USCSC, *Thirty-seventh Report*, 1920, p. xiv.
53 For other details, such as credit for military experience, reinstatement, apportionment, etc., see USCSC, *History of Veteran Preference in Federal Employment*, as cited in footnote 48, pp. 6–14.
54 This estimate is by the Chief Examiner of the Civil Service Commission, April 12, 1934, as quoted in Commission of Inquiry on Public Service Personnel, *Problems of the American Public Service* (New York: McGraw-Hill Book Co., Inc., 1935), p. 277.

of the effects of veteran preference upon the nature of the government service, but most of these indicate no more than that a number of types of positions have been largely occupied by veterans.[55] The results in terms of morale and efficiency have not been measured. It is questionable if they could be, and with the influx of veterans from World War II it is unlikely that the full effects of the preference resulting from the First World War will ever be determined.

From a chronological standpoint, veteran preference has antedated the merit system in most governmental jurisdictions. However, a full application of veteran preference is possible only under a centralized personnel system, and the two have developed hand in hand. The principal impetus for the preference system seems to have arisen from a combination of humanitarianism and recognition of the importance of veteran voting power. In 1920 preference aided the civilian relocation of veterans by providing an additional source of employment for ex-military personnel. At the same time it also provoked additional administrative friction and dislocation in a government service already suffering from an increasing turnover in personnel. As preference came more into prominence, merit probably tended to retreat, for the two have seldom been synonymous. However, there is very little evidence from which to draw satisfactory conclusions for the period between the two World Wars.[56]

Family Squabbles

During the period of reconversion of the public service, the Civil Service Commission became the center of a public display of recrimination such as never before or since has affected the reputation of that agency. That personal incompatibilities existed has already been suggested. Other evidence is scanty. The National Civil Service Reform League had for some time, publicly and in private communications to President Wilson, advocated the reorganization of the Commission. The League felt that the Commission had supported partisan politics in the postal service and that it had impeded the war effort through its failure quickly to adjust to wartime problems.[57] As early as February, 1918, the League noted in its official organ that it

[55] See, for example, the statistics on veterans contained in the Commission's *Forty-eighth Report*, 1931, pp. 10–11, and 96.

[56] For a comparative study of veteran preference here and abroad, see Albert G. Huegli, "A Study of Veterans' Preference in the Civil Service" (unpublished Ph.D. dissertation, Department of Political Science, Northwestern University, 1944). See also John P. McCarthy, "Veterans' Preference in Public Employment" (unpublished Master's thesis, Department of Political Science, University of Chicago, 1947).

[57] See, for example, "Reorganization Demanded," *Good Government*, XXXV (December, 1918), 184–90; and a copy of a letter from C. C. Burlingham of the League to Colonel E. M. House, February 5, 1918, NCSRL Papers, IV, Jb5.

had verified that Wilson was looking for a successor for Commissioner McIlhenny.[58] The *Boston Herald* later reported that his position had been offered to two or three other persons and that they had declined.[59] Though evidently notifying the Reform League as early as April, 1918, that there would be a change, Wilson did not accept McIlhenny's resignation until February, 1919. The President then appointed him as a financial advisor to Haiti at a yearly stipend of $10,000, twice his former salary. Early in March, the President demanded the resignations of the other two commissioners. Craven's resignation he accepted almost immediately. Galloway's he held until fall.

The sharpness of the presidential action, involving all three of the commissioners, brought forth considerable press comment. Meanwhile, Craven was in May, 1919, made Chief Clerk for the Republican members of the Senate, while Galloway remained temporarily with the Commission, his resignation in Wilson's hands. Speculation continued to mount as the commissioners refused to talk. Apparently neither Craven nor McIlhenny ever made any significant public statements on the questions at issue.[60] But when Galloway was finally retired on the 7th of September, 1919, he let forth a blast to the press, which, among other things, alleged, "My resignation was forced because I would not cooperate with Postmaster General Burleson in debauching the Civil Service and making a sham of the merit system." [61] The argument was, according to Galloway, over the question of the selection of postmasters under the regulations which Taft and Wilson had previously ordered. Galloway charged that Burleson and McIlhenny desired to overly emphasize the reports of post office inspectors as to an incumbent's efficiency, while he claimed that he and Craven favored more reliance on straight examinations on which no influence could be brought to bear. A little earlier it had been alleged that Burleson was holding up postmaster appointments until Galloway was out of the Commission and Burleson could do as he pleased.[62]

Immediately a political tempest arose in Congress, for the disposition of postmasterships is always a touchy subject. The House voted an inquiry on September 11, 1919. Senator George W. Norris of Nebraska introduced a resolution, later adopted, for an investigation of Burleson and alleged that it would show grounds for impeach-

58 "McIlhenny to Quit," *Good Government*, XXXV (February, 1918), 27.
59 August 28, 1919. See also miscellaneous correspondence in NCSRL Papers, IV, Jb5.
60 However, Craven is mentioned by the *Boston Evening Transcript* of September 22, 1919, as supporting Galloway.
61 *New York World*, September 7, 1919.
62 *Boston Herald*, August 28, 1919.

ment. Meanwhile, Burleson protested that he had never tried to influence the Commission "improperly." [63] A few days later the First Assistant Postmaster General, J. C. Koons, and the new President of the Civil Service Commission, Martin A. Morrison, both denied that the Post Office Department was involved.[64] Much political sniping at Burleson and others followed, but no real investigation was ever made. After waiting for more details the National Civil Service Reform League finally concluded at its annual meeting on February 26, 1920, that the committees of Congress were too political to get a "clear judgment of the merits." [65]

Two new commissioners were appointed almost immediately, one of them the former Chief Examiner of the Commission, George R. Wales. The third vacancy was not filled for several months. After partially recovering from his illness, President Wilson chose a woman for this position. Thus, Mrs. Helen Hamilton Gardner, once a militant suffragette, became the first female civil service commissioner. The new Commission apparently functioned without internal difficulty.

Problems of "Superorganization" [66]

As the demands of reconversion were being met and the Commission was undergoing a change of top personnel, the problems of the individual employees in the form of pay, hours, retirement, and the like were becoming more and more a matter of widespread concern. The difficulties have already been suggested. They had been noted by the Keep Committee, the Commission on Economy and Efficiency, the Civil Service Commission, the employee unions, and many others during the years prior to the First World War, but little had been done. The Civil Service Commission still examined and certified applicants. The departments did the rest under little or no guidance. There was still no comprehensive personnel policy for the federal civil establishment nor any agency with power to develop one.

Unionization. The next effort to improve federal personnel practices came from the public employees themselves. The postal unions had been successful in the early years of the century in obtaining for themselves special legislation alleviating some of the worst of their

---

63 *New York Post*, September 10, 1919.

64 *Philadelphia Public Ledger*, September 20, 1919.

65 The two congressional investigations ended as political maneuvers directed at the Postmaster General and almost completely ignored the Commission. See, for example, the *Congressional Record*, 66th Cong., 1st Sess., pp. 5904-11, September 25, 1919, for part of the Senate debate and for further details of the squabble.

66 This is a term used by William E. Mosher in his discussion of the state of the public service in 1920, "A Federal Personnel Policy," *Monthly Labor Review*, XI (July, 1920), p. 23.

grievances. Of the public employee groups, they were the most actively involved in support of the Lloyd-LaFollette Act in 1912. Outside the postal service only a few, mostly local, unions of public employees had been organized in the early years of the twentieth century. In other departments there was seldom the real unity or similarity in interests which promotes the formation of employee unions. To be sure, skilled laborers had for many years been members of the usual craft unions, but before World War I there were no important white-collar employee unions to promote the interests of all public employees in an aggressive manner.[67]

The passage of the Lloyd-LaFollette Act prepared the way for extensive unionization by rescinding the Gag Orders, by tightening the removal restrictions, and by formally legalizing the right to organize on the part of postal workers and, by implication, the rest of the service. But it was not until the First World War that an issue of sufficient importance arose to cause, almost overnight, the formation of a militant employee organization which in its membership crossed departmental as well as professional and craft lines.

The catalytic event which provoked a new unionization movement among public employees was the proposal by Representative William P. Borland of Missouri, late in February, 1916, that the government increase the daily working hours of public employees from seven to eight. This would have meant not only an hour more a day, but probably overtime as well, without additional pay. Of course, the employees vehemently protested. The American Federation of Labor became an interested party, since an increase in federal working hours might have an important bearing upon the future of organized labor. After considerable argument and much pressure from all sides, Congress defeated the measure.

Almost immediately after Borland brought forth his proposal, a small group of clerks in the office of the Quartermaster General of the War Department began to organize. They and a group unionized earlier in the Bureau of Printing and Engraving requested and received a charter from the AF of L. The action of this national labor group was unusual in that it recognized a type of unionism which cut across craft and professional lines, a decision which caused both the AF of L and the new union considerable difficulty later on. This

67 There is no history of government employee unionism as a whole, but for brief treatments of the period before 1916 see Harvey Walker, "Employee Organizations in the National Government Service: The Period Prior to the World War," *Public Personnel Studies*, X (August, 1941), 67–73; Sterling Spero, *Government as Employer* (New York: Remsen Press, 1948), Part II; and Morton R. Godine, *The Labor Problem in the Public Service* (Cambridge, Mass.: Harvard University Press, 1951), scattered.

union was first known as the Federal Employees Union. It organized mass meetings, commenced to publish *The Federal Employee*, and began to promote the further organization of civil servants. Within a year—by February, 1917—about thirty similar bodies had been formed. By September, 1917, when the number of local organizations had increased to nearly seventy, the entire group petitioned the AF of L for a charter as a federation. It was granted and the National Federation of Federal Employees, popularly known as the NFFE, came into being.[68]

The new organization was granted a "jurisdiction broader than that of any other unit in the American Federation of Labor."[69] Through a membership drive the union was successful in increasing from 10,000 members in October, 1917, to 50,000 by June, 1919. By that time, it was the largest single union of government employees, larger even than any union in the Post Office Department.[70] A second unsuccessful attempt by Borland to bring forth his eight-hour proposal in 1918 only aided the membership drive, and eventually the opposition of all organized labor was instrumental in Borland's defeat for reelection.[71]

Several other problems stemming from the war intensified the employees' desire for concerted activity to improve their situation. Prices were still rising. The pay position of government workers in 1916 has been described in the previous chapter. It continued to worsen during the war. Congress, after considerable pressure from organized labor outside the government as well as from the newly-formed federal employee unions, finally passed a bonus bill for the fiscal year of 1917. This same type of legislation was enacted yearly up to and including the fiscal year of 1924, when the Classification Act of 1923 came into force. In amount the bonus varied in different years from 10 per cent of the basic salaries of those receiving less than $1,200 to a flat bonus of $240 for those receiving under $2,500. By 1919, government employees in Washington were receiving an

---

[68] For the formation of the NFFE see Harvey Walker, "Employee Organizations in the National Government Service: The Formation of the National Federation of Federal Employees," *Public Personnel Studies*, X (October, 1941), 130–35; Eldon L. Johnson, "General Unions in the Federal Service," *Journal of Politics*, II (February, 1940), 23–27; Sterling Spero, as cited in footnote 67; and Geniana R. Edwards, "Organized Federal Workers: A Study of Three Representative Unions" (unpublished Master's thesis, Department of Economics, The George Washington University, 1939), pp. 15–26. The last study contains the best discussion of the pressures brought to bear on Congress by the employee unions and the AF of L.

[69] Johnson, as cited in footnote 68, p. 26.

[70] Same, p. 27.

[71] Under the guise of a wartime measure the second Borland Bill got as far as the President, who vetoed it.

275

average of $1,494 a year. However, wages in private industry had also considerably increased, and the government service was still suffering by contrast.[72]

Retirement. Agitation for a retirement plan was a primary plank in the program of the new employee unions. In 1917 the Federal Employees Union promoted the introduction of a bill based on a half-and-half plan—that is, contributions would be half by employees and half by the government. The bill failed but was introduced a second time in 1918, when it again was lost under the pressure of other business. However, public opinion was slowly changing and civil pension legislation became one of the recommendations of the Joint Commission on Reclassification of Salaries early in 1920. At this time several bills were discussed, but the Sterling-Lehlbach measure, introduced by the chairmen of the congressional civil service committees, finally won approval and became law on May 22, 1920.[73]

Several revisions were later necessary in the new law because it did not provide a completely satisfactory financial base for the pension system. To pacify the congressional economy bloc and to make possible the passage of any law at all, certain costs were deferred to a later date, thus making the immediate outlay from taxation almost nothing. As one commentator remarked:

. . . The opposition of Congress to expenditures by the government for retirement was appeased by providing that for the first few years all the expenditures for retirement should be met by using the monies supplied by the contributions of the employees.[74]

Approximately 7,000 employees took advantage of the provisions of this act the first year. However, as it was not an overly generous act, many still found it more desirable to continue in active service as long as possible. The law was also criticized for not always providing benefits in proportion to contributions. These objections were finally met to some extent by two amendments, passed in 1926 and 1930, which made retirement more nearly compulsory than it had been

---

72 U.S. Congress, House, Committee on Civil Service, *Salary Increase for Certain Civil Service Employees—Welch Increase Salary Bill,* Hearings on H. R. 6518, March 19, 20, 21, 22, and 29, 1928, 70th Cong., 1st Sess. (Washington: Government Printing Office, 1928), pp. 15–35. These figures are from the testimony of Paul H. Douglas.

73 41 U.S. Statutes 614. For details of the enactment and a curious reversal of testimony by the Bureau of Efficiency—at first for and then against a retirement plan—see Edwards, as cited in footnote 68, pp. 33–36. For a contemporary discussion of the law by the Secretary of the Civil Service Commission, see John T. Doyle, "The Federal Civil Service Retirement Law," *The Annals,* CXIII (May, 1924), 330–38.

74 Paul Studensky, "Pensions in Public Employment," *National Municipal Review,* XI (April, 1922), 100.

before but which liberalized the payments and terms.[75] The administration of the act was first divided between the Bureau of Pensions in the Department of the Interior and the Civil Service Commission. In 1927 the Veterans Administration was substituted for the Bureau of Pensions, and in 1934 President Franklin Roosevelt placed the complete administration of the Retirement Act under the Civil Service Commission.

Paid advertisement from *Chicago Tribune*, March 28, 1920.

Demoralized Mail Service Preferred to Living Wages

Congress Fails to Heed Postal Needs

The Mail Service is demoralized because living wages are denied. The Sixty-Sixth Congress, seemingly indifferent as to this deplorable state of affairs, ignores postal needs rather than pay living wages. Congress is not concerned, because the Public or the Business World (the victims of an unreliable, incompetent and badly abused Postal Service) show no concern anent this gross lack of attention to their vital interests.

An Undeniable Injury to Public and Business Interests

Because Congress refuses adequate pay to post office clerks, an inadequate force cannot dispatch your mail in time. Delay of your mail, in many instances, is harmful—the direct results of that peculiar brand of economy which cheats the business man out of prompt transaction of his affairs. The shortsighted, penurious policy of denying living wages is a far greater loss to the Public and Business World that the ill-advised gain the U. S. Treasury derives therefrom.

Stealing the Crab's Thunder — Advancing from 60c to 41c Per Hour

Gaze at the following unique wage scale for postal employes—a crab-like advance which means reduction in pay in case of promotion:

Substitutes or Beginners	60c per hour
Experienced Clerks (After Years of Home Study)	41c per hour
Maximum Pay for Experienced Clerks	57c per hour
Minimum Pay for Beginners	60c per hour

A clerk may work in the service ten years or more and still receive less pay than during his first year. Only when he is classified as an expert will he receive as much as the beginner. At no time, however, will he be granted a living wage. If he becomes a superior he will be somewhat closer to the pay of unskilled labor.

According to authentic government statistics, emphasizing that the cost of living has advanced 104% since 1913, the actual present buying power of a clerk's maximum pay (a clerk classified as an expert) is but $875.00 a year.

Such is a postal employe's compensation—not at all disapproved by the very authorities who have repeatedly advocated a subsistence in reasonable health and comfort for every toiler in the United States.

Do Not Be Misled

Do not be deceived by misleading reports. Congress to date has not granted post office clerks an increase in pay for the coming fiscal year. Any report to the contrary is viciously false. The House of Representatives merely has continued a totally inadequate wage which includes a meager bonus for the ensuing year. According to all indications, the Senate will not alter this "low pay" imposition.

First Aid by Wage Commission Not Ready After More Than a Year of Its Existence

The Congressional Joint Postal Wage Commission, after having investigated wages and conditions in the Postal Service since February 28, 1919, is not as yet ready to give First Aid to the Postal Employes. With terrific speed it will submit its Tentative Report of its investigations in the near future (but 14 months after it began to investigate). According to certain members of this Wage Commission, no legislative action will be taken until December, 1920. Therefore, there could be no relief until July, 1921. They bring the pulmotor two years after the cry of distress—the well founded appeal for help.

Poor Pay—Poor Work—Poor Service

Public and Business Interests can command the Postal Service they need. Assert yourself and insist upon a mail service that serves your interests. Poor pay, at present, results in poor work and poor service. If the mail service remains as poor as it is today, you are responsible for it. This means the public and business interests as well.

Chicago Local No. 1
National Federation of Post Office Clerks

Position-classification. In 1917 Congress had requested that the Bureau of Efficiency investigate the compensation rates of private industry and that it report back to Congress on the problem of pay and position-classification within one year. Busy with wartime work, the Bureau did not fulfill its legislative mandate. In addition, it had

---

[75] For a short resumé of the development of retirement legislation from 1920 to 1933, see Carroll H. Wooddy, *The Growth of the Federal Government* (New York: McGraw-Hill Book Co., 1934), pp. 55–57.

opposed the retirement legislation and seemed to be allied with the congressional elements which did not favor any liberalization of benefits to government employees.[76]

Therefore, on March 1, 1919, Congress approved the appointment of a Joint Commission on Reclassification of Salaries, composed of three senators and three representatives, and requested that the long-deferred pay and classification study—on the departmental service only—be completed by January, 1920. The Commission tackled this difficult problem in a comprehensive and thorough manner, and issued a lengthy report consisting of findings and proposed legislation in March, 1920.[77]

The report called attention to and illustrated the appalling inequalities of the federal government in the matter of equal pay for equal work. It condemned certain restrictive and inconsistent policies of the departments toward matters of hours, leave, transfers, outside activity, health, safety, and the like. It outlined a complete set of class specifications for the federal government and suggested that they be enacted by reference in the English manner. It recommended that the departments organize personnel sections on a modern basis, under the general guidance of the Civil Service Commission. It then proposed a rejuvenated and expanded Commission with central control of the position-classification scheme and with all the powers and duties of a central employment agency in a great organization.

The report, however just and accurate it may have been—and it was extremely well received throughout the country by those acquainted with the personnel problems of the government—touched off a set of fireworks in Congress which did not subside into legislation until 1923. The Republican leader in the Senate, Senator Reed Smoot of Utah, who was directing an economy drive at the time, accused the Commission, even before the appearance of its report, of exceeding its instructions, of conspiring to make employees dissatisfied with their wages, and of failing to recognize that the "introduction of labor-saving devices . . . has diluted the labor force by making it possible to utilize low-paid clerical labor." [78] Under this and similar barrages, the position-classification legislation was tem-

---

[76] Edwards, as cited in footnote 68, pp. 24–25. Senator Kenneth D. McKellar of Tennessee charged on the floor of the Senate, February 24, 1920, that Herbert D. Brown, head of the Bureau of Efficiency, was lobbying against the retirement legislation. Same, p. 35. It has also been alleged that there were close relationships between Senator Reed Smoot of Utah and Brown. The Senator was chairman of the Senate Appropriations Committee and a stout partisan of economy.

[77] U.S. Congress, House, Joint Commission on Reclassification of Salaries, *Report*, 66th Cong., 2d Sess., House Doc. 686 (Washington: Government Printing Office, 1920). For a discussion of the way the Commission went about its investigations, see Edwards, as cited in footnote 68, pp. 36–42. See also the "supplementary notes" to ch. xii.

[78] *Congressional Record*, 66th Cong., 2d Sess., p. 1096, January 6, 1920.

porarily sidetracked. It was almost four years before an acceptable compromise could be worked out, and the final solution was one of a much more limited scope than that originally proposed. Nevertheless, Congress finally had a plan before it, whether or not it liked it, and the principles of that plan had the backing of much of organized labor and of those interested in more effective personnel management for the federal government.[79]

Public and Private Personnel Management

For many years before World War I the administrative worlds of business and public affairs, despite a considerable interchange of personnel, had remained largely apart. In so far as there were influences of one on the other, business methods were applied to government and rarely vice versa. For the first time in our history, World War I seriously interrupted this one-way flow of ideas and brought the relationship into at least a partial equilibrium.

The military departments, a main reservoir of large-scale managerial experience, were from this point on to furnish increasing increments of executive talent to commerce and business.[80] With them they brought the concept of the general staff, which had also come to the attention of many of the civilians associated with the military, in uniform and out, during the war. Though not always well understood or applied in the industrial world, line and staff concepts were to be increasingly influential, with the end not yet in sight, in solutions of the growing organizational problems of big business.

Beyond this, many representatives of private enterprise began to comprehend the potentials of public employment procedures, especially the value of the testing systems of the Civil Service Commission and the War Department. Private industry was adopting variations of the government's examination and selection procedures by 1918, and a number of firms had come to the Commission for assistance in the organization of central employment bureaus.[81] Commissioner Wales said in 1919 that many of the wartime difficulties of the Commission had arisen from the attitude of businessmen who came to Washington feeling that ability could not be tested. Yet, argued the Commissioner, employee turnover within the government, even during wartime, was considerably less than that of many in-

---

[79] For a brief history of the classification movement at this time, see Fred Telford, "The Classification and Salary Standardization Movement in the Public Service," *The Annals*, CXIII (May, 1924), 206.

[80] See, for example, Frank Freidel, *Franklin D. Roosevelt: The Ordeal* (Boston: Little, Brown and Co., 1954), p. 22.

[81] USCSC, *Thirty-fifth Report*, 1918, p. xxx.

dustrial concerns. Perhaps, he suggested, there was a lesson involved.[82]

More impressive in its recognition of the early leadership of the government in the field of personnel testing is the testimony of the well-known psychologist, L. L. Thurstone, who, as early as 1923, told the American Management Association:

> I want to take this opportunity to describe my recent experience with civil service tests. Until last January I knew little about civil service examinations. . . .
> I will say very frankly that I came into that work with the impression that civil service tests were probably very poor. Somehow they have that reputation. But after working with them as well as with tests in private employment, I am convinced that civil service tests are in general far superior to the tests that are used in private industries, and I am saying this as a frank evaluation of civil service test procedure. I am not a civil service examiner, but I have found occasion to change my own opinion about civil service examinations on account of my work with the commissions.
> I want to suggest that those of you who are interested in employment test methods will find a mine of very interesting and useful material and very excellent ideas if you consult the practices of some of the best known civil service commissions.[83]

In 1927 the National Civil Service Reform League, after an investigation of a hundred corporations, came to the conclusion that the government was still ahead in its testing and recruiting system but that industry was rapidly catching up. The President of the League then concluded:

> To those who ask "why doesn't the Government adopt the business methods of successful corporations?" we may answer, "It does; in fact, it has shown the way to private business so far as it has applied the Civil Service Law to its employees." [84]

The view that in some things the government was more efficient than private industry was radical doctrine even to the civil service reformers. A paragraph from the annual report of the Chief Examiner of the Civil Service Commission for 1918 provides an enlightening example of the attitudes then current concerning the relative merits of public and private endeavor:

> To some of us who have been in active civil-service work for years and have had opportunity to observe its effects from the inside, has come an

---

82 NCSRL, *Proceedings*, 1919, pp. 15–17.
83 As quoted in Albert Smith Faught, "Employment Tests in the Public Service," *The Annals*, CXIII (May, 1924), 311–12.
84 NCSRL, *Proceedings*, 1927, p. 30.

abiding belief in the "good business" of the merit system. At the time of its adoption 45 years ago and ever since, its supporters have in the main been apologetic; they firmly believed that it was much better and more efficient and economical than the spoils system it supplanted, but, so they seemed to feel, it was an expensive way of securing help when measured by the methods used in the commercial world. The commercial world, however, has now adopted the civil-service system.[85]

Of equal importance in its stimulation of applied psychology everywhere was the experience of the military with the classification of individual abilities through mechanisms such as the Army's Alpha and Beta tests. While from 1919 to 1940 the Army largely ignored its own pioneering efforts, the leaders of commerce and industry were, as one brief history of applied psychology has put it, "greatly impressed by the Army reports of the achievements of applied psychology (1) in rejecting unworthy applicants and (2) in selecting, assigning, and promoting the most worthy candidates." [86] Under the dual stimuli of military and civil public experience, the whole field of private personnel management was to undergo almost a revolution within the next twenty years. Even the famous Hawthorne experiments in worker motivation, conducted at the Chicago plant of the Western Electric Company, can be traced back to the wartime experiments of the British with respect to fatigue.

As the reverse of the coin, the public service of 1920 had yet much to learn from private industry concerning employee welfare and union-management relations, and from both private industry and the military about training.[87] With respect to retirement, efficiency ratings, and some aspects of position-classification, the military was on firmer ground than either private industry or civil government, but no one was very satisfied with developments in the latter two realms.

On the more inclusive question of the over-all efficiency of government as compared to private industry, the war left few objective bases for comparison. Wilson's Secretary of Commerce, William C. Redfield, himself a businessman, concluded after the war: "The entire body of employees [of the government] would compare favorably in character and in quality of service with any equal number of men and women in corporate employ." [88] Franklin D. Roosevelt, then Wilson's As-

---

85 USCSC, *Thirty-fifth Report*, 1918, p. xxx.

86 Walter Dill Scott, Robert C. Clothier, and William R. Spriegel, *Personnel Management* (5th ed.; New York: McGraw-Hill Book Co., 1954), ch. xv, "The First Fifty Years of Applied Psychology," p. 248.

87 For a comparison of the scope of public and private personnel management shortly after World War I, see Leonard D. White, *Introduction to the Study of Public Administration* (New York: The Macmillan Co., 1926), pp. 216–18.

88 As cited in footnote 25, p. 125.

sistant Secretary of the Navy, did not entirely agree, but put the blame squarely on the shoulders of Congress for refusing to raise wages, establish pensions, and encourage promotion only for merit. Before a group of businessmen he concluded:

> . . . Any man with common sense could save 10 per cent of our government expenses, and based on even the old figures this would mean an annual savings of one hundred million dollars. You are paying for it in taxes and you will continue to do so until you put your government on a business basis.[89]

However this may sound in light of Roosevelt's later record, he was reflecting widely held opinion of the day. The prestige of the public service was vastly improved over the days of General Grant, but it was as yet by no means on a par with private industry.

Past is Prologue

The federal government had felt the impact of the greatest expansion in its history under Woodrow Wilson, an expansion not only in numbers but also in variety and scope of functions. Under the guidance of the positive state not only had much of the Progressive program come to fruition but a war had been won. Despite the return of Old Guard Republican views of the proper place of government in economic affairs, a subtle and suggestive idea had been firmly planted. This was the explosive thought that under the proper organization of social endeavor it was possible for the American people to produce almost anything they saw fit, once the objectives were agreed upon. If the Wilsonian period left evidences of waste and frustration, it also left many satisfying memories of effective collective endeavor under the aegis of government. When the times would be more propitious, during the Depression and Second World War soon to follow, these memories, and the governmental mechanism and the administrative experiences upon which they were in part based, were to return in new forms and under new auspices.

SUPPLEMENTARY NOTES

There is an astonishing scarcity of data concerning civilian personnel management in the federal public service of the First World War. The annual reports of the Civil Service Commission for the years involved are useful but usually limited in scope compared to those of many earlier years. The National Civil Service Reform League's publications and records

[89] Quoted in Freidel, as cited in footnote 80, p. 35.

are of some value in the indication of trends, but, as the Reform League had already clashed with the Commission earlier in Wilson's administration, some of the lines of thought indicated in the League's reports are open to question. The author has interviewed several wartime employees of the League and of the Civil Service Commission. Their views on a number of matters do not entirely coincide. The author has, in addition, consulted the librarian of the Civil Service Commission in an endeavor to discover what World War I records might remain in its files or elsewhere. The library has next to none and the librarian doubts if any are in existence. The same question—of First World War experience—arose at the beginning of World War II and a thorough search by the Commission's own staff revealed few illuminating materials. Quantities of secondary sources which might have been expected to refer in passing to the work of the wartime Commission have been searched to little avail. Only Matthew F. Halloran's sentimental reminiscences have yielded anything very specific about the Commission's work from 1916 to 1919. Concerning the personnel policies of other governmental agencies, a few memoirs, such as those by Herbert Hoover and William Gibbs McAdoo, are modestly helpful. The newspaper and periodical press is almost void of discussion of the operations of the wartime Commission, as an examination of the periodical indexes and of the Commission's own extensive press clipping files clearly shows. The *Congressional Record* is no more helpful. The interpretation in this chapter is, therefore, the best that can be pieced together from a jigsaw puzzle for which some of the pieces may be missing.

CHAPTER 12

"The Business of America Is Business"[1]

1921–1933

With the end of the war, the administrative machine built up for military purposes deflated as rapidly as it had been expanded. Dollar-a-year men returned home. Many government employees accepted attractive offers from private industry. Still others, facing federal employment conditions which were anything but utopian, simply left to look for work elsewhere.

Due in part to the absence of President Wilson in Europe and his later serious illness, there was no particular system to the demobilization of civilian workers. This does not mean that the federal administrative machinery fell apart, or that the Civil Service Commission did not do a capable job in terms of its limited authority. But the same symptoms of disorganization arose that developed after the Second World War; only they came more rapidly and with less organized endeavor to prevent them.

Back to Political Normalcy

After a brief wartime moratorium, the public service again found itself to be a major political objective. Congress quickly decided that the greater portion of the 1920 census employees should be selected through traditional procedures rather than through any sort of merit system. To this Wilson acquiesced, despite a protest from the

---

1 Calvin Coolidge in an address before the American Society of Editors, Washington, D.C., 1924, as quoted in William Allen White, *A Puritan in Babylon* (New York: The Macmillan Co., 1938), pp. 264–65.

National Civil Service Reform League. Representative Andrew J. Volstead's opposition to the merit system and the Anti-Saloon League's indifference encouraged Congress to exclude the employees of the newly-created Prohibition Bureau from the classified service. The Treasury was accused of circumventing the civil service regulations in the appointment of employees in the War Risk Insurance Bureau. As discussed in the previous chapter, the preference rights of veterans were quickly expanded and strengthened. The Reform League concluded that the first year of the post-war period showed "a marked diminution of the spirit of unselfish devotion to the public interest and . . . the same old problems of personal and political selfishness." [2]

Nor did Congress limit itself to these more conventional types of activities. The political tension stemming from the post-war radical witch hunts and a conservative reaction against labor union activities had its effects upon the organizations of public as well as private employees. The Boston Police Strike of 1919 heightened fear of a radical labor "conspiracy" and provoked the first federal anti-strike legislation aimed at unions of civil servants. By acts of December 5, 1919, and January 24, 1920, Congress hastily forbade the members of the police and fire departments of the District of Columbia to strike on penalties of discharge, fine, or prison, and prohibited affiliation with outside labor organizations. The police were not even permitted to resign with less than one month's notice. Meanwhile, Governor Calvin Coolidge's terse declaration, "There is no right to strike against the public safety by anybody, anywhere, at any time," had caught the mood of the day and was to be largely responsible for his selection a few months later as the Republican vice-presidential candidate.[3]

As the campaign of 1920 progressed, even the Civil Service Commission seemed to go out of its way to keep the growing public employee unions from exerting any influence. In a letter to the Post Office Department, the Commission declared that the political activity of *wives* of employees could be considered "collusion" under the Act of 1883.[4] When this attitude was criticized, the Commission implied that it did not quite mean what it said, but shortly before

---

[2] NCSRL, *Proceedings*, 1920, p. 39.

[3] See Sterling D. Spero, *Government as Employer* (New York: Remson Press, 1948), ch. xii, "The Rise, Fall and Revival of Police Unionism."

[4] USCSC, *Thirty-eighth Report*, 1921, pp. 139–40. Luther C. Steward, long-time President of the NFFE, has told the writer that it was not until 1930 that the civil service unions received anything like assistance from the executive branch. Civil Service Commission Secretary John T. Doyle, remarked Steward, looked upon him as "a wayward son going to hell." Incidentally, Steward was refused membership in the National Civil Service Reform League in 1918. From a personal interview, September 2, 1948.

the election it reaffirmed the greater part of its original letter.[5] During the campaign the Commission formally reprimanded the editor of the *Federal Employee* for reprinting an article from a Georgia paper which censured Senator Hoke Smith—up for re-election—for his opposition to a minimum-wage bill.[6] In addition, the Commission was continuing to reject applicants on the grounds of "disloyalty."

In the campaign of 1920 government officials played their usual roles. Wilson himself evidently made no effort to control the Democratic convention, but one writer has reported that McAdoo and a "crowd" of Treasury officials, along with A. Mitchell Palmer and many others from the Department of Justice, were there in full force.[7] Their efforts were in vain, however, and Governor James M. Cox of Ohio received the nomination. The details of Senator Warren G. Harding's nomination on the Republican ticket and his subsequent overwhelming election are well known. One need underscore only that "normalcy," not reform, was the principal issue.

Personal Honesty is Not Enough

Characteristically, Harding has been given credit for making both some of the best political appointments and also some of the worst. Hughes, Hoover, and Hays—the three "H's"—were unquestionably topnotch and their departmental administrations were on the whole enlightened. For the rest, they might be said to be more characteristic of the Grant era than of the twentieth century.

Though the clamor was modest compared to that of previous political turnovers, the Republicans soon found themselves involved in the usual type of rush for the offices. The *Washington Star* noted on March 10, 1921, that two-thirds of Harding's appointment hours were taken up by office seekers. On April 5 the *Indianapolis News* remarked that the pressure on Postmaster General Will Hays, a native Hoosier, was increasing. Said Representative Thomas S. Williams of Illinois a month later:

. . . History will record that Roosevelt had his Cortelyou, that Taft had his Hitchcock, that Wilson had his Burleson, and I hope—well I don't want to be disrespectful, but I hope that our great President Harding will be properly served by his Postmaster-General.[8]

5 For details of the action and for press comment, see "Political Activity of Relatives of Federal Employees," *Good Government*, XXXVII (October, 1920), 154–57.

6 USCSC, *Thirty-seventh Report*, 1920, pp. 105–106.

7 Arthur W. Dunn, *From Harrison to Harding* (2 vols.; New York: G. P. Putnam's Sons, 1922), II, 409.

8 *Boston Post*, May 5, 1921.

Evidently Harding quickly decentralized his patronage responsibilities, for by early summer it was clear that Hays, Attorney General Harry Daugherty, and John T. Adams of Iowa, the Chairman of the Republican National Committee, were dispensing the bulk of the patronage. When the perennial question of the disposition of postmasterships arose, Harding was persuaded to return to the "rule of three," thus rescinding Wilson's instructions that the man at the top of each list should be selected automatically. Postmaster General Hays shortly thereafter avowed his support of the merit system. Nevertheless an investigation by the National Civil Service Reform League resulted in a series of four reports quite critical of Republican postal appointment policies.

By the middle of the summer of 1921 the spoils efforts of the Republicans began to assume the proportions of a sizable if not full-scale raid.[9] Many Republicans publicly asserted that civil service reform had gone too far. Shortly after taking office, Secretary of Labor James J. Davis wrote, "The simple fact is that I am powerless to enforce changes which I desire because I am powerless to put in charge of these places individuals in sympathy with such changed policies."[10] Davis concluded that the classified service extended too far up in his department. Mark Hanna's former secretary, Elmer Dover, now an Assistant Secretary of the Treasury, let it be known upon his arrival in Washington that, if Hays intended to "humanize" his department by postal reforms and welfare work, he intended to "Hardingize" his. He promptly began to look for ways to make inroads into the classified service. And Attorney General Daugherty, who was then engaged in "reconstructing" the Prohibition Bureau, stated publicly before the House Committee on Appropriations that "civil service" was a "hindrance to the government."[11]

In late March, 1922, President Harding, by an executive order, removed thirty-one employees in the Bureau of Printing and Engraving without offering any reason other than "the good of the service," and even abolished the positions themselves. Then he created new positions, which were immediately filled by new appointees. The President was widely censured for cruelty to the employees. Since Congress had created some of the positions by statute, the legality of the President's action was questioned as well.

---

[9] The most complete history of this spoils attempt is contained in Frank M. Stewart, *The National Civil Service Reform League* (Austin: University of Texas, 1929), pp. 161–68. See also Harry W. Marsh, "The Recent Spoils Raid in Washington," *National Municipal Review*, XI (September, 1922), 269–74; and the NCSRL Papers, File Sa3.

[10] Marsh, as cited in footnote 9, p. 269.

[11] "Daugherty Attacks the Merit System," *Good Government*, XXXIX (April, 1922), 41.

Even the Civil Service Commission became indirectly involved. In July, 1921, Harding had appointed John H. Bartlett of New Hampshire as president of the agency. Evidently restive in this largely non-political post, Bartlett soon found a new position as First Assistant Postmaster General. He had hardly taken this post before he issued a press release stating that the merit system had gone too far by including $5,000 jobs, when, in his opinion, the Act of 1883 had only intended that offices up to $1,800 be included. He continued to argue that the new administration should have a free hand in selecting officials for all types of positions in which executive discretion was necessary. Finally Postmaster General Hubert Work, who had succeeded Hays in early 1922, declared that postmasters should be examined by the Post Office Department and that the Civil Service Commission ought to have no part in the process. He indicated that, in any event, a Republican would always be chosen if he were among the highest three.

As a result of these public statements and actions, the National Civil Service Reform League felt compelled to call a mass protest meeting in Washington on April 27, 1922. A large audience heard former Civil Service Commissioner William Dudley Foulke, himself a Republican, excoriate the administration's partisan patronage policies as well as those of Assistant Postmaster General Bartlett, who had come to the meeting to defend the administration. What, if any, causal relationship there was between the overwhelmingly favorable press response which the meeting engendered and the subsequent decline of the spoils raid will never be known. But Secretary Andrew Mellon shortly thereafter received Elmer Dover's resignation, and the movement to revive the spoils system collapsed.

At its annual meeting in late 1922 the Reform League praised the work of Secretary of State Hughes in the organization of the foreign service; but, deprecating the operation of the Prohibition Service, the Post Office, the Treasury, and the Department of Justice, the League concluded:

. . . It is doubtful if, since the passage of the United States Civil Service Law in 1883, there has been a more insistent effort made on the part of party spoilsmen to overthrow the merit system in the Federal civil service than has been made in the last year and a half.[12]

The League overstated its case, but a spoils raid of considerable force and proportions had undoubtedly been under way.

[12] NCSRL, *Proceedings*, 1922, pp. 3–17.

Within another year, during which the administration confined itself to manipulating the unclassified service, comprising 20 to 30 per cent of the total civil employment, President Harding died and Calvin Coolidge took the oath of office. There had been, of course, no extension of the merit system under Harding. But it should not be assumed that the disruption of the public service through legislative action was as great as that accomplished during the years of the Wilson administration. The difference can be accounted for partly by the fact that the voting public by this time had begun to realize the value of the merit system. But, more important, the Republicans were functioning in a period of relative prosperity, had more financial resources as a party than did the Democrats, and their president had no great economic program to force through a reluctant Congress.

By the time of the President's death, the gross fraud and corruption which permeated his ineffective and overly amiable administration had not yet come to full public notice. No one has ever successfully accused Harding of personal peculation. How much he knew when he died of what had been done under his aegis no one knows, but near the end Harding cried out to William Allen White:

My God, this is a hell of a job! I have no trouble with my enemies. I can take care of my enemies all right. But my damn friends, my Goddamn friends, White, they're the ones that keep me walking the floor nights! [13]

Within a few months the Teapot Dome oil scandal burst into full light, and before long Harding's Secretary of the Interior and his head of the Veterans' Bureau were convicted and sent to jail, his Attorney General had been indicted for fraud, and his Secretary of the Navy, Alien Property Custodian, and a long list of other officials discredited.[14]

Silent Politics

Coolidge records in his autobiography that, after an appropriate telegram to Mrs. Harding, he firmly announced that there would be "no sweeping displacement of the men then in office," and "no violent changes in the administration of affairs." [15] Nevertheless, patronage

---

[13] *The Autobiography of William Allen White* (New York: The Macmillan Co., 1946), p. 619.
[14] See Samuel Hopkins Adams, *Incredible Era* (Boston: Houghton Mifflin Co., 1939); and M. R. Werner, *Privileged Characters* (New York: Robert M. McBride and Co., 1935).
[15] Calvin Coolidge, *The Autobiography of Calvin Coolidge* (New York: Cosmopolitan Book Corp., 1929), p. 175.

problems intruded even on the quiet of the funeral train from Washington to Marion, Ohio. When Coolidge returned to the capital he found that he had to give up his usual morning walk because "crafty patronage seekers" would try to join him.[16]

Despite some protests by the press, he selected C. Bascom Slemp, a Virginia congressman, to serve as his private secretary. An able partisan, Slemp could be expected to organize and control the southern delegates to any Republican convention and to function as a competent political adviser. William Allen White later observed, "When he chose Bascom Slemp as his Secretary, the choice was an announcement" of his intention to have a term in his own right.[17] In the Cabinet, Coolidge retained the incumbents he inherited from Harding. As public clamor grew in the wake of the Teapot Dome scandals, he soon asked for Daugherty's resignation. But, for a while he resisted congressional pressure that he dismiss Secretary of the Navy Edwin Denby. Feeling no admiration for Denby's role in connection with the oil reserves, he nevertheless disliked legislative interference in what he conceived to be an executive matter. In minor appointments Coolidge recognized a legitimate congressional claim. He is quoted as saying that "he had to deal with the situation as he found it."[18] Within the unclassified service Coolidge seldom acted without full consultation with legislators, cabinet members, and other political leaders interested in the future of the Republican party.

Still, in his first message to Congress, Coolidge recommended the merit system for postmasters and the prohibition force. He even went so far as to state: "The best method for selecting public servants is the merit system."[19] He must be given credit for supporting these early statements of policy with considerable positive action. He refused to countenance any interference with the classified service. He encouraged the legislation which removed the prohibition force from its chaos of spoils. If he did not actually support, neither did he oppose such basic administrative reforms as those involved in the Classification Act of 1923. And, in his determined and largely successful efforts to lift his regime from the morass of corruption in which Harding had left it, it may be said that he demonstrated political courage of a very high order. There is general agreement among those who knew Calvin Coolidge that there was little scandal of the Harding variety ever involved in his administration and that

16 Claude M. Fuess, *Calvin Coolidge* (Boston: Little, Brown and Co., 1940), p. 325.

17 As cited in footnote 1, pp. 251 and 261. See also Guy B. Hathorn, "C. Bascom Slemp —Virginia Republican Boss, 1907-1932," *The Journal of Politics*, XVII (May, 1955), 248.

18 Letter from Everett Sanders to William Allen White, March 9, 1937, quoted in White, as cited in footnote 1, p. 286.

19 *Congressional Record*, 68th Cong., 1st Sess., LXV, p. 98.

he was an astute if not entirely orthodox politician. Inheriting a divided party reeking with scandal, the new president reorganized it in a little over a year, made it respectable, and won a presidential nomination in his own right with little more difficulty than Theodore Roosevelt had in 1904. This was the work of no bumbling hack. This was purpose and action.

But, if the action was clear, the purpose was not. It is with respect to the ultimate ends of the Coolidge administration and the Coolidge appointments that there has been most disagreement. One Coolidge biographer, Claude Fuess, has concluded that "Coolidge was an unusually shrewd judge of men and their motives and saw through all those who attempted to exploit him." "Few Presidents," he flatly states, "have set for themselves higher standards for appointees or acted more independently of solicitors." [20] However, Chief Justice Taft so despaired of the improvement of the federal judiciary that he wrote Learned Hand, "His one weakness is his lack of judgment in the selection of competent persons for office." [21] In the muck-raking *Mirrors of 1932* both Coolidge and his appointees were viciously pilloried. "The federal officials named by Mr. Coolidge are of a low order unexampled," emphatically stated the then-anonymous author.[22] Only William Allen White took no position at all. A bit out of character here, he merely presented evidence which might be interpreted in favor of any of the preceding types of conclusions.

As several students of the politics of reform have pointed out, the Progressives believed in the power of a positive state.[23] The keystone of their organizational system lay in the concept of the *regulation* of business affairs in the name of the people. Between 1900 and 1920 much of the structure of the independent regulatory commissions was erected and roofed. But the Progressive doctrine had not anticipated that its organizational fortress might be manned against it.

This, however, was exactly what Calvin Coolidge and his chief ideological architect, Secretary of Commerce Herbert Hoover, were busily doing. While Coolidge declared the "business of America is business," Hoover was equally insistent that the future of America lay in a move away from an extreme competitive individualism of the McKinley variety and toward a concept resembling the New Nationalism of Theodore Roosevelt. Favoring the development of private

[20] Fuess, as cited in footnote 16, pp. 479 and 366.
[21] Taft to Judge Learned Hand, May 3, 1927, as quoted in White, as cited in footnote 1, p. 414.
[22] Ray Thomas Tucker, *The Mirrors of 1932* (New York: Brewer, Warren and Putnam, 1931), p. 63.
[23] See especially Eric Goldman, *Rendezvous with Destiny* (New York: Alfred A. Knopf, 1952), pp. 306–19.

enterprise through what he termed "associational activities," Hoover desired to devote the new Progressive state which Coolidge and he had inherited to the facilitation rather than the limitation of the ends and energies of corporate capitalism. In these terms, it was possible to conceive of Andrew Mellon as the greatest Secretary of the Treasury since Alexander Hamilton, of Herbert Hoover as the great organizational engineer, and the conservative William E. Humphrey, of *Humphrey's Executor* fame, as an eminently suitable candidate for membership on the Federal Trade Commission.

On the other hand, to an unreconstructed Progressive the Coolidge and Hoover appointments must frequently have seemed almost like treason. Even to the conservative Taft, to whom impartiality meant perhaps more than anything else, the judicial prospect was peculiar to say the least. As Eric F. Goldman has rightly concluded:

. . . What the conservatives did do was to staff the commissions, the antitrust enforcement division, and the courts with men sympathetic to corporations—to 'bore from within,' in the angry phrase of Senator Norris . . . [so that] business was more immune than ever.[24]

This is not to say that these men were either dishonest in the traditional sense or inefficient in the conduct of public affairs. They were, from a Progressive and liberal point of view, deadly effective. We may only conclude, therefore, that in the orientation of the public service of the nineteen twenties Coolidge and Hoover knew exactly what they wanted and largely accomplished their aims.

Controlling the party. As with both Harding and Hoover, Coolidge's main problems lay not with the Democrats but with his own rebellious left wing. With a legislative program expressed largely in terms of inaction, these problems were less difficult than if he had been trying to turn the clock back to 1900. With modest success he attempted to heal the breach between the Progressives and the Republican Old Guard. He would not, however, tolerate complete apostasy. During the period of Robert LaFollette's candidacy for the Presidency on the third-party Progressive ticket, the Wisconsin senator and his supporters were politically punished in the usual manner. After the 1924 campaign, LaFollette nominally returned to the Republican fold. Still Coolidge did not extend the olive branch of federal patronage until 1926, when he thought that the results of the forthcoming congressional elections might seriously weaken the hitherto fairly solid Republican front.[25]

24 Same, p. 307.
25 Alfred Lief, *Democracy's Norris* (New York: Stackpole Sons, 1939), pp. 285 and 289.

The uncontested nomination of Coolidge in 1924 is strong evidence of the success of the President's patronage practices as well as of the acceptability of his big business policies. The Harding scandals had been handled so adroitly, the Democrats were so divided, and confidence in prosperity so widespread that the voting population confirmed Coolidge's leadership by majorities almost equal to those of 1920.

During Coolidge's full term of office there were few unusual incidents involving the patronage, except that the President became the first chief executive since Grant for whom a cabinet nomination was turned down by the Senate—not once this time, but twice. At such an affront, Coolidge modified his usually conciliatory practice and took his revenge on several senators by making it a point to confer with members of the House of Representatives on patronage matters.[26]

Though in an excellent position to seek a third term, Coolidge, by not "choosing" to run, played an ambiguous role in the months prior to the election of 1928. But he did not interfere, as he very well could have, with the extensive maneuvers of Hoover's managers in corralling southern delegates to the Republican national convention. The nomination of Hoover was a foregone conclusion, although there was a flurry of accusations of graft and corruption within southern Republican ranks. A congressional committee was appointed to investigate further. Conveniently reporting *after* the election, it substantiated a considerable number of charges. Hoover promised to make the necessary reforms, and he evidently did so to some extent.

Engineering the Offices

Herbert Hoover has been one of the few presidents since the Virginia Dynasty to accede directly to the Presidency from the Cabinet. He also possessed the least partisan political experience of any president since Taft and possibly Grant. Hoover's relationship to the public service can best be compared to that of Taft, whom he resembled in many other ways as well.

Most analyses of Hoover's political career have been somewhat confused by an over-emphasis upon Hoover's economic individualism, a topic about which he has been exceedingly vocal. However his real contribution as president was of a more radical sort. Unquestionably a proponent of private enterprise, Hoover, nevertheless, was no

---

[26] Richard L. Neuberger and Stephen B. Kahn, *Integrity: The Life of George W. Norris* (New York: The Vanguard Press, 1937), pp. 159–61.

disciple of those who conceived of economics in terms of unbridled competition. His tidy engineer's mind quickly perceived that much economic waste could be eliminated by trade associations, by codes of ethics, and by proper governmental supervision and encouragement of business, especially big business. Like Coolidge, his appointments as well as his policies reflected these concepts.

Unlike Coolidge, he was never able to stay on the top of the political pyramid with any sense of assurance. Representing the conservative interests of eastern Republicanism, Hoover, even more than Coolidge, found it difficult to reach a common meeting ground with the liberal and largely western wing of the party. When this was combined with an inability to conceive of the Presidency as a positive political post, Hoover's impasses multiplied. Though undoubtedly an expert in management, Hoover conceived of administration in the limited terms of organization and methods. The Great Depression only underscored the fact that truly effective public administration is, above all, dependent upon effective political action at the policy level. William Allen White concluded late in 1929 that Hoover "can plow the ground, harrow it, plant the seed, cultivate it, but seems to lack the power to harvest it and flail it into a political merchantable product." [27] In his own memoirs the ex-President has a bit plaintively noted:

I was convinced that efficient, honest administration of the vast Federal government would appeal to all citizens. I have since learned that efficient government does not interest the people as much as dramatics. Holding to this conviction, I was a strong supporter of the Civil Service.[28]

Hoover was quite right in describing himself as a friend of the merit system. Nevertheless, there was in his use of the offices a little of the same sort of uncertainty which plagued President Taft. Soon after his inauguration Hoover told the New York Bar Association that he would follow merit principles in his appointments.[29] A stout partisan of executive reorganization, he supported the Civil Service Commission as a presidential staff agency. In the higher levels of the civil service he made a signal departure from previous practice by appointing all the heads of scientific bureaus by promotion from within the service. He was as energetic as Coolidge in ferreting out

27 Letter of White to David Hinshaw, December 3, 1929. Walter Johnson (ed.), *Selected Letters of William Allen White* (New York: Henry Holt and Co., 1947), p. 299.

28 Herbert Hoover, *The Memoirs of Herbert Hoover* (3 vols.; New York: The Macmillan Co., 1952), II, 279.

29 William Starr Myers and Walter H. Newton, *The Hoover Administration* (New York: Charles Scribner's Sons, 1936), p. 378.

wrongdoing among civil employees, and he generally supported those department heads who felt as he did about the permanent service. He left the classified service inviolate and even extended it to its greatest proportions in our history prior to 1940.

On the other hand, he lost the tariff reduction by one vote, when patronage, properly distributed, could undoubtedly have swayed the balance the other way. With his political philosophy closely akin to that of Coolidge, he, too, selected conservatives for appointments within the unclassified service, thereby subjecting himself to the same types of criticism. While he nominated for the Supreme Court the distinguished Hughes, Cardozo, and Roberts, and sought to improve the judiciary at all levels,[30] William Allen White pointedly protested to Attorney General William D. Mitchell:

This letter is about the Kansas Judgeship, and I hope you will bear with me while I discuss the theory of appointing Federal Judges outside politics. The theory looks like copybook perfection. But this Kansas case affords a perfect example of the fallacy of the hypothesis. What you are getting is something worse than political endorsements, and what you will get if you entirely neglect political endorsements, is the endorsements of interested litigants.[31]

When Hoover endeavored to reenforce his party position in anticipation of the next campaign, he was accused of appointing more lame ducks and "discarded party-hacks" than any previous president.[32] While after his election he had publicly admitted corruption in the southern Republican ranks, and had to some extent taken the matter in hand, the process was nevertheless largely repeated in 1932. Postmaster General Walter F. Brown, Hoover's political chief, pulled all stops in his effort to line up the postmasters and all their adherents in the election conflict to come.

The power of the patronage, wielded even with the finesse of a Theodore Roosevelt, could not have stayed the anti-Republican tide in 1932. Hoover had a point when he claimed, "It is a handicap to any man to succeed a member of his own party as President. He has little patronage with which to reward his personal supporters. This was especially true in my case as Mr. Coolidge had with few exceptions left me a most able body of public servants." [33] But Hoover was not able to utilize even the few weapons at his disposal to any-

---

[30] Harold Wolfe, *Herbert Hoover* (New York: Exposition Press, 1956), p. 149.
[31] Letter from White to Mitchell. Johnson, as cited in footnote 27, p. 293.
[32] For the only analysis of Hoover appointments see the vitriolic volume by Drew Pearson and Robert S. Allen, *More Merry-Go-Round* (New York: Liveright, Inc., 1932), pp. 419–30 and elsewhere.
[33] Hoover, as cited in footnote 28, II, 217.

thing like their maximum strength. A bit the virtuous political man of a Cleveland stripe, Hoover's essential failing was that of all men of this sort. This, to quote the perceptive White again, may be summed up as follows: "Politics after all is one of the minor branches of harlotry, and Hoover's frigid desire to live a virtuous life and not follow the Pauline maxim and be all things to all men, is one of the things that has reduced the oil in his machinery and shot a bearing." [34] Certainly the hitherto formidable Republican juggernaut of the twenties ground to an abrupt halt in 1932.

The Classification Act of 1923

Despite its early lack of promise for the development of the merit system and, indeed, for the maintenance of any standards of honesty and integrity within the public service, the period of the twenties was one of considerable advancement toward a more centrally organized and coordinated public personnel system. Yet progress did not come all at once. The frustrating struggle over the Classification Act of 1923 is typical of the fundamental problems of the public service of this period.

Background. The report of the Joint Commission on Reclassification of Salaries had been effectively shelved at the time of its issuance in 1920. Then and during the decade immediately following, the political climate was hardly favorable to any kind of governmental reform except that clearly oriented toward the more traditional doctrines of economy and efficiency. The passage of civil pension legislation by a Republican Congress in 1920 may seem incompatible with this conclusion, but it must be remembered that the Retirement Act was so designed as to cost the government almost nothing until 1929. Pensions were far from generous, and the employees' contributions more than paid for the demands on the funds during the first decade of the law's operation.

As rapidly as the developing prosperity of the twenties made them again seem valid, the Old Guard Republican views of the proper place of government in relation to business returned to the fore, with the sharp economic decline in 1921 only reenforcing the idea of economy in public affairs. Congress was now struggling to emphasize private enterprise not only by turning the Progressive governmental machinery of the decade before World War I to the ends of commerce and business, but also by reducing its overhead costs. This meant, in turn, the reduction of the federal civil establishment in terms of size, function, and per unit expenditure. While many

34 White to Vernon Kellogg, April 4, 1931. Johnson, as cited in footnote 27, pp. 311–12.

296

proponents of these views interpreted their concern with the public service as contributing to both economy *and* efficiency, this was efficiency largely defined to reflect current, out-of-pocket dollars and cents.

Unfortunately for their immediate enactment, the proposals of the Joint Commission were more in accord with the mood of an out-dated Progressivism than with that of an all-powerful Senator Smoot. At the same time, the Commission's suggestions ran afoul of the normal congressional opposition to an implicit increase in executive power. The refusal to give the Civil Service Commission the authority necessary to become a central personnel agency and to operate as an integral arm of executive management was typical of Congress' aversion to attempts to interfere with historic legislative prerogatives in personnel matters. Congress in 1920 did not trust—whether it could or should have then is open to question—the executive branch of the government any further than absolutely necessary. The mutual recriminations between Congress and President Wilson and the ineffectiveness and downright dishonesty of the Harding executive staff did little to allay such distrust at this time.

The Budget and Accounting Act of 1921. The principal administrative accomplishment of the Harding regime lay in the passage and implementation of the Budget and Accounting Act of 1921. First approved by both houses of Congress under Wilson, the new fiscal proposal had been vetoed because it provided that the Comptroller General could be removed by Congress alone and without presidential concurrence. With this provision modified, the bill was again passed under Harding and this time approved.

One of the administrative innovations of the first Bureau director, General Dawes, was the establishment of what became known as the "Business Organization of the Government." This was a coordinating device, the keystone of which was a semiannual meeting of one to two thousand major departmental officials for the purpose of information and education on budgetary matters. This was buttressed by a nation-wide field organization of Business Associations, composed of local federal officials and functioning under the supervision of nine Area Coordinators. While the semiannual meeting was discontinued by President Hoover in 1929, the local organizations survived, some even into the fifties. By December, 1932, there were 269 of these groups which, among other things, considered personnel problems. There has been little study of this coordinating device,[35] but there can be no doubt that it furthered the personal acquaintance and the habits of

---

[35] The principal discussion is contained in Carroll H. Wooddy, *The Growth of the Federal Government* (New York: McGraw-Hill Book Co., 1934), pp. 28–29. See also USCSC, *Forty-first Report*, 1924, p. v.

297

cooperation which are essential for the efficient operation of a far-flung institution.

From the beginning the Bureau of the Budget tended to emphasize economy at the expense of almost everything else. But the pressing need for careful estimates of personnel and personnel costs, if any budget was really to mean anything, also stimulated further concern with the standardization, if not the liberalization, of federal wages and functions. Both Congress and the executive branch soon found themselves sharing the Joint Commission's concern for any device which would bring some order out of the chaos of job titles and pay scales. At the same time the growing public employee unions as well as a considerable number of legislators were more than ever concerned with attempts to revive the position-classification measures introduced and shelved in 1920.

The Classification Act. However, a large bloc in Congress, led by Senator Smoot, the powerful chairman of the Senate Appropriations Committee, and aided by information provided by the Bureau of Efficiency, still opposed any such comprehensive scheme as that originally recommended by the Joint Commission on Reclassification. With Presidents Harding and Coolidge largely on the sidelines except as they expressed the need for some sort of action, the final product was a compromise known generally as the Classification Act of 1923.[36]

The extent of the compromise is indicated by several key provisions of the act. The application of the law was limited to the departmental service in Washington. The law prescribed exact salary ranges and distinctly limited the raises which could be made under them. Finally, the administration of the act, instead of being placed under the unqualified supervision of the Civil Service Commission, was made subject to a specially created Personnel Classification Board. This was to be a tripartite *ex officio* body composed of one representative each from the Bureau of Efficiency, the Bureau of the Budget, and the Civil Service Commission. Nevertheless, the measure gave some promise of change. As summarized by the late Ismar Baruch, for many years the chief authority on position-classification in the federal government, the new law contained, in addition to those pointed out above, the following distinctive features:

---

[36] 42 U.S. Statutes 1488, approved on March 4, to take effect on July 1, 1924. For the few earlier attempts at position-classification under limited discretionary powers granted by Congress to particular federal agencies, especially the Post Office Department, see Ismar Baruch, *History of Position-Classification and Salary Standardization in the Federal Service, 1789–1941* (2d ed., P.C.D. Manual A-2; Washington: U.S. Civil Service Commission, 1941), pp. 38–49.

1. Very broad occupational divisions, called "services," were established. These services were defined in the act and designated as the Professional and Scientific Service; the Subprofessional Service; the Clerical, Administrative and Fiscal Service; the Custodial Service; and the Clerical-Mechanical Service.

2. Each service was subdivided into a number of "grades" or levels of importance, difficulty, responsibility, and value of work.

3. Uniform compensation schedules consisting of these services and grades were enacted into the law, each grade having a salary range fixed by Congress, and a short, very general description of the kind of work falling in each grade.

4. The pay of individual positions was to be determined through a process known as "allocation," *i.e.*, a determination of which grade covered the duties and responsibilities of the position to be allocated; or, in other words, an appraisal of the duties and responsibilities of an individual position according to general standards of appraisal (grades) set by Congress. When a decision was reached that a position was of such difficulty, responsibility, and importance as to bring it within a particular grade, the salary range stated in the statute for that grade would mandatorily attach to the position.

5. As a mandate for the uniform interpretation and application of the compensation schedules, and as a guiding principle for the process of "allocation," the policy that equal pay for equal work, irrespective of sex, should be observed, was expressly written into the statute.

6. "Classes" of positions were authorized to be established within grades, each class covering positions substantially alike as to character, difficulty, importance, responsibility, and value of work; and descriptions of those classes, known as "class specifications" were authorized to be written, to serve as administrative guides.

7. A central classifying agency, designated as the Personnel Classification Board, was established to administer the act, and especially to "review" and "revise" allocations made by departmental officials.

8. The allocations made by the Personnel Classification Board were to be "final." [37]

As both blue collar jobs not of a custodial or maintenance character and field service positions were excluded, the act applied in total to barely 10 per cent of the federal service. However, the new law required the Personnel Classification Board to study the field service and to report to Congress at its next regular session concerning the applicability of the new statute to this major segment of the public service.

From a comparative point of view it should also be noted that the new law followed the American custom of placing "rank in the job" rather than the European tendency to emphasize "rank in the man." Further, in the large number of different categories of positions for which it provided, the law reflected the extensive specialization and

37 Same, pp. 50–51.

emphasis on personal skills acquired before individual employees entered the public service, which had long been typical of American employment practices in private industry as well as the government service. The Classification Act of 1923 merely systematized rather than modified some of the fundamental characteristics of American public management.

Controversy. No sooner was the new law on the statute books in the spring of 1923 than the controversies which had plagued the discussion of position-classification legislation since 1920 arose anew. The idea of granting power to an executive agency to tamper with wages was still looked upon with considerable legislative suspicion. The general political emphasis on economy in government, as well as the terms of the act itself, meant that the salary increases anticipated by civil employees and much of the public would not be forthcoming. And, as if these were not enough troubles, there were at least two major schools of thought as to how the powers of the new Personnel Classification Board should be administratively implemented. Almost from the beginning there was disagreement between the Civil Service Commission and the Bureau of Efficiency, with the Bureau of the Budget holding the balance of power, which it wielded first in one direction and then in another.[38]

The quarrel between the Civil Service Commission and the Bureau of Efficiency was over the manner in which position-classification and pay problems in the federal service should be approached. The Commission wished immediately to develop detailed class specifications based on the work of the earlier Joint Commission on Reclassification. These specifications would then be adjusted to the terms of the pay grades established in the act. After this was done, existing positions would be placed in the proper classes by the agencies working under Board supervision. Under this plan the newly created Board would exercise the initiative in developing a position-classification plan for the federal service and would maintain effective control over its administrative implementation. On the other hand, the Bureau of Efficiency desired to leave to the departments, relatively unsupervised, the power to allocate all their positions to its pay schedule, a plan which had previously been rejected by Congress. The new Board

---

38 The heads of these three agencies consistently designated alternates to act for them as members of the Personnel Classification Board. During the first few years of the Board's existence the principal alternates were Guy Moffett, representing the Civil Service Commission; Harold N. Graves and William H. McReynolds, representing the Bureau of Efficiency; and W. W. Warwick and F. J. Bailey, representing the Bureau of the Budget. For a discussion of sources relating to this controversy, see the "supplementary notes" to this chapter.

then would gradually establish class specifications and standards bit by bit some time in the future. In the view of the Civil Service Commission, making salary allocations before position-classifications was putting the cart before the horse. Under the Bureau's plan, which was the plan actually put into effect on May 5, 1923, with the concurrence of the Bureau of the Budget, it was only gradually possible to produce any adjustment of existing inequities in the relationship of pay to duties and responsibilities. This reduced the expenses of the government for salary increases. In this fact lay the cause of many employee, employee union, and congressional complaints, for it had been generally assumed that the Classification Act would immediately remedy salary inequities and provide needed salary increases for at least the departmental employees in the District of Columbia.

In all fairness to the Bureau of Efficiency, it should be noted that there is, and was in 1923 and 1924, some question as to whether the Civil Service Commission's plan would have allowed matters to proceed much faster. The development of detailed specifications, the allocation of positions to these specifications, and the obtaining of the necessary appropriations was not a simple process. Moreover, there was some need for haste so that the new pay scales could be incorporated in the budget for the fiscal year of 1925. Nevertheless, the onus of the argument must be borne by the Bureau of Efficiency and to some extent the Bureau of the Budget because their plan was clearly contrary to the intent of the Classification Act itself.

As regards the other principal requirement of the Classification Act, a survey of the field service and a report to Congress, the Bureau of the Budget at first voted with the Civil Service Commission in favor of proceeding to implement the act. A staff was gathered for a field division and tentative class specifications and compensation schedules were prepared by September 15, 1923, in time for possible use in connection with the preparation of the budget for the fiscal year of 1925. However, in late October the Bureau of the Budget reversed its previous decision to use these preliminary specifications in its budgetary planning for 1925; and on November 12 the Bureau of the Budget and Bureau of Efficiency decided, over objections by the Civil Service Commission, to abolish the field division and to scrap the work already accomplished. At the same time the Board directed the heads of field agencies to allocate their positions to the same general salary schedules already applied to employees in the District of Columbia.

For the Washington area the Board approved the allocations made by the agency heads without any extensive review. For the

301

field service the full analysis apparently contemplated by the Act of 1923 was never made.[39] After much criticism the Board later developed a small 156-page class specification manual for positions in the District of Columbia.[40] But this manual provided nothing like a full set of class specifications and no attempt to develop such a set for the departmental service was made until after World War II. While salaries were gradually and reluctantly raised both within and without the District, the actions of the Board generally favored the maintenance of the status quo, though it presumably was the intent of the Classification Act of 1923 to bring about change. Senator Smoot, leader of the congressional economy bloc, apparently was not only able to influence the act itself, but also was able to control the administrative development of the new law through his influence with the Bureau of the Budget and, especially, the Bureau of Efficiency.[41]

Of course, all this pulling and hauling over the Act of 1923 did not pass unnoticed. The public employee organizations were bitterly and publicly disappointed and critical of the work of the Personnel Classification Board. The House, by resolution, called for the minutes of the Board and referred them to the chairman of the House Committee on Reform of the Civil Service, Congressman F. R. Lehlbach of New Jersey, who had been instrumental in the passage of the Classification Act. Lehlbach, in turn, referred the papers to Lewis Meriam of the Institute for Government Research for analysis. Meriam confirmed the general impression that the Bureau of Efficiency had been instrumental in undermining the intent of the Classification Act. In presenting Meriam's report to Congress, Lehlbach publicly accused Herbert Brown, director of the Bureau of Efficiency, of sabotage, saying, "In this as in his other manipulations he has had highly influential support." [42] Following a series of hearings during the spring of 1924, the House approved a bill to abolish the Personnel Classification Board, which, though reported favorably to the Senate, was blocked largely through the efforts of Senator Smoot. There the matter rested until 1928.

39 A token report, in which the Civil Service Commission did not concur, was, however, made in May 1924.

40 *Class Specifications for Positions in the Departmental Service*, P.C.B. Form 12 (Washington: Government Printing Office, 1924). Actually this manual was much smaller and considerably less complete than the compilation of specifications originally offered to Congress for consideration by the Joint Commission on Reclassification in 1920.

41 These conclusions were confirmed by William H. McReynolds in a personal interview on April 23, 1947, and by Kenneth C. Vipond and Luther C. Steward in personal interviews on September 2, 1948.

42 For the full context of Lehlbach's remarks together with Meriam's report, see the *Congressional Record*, 68th Cong., 1st Sess., February 12, 1924, pp. 2290–2310. In his reference to "support," Lehlbach obviously meant Senator Smoot.

Whatever subterranean political forces were working—and the story is yet far from clear in all its details—the result was that salaries were only gradually and grudgingly raised and the implementation of the doctrine of equal pay for equal work was a long time in coming. By the beginning of the fiscal year of 1925 it appeared that salary increases would still be primarily dependent upon what the *departments* chose or were able to give and upon the pay grade to which a *department* allocated an employee's position. The Board controlled the final decisions concerning such allocations, but it might be several years before a given employee's position was carefully considered. In the field service, representing nearly 90 per cent of the federal establishment, the Board was almost powerless. And its failure to undertake the full study of the position-classification requirements of the field service, which the Act of 1923 had directed it to initiate, left the Board and the two Bureaus subject to still further criticism.

Altogether, these interpretations of the Classification Act of 1923, while they were an improvement over previous legislation, by no means removed all causes for dissatisfaction with the pay policies of the federal government. In addition, the cost of living was still rising. After a carefully planned union campaign Congress finally in 1928 amended the Classification Act of 1923 by passing the Welch Bill. This act granted further general salary increases and specifically required the Board to commence the intensive survey of the field service which it had laid aside amid controversy a few years earlier. A full report on the field service eventually appeared in 1931.[43] Though the specifications contained in this volume never became official, they served, together with those first prepared by the Joint Commission on Reclassification, as the principal examples available for the guidance of federal personnel officers until the end of World War II. They are to some extent still used.

The reluctance of several departments to use their money for salary increases and the fact that these increases were by no means mandatory, together with a series of confusing decisions by the Comptroller General as to the authority of the Personnel Classification Board, made the effects of the salary legislation of 1928 also somewhat inconsistent. This led to another amendment of the Classification Act of 1923 in the form of the Brookhart Act of July 3, 1930. This contained the compensation schedules which remained in effect up to World War II and which finally enabled the Personnel Classification Board to employ its own staff. Up to this time it had been relying

---

[43] See U.S. Congress, House, *Preliminary Class Specifications of Positions in the Field Service*, prepared by the Field Survey Division, Personnel Classification Board, 71st Cong., 3d Sess., House Doc. 772 (Washington: Government Printing Office, 1931).

303

largely upon details from the three agencies which together directed its policy and operations.

The Classification Act of 1923 had also required that the Personnel Classification Board review the efficiency rating functions of the Bureau of Efficiency. In 1924 what has been known as the "graphic rating scale" was approved and put into use in a number of agencies. This stemmed from military experience during the war. The device was considered a great improvement over the minutely numerical system which had been set up by the Bureau of Efficiency in the Post Office Department before the First World War and in other departments after the war. The graphic rating scale was retained until 1935.[44]

Altogether, the Classification Act of 1923, though reluctantly and indifferently implemented for a number of years, marked a major milestone in the development of federal public personnel administration. Amendments of some importance were made to this act on a number of different occasions, but it was not finally supplanted by a completely new statute until 1949.

Further Research and Analysis

Though the Personnel Classification Board's conduct was in many ways open to question, the Board eventually produced between 1929 and 1931, under authority of the Welch Act, the first and only careful analysis of federal wage and related policies ever made. The Board's study brought to the attention of Congress and the general public a number of interesting findings which provide an illuminating insight into the fundamental character of the public service of the late twenties. As regards the relative wage position of the public service compared to private industry, these findings are considered as still largely valid. In the words of the Board itself, its conclusions may be summarized as follows:

1. The authority granted to the departments . . . to adjust pay rates in the field service "to correspond, so far as may be practicable," to the rates established by the classification act, as amended, for like positions in the departmental service in the District of Columbia, has resulted in an improvement of pay conditions in the field service, but not to a degree that represents the existence of a consistent and equitable system of allocations and pay for positions involving the same work.

2. Employees in the field service doing work of the same kind and value

[44] See U.S. Bureau of Efficiency, *Annual Report for 1923–24* (Washington: Government Printing Office, 1924), pp. 4–18, for the details of the new system.

have been administratively allocated to different grades and are paid at widely varying rates.

3. Titles of positions in the field service are in the main unstandardized, particularly across departmental lines, and are inadequate and sometimes misleading for purposes of budgeting, appropriating, and paying for personnel services, recruiting qualified employees, keeping meaningful records, and preparing correct and adequate communications and reports.

4. The prompt and scientific recruiting and selection of field employees is difficult under existing conditions.

5. There is no uniform plan in the field service for regulating increases in pay of employees who have gained in experience and usefulness in a given class of work.

6. For positions in the clerical, administrative, and fiscal and the subprofessional services, the Federal pay scale below the $2,000 level is more liberal than the average pay for similar non-Government positions, and for those above the $2,000 level it is less liberal; however, there is a considerable number of employers who pay higher rates than the Federal scale even in the lower grades.

7. The Government pay scale for positions in the custodial service is generally somewhat lower than the average pay for similar non-Government positions both above and below the $2,000 level.

8. The Government pay scale for positions in the professional and scientific service compares favorably with the average pay for similar non-Government positions below the $3,800 level, but above the $3,800 level the Government pay scale is lower and the discrepancy becomes greater as the importance of the work increases.

9. For professional and scientific positions the Government salary scale is generally more liberal than the average salaries for similar positions in the large colleges and universities (not including extracurricular income), although these same positions command a considerably higher rate in some of the institutions in question.

10. The salaries paid by private concerns to their major executives exceed those paid by the Federal Government to positions of similar responsibility anywhere from 100 to 500 per cent.

11. There does not appear to be justification on the basis of comparison with non-Government practice for establishing a different level of pay for similar work in different localities.

12. As a group Federal employees compare quite favorably as to stability with private employees of comparable character, but the Federal personnel is now much less stable than it was during the first decade of this century and the stability is greater in the departmental than in the field service.

13. The experience of private concerns with rating scales in selecting employees for salary increases has not been encouraging and several concerns report that they have discontinued them because of the difficulty of educating the supervisory force to use them properly.

14. The hours of work . . . compare favorably with those in general commercial practice, except that the practice of not working Saturday afternoons is more prevalent in private industry.

15. The leave privileges . . . are generally more liberal than those in private employment.

16. Non-Government employers do not generally provide retirement systems, but in some cases systems even more liberal than the Federal retirement plan are provided, such as group insurance and cooperative stock purchasing plans.

17. The civil-service requirements for employment in the Federal service are more exacting and thorough than entrance requirements generally for non-Government employment.[45]

The reports by the Personnel Classification Board were, in turn, utilized in 1931 by Herman Feldman, then Professor of Industrial Relations in the Amos Tuck School at Dartmouth, when he prepared one of the most complete analyses of the federal service ever made. In many ways this study by Feldman, employed as an outside consultant by the Field Survey Division of the Personnel Classification Board, has never been equaled in either depth or breadth of approach to the personnel problems of the federal government. It is still a useful and provocative document.[46]

Feldman's answer to the question: "To what degree has the magnitude of the Government personnel problem been met?" was

. . . that in spite of gratifying progress in certain fields of employment, the Government has neglected many aspects which have long required attention. In several aspects of employment, no authority exists to carry on the required activities. As an instance, the present survey has been unable to discover from any central source what the sanitary conditions as a whole are in offices and buildings occupied by field services throughout the country. Furthermore, there seems to be no one charged with responsibility to report to the Executive or Congress upon the accident hazards of these buildings. There is no agency charged with an educational program of training for Government employees. The lack of leadership or authority for other necessary functions of a Government personnel program will be a recurrent complaint throughout the report.

45 U.S. Congress, House, *Closing Report of Wage and Personnel Survey*, prepared by the Personnel Classification Board, 71st Cong., 3d Sess., House Doc. 771 (Washington: Government Printing Office, 1931), pp. iii–v. For the preliminary report see U.S. Congress, House, *Report of Wage and Personnel Survey*, prepared by the Field Survey Division, Personnel Classification Division, 70th Cong., 2d Sess., House Doc. 602 (Washington: Government Printing Office, 1929).

46 U.S. Congress, House, *A Personnel Program for the Federal Civil Service*, a report prepared by Herman Feldman, transmitted by the Director of the Personnel Classification Board, 71st Cong., 3d Sess., House Doc. 773 (Washington: Government Printing Office, 1931). Mention should be made of the earlier study by Lewis Mayers, *The Federal Service* (New York: D. Appleton and Co., 1922). Somewhat better than Feldman's with respect to the elimination of patronage and the handling of employee-management relations, Mayers' study is much less effective in terms of the comparison of public and private personnel practices and in presentation of a full-scale program of recommendations. Mayers also did not have the benefit of the Personnel Classification Board's vast quantity of wage and salary data.

Mayers' study was made under the auspices of the Institute for Government Research, a nonprofit organization created in 1916 and aimed at the study of administration from a more objective and scientific point of view. For an understanding of public administration in the twenties, the Institute's shelf of studies is essential.

In particular, on matters of wage legislation, changes come as a result of the energetic efforts of various groups to attract attention to their conditions and to secure special measures. Except as called for by a specific act of Congress, the proper kinds of wage data are not kept and, therefore, are not available to those concerned in the Government wage policy. In this and other matters dissatisfaction with various aspects of conditions of employment has been voiced for years, and the complaints may be justifiable, without adequate official action in any responsible quarter. The delay has made the solution of many personnel problems increasingly difficult because of the states of mind it has fostered and the habits it has encouraged.

There is little doubt but that an important cause of this situation is the lack of coordination and leadership in personnel activities. On the congressional side, legislation applying to Federal service is a patchwork with many large holes. On the administrative side, responsibility for personnel activities is divided among at least seven major commissions, boards, and bureaus, and among other bodies of a minor character. Things seem to have been allowed to drift, each agency doing only what the law specifically authorizes and being prevented by lack of power or funds from going beyond the bare outlines of its minimum activities.

To institute coordination and leadership in personnel activities in a broadened personnel program becomes the needed logical step in civil-service progress. A central authority with certain broad powers and with at least the responsibility for informing the Executive, the public, and Congress with regard to the major aspects of Government employment, would have the opportunity to reestablish, or perhaps more properly, for the first time establish, prestige for the civil service. It could inaugurate policies and methods which would improve the contentment and efficiency and the loyalty of all engaged in the Government employ. Not the least of its functions would be the development of a definite wage policy and the outlining of methods for adjusting wages to changes in conditions. It could become a source of vital information to the various departments of the Government concerning the newest and best practices of the various units and the most modern methods of private industry, and thus be a stimulating influence in promoting economical administration.[47]

Feldman's recommendations were based on the concept of the Civil Service Commission as a central personnel agency, the lack of which he felt was at the bottom of much of the difficulty. He went so far as to speak favorably, and in some detail, of a proposal for the establishment of a "Service of Administration," then sponsored by The Brookings Institution, the Bureau of Public Personnel Administration, the National Civil Service Reform League, and others. Under this plan a Secretary of Administration would coordinate the efforts of the Bureau of the Budget, the Civil Service Commission, the

---

[47] *A Personnel Program for the Federal Civil Service*, as cited in footnote 46, pp. 8–9. For an earlier statement along similar lines, see Herbert A. Filer, "The Need for Correlation of Personnel Activities in the Federal Service," *The Annals*, CXIII (May, 1924), 220.

Bureau of Efficiency, the Personnel Classification Board, the General Supply Committee of the Treasury Department, and, perhaps, the Bureau of Pensions, the Federal Employees' Compensation Commission, the Office of Public Buildings and Public Parks, and the Government Printing Office.[48]

This was, of course, radical doctrine. As Feldman noted, one of the more salient criticisms of the concept of a Service of Administration came from those who still felt that the patronage policing functions of the Civil Service Commission were not yet outdated. These critics feared the submersion of the Commission within a larger and less independent executive agency. The events of the thirties were to demonstrate that such fears were by no means groundless. In 1949 a General Services Administration was established, but it bears little resemblance to the all-inclusive, general staff type of organization envisioned by Feldman.

Unfortunately, Feldman's report became public at the worst possible time, in the depths of the Great Depression and just prior to the election of 1932. Times were anything but propitious for careful consideration of a detailed report on the civil service. Nevertheless, his study unquestionably assisted in stimulating the administrative and legislative actions which granted the Civil Service Commission a more inclusive jurisdiction during the early years of the thirties.[49]

Progress Report for the Twenties

Despite the clash of dollars-and-cents economy with a more inclusive concept of administrative efficiency, the Retirement Act of 1920 and the Classification Act of 1923 were major accomplishments. Nor were these the sole efforts toward the improvement of the public service during this period of Republican supremacy.

Extension of the merit system. By 1923 the momentum of the Republican spoils raid was largely gone. Though the additional offices which could legally be placed under full merit system procedures were not great in number, there were steady additions to the classified list throughout the administrations of Coolidge and Hoover. Under

48 *A Personnel Program for the Federal Civil Service,* as cited in footnote 46, pp. 256–59.
49 Of growing influence also, especially within the educational world, was the gradual increase in the number of studies of public personnel administration made largely under private auspices. See, for example, the first edition of Leonard D. White's *Introduction to the Study of Public Administration* (New York: The Macmillan Co., 1926), much of which was devoted to public personnel administration, and the publications of the Institute for Government Research, the Bureau of Public Personnel Administration, founded in 1923, and the growing number of official and quasi-official organizations of public officials such as the National Assembly of Civil Service Commissions and the City Managers' Association.

Hoover the portion of the offices under the merit system finally reached a peak of approximately 80 per cent. The most spectacular classification was that of the Prohibition Bureau in 1927. Of equal importance was the Rogers Act of 1924, which provided a firm legislative base for a career system for all but top diplomats in the Department of State. The Civil Service Commission did not have charge of the operation of this system, but it was officially represented on the governing board of examiners.

The Commission. The position of the Civil Service Commission itself was considerably improved during the twenties, in terms of both personnel and available funds. In 1920 its relationship with the Department of the Interior was terminated and the Commission was master of its own quarters and in control of its own funds for supplies and printing. By 1923 it had control over its entire field force and no longer had to depend upon details from the various departments. The funds at its disposition jumped from around $640,000 in 1920 to about $1,850,000 in 1932. After severe cuts for the fiscal years of 1933 and 1934, funds jumped back again to nearly $2,000,000 in 1935 and rose steadily thereafter.[50] On the whole, the Commission fared as well as any other agency during the decade or so after 1920.

The Commission survived three investigations with little difficulty, two by Congress and one by the critically disposed Bureau of Efficiency.[51] By 1930 its reputation, in comparison with that of the Bureau of Efficiency and the Personnel Classification Board, was well on the upgrade. During the entire period it had the full support of the employee unions as well as the National Civil Service Reform League.

In technical matters, the most important contribution of the Civil Service Commission was the improvement of examination techniques through the refinement and more extensive utilization of advanced testing methods. Psychological testing had been given a great impetus by the success of the Army's program in World War I. In 1922 the Commission introduced short-answer examinations into the junior technical, scientific, and professional fields. It greatly revised its tests to determine the equivalent of a high school education, and it commenced new research on the problems of detecting mental capacity and the standardization of test items. In 1923 it acquired the services of Dr. L. J. O'Rourke, formerly of the War Department, to

---

50 See the Commission's annual reports for the years in question.
51 See USCSC, *Thirty-ninth Report,* 1922, p. xxxix; Agnes Wright Spring, *William Chapin Deming of Wyoming* (Glendale, Calif.: Arthur H. Clark Co., 1944), pp. 275–82; and U.S. Bureau of Efficiency, "Report on the Methods of Transacting the Public Business in the United States Civil Service Commission," April 7, 1922 (Typed copy in the Library of the U.S. Civil Service Commission, Washington, D.C.).

head a technical research section within the Commission.[52] In the late twenties O'Rourke outlined a new and broader program of general research into personnel testing and secured the cooperation of a large number of industrial concerns in an attempt to set up national testing standards for certain occupations. In the testing field the Commission was still more than abreast of the times.

Since 1915 the Commission and the Public Health Service had cooperated in the physical examination of a limited number of applicants to discover disabilities. But physical examinations were not generally required for all prospective employees until 1923, when President Harding made possible a more full-scale program.[53] Fingerprints were first extensively taken in the course of the 1927–28 investigation of the personnel of the Prohibition Bureau. One out of thirteen of the Bureau's employees was found to have had a police record. Thereafter it was decided to accomplish such a check for all similar types of positions.[54]

On the whole, the Commission kept itself up-to-date. Private industry, however, was rapidly advancing into what may be called its "personnel age." This was characterized by the wide repercussions of Western Electric's Hawthorne experiment in human relations and counseling, the refinement of employee welfare programs, the rise of new union-management relationships, the improvement of supervision and training, and the consolidation of central personnel systems. In terms of personnel management as a unified whole, the relative position of the federal service was slipping compared to private industry. Part of the difficulty has already been discussed. Other complications stemmed from the very size of the federal service and our democratic reluctance to emphasize what were still to many merely managerial "frills."

Centralization at last. Some tentative efforts at interdepartmental cooperation were made in the early twenties under the stimulus of the Bureau of the Budget. The Director of the Bureau was instrumental in 1921 in the formation of a Federal Personnel Board composed mainly of the appointment clerks of the various departments and operating under the guidance of the Civil Service Commission.[55] This was of some assistance to the Commission. But the departments themselves were not well organized to handle their own personnel matters, let alone to cooperate extensively for the development of any

52 For these developments, see especially USCSC, *Fortieth Report*, 1923, pp. xli–xlvii and l–c.
53 Same, p. vi; and USCSC, *Thirty-third Report*, 1916, p. xxxi.
54 USCSC, *Forty-sixth Report*, 1929, p. 42.
55 See "A Federal Personnel Board Established," *Good Government*, XXXIX (January, 1922), 4–6; and USCSC, *Fortieth Report*, 1923, p. xxi.

more comprehensive plans. The first department to initiate a personnel system in the full sense of the word was the Department of Agriculture in 1925. This was followed later by more or less formal organizations in the Treasury and Interior departments.[56] In the remainder, the tendency still was to retain such matters under the control of the chief clerk or some similar line official. Outside the departments the Commission was cooperating in personnel matters as much as possible prior to 1930 with the Bureau of Efficiency, the Personnel Classification Board, the Bureau of the Budget, the Bureau of Pensions, the Federal Employees' Compensation Commission, the State Department, and the General Accounting Office, all of which had official functions vitally related to personnel management.

It took the Great Depression and the efforts of President Hoover for economy and efficiency in administration to force consolidation of the major personnel functions of the government under the direction of the Civil Service Commission. The first important action was the creation by an executive order of April 25, 1931, of a new Council of Personnel Administration, with the president of the Civil Service Commission as chairman and Dr. L. J. O'Rourke as director of the Council's activities. Its objectives were broad, and, almost immediately, advisory committees were designated to work on a group of special projects. Among the first were studies of transfers and training methods, neither of which had received much attention for years. In one form or another such a council has functioned ever since.

As a result of the Economy Act of June 20, 1932, the Personnel Classification Board was abolished. Its two main functions, position-classification and the supervision of efficiency ratings, were transferred to the Civil Service Commission. The following year the Bureau of Efficiency was also legislated out of existence. The chief antagonist of the Commission was gone. By executive order in 1934 the Commission received full jurisdiction over the operations stemming from the Retirement Act.

The economy legislation vitally affected public employees in other ways, too. It drastically curtailed salaries, leaves, promotions, and miscellaneous privileges. Had the principal employee union, the National Federation of Federal Employees, not split at this time with the American Federation of Labor, the restrictions might not have been quite so severe. The full effects of this legislation were not felt until the very end of the Hoover administration, but by 1932 the future was most uncertain for many members of the public service, despite

[56] See Leonard D. White, *Trends in Public Administration* (New York: McGraw-Hill Book Co., 1933), pp. 166–69, for a more complete chronology of such developments.

the centralization of many personnel functions within the Civil Service Commission.

The End of an Era

The First World War stimulated an appreciation by private industry of the government's success in the centralized recruiting of personnel. It also stimulated the government to adopt new personnel procedures relating to retirement and position-classification. But the prosperity of the twenties and the narrow dollars-and-cents view of economy and efficiency taken by the Republican administration effectively delayed the full implementation of these new devices whenever they tended to increase the current costs of government. The real contribution of the twenties to public personnel administration thus was to put into legislation the essentials for an up-to-date personnel program, even if the tools were not effectively wielded at first.

By 1930 the merit system seemed as firmly entrenched as it had appeared to be in 1913. More than 80 per cent of federal public employees occupied competitive positions within the classified service, leaving only 100,000 or so positions outside the merit system. This group represented both the highest and the lowest of the federal positions, with the bulk of the exempt positions specifically excluded from the merit system by the terms of the Pendleton Act.

During this period the traditional view of civil service reform as a remedy for political corruption had faded into the background. The old words and phrases tuned to an older morality had lost their appeal, as the National Civil Service Reform League had discovered just before the First World War. During and after the war the League found that it was necessary, if for no other reason than to obtain funds for its work, to advocate the merit system as a means of promoting efficiency and economy in terms of dollars and cents. Through these years civil service reform itself was not important as a political issue; but efficiency and economy, of which it was an integral part, were of major concern in 1920, 1924, and 1932, and to a somewhat lesser extent in 1928. The merit system continued to develop as an adjunct to the broader movement for the modernization of governmental as well as industrial administrative machinery.

However, the depression and the election of 1932 introduced elements of decided uncertainty into what otherwise had appeared to be a secure future for the merit system and personnel administration in general. Tremendous economic and political pressures were asserting themselves in preparation for a disavowal of a government primarily oriented toward the desires of the business community.

312

THE GUMPS—SUPERSALESMEN

From *Chicago Tribune*, June 22, 1925.

If the righteousness of the moral political man had failed to solve the ills confronting the nation during the nineteenth century, the revision and reorientation of our governmental and administrative machinery had been no more effective in the first three decades of the twentieth. Civil service reform had prospered in its close relationship to both of these movements. Now arose the question of its relationship to those more fundamental forces which govern society in a time of major domestic crisis and conflict.

After 1932, the business of government would be business, to be sure; but the result would be something far different from that envisioned by Calvin Coolidge nearly a decade before. As the nature of our government changed, public personnel administration and the civil service it represented would inevitably face the problem of readjustment to the whole of which they were part.

SUPPLEMENTARY NOTES

The struggle over position-classification. The story of the position-classification controversy deserves a more extensive treatment than that possible here. Its major significance lies in the fact that the decisions reached at this time affected the trend of the pay and position-classification structure of the federal government for the next three decades. It is also an intriguing example of sabotage of declared legislative intent by administrative agencies supported by an influential legislative bloc. The interpretation here is based upon a wide range of miscellaneous materials of which the following are the more important: Baruch, *History of Position-Classification and Salary Standardization in the Federal Service, 1789–1941*, as cited in footnote 36, pp. 48–49; "The Work of the Personnel Classification Board," *The Public Business*, II (December 1927–January 1928), pp. 1–20; "The Personnel Classification Board," a report by a special committee of the National Civil Service Reform League, December 7, 1923; Pearson and Allen, *More Merry-Go-Round*, as cited in footnote 32, pp. 323–31; the *Congressional Record*, scattered, from May 1923 through the following year; together with almost all the issues of *Good Government*, the organ of the National Civil Service Reform League, and the *Federal Employee*, that of the National Federation of Federal Employees, from 1920 up to 1928. These sources were supplemented by information gained from interviews with several participants and interested onlookers, among them Luther C. Steward, Guy Moffett, and William H. McReynolds. Paul V. Betters' study of *The Personnel Classification Board* (Washington: The Brookings Institution, 1931) is of use only with respect to legal and organizational matters.

CHAPTER 13

Challenge and Response: 1933–1940

The federal civil service of the nineteen thirties presents a study in contrasts. At first the disintegration of fifty years of experience seemed almost complete; but by 1940 an astonishing degree of order had appeared on the scene. It is these opposites which make the study of the American public service in the depression era so challenging and which have made the figure of Franklin D. Roosevelt so controversial.

The New Gold Rush [1]

The public service of President Hoover was in dire straits by 1933. The depression, the economy acts, and the impending change of party control together produced in the bureaucracy a state of mind even more pessimistic than in the nation at large. Nor was this state of mind entirely unwarranted. The federal civil service was soon to become the scene of one of the most spectacular resurgences of the spoils system in American history. Much of this story is well known. But there was more method to the manipulation than was often apparent. It is this underlying pattern rather than the more lurid details that is analyzed here.

At its annual meeting for 1934 the Council of the National Civil Service Reform League concluded that the pledge of the Democratic party for economy and the party's need to satisfy its more importunate partisans were the more obvious causes of the temporary eclipse of civil service reform.[2] The Council was generally correct in its

---

[1] Herbert S. Hollander in *Spoils* (Washington: William Ullman, 1936), p. 23, applied this title to the first years of the Franklin D. Roosevelt regime.

[2] NCSRL, *Proceedings*, 1934, p. 8.

analysis if, in addition, one keeps in mind the impact of the largely Republican sponsored economy measures of 1932–33 upon the activities of the Civil Service Commission. It is questionable if the Commission of 1933–34 with its existing staff and budget could have fully met the current employment requirements of the federal government. On the other hand, the Roosevelt administration certainly did not rush to the financial aid of its central personnel agency. For the deliberate patronage politics marking Franklin D. Roosevelt's first term in office, the party of Jefferson, Jackson, and William Jennings Bryan must be given the lion's share of the credit.

The preliminary. One particular legislative action in the fall of 1932 presaged the trend of events. At the suggestion of Democratic Senator Kenneth D. McKellar of Tennessee, Congress led off with a traditional request for the compilation and publication of the famous "Plum Book" of 1933 in which were listed all the federal civil offices for which examinations were not required for appointment.[3] At stake were more than 100,000 positions. Some 20,000 of these were of more than average significance: postmasters of the first, second, and third classes; collectors and deputy collectors of internal revenue; collectors and deputy collectors of customs; surveyors, special examiners, appraisers, and naval officers in the Customs Service; registers, receivers, and surveyors general of the Land Office; superintendents of mints and assayers in mints; supervising inspectors in the Steamboat Inspection Service; commissioners of immigration and naturalization; attorneys of nearly all types; United States marshals and deputies; the Foreign Service and diplomatic corps; assistant secretaries and undersecretaries of departments; heads of most of the bureaus of the departments at Washington; and the heads of nearly all agencies at home and abroad. Such was the political pie in early 1933.

Presidential decisions. The actions of the President-elect and his chief advisers during the first few weeks after the decisive election gave little indication of the deluge to come. According to James A. Farley, he had made it clear to Governor Roosevelt before the election that he "had been most careful not to embarrass him by promising positions or appointments to anyone, either during the Chicago Convention or after it." Roosevelt replied that "he appreciated that attitude and that

---

3 This included all the unclassified offices as well as those which were classified but excepted from examination under *Schedules A* and *B* or other provisions of the civil service rules. U.S. Congress, Senate, *Positions Not Under the Civil Service*, 72nd Cong., 2d Sess., Senate Doc. 173 (Washington: Government Printing Office, 1933); and its companion piece, U.S. Congress, Senate, *Presidential Post Offices*, 72nd Cong., 2d Sess., Senate Doc. 176 (Washington: Government Printing Office, 1933). As usual the Civil Service Commission prepared these lists.

he had pursued the same policy himself." [4] For other than his Cabinet and the inner circle of the so-called Brain Trust, Roosevelt indicated few choices before his arrival in Washington for the inauguration on March 4, 1933.

Nor was this early paucity of patronage promises the result of mere chance. Rather it was part of a carefully planned policy. Raymond Moley has told one version of the story of the essential decision which occasioned a deliberate withholding of the patronage until future necessity should point the way to its most effective use. The decision was evidently made at a conference of Farley, Edward J. Flynn, Frank C. Walker, Louis Howe, and Roosevelt himself at Warm Springs, Georgia, in February, 1933. While, as Moley said, the policy worked, it also meant that "we stood in the city of Washington on March 4th like a handful of marauders in hostile territory." [5]

During the remarkable Hundred Days, Roosevelt continued his "calculated delay" [6] in rewarding the faithful. The patronage was to be used, "if not as a club, then as a steel-pointed *pic*." [7]

The system. Farley, as Postmaster General, continued in the central position as chief dispenser. In this he was ably assisted by Flynn, Walker, Homer S. Cummings and Daniel C. Roper. Despite Farley's famous political clearance system for appointments to public office and the organization of his semi-official political employment agency, managed by Emil Hurja,[8] neither Farley nor anyone else expected quite the rush that occurred. As he admitted, there was not even a possibility of a job for more than one person in twenty.[9] Of course, critical salvos were constantly fired at the whole procedure in the press, and Farley became known as the boldest and frankest patronage dispenser in the recent history of the United States. But he stoutly maintained that the only difference between his and his predecessors' points of view on the offices was that he admitted he believed in patronage. Moreover, in his opinion, the policies of patronage and

---

[4] James A. Farley, *Behind the Ballots* (New York: Harcourt, Brace and Co., 1938), p. 183. See also Raymond Moley, *After Seven Years* (New York: Harper and Bros., 1939), p. 109.

[5] Moley, as cited in footnote 4, pp. 127–28.

[6] As labeled by Alfred Lief in *Democracy's Norris* (New York: Stackpole Sons, 1939), p. 414.

[7] Moley, as cited in footnote 4, p. 128.

[8] Farley, as cited in footnote 4, pp. 223–38; and James A. Farley, "Passing Out the Patronage," *American Magazine*, CXVI (August, 1933), 20 ff. See also Charles Michelson, *The Ghost Talks* (New York: G. P. Putnam's Sons, 1944), pp. 46–47; the "Unofficial Observer," pseudonym of John Franklin Carter, *The New Dealers* (New York: Simon and Schuster, Inc., 1934), pp. 234 and 244–47; and Rexford G. Tugwell, *The Democratic Roosevelt* (Garden City, N.Y.: Doubleday and Co., 1956), p. 266.

[9] Farley, as cited in footnote 4, p. 36.

merit could, and should, exist side by side.[10] Farley may well be given credit for originating the view, more recently emphasized by such persons as Paul Appleby, that patronage and politics have a legitimate place in governmental administrative affairs if they are properly handled.[11]

It should not be assumed that the distribution of offices was as completely systematic as the reference to Farley's employment office might imply. While the Postmaster General was usually consulted on appointments, this was by no means always the case. "I can remember," says Donald R. Richberg, then general counsel for the National Recovery Administration, "the somewhat pathetic appeals of Jim Farley for notification at least of our intention to appoint someone so that he might clear it with the appropriate politician who would like to get the credit even for an appointment to which he was personally opposed." [12] Moreover, it was frequently extremely simple to obtain a political clearance. One Civil Service Commission official familiar with Washington in the middle thirties has observed that "Congressmen and Senators from the district or state from which these prospective job seekers arrived wrote letters of endorsement practically upon request." [13] The system certainly favored the Democrats but it did not preclude Republicans or those who were essentially neutral. Nor did it prevent thousands of extremely competent individuals from seeking employment under the federal aegis, many of whom were as much motivated by a relatively nonpartisan sense of urgency as by a more mercenary and clearly personal political self-interest. The great influx of personnel into the federal government in the thirties contained a smaller than usual proportion of ex-precinct workers, party hacks, and unemployables. In this respect the "gold rush" of 1933 differed considerably from those of previous years.

Still, the civil service of the early and middle thirties was heavily stamped with a partisan political imprint. By the fall of 1933 the National Civil Service Reform League warned, "Not since Grover Cleveland's administration has the merit system had to face such a serious challenge to its existence as it faces now upon the late change of administration." [14] Shortly before this the League had received a

10 Same, pp. 224–25; and James A. Farley, *Jim Farley's Story* (New York: McGraw-Hill Book Co., 1948), p. 35.

11 Paul H. Appleby, *Big Democracy* (New York: Alfred A. Knopf, 1945), pp. 144–55. Appleby is, however, much less sweeping in his support of patronage, emphasizing mainly the need for each department head to have a number of top positions always available for political appointment. This would follow French practice.

12 Donald R. Richberg, *My Hero* (New York: G. P. Putnam's Sons, 1954), p. 236.

13 Letter to the writer, dated October 10, 1951. Its author, a government official, prefers to remain anonymous.

14 NCSRL, *Proceedings*, 1933, p. 11.

reply from Roosevelt to its inquiry as to his intentions toward the classified service. With the ingenuousness of Taft and T. R. the President had written, "May I assure the members of your League that the merit system in civil service is in no danger at my hands; but on the contrary I hope that it will be extended and improved during my term as President." [15] The League had not been impressed.

From the point of view of public personnel administration, President Roosevelt appeared at this time in one of his more ambiguous roles. Leonard D. White, himself a civil service commissioner from 1934 to 1937, has emphasized that F. D. R.'s public statements consistently upheld the theory of merit.[16] That his initial tactics tended

Big Jim, the Spoilsman

"SPOILSMAN, SPOILSMAN, SAVE THAT TREE."
From *Washington Times*, August 11, 1936.

[15] "The Civil Service Under the New Administration," *Good Government* (December, 1933), 26.
[16] Leonard D. White, "Franklin Roosevelt and the Public Service," *Public Personnel Review*, VI (July, 1945), 139-46.

to belie his remarks is an understatement. Nevertheless he was no William Jennings Bryan, from whom neither words nor actions offered any promise for civil service reform. The unusual progress in public personnel administration during F. D. R.'s second term supports White's thesis that Roosevelt's "declarations of faith" in the principles of civil service reform were more than transitory press releases for partisan purposes.

Trained early in the back yard of his cousin, T. R., and in the sub-cabinet of President Wilson, Franklin D. Roosevelt fully understood the intricate relationship of party, program, and patronage. As Governor of New York he had found it painfully obvious that control of his party was essential to execute any political program. With a Congress hungrier than usual for patronage, the present opportunity was one that no master politician could afford to ignore.

The President, therefore, seldom disapproved congressional exemptions of newly created alphabetical agencies from the classified service. As these exemptions increased, the jobs proliferated and the appointive power of the President was accordingly greatly expanded. In the same manner as Wilson, Roosevelt rewarded and punished to support his social program and to bind together the discordant party he had inherited. The nature of the emergency was probably the essential moving force behind the unusual subservience of Congress in 1933. Nevertheless the patronage was used for all it was worth to further the President's aims. Its importance can be gauged by the concerted and successful efforts of Congress to prevent the extension of the merit system during the middle thirties.

The alphabetical agencies. By the end of 1934 Congress had exempted from merit system regulations the personnel of almost sixty new agencies, totalling approximately 100,000 offices, and had placed only five agencies under the jurisdiction of the Civil Service Commission. The result was a public service in which the proportion of offices under the merit system rapidly declined from its previous peak of around 80 per cent under President Hoover. By 1936 only about 60 per cent of a total federal public service of more than 800,000 was on the classified list. The lowest percentage recorded since Theodore Roosevelt's first term in office more than thirty years before, it was to be the lowest recorded under Franklin D. Roosevelt as well.

Of course, the President could not begin to confer with Farley on all the jobs to be filled. Despite Farley's clearance system, the recruitment for political plums became largely decentralized, with only an ultimate control held at the top. As the new agencies grew, their heads in some instances had as much money and patronage at their disposal as many former chief executives had once enjoyed.

From the standpoint of administrative effectiveness and efficiency political recruitment was by no means always unfortunate. The phenomenally small organization, "consisting of 121 people with a total payroll of $22,000 a month," with which Harry Hopkins administered the first year of his relief work and spent a billion and a half dollars, has been vividly described by Robert E. Sherwood. As Sherwood justly remarked, "To anyone in any way familiar with the normal workings of government, the lowness of those figures is well nigh incredible. But Hopkins managed to obtain people to whom a sixty-hour work week would be a holiday." [17] There was a similar esprit de corps in many sections of the Department of Agriculture. "Never in my 16 years of service have I witnessed such production records as I did in the old Agricultural Adjustment Administration during this period," wrote a former employee of this agency a few years ago.

. . . Moreover, much of the work was done at an absolute minimum cost so far as salaries are concerned. In one particular operation, for example, the supervisor of approximately 500 employees in an IBM operation, resigned his position to accept an appointment as District of Columbia policeman because the latter job offered a higher salary than he was getting as a supervisor.[18]

But there was a darker side, too. The Home Owners' Loan Corporation, for example, had to be reorganized after spoils policies had brought it almost to its knees. Far more damning were the widespread charges, many quite true, of local political corruption in the use of relief funds, relief jobs, and the moneys allocated for public works. However, considering the tremendous efforts involved and the short time in which most of the agencies had to organize and to spend their appropriations, fraud and corruption, while unquestionably present, were surprisingly negligible.[19] They did not compare to the wholesale knavery under Grant and Harding.

In the opinion of Samuel H. Ordway, Jr., a civil service commissioner from 1937 to 1939, Secretary Frances Perkins of the Department of Labor was more constant than any other of Roosevelt's cabinet officers in her support of the merit system. Ordway credits the Department of Agriculture with the most competent personnel department, and, during his period as commissioner, the War Department and

[17] Robert E. Sherwood, Roosevelt and Hopkins (2 vols.; New York: Bantam Books, Inc., 1950), I, 59.

[18] Letter to the writer, dated October 10, 1950. See note 13.

[19] For views and opinions of the competency and the patronage policies of Hopkins, Ickes, Wallace, and others, see, e.g., Carter, as cited in footnote 9; Frank Kent, Without Gloves (New York: William Morrow and Co., 1934); and Raymond Clapper, Watching the World Go By (New York: Reynal and Hitchcock, 1943). See Sherwood, as cited in footnote 17, chs. iii and iv, for the most complete discussion of "The Relief Program."

the Department of Justice with a tie for the worst.[20] Actually, as former Commissioner White has noted, the old-line departments were often outshone by the New Deal agencies in many aspects of personnel management:

. . . It is significant that at a time when the U.S. Civil Service Commission had never held an examination for personnel officer, and when the Commission, like most other agencies had no personnel office other than that of chief clerk (Dr. W. W. Stockberger in the Department of Agriculture excepted), the Farm Credit Administration, the Home Owners' Loan Corporation, the Agricultural Adjustment Administration, and other New Deal agencies were setting up personnel offices staffed with an alert group of industrial personnel men who saw much more in their tasks than merely keeping employment records. These men brought a fresh and invaluable contribution to the federal service; their concept of personnel work has become standard in the federal service, although not always fully realized in practice.[21]

Thus it cannot be assumed that the free and easy appointment policies of the New Deal were fully incompatible with the advance of public personnel administration.

Moreover, as an unusual experiment, the new Tennessee Valley Authority was permitted in 1933 to operate its own personnel system. This was developed under the cover of a specific legal requirement:

In the appointment of officials and the selection of employees for said corporation, and in the promotion of any such employees or officials, no political test or qualification shall be permitted or given consideration, but all such appointments and promotion shall be given and made on the basis of merit and efficiency.[22]

While Congress had expressly authorized the new agency to by-pass the regular civil service procedures,[23] there had been no intent to permit the ignoring of merit principles. Under the auspices of its first directors, the T.V.A. oriented itself firmly toward the merit requirements of the law creating it, despite the strong pressures constantly brought to bear upon it, particularly by the senior senator from Tennessee, Kenneth D. McKellar.

Under a tradition-shattering management the T.V.A. soon created an unusually positive type of personnel management rivaling that of the more advanced business concerns and serving as a model for some

---

20 Statement in a personal interview, April 28, 1947.
21 As cited in footnote 16, p. 141.
22 Sec. 6 of the act creating the T.V.A., 48 U.S. Statutes 58 (May 18, 1933).
23 Same, sec. 3, includes the phrase "without regard to the provision of Civil Service laws."

of the more innovative developments in public personnel administration in general. To this day the T.V.A. has maintained its separate and unique personnel system. The core of the system has been a centralized personnel office which operated in a decentralized manner in an effort to provide personnel staff services for the maximum benefit of the line operating divisions. Utilizing from the beginning the highly flexible devices of relatively "unranked registers" and "selective certification," [24] and promoting the development of unusually close employer-employee relations, the T.V.A. early set a remarkably forward-looking personnel standard for other governmental units.

Its immunity from veteran preference and apportionment legislation made its problems somewhat simpler, of course.[25] That its relatively free and easy recruitment and certification procedures left it open to personal influences not entirely consistent with the merit system was also true. Nevertheless, from the beginning the T.V.A. more than lived up to the hopes of its political sponsor, Senator George W. Norris of Nebraska. It is only fair to add that there is no evidence that President Roosevelt ever wavered in his backing of the directors of this unique organization in their efforts to follow the spirit as well as the letter of their guiding statute.[26]

Under more orthodox legislation and management, the Social Security Administration became one of the few new agencies besides the T.V.A. to be placed under the merit system by congressional action during the first term of Franklin D. Roosevelt. A few others not specifically exempted by law, such as the Farm Credit Administration, were placed under the jurisdiction of the Civil Service Commission by executive order. But, despite these actions, the result was still a decline in the percentage of federal employees under the merit system to its lowest point in our recent history.

As is often the case, periods of rapid change bring with them great improvements as well as great evils. Certainly the New Deal produced a political manipulation of public office, the like of which this country had not seen in the twentieth century. But at the same time, some of the more hidebound rigidities in the federal civil service gave way to

---

[24] Under a system of "unranked registers" applicants are still ranked, but only in broad groupings or categories such as "Outstanding," "Well Qualified," "Qualified," etc. With selective certification it is possible to give examinations for relatively broad categories of skills. Then the appointing officer may be permitted to prescribe more detailed requirements for individual positions, followed by a "selective certification" of those with the needed specialized qualifications by the personnel agency from the registers of more generally qualified candidates.

[25] Preference was, however, applied to the T.V.A. in 1944.

[26] For further details on T.V.A. personnel policies, see the "supplementary notes" to this chapter.

the pressures of the times. The insurge of new faces, the growth of new tasks, the reorganization of functions, and the general abundance of funds forced changes in the administrative as well as in the political scheme of things.

"Ideological Patronage"

Among the phenomena brought about by the social politics of the New Deal was the rapid development of a new type of patronage, which may be termed "ideological patronage." It developed in its most refined form under F. D. R., though the same type of phenomenon occurred to a very limited extent before 1900 and, to a much greater extent, under Presidents Theodore Roosevelt and Wilson.

A crucial decision of 1932. The introduction of this type of patronage in the thirties can in a general way be traced to an unusual decision made by Franklin D. Roosevelt in the 1932 campaign and reported by Raymond Moley. It seems that F. D. R. instructed Moley to go ahead and work on the main campaign issues while Roosevelt took a short trip early in July, 1932. In the course of the conversation Moley asked, "You mean to go on keeping the policy job and the other separate?"

"Definitely," Roosevelt answered.

"And I'm to head up through to you on policy?"

"Yes."

"And authorization for the same piece of work won't be scattered around? This isn't Louis [Howe], now, I'm thinking about. It's Jim Farley and the senators and the contributors."

F. D. R. then spoke plainly, "There'll be no drafts or suggestions or proposals that aren't cleared through you. I give you my assurance." According to Moley this promise was kept "without exception" and was confirmed by Farley a week later when the latter acknowledged, "I just want you to know that I'm interested in getting him the votes —nothing else. . . . Issues aren't my business. They're yours and his. You keep out of mine, and I'll keep out of yours." [27]

Effects. The result of this decision was to separate in a way that had not been so thoroughly done before in American history intellectual policy-making from political policy-selling. First manifested through the Brain Trust, brought together largely from the universities in

---

[27] Moley, as cited in footnote 4, p. 36. See also Samuel I. Rosenman, *Working with Roosevelt* (New York: Harper and Bros., 1952), p. 201; and Farley, as cited in footnote 10, p. 38.

1932,[28] policy-making later fell to that loosely knit organization of "kitchen cabinet" members vaguely described as the New Dealers. Moley has noted the types of administrative personnel available to the Democratic party in 1932. In his opinion that which was left over from Wilson was for the most part too old. Much of the rest was too politically partisan, or with no comprehension of the problems of the day. As F. D. R. could not seem to bring himself to trust many of the businessmen who wished to help, he often turned to representatives of the universities and to young lawyers for crucial intellectual contributions. Delighted to find themselves called to the center of political power for the first time in our history, they in turn encouraged their friends and those who thought as they did. With unprecedented opportunities for action and for contribution to the affairs of the nation, the lure was irresistible to many of these highly intelligent and well educated but, in the old-time partisan sense, politically detached individuals. As one of their number, who himself later became a presidential assistant, wrote at the time:

. . . An entirely new type of public servant came storming into Washington —young, enthusiastic, idealistic, able and hard-working. He knew the difference between fudge and a fugue, had read books, could talk intelligently, and had ideas. He spent long hours at his desk, scorned the clock-watchers of the old Civil Service, drank hard, played hard, talked hard, and got hard things done. For the first time, short of war, the government had tapped the moral and intellectual energies of the college-bred middle classes. It was a psychic "blood-transfusion," which invigorated political administration beyond belief. It frightened the politicians and the bureaucrats and, through the newspapers, amused and puzzled the public.[29]

The most startling break from the past lay in the separation of the idea men from the political organizers in the preparation of legislation for submission to Congress. Especially during the famous Hundred Days, Congress frequently received its legislation already fully drawn up by the White House staff and usually passed it without substantial change. This phenomenon of the division of labor be-

28 The origin and workings of the Brain Trust (first known as Brains Trust) are best described in Rosenman, as cited in footnote 27, pp. 56–59, 80–81, 87–89, and elsewhere. See also Moley, as cited in footnote 4, pp. 128–31; and Tugwell, as cited in footnote 9, pp. 214–19.

29 John Franklin Carter, *1940* (New York: The Viking Press, 1940), pp. 31–32. In a sense Carter is wrong about this being the "first" time for such an invasion. Lord Bryce had noted the same sort of manifestation under Theodore Roosevelt, and some other "kitchen cabinets" had tended in this direction. But, in terms of the size, importance, and systematic character of the movement, nothing like it had existed before. See also Edward S. Corwin, *The President: Office and Powers* (3d rev. ed.; New York: New York University Press, 1948), pp. 517–18.

tween the intellectuals and the politicians arose in part out of the tremendous pressures of the times, pressures which demanded extraordinary political and social inventiveness. The old-line politicians simply could not supply the ideas. Neither could the permanent civil service, for it had only rarely been encouraged to do the type of thinking needed in 1933. As for calling in a bevy of businessmen to assist, Rosenman argued before F. D. R.:

> Usually in a situation like this a candidate gathers around him a group composed of some successful industrialists, some big financiers, and some national political leaders. I think we ought to steer clear of all those. They all seem to have failed to produce anything constructive to solve the mess we're in today. Why not go to the universities of the country? [30]

Roosevelt did, and to all other sources from whence new ideas might come. As these ideas became incorporated into the expanding New Deal, their authors too became integrated into the public service through the encouragement of Roosevelt and those who could understand their importance and function.

The administrative problem. The advent of the New Dealers was an implicit recognition of the importance of research in modern decision-making. First recognized by Theodore Roosevelt, the problem was then met by the appointment of so many advisory committees that Congress formally objected. His successors largely followed T. R.'s type of solution. Under considerably more compulsion for speed in decision and action than his predecessors, F. D. R. would probably have found the advisory commission mechanism impossibly slow, even if he had seriously considered it in 1933. He did, however, depend upon it considerably more as time passed.

The peculiarities of the relationship of the president and his cabinet also explain the need for brain trusters. It is often impossible for a president fully to utilize his cabinet as a collective advisory body.[31] Cabinet members may or may not be placed in the cabinet for reasons bearing any relationship to their ability either as administrative and idea men or as political leaders. As a rule the cabinet is strictly an amorphous body with almost none of the collective functions of its British counterpart. With decision-making becoming more and more a matter of both extensive research and extensive coordination, a more formal administrative solution to the need for presidential advice was eventually to arise in the form of a vastly augmented White

---

[30] Rosenman, as cited in footnote 27, p. 57.

[31] President Eisenhower's use of his cabinet as a collective device for decision-making is the outstanding exception to the normal role of the cabinet in our history, and there is much speculation today as to whether such use can be institutionalized.

CHALLENGE AND RESPONSE: 1933–1940

House staff. But in 1933 times would not wait nor did Roosevelt choose to be bound by the past. The immediate answer to the practical problem of designing a program to save the nation in 1933 came in the form of New Dealers.

The political problem. From a political point of view this resulted, in turn, in the development of another kind of patronage, a sort of intellectual and ideological patronage rather than the more traditional partisan type. Of the appointment practices of Harry Hopkins, Charles Michelson has written: "Actually it must be assumed that he was politically nonpartisan in these matters and named his individual friends and associates—which may or may not be an improvement on the more conventional spoils system." [32] Ickes, Wallace, Corcoran, Frankfurter, Moley, Arnold, Cohen and many others tended to operate in similar fashion. The influx of their appointees continued apace throughout almost the entire period of Franklin D. Roosevelt's term of office. Many of these men remained in government employment, and by the beginning of World War II the federal public service was an inextricable intermixture of the old and the new. Undoubtedly, F. D. R.'s "young men" gave a lift to administration which it had not felt since the relatively brief emergency period of the First World War.

But, whatever the motives and whatever the length of hours they labored, the new patronage was still patronage and it was often bewailed and resented by the old-line Democratic politicians who knew it for what it was, even if the general public did not. David Lilienthal, himself an outstanding product of the loose recruitment procedures of the early days of the Roosevelt period, has said:

. . . "Taking care of the boys" is an evil in any guise, whether it is on the basis of personal friendship, business or social ties, or some amateur political notion about an "elite of brains" (self-selected), a kind of Phi Beta Kappa version of Tammany Hall.
The usual forthrightness of Congressmen is wholesome compared with the "holier-than-thou" attitude toward politicians of those who occasionally practice their own personal brand of politics.[33]

Had the so-called New Dealers been more careful of party sensibilities and more concerned with the development of grass roots support, they might have formed, as more traditional politicians sometimes feared, the nucleus of a new party structure in this country. But, usually more interested in action than in the political minutiae inevitably connected with large-scale political organization, they, as a

---

[32] As cited in footnote 9, p. 189. For further references, in part of a similar character, to Hopkins' appointments see Sherwood, as cited in footnote 17, 1, 60, 83–84, and elsewhere.
[33] *TVA: Democracy on the March* (New York: Harper and Bros., 1944), p. 184.

group, failed to take firm political root. Perhaps this was just as well. For the ideological recruitment of the New Deal seemed to portend much more than mere reform: perhaps even real revolution. It was this implication which was sometimes feared, if not always rationally well understood.

The new recruitment resembled in form and tendency some of the more violent manifestations of European civil service reorientations since World War I. That it went no further than it did is a reflection that our "social revolution" of the thirties was not really a full revolution. As the New Deal embodied a more positive attitude toward the function of government in American society, so the ideological recruitment of these years brought into government persons who were willing and able to turn that attitude into more of a reality than the traditionalists cared to envision. Hence the "frightening" of the politicians, the fear of a "new" and peculiar phenomenon, and the outcry from many directions against a bureaucracy which did more things and sometimes did them better than many liked to see.

Much of the criticism of the New Deal public service arose from that deep-seated tendency of the American people to consider the proper sphere of government to be a negative one. The effects of the Great Depression were to change that point of view in some measure. But it was only a partial change, accompanied by all the conflicts inherent in a split personality concerning the proper role of government in human affairs.

While the new recruitment caused some fear and suspicion on the one hand, many of the new officials it represented unquestionably left lasting imprints upon the federal civil establishment by their example, their ideas and their energy. They gave it an intellectual respectability which helped to recruit greater numbers of public servants from the more educated ranks of American society. The free and easy days of this period of personal and ideological recruitment were largely over by 1940, but the American national service will reflect their influence for years to come.[34]

A Career System

The necessity for the recruitment of "idea men" from outside the party ranks and the permanent public service emphasized the lack of any system for attracting to the American national scene individuals capable of the type of intellectual effort which has so often been con-

---

[34] For one of the very few thoughtful contemporary discussions of the necessity for and the function of the "New Dealers" in the Roosevelt administration, see Joseph Alsop and Robert Kintner, *Men Around the President* (New York: Doubleday, Doran and Co., 1939).

sidered the principal achievement of the British civil service. That President Roosevelt recognized the weakness of the American public service in this respect is clear, for he endeavored to remedy the situation in at least two ways.

In the first place, he encouraged the ideological recruitment mentioned above. He even went so far as to try to reorient the Democratic party to include the newer intellectual elite. The attempted "purge" of 1938 was at least in part the result of Roosevelt's belief that the New Dealers would die unless they devised a new or captured an old political organization.[35] The formation of a New Deal party would not, of course, have guaranteed a real career system in the public service, but it would have perhaps tended to perpetuate a recognition of the value of such men to the public service.

Roosevelt also comprehended the fundamental need for modification of the traditional civil service procedures to provide attractive careers for top brains. As have few other presidents before him, he understood the operation not only of the American public service but also of its English and continental counterparts. Leonard D. White has maintained, "One of his long-range objectives was to develop a career service in all phases of government work, and in his first conversation with me he invited me in general terms to give attention to this problem." [36] Moreover, according to White, the President desired to avoid the inflexibility and class orientation of the British recruitment system. "He wanted a system with no barriers to the recognition of men and women of capacity. He also wanted a system that would automatically eliminate its own deadwood." [37]

If this were to be the goal, what then was accomplished by 1940?

The twenties had provided many of the fundamental requisites for a type of public personnel administration which might encourage a career system. Position-classification, retirement, more liberal pay, and a certain amount of centralization were already facts by the time Roosevelt took office. However, a fully classified service, a recognized method of entrance into the service for those desiring careers, and a well-developed in-service training program, as well as properly organized agencies for their supervision and guidance, simply did not exist in 1933. Instead, from 1933 to 1937 the Civil Service Commission labored under severe handicaps and kept its head above water only with difficulty.

---

35 For instance, see same, pp. 7–8; James A. Farley, "Why I Broke with Roosevelt, Part II: Revolt in the Party," *Collier's*, CXII (June 28, 1947), 20 and elsewhere; and Farley, as cited in footnote 10, chs. xiii and xiv.
36 As cited in footnote 16, p. 144.
37 Same.

The most frustrating obstacle during most of this period was a lack of funds. The economy acts crippled the Civil Service Commission as well as the remainder of the public service at a time when the Commission was receiving more applications for jobs and more calls for employees than it had ever received in its previous history except during the First World War. In 1936 the Commission stated in its annual report that, despite improvement in examining techniques and in the system of rating papers, one-third of its nearly seven hundred registers were more than two years old, with more than a hundred registers over four years old. It regretted that its funds were not adequate to enable it to employ the necessary personnel and predicted that, if it were not given more assistance, its position might grow steadily worse.[38]

The Commission's program. Commission President Harry B. Mitchell and his two associates made what progress they could under the circumstances and planned for a time when the temper of the legislative branch and the character of the political milieu might change. In an address before the Civil Service Assembly in 1934 Commissioner White outlined the constructive program of the Civil Service Commission. It included bringing the registers up to date, advanced testing research, study and improvement of efficiency ratings, the requesting of authority to apply position-classification to the field services, decentralization of certification with a goal of twenty-four-hour service, the affirmative use of the probationary period, recruitment in colleges and universities, improvement of promotion and transfer regulations, and the development of in-service training. In addition, he stated that the Commission felt effective departmental personnel staffs were necessary if the best work were to be done. It was much interested in their improvement and was often sending its own people to consult with them.[39]

After a study by Lewis Meriam of The Brookings Institution, the Commission reorganized its own internal procedures, thus logically starting toward the accomplishment of its objectives by first reorganizing itself. A full-time personnel officer was installed for the first time. A partial division of functions was then instituted, with Commissioner Lucille Foster McMillin concerning herself especially with the problems of women and President Mitchell functioning primarily as a liaison agent with Congress, while Commissioner White devoted a large part of his efforts to publicizing the aims, activities, and needs of the federal personnel agency and the service itself. President

---

[38] USCSC, *Fifty-third Report*, 1936, p. 2. By 1936 the Commission's funds were again as great as before the economy cuts, but the requirements were much greater.
[39] Civil Service Assembly, *Proceedings*, 1934, pp. 113–18.

Roosevelt seems to have frequently relied on Republican Commissioner White, as he later relied on Commissioners Ordway and Flemming, also Republicans, to be the guiding and inspirational force behind the technical advances of the agency. However, the entire Commission was usually in full agreement and harmony on policies for improving federal personnel management during the period from 1933 to 1940.[40]

Results. One of the major achievements of the Civil Service Commission of 1933 to 1937 lay in the development of the junior professional and managerial examinations. First applied in the form of tests for the position of junior civil service examiner, an attempt was made to adjust examinations to the education and interests of young men and women about to graduate from college. As early as 1934, Commissioner White had publicly deplored the need to bring brain trusters in from the outside during political emergencies.[41] He declared, "I am anxious to make it possible for some of the best brains of each academic generation to find a career in the public service, in the hope that we may thus build a strong and wiser Government." [42] The idea was not an original one,[43] but its actual application in practice was a new departure of major importance. By 1937 the Commission was prepared to give junior professional and scientific examinations based on tests of specific information concerning various optional fields of knowledge. In 1939, for example, approximately 44,000 students and others applied for permission to take these examinations.[44] From the registers thus developed almost yearly ever since, the departments and other agencies have taken into the public service more of the most competent products of the country's educational system than ever before. Still unsolved, however, were the perplexing problems of determining the qualities needed for junior executives and of devising appropriate selection methods.

In keeping with the increased interest in the public service as a career came a proliferation of university courses in public administration and the publication, in 1936, of the first college text devoted entirely to personnel management in the public service—Mosher and Kingsley's study, *Public Personnel Administration*.[45] University conferences on training for the public service, held at the University of

[40] The author has had the opportunity to confirm this view, through interview or by letter, with three of the four commissioners who served during this period.

[41] *Washington Star*, August 28, 1934.

[42] *Washington Post*, June 2, 1934.

[43] See, for instance, USCSC, *Forty-sixth Report*, 1929, pp. 6-7, for earlier ideas and efforts.

[44] USCSC, *Fifty-sixth Report*, 1939, p. 12.

[45] William E. Mosher and J. Donald Kingsley (1st ed.; New York: Harper and Bros., 1936).

Minnesota in 1931, the University of Chicago in 1934, and Princeton University in 1935, provided meeting grounds for public servants and members of the educational profession. There developed not only an increase in the number of students preparing for the public service, but also an increasing tendency toward greater training and professionalization in the whole field of personnel management, private as well as public. This was further encouraged by a reorganized Civil Service Assembly of the United States and Canada and by the newly formed (1937) Society for Personnel Administration, as well as by the impetus of the readily observable progress of personnel administration in private industry.

Despite these promising developments, the period of Franklin D. Roosevelt's first term must be considered anything but favorable to administrative reform. At times the efforts of the Commission to accomplish even its traditional tasks seemed completely in vain. But, if progress were to be made, someone had to educate and to advertise, and this was done to the best of the ability of the commissioners and others interested in civil service reform during this period. Samuel H. Ordway, Jr., once remarked to the author that Leonard D. White often felt that his educational efforts concerning the need for and potentialities of personnel administration as a tool of management were constantly being thwarted by a lack of understanding and by the politics of the times. White could not know then how well he had actually built. In Ordway's opinion White was instrumental in preparing the way for the executive orders and the legislation which appeared almost as if out of nowhere in the late thirties.[46]

Turning Point—The Election of 1936

By 1935 the Civil Service Commission noted "with interest the increase in public sentiment . . . in favor of the merit system." [47] In March, 1936, a Gallup poll presented this question: "Should government positions, except those which have to do with important matters of policy, be given to (1) those who help put their political party in office, or (2) those who receive the highest marks in Civil Service examinations?" The poll uncovered the information that 88 per cent of the public seemed to favor the merit system to 12 per cent favoring the spoils system.[48] While the Democratic party under Franklin Roosevelt had reintroduced the spoils system to an extent unprecedented

46 Statements by Ordway in a personal interview, April 28, 1947.
47 USCSC, *Fifty-third Report*, 1935, p. 5.
48 George Gallup and Saul Forbes Rae, *The Pulse of Democracy* (New York: Simon and Schuster, Inc., 1940), p. 296.

in recent American history, there were by the end of Roosevelt's first term signs of other tendencies and other pressures at work. First of all, there was simply the normal reaction of the body politic to the excesses of spoils which no apologetics could cover up. The public was to some extent reacting in the same way and to the same ends as it had reacted for fifty years. But there is more to the story. In 1933 the Social Science Research Council, with the permission of President Roosevelt, appointed a Commission of Inquiry on Public Service Personnel financed by the Spelman Fund. A number of well-publicized hearings were held around the country during 1934, and by 1935 a series of important monographs was published.[49] All this brought the problems of the public service to the attention not only of the general public but also the educational world. On a more limited scale, and with special attention to members of Congress, were the continuing efforts of the public employee unions to eliminate the last vestiges of the economy acts. Pay scales were returned to normal, payless furloughs ended, and leave privileges restored by 1936. Equally important in its bearing on future legislation was the accession of Congressman Robert Ramspeck of Georgia to the chairmanship of the House Civil Service Committee, a position which he held until 1945. Ramspeck was an announced advocate of civil service reform who later became the head of the Civil Service Commission.

Ramspeck's role as a champion of the merit system signified that even the South was beginning to reconsider its post-Civil War antipathy to civil service reform. It has been unusual since 1865 to find a southerner greatly concerned with the merit system either in the southern state governments or in the federal government. While the South was the section least touched by spoils politics before the Civil War, it has been the most reticent to support reform since then. If aristocracy was the key to an interpretation of the earlier period, the Negro and states' rights must be considered as basic to the more recent developments. A completely competitive and nonpolitical federal or state civil service in which a Negro might reach a place of power and prominence could not be considered. Moreover, a non-

49 The final report of the Commission appeared under the title of *Better Government Personnel*. This volume together with another entitled *Minutes of Evidence* and twelve monographs on various aspects of public personnel administration were published by the McGraw-Hill Book Co. in 1935. The monographs are as follows: (1) *A Bibliography of Civil Service and Personnel Administration*, by Sarah Greer; (2-5 in one volume) *Civil Service Abroad: Great Britain, Canada, France, Germany*, by Leonard D. White, Charles H. Bland, Walter R. Sharp, and Fritz Morstein Marx respectively; (6) *Training Public Employees in Great Britain*, by Harvey Walker; (7 to 11 in one volume) *Problems of the American Public Service*, with studies on municipal civil service problems, veteran preference, etc., by Carl J. Friedrich, William C. Beyer, Sterling D. Spero, John F. Miller, and George A. Graham; (12) *Government by Merit: An Analysis of the Problem of Government Personnel*, by Lucius Wilmerding, Jr.

political federal bureaucracy, not subject to checks by southern senators and congressmen, might endanger the political stability of the area. Merit principles were applied in the Tennessee Valley Authority in spite of Senator Kenneth McKellar. Moreover, the extension of the merit system into southern state and local government lagged markedly in comparison to the rest of the nation. After discussing a breakdown of northern and southern votes on civil service legislation in his study of federal civil service developments between 1933 and 1947, Ralph S. Fjelstad has concluded:

. . . Such evidence seems to indicate a regional protest against the extension of the merit system that is not typical of any other section of the country. That the South is more interested in the political purposes to which government offices can be put is one explanation for the actions of the Southern Democrats. That the South is hesitant about accepting any system that would provide for equal opportunity for all persons in securing governmental positions may well be another.[50]

Nevertheless, the T.V.A. personnel system survived and gradually gained wide acceptance. And, finally, in 1937 Tennessee itself became the first southern state to adopt a formal merit system. By this time the exigencies of the depression and the need to rationalize even state and local administration in order to meet the demands being placed on modern government were becoming evident throughout the South as well as the North. Though civil service reform still lags in the South, from this point on the gap between it and the rest of the nation began to close.

In addition, the National League of Women Voters launched in 1934 one of the most extensive anti-patronage campaigns ever conducted in the United States. Apparently influenced by their concern for efficient administration of welfare legislation, as well as by a general appreciation of personnel standards, the League members, under the slogan "Better Government Personnel," delved into the intricacies of the civil service for a period of two years between 1934 to 1936. Thousands of meetings, hundreds of broadcasts, and endless reams of publicity testified to their earnest endeavors.[51] In this move-

50 Ralph S. Fjelstad, "Congress and Civil Service Legislation, 1933–1947" (Unpublished Ph.D. dissertation, Department of Political Science, Northwestern University, 1948), pp. 448–49.

51 For a summary of this campaign, see Katharine A. Frederic, "Changing the Public Mind about Patronage," The Public Opinion Quarterly, I (January, 1937), 119–23. Miss Frederic was also the author of the League's principal pamphlet used in the campaign, Trained Personnel for Public Service, published by the League in 1935. See also, for example, "League of Women Voters Holds Chicago Conference on Better Personnel," Good Government, LIV (February, 1937), 11–12.

ment they were assisted by a similar effort on the part of the Junior Chamber of Commerce of the United States.

These manifestations of public interest forced civil service reform to the fore as a separate and distinct campaign issue for the first time since 1916. Despite the obvious reluctance of his party, the Republican candidate, Governor Alfred M. Landon of Kansas, came out flatly for civil service reform and endeavored to press the issue. He even went so far as to advocate the placing of postmasters on the classified list.[52] Roosevelt, realizing his vulnerability on this issue, replied with a precedent-breaking executive order on July 6, 1936, requiring all unclassified employees who *thereafter* might be placed within the classified service to pass at least a noncompetitive examination. This minimum requirement had hitherto not been customary for incumbents of positions moved from the unclassified into the classified service. Then, through another order of July 20, 1936, he returned to Wilsonian practice and again made it mandatory for the highest man on a postmaster register to be appointed. Of course, both these orders, while reenforcements for the merit principle, were of relatively little importance in light of the fact that there were still great numbers of alphabetical agencies outside the merit system. Moreover, neither order affected very many persons or positions in any immediate fashion. Roosevelt himself allegedly remarked that the Republicans failed to make good their attack where his party was most vulnerable, namely, its civil administration.[53]

Renaissance

The election was decided in favor of the Democrats on the basis of economic rather than administrative reform. Nevertheless, the matter of governmental reorganization and renovation, including civil service reform, remained on the public mind. As it became more apparent that the complete success of the economic and other New Deal measures might be dependent upon their efficient administration and as the dangers of uncontrolled partisan and personal manipulation of tremendous powers and appropriations were realized by greater numbers of citizens, the public interest in such affairs slowly but surely increased. A number of political scandals associated with the administration of relief served to focus public attention even more, while the fact that the Democrats had had ample time to fill the available offices made them less reluctant to appear in an ascetic political garb.

---

[52] See NCSRL., *Proceedings,* 1936, pp. 14–25; and Lief, as cited in footnote 6, pp. 479–80.
[53] Wilfred E. Binkley, *The Powers of the President* (New York: Doubleday, Doran and Co., 1937), p. 236.

Even so, 1937 was destined to represent the low point for the merit system in the administrative cycle of Franklin D. Roosevelt's first years in office. This year saw even the Supreme Court and the federal judiciary subjected to immense political pressure to bring them into line with New Deal concepts. On February 5, 1937, the so-called "Court Packing Plan" was introduced to a startled Congress, and for the better part of a year this controversial legislation obscured nearly all other reform measures. Moreover, in calculated efforts to push the plan through a reluctant legislature, the President wielded all the patronage pressures at his command. On February 11 Roosevelt outlined his strategy to Jim Farley:

"First off," continued the President, "we must hold up judicial appointments in states where the delegation is not going along. We must make them promptly where they are with us. Where there is a division, we must give posts to those supporting us. Second, this must apply to other appointments as well as judicial appointments. I'll keep in close contact with the leaders." [54]

But the patronage, even combined with the great prestige of the President, was not enough. The scheme foundered amidst a welter of conflict and cries of "dictatorship."

The President's Committee on Administrative Management. Meanwhile, however, the so-called Brownlow Committee, composed of Louis Brownlow, Charles E. Merriam, and Luther Gulick and assisted by a corps of experts, was working by presidential direction on a plan for the full-scale reorganization of the executive branch, with special attention to the civil service. Unfortunately, the President's Committee on Administrative Management, as it was formally known, reported almost exactly at the time the President introduced his court reform bill. Nevertheless, by carefully formulated proposals and well-marshalled arguments the committee did much to consolidate opinion and focus attention upon the condition of the public service. While many of the committee's suggestions were lost amidst the political ill-will generated over the court fight, the upswing in needed civil service legislation which characterized the remaining pre-war years of the Roosevelt administration may be dated from this report.[55]

In the sections of its study devoted to the merit system, the President's Committee advocated the reorganization of the Civil Service Commission into an agency headed by a single administrator and advised the extension of the merit system "upward, outward, and

54 Farley, as cited in footnote 10, p. 74.
55 The President's Committee on Administrative Management, *Report with Special Studies* (Washington: Government Printing Office, 1937), pp. 7–14 and 59–133.

336

downward to include all positions . . . except those which are policy-determining." Strongly urging a more "positive" integration of personnel management with general management, it recommended once again that the Civil Service Commission be clearly designated the central agency for the supervision of all aspects of federal public personnel management. The committee's report brought the problem of the chaotic organizational structure of federal administration, including personnel administration, systematically to the attention of the one agency besides the Chief Executive whose cooperation was absolutely essential for any conclusive remedy: namely, the Congress.

The recommendation to replace the tripartite Commission with an administrator failed, but the other proposals of the Committee were partially implemented by a mixture of legislative and executive action. Even in regard to the suggestion of a single administrator, the President gained a limited victory with the appointment in 1939 of William H. McReynolds, a long-time and experienced civil servant, as his administrative assistant in charge of personnel, with the title of Liaison Officer for Personnel Management. Thus the President recognized the importance of the personnel function by according it status at the highest staff level, a status which was to be maintained during the next two decades.

The Postmasters. The first legislative manifestation of the interest being generated in the state of the public service was the passage of the Ramspeck-O'Mahoney Postmaster Act on June 25, 1938.[56] While this new law did not provide anything like a nationwide examination system for the selection of postmasters comparable to the merit system applied to other offices, it did represent a considerable departure from previous custom in the direction of merit. Four-year terms of office were abolished and indefinite tenure established. Noncompetitive examinations for incumbents were administered by the Civil Service Commission; and delivery-area-wide examinations under standard merit system provisions were required for new appointees to some 14,800 first, second, and third class postmasterships. Soon afterward, the Civil Service Retirement Act was applied to postmasters. Of course, the local residence requirement and the need for senatorial confirmation, which were untouched, left open several means by which political considerations might still enter into postal appointments. Purists criticized the Civil Service Commission for taking a positive part in supporting such legislation. But the new system did provide a means for the development of a partial career service in what has historically been the largest and most partisan of our govern-

[56] 52 U.S. Statutes 1076 (1938).

mental institutions. By 1958 this act was still the principal governing statute for appointments to postmasterships.[57]

The executive orders of 1938. Concurrently with the signing of the Ramspeck-O'Mahoney Act, President Roosevelt, at the instigation of the Civil Service Commission, and Commissioner Ordway in particular, extended the classified service by an executive order of June 24, 1938, to the maximum consistent with the legal restrictions then in force. On the same day he also promulgated the first thorough revision of the civil service rules since 1903.[58]

However, two further actions limited the inclusiveness of the extension directive. After it was issued, the President had been besieged on all sides to make exceptions for political reasons. On January 31, 1939, the day before the order was to go into effect, Roosevelt modified his proposal so as to exclude from the classified service a considerable number of the higher administrative and professional posts pending further investigation of the advisability of their inclusion under the merit system. A special committee was then appointed to look into the matter. This group, under the chairmanship of Supreme Court Justice Stanley Reed, and known as the Reed Committee, made its final report in early 1941.[59] As a result of its recommendations, the offices previously excluded, with the exception of attorneys' positions, were placed under the merit system in 1941. The committee itself was divided over whether attorneys should be selected through traditional procedures or by a separate system. The President accepted the latter proposal and set up a Board of Legal Examiners by executive order. This plan was soon thwarted by congressional disapproval and legal positions were in 1958 still subject to few competitive regulations.

Congress also effectively modified the proposals of the summer of 1938 by requiring in a Deficiency Appropriation Act of February 4, 1939, that employees of the Works Progress Administration, about 36,000 in number, who were to have been covered into the classified service by the President's order, were no longer to be paid from federal funds if the jobs were classified. But, despite these deletions, the executive order of 1938 constituted a major extension of the merit system and "covered-in" well over 20,000 positions.

The orders of June 24, 1938, also provided for the establishment of modern personnel sections in all departments and separate agencies.

57 See Joseph P. Harris, *The Advice and Consent of the Senate* (Berkeley and Los Angeles: University of California Press, 1953), pp. 344–55, for a history of the effects of this and prior postal appointment procedures.

58 Executive Order 7916 and 7915, respectively.

59 U.S. Congress, House, *Report of President's Committee on Civil Service Improvement*, 77th Cong., 1st Sess., House Doc. 118 (Washington: Government Printing Office, 1941).

A new competitive promotional examination and transfer system was to be established and in-service training courses were to be developed. All these activities were to be coordinated by the Civil Service Commission, whose internal operations were also modernized by the new rules, and whose supervisory powers over such matters as probation were tightened.[60] Further, the orders provided for the creation of a revitalized Council of Personnel Administration, to consist of the new departmental and agency directors of personnel together with representatives of the Bureau of the Budget and the Civil Service Commission. Attached directly to the Civil Service Commission in July, 1940, the Council served as a research, advisory, and coordinating body. However, Congress refused at this time to grant additional appropriations for the creation of the departmental personnel offices. Equally frustrating was the reluctance of some of the old-line agencies to modify personnel systems still reminiscent of the Cleveland era. The development of the personnel programs envisaged by the executive orders of 1938 was thus slowed up but by no means entirely stopped. Under executive pressure much was accomplished by the beginning of World War II.

The Hatch acts.[61] While the period of the thirties brought with it systematic manipulation of the federal public service under the political aegis of the Democratic National Committee, these years also produced the most systematic revision of the political activity regulations binding upon public employees since the passage of the Pendleton Act of 1883. Under the provisions of the Pendleton Act, the Civil Service Commission had developed well defined principles concerning the control of the political activity of classified employees. Moreover, a few of the act's provisions, especially those relating to political assessments, had been effective in controlling the actions of even senators and representatives as well as unclassified employees. But the Pendleton Act had many loopholes, its interpretation was largely dependent upon presidential attitudes, and the enforcement powers it conferred were by no means stringent. Unclassified employees were still relatively free to carry on as they pleased in political affairs, except for limitations on the solicitation of political contributions and except for practices proscribed under the "conflict of interests" and the "corrupt practices" acts.[62]

---

[60] For a discussion of the new rules by a member of the Commission, see Samuel H. Ordway, Jr., "Meaning of the Executive Orders of June 24, 1938," *Good Government*, LV (December, 1938), 61–63.

[61] For relevant literature, see the "supplementary notes" to this chapter.

[62] The conflict of interests statutes were then and still are a hodge-podge of legislation designed to insure that the actions of public employees at all levels are impartial and not prejudiced by, for example, such matters as the ownership of stocks in companies with

By 1939 the creation of the New Deal agencies had left nearly 40 per cent of the federal public service of some 850,000 employees subject to few political activity regulations. The same freedom was enjoyed by thousands of state employees of emergency relief agencies who were paid in full or in part by federal funds. This in itself would not have stimulated the enactment of additional political activity legislation had there not come to light at this time spectacular evidence of patronage politics involving these offices during the 1938 congressional campaigns. Major cases in point were the scandals resulting from the political struggle between Senator Alben W. Barkley and Governor A. B. "Happy" Chandler in Kentucky, which were highlighted both by a series of articles in the Scripps-Howard press and by a full-scale Senate investigation.[63]

Perhaps even more important was the congressional reaction to the presidential patronage manipulations during F. D. R.'s attempted "purge" of Congress in 1938. Irritated at a lack of legislative support for many of his proposals, the President had decided to work actively for the defeat of a number of recalcitrant Democrats during the midterm elections. The patronage was again a principal weapon. In early 1938, according to Farley, F. D. R. "went over the whole political field as he prepared to distribute patronage rewards for 'going along' and punishments for not 'going along' to twenty-seven Senators and some three hundred Representatives."[64] Still others were concerned about the President's third-term intentions. Samuel Lubell's conclusion that "Garner contrived the Hatch Act" in an attempt to bar federal office-holders from the 1940 convention is too sweeping in its causal suggestion.[65] But congressional leaders as well as the public were gravely concerned about the patronage and its use and implications. By 1939 they were ready to control what six years before they had been so eager to free. Thus the partisan "binge" of the early thirties brought in its wake its own peculiar purgative in the form of the Hatch acts of 1939 and 1940.

Becoming law on August 2, 1939, the first Hatch Act basically

---

whom the employees are doing official business. The corrupt practices acts have regulated the amount of money which may be spent in campaigning for federal office, prescribed how money received for political campaigning shall be accounted for, and prohibited certain kinds of political contributions, especially from corporations and labor unions. The laws relating to potential criminal acts, sabotage and subversion, and the over-stepping of official authority have some "political activity" connotations but for the most part are not relevant to the discussion here.

63 U.S. Congress, Senate, Special Committee to Investigate Senatorial Campaign Expenditures, *Investigation of Senatorial Campaign Expenditures and Use of Government Funds*, 76th Cong., 1st Sess. (Washington: Government Printing Office, 1939).

64 As cited in footnote 10, pp. 121–22.

65 *The Future of American Politics* (2nd ed., rev.; New York: Doubleday and Co., 1956), p. 14.

applied the restrictions on political activity effective for classified employees to unclassified employees other than those in top policy determining posts.[66] In addition, the act strengthened existing regulations by further extending the definition of prohibited political activities to include those especially related to the administration of public welfare and relief. The penal provisions against pernicious political activity were reenforced by fines and imprisonment. Enforcement authority was placed in the hands of the Department of Justice with the Civil Service Commission acting mainly as an investigating and supervisory agency.

All employees covered by the Act of 1939—and nearly all the federal service was covered—were prohibited from using their "official authority or influence for the purpose of interfering with an election or affecting the result thereof." [67] The Hatch Act of 1940 clarified the meaning of this provision and stated that the intention of the Act of 1939 was to apply the existing political activity rules of the Civil Service Commission to the unclassified—except policy posts—as well as the classified service.[68] In an unprecedented provision, the 1940 law extended the prohibitions against political activity to state and local employees paid in full or in part by federal funds. The supervision of the political activities of state and local as well as federal employees was assigned to the Civil Service Commission. Up to 1950 removal of federal officials was mandatory following the determination of a violation. An amendment to the Hatch Act, approved on August 25, 1950, now permits the Commission, when it "finds by unanimous vote that the violation does not warrant removal," to assess a lesser penalty upon a federal official, provided that "in no case shall the penalty be less than ninety days' suspension without pay."

Prior to 1938, the Commission had lacked full authority to require department heads to carry out its political activity policies and decisions. In most cases the best the Commission could do was to investigate and report to either the President or the agency head or to both. Action was then up to the administrative officers concerned, and enforcement was, of course, most uneven. The new statutes required all disbursing and auditing officers to withhold payments to public employees judged guilty by the Commission of violation of the anti-political activity rules. The passage of the Hatch acts thus represents a considerable extension and tightening up of the

---

66 53 U.S. Statutes 1147 (1939).

67 Same, sec. 9.

68 54 U.S. Statutes 767 (1940), an amendment to the 1939 act. A 1942 amendment removed personnel employed in educational and research institutions from among those covered.

political activity rules for many state and local as well as federal employees. Ordinary expressions of opinion are permitted as well as voting and the joining of nonpartisan organizations working for good government. But overt partisan activity is forbidden except by policy-making officials.

The legal regulations on the subject of partisan political activity are as strict in the American national civil service as in any country in the world and far more so than in most European countries.[69] Nor has our record of enforcement of these provisions been lax. The standards of the Civil Service Commission had been developed for the classified service over a long period of time—since 1883—and were ready for immediate application to the remainder of the public service. Moreover, as neither the motives nor the actions of the Commission in enforcing the Hatch acts have been suspect, little complaint has been made that the intent of the law has been evaded. Though the acts have been upheld by the courts as not infringing on the civil rights of public employees,[70] most objections have raised the question of whether the law is too inclusive and restrictive, especially in light of the increasing percentage of the population associated with the public service.[71]

Pressures for the relaxation of the Hatch acts have come primarily from the state political organizations and from those who are in general concerned about any limitations of essential civil and political rights. But the civil servants themselves and their employee unions have not responded, fearing, perhaps rightly, that any modification of the Hatch acts in favor of an expanded concept of allowable political endeavor might well mean only the reintroduction of the old patronage system in one form or another. Nevertheless, in late 1957 a House subcommittee, financed by a special appropriation of $50,000, began to study these statutes with a view to recommending changes. Where this report together with a possible recommendation by the Civil Service Commission for the reduction of the penalties for Hatch Act violations may lead is impossible to determine at the time of writing. In light of the opposition of public employees themselves, it is unlikely that major changes will develop for some time.

Of special importance just prior to World War II was a provision

---

[69] See, for instance, Leon D. Epstein, "Political Sterilization of Civil Servants: The United States and Great Britain," *Public Administration Review*, X (Autumn, 1950), 281; and Richard Christopherson, *Regulating Political Activities of Public Employees* (Chicago: Civil Service Assembly, 1954), p. 48.

[70] See especially Dalmas H. Nelson, "Public Employees and the Right to Engage in Political Activity," *Vanderbilt Law Review*, IX (December, 1955), on this question.

[71] For typical criticisms and suggestions see Gustav C. Hertz, "Does the Hatch Act Need Revision?" *Personnel Administration*, XII (September, 1949), 29.

of the 1939 Hatch Act, which forbade the employment of individuals advocating the overthrow of the government by violence. Representing one of the first modern attempts by the American national government to extend the control of subversive activity to the field of "words" as differentiated from "acts," this provision formed the basis for the early loyalty investigations of the Civil Service Commission during the emergency preceding World War II. These in turn, served to provide the foundation for more current law and practice. Interestingly enough, the passage of this early legislation caused relatively little comment or objection in 1939, although it seriously modified the traditional merit system rules against discrimination because of political opinions or affiliations.

The Social Security Amendment of 1939. At this time Congress also saw fit to amend the Social Security Act of 1935 and to set unprecedented standards for state and local personnel administration under federal supervision. The most far-reaching requirements were those which compelled states desiring to receive federal welfare funds to develop state merit systems for employees paid in whole or in part by those funds. Approved overwhelmingly by Congress, the amendments became effective on January 1, 1940. After considerable consultation with state and local officials, the Social Security Board formulated its "Standards for a Merit System of Personnel Administration." The State Technical Advisory Service was organized to assist the states in developing their merit systems and the eventual successor to this agency, the Division of State Merit Systems within the Department of Health, Education, and Welfare, has provided the federal government with nearly the equivalent of "another Civil Service Commission" with a nation-wide impact.

That the federal supervision of state welfare employment practices has been generally accepted is clear, and there seems to be agreement that a desirable and effective control and coordination have been achieved.[72] This pattern of federal supervision of state activity, at first applied only to employees involved in state public assistance and state employment security agencies, was extended after World War II to the personnel of two other grant-in-aid programs through the Public Health Act and the Hospital Survey and Construction Act. Outside the public health and welfare fields the pattern had by 1958 not yet been imitated. The arrangement has set a most important precedent which one may expect will eventually be followed in connection

---

[72] For references relating to the work of the Division of State Merit Systems, see the "supplementary notes" to this chapter under the heading of "Federal supervision of state merit systems."

with other grant-in-aid programs besides those relating to the social services.

The Ramspeck Act of 1940. The culmination of this almost convulsive movement to renovate the civil service system of our national government was reached in the passage of the Ramspeck Act of November 26, 1940.[73] Though President Roosevelt supported this legislation, the immediate reasons for the congressional approval of a law which repealed most of the previously enacted limitations on application of the merit system to federal agencies are not entirely clear. As with the other new merit system legislation, much of the impetus came from a welter of sources and motives. Perhaps most important in this case was the fact that the Democratic party had by now become thoroughly established in the agencies "covered-in" by the act. This "covering-in" of the personnel in unclassified offices has been a typical feature of the development of the American public services during the closing years of the incumbency of either political party. But the greater number of offices involved at this time plus certain other provisions of the new law combined to make it one of the landmarks of civil service reform in our national government.

Altogether, the Ramspeck Act authorized the extension—typically, it did not require it—by the President of the merit system rules to nearly 200,000 positions previously exempted by law. Contrary to previous custom, the law required incumbents to pass noncompetitive tests before they received permanent status in the federal public service. This provision must be considered, from the point of view of civil service reform, an improvement on earlier directives, which, almost without exception, had permitted employees to be "blanketed-in" without benefit of any examination whatever. Only employees of the T.V.A. and the Works Projects Administration, those in positions subject to appointment by the President and to senatorial confirmation, and assistant United States district attorneys were still excluded from any presidential application of merit system procedures. The new law even modified the original Pendleton Act by permitting the extension of the classified service to include unskilled laborers.

Through a series of executive orders starting with No. 8743 of April 23, 1941 (effective January 1, 1942), the President began to take full advantage of the authority granted him. By 1943 approximately 95 per cent of the nearly 2,000,000 federal employees occupied positions under the "jurisdiction" of the Civil Service Commission. At least 85 per cent of all federal personnel were within the permanent service, though only 72.9 per cent of the positions were subject to

[73] 54 U.S. Statutes 1211 (1940).

full competitive requirements.[74] Adding those employees occupying positions covered by other types of merit or semi-merit systems, such as that of the T.V.A. and the Department of State's Foreign Service, the percentage of the service under some sort of merit system jurisdiction by the early months of World War II undoubtedly hovered around 90 per cent.

The Ramspeck Act also made significant extensions of the authority of both the President and the Civil Service Commission in the crucial field of position-classification. The Classification Act of 1923 had provided a basis for pay allocations in much of the federal civil service, particularly that portion in Washington. But the first emergency enactments of the thirties had so complicated and confused pay scales and job titles that in late 1933 and early 1934 President Roosevelt had outlined by a series of executive orders special salary schedules to apply to the newer agencies in order that some uniformity might prevail. The across-the-board pay cuts enforced by the cost-of-living requirements of the economy acts from 1933 to 1935 increased the salary confusion. And the fact that departments and agencies were strictly held to the terms of the Classification Act of 1923 only for their employees in Washington, D.C., while the field service was obliged only to follow the Act "so far as may be practicable," meant that there was often wide discrepancy in the salary scales of the federal field service. Nor was the Civil Service Commission allowed more than a most nominal kind of supervision to ensure compliance.

Title II of the Ramspeck Act authorized the President to request the Civil Service Commission to make compensation studies of many of the departmental agencies previously excluded from the Classification Act of 1923. If, upon the consideration of the Commission's reports, he felt that the provisions of the Act of 1923 should be made mandatory upon the establishments concerned, he might by executive order accomplish the change. The President was also given some authority to make limited modifications of the existing pay and allocation standards provided there was no discrimination on the basis of race, creed, or color. Apparently this is the first federal law in which such a non-discrimination provision was enacted to apply to the federal service in general.

The Civil Service Commission had consistently since 1923 advocated the extension of the Classification Act of 1923 to the field services and

---

[74] For these three percentages see, respectively, USCSC, *Sixtieth Report*, 1943, p. 1; Joseph E. Evans, "Growth of the Federal Civil Service," *Personnel Administration*, IV (June, 1942), 8; and USCSC, *Sixty-eighth Report*, 1953, p. 79. Evans was then employed in the Information and Recruitment Division of the Civil Service Commission.

Congress had finally provided the legal means for ironing out many of the existing salary inequities in that part of the federal service which was not covered by the postal classification laws, the wage board system, or such special systems as that affecting the Foreign Service of the Department of State. Nevertheless, despite the legislation of 1940, salary standardization in large segments of the federal public service continued to lag. The press of the rapidly expanding war emergency, commencing almost with the enactment of the 1940 legislation, effectively prevented the Civil Service Commission from fully exercising its newly won authority. Not until well after World War II did the problem of position-classification in our national government receive the consideration that it undoubtedly needed.[75]

Finally, Section 9 of the Ramspeck Act of 1940 provided for a revision in the administration of efficiency ratings, upon which, by this time, many other personnel actions such as promotions and demotions were often by law dependent. Departments and other agencies were for the first time required to set up boards to review, hear, and decide appeals against efficiency ratings. In addition to the agency concerned, the Civil Service Commission and the employees themselves were to have representation on these boards which were empowered to hear appeals made by employees and to make suitable adjustments.

Since the first general efficiency rating legislation in 1912, the whole problem of the rating of employee performance had been subjected to approximately the same kind of treatment as had been accorded position-classification. During the twenties this personnel function had been allocated to the separately organized Bureau of Efficiency, over which the Civil Service Commission had even less control than it did over the separate Personnel Classification Board. But the Bureau of Efficiency, like the Classification Board, possessed authority only over the employees residing in Washington. The result was, of course, the same confusion in efficiency rating procedure as was found in salary classification.

The Ramspeck Act of 1940 provided for further refinements in the system to be followed for employees in Washington. But it was not until a supplementary act had been passed on August 1, 1941,[76] that

75 For further details see Fjelstad, as cited in footnote 50, chs. ii and vi; and Ismar Baruch, *History of Position-Classification and Salary Standardization in the Federal Service, 1789–1941* (2d ed., P.C.D. Manual A-2; Washington: Civil Service Commission, 1941), pp. 60–84. In 1933 approximately 26 per cent of the executive civil service of over 550,000 positions had its pay determined by the Classification Act of 1923; 15 per cent by wage boards; 48 per cent by the special Postal Reclassification Act of 1925; and 11 per cent by miscellaneous provisions. As quoted in Fjelstad, as cited in footnote 50, p. 319.

76 This act also provided for certain badly needed reforms in "within-grade" salary schedules.

the various governmental agencies were required to extend the efficiency rating provisions of previous legislation and the Ramspeck Act to employees outside Washington—again under the general supervision of the Civil Service Commission.

Postal employees, and the employees of certain agencies such as the Foreign Service and the T.V.A. were generally exempt from Commission supervision. Nevertheless, through the passage of the legislation of 1941, the federal government was for the first time able to systematize its efficiency rating procedure for at least the positions covered by the Classification Act of 1923. With the assistance of the Federal Personnel Council the Commission then devised a "Uniform Efficiency Rating System." It was based upon the judgment of rating officers concerning various work operations, duties, or other "factors," and culminated in one of five standard adjectival ratings: Excellent, Very Good, Good, Fair, or Unsatisfactory. This system was then applied in many agencies, though often with considerable modification and in co-existence with a number of other rating systems.[77] Not for another decade would the efficiency rating or the position-classification schemes be significantly revised.

Employee Relations

The new legislation of the late thirties and early forties greatly revised and expanded the concept of federal public personnel administration in favor of a "positive" rather than "negative" type of personnel management. Certainly the "employer" was undergoing a transformation both in organization and also in the application of the newer concepts of personnel work. During the twenties and early thirties there had developed within the public service, as well as in industry, a frequent tendency to consider that all the differences of labor and management could be settled simply by the construction of better washrooms and by the printing of more and better employee news letters. There is unquestionably some merit in the "welfare" conception of personnel administration, especially in a public service in which employee relations are subject to limitations not found in private industry. But the development of a satisfactory relationship between employer and employee is a two-way operation. Even in the public service, there have been since the First World War employee unions carrying with them the implicit power of the strike.

77 This system was essentially a modification of a plan worked out by the Civil Service Commission and the old Council of Personnel Administration in 1935, which also used a five-adjective rating system.

If the concept of the proper organization and role of the chief federal public personnel agency, representing essentially the viewpoint of management, was changing in the thirties, what of the organization and role of the employees? Theories of the sovereignty of the state have long tended to obscure what is fundamentally a problem compounded of a mixture of civic duty, civil rights, and political power. Not until relatively recently have any careful studies of the unionization of American government employees appeared.[78] This is in contrast to most European countries, where the implications of public employee unionism have for many decades received open and frank public and legislative consideration. But then, our general labor union movement has been characterized by a unique non-European bent, and the unionization of American public employees has resembled that of the larger movement.

Modern public employee unions. Though postal unions have existed in the United States for many decades and government workers in the skilled trades have participated in craft union organizations for a century, the first significant vertical unionization in the American public service had come during and immediately after the First World War. For fifteen years the National Federation of Federal Employees (NFFE) maintained itself as the major union of government employees. Under the terms of an unusually broad charter, it had quickly affiliated with the American Federation of Labor and carried the brunt of the employee position during the political in-fighting over the Retirement Act of 1920, the Classification Act of 1923, and the Welch Act of 1928.

When the Classification Act, which it had so strongly supported, failed to effect any substantial increases in pay, the NFFE suffered a loss of prestige, but regained it with the passage of the Welch Act. By the early thirties its membership had increased to well over 50,000. The depression then subjected it to the usual stresses and strains. In addition, there was a growing suspicion on the part of the AF of L's craft unions that the NFFE's service-wide membership authorization had really promoted an industrial-type union which would lead to jurisdictional problems. The issue came to a head when the NFFE approved a report of the Personnel Classification Board, which, had it been adopted, might well have subjected some craft union members to the wage determination methods of the Classification Act. When the AF of L voiced its official opposition to the classification procedures deemed essential to the betterment of public employment conditions, the NFFE withdrew from the AF of L in 1931 amidst a blaze of

---

[78] See the "supplementary notes" to this chapter.

mutual recrimination. Whether the break might have been prevented by less intransigence on both sides is arguable.

No sooner had the ties of nearly fifteen years been severed than the American Federation of Labor, in an unusual move, proceeded in 1932 to create the dual unionism it usually excoriates, by chartering a group of NFFE secessionists who felt that affiliation with a national labor organization was essential for the progress of public employee unionization. The problems raised by the economy acts, the decline in general employment, and the influx of new workers into Washington, D.C., made it possible for the new union to survive and to grow in four years to more than 35,000 members, including state and local affiliates. The new organization, known as the American Federation of Government Employees (AFGE), surrendered its state and local jurisdiction and a third union, known as the American Federation of State, County, and Municipal Employees, was created in 1936. The formation of the Congress of Industrial Organizations on the national scene and internal quarrels within the existing unions, particularly those associated with the AF of L, led to still further fragmentation and the formation in 1937 of the United Federal Workers of America (UFWA) and of the State, County and Municipal Workers of America, both affiliates of the CIO. The break-up of the once fairly solid federal government employee unionization front was thus completed in a little over five years.

During World War II the employee union movement retained its prewar outlines. After the conflict it was felt that the dual organization of federal and local public workers was contrary to CIO policies, and the two CIO affiliates merged in 1946 into the United Public Workers of America (UPWA). Four years later, however, this union was expelled from the CIO for alleged Communist elements within its leadership, and the union is now defunct. The CIO has since formed a Government and Civic Employees' Organizing Committee for government workers, with the organization for federal workers known as the Government Workers Union (GWU). In 1955 plans were initiated to merge the GWU and the AFGE. There are, in addition, still the postal unions and a number of other independent departmental, professional, and craft unions such as the National Customs Service Association, formed in 1925.

Undoubtedly this proliferation of unions has impaired their effectiveness in promoting the interests of the public employees they represented. While the unionization movement contributed to the sympathetic attitude of Congress toward the merit system from 1938 to 1940, its influence was certainly not paramount. The same fractionalism which has discouraged labor cooperation in private industry has been even more apparent in the public service. However, by 1940 over a third of the federal civil employees were unionized. This corresponds favorably to unionization in private industry.[79]

The strike. A by-product of the internecine warfare incidental to the formation of these different employee organizations came in the form of an unusual amount of public discussion concerning the propriety of the aims and philosophy of employee unions in the public service. The central question which always arises in discussions of unions of public employees concerns the right to strike. Until recent years, the legislative policy of the federal government avoided the issue wherever possible. In a letter to Luther C. Steward, head of the NFFE, President Roosevelt, himself a former member of the NFFE, stated the policy of the executive branch of the government in 1937 as clearly as anyone had done up to that time. Though encouraging employee unionization in general, Roosevelt warned that "meticulous attention should be paid to the special relationships and obligations of public servants to the public itself and to the Government." He continued, more specifically:

All Government employees should realize that the process of collective bargaining, as usually understood, cannot be transplanted into the public service. It has its distinct and insurmountable limitations when applied to public personnel management. The very nature and purposes of Government make it impossible for administrative officials to represent fully or to bind the employer in mutual discussions with Government employee organizations. The employer is the whole people, who speak by means of laws enacted by their representatives in Congress. Accordingly, administrative officials and employees alike are governed and guided, and in many instances restricted, by laws which establish policies, procedures, or rules in personnel matters.

Particularly, I want to emphasize my conviction that militant tactics have no place in the functions of any organization of Government employees. Upon employees in the Federal service rests the obligation to serve the whole people, whose interests and welfare require orderliness and continuity in the conduct of Government activities. This obligation is paramount. Since their own services have to do with the functioning of the Government, a strike of public employees manifests nothing less than an intent on their part to prevent or obstruct the operations of Government until their demands are satisfied. Such action, looking toward the paralysis of Government by those who have sworn to support it, is unthinkable and intolerable. It is, therefore, with a feeling of gratification that I have noted in the constitution of the National Federation of Federal Employees the provision that "under no circumstances

79 O. Glenn Stahl, *Public Personnel Administration* (4th ed.; New York: Harper and Bros., 1956), pp. 281–82, contains a summary of government employee union membership figures for various years as well as comparisons to similar figures within private industry. The postal service is the most highly unionized segment of the federal government with 455,000 union members, or 90% of the eligible postal employees.

shall this Federation engage in or support strikes against the United States Government." [80]

This statement of policy, issued unilaterally by the President reflected the traditional theory of the superior rights of the state. In general conformity with this theory, all the public employee unions have in their constitutions either denied the right to strike or indicated in various ways that they would strike only under extreme provocation. All have also avoided any automatic commitments for sympathy strikes, boycotts, and the like, which might result from any affiliation with national industrial or craft unions. Thus, the traditional policy on this matter has been one of legislative, and usually executive, restraint on the part of the government and of caution on the part of the unions. Nor were there for many years any particularly serious labor difficulties to break what might be considered a gentleman's agreement.

However, the ambiguous wording of a provision of the constitution adopted by the comparatively militant UPWA at Atlantic City in 1946 aroused considerable discussion. It appeared that the union was endorsing the right to strike. Despite the union's denials, Congress immediately attached riders to appropriation bills forbidding the payment of wages to anyone engaged in a strike against the government or belonging to an organization which asserted the right to strike against the government. In addition, each government employee has, since 1946, been required to sign an affidavit repudiating the right to strike and indicating that he does not hold membership in and will not join any organization asserting the right to strike.

Finally, the passage of the Taft-Hartley Act of 1947 indicated a clear desire on the part of Congress to define the position of the government more precisely and in the form of permanent legislation. As a result, Section 305 of this controversial statute reads:

It shall be unlawful for any individual employed by the United States or any agency thereof including wholly owned government corporations to participate in any strike. Any individual employed by the United States or by any such agency who strikes shall be discharged immediately from his employment, and shall forfeit his civil service status, if any, and shall not be eligible for reemployment for three years by the United States or any such agency.

The anti-strike legislation appearing regularly in appropriation acts was finally codified in permanent form in 1955. This legislation has

---

[80] "The President's Letter," *The Federal Employee*, XXII (October, 1937), 7.

gone even beyond the Taft-Hartley Act and prohibits employment by the government of persons who are disloyal or who believe in the right to strike against the government.

The philosophy expressed by these acts is diametrically opposed to that of the French parliament, which in 1947 granted public employees essentially the same right to strike as private employees.[81] What the ultimate effects of either approach are, remains to be seen. As David Ziskind has pointed out, strikes by American public employees have seldom occurred except under what might be called extreme provocation.[82] That the Taft-Hartley Act would be a real bar to action under such conditions seems unlikely, for much of the penalty which it imposes has always been ultimately available to administrative officers. Thus at the present time there are on the statute books both the Lloyd-LaFollette Act of 1912, which was designed to encourage public employee unionization, and the Taft-Hartly Act, which does not ban unions but which places a severe limitation on what is considered to be the principal weapon available to them.

Collective bargaining. On the matter of bargaining, American law and practice are less restrictive. For more than a decade, the T.V.A. has engaged in a modified form of "collective bargaining," especially with the craft unions active in its area, and there are a number of similar cases involving other federal agencies.[83] One of the more interesting examples has been furnished by the National Labor Relations Board. While the NLRB has, as a result of its peculiar functions, required its employees to refrain from affiliating with national labor unions, it has signed several agreements with its public employee unions and frequently has discussed employee policies with union representatives. The increasing acceptance and effectiveness of collective bargaining will go far to relegate the issue of the strike into the background. The process of bargaining is made difficult by the inherent nature of government and the requirement of prior legislative enabling acts. Separation of powers within the government compounds the problem. Further, neither Congress nor the executive branch has ever accepted the right of any particular union, no matter how strong, to speak for all public employees either in general or in a particular agency. Nevertheless, Congress in 1956 and both Congress and the executive branch in 1957 considered official "recognition" of government employee unions for discussion and bargaining purposes.

81 For a comparison between American and foreign governmental attitudes toward the unionization of public employees see Leonard D. White, "Strikes in the Public Service," *Public Personnel Review*, X (January, 1949), 3.

82 *One Thousand Strikes of Government Employees* (New York: Columbia University Press, 1940).

83 Sterling Spero, *Government as Employer* (New York: Remsen Press, 1948), ch. xv.

It is probably in this direction that the government's labor policy will change most decisively in the next decade.

Other issues. On other typical labor relations matters the policy of the government is similarly ambiguous compared with industry and for similar reasons. *Arbitration* occurs infrequently in the federal service and almost always in agencies containing large numbers of employees belonging to the old-line craft unions. The limits of governmental administrative discretion make the process a shadow of what it is in private industry. Nevertheless, the formation of civil service Boards of Review and Boards of Appeals, and the development of various types of grievance mechanisms have tended to make arbitration a reality of sorts, at least in modified forms. Under various legislative and executive actions, appeals have been made possible on matters relating to efficiency ratings, position-classification, loyalty, retirement, veteran preference, reemployment rights, disciplinary actions, and discrimination based on race, color, religion, or national origin. Machinery for the handling of other and more miscellaneous employee grievances was first set up under regulations of the Civil Service Commission issued in 1941, pursuant to Executive Order No. 7916. Substantially the same in 1958, they require each agency to establish a grievance procedure in accord with broad standards laid down by the Commission. These standards also recognize the right of employees to join or refrain from joining unions. In most cases employees may make a final appeal to the Commission itself.

In the process of *wage determination* there is a very limited scope for maneuver and bargaining, primarily in the handling of the wage-board system used for blue collar workers. In most agencies, however, this system represents little but an administrative determination of fact, rather than any really meaningful wage discussion or bargaining. Only a few governmental units like the T.V.A., which employs members of unions representing both government and private workers, have enough administrative discretion to permit something resembling a genuine bargaining process over wages. But these are the exception rather than the rule. Congress is extremely reluctant to relinquish a power so closely related to its constitutional prerogatives over appropriations.

On the matter of the *closed shop*, public employee unions have been almost uniformly unsuccessful. Here union policy runs into the well-accepted theory of the merit system: namely, that all shall have an equal right to public employment if they possess the requisite qualifications. The issue, which first came to a head under Theodore Roosevelt in connection with the Miller Case involving the Government Printing Office in 1903, was decided against the closed shop in spite of the personal protest of Samuel Gompers.[84] Even the T.V.A., whose employment policies come closest to those of a private industry, explicitly guarantees its employees against discrimination as a result of either membership or non-membership in a union. The union shop has sometimes been recognized in an independent agency. Such was the case with the Inland Waterways Corporation before its sale to a private concern in 1953. The general tendency has, however, been heavily against such developments.

Of *picketing* and *boycotts* there have been a few cases. One of the more well-known was the "Donovan Case" which involved the dismissal in 1934 of an active member of the AFGE by General Hugh Johnson, head of the National Recovery Administration. The quarrel was all the more spectacular because the NRA was supposedly dedicated to the prevention of anti-union activity. Charges of picketing and undue militancy were leveled against the union on the one hand, while, on the other hand, General Johnson was accused of betraying labor. Finally, the dispute was mediated by the National Labor Relations Board and Donovan was reinstated. Despite their reluctance fully to renounce all of the more typical union tactics, most of the public employee unions, with the occasional exception of the UPWA before its disintegration in the early fifties, have been extremely cautious in applying them; and the tactics of the Donovan partisans received considerable criticism. Nevertheless, the legal regulation of such activity has never been systematically considered, and the limits of public employee union activity of a character less controversial than the strike were still most unclear by early 1958.

Trends. In general, the government employee unionization movement in the United States reflects a recognition of the special place of government in a democratic society and of the viewpoint that civil servants have an exceptional obligation to the public as a whole. Still, there has been an increasing recognition of the so-called "rights" of public employees, and increasing efforts to improve employee relations policies in federal agencies. Unquestionably the T.V.A. and the newer alphabetical agencies of the thirties have led in this respect. One has only to read the literature in the field of public personnel administration to see the gradually developing interest in "employee relations," which has paralleled a similar, though more advanced and inclusive, tendency in private industry.

Nevertheless, as yet the American government is by no means the "model employer" that some would have it be. Increasing employee unionization is itself an indication that many public employees

84 See above, ch. viii, p. 188.

are not satisfied with things as they are. Affiliation with a national labor organization is regarded by many as a distinct benefit when it comes to the all-important matter of pressure upon the governmental mechanism. Certainly the AF of L played a vital role in defeating the Borland proposals which had stimulated the formation of the NFFE during World War I, and public employee union pressures have clearly been helpful in the furthering of legislation they desired.

From time to time, it has been recommended that the federal government establish some type of agency similar in form and authority to the well-known Whitley Councils of the British public service, in which the "staff," as opposed to management, has an authoritative bargaining representation almost unknown in this country.[85] Most such recommendations have, however, ignored the basic differences between the parliamentary and the presidential systems of government. The administrative branch in a parliamentary system truly represents the legislative branch, and it is possible for employees to bargain with administrators who can guarantee the integrity of a contract. No such contractual relationship can be easily guaranteed under a constitutional separation of powers, unless the legislative branch first outlines the limits within which the administrative branch may have discretionary power. This is to some extent possible. But it is a fact of our constitutional history that the setting of limits wider than traditionally customary may be challenged as "delegation run riot."

Still, the discretionary powers of administrative officials in the field of employee relations have been increasing in recent years. A more systematic solution to the governmental employer-employee relationships was established in the Civil Service Commission itself during World War II. Through this period a Labor-Management Advisory Committee, consisting of six employee union officials and six representatives from the operating departments met under the chairmanship of a member of the Civil Service Commission. As described in an annual report of the Commission:

. . . The committee's functions were to initiate and recommend policies which would expedite the Government's part in the war program by the effective utilization of personnel. The Commission placed proposed personnel policies before this committee for discussion in order to benefit from the committee's advice before taking final action. In some cases, the committee itself initiated suggestions for policies that would improve Federal personnel management.[86]

---

85 See, for example, Wilmerding, as cited in footnote 49, p. 253.
86 USCSC, *Sixty-second Report*, 1945, p. 45.

During the war similar committees, known as Victory Councils, were established in a number of other departments and agencies at several administrative levels.[87] However, few of these wartime attempts to bring governmental management closer to its workers survived the post-war period. Even the post-war annual reports of the Civil Service Commission itself, while replete with suggestions for the improvement of the civil service in other directions, contain almost no references to the knotty problems involved in governmental employee relations.[88]

Certainly, if the human relations research into private industrial employer-employee relations even approaches the validity which has been generally conceded since World War II, the public service is bound to suffer in the long run from any continued failure to tap, other than through written suggestion systems, the ideas and energies of its employees in a systematic fashion. While by early 1958 both Congress and the executive branch were seriously considering a more official recognition of unions for bargaining purposes, there was no overall solution to the "employee relations" problem on the horizon at this time.[89]

Because our separation of powers and federalistic governmental arrangement have tended to intensify the political use of the patronage, the American public service has never had the security from political manipulation long taken for granted on the English and some of the Continental scene. Much of the force of American unionization has therefore gone into the struggle for the advancement of the merit system. In several European countries, where the threat of partisan orientation of the public service has been negligible, the same efforts have been directed to far more militant demands. Thus the American public servant has in part been caught between his dislike of the curtailment of his political and union privileges under a fairly rigid interpretation of the concept of political neutrality and his fear of a return to the days when the spoils system provided the accepted method for recruitment of public servants.

87 Emmett R. Rushin, "A New Frontier for Employee-Management Cooperation in Government," *Public Administration Review*, III (Spring, 1943), 158.

88 That some of these problems can be attacked successfully, even within the framework of a military agency, is evident from the discussion of the function of the Civilian Advisory Staff of the Sacramento Air Material Area, then (1947) part of the Army Air Corps, by Col. A. W. Vanaman, commanding officer of the area, under the heading of "Democratic Management," *Personnel Administration*, IX (July, 1947), 10.

89 See Morton R. Godine, *The Labor Problem in the Public Service* (Cambridge: Harvard University Press, 1951), ch. xi; and Joseph P. Goldberg, "The Government's Industrial Employees, Part II: Consultation, Bargaining, and Wage Determination," *Monthly Labor Review*, LXVII (March, 1954), 249, for discussions of the potentialities of "collective negotiation" in the federal civil service. For another estimate of the possible directions in which American experience may turn, see Leonard D. White, as cited in footnote 81.

All this is not to say that the conditions of public employment have produced any more strain than is prevalent in private employment—if anything they have produced much less. Since the early and middle thirties, the problem of employee relations in the federal service has not been nearly as insistent as many other political problems before the government. Certainly we have never been threatened with general strikes of public employees such as France has faced in recent years. Even the Civil Service Commission, in an unusually buoyant if somewhat patronizing statement, reported in 1938:

> The Commission has noted with real satisfaction the constructive work of organized groups of employees in improving personnel practices.
> Leadership of employee unions has been responsible and intelligent. Cooperation from employee groups has been outstanding. The Commission believes that the maintenance of a close cooperative relationship with employee organizations is an assurance of progress in the field of personnel administration, and an assurance against friction and misunderstanding preventable wherever enlightened personnel management exists.[90]

"Upward, Outward, and Downward"

The civil service of the first two terms of Franklin D. Roosevelt's administration is likely to be remembered for years to come for three principal reasons: (1) the magnitude of its partisan manipulation in the middle thirties, (2) the equally impressive magnitude of the merit system reforms in the years immediately preceding World War II, and (3) the emergence of a portion of the civil service as a prime force in the realm of political power. What influence did these trends have on the general character of the American civil service?

The functions of patronage. In America the spoils system has not only provided for partisan gain. It has also served to keep the bureaucratic bonds of custom and habit, inevitably present in all types of large scale endeavor, from crystallizing in the more rigid European pattern. One of the major effects of the free and easy appointment policies of the period from 1933 to 1937 was just such a breaking up of old rigidities. The times demanded administrative, as well as legislative, innovation. That the resulting pattern was often imperfect was not surprising, for the problems to be faced were anything but traditional. During the first term of Franklin D. Roosevelt there was an administrative drive, a desperate energy, which aroused bitter political opposition but which did produce a governmental and economic machine capable of weathering the Great Depression and the crushing blows of the series of international crises after 1938.

90 USCSC, *Fifty-fifth Report*, 1938, p. 27.

Certainly no one since Theodore Roosevelt or perhaps since Lincoln better understood the relationship of patronage to political power or wielded them both more astutely than F. D. R.

Civil service reform. Not quite so much can be said for Franklin D. Roosevelt as regards administrative and merit system reform, though he stands well ahead of most presidents. As an administrator, without consideration of the manipulation of public policy, Washington, T. R., Taft, Hoover, and Eisenhower clearly outshine him, with Polk and Truman almost his equal. But in comprehension of both administration and the relationship of administration to public policy and political power, only T. R. and perhaps Washington rank with Franklin D. Roosevelt.[91] Nevertheless, whatever F. D. R.'s place in these matters, there was a great deal accomplished for the renovation of public administration in general, and the merit system in particular, during the late thirties.

Certainly the recommendations of the President's Committee on Administrative Management to extend the limits of the classified service "upward, outward, and downward" became a reality far more quickly than had seemed even remotely probable in 1937 when the Committee issued its report. While the tendency toward centralized personnel management, recommended more than twenty years earlier by Taft's Commission on Economy and Efficiency, was seemingly submerged under the proliferation of exempt alphabetical agencies, it burst forth again by 1940 with profound changes for the federal public service. The influx of new faces and new talents under the New Deal, the loosening of bureaucratic bonds, and the general willingness to consider new administrative devices was forcing traditional civil service reform, with its emphasis on examining and policing functions, into something of a more inclusive and positive nature.

Congress, too, loosened its grip upon the spoils of office and provided the legislative wherewithal for a general renovation of personnel procedures. The examples of the highly developed and well-respected merit systems of the Social Security Board and the Tennessee Valley Authority provided much needed stimuli to the traditionalism of the old-line agencies at both federal and state levels.

Moreover, private industry, under the dual pressures of an increasing unionism and of a realization of the beneficial effects upon the balance sheet of a well-developed employee relations system, was expanding its whole labor relations program. The newer govern-

91 None of these rankings involve judgments as to the ends toward which particular presidents aimed, nor do they recognize the ultimate political and ideological contributions of men such as Wilson and Jefferson.

mental agencies and the newly-organized public employee unions reflected this increased interest in more modern and more positive personnel techniques.

The Civil Service Commission itself typified the transition from the quiescent policies of the twenties to the turbulent renovations of the thirties. There were times when the Commission's funds were insufficient for its legal duties, let alone its hopes and aspirations. Nevertheless, the Commission tried to do as much as possible. The tenor and scope of, for instance, the annual reports of the Commission under Franklin D. Roosevelt make quite a contrast to the efforts of many preceding Commissions. There is considerable justice in Samuel H. Ordway, Jr.'s, characterization of Leonard D. White's, his own, and Arthur S. Flemming's periods of service on the Civil Service Commission as, respectively, periods of preparation, action, and administrative consolidation of the Commission.[92]

Prestige and power. Of prime importance was the infusion of new blood into the bureaucratic organism. Certainly, as a result of the myriads of opportunities and the challenging magnitude of the tasks to be performed in the thirties, the prestige of the public service as a career rose immensely as compared with the early twenties. With the development of special examinations geared to college programs and with the expansion of the classified service to include many important positions, the influx of trained personnel rapidly expanded in numbers as well as in influence. With public administration by now a recognized professional subject of study, with the tapping of the energies and ideas of the nation's great institutions of learning, and with a return to some of the older concepts of service as a worthy occupational aim, a relatively firm base for the future was also laid.

By 1940 the civil bureaucracy had reached a hitherto unknown peak of power. The bitter attacks on the service—now as "bureaucratic" rather than "aristocratic"—are symptomatic of the position it enjoyed. The positive state had come into its own, at least as conceived in American terms. This fact of real political power, in turn, meant further prestige. Moreover, it appeared likely that, this time, the state would endure. Offering the trilogy of "tenure," "service," and "power," the public service was then and would continue to be hard to resist for many men of restless energy and intelligence, whatever the mores might formally prescribe concerning the prestige of the commercial and industrial worlds.

Some final comparisons. The expansion of the classified executive civil service to a new high coincided with the political neutralization

[92] Statement in a personal interview, April 28, 1947.

of that service by the unprecedentedly comprehensive regulations of the Hatch acts, which dipped down to touch even the political behavior of many state and local governmental employees. By 1940 it could truly be said of the American national public service that civil service reform seemed less a mirage than ever before. The implicit promise of the Pendleton Act appeared to have been largely fulfilled. The basic criteria of the merit system—(1) selection by examination, (2) tenure for good behavior, and (3) political neutrality—had been met for most of the federal service.

With the rest of American society, the national public service too had undergone an almost violent transformation: not violent in the sense of Old World reorientations of the Nazi or Fascist variety, but frequently far from polite in its shaking up of established structure and custom. But, while the movement within the framework was staggering in terms of its historical perspective, the precise direction of the motion was less clear. For the basic theory of the public service of 1940 was either so little at variance with that of the Pendleton Act of 1883 as strengthened by the movements for economy and efficiency, or was so submerged as to be yet undecipherable.

What distinguished, for our purposes here, the first two terms of Franklin D. Roosevelt from those of his predecessors was that the public service became, at one and the same time, the focus of all three of the predominant reform tendencies evident in recent American history. The forces of morality, preeminent in the last decades of the nineteenth century, came to the fore again in the middle thirties. The Progressive organizational movement along with businessmen's concepts of economy and efficiency were perceived once more in the reports of the Commission of Inquiry on Public Service Personnel and the President's Committee for Administrative Management. And the violence of the economic and political transformation to suit the changing ethics of our modern industrial society exceeded in their force even the most optimistic hopes of the exponents of the New Nationalism or the New Freedom of Theodore Roosevelt and Woodrow Wilson. In past administrations only one or at the most two of these movements had been brought to bear upon the federal service. But in the thirties all three combined to produce the peculiar convolutions of theory and practice so typical of the strenuous days of the heyday of the New Deal.

Yet, by the late thirties there was tension in the air. Hardly had the ink of the presidential autograph dried on the public personnel legislation of 1940 before the demands of a new, and even greater, emergency threatened the integrity of the system. Hardly had the Civil Service Commission fully comprehended the import of the legislative and executive authority placed at its command between 1938 and 1940 before new demands and new burdens were thrust upon it.

SUPPLEMENTARY NOTES

The T.V.A. There is a vast literature on the T.V.A. in general and its personnel practices in particular. But for highlights and many details see especially Leonard D. White, "Survey of the Personnel Department, Tennessee Valley Authority," in U.S. Congress, Senate, *Reports and Exhibits of the Joint Committee Investigating the Tennessee Valley Authority,* 76th Cong., 1st Sess., Senate Doc. 56, Part II (Washington: Government Printing Office, 1939), pp. 65–86; C. Herman Pritchett, *The Tennessee Valley Authority* (Chapel Hill: University of North Carolina Press, 1943), ch. ix; Robert Avery, *Experiment in Management: Personnel Decentralization in the Tennessee Valley Authority* (Knoxville: University of Tennessee Press, 1954); and Harry L. Case, *Personnel Policy in a Public Agency: The TVA Experience* (New York: Harper and Bros., 1955).

The Hatch acts. For legal cases and Civil Service Commission actions stemming from the "political activity" (not the "loyalty") provisions of the Hatch acts, see James W. Irwin, *Hatch Act Decisions of the United States Civil Service Commission* (Washington: Government Printing Office, 1949). Historical matters and the constitutional and legal theories behind the Hatch acts are discussed in Otto Kirchheimer, "The Historical and Comparative Background of the Hatch Law," *Public Policy,* Vol. II, Yearbook of the Graduate School of Public Administration, Harvard University (Cambridge: The Graduate School, 1941), pp. 341–73; Ferrell Heady, "The Hatch Act Decision," *American Political Science Review,* XLI (August, 1947), 687; Dalmas H. Nelson, "Public Employees and the Right to Engage in Political Activity," as cited in footnote 70, p. 27; and James W. Irwin, "Public Employees and the Hatch Act," *Vanderbilt Law Review,* IX (April, 1956), 527. For state and local practice see Richard Christopherson, *Regulating Political Activities of Public Employees,* as cited in footnote 69.

Federal supervision of state merit systems. There has been astonishingly little criticism and few studies made of the work of the Division of State Merit Systems of the federal Department of Health, Education, and Welfare. For a statement of the initial problems encountered, see Albert H. Aronson, "Merit Systems Under the Social Security Act," *Public Personnel Review,* I (April, 1940), 24. For a more comprehensive analysis of early accomplishments, see Jean Charters Graham, "Merit Systems in Social Security: A Study of the Administration of Personnel Amendments to the Social Security Act" (unpublished Ph.D. dissertation, Department of Political Science, University of Chicago, 1942). A summary of the first ten years of experience under the 1939 amendments to the Social Security Act is contained in Albert H. Aronson, "Merit System Objectives and Realities," *Social Security Bulletin,* XIII (April, 1950), 3. The most recent summary, also by Aronson, the director of the agency since its inception as well as the first director of personnel of the Social Security Board, contains references to such few formal evaluations of the work of this agency as have been made. See Albert H. Aronson, "Merit

361

Systems in Grant-in-Aid Programs," *Public Personnel Review*, XVII (October, 1956), 231.

Public employee unions. Sterling D. Spero's study of unionization in the postal service pioneered on this subject. *Labor Movement in a Government Industry* (New York: George H. Doran Co., 1924). Spero followed this with his monograph, cited in footnote 49, for the Commission of Inquiry on Public Service Personnel. More recently his *Government as Employer*, as cited in footnote 83, has provided a much-needed historical survey of government labor problems at both the national and local levels. The first full discussion of practical policy and administrative questions was prepared by a special committee of the Civil Service Assembly under the chairmanship of Gordon Clapp, then of the T.V.A., *Employee Relations in the Public Service* (Chicago: Civil Service Assembly, 1942). A more analytical study is Morton R. Godine's *The Labor Problem in the Public Service* (Cambridge: Harvard University Press, 1951). Useful current treatments are found in a "note" on "Union Activity in Public Employment," *Columbia Law Review*, LV (March, 1955), 343; Joseph P. Goldberg, "The Goverment's Industrial Employees, Part I: Extent of Employment, Status, Organization," *Monthly Labor Review*, LXXVII (January, 1954), 1, along with "Part II: Consultation, Bargaining, and Wage Determination," *Monthly Labor Review*, LXVII (March, 1954), 249; and Rollin B. Posey, "Employee Organization in the Public Service," *Public Personnel Review*, XVII (October, 1956), 238. Union publications are brought into focus for two decades by Geniana R. Edwards' study, "Organized Federal Workers: A Study of Three Representative Unions" (unpublished Master's thesis, Department of Economics, The George Washington University, 1939); and Eldon Johnson's "Unionism in the Federal Service" (unpublished Ph.D. dissertation, Graduate School, University of Wisconsin, 1938). Additional important material concerning postal working conditions over decades is presented in Karl Baarslag's *History of the National Federation of Post Office Clerks* (Washington: National Federation of Post Office Clerks, 1945).

CHAPTER 14

Total Civil Service: 1940–1945

By 1940 the civil service system of the United States was, for the first time in its history, potentially centralized. The Civil Service Commission possessed most of the authority which official and unofficial critics of the federal service had recommended for more than twenty-five years. But before it could make full use of its new powers the entire governmental personnel system was subjected to a succession of civil and military crises. During the period from 1940 through 1945, personnel administration in the federal government not only had to readjust to the epoch-making legislation and executive orders of the thirties, but also to the massive urgencies of total war.

In Retrospect and Anticipation

The magnitude of the task. To complicate its task just prior to World War II, the Civil Service Commission was woefully lacking in funds and personnel. Between 1931 and 1939 the agency's appropriations had doubled but its responsibilities had increased several fold. The depths of the problem were thoroughly plumbed in the forthright annual report of the Commission for the fiscal year ending June 30, 1939:

1. At the close of business on June 30, 1939, the Examining Division of the Commission had on hand more papers to be graded than it had been able to grade throughout the entire fiscal year.
2. The Commission has been compelled to authorize thousands of temporary appointments pending the establishment of registers. . . .
3. In many parts of the country the Commission's Investigations Division is approximately 7 months behind in its work. . . .

4. . . . the division in the Commission charged with the administration of the Classification Act of 1923 . . . now finds itself facing an arrearage of approximately 2,500 cases a month.

5. In certain aspects of its work the Commission's Board of Appeals and Review is from 7 to 9 months behind.

6. Reports from the Commission's field offices show that at the rate of current operations a total of 8,736 registers will be 3 years old or more during the fiscal year 1941. Over 3,000 will be 5 years old or more.[1]

It is hardly surprising that the Commission's first recommendation at this time was for the "provision of adequate funds and personnel which will bring the Commission abreast of its current operations, and enable it to discharge the additional responsibilities growing out of present world conditions." [2]

By this time federal civil employment totals had already exceeded those at the height of World War I, and there was no end in sight. As the magnitude of the personnel operations ahead became even more apparent in 1940, it might have seemed to a superficial observer that an understaffed and overworked Civil Service Commission was faced with an impossible task. The acute demand for personnel during the next few years was to call for administrative inventiveness of a far different order from that required in 1917 and 1918.

The situation was further complicated by the more traditional problems arising from the continual press for administrative speed and procedural short circuits, the housing and equipment shortages, and the investigations of the loyalty of current and prospective employees. About the only problem which the Commission of 1918 faced, which was spared its successor in World War II, was a disastrous influenza epidemic.

Compensatory factors. Had Commissioners Mitchell, McMillin, and Flemming [3] been forced to face World War II with the administrative weapons and experience of 1917, the breakdown might have been complete. However, certain compensating factors intervened to ease the initial impact if not to absorb the full shock of the new emergency.

First of all, the example of the First World War itself, though poorly documented, left a legacy of method and improvisation still within the memory of many of the employees of 1940. What had been faced before could be faced again. There were precedents for action which had not been available in 1917.

These precedents were reinforced by the series of renovations in personnel management which had been undertaken in the twenties

1 USCSC, *Fifty-sixth Report,* 1939, p. 3.
2 Same, pp. 5–6.
3 Arthur S. Flemming had been appointed on July 8, 1939, to succeed Samuel H. Ordway, Jr., who had resigned on May 31, 1939.

and thirties. Position-classification and the general improvement and standardization of salaries forestalled some of the worst labor pirating and some of the more frustrating inter- and intra-departmental inequities which had plagued civilian organization and morale during and after World War I. The Commission's own organization and authority in personnel matters had been greatly fortified. The development in many departments and agencies of more or less full-scale personnel units enabled the Commission to devolve upon administrative agencies functions which it had not always been feasible to delegate in earlier years. The creation of the White House Liaison Office for Personnel Management and the revitalization of the Council of Personnel Administration in 1939 completed the basic framework. Organization-wise, thanks to the foundation of legislation and executive orders in the late nineteen-thirties, the personnel system of the United States government was in good condition to meet a full-scale emergency head-on.

In addition, the Civil Service Commission itself faced its perplexities with a united front and with a clearly designated director of its wartime and emergency activities. Almost from the beginning of the defense emergency, Commissioner Arthur S. Flemming undertook, with the full approval of his fellow-commissioners and President Roosevelt, the responsibility for meeting the emergency problems confronting the agency. Thus were avoided the personal conflicts which had complicated the efforts of the 1917 commissioners. Many of the advantages of a single administrator were gained at a time when administrative flexibility and rapidity of decision were essential.

Of equal assistance was the experience gained from facing and meeting the enormous governmental problems of the depression. Out of this experience there had come a willingness to reevaluate, reconsider, and reorganize traditional procedures in terms of the complications of a modern industrial society in a time of stress. Some of the difficulties facing the Civil Service Commission of 1917–18 had stemmed from a reluctance to meet emergency with innovation. In 1940 such hesitation seldom clogged the administrative channels of personnel administration. The reports of the Civil Service Commission for the period just before and during World War II reflect a much greater concern over flexibility than do the more staid and traditional documents of World War I. From the very beginning, despite a crippling lack of funds, the Civil Service Commission and most of the departmental personnel agencies were generally aware of both the potential magnitude of the problems they faced and the administrative ingenuity that was needed.

Above all, the Commission of 1940 had time in which to prepare.

The gradual development of the wartime emergency through 1938, 1939, and 1940 permitted the Commission and others in the federal government to ready themselves much less convulsively than in 1917 when only a few days elapsed between a presidential warning of the imminence of war and the actual declaration.

Problems to be faced. The Civil Service Commission of 1940 faced five major war problems: (1) defining its wartime role and securing commensurate funds and personnel; (2) procuring and initially allocating civilian manpower in a period of manpower shortage; (3) providing for proper manpower utilization and control; (4) controlling decentralization of authority over personnel practices and procedures; and (5) assuring administrative responsibility and loyalty during a period of bitter ideological conflict.

There were other problems, of course, involving such traditional matters as efficiency ratings, examinations, position-classification, and the like. But these were, almost without exception, subordinate during these years to the more fundamental concerns outlined above.

Mission, Funds, and Reorganization

The most pressing urgency confronting the Commission in 1939 and 1940 was the necessity of putting its own house in order. Its ability to do this would not only enable it to carry its greatly enlarged responsibilities, but would also affect the imminent political decision as to the place of the Commission in relation to the new agencies springing up in response to the developing world-wide conflict.

The decision of 1940. In the early and middle thirties the personnel requirements of the emergency alphabetical agencies had largely been met through bypassing the merit system and the Civil Service Commission. With the Commission well behind in its work even in peacetime, it is no wonder that Congress seriously considered applying the same type of solution to its personnel problems of 1940.

The story of the crucial "decision of 1940" [4] has been related briefly in Commissioner Flemming's testimony before the House Committee on the Civil Service in March 1943:

. . . the Military Affairs Committee of the House of Representatives [in the spring of 1940] . . . was considering legislation for the War Department, designed to expedite the conduct of what was then the defense program. The bill, in one form, contained a general exemption from civil service. Natu-

---

4 So titled by Gladys M. Kammerer in her excellent and comprehensive study of the activities of the wartime Commission entitled *Impact of War on Federal Personnel Administration, 1939-1945* (Lexington: University of Kentucky Press, 1951), p. 14. For further sources for the wartime period, see the "supplementary notes" to this chapter.

rally we [the Civil Service Commission] protested because we realized that if a bill of that kind should pass at that particular time it would start the ball rolling in the wrong direction and the Civil Service Commission from that point on would probably have very little to do with the war program.

It so happened that I was asked to appear before the committee in support of our point of view. I may say very frankly that the committee, generally speaking, was not at all enthusiastic about the idea of the Civil Service having anything to do with the recruitment of personnel for the defense program. I found that they were anything but happy over the thought. . . .

We were told that we were bogged down with red tape; that we would slow up the defense program, and that it might be all right to fool around with us and our procedures and so forth in normal times, but in times such as confronted the Nation at that point, we just did not have any business trying to recruit personnel.[5]

At this point the future of the Commission seemed more bleak than at any time during World War I. However, Flemming was able to reassure the congressional committee and by guaranteeing a certain flexibility in the rules and regulations of the Commission was able to prevent the proposed exemption of wartime employment from the control of the Commission.[6] As Flemming said:

. . . I assured the Military Affairs Committee of the House of Representatives, in response to those allegations: That we would see to it that our procedures did not get in the way of the expeditious handling of the defense program, that we would see to it that, if we could not solve a particular recruiting problem, and someone else felt that they could we would give them the opportunity to work on it, keeping in mind the fact that at all times we would pass on the qualifications of the person concerned. In other words, I assured the committee that if we could not recruit we would not stand in the way of a defense agency obtaining qualified personnel for themselves.

Flemming concluded his story with this observation:

. . . I will have to admit that certainly everything that I have done in connection with our part in this war program has been conditioned somewhat by the experience I had before that committee. In other words, our system of checks and balances is all right, and it does us bureaucrats good to have a standard of performance of that kind set for us, now and then. But, from that point on we proceeded to do the things which we felt it was absolutely

---

[5] This and the following remarks of Flemming are from U.S. Congress, House, Committee on the Civil Service, *Investigation of Civilian Employment*, 78th Cong., 1st Sess., Hearings pursuant to H.R. 16, Part I, March 1943 (Washington: Government Printing Office, 1943), pp. 21–23. This is hereafter cited as *Investigation of Civilian Employment*. This 746 page set of well indexed hearings is one of the most illuminating documents on the operation of the civil service during World War II.

[6] Even such few exemptions as Congress eventually permitted were seldom made use of by the operating agencies.

necessary for us to do in order to render the service which we promised to render.

By November, 1940, the Commission was able to report that it "had been provided with additional funds and personnel" and that "both the executive and legislative branches of the government have decided not to permit the mixing of politics with defense and have turned over the recruiting of civilian personnel for the defense program to the Commission's experienced staff." [7]

The Commission had received its "go-ahead signal" from President Roosevelt in September 1939,[8] and, with the additional support of a now firm congressional concurrence, proceeded rapidly to adjust its organizational and procedural mechanism to the demands of the growing conflict and to exert its full authority on the personnel scene. This was not done without some objections, of course. All agencies were under great pressure to accomplish Herculean tasks; and controls and directives, no matter how well meant, were not always received with open arms.

Administrative officers continually complained, especially about the system of position-classification. The Commission was particularly adamant in maintaining its detailed authority in this field because it involved the crucial matter of job allocation and pay. Its detailed requirements concerning the allocation of positions, the demand that nearly all positions in Washington be audited by Commission personnel, and the lack of "type" classifications for the guidance of departmental agencies were sore points during almost the entire war.[9] On the whole, however, nearly all the departments and agencies were quite prepared to accept the central role in federal personnel management which the legislation of the thirties and the "decision of 1940" had delegated to the Commission and which it played with

---

[7] USCSC, *Fifty-seventh Report*, 1940, p. vii. For the most complete story of the "decision of 1940" see Ralph S. Fjelstad, "Congress and Civil Service Legislation, 1933–1947" (unpublished Ph.D. dissertation, Department of Political Science, Northwestern University, 1948), pp. 209–12. From an appropriation of $3,316,750 for 1939 the sums allotted to the Civil Service Commission for operating expenses by the Congress increased to over four millions of dollars for the fiscal year of 1940, to nearly nine millions for 1941, to nearly fourteen millions for 1942, and to a plateau averaging twenty millions or so for the period from 1943 through 1946. During the same period the Commission's personnel, excluding WOC's (without compensation) and dollar-a-year men, increased from about 1200 for the fiscal year of 1938 to nearly 1800 in 1939, to nearly 2800 in 1940, and to a figure averaging nearly 7000 for the years 1941 through 1945. These data are from various annual reports of the Commission, as corrected for the writer by the Employment Statistics Office of the Commission.

[8] Executive Order 8257, September 21.

[9] See, for example, Leonard D. White, "The Scope and Nature of the Problem," in Leonard D. White (ed.), *Civil Service in Wartime* (Chicago: University of Chicago Press, 1945), p. 15.

increasing effect through the so-called "defense period" and on into wartime proper after December 7, 1941.

Reorganization. Organizational and procedural changes based on the revised civil service rules of 1938 were made in rapid succession. Junior management examinations were developed to introduce college trained personnel in greater numbers into the civil organization. Recruiting was stepped up. The mechanization of basic records was undertaken on a large scale. A number of improvements in the retirement system, authorized by legislation in 1940, were put into effect. The Commission's 13 district offices, 5000 local boards, and 150 special rating boards at large government industrial establishments were prepared for a decentralization of recruitment and examination. The training mission of the Commission, outlined in Executive Order 7916 of 1938, was recognized by the creation of a Coordinator and Director of Training. Organization of special committees and conferences followed. The new political activity authority under the Hatch acts was systematized and applied. The creation of a Division of Personnel Supervision and Management to aid line administrators, and a Division of Information to assist the general public, helped round out the new organizational system.

By June, 1940, the Commission's recruiting methods were becoming increasingly positive. Liaison officers were placed with national defense agencies in order that plans and programs could be approved on the spot. Eligibles were supplied upon twenty-four-hour notice. A coding system was applied to the qualifications of several hundred thousand current government employees in order to streamline transfer procedures. Executive and scientific and technical recruiting plans were well under way. All in all, the Civil Service Commission was undergoing a considerable internal overhauling.

The War Service Regulations. As 1940 moved into 1941 the Commission continued to streamline its rules and procedures. By Executive Order 8257 of September 21, 1939, President Roosevelt had, at the Commission's request, permitted the relaxation of competitive requirements subject to the Commission's approval. However, persons appointed under this authority could not receive a permanent classified status. This action helped to forestall some of the complications inevitably arising at the end of the war from the introduction of thousands of new employees into the permanent civil structure of the national government. It also took into account the fact that the reinstatement requirements of the Selective Service Act of 1940 applied to government as well as to industry. Many government employees inducted into the armed services would be returning to their original positions after the war and places would have to be found for them. But the Commission soon learned that it needed further powers to permit the expeditious handling of defense affairs. Accordingly, an executive order of October 8, 1940, permitted the Commission even more latitude in immediate hiring but stipulated that appointments under this order were to be for the duration of the emergency only.

Even more basic changes in the civil service regulations were promulgated by the Commission under the authority of Executive Order 9063 of February 16, 1942. The order, which provided the legal authority for the War Service Regulations of March 16, 1942, required that "persons appointed solely by reason of any special procedures adopted under authority of this order to positions subject to provisions of the Civil Service Act and Rules shall not thereby acquire a classified [permanent] civil-service status, but, in the discretion of the Civil Service Commission, may be retained for the duration of the war and for six months thereafter." Up to this time, as Commissioner Flemming later remarked, the Civil Service Commission had been "operating two assembly lines." [10] Henceforth the assembly line leading into the permanent service would be almost completely closed. The great bulk of the public employment then being anticipated and encouraged would be temporary in nature.

Under the new regulations the Commission was to announce competitive examinations only "when the supply is ahead of the demand," [11] a generally infrequent occurrence in 1942. In the absence of competitive examinations, noncompetitive examinations were authorized. A simple determination of minimum qualifications was to be made. Age limits were waived for most positions. Physical requirements were lowered to the point where it was stipulated merely that the applicant "not be a menace either to himself or to his fellow workers."

The new regulations loosened certain procedures, but they tightened others. All government agencies were ordered to supply the Commission with much-needed personnel estimates for advance planning. Their own plans for the recruitment of personnel and the development of sources of manpower supply were to be coordinated with those of the Commission. Separate departmental programs were to

---

10 *Investigation of Civilian Employment,* as cited in footnote 5, p. 25.
11 This and the immediately following quotation as well as the general summary of the regulations are taken from the testimony of Commissioner Flemming, same, pp. 25–30. See also Arthur S. Flemming, "Emergency Aspects of Civil Service," *Public Administration Review,* I (Autumn, 1940), 25; Arthur S. Flemming, "The Recruitment of Civilian Employes for War Agencies," *Good Government,* LIX (March–April, 1942), 12; and Civil Service Assembly, *Wartime Policies of the United States Civil Service Commission* (Chicago: Civil Service Assembly, 1942).

continue only with the express authorization of the Commission, and all programs for publicizing personnel requirements were to be cleared with it also.

The overall effect of the regulations was to consolidate the Commission's position as the director of the civilian manpower activities of the federal government. At the same time the Commission endeavored to work as closely as possible with the defense agencies in order that control might not mean irresponsible rigidity.

It also tried to prepare for the inevitable peacetime demobilization of the executive civil establishment. One of the worst problems following World War I had arisen from the necessity to prune and pare the civil service in a most unsystematic fashion hardly conducive to the development of morale, a career service, or administrative efficiency. As Flemming put it, the War Service Regulations said in effect:

We [the Civil Service Commission] will not follow the procedures we normally use in administering a civil service system; and because we are not going to follow the normal procedures—we will not give anyone a classified or competitive civil-service status.

Furthermore, to be perfectly frank, we will make sure of the fact that no misunderstandings develop, and we will tell the persons that we recruit from now on that their appointments are only for the duration of the war.

We will continue to determine whether or not persons are qualified before we permit them to go to work in particular agencies; also we will avoid duplication of effort in carrying on recruiting activities, and we will continue to draw on the specialized recruiting skills which have been developed over a period of time, by channeling recruiting activities through the central personnel agency of the Government, namely, the Civil Service Commission.[12]

Thus the crucial groundwork was laid for a far more equitable and systematic reduction-in-force than had been possible after the First World War. Demobilization was not to proceed without complications, but these were to prove far less disrupting than had previously been the case. The War Service Regulations of 1942 represented a major administrative innovation suitable for emergency purposes. In effect until 1946, they provided the example for similar regulations later put into use during the Korean conflict.

Other developments. By 1943 the problems of manpower allocation and manpower control were coming to a head. Congress turned its attention to these matters through a general investigation of the operation of the civil service by the House Committee on the Civil Service, under the chairmanship of Robert Ramspeck of Georgia.

12 *Investigation of Civilian Employment,* as cited in footnote 5, p. 28.

Concurrently, the Civil Service Commission and a number of defense and other establishments began to undertake surveys of manpower utilization, and the Bureau of the Budget commenced to interest itself more extensively in the problems of management control within the civil establishment. From these efforts came the first wartime drop in the total number of civilians employed within the continental limits of the United States. At the same time, however, employment outside the continental limits was rising and the overall employment total was passing the 3,000,000 mark.

In late 1942, the Commission began to survey the use of manpower within its own agency as well as to encourage such surveys in other agencies. As a result, a number of transfers were made, promotion policies were strengthened, work standards and guides were developed, and several training programs were undertaken. A study of federal personnel procedures as a whole was then made and a general codification of the Commission's instructions and policies was started. This was the forerunner of the well-known *Federal Personnel Manual*, a loose-leaf guide for personnel administrators throughout the federal government. Other administrative improvements affected the Commission's own Personnel Office, the Service Records Division, and the general relations between the operating divisions and the Executive Director and Chief Examiner.

The period from the end of 1943 to 1945 represented primarily a consolidation of the experience of the previous three years, complicated by only a few additional problems. Pay scales needed revision to accord with rises in the cost of living. Veteran preference legislation was destined for a major overhauling with many implications for the peacetime civil service structure. Manpower allocations were continually disturbed by shifts in military requirements reflecting the changing state of the war. And, as the end of the worldwide conflict became increasingly evident, the problem of maintaining an effective civil establishment during a rapid demobilization began to receive further attention. On most of these topics the Civil Service Commission had prepared recommendations and actively sought legislative and executive solutions to implement them. Since some of these problems involved long-range planning for the postwar years, they will be discussed more in detail in the following chapter.

"Beating the Bushes" [13]

Even more important than obtaining the funds and personnel with which to meet its assigned mission, was the Commission's success or

---

[13] A term used by the Commission itself to describe its wartime procurement of personnel. USCSC, *Fifty-seventh Report,* 1940, p. x.

failure in terms of that mission. Congressman Jennings Randolph of West Virginia bluntly inquired of Commissioner Flemming in 1943, "Mr. Flemming, as of today, have the assurances you gave the House Military Affairs Committee been kept by the Commission?" [14]

The principal assurances concerned, of course, the procurement of manpower. In comparison with past needs, the wartime requirements for public employees, both civilian and military, had reached stupendous proportions. The first duty of the Commission was to produce that manpower when and where desired, and from the beginning the efforts of the Commission to reorganize and simplify its procedures were aimed primarily at supplying the seemingly insatiable demands for personnel.

The demand. During the "defense period" from early 1939 through December 1941, civilian employment in the executive branch nearly doubled, from more than 900,000 to almost 1,800,000 individuals.[15] This represented a rate of increase of more than 35,000 employees per month. From the time of Pearl Harbor to the end of the calendar year 1943, the civil establishment of the federal government at home and abroad, excluding only dollar-a-year and "without compensation" (WOC) personnel, almost doubled again and soared well beyond the 3,000,000 mark. This cumulative total rose slowly during the next year and a half, principally through an increase in the number of employees outside the continental United States, to its maximum height of more than 3,800,000 full time employees plus over 330,000 WOC's and dollar-a-year men by July of 1945.[16]

Federal employment totals rose, on the average, from the 35,000 per month of the defense period to nearly 90,000 per month after Pearl Harbor. But these totals provide an inadequate index of the personnel procurement problem. For instance, during the early months of 1942, the turnover rates forced the Civil Service Commission to make more than 150,000 placements per month to insure the 90,000 monthly additions to the total federal civil work force. Under

---

[14] *Investigation of Civilian Employment,* as cited in footnote 5, p. 22.

[15] These and the other figures immediately following are summarized from several sources including the annual reports of the Civil Service Commission for the years concerned; Table I, "Growth in Federal Civilian Employment, Selected Months, 1939–45," in Kammerer, as cited in footnote 4, p. 17; and a series of articles appearing in the *Monthly Labor Review* for January, June, and December of 1941, August of 1942, March of 1943, and April of 1944. Several of these articles in the *Review* represent the joint efforts of the Civil Service Commission and the Bureau of Labor Statistics. In most cases the figures have been rounded off to the nearest hundred thousand, anything more precise representing only an artificial exactness.

[16] To place these figures in proper perspective, it should be noted that the total American labor force approximated 65 million workers in 1945. Of this total about 45 per cent were enrolled in the military services (more than 12 million) or engaged in war production. Adding the persons in the military services to those in the federal civil establishment, approximately 25 per cent of the available manpower was working directly for the federal government in 1945.

the limited draft exemption policy of President Roosevelt few federal employees eligible for military duty were excused.[17] The federal service suffered from the same problems as did private industry when it came to wartime personnel dislocations of all varieties. During the latter half of 1942 the monthly turnover rate was over 5 per cent, compared to 2 per cent just before Pearl Harbor and 2 to 4 per cent during the middle thirties.[18] High as the wartime civil service turnover figures were, they were constantly exceeded by those of private industry. Labor turnover in manufacturing industries during the same period averaged from 5 to 9 per cent. The case of the Boeing aircraft plant in Seattle, which employed a total of 250,000 people from June 1940 through June 1943, but had only 39,000 workers on the latter date, was by no means unusual.[19]

Altogether, from June 1, 1939, through June 30, 1945, about 8,900,000 placements were made within the executive civil service, the largest number occurring between July, 1942, and June, 1943, and totalling approximately 2,700,000. More than 1,500,000 placements were made yearly from 1942 through 1945.[20]

The supply. The story of the recruitment of nearly 9,000,000 individuals for the civil service of World War II is a complex one which can only be summarized here.[21] From the beginning of the defense period the Commission was forced into the positive recruiting that had been necessary only once before in American history—during the First World War. All media of communication were used; the cooperation of countless private agencies and associations was eagerly sought and exploited; and the facilities of the Commission's own numerous field agencies and liaison officers as well as those of the departments and agencies were utilized to the maximum. Twenty-four-hour service to defense agencies became common rather than exceptional. In Washington itself a central interviewing unit referred individuals immediately to prospective employers. Potential employees, particularly for the skilled trades, were recruited everywhere and signed, sealed, and delivered across the continent in all directions.

---

17 See L. Vaughn Howard, "War and the Federal Service," *American Political Science Review*, XXXVI (October, 1942), 917.

18 From data supplied to the writer by the Employment Statistics Office of the Civil Service Commission. For an analysis of wartime turnover problems and statistics see John W. Mitchell, "Personnel Turnover in the Federal Government," *Personnel Administration*, V (May, 1943), 12. This turnover rate is essentially an average of the accession and separation rates.

19 For private industrial turnover data, see U.S. Bureau of the Budget, Committee on Records of War Administration, *The United States at War* (Washington: Government Printing Office, 1947), pp. 432 and 438.

20 USCSC, *Sixty-second Report*, 1945, pp. 31 and 37. This report summarizes much of the Commission's wartime recruitment and placement activity.

21 For greater detail see, for instance, Kammerer, as cited in footnote 4, ch. iii.

An early example of the type of service constantly required (and normally furnished) is the following incident:

. . . It was a Saturday morning early in October, 1940. A high-ranking naval officer visited us. Here is the deadline he gave us: Recruit, examine and investigate approximately 1,000 workers for the Pearl Harbor Navy Yard and have them on the West Coast ready to sail in three weeks. Our 13th district offices went to work that Saturday afternoon. They continued to work day and night for the next three weeks. They met the deadline. The thousand workers were on the coast ready to go. We received the commendation of the Secretary of the Navy.[22]

The Commission was naturally desirous of meeting the needs of the War and Navy Departments especially. From June 1, 1940, through December 31, 1944, more than 5,000,000 employees were appointed to the field establishments of these departments alone.[23] As usual, the great bulk of the federal service was employed outside Washington, D.C. The proportion was even greater than the normal 10 to 1. Of all new employees, those attached to the two great defense agencies were by far the most numerous. During early 1942, for instance, of every 100 new civilian jobs 57 were in the War Department and 28 in the Navy Department, primarily in the field. Only 7 were in other defense organizations and 8 in the remaining federal agencies.[24] This proportion remained fairly constant throughout the war.

Of special importance in a world of science and technology was the recruitment of highly trained personnel. Early in the defense effort the National Resources Planning Board initiated a National Roster of Scientific and Specialized Personnel at the instigation of a group of scientific and professional societies. About 400,000 persons were listed.[25] Under the joint jurisdiction of the Civil Service Commission and the Planning Board the Roster proved a useful source for the recruiting of technical personnel, demonstrating at the same time the dearth of professionally trained workers necessary for a modern all-out war effort. Later the Roster was transferred to the War Manpower Commission, which continued to cooperate with the Civil Service Commission on the project. Altogether, it is estimated that at least 180,000 referrals and 50,000 placements were made from

22 H. E. Kaplan, "Our Merit Systems Meet the Test of War," *Personnel Administration,* IV (February, 1942), 5–6.

23 See Arthur S. Flemming, "The Mobilization of Personnel for the Field Establishments of the War and Navy Departments," in White, as cited in footnote 9, ch. vi.

24 K. R. Murphy and Simon Krixtein, "War and the Increase in Federal Employment," *Monthly Labor Review,* LV (August, 1942), 217.

25 Frances Cahn, *Federal Employees in War and Peace* (Washington: The Brookings Institution, 1949), p. 46.

the Roster.[26] It has been maintained in one form or another ever since and is now in the hands of the National Science Foundation.

Much less successful was the War Manpower Commission's effort to secure full utilization of younger scientists and technicians through either draft deferments or special military assignments. The fundamental difficulty lay in the general failure at this time to assess and provide for the long-term needs of the nation for scientific and technical personnel. Some of the effects of this shortsightedness became painfully evident in the grave shortages of engineers, for example, which had appeared by the mid-nineteen fifties. Our educational system at the graduate level ground almost to a halt during the war while the demands for highly skilled scientific personnel continued to rocket.

Also crucial to the defense effort was the demand for top-level executive personnel. With the passage of the merit system legislation of the late thirties and with executive implementation of the recommendations of the Reed Committee of 1941, the career civil service by 1942 included many top positions. In addition, the provision that the staffing of the new defense agencies would be within the general rules of the merit system, as modified by the wartime regulations of the Civil Service Commission, necessitated the emergency procurement of a type of administrative personnel which the Commission had seldom heretofore been required to locate.

In December, 1941, the Commission organized a Committee on Administrative Personnel which supervised the recruitment of top-level civil servants of all varieties.[27] Nevertheless, the Commission was in no position to obtain the great numbers of such individuals needed. Long before the efforts of this committee were effective the defense agencies had been compelled to move far outside the normal civil service channels for their administrative and technical personnel. In 1940 Congress permitted, though with some misgivings,[28] the revival of the "dollar-a-year" technique of the First World War. In addition, the 1940 legislation authorized a new category of "without compensation" employees. While the legislative distinctions between the two categories were negligible, administrative practice resulted in the utilization of dollar-a-year men largely in full-time executive or administrative positions, with WOC's serving primarily as consultants without full executive authority. At the peak of the war effort over

26 See Leonard Carmichael, "The Nation's Professional Man-power Resources," in White, as cited in footnote 9, ch. v; and Cahn, as cited in footnote 25, pp. 42–48.

27 Emery E. Olson and Ross Pollock, "Staffing and Training for Administrative Competence in the Federal Government," *Personnel Administration*, VIII (September, 1945), 8.

28 The Special Committee Investigating the National Defense Program, popularly known as the Truman Committee, was especially concerned over this matter.

330,000 persons were serving in these two categories. There were in addition the usual types of volunteers associated with the Selective Service System, the rationing boards, and the many other similar agencies.[29]

While executives were to some extent recruited by various means from within the existing governmental establishment, this source of supply was on the whole most inadequate. The case of the War Production Board is typical of most of the defense agencies. By February, 1943, 853 dollar-a-year men and 91 WOC's were working for the Board. At the same time 260 executives received $8,000 a year, then the top salary in the career service. Many of the latter, however, came from sources other than the public service, and it has been estimated that probably less than 10 per cent of the Board's executive personnel represented the traditional civil service.[30]

The wartime experience emphasized the needs of the career service at the top levels of the federal government as well as the fact that salaries were too low at these levels to encourage executives from private industry to enter the public service except under emergency conditions. In wartime, however, even a full-scale career service would not have been adequate. There will always remain the problem of the mobilization and demobilization of public servants for emergency purposes. This problem is particularly perplexing at executive levels, and more than a decade after World War II we had only begun to face up to it.

Tapping new sources. Not only were efforts made to attract persons with established work records, from skilled laborers to executives, but attempts were also made to tap sources of relatively unused manpower. The employment of women, for instance, rose rapidly, especially in Washington. By July, 1944, nearly 40 per cent of all civil employees of the federal government were women, as compared to 19.5 per cent in 1938. This figure had dropped back sharply to a near normal of 25.9 per cent by 1947.[31] In general the employment of women closely followed the pattern of the First World War. During the more recent conflict, however, the number of women in ar-

---

[29] For further information see Cahn, as cited in footnote 25, pp. 38–42; U.S. Congress, House, Antitrust Subcommittee of the Committee on the Judiciary, *Interim Report on WOC's and Government Advisory Groups*, 84th Cong., 2d Sess., April 24, 1956 (Washington: Government Printing Office, 1956), pp. 4–7; James A. MacAleer, *Dollar-A-Year and Without Compensation Personnel Policies of the War Production Board and Predecessor Agencies, August 1939 to November 1945* (Washington: Civilian Production Administration, 1947); and Imogene H. Putnam, *Volunteers in OPA* (Washington: Government Printing Office, 1947).

[30] Herbert Emmerich, "The Search for Executive Talent," in White, as cited in footnote 9, p. 37.

[31] Cahn, as cited in footnote 25, p. 6.

senals and other manufacturing establishments of the defense agencies was considerably greater than ever before.

To some extent, particularly in Washington as a result of the composition of the local population, the employment of Negroes also increased—from over 80,000 in 1938 to a peak of about 300,000 in 1944, representing a percentage shift of from 9.8 per cent of the federal service to 11.9. However, Negro employment largely represented additions to the working force in the lower echelons. This reflected in part comparative educational levels, and in part discrimination. Nevertheless, there is evidence that the overall position of the Negro employee improved during this period. One study, made during the war, estimates that the proportion of Negroes employed in clerical, administrative, and professional positions within Washington, out of the total number of Negro civil servants employed in the capital, rose from less than 10 per cent in 1938 to something under 50 per cent by the end of 1942. This does not mean that Negroes were shifting into the higher posts in any marked degree, but that they were moving gradually into employment categories other than those of the traditional custodial group.[32]

Undoubtedly the efforts of the Committee on Fair Employment Practice and the Civil Service Commission to avoid discrimination within the classified service on the grounds of race, as well as politics and religion, were to some avail. But the shortage of manpower probably provided the underlying cause for the utilization of Negroes to an unprecedented extent. Not until this wartime period did the Negro begin to receive any appreciable consideration in public employment over and beyond that which had been traditionally his. Even the palmiest days of the New Deal had meant relatively little for the Negro worker in terms of higher pay or advancement in the federal public service.[33] Progress since 1940 has been considerable; and, as long as manpower shortages exist, one can expect that the improvement will continue at a relatively rapid rate.[34] What a depression would bring—besides its tendency to aggravate interracial conflict—is hard to tell.

---

[32] Same, pp. 6–7; and "Employment of Negroes by Federal Government," *Monthly Labor Review*, LVI (May, 1943), 889.

[33] Laurence J. W. Hayes, *The Negro Federal Government Worker* (Washington: Howard University, 1941), p. 104 and elsewhere; and John A. Davis, "Nondiscrimination in the Federal Service," *The Annals*, CCXLIV (March, 1946), 65.

[34] Due to the difficulty of collecting data, as a result of the elimination of racial questions on employment forms in the government, there is little precise information on this matter at the time of writing. For an indication of the trend, however, see U.S. Department of Labor, Bureau of Labor Statistics, *Negroes in the United States: Their Employment and Economic Status* (Washington: Government Printing Office, 1952), p. 16 and elsewhere.

Another source of untapped labor consisted of the physically handicapped. The Civil Service Commission and the Selective Service System constantly suggested the use of such persons. An interdepartmental committee representing such agencies as the Commission, the Veterans Administration, and others assisted. Between October 1, 1942, and June 30, 1947, nearly 90,000 placements of physically handicapped persons were made, of whom less than a third were veterans.[35]

Augmentation by transfer and training. Nevertheless, even with the maximum utilization of available labor outside the government, the shifting requirements of a wartime emergency could not be adequately met. Transfer and re-training of persons already in the federal service became a necessity. Early in 1939 the Bureau of the Budget rescinded a directive of 1934 which had required the consent of the employing agency before another agency might negotiate for the transfer of a civil employee. This prepared the way for facilitating the horizontal movement among federal personnel.[36]

In the summer of 1940 the Civil Service Commission organized the Interdepartmental Placement Service which attempted, not too successfully, to code the qualifications of several hundred thousand employees on punch cards in order to make such information generally available to interested agencies. Later, through the War Transfer Unit, the Commission endeavored to control the transfer process, but still with indifferent success. Shortly after the declaration of war, the Commission, in desperation, froze transfers again by requiring the consent of the employing agency. Finally in 1942 the Bureau of the Budget set up a series of priorities for the personnel requirements of various types of government agencies. Later the War Manpower Commission was given the duty of administering the priorities but quickly transferred it back to the Civil Service Commission. The priority system, a partial and moderately effective solution, was maintained until the end of the war.[37]

Fortunately the pay structure in World War II was far more equitably arranged as among the various departments and agencies than had been the case in 1917, and labor pirating based on inequitable pay differentials had been somewhat discouraged. Nevertheless, the transfer problem—and along with it the promotion problem—was never completely solved during World War II or the subsequent Ko-

---

[35] Cahn, as cited in footnote 25, pp. 7–8.
[36] USCSC, *Fifty-sixth Report*, 1939, p. 7.
[37] On transfer and promotion policies see Kammerer, as cited in footnote 4, ch. ix; and Cahn, as cited in footnote 25, ch. vii. The agency priority system is outlined briefly in Howard, as cited in footnote 17, pp. 926–27.

rean conflict. Nor in all likelihood can it be fully solved in a time of manpower shortages. The problem was even further complicated by the desirability of moving classified employees into temporary jobs and, eventually, back again. The existence of a public service in which rank is inherent in the position—in contrast to some of the European public services—may be a deterrent to mobility within the service under some circumstances.

The final attempt to solve wartime recruitment problems came through training. Before 1940 training had not been a strong point of the federal service, for the excess of applicants compared to available jobs had suggested to both Congress and many administrators that extensive in-service training programs were essentially wasteful. But the manpower crisis which had clearly appeared by 1942–43 forced a rapid revision of this traditional attitude. Despite the frequent installation of mass production techniques permitting the utilization of less skilled employees, there were still not enough people to go around. It became necessary to re-train personnel. The federal government's relatively new concern and experience with training and management development of all types since World War II may be dated from this point.

As is often the case with a new function, there was considerable confusion over responsibility for the supervision of training programs. Nor was the need always fully understood by administrators on down the line. In 1940 the Frankford Arsenal, for example, was turning away competent machinists because they could not read blueprints and handle certain types of precision instruments. Commissioner Flemming visited the arsenal, where manpower requirements were rocketing, and persuaded its officers to accept these applicants and train them in a school set up for the purpose.[38] Except in a very few federal agencies, such as the Department of Agriculture, a whole new attitude toward both the need for and the potential effectiveness of training programs had to develop.

The Civil Service Commission modified and sponsored for clerical and other government purposes the Training Within Industry (TWI) techniques of the War Manpower Commission. These were widely used and supplemented by the more specialized efforts of the line agencies. The War and Navy Departments, in the end, produced notable programs. On the whole, however, the training effort was spotty and directed primarily to the lower echelons of the service and to types of positions for which shortages of trained personnel were periodically reported. The full acceptance of training as a basic

38 Kammerer, as cited in footnote 4, p. 141.

and continuing activity of management and the design of permanent supervisory and management development programs would be another decade in coming.

Overall standards. Even these efforts failed to produce personnel of the required skills and experience. The inevitable result, most evident in 1943 and 1944, was a limited yet observable dilution of the general efficiency of the federal service. The Civil Service Commission itself felt the pinch. By 1944 the agency's 1939 workforce of less than 2,000 had trebled. A large number of the Commission's own experienced employees had left for the military, been transferred to other agencies, or been up-graded into higher positions. These developments, when combined with the pressures of time which made every attempt at orientation and training seem like an unnecessary delay, resulted in a certain amount of administrative confusion typical of most federal agencies. The problem became less acute by 1945, as many persons grew accustomed to their work and as teamwork developed.[39]

As a whole, the federal government met with considerable success in its recruitment of personnel for the wartime civil service, especially considering the magnitude of the problem. In general control was the Civil Service Commission, though, in keeping with its guarantee to the House Military Affairs Committee, it seldom stood in the way of other agencies when it could not itself furnish the necessary eligibles. The fact that nearly 9,000,000 placements were made under Commission auspices during the war is certainly an index of considerable accomplishment. Commissioner Flemming was able to answer Congressman Randolph's query in the affirmative: "On an over-all basis I feel that it [the Commission's promise to the House Committee in 1940] has been kept." [40]

Manpower Control and Utilization

Historically, a principal function of the Civil Service Commission has been to produce qualified personnel in accord with legislative and executive mandates. At no time has the Commission been designated as the sole or even the principal agency to exercise any overall control of either the manpower required for the federal service or its efficient utilization. Throughout most of its career the Commission has been mainly a "central service" type of agency. Only in a limited sense has it functioned as a full-scale partner in the execu-

[39] The principal discussion of wartime training problems and policies is contained in same, chs. vii and viii.

[40] *Investigation of Civilian Employment*, as cited in footnote 5, p. 22.

tive staff. Manpower controls, when they existed at all, have been mainly in the forms of financial controls—with only indirect effects upon manpower utilization—exerted by the Bureau of the Budget, investigative and financial controls sporadically exercised by Congress, and administrative controls maintained by the President and the heads of departments and agencies. Over all this rests the control implicit in the range of restraints which public opinion is prepared to accept.

One of the penalties of the growth of big government has been a rapid decline in the utility of common sense and casual observation as means for any effective legislative or executive direction of our far-flung federal establishment. Nor during wartime is it always feasible to investigate our national government with the leisurely thoroughness of a Hoover Commission. Nevertheless, the astounding costs of the war and the increasing pinch on the nation's manpower felt through the expanding requirements of the military as well as civil government and private industry, forced the attention of Congress and others toward the mushrooming executive establishment.

Manpower allocation. In the early days of the war, the Civil Service Commission, as the chief source of federal civilian manpower, attempted to police its procurement through such limited means as refusing to recruit for specialists who were obviously not available. Not until the creation of the War Manpower Commission by executive order in April, 1942, was there anyone to referee the three-way scramble for personnel among the military, the civilian governmental establishment, and the rest of the nation. The Civil Service Commission, a statutory agency, thus found itself in the novel position of being subordinate to an agency created by executive order. However, as the War Manpower Commission quickly delegated its authority concerning federal civilian employment to the Civil Service Commission, the position of the Civil Service Commission as the central personnel agency of the federal government was confirmed in the most forthright terms in our history up to this time. Throughout the country the representatives of the Civil Service Commission sat as advisors to local manpower agencies on federal civilian manpower problems. With the demise in 1943 of the Division of Central Administrative Services within the Office for Emergency Management, the Commission's control over the recruitment of civilians was almost as complete as it cared to enforce.[41]

---

41 The Division of Central Administrative Services had considered itself a central personnel agency for the defense agencies grouped under the loose aegis of the Office for Emergency Management. This led to considerable conflict with both the Civil Service Commission and the agency personnel staffs. CAS leaders were charged with intent to ex-

This did not mean that the Civil Service Commission possessed absolute powers. Nor did the Commission ever request them. Until the summer of 1943 the manpower problem had not been acute on a national scale. Then a sharp political conflict over the question of manpower control methods developed. The military departments strongly supported the concept of an American equivalent to the British national service legislation. They were opposed by both management and labor. Nevertheless, in his message to Congress on January 11, 1944, President Roosevelt firmly plumped for controls of both industry and labor modelled on the British example. An unexpected easing of the draft situation and the concerted opposition of labor, industry, and agriculture kept any measure from being reported out of committee. After the spring of 1944 more restrictive manpower control legislation was not seriously considered.[42] Thus, manpower controls remained essentially voluntary during the entire war. The Civil Service Commission's powers of persuasion were enhanced by support from the Bureau of the Budget, whose very real power lay in its appropriation monitoring function. Moreover, the cooperative geographic, occupational, and agency priorities which were gradually put into effect did mitigate the sharpness of the struggle for the available personnel resources during the latter years of the war.[43]

Manpower utilization. An allocation of manpower, based primarily on the refereeing of competitive demands for personnel, did not solve the increasingly important problem of manpower utilization. The insatiable demands for personnel and the swollen civil and military bureaucracy stimulated criticism on this score as early as 1941 by the Joint Committee on Reduction of Non-essential Federal Expenditures, known as the Byrd Committee. In 1941 and several times later this

---

pand their agency into a general service organization for the whole government. As such, CAS would handle all central personnel activities (including those of the Commission) plus the fiscal activities of individual agencies and the purchasing functions of the Procurement Division of the Treasury Department. This view may or may not be correct, but the growing staff and absorption of functions by CAS unquestionably disturbed a number of people. The whole story deserves more attention, though much of the personnel conflict is documented in Russell P. Andrews, "The Personnel Function and Its Relation to Management," Case 110 in *Case Reports in Public Administration* (Chicago: Public Administration Service, [1945]).

[42] See Samuel I. Rosenman, *Working With Roosevelt* (New York: Harper and Bros., 1952), pp. 419–27; U.S. Bureau of the Budget, as cited in footnote 19, ch. xiv; and Henry L. Stimson and McGeorge Bundy, *On Active Service in Peace and War* (New York: Harper and Bros., 1947), pp. 480–88. John J. Corson, *Manpower for Victory* (New York: Farrar and Rinehart, 1943), pp. 218–19, contains a brief analysis in chart form of American, British, and Canadian manpower controls and organization in 1943.

[43] On the subject of manpower controls, see also Kammerer, as cited in footnote 4, ch. xii; Cahn, as cited in footnote 25, ch. vii and elsewhere; and Edgar B. Young, "The Control of Government Employment," in White, as cited in footnote 9, ch. viii.

committee called for the reduction of federal personnel. But the Byrd Committee's approach was essentially that of the ax. This resulted mainly in some fairly arbitrary appropriation ceilings for many federal agencies. The Committee failed to tackle forthrightly the difficult problem of analytically assessing the overall management and utilization of civilian personnel.

With the well-known Truman Committee concentrating upon the problems of defense organization and the activities of dollar-a-year men, it was left to the House Committee on the Civil Service, known as the Ramspeck Committee, to consider this matter. Authorized on October 15, 1942, the Committee proceeded before long to an extensive, if far from complete, inquiry into manpower utilization and control within the federal civil and military establishments.

In testimony before the Ramspeck Committee the Civil Service Commission described its personnel control problems, but did not recommend that it be given the overall authority to remedy the situation. The Commission's view of its proper position is well stated in an excerpt from one of the Ramspeck hearings in which Congressman Charles W. Vursell of Illinois inquired of Commissioner Flemming:

> I would like to clear something up, in my mind. I am not familiar with all the procedure, but suppose an agency has 500 employees more than they need, and suppose the head of the department wants to keep his department large in numbers.
>
> Do you recommend to him that he has too many employees, or have you any power to, or, who has the power to get that department to fire 500 employees blanketed in under Civil Service, that he does not need?

Flemming replied:

> Congressman, as I indicated a few days ago, in our judgment, whatever authority along that line there is, outside of the head of the agency, rests with the Bureau of the Budget, under the Budget and Accounting Act.
>
> There is no authority existing outside of that, that I know of.[44]

The next day Commissioner Flemming outlined the Commission's attitude toward the whole problem of controls:

> We do not believe that any over-all management controls should be placed in the Civil Service Commission.
>
> Whatever additional controls of this character may be needed should, in our judgment, be placed in an agency such as the Bureau of the Budget,

---

44 *Investigation of Civilian Employment,* as cited in footnote 5, p. 54.

384

subject, of course, to the general direction of the President of the United States.[45]

Flemming emphasized that the information and resources available from the Civil Service Commission should be used in determining the extent and nature of controls; and he requested that the Civil Service Commission be directed to work with the departments and agencies "in the interest of bringing about a better utilization of personnel now on the pay roll." Beyond this the Commission requested a legal formalization of its practice of refusing requisitions for personnel when it was patently impossible to fulfill them, as well as a legislative authorization to apportion the available manpower as best it could among the requisitioning agencies. The Ramspeck and Byrd investigations brought to light considerable evidence of manpower waste, pirating, and underutilization, some of which was remedied. But they also illustrated the difficulty of attacking a huge and interlocking administrative system by an essentially piecemeal approach.

The first proposals to limit the number of federal employees in some specific fashion were enacted as part of the First Wartime Pay Act of 1942. Aimed at the establishment of personnel ceilings, they required many of the departments and agencies to report and justify certain types of personnel needs to the Bureau of the Budget. The Bureau was authorized to approve or disapprove. In the case of noncompliance the overtime pay provisions were to be inapplicable to the agency concerned. Similar requirements were enacted in 1943 and in a more permanent form in 1945.

Following the passage of the First Wartime Pay Act, President Roosevelt directed all governmental establishments to consider carefully their management control programs. The Civil Service Commission commenced a government-wide personnel utilization program in 1943. In endeavoring to encourage other agencies to take the same type of action, the Commission assisted the Bureau of the Budget which was trying to stimulate a general improvement in agency management through management surveys, work simplification programs, and more careful budgetary planning. In the War Department a special Manpower Board, known originally as the Gasser Board, conducted one of the most extensive investigations of manpower utilization made in any governmental establishment during the war.[46] A lesser program was undertaken by the Navy.

After the war Congress continued its interest in overall management

---

[45] For these and the following quotations see same, p. 89.
[46] See George W. Peak, "The War Department Manpower Board," *American Political Science Review*, XL (February, 1946), 1.

supervision, and the executive branch so developed its management control activities that this special type of administrative effort became known as Organization and Methods work, commonly referred to as "O&M work" (a term borrowed from the British, who had found themselves facing similar problems at about the same time) or "management analysis." These techniques, which have been considerably refined and frequently merged with private industrial "management engineering" approaches during the decade since World War II, represent a significant addition to those long since developed for the analysis and control of more purely fiscal matters. They also provide further evidence of the growing integration of personnel administration with the fibre of public administration as a whole.

Centralization and Decentralization

While on the one hand the Civil Service Commission's overall supervision of personnel administration during World War II represented a long-sought centralization of final *authority,* on the other hand the same forces which brought about the centralization simultaneously operated to cause a greater degree of decentralization of *personnel activity* than had been in effect at any time since the days of William McKinley. However, the decentralization of the eighteen nineties differed greatly from that of the Second World War. The former was characterized by a lack of control, while the latter was much more systematically approached through explicit delegations of authority guided by minimum standards. In a sense the events of World War II illustrated the old administrative adage that, if the administrative relationships of superior and subordinate agencies are to be effectively delimited, it is often necessary to centralize first in order to decentralize later.

Recruitment and examination. From the beginning the Civil Service Commission found it impossible to serve as the direct source of supply for all the principal personnel requirements of the federal government. The entire recruitment struggle continually emphasized this fact. As mentioned earlier, the Commission quickly delegated much of its field authority to its regional offices and to its hundreds of local boards. These, in turn, were greatly augmented. Altogether, the field establishments of the Civil Service Commission increased from a little over 5,000 in number to nearly 9,000 by the end of the war. These figures include 13 district offices, the post office boards which increased from about 5,000 to nearly 8,000 in number, and the special departmental boards of examiners which increased from a little over 100 to nearly 800.[47] At the same time the proportion of the Commission's staff engaged in field activities increased from 21.5 per cent in 1939 to 53.8 per cent in 1943, near which figure it remained for the rest of the war.[48]

Delegation to the field by the Commission called for a similar delegation by administrative agencies, and one of the principal problems facing the Commission was to encourage operating agencies to match its delegations of authority. In 1940 the Commission formally noted that it could "not, in many instances, delegate authority to act to its field representatives unless the Government agencies which the Commission serves are willing to do likewise." [49]

Considerable progress was made as the departments and agencies developed their own personnel offices under the requirements of the executive orders of 1938. From 300 to 600 Commission representatives were stationed at points where they could give prompt service to the federal field offices. These men were given wide latitude in nearly all personnel matters. Joint recruiting teams, composed of agency and Commission representatives, made special trips to look for and to place qualified personnel.[50] Shortcuts of all kinds, facilitated by liaison officers acting on the spot, were especially successful in dealing with the complex personnel problems of the field establishments of the War and Navy Departments.

The responsibility for conducting examinations, the rating of papers, and the placing of applicants was for the most part also delegated to the Commission's field establishments, especially the district offices. Instead of maintaining the usual central, ranked registers in Washington, the Commission authorized its field establishments to rate applicants promptly as "eligible" or "ineligible" and to refer them as quickly as possible to potential employers. As the manpower shortage made it almost certain that all the "eligibles" would be employed, the process saved time for all concerned.

Position-classification. Even in the controversial field of position-classification the Commission delegated some of its central authority to resident classifiers in the departments and agencies subject, however, to considerable review. In some emergency situations the agencies in Washington were permitted to take an initial action in allocating positions, subject to a postaudit. Still, position-classification continued

---

[47] USCSC, *Fifty-eighth Report*, 1941, p. 1; and *Sixty-third Report*, 1946, p. 13.
[48] Kammerer, as cited in footnote 4, p. 19.
[49] USCSC, *Fifty-seventh Report*, 1940, p. ix.
[50] See USCSC, *Sixty-second Report*, 1945, pp. 38–40; and H. L. Buckardt, "The Liaison Service of the U.S. Civil Service Commission," *Personnel Administration*, VII (May, 1945), 4.

all through the war to remain a major bone of administrative contention between the Commission and nearly all government agencies. But there is no evidence that the inequities in pay and position during World War II even approached those of World War I. An extensive examination of the classification actions in the Washington offices of the emergency agencies revealed substantial compliance with the intent of the Classification Act. Not so much could be said for the field services, however.[51]

To be fair, the fault did not lie entirely with the Commission, for it had never possessed full authority to control the classification of field positions. The Ramspeck Act of 1940 had authorized the President to confer such authority upon the Commission's recommendation. But the war had intervened before much could be done. Nor was the Commission in any position to enforce rigid standards during a period when administrative flexibility was the *sine qua non* of all action. Even more disruptive was the constant pressure from all sides to upgrade positions, hence pay and prestige, in the competitive struggle for manpower.

The Commission had been negligent in developing standards. Had there been available in 1940 the "type" position descriptions originally called for in 1923 by the Classification Act, a more orderly delegation of authority to departmental and field agencies would have been possible. Not until 1943, and then under the impetus of an executive order and a War Manpower Commission directive, did the Commission undertake to fulfill its responsibilities for the publication of position-classification standards. The same directives required the heads of agencies to classify field positions in accord with the standards and to refer unsettled problems to the Commission. At the same time the Commission was directed to postaudit field positions and report erroneous allocations to the head of the agency concerned for correction. Even then, the Commission's effective control was severely limited by a lack of authority to enforce its decisions.

While 147 standards covering 35,000 departmental and 70,000 field positions were published during the fiscal year of 1944, they were to prove of more use in controlling downgrading after the war than

---

51 On this subject see the detailed discussions of Kammerer, as cited in footnote 4, ch. xi; and Cahn, as cited in footnote 25, ch. ii; along with Ismar Baruch, *History of Position-Classification and Salary Standardization in the Federal Service, 1941–1944* (Washington: U.S. Civil Service Commission, 1945). The latter is a supplement to the earlier history covering the period from 1789 to 1941. For a description of the effect of the classification program within one of the emergency agencies, see Richard W. Cooper, "Position Classification in the War Program," *Personnel Administration*, IV (April, 1942), 1. *Personnel Administration*, the journal of the Society of Personnel Administration, primarily an association of public personnel administrators in Washington, was replete during the war period with articles critical of classification procedures.

in the war effort itself. A new executive order issued on January 16, 1945, somewhat extended the authority of the Commission. Under this mandate approximately 50 per cent of the necessary standards, covering about 75 per cent of the federal field personnel, were developed within two to three years after the war.

Coordination and control of the system. Gradually the Commission turned over large portions of its authority over position-classification to its own field establishments and to the developing personnel sections in the departments and agencies. It was not, however, until after the war that the decentralization was fully institutionalized and an "inspection" service organized to maintain the integrity of the system.[52] During the war the Commission functioned primarily through its liaison officers, through its departmental personnel management advisory service, through special investigations, and through its district supervisors. Decentralization may easily become anarchy. That it did not become so during the war years is another measure of the Commission's wartime effectiveness.

In quite another way it is possible to say that the personnel activities of the federal government were to some extent decentralized, though perhaps "coordinated" is a better word. The liaison with the War Manpower Commission and the Bureau of the Budget, the development of an effective Council of Personnel Administration, the association with the National Resources Planning Board and its Roster of Scientific and Specialized Personnel, and the effective relationship with the Presidential Liaison Office for Personnel Management, together with the creation of several different types of advisory and coordinating committees, meant that personnel management in the federal government, while centralized in one respect, was also becoming the business of an increasingly interlocking mechanism involving many individuals and organizations besides the Civil Service Commission. Yet the Commission was able at the same time to maintain a kind of supervisory control over the developing structure.[53] This was not disintegration but coordination and decentralization with a purpose.

In particular, the Council of Personnel Administration served an extraordinarily useful purpose throughout the war, and it has continued to function in one form or another throughout the postwar period. Representing the horizontal type of cooperative arrangement, the Council worked with the full support of the President, the

---

[52] A full-time inspector of the Commissioner's district offices was, however, appointed before Pearl Harbor.

[53] See John McDiarmid, "The Changing Role of the U.S. Civil Service Commission," *American Political Science Review*, XL (December, 1946), 1067.

Civil Service Commission, the Liaison Office for Personnel Management, and the departmental personnel sections. The full record of its accomplishment has never been systematically outlined, but among its effective wartime interests were the development of a standard application form,[54] the simplifying of leave regulations, the improvement of efficiency rating systems, and the development of field personnel councils. The Council conducted a drive for safety and health programs, furthered the improvement of within-grade promotion procedures, encouraged interdepartmental cooperation on housing, transportation, and carpooling, and assisted in the development of the exit interview. In its encouragement of top agency officials in the development of full-scale positive personnel programs, and in its effective liaison between the Civil Service Commission and the personnel offices of the operating agencies, the Council performed unique and constructive functions.[55]

The problem of basic administrative relationships between the Civil Service Commission and its developing departmental counterparts was less well resolved. The difficulty during the early months of the war has been described most bluntly by George C. S. Benson, then Director of the Administrative Division, Office of Price Administration, when he stated in 1942, "What is needed is recognition by the Commission that departmental personnel offices are necessary allies and not rivals in the main purpose of building up a sound Federal personnel program." [56] As Benson noted, the Commission frequently dealt directly with administrative officials concerning their needs for personnel, thereby bypassing rather than working with and strengthening departmental personnel agencies. The fact that, despite its recruitment decentralization, the Commission continually insisted upon approving the great bulk of personnel placements—particularly in the higher grades—left the departmental agencies bereft of one of the most important personnel tasks.

The problem of staff coordination among different operating levels and of establishing both horizontal and vertical administrative relationships is admittedly difficult. The War Department took almost two decades to work out the complicated mechanism of the General Staff, and the Bureau of the Budget has worked since 1921 to develop its fiscal system. That the Commission has had trouble equaling these efforts is not surprising. Yet decentralization is one of these perplex-

---

54 This is the well-known "Form 57."
55 For one description of its operations see Frederick M. Davenport, "Let's Look at the Record," *Personnel Administration*, VI (January, 1944), 5.
56 "Central Control Agencies with Special Reference to Personnel," *Personnel Administration*, V (October, 1942), 7.

ing administrative problems common to all large scale operations, which sooner or later must be solved or the entire structure suffers. As of 1945, this matter clearly had to be classified under the heading of "unfinished business." [57]

The Political Front

The political milieu in which the merit system was required to function was in many ways more favorable in the forties than in the preceding decade. By 1940 Congress had acquiesced at the inclusion within the classified service of the great bulk of all federal civilian employees. At the same time Franklin D. Roosevelt had clearly given the system his blessing.

The 1940 campaign. Still, all was not as well as it might have been. During F. D. R.'s terms in the White House the phenomenon described first as the Brain Trust and later as the New Dealers or, more cynically, as the "palace guard," had always provoked considerable uneasiness even within the ranks of the Democrats. Harry Hopkins' lashing of the professionals at the 1940 Democratic national convention, to keep them in line for the nomination of Henry A. Wallace as Vice-President, did little to ease any tension. At this time even "the Democrats knew, too," states the author of *The Roosevelt Leadership, 1933–1945*, "that long years in office had produced a tremendous opposition, not so much to the party or to its candidate as to the array of personal adherents of the President." [58] To some extent Wendell L. Willkie, the Republican candidate in 1940, endeavored to capitalize on these fears and on the distrust in many quarters of the expanding bureaucracy. The merit system itself received little attention in the 1940 campaign, though it is likely that a Republican victory in 1940 would have meant more substantial changes in the upper reaches of the federal career service than were attempted in 1953. But the really live issues lay in foreign affairs and F. D. R. broke the third-term tradition with considerable ease.

Congress and the civil service during the war. The attitudes of Congress toward the federal service during the war were ambivalent. The suggested disregard of merit system procedures in 1940 and the later investigations by the Byrd, Ramspeck, and Truman Committees have already been mentioned. Looking askance at the giant of its own creation, Congress from time to time sought some means of controlling

---

[57] For a more recent and more generalized statement of the problem see Willard N. Hogan, "A Dangerous Tendency in Government," *Public Administration Review*, VI (Summer, 1946), 235.

[58] Edgar E. Robinson (Philadelphia and New York: J. B. Lippincott Co., 1955), p. 253.

the growing public service. Nevertheless, the legislative efforts were fragmentary and frequently diffused in verbal meanders, especially as Congress under the pressures of circumstance continued to appropriate as fast or faster than it pruned. There is something a little desperate and melancholy in the efforts of the wartime Congress to take on the administrative Goliath.

There was, however, one substantial accomplishment of crucial importance, though Congress alone does not deserve all of the credit. While the President rejected the Truman Committee's critical view of dollar-a-year men drawn from business and industry, he welcomed and firmly supported the Committee's conclusion that the frequent requests for complete military control of the national economy should be firmly denied. As the authors of the principal study of the top administration of the American defense effort specifically note, "the military leaders . . . never abandoned the sincere conviction that they could run things better and more expeditiously than could the civilians." [59] To deny this conviction all through the war took considerable courage on the part of both Congress and the President. But deny it they did, with tremendous implications for the future of a democratic system of government.

The remaining efforts of Congress vis-à-vis the federal service are a phase of the perennial conflict between the legislative and executive branches of the government. Despite the tendency of the war to discourage the more open forms of internecine political warfare, from time to time they cropped out. From the standpoint of the career system the most ominous congressional move was the effort of the Senate, spear-headed by Senator McKellar of Tennessee in 1943, to enact a comprehensive requirement that any civil servant "receiving compensation at a rate in excess of $4,500 a year for his services . . . be deemed an officer of the United States, to be appointed . . . by and with the advice and consent of the Senate, and shall not be deemed to be an inferior officer who may be appointed by the President alone or by the head of a department." [60] Such a confirmation requirement had been successfully applied to the War Manpower Commission in 1942, and many legislators were anxious to see it applied to the entire executive establishment.

Back of the proposal lay a number of factors, some obvious and some more or less veiled. In the first place the reference to an "officer

59 U.S. Bureau of the Budget, as cited in footnote 19, p. 281; for the position of the Truman Committee, see p. 280.
60 Quoted from the original bill, S. 575, as introduced by Senator Kenneth McKellar on January 25, 1943.

of the United States" was meant to bring into operation the terms of the Constitution, which require that "officers" be confirmed by the Senate. Never in our constitutional history has there been a definition of "officer" which all concerned have accepted, and McKellar and his associates were prepared to clear up the point. Again the old conflict over the division of the appointing power rose to the fore. This time Congress was using another constitutional technique to accomplish its aim. The immediate quarrel of Congress, particularly the Senate, with the administrative branch was over the distribution of the public offices within the rapidly expanding civil establishment, magnified by a "jealous zest . . . to participate in vast powers that it dared neither to withhold nor to withdraw." [61] Politically imprudent recruiting by many of the defense agencies, particularly in their field establishments close to the legislative grass roots,[62] and the lack of any confirmation at all for many top positions in the emergency organizations established by executive order, left the legislative branch on the sidelines and rewarded the friends of the administrative branch where anyone at all was rewarded. Representative John Tabor of New York declared that "at the present time the agencies of government have been filled up with appointments of the type that Harry Hopkins, Benny Cohen, and David K. Niles have dictated." [63] The ideological patronage of the thirties continued to be objectionable to the partisans of the more traditional variety in the forties. The entire executive establishment seemed, from a legislative point of view, to be completely out of hand.

The McKellar bill proved the climax if not the end of legislative efforts greatly to expand the practice of senatorial confirmation.[64] The bill passed the Senate by a considerable margin and was defeated—on more than one occasion, as it was introduced again—only when the House refused to accede to the Senate position in conference committee. Altogether the battle raged for more than six months, with the President intervening to denounce the bill as something which was "the very antithesis of the merit system" and which "would sweep away years of civil-service progress." [65] Against the bill was arrayed a

---

61 Arthur W. Macmahon, "Senatorial Confirmation," *Public Administration Review*, III (Autumn, 1943), 289. For the details of the conflict over the confirmation bill of 1943, see this article together with Joseph P. Harris, *The Advice and Consent of the Senate* (Berkeley and Los Angeles: University of California Press, 1953), pp. 368–74.

62 See, for instance, testimony in *Investigation of Civilian Employment*, as cited in footnote 5, pp. 43–46.

63 *Congressional Record*, 78th Cong., 1st Sess., 1943, LXXXIX, Part 6, 7570.

64 See Macmahon, as cited in footnote 61, pp. 284–87, for a summary of the earlier efforts from 1935 to 1942.

65 *Congressional Record*, 78th Cong., 1st Sess., 1943, LXXXIX, Part 1, 1176.

constellation of forces, including, besides the President, the Civil Service Commission and the public employee unions. A number of civic associations, such as the National Civil Service Reform League, also protested.[66] But in all probability the principal barrier was manned by the members of the House Committee on the Civil Service, who did not always look with favor upon senatorial pretensions and who included such firm supporters of the merit system as Congressman Ramspeck. Still others were impressed by the veritable Pandora's Box of administrative, legislative, and even judicial problems the legislation might pose if it were passed. Fortunately, too, a simultaneous tightening up of controls on promiscuous personal and agency recruitment by the Civil Service Commission via the War Service Regulations made the Senate's complaints somewhat less relevant.

The Civil Service Commission and Congress. No doubt one of the deterrents to further congressional concern with the operations of personnel management was the effective legislative relationship which the Commission developed during the wartime period. Even before the war it had appointed a liaison officer to the Hill. The efforts of the Commission to publicize its problems, not only before the general public but with individual legislators as well, had proved fruitful in the Ramspeck and other enactments of the late thirties. During the war the most effective demonstrations of the Commission's relationships with Congress were shown in the legislative agreement to give the Commission control over emergency recruiting and in the confirmation of the arrangement by both the Byrd and the Ramspeck Committees.[67] Most of the congressional investigative criticism was levied at the operating agencies and relatively little at the Civil Service Commission except on the matter of classification. The Commission was not equally successful in all its efforts to influence Congress, but on the whole the Commission, especially Commissioner Flemming, received more respectful treatment than most government agencies.[68] At least the wartime period passed with the merit system grounded more firmly than ever before.

Presidential support. During the war the merit system and the Civil Service Commission received unqualified support from the Chief Executive. While F. D. R. did not often concern himself directly with the career service system, in the way that he had occasionally done in the past, there is no record of his refusing the Commission any major

---

66 During World War II the Reform League had little but praise for the Commission. By 1940, in view of federal progress, the League had turned a great deal of its attention to relatively virgin state and local territory.

67 See, for example, *Investigation of Civilian Employment*, as cited in footnote 5, p. 238.

68 See McDiarmid, as cited in footnote 53, pp. 1074–78, for a discussion of the Commission's legislative relations during the war.

request.[69] Executive order followed executive order at the Commission's suggestion, and, finally, under the directive authorizing the War Service Regulations, the President said in effect, "Write your own ticket." The delegation of authority could hardly have been more complete. Former Commissioner Leonard D. White has reported that:

. . . members of the United States Civil Service Commission, dealing with Franklin Roosevelt in the White House on matters which required his attention, were deeply impressed with his extraordinary grasp of principle and detail. Nothing in the civil service field seemed unfamiliar to him and his capacity to catch the essential point of a complicated situation and relate it to general policy was impressive.[70]

Certainly, not since the time of T. R. had a Civil Service Commission put itself on record in such terms as did the Commission of 1944 when it concluded the letter transmitting its annual report for that year to the President with, "No Civil Service Commission has ever received finer support from a President of the United States than we have received from you during these very difficult years." [71]

The Problem of Loyalty

Loyalty represents one of the basic manifestations of the roots of political power and in times of great political stress receives, both in the abstract and in the particular, unusual public attention. This has been true during and after all our great conflicts, but World War II was distinguished on the whole by the care with which administrative procedures were established to handle the problem. Whatever the critics may say—and they have been many—the "witch hunting" of the nineteen forties did not compare to that conducted under the authority of the Alien and Sedition Acts or the Civil War test oaths, or by Attorney General Palmer in the last years of the Wilson regime. Both public opinion and administrative action were more discriminating (in the best sense of the word) than ever before. As described by the New York City Bar Association's Special Committee on the Fed-

---

[69] Leonard D. White states, "He approved the basic War Service Regulations effective March 16, 1942. He integrated the work of the Civil Service Commission with that of the War Manpower Commission. He endorsed the decision of the Civil Service Commission itself to turn over the initial conduct of defense and war civil service matters to the minority member of the Commission, again confirming his preference for a single head of the central personnel office." "Franklin Roosevelt and the Public Service," *Public Personnel Review*, VI (July, 1945), 143.

[70] Same, p. 146.

[71] USCSC, *Sixty-first Report*, 1944, p. ii.

eral Loyalty-Security Program, "These older measures . . . were predominantly punitive rather than preventive in character. The recent totalitarian movements, Communism, Fascism, Nazism, and World War II, have led to the adoption, step by step, of an essentially new type of measure, a broad personnel security system." [72]

Except for a brief period during World War I, the matter of loyalty had seemed to be beyond the scope of legitimate administrative inquiry, at least within the classified service, between the Civil War and the passage of the Hatch Act of 1939. The main purpose of the Pendleton Act had been to exclude political affiliation from consideration in the selection of permanent civil servants.[73] Even President Wilson had been cautious in the handling of his loyalty instructions to the Civil Service Commission during the First World War. The provision of the Hatch Act which forbade the payment of salary to any federal employee belonging to an "organization which advocates the overthrow of our constitutional form of government" was, in reality, an amendment to the Pendleton Act as well as to the Lloyd-LaFollette Act of 1912, which outlined removal procedures.

Since 1941 there has also been added to all appropriation acts a proviso forbidding the payment of salary or wages to any person who advocated or who was a member of an organization which advocated the overthrow of the United States government by force or violence. Under the authority of these statutes and its traditional power of investigation the Civil Service Commission modified its application forms to inquire into an applicant's loyalty, for the purpose of refusing employment if "the existence of a reasonable doubt as to his loyalty to the Government of the United States" were established. This standard was in 1942 incorporated into the new War Service Regulations of the Commission and remained in effect throughout the war.

Beginning in 1940 the Civil Service Commission refused to certify for employment members of the Communist Party, the German-American Bund, and similar organizations. It also commenced to

---

[72] *Report of the Special Committee on the Federal Loyalty-Security Program of the Association of the Bar of the City of New York* (New York: Dodd, Mead and Co., 1956), p. 51. For additional references on the loyalty-security problems of the wartime period, see the "supplementary notes" to this chapter.

[73] Civil Service Rule VIII, approved in 1884 and continued substantially unchanged until the time of writing (see, for example, sec. 04.2 of Rule IV in the Civil Service Rules as published in the Commission's February, 1955, edition of its Pamphlet 2), reads as follows: "No question in any examination, or proceeding by, or under, the Commission or examiners, shall call for the expression or disclosure of any political or religious opinion or affiliation, and if such opinion or affiliation be known, no discrimination shall be made by reason thereof by the examiners, the Commission or the appointing power. The Commission and its examiners shall discountenance all disclosure, before either of them, of such opinion by or concerning any applicant for examination or by or concerning any one whose name is on any register awaiting appointment." USCSC, *First Report*, 1884, p. 47.

tighten up its investigative procedure and to expand its organization. From 1939 to 1944 the Commission's staff of investigators increased from 39 to 727. The number of persons investigated·increased from 7,806 in 1939 to 118,036 in 1945. Altogether, from July, 1939, to July, 1945, investigations of 356,537 persons were made. Approximately 11 per cent of the individuals were found ineligible for employment for one reason or another, but less than one-half of 1 per cent of those investigated were disqualified on the grounds of loyalty.[74] These investigations admittedly did not cover all applicants. The Commission spoke, for instance, in 1946 of its "limited number of personal investigations" and regretted the effect of its "reduced resources."[75] Considering that the Commission made or assisted in making about 9,000,000 placements during the wartime period, the number of applicants investigated was not large.

Responsibility for investigating the loyalty of civil servants already in office was primarily in the hands of the Attorney General and the Federal Bureau of Investigation, with certain of the military agencies cooperating with respect to uniformed and other personnel in the defense departments. The latter were also relieved, by legislation in 1940 and 1942, of the necessity of following Lloyd-LaFollette Act procedures in the case of employees whose dismissal was sought on the grounds of security. By 1942 cases unearthed by the FBI went before an Interdepartmental Committee on Investigations set up by the Attorney General and by 1943 to a similarly-titled agency designated by executive order. This committee developed procedures, considered the evidence, and brought the information at its disposal to the attention of appointing officers. Final action was, however, up to the latter. This system lasted until the institution of what became known in 1947 as President Truman's loyalty program. Though the record is anything but clear, out of something over 6,000 persons investigated by the FBI between July 1942 and June 1946, perhaps 100 to 200 were discharged as subversive.[76] On the whole, the loyalty-security system received general approval except from a sizable bloc in Congress, which considered it so protective of the rights of employees and prospective employees as to endanger the safety of the government.

---

[74] USCSC, *Sixty-second Report*, 1945, p. 46; Arthur S. Flemming, "Of 31,359 Found Ineligible for Federal Employment, About 1,000 Were Disloyal," *Victory Bulletin*, V (May 24, 1944), 3; and USCSC, *Sixty-third Report*, 1946, p. 20.

[75] USCSC, *Sixty-third Report*, 1946, p. 20.

[76] See especially Thomas I. Emerson and David M. Helfeld, "Loyalty Among Government Employees," *The Yale Law Journal*, LVIII (December, 1948), 53–56; and the President's Temporary Commission on Employee Loyalty, *Report* (Washington: The Commission, 1946).

397

Such was, in effect, the attitude of the influential House Committee on Un-American Activities, inaugurated in 1938 and popularly known as the Dies Committee. The inquiries of this committee paralleled and to some extent stimulated the activities of the executive branch. Though utilizing the results of several investigations by the FBI, the Committee also did considerable work on its own. Its most spectacular product was the well-known rider to the Urgent Deficiency Appropriation Act of 1943, forbidding the payment of salaries to three, specifically-named, civil employees. After the rider was struck down by the Supreme Court as a bill of attainder, this type of legislative control was dropped. Much of the difficulty stemmed from the fact that, while many members of Congress felt the executive branch was "soft" on the loyalty question, Congress all through the war failed to outline any precise loyalty or security standards except those normally associated with treason, espionage, and the like. Not until 1947 was the system substantially changed. By this time the loyalty-security problem with respect to government employees had become part of the much larger and extremely complicated issue of civil rights in general.

From the standpoint of public employees, the principal loyalty-security policy question is similar to that underlying arguments over the right of civil servants to strike. That is, to what extent does public employment negate the normal civil and political rights and privileges of the individual citizen? While no generally approved answer to this perplexing query was forthcoming during World War II (nor was it clearly on the horizon at the time of writing), the experience of the wartime years with subversive controls was sufficiently satisfactory to discourage a return after the war to the hysterical repression associated with the Red Scare of the twenties: In all, a net gain of considerable proportions.

The End of the Roosevelt Era

The election of 1944 and the death of the President. From the standpoint of the civil service the campaign of 1944 resembled those of 1936 and 1940. The same arguments were raised over the President's personal staff, over the swollen civil and military establishment, and over the general merits of government ownership, controls, and red tape. But again, the principal issues were international rather than national and the President was returned for a fourth term by margins almost as great as before.

A truly national leader in the thirties, Roosevelt had become a major symbol of democracy throughout the international scene in the forties. With his death in the spring of 1945 there was almost universal sorrow of unusual depth. While the war continued on to a successful conclusion under the guidance of President Truman, it was clear that something was missing. There were people, of course, who had no regrets. But in the public service, as elsewhere, there was a certain sense of depression and a little uncertainty which had not been there before, for the political milieu as a whole was rapidly changing.

Gains and losses. The civil service of Franklin D. Roosevelt had much for which to remember him. Above all, the merit system had met the most urgent personnel needs of the war. It had survived the conflict intact and in many ways strengthened. By 1945 public personnel administration was more thoroughly integrated with governmental administration in general than ever before. The Pendleton Act of 1883, for constitutional reasons, envisioned the Civil Service Commission as legally an agent of the President, though its bipartisan nature and the legislative debate over its creation indicate that it was to be set apart to some extent from the usual run of executive agencies.[77] Whether the development after 1883 followed the legislative intent or not, the Commission had frequently seemed an agency off by itself solely occupied with policing the remainder of the executive establishment. Previously, only under Theodore Roosevelt could the Commission have been considered as anything resembling an executive staff agency. During World War II it finally blossomed out into something more than an administrative provost-marshal, becoming a full-scale coordinating agency of a truly staff character without entirely shedding its control responsibilities—a difficult task at best and a tribute to the public acceptance of the merit system. By the end of the war the American national government could be said to have a personnel system in the full sense of the phrase.

Even more important for the civil establishment as well as for the national future was the decision to retain control of the national economy in the hands of civilians, thus utilizing essentially voluntary as opposed to compulsory means for the mobilization of the national effort. Efficiency is an attribute more often associated with dictatorial governments than with democracies. World War II demonstrated, however, that administrative planning for an all-out mobilization of national resources could be done even more effectively in a democratic than in a totalitarian regime. On this point the war historians of the U.S. Bureau of the Budget have concurred without reservation:

[77] The author rejects the thesis—stated in 1941 by William H. McReynolds and again in 1946 by John McDiarmid—of the purely executive position of the Civil Service Commission, as drawn solely from an analysis of the Pendleton Act and without a full consideration of the legislative intent quite evident at the time the act was passed. See William H. McReynolds, "The Liaison Office for Personnel Management," *Public Administration Review*, I (Winter, 1941), 121; and McDiarmid, as cited in footnote 53, 1079.

Long before they entered the war, both Germany and Japan had developed administrative machinery designed to expand their economic capacity, particularly that which was useful in war. Such machinery was established within the framework of sharply limited objectives as well as available resources. In the case of Germany, it is clear that the organizational and administrative problems of war were underestimated. No thought was given to the possibility that the existing machinery might prove inadequate. As the requirements of the war mounted beyond the ability of the established governmental machinery to handle, it displayed marked inflexibility and resistance to change—the typical marks of a senile bureaucracy. The situation in Japan was perhaps even worse.[78]

Certainly the American bureaucracy, either civil or military, could not be accused of resistance to change during the Second World War. Under the critical eye of public opinion and political groups of all sorts and descriptions, the administrative mechanism of the war was constantly remolded and had barely solidified into a generally acceptable pattern by the end of the war. Again to quote the historians:

The record dispels the notion that government in a time of stress is best conducted by autocrats. Our superiority in resources would have been of little significance without a parallel superiority in the ability to organize our efforts for the exploitation of these resources. Administrative personnel brought to the war agencies from business, from the colleges and universities, and from the permanent civil service demonstrated the existence of a reservoir of organizing talent superior to that of the dictatorships.

In the determination of our goals, free discussion occasionally brought delays—even dangerous delays—yet open debate operated to bring error into the open where it could be seen and corrected. The continuation in time of war of the politics of democracy occasionally enabled the advocates of private group advantage to threaten the general good, yet the give-and-take of the democratic process provided ways in which these tensions could be resolved before the war effort was seriously crippled. Our reluctance to establish even the semblance of autocratic rule may have been partly responsible for our constant struggle to coordinate or harmonize a mobilization effort made up of many separately operating parts, but problems of coordination do not disappear even in an autocratic administration and we developed methods that produced effective end results. Finally, freedom of expression and the absence of severe restraints on civil liberties aided mightily in enlisting the energies and loyalties of the people in the creation and supplying of a great war machine.[79]

Above all, the regime of Franklin D. Roosevelt must, as far as the public service is concerned, be associated with flexibility, the bringing in of new talent, and administrative innovation and reorganization on a grandiose scale. Henry L. Stimson is not too unjust in describing

78 U.S. Bureau of the Budget, as cited in footnote 19, p. 511.
79 Same, pp. 518-19.

President Roosevelt as "the poorest administrator I have ever worked under in respect to the orderly procedure and routine of his performance." [80] And in no respect can the top leadership of the Roosevelt period be described as a "team." Yet F. D. R. unquestionably was, as characterized by his Director of the Budget, Harold Smith, "an *artist* in government." [81] Credit for the creation of the greatest peacetime as well as wartime mobilization of material and human resources in our national history must in large part be laid at his door.

To be sure, there were many things left unsettled at the end of the war, not only with respect to the nation at large but also with respect to its federal service. The problems of manpower utilization and control, demobilization of both the civilian and military establishments, veteran preference, position-classification and wages, and loyalty and security were left open-ended and would continue to press for solution in the decade to come. But a war had been won, and, if an era had ended, it had on the whole ended well.

SUPPLEMENTARY NOTES

The civil service in World War II. Compared with the data available for World War I, those relating to World War II are overwhelming. The principal secondary studies are those by Kammerer, *Impact of War on Federal Personnel Administration, 1939–1945*, as cited in footnote 4; Leonard D. White (ed.), *Civil Service in Wartime*, as cited in footnote 9; Cahn, *Federal Employees in War and Peace*, as cited in footnote 25; Fjelstad, "Congress and Civil Service Legislation, 1933–1947," as cited in footnote 7; and McDiarmid, "The Changing Role of the U.S. Civil Service Commission," as cited in footnote 53. Basic also are the reports of the Civil Service Commission, the reports of the Byrd, Truman, and Ramspeck congressional investigating committees, and the many wartime historical monographs cited in the *List of World War II Historical Studies Made by Civilian Agencies of the Federal Government* (Washington: Government Printing Office, 1951). The important journals are *Personnel Administration, Public Personnel Review,* and *Public Administration Review.* Few memoirs or biographies are very helpful.

Military personnel developments during the war. In some ways the military was ahead of civil government and private industry in its personnel developments during World War II. This was especially true in the testing and examination field. Many other types of personnel research were also fostered by the military services. In the post-war period the scientific investigations into human relations and personnel problems, which have been supported by agencies in the Department of Defense, have been probably the most extensive and advanced undertaken anywhere.

For the Army and Air Force military personnel system at the beginning of the war see Paul P. Van Riper, "Personnel Administration in the United

---

[80] As quoted from Stimson's diary in Stimson and Bundy, as cited in footnote 42, p. 495.
[81] As quoted in Robert E. Sherwood, *Roosevelt and Hopkins* (2 vols.; New York: Bantam Books, Inc., 1950), I, 89.

States Army," *Public Personnel Review,* II (July, 1941), 199. For a brief summary of military personnel research in one department see, C. D. Leatherman, "Army Personnel Research," *Public Personnel Review,* IX (July, 1948), 115. For some contributions of wartime military personnel experience, see Ernest Engelbert, "The Army Personnel Process: Trends and Contributions," *Public Administration Review,* IV (Winter, 1944), 51. For an analysis of the frontiers opened up by the unique studies of *The American Soldier* by Samuel A. Stouffer and others, see Robert K. Merton and Paul F. Lazarsfeld (eds.), *Studies in the Scope and Method of "The American Soldier"* (Glencoe, Ill.: The Free Press, 1950).

The loyalty-security program. By 1958 there was as yet no general history of the federal loyalty-security program of the forties, though a great mass of material had appeared on various aspects of the topic. For the period from 1939 through 1945, see especially the systematic compilation of references to laws, hearings, and actions prepared by Dorothy C. Tompkins, *Loyalty-Security Programs for Federal Employees: A Selected Bibliography* (Berkeley: Bureau of Public Administration, University of California, 1955). Important substantive items are Robert E. Cushman, "The Purge of Federal Employees Accused of Disloyalty," *Public Administration Review,* III (Autumn, 1943), 297; Kendrick Lee, "Loyalty in Government," *Editorial Research Reports,* II (September 11, 1946), 613; Emerson and Helfeld, "Loyalty Among Government Employees," as cited in footnote 76, together with J. Edgar Hoover's reply in the February, 1949, issue of the same journal; Kammerer, as cited in footnote 4, ch. vi; Eleanor Bontecou, *The Federal Loyalty-Security Program* (Ithaca, N.Y.: Cornell University Press, 1953), ch. i; and Robert E. Cushman, *Civil Liberties in the United States* (Ithaca, N.Y.: Cornell University Press, 1956), ch. vii. Historical summaries are also contained in U.S. Congress, Senate, Report of a Subcommittee of the Committee on Post Office and Civil Service, *Administration of the Federal Employees' Security Program,* 84th Cong., 2d Sess., Senate Committee Print (Washington: Government Printing Office, 1956), pp. 9–22; and Commission on Government Security, *Report* (Washington: Government Printing Office, 1957), especially pp. 3–22.

CHAPTER 15

Cold War on the Personnel Front

1945–1953

Under the jubilation of V-J Day, August 14, 1945, lay a distinct current of anxiety. The sudden death of President Roosevelt, the breathtaking inauguration of the atomic age, the revolutionary temper of much of the world, and the perplexing difficulties of foreign policy combined to dampen the mood of the day. Nor were the memories of the aftermath of World War I at all reassuring.

All this was to have its repercussions on the federal service. As Americans reluctantly adjusted themselves to a new world from which they could not this time retreat, no matter how desperately they might wish to, the American civil establishment was to suffer a sort of sympathetic malaise.

Politics and Personalities

Above all, the New Deal was dead! Primarily designed for a period of grave domestic upheaval, the Rooseveltian program had been shelved at the beginning of the war. Actually the last major piece of New Deal legislation which Franklin D. Roosevelt had been able to push through Congress was the Wages and Hours Law of 1938. By 1943 the conservatively inclined Southern Democrats held the balance of power. At the end of World War II, the nation was politically restive. There was a distinct, if vacillating, tendency to turn to the Right in a search for an acceptable economic and political program, though there was little widespread agreement as to the precise shape

403

such a program should take. In this void Harry S. Truman was catapulted into the Executive Chair.

"**The man who bought time.**"[1] That President Truman, himself a border state politician owing his elevation to his acceptance within both the North and South wings of the Democratic party, should not unduly upset the political balance is hardly surprising. His actions, however, were not those of a Harding, who had been a political vacuum. Instead, Truman lashed first one way and then the other in bold strokes, but strokes which often canceled each other out or, as in Korea, led to a policy of limited action.

Truman's public pronouncements and papers, especially his first message to Congress on September 6, 1945, and his nomination acceptance and whistle stop speeches in 1948, echoed the New Deal with sharp emphases. But his administration was not characterized by continued reform. Nor was there the congressional support for social reform, even if the President had bent every effort in such a direction. Rather, to use Truman's own term for his program, the President administered a Fair Deal in which he frequently pushed and prodded for action in a true partisan manner but over which, in fact, he largely presided as an umpire among discordant factions both within his own party and the nation at large.

Nevertheless, President Truman succeeded in preserving something of the flavor, if not the fact, of reform. In so doing, he also preserved, though decreasingly so as time passed, some of the drive and force which had characterized the administration of Roosevelt. His moves to organize his staff and the cabinet more as a team, his continued support of the concept of civilian control of the military, and his loyalty to subordinates were especially notable. When one also considers the work of the First Hoover Commission, the unification of the armed services, the formation of the Atomic Energy Commission, the inauguration and carrying through of the Marshall Plan, and the successful management of a major military effort, one must rank Harry S. Truman well up on the list of presidents as regards administrative and legislative accomplishments.

Truman and the public service. In his support of the public service in general, as well as the merit system, Truman was forthright and constant. His loyalty program in no way resembled a witch hunt, and he maintained a careful line between the patronage and the permanent service. Political appointments cleared either through the Democratic

---

[1] This is Samuel Lubell's characterization of President Truman in a chapter of this title in *The Future of American Politics* (2d ed., rev.; New York: Doubleday and Co., 1956), ch. ii. For a similar estimate, see Eric F. Goldman, *Rendezvous with Destiny* (New York: Alfred A. Knopf, 1952), ch. xvii.

404

National Chairman or through executive assistants such as Donald S. Dawson. During the latter part of the Truman administration, Dawson became in effect the presidential Liaison Officer for Personnel Management. But the title lapsed and Dawson's functions were expanded to include political liaison with special reference to the presidential patronage. Though there were fewer offices to dispose of than in the thirties, President Truman managed them to political advantage. His renomination in 1948, despite his decline in popularity both in his party and elsewhere, was in part due to his skill in this matter.

The President withdrew no offices of any number or consequence from the classified service. Toward the end of his term in office he placed some within it, notably the top personnel of the Bureau of Internal Revenue.[2] Truman continued Roosevelt's support of Civil Service Commissioner Arthur S. Flemming and left him in fact, if still not in title, largely in charge of the government's personnel program. The President's appointment of Frances Perkins, former Secretary of Labor, to succeed Lucille Foster McMillin in 1946 brought the talents of an experienced administrator to the Commission. His decision to appoint James M. Mitchell, former Executive Director of the Civil Service Assembly, as a Republican member and successor to Flemming in the fall of 1948 maintained the tradition of expertise in the minority party appointment to the Commission. These two well-received appointments were climaxed in 1951 by the selection of former Representative Robert Ramspeck of Georgia, a long-time supporter of the merit system and author of the civil service acts of 1938 and 1940 which bear his name, to head the Commission upon the resignation of Harry B. Mitchell. Truman's commissioners were as competent as those appointed by any president, and they compared well to those of Theodore Roosevelt in terms of the program they developed and undertook after World War II. For their program, one of the most complete ever devised, they received the full support of the President.

The White House staff and the Cabinet. Though a shrewd and often hard-hitting politician, Harry S. Truman lacked that touch of intellectual perception, that spark of leadership genius, which is essential to the full invigoration of any social movement or organization, particularly in time of crisis. Neither an accomplished orator and writer nor an intellectual, Truman's appeal lay in his personification of the average man writ exceedingly large. Nowhere was this more apparent than in the men whom he drew around him, especially in his immediate White House entourage.

---

[2] This was accomplished in 1952 through Reorganization Plan No. 1 of that year.

President Truman retained the mechanism of White House assistants and secretaries as developed and expanded under Franklin D. Roosevelt.[3] But the personnel rapidly changed both in name and in characteristics. Robert S. Allen and William V. Shannon have described the period of 1945–47 as "the years of the flight of the intellectual." [4] Though their vitriolic portrayal of postwar White House personalities is overdrawn, there is some truth to the conclusion. Of the many distinguished Roosevelt advisers only David K. Niles, a specialist on minority problems, and Fleet Admiral William D. Leahy, personal Chief of Staff to the President and then over seventy, remained in a position to influence policy on a national scale. The new White House staff contained a few persons—Clark M. Clifford,[5] for example—who could reasonably be described as "idea men," but they were rare.

The kindest published estimate of Truman's collection of White House personnel was by Jonathan Daniels, himself an associate of the President in the 1948 campaign:

Truman used fewer free-lance assistants than Roosevelt. He had divested himself of those who came in with lightning-like or maybe just hit-and-run wisdom. There is no man approximating either . . . Harry Hopkins or . . . Colonel House. . . . Truman seems, indeed, to have a predilection for not very dramatic but industrious men in his Secretariat.[6]

Others dubbed these same men as "The Missouri Gang" or "The Truman Gang" and described them as:

. . . an extraordinary group, unparalleled in the history of the White House. Never was there such a large, weirdly assorted, and variegated crew, and never one which ran so instinctively and unerringly to the banal and second rate. . . .

But the worst thing about the Truman gang is their complaisance, their lush sense of self-satisfaction, and their utter lack of any sense of moral commitment, personal urgency, or intellectual fervor.[7]

3 In comparison, President Hoover's personal staff totalled about 40 persons. By 1939 the White House payroll listed more than 100 persons, and by 1950 nearly 250.

4 Robert S. Allen and William V. Shannon, The Truman Merry-Go-Round (New York: The Vanguard Press, 1950), p. 48.

5 Clifford was the President's Special Counsel from mid-1946 through early 1950.

6 The Man of Independence (Philadelphia: J. B. Lippincott Co., 1950), p. 307.

7 Allen and Shannon, as cited in footnote 4, pp. 88–89. For other analyses of the Truman White House staff see Jonathan Daniels, Frontier on the Potomac (New York: The Macmillan Co., 1946), ch. iv; Tris Coffin, Missouri Compromise (Boston: Little, Brown and Co., 1947), pp. 3–45; "Role of President's Advisers," The United States News, XXI (October 4, 1946), 16; "The White House Team," Kiplinger Magazine, II (May, 1948), 30; and "Mr. Truman, Chairman of the Board," U.S. News and World Report, XXVII (November 25, 1949), 17.

The truth is yet somewhat obscure, but certainly the influx of young men with ideas, vigor, and a zeal for reform, which had characterized the Roosevelt period, was notable for its absence under President Truman. Moreover, many of the abler New Dealers who had risen to the top since 1933, such as Wilson Wyatt and Paul Porter,[8] resigned in discouragement. At the more anonymous levels the bright young men were "packing their bags by the scores" in 1947.[9] The astonishing postwar prosperity and easy availability of well-paying jobs outside the government for the first time in a generation accounted for some of the movement. But this was not the only influence at work. "There isn't any fun working for the government any more," a New Dealer told news analyst Tris Coffin at lunch, "No inspiration. No one to demand you do the impossible, and giving you confidence you can. No bold adventures." [10]

At the cabinet level the exodus was equally obvious, climaxed by the quarrels involving Secretary of Interior Ickes and Secretary of Commerce Wallace, both landmarks of the Roosevelt period. The Truman Cabinet included at various times such outstanding personalities as James F. Byrnes, Fred M. Vinson, W. Averell Harriman, James Forrestal, General George C. Marshall, and Dean Acheson. But it was hardly a crusading cabinet. It was also, as Truman preferred, for the most part frankly partisan, with more emphasis on prior governmental and political experience than sought under F. D. R.[11]

On the whole, men with amorphous political philosophies like Major General Harry H. Vaughan, James K. Vardaman, Jr., Leslie Biffle, John W. Snyder, Edwin H. Pauley, George E. Allen, John R. Steelman, and Donald S. Dawson, rather than, say, Acheson or Byrnes, set the tone of federal management during the Truman administration. Many professionals in both Congress and the departments were frankly pleased to see the New Dealers gradually drop out of sight, for they were not always comfortable to live with. Whether the result was an improvement from the point of view of the efficiency and effectiveness of the federal service is questionable.

Other forces at work. When one adds to the picture a typical postwar resurrection of congressional power, the resurgence of a deeply divided Republican party, and the quarrels of the President with the famous Eightieth Congress of 1946-48, the prospects for the development of even a moderately unified program at the national level were

---

[8] Wyatt and Porter were, respectively, Housing Expediter and OPA Administrator during the war.

[9] Coffin, as cited in footnote 7, p. 64.

[10] Same.

[11] See Harry S. Truman, *Memoirs: Year of Decisions* (Garden City, N.Y.: Doubleday and Co., 1955), p. 328.

discouraging at best. The federal service was one of the casualties, for administrators and bureau chiefs were constantly caught in the midst of the no-holds-barred political in-fighting characterizing the postwar years under President Truman. In turn, a steady decline in the formerly high *esprit de corps* of the service commenced almost immediately after World War II, with three other developments precipitating the drop between the late forties and 1952.

The traditional bureaucratic fear of a change in administration was especially pervasive between 1946 and 1952. The Truman administration was operating on a shaky political base and Republican spokesmen, especially Senator Robert A. Taft of Ohio, promised a major house cleaning for the federal service. At the same time the loyalty program was accompanied by stinging and often indiscriminate attacks on the integrity of many in the civil establishment, both high and low. Finally, there came the rising crescendo of charges of dishonesty and corruption in office. The Reconstruction Finance Corporation became associated with mink coats, the Bureau of Internal Revenue with embezzlement and the favored treatment of selected taxpayers, and Truman's staff with "deep freeze" and "five per cent" deals.[12]

A traditional postwar letdown in moral standards had become evident both in the government and in the country at large.[13] For better or, frequently, for worse, the President largely stood by his political friends, whatever their actions, and refused to recognize much responsibility for ethical standards in the federal service. True, the RFC and the Bureau of Internal Revenue were eventually reorganized, but only after considerable pressure and with much of the impetus given by the First Hoover Commission and the general public.

The succession of scandals encouraged the Senate for the first time in history to authorize a special investigation, directed in 1951 by Senator Paul H. Douglas of Illinois, into the general problem of ethical standards in government. Unfortunately, few congressmen paid serious attention to the committee's recommendations for much new legislation and for the creation of a regular Commission on Ethics in Government.[14] Equally frustrating was the tendency of the Senate, bent on reestablishing its power, to make life as difficult as possible for a con-

12 For a critical summary of these and similar incidents see Blair Bolles, *How to Get Rich in Washington* (New York: W. W. Norton and Co., 1952).
13 See for instance, Eric F. Goldman, *The Crucial Decade* (New York: Alfred A. Knopf, 1956), pp. 186–98.
14 For the work of the Douglas Committee see U.S. Congress, Senate, Subcommittee of the Committee on Labor and Public Welfare, *Hearings: Establishment of a Commission on Ethics in Government*, 82d Cong., 1st Sess., June and July, 1951 (Washington: Government Printing Office, 1951); and U.S. Congress, Senate, Subcommittee of the Committee on Labor and Public Welfare, *Report: Ethical Standards in Government*, 82d Cong., 1st Sess., Committee Print (Washington: Government Printing Office, 1951).

408

siderable number of presidential nominees to political executive posts. The confirmation fights over the nomination of former Senator Abe Murdock of Utah to the NLRB, of Dean James Boyd of the Colorado School of Mines to be Director of the Bureau of Mines, and of Leland Olds for a third term on the Federal Power Commission were prime cases in point. Despite his previous experience in the Senate, President Truman probably faced even more contests with that body over appointments than President Jackson. While some of the contests were clearly deserved from almost any point of view, many were not, and the public service again found itself betwixt and between.[15] Almost no one's reputation seemed safe from attack.

Political stalemate. To give Harry S. Truman his due, he faced political issues of a magnitude and complexity with which F. D. R. might well have had trouble in coping. The old ethical imperative of individualism was, as has traditionally been the case during prosperity, regaining support; but the deep impact of the New Deal, the still potent fear of depression, and the requirements of cold war foreign policy were too strong to permit a forthright return to the type of domestic normalcy which had characterized the twenties. By the forties William McKinley's economic doctrines seemed quaint and totally unrealistic except to the most hardened of the business community. But the example of Fascist Germany and Communist Russia provided an antidote to any tendency for indiscriminate reliance on government controls. The impossibility of withdrawal from the international scene frequently frustrated both the Left and the Right and further confused and fragmented traditional political alignments. Yet in the immediate postwar years no one was ready for compromise, and no Henry Clay appeared on the scene with a solution in mind or in hand. There seemed to be no end in sight to the postwar political stalemate in which conservative and liberal, internationalist and isolationist forces were locked after 1945.

It was to be the fate of the Truman administration and its federal service to find themselves in the middle of a blind and bitter resolution of political, economic, and ethical forces the like of which has occurred only twice before in American history—just before the Civil War and again during the era of President Cleveland. The civil establishment has always come to some grief under such circumstances, if only from the lack of any firm policies to guide or inspire it. It was to suffer again. How did the personnel of the federal government and personnel management fare in the fight?

---

[15] See Joseph P. Harris, *The Advice and Consent of the Senate* (Berkeley and Los Angeles: University of California Press, 1953), chs. xi and xii.

Civil Demobilization and Reconversion

With the advent of peace, one of our chief domestic problems centered about the reduction and reconversion of an immense wartime governmental establishment. In a general way the experience of 1945 to 1947 paralleled that of 1918 to 1920, but there was considerably more advance planning for the more recent readjustment.[16]

Governmental reorganization. All through the war the Bureau of the Budget had from time to time reviewed the organization, personnel and activities of governmental agencies. Several war agencies, among them the Office of Civilian Defense, for example, were terminated long before the cessation of hostilities. A new impetus to reconversion was provided when in late 1944 President Roosevelt directed the Bureau to examine the entire wartime establishment and to prepare recommendations for "the liquidation of war agencies," "the reduction of Government personnel to a peacetime footing," and the "adaptation of the administrative structure to peacetime requirements." [17] At the same time Congress requested the new Office of War Mobilization and Reconversion to consider these matters.[18] To avoid duplication the OWMR designated the Bureau as its agent too.

In late August, 1945, President Truman followed up these efforts with the appointment of a special committee, consisting of Judge Samuel I. Rosenman, together with the Director of the Bureau of the Budget and the Director of OWMR, to make further recommendations concerning the reduction of the civil establishment. The President accepted most of the proposals, and by the end of 1945 nearly twenty major wartime agencies had either been abolished or their functions transferred to established agencies of the government, especially the Departments of Labor, Commerce, and State. Nearly all of the remaining wartime agencies were gathered under the wing of the OWMR. By early 1946, less than a year after the end of hostilities, the structure of the federal government had in main outline reverted to that of the late thirties.

The magnitude of the postwar personnel problem. Such a convulsive shedding of wartime functions and agencies demanded at the same time a drastic pruning of both the military and the civil services. By June 30, 1946, the armed forces had released to civil life approximately eight million persons, while the civil government had released

16 For a summary of reconversion plans and operations, see U.S. Bureau of the Budget, Committee on Records for War Administration, *The United States at War* (Washington: Government Printing Office, 1947), pp. 459–501.

17 From a letter by President Roosevelt to the Bureau of the Budget, September 18, 1944, as quoted in same, p. 498.

18 On October 3, 1944, this statutory agency replaced the Office of War Mobilization, established by executive order in May, 1943.

more than one million. During the next year an additional two millions of military personnel were demobilized along with another half million civilian employees. Altogether, between eleven and twelve million persons were released from the federal service in the two years after V-J Day. By June 30, 1947, paid employment in the executive civil establishment alone had dropped from a wartime peak of nearly 3,800,000 to a postwar normal of about 2,100,000.[19]

These simple totals do not, however, indicate the full kaleidoscopic pattern. While hundreds of thousands of persons were leaving the service, many more thousands were either returning to their old positions or entering the service for the first time. For instance, within the continental United States alone, from June, 1946, through June, 1947, 1,200,000 persons were separated from the service and 750,000 entered: nearly 2,000,000 personnel changes to accomplish a reduction-in-force of less than 500,000.[20]

One result of all this movement of personnel was an incredible amount of paper work. During fiscal year 1945, a *monthly* average of 850,000 reports of various personnel actions was received by the Civil Service Commission for processing to individual service record cards. This was an increase of 1500 per cent over the 1939 calendar *year* total of 661,800.[21] Also during 1945, some 3,700,000 records of temporary employees were consolidated with the master service records of other federal employees.[22] Since this peak year, it has taken approximately 5,000,000 personnel actions to service annually a civil service system of 2,000,000 persons. This mass processing of personnel reports, inquiries, investigations, and other records concerning individual civil servants constitutes one of the most frustrating and time-consuming of federal personnel functions. Much has been done to simplify the mammoth problem through punch card systems and mechanization,

[19] These figures are derived from Frances T. Cahn, *Federal Employees in War and Peace* (Washington: The Brookings Institution, 1949), pp. 156–58; Solomon Fabricant, *The Trend of Government Activity in the United States Since 1900* (New York: National Bureau of Economic Research, 1952), pp. 182–83; and from data supplied to the writer by the Employment Statistics Office of the U.S. Civil Service Commission.

[20] These totals are calculated from tables in USCSC, *Sixty-fourth Report*, 1947, pp. 77–78. They include transfers but do not include the several hundred thousand overseas accessions and separations. The single agency most affected was the War Department. See U.S. Department of the Army, Office of the Chief of Military History, *The United States Army in World War II, Statistics: Civilian Personnel*, prepared by Amanda Tichenor under the direction of Theodore E. Whiting (Washington: Office of the Chief of Military History, 1953), pp. 34–35. For a general commentary on the War Department's civilian demobilization experience see Matthew R. Gray and Walter F. Meyer, "Separating One Million Employees," *Personnel Administration*, X (May, 1948), 30. A comparable summary of Navy experience is contained in Robert E. Kronemeyer, "Manpower Problems in Demobilizing the Navy," *Personnel Administration*, IX (May, 1947), 32.

[21] From May, 1942, through July, 1945, more than 25,000,000 individual personnel action reports were filed.

[22] USCSC, *Sixty-second Report*, 1945, pp. 58–59.

411

but the many transactions which demand judgment on the part of someone make the system anything but self-operating. In late 1954 the Commission abolished its Service Record Division and delegated responsibility for maintaining employee records to the various agencies and departments in the case of present employees, and to the General Service Administration's Record Center at St. Louis, in the case of separated personnel. Though preventing some duplication, this action merely transferred much of the problem to the operating agencies.[23]

The postwar federal service was the scene of a gigantic reshuffling of personnel unparalleled in its history. That private industry was undergoing a similar strain, frequently characterized by even greater turnover rates than those in the federal government, further testified to the general difficulty during the middle and late forties of maintaining stable work-forces in either public or private organizations.[24]

Reduction-in-force policies. Prior to World War II the lay-off procedures of the federal government were relatively simple, because they were designed for a peacetime situation in which contraction of the service was the exception rather than the rule. There were legal requirements relating to veteran preference and executive orders directing that preference in reductions be granted on the bases of tenure of employment, length of service, and efficiency ratings. But the Commission's regulations, except for those relating to veteran preference, applied mainly to employees working in the District of Columbia.[25]

New reduction-in-force (RIF) regulations, covering the entire service, were issued in August, 1945, to be put into effect as promptly as possible. At the same time the reinstatement provisions of the Selective Service and Training Act of 1940 and related legislation, which protected the reemployment rights of all persons called into the service, also became operative on a large scale throughout the federal civil service.

In anticipation of postwar reconversion problems, new employees had been granted since 1942 only a "war-service" or temporary status under which the maximum guarantee was employment for the duration plus six months. The positions of the war-service and temporary employees were reserved for those veterans who desired to return to the service. Civil servants who had transferred from their permanent posts to the war agencies for the benefit of the service enjoyed similar

---

23 Much of the record keeping is, of course, required by legislation for the adjudication of appeals and the determination of reduction-in-force priorities, retirement and preference equities, and the like.

24 For a comparison between the turnover rates of the War Department and those of manufacturing industries for 1945 and 1946, see U.S. Department of the Army, as cited in footnote 20, pp. 11–12.

25 USCSC, *Sixty-second Report*, 1945, pp. 57–58.

reemployment rights. On February 26, 1944, President Roosevelt designated the Civil Service Commission "as my representative" to supervise compliance with the Selective Service and Training Act. The creation of the Office of War Mobilization and Reconversion later in 1944 notwithstanding, the great burden of supervising civilian demobilization and RIF procedure was left primarily in the hands of the Civil Service Commission and the operating authorities.

A noteworthy development within the operating agencies, especially the temporary ones undergoing liquidation during 1945 and 1946, was the frequent reconversion of personnel offices into outplacement offices to take care of personnel about to be separated. An Inter-Agency Committee on Administrative Placement assisted. The program of the Office of Price Administration was especially effective and indicated that an agency could, if it wished, do much to reduce the impact on its employees of a reduction-in-force. Since World War II a number of permanent agencies have used outplacement procedures to assist their employees in the wake of economy moves, and after the Korean conflict the technique became an accepted personnel practice.[26]

More important, however, for the long-run future of the service was the gradual development of an increasingly complex system, unprecedented in the history of the federal service, of RIF and employment priorities. Under these provisions the great bulk of the veterans who desired to return to their former civil service posts and most of the displaced career civil servants from the war agencies were able to obtain permanent positions again. However, it became clear by early 1947 that there were not enough jobs for all of those seeking, and entitled to, reinstatement and that voluntary programs for displaced career employees were not adequate. Many operating officials were understandably loath to release efficient and experienced war-service employees who wished to remain in the service with persons who, however deserving, were to the agencies in question now merely "new" employees. The fact that peace had not been formally declared negated much of the intended effect of the "duration plus six months" tenure provision applying to the war-service and temporary employees and further complicated the reconversion.

To cope with the problem the Commission proceeded in the summer of 1947 to inventory all the positions held by war-service and temporary personnel. The Commission then assigned to the various agencies quotas of displaced career employees seeking and entitled to reemployment. To provide positions for these persons, it required that

---

[26] See Walter G. Kealy, "Outplacement Programs of the Federal Government," *Personnel Administration*, X (September, 1947), 30; and Mario P. Canaipi, "The OPA Employment Security Program," *Personnel Administration*, IX (July, 1947), 19.

the necessary numbers of non-status employees in appropriate categories be dismissed. The Commission was determined, stated Arthur S. Flemming before the Society for Personnel Administration on October 27, 1947, that "the career civil service system is going to emerge from this transition period with more meaning behind it than ever before in the history of our government." [27] More than 11,000 former career employees were placed through this program during the fiscal years of 1947–48.[28]

By 1949 this type of personnel problem was largely solved, but at a price. While the numbers of non-status employees who were actually forced from the service to make room for displaced career personnel were never large, the atmosphere created by forced placement frequently impaired the morale of both the returning careerists as well as the many other employees who were continually threatened by removal and displacement from 1945 through 1949. Equally important was the fact that by 1947–48 the Civil Service Commission was, in effect, treating the federal service as a single entity in its displaced career service program. This denied to individual agencies their traditional authority in the realms both of removals and of selection and placement. What the career service had gained in security, the individual agency administrator had lost in control of his staff. Whether the forced placement of the last few thousands of displaced careerists, at a time when alternative employment possibilities were legion, did anything for the overall efficiency of the service is very doubtful.

Demobilization in perspective. Judged in terms of previous experience, especially that of World War I, the civilian demobilization of 1945–47 was well managed. The relative prosperity of private industry aided the process considerably. The government must be given credit for anticipating many postwar problems through its War Service Regulations and demobilization planning. Certainly the career concept survived a major test relatively unscathed.

The unprecedented peacetime size of our armed forces after World War II meant that federal civil employment figures would remain almost 100 per cent above prewar levels. It also threw out of balance the historic relationship of the military to the civil service in the federal government. Not only was the complement of uniformed military personnel much larger during the middle and later forties than in any prior peacetime period, but over 40 per cent of the civil service

---

27 Quoted in Cahn, as cited in footnote 19, pp. 163–64.
28 USCSC, *Sixty-fifth Report*, 1948, p. 23. For a more extended analysis of federal layoff policies at this time, see Cahn, as cited in footnote 19, pp. 156–64. The Commission's authority was based upon an executive order fortified later by the Selective Service Act of 1948.

was employed by the War and Navy Departments and operated under military rather than civil control. The full implications of a gradual but clear overshadowing of the federal civil service by its military counterpart were not realized in the late nineteen forties. One can look in vain among the official statements of the Civil Service Commission during this period, in the report of the First Hoover Commission of 1949, and in the general literature on the subject of public personnel administration before 1950 for any recognition of the existence of even a potential civil-military personnel problem of more than incidental import. Neither the Civil Service Commission nor, to be fair, anyone else prepared the federal civil service for the Korean conflict soon to come, let alone for a future which might envisage a more or less permanent garrison state.

The Peacetime Personnel Program

The Civil Service Commission's foresight lay in other directions. Its annual report for the fiscal year 1945 is unique among the agency's documents in its comprehensive outline of a peacetime personnel program for the federal service, moving far beyond the obvious requirements of demobilization. That the Commission and, indeed, the federal government as a whole have in the decade or so since 1945 largely followed the general guidelines of this program makes it even more significant.

Unlike its predecessor of World War I, the Commission of 1945 was extremely desirous of incorporating some of the wartime innovations into the postwar structure of federal personnel management. In particular, it wished to retain its policy of "close cooperation with operating agencies in meeting their personnel needs." [29] In the fulfillment of this policy "the Commission desires to eliminate all unnecessary paper work and red tape, to make operating agencies the partners of the Commission in the performance of its service functions, and to delegate to agencies responsibilities for taking personnel actions without the prior approval of the Commission so long as there is adherence to basic standards." Wartime innovations were to be continued "in matters of recruitment; fitting workers to jobs; and obtaining maximum utilization of manpower through improvements in employee training, safety, health, working conditions, incentive systems, and mechanisms for employee-management cooperation."

Above all, the Commission reemphasized the importance of a ca-

---

[29] This and the quotations immediately following are from USCSC, *Sixty-second Report*, 1945, pp. 7–8.

reer service, and outlined six "Essential Policies" to achieve it. It would be necessary:

(1) To place in the career public service all positions not of a high policy-making nature.

(2) To recruit and select the best qualified and available persons for such positions on the basis of open competition when well-qualified persons are not available from within the service.

(3) To provide for the development of employees to meet current and future needs of the Federal Government when such needs can best be met by transfer, promotion, or reassignment, and thereby to provide such opportunities for reasonable growth and advancement as will help to assure the retention in the service of competent and willing workers.

(4) To provide that employees who are in the career public service shall have protection as to tenure, subject to the limitations of available funds and the quality of their performance.

(5) To provide compensation and working conditions designed to make the public service a desirable endeavor to which to devote a career.

(6) To provide a reasonable degree of freedom from economic hazard resulting from injuries or illness and from unemployment, old age, or death.

To make these general concepts meaningful in terms of action the Commission broke down its program into the following elements, each of which was to be implemented through more specific policies and procedures: [30] (1) the development of a new set of civil service rules emphasizing decentralization, (2) the preservation of the career service during demobilization and its revitalization through a new competitive recruitment, examination, and placement program, (3) the development of a more adequate pay and position-classification structure, (4) an emphasis on promotion, transfer, training, performance rating, and separation procedures to improve the service from within, (5) the support of an enlarged welfare program and of improved employee-management relations, and (6) the extension of the merit system itself.

While this comprehensive blueprint did not anticipate all problems to come and largely ignored the impact of the military, it was still remarkably complete and thorough in its planned consideration of postwar federal personnel problems, especially when compared to the lack of advance personnel planning characterizing most decades in our government's history. How successful was this program from 1945 to the advent of the Korean crisis in mid-1950? [31]

---

[30] In the following listing the writer has synthesized, condensed, and rearranged the Commission's much longer presentation in its 1945 report.

[31] In a few cases the period dealt with will include the years up to 1952 or even later.

Decentralization and Reorganization

Immediately after V-J Day a "steering committee" was organized within the Civil Service Commission to revise the civil service rules. A set of transitional regulations, developed to bridge the gap between wartime and full peacetime personnel requirements, was promulgated by the President on February 4, 1946.[32] On February 9 he presided at a White House meeting of departmental and agency heads and gave his personal accolade to the Commission's new program.[33] These Temporary Civil Service Regulations remained in effect until May 1, 1947, when they were superseded by a more permanent codification which remained in force until substantially amended in the fall of 1950 as a result of the Korean hostilities.

The rationale of decentralization. The most innovative, as well as the most crucial, of the Commission's new policies lay in its forthright espousal of decentralization. In this decision lay a distinct break with the past. What were the factors involved?

First of all, by 1945 most of the government departments and agencies contained fairly well-developed personnel staffs with a wealth of experience. Secondly, the postwar civil establishment was more than double the size of its counterpart of the thirties. Finally, the Civil Service Commission was simultaneously faced not only with the usual postwar decline in appropriations and staff,[34] but also with greatly expanded personnel control functions. Slowly but surely, through the late thirties and early forties, the Commission had become in fact as well as in name the central personnel agency of the federal government, with a constantly expanding range of duties and responsibilities in personnel matters. In 1946, John McDiarmid, a former official of the Commission, summarized the Commission's control responsibilities:

. . . Jurisdiction over initial appointments grew "upward, outward, and downward" with successive recent extensions of the coverage of the Civil Service Act. A tremendous jump took place in the number of suitability investigations, with authority to order removal of those who had been appointed to war jobs "subject to investigation" should the check-up prove

---

[32] Harold H. Leich and Stephen P. Ryder, "From War Service to Civil Service," *Personnel Administration*, XI (July, 1949), 8.

[33] See John McDiarmid, "The Changing Role of the U.S. Civil Service Commission," *American Political Science Review*, XL (December, 1946), 1083.

[34] Appropriations declined from a wartime high of $23,166,980 in 1945 to $15,410,381 in 1947; and personnel declined from a peak of 7832 in 1942 to 3408 in 1947. The Korean crisis and the assumption of additional functions brought the level of appropriations up to an average of 18 to 19 millions and the Commission's staff to an average of approximately 4500 during the fifties.

unfavorable. In inter-agency transfers, the Commission's control became practically absolute during the war, with authority of approval or disapproval on either or both grounds of unsatisfactory qualifications or contribution to the war effort. Decision on withholding or conferring permanent civil service status in a wide variety of cases, though nothing new, assumed enlarged proportions after 1944. Authority to set standards, and to permit or refuse individual agency requests in the field of internal promotions, was conferred, and its exercise increased noticeably in 1943.

A measure of Commission control over position classification was extended to the field service of the emergency war agencies in 1943, and to the federal field service generally in 1945. Executive Order 9414 directed the Commission to promulgate regulations controlling the administration of annual and sick leave throughout the executive branch. The Hatch Acts of 1939 and 1940 gave a statutory basis for Commission efforts to prevent undue political activity of civil servants.

Efficiency rating regulations and the rules governing the order of lay-offs during reductions in force have both been issued under earlier authority, but toward the close of the war and during the demobilization period they assumed major significance as limitations on departmental discretion.

The Commission's general oversight of the reemployment of returning veterans who had left the civil service has included several control aspects. Also, the Veterans Preference Act of 1944 assigned to that body a number of specific enforcement responsibilities, along with general power to issue regulations carrying out the intent and purpose of the act. In the procedural realm, the Commission's power to prescribe forms and methods has cut a wide swath since 1941—embracing forms and procedures in application, appointment, promotion, status change, classification, leave administration, and reporting of personnel statistics.[35]

Considering the magnitude of the Commission's post-war task in light of its available resources, decentralization represented the only practical policy. However, the decision to decentralize was not forced on the Commission. Rather, the Commission had reached its decision before the war ended and made its position clear in its 1945 annual report. A year later McDiarmid described the emerging pattern as the "setting of standards by the Commission, delegation of authority to the departments to administer those standards, occasional Commission spot check."[36] Strictly speaking, the Commission was not just decentralizing but striving to strike a *balance between centralization and decentralization.*

Reorganization. To accomplish this most difficult of management tasks required first some reorganization within the Commission. Most important was the Commission's delegation of further authority to a redesigned system of fourteen regional offices and to a considerably

35 McDiarmid, as cited in footnote 33, pp. 1084–85.
36 Same, p. 1086.

418

expanded network of local boards of examiners.[37] These boards included nearly 8,000 of the traditional post office boards which operated only intermittently, and more than 500 "establishment boards" operating more or less continuously within other governmental agencies. The post office boards administered the more general types of examinations on behalf of the Commission, such as those for clerical workers. The establishment boards administered examinations especially designed to produce personnel for particular departments and agencies, and were considered as much adjuncts to departmental and agency personnel offices as to the Civil Service Commission. Through these field agencies and with the further assistance of a considerable number of committees of expert examiners functioning intermittently through the Commission's central and regional offices, the Commission was able to decentralize many activities, particularly in the examining field which carried an especially heavy postwar workload.

The Federal Personnel Council remained as an extremely important agency in Commission-departmental cooperation, and its functions were strengthened in the rules revision of 1947. Composed of the directors of personnel of the departments and agencies and of representatives from the Commission and the Bureau of the Budget, the Council provided a continuing interdepartmental advisory body which not only initiated and developed plans but spread throughout the service information about personnel practices. Under the guidance of experienced Frederick M. Davenport, the Council continued its extensive coordinating committee system as well as the field personnel councils. This mechanism also provided a most valuable departmental sounding board for Commission policy.[38]

The creation in 1946 of an Inspection Division within the Commission's central office and of counterpart divisions in the regional offices completed the main outlines of the new organizations.[39] The new inspection service supervised delegations of authority to the operating agencies, advised and assisted these agencies, reported to the Com-

---

[37] While economy measures after the war necessitated a reduction in the Commission's field personnel and field stations, the number of regional offices was increased from thirteen to fourteen in 1946 and their authority greatly expanded. USCSC, *Sixty-third Report*, 1946, p. 14. The increase in the number of local boards of examiners helped to compensate for the loss of full-time Commission employees. The number of post office boards increased roughly 50 per cent, while the establishment boards tripled.

[38] For the accomplishments and operating procedures of the Council during the Truman administration, see, for example, Federal Personnel Council, *Committee Work in the Federal Personnel Council System*, Pamphlet 25 (Washington: The Council, 1952); and T. Roy Reid, *Report on Organization of the Council* (Washington: The Federal Personnel Council, 1951).

[39] Some additional advisory committees were utilized. These will be mentioned later at appropriate points.

mission concerning the effectiveness of agency personnel offices, and encouraged the improvement of personnel management in the federal government.[40] By this time about half of all personnel actions concerned delegated matters. During the initial two-year period of the inspection service's operations, approximately 150,000 such actions were checked by controlled sampling techniques in the course of about 3,000 inspections. The percentage of violations discovered was reported as 2.9. Since "willful" intent to violate was rare, stringent sanctions, such as the withdrawal of delegated authority, were almost never applied.[41]

This crucial control mechanism, devoted to the development of adequate personnel standards throughout the federal service, became a permanent fixture on the federal scene and has been considered a success. The major criticism levied against the inspection service has been its inability to provide an equally competent advisory service to departmental personnel staffs.[42] However, there is no question but that the inspection service has served a necessary function. Decentralization with standards requires some check on compliance.

Decentralization as a statement of policy. During the war it had been necessary to delegate to the line agencies many minor functions which had formerly been handled by the Commission itself, often through its central office in Washington. This type of delegation continued after the war and encompassed such activities "as the determination of an employee's physical fitness for a position, check of members-of-family and citizenship requirements, verification of his eligibility to receive 5-point veteran preference, determination of status and qualifications for reinstatement, reappointment, transfer and promotion, and authority to grant within-grade promotions because of superior accomplishment, etc." [43] But the Commission did not stop here. It stated its determination to apply its concept of decentralization, as it had developed during the war, to fundamental personnel matters also. How well did it succeed?

Recruitment, Examination, and Placement

We now turn to a more detailed examination of the Civil Service Commission's postwar personnel program. At the end of the war the

---

40 These were the goals of the inspection service as stated by a former chief of the division, F. W. Luikart, in "An Inspection Program to Improve Personnel Administration," *Public Personnel Review*, X (April, 1949), 74.

41 Same, p. 75. For summaries of the activities of the inspection service see the annual reports of the Civil Service Commission from 1947 on.

42 This is the view of a number of agency personnel directors as given to the writer during the period from 1951 through 1956.

43 USCSC, *Sixty-third Report*, 1946, p. 13.

Commission concluded that it was necessary quickly to reinstitute a competitive system of recruitment, examination, and placement. The continuing manpower shortages only underscored the need for dependable sources for skilled personnel.

Decision as to approach. The main problem, in the Commission's opinion, was how to be fair to three competing groups: the two million war-service appointees,[44] the returning veterans, and members of the general public who were interested in federal positions. "The easiest and cheapest way for placing the Federal service on a permanent basis," the Commission later explained, "would have been to blanket in, by Executive order, all war-service appointees remaining on the rolls after the postwar reductions in force."[45] But this would have discriminated against returning veterans and the general public. Therefore:

The solution adopted was to plan a program of open competitive examinations in which returning veterans, war-service appointees, and the general public could compete, and to use the resulting registers of eligibles to displace war-service incumbents or to convert them to permanent status if their ratings were sufficiently high.

The Commission's resources did not permit carrying on recruiting and examining programs both for the current needs of agencies and for reconversion. Therefore, authority was delegated to agencies to make temporary appointments, under general standards established by the Commission, pending the establishment of registers of eligibles for probational appointment.

Examination and placement. In converting the service again to a fully competitive system the Commission faced a task of first magnitude. There were almost no usable registers of eligibles on hand anywhere in the federal service in the spring of 1946.[46]

Basing its calculations upon an estimated peacetime civil employment total of 1,500,000 with an anticipated monthly turnover rate of 2.5 per cent, the Commission planned to reinstitute a full-scale examination program and to reestablish a comprehensive battery of registers of eligibles for most federal positions by July 1, 1949.[47] Despite the facts that the federal service never declined below a total of nearly 2,000,000 employees and that the turnover rates exceeded 3.5 per cent for some months of the demobilization period, the Commission substantially reached its goal by the target date. In so do-

---

[44] By 1946, when the Commission actually got its program under way, this total had reduced itself to about 1,000,000 as a result of normal postwar reductions-in-force. However, many former war-service employees took the examinations and some returned to the service.

[45] This and the following quotation are from USCSC, *Sixty-sixth Report*, 1949, pp. 14-15.

[46] Leich and Ryder, as cited in footnote 32, p. 9.

[47] Same.

ing, the Commission expanded its own examining staff. During 1947, 1948, and 1949 it offered through its central office in Washington an annual average of more than 4,000 examinations for an equivalent number of registers for positions common to all the service. Through the Commission's field agencies and various types of examining boards, it scheduled an annual average of an additional 30,000 examinations during the same period.

The success of the program is best evidenced by the fact that over the three year period the percentage of federal civil employees with permanent status obtained primarily through the passing of appropriate examinations increased from 33 to 81 per cent. To accomplish this feat in a civil service of 2,000,000 persons, the Commission had had to announce 104,413 examinations, process 4,769,735 applications, and make 1,348,470 placements.[48] Examinations had been held for more than 90 per cent of the job categories in the competitive service. This meant that the great bulk of the war service and temporary employees had been given the opportunity of competing for permanent positions before 1950.

Recruitment. To produce qualified applicants for this immense program of examinations, the agencies continued much of their wartime separate recruitment activities. The Commission not only prepared its usual promotional literature issued with examination announcements, but it also tried to enhance interest in federal employment among several especially important groups of potential employees.

Recruitment of recent college graduates for the lower entrance levels was fostered by the development of Joint College-Agency Federal Service Councils within nearly all of the Commission's regions and the revision and expansion of the Junior Professional Assistant, Junior Management Assistant, and Junior Agricultural Assistant examination programs. Student-aid trainee programs, through which students were brought into the service on a part-time work-study basis, and special recruiting trips to colleges and universities by agency and Commission representatives rounded out this effort.

Upper level recruitment had not generally been a function of the Civil Service Commission before the war, since many top positions were not placed under the merit system until the reforms of 1938-40. The war emphasized the need for able candidates for major positions and spotlighted the Commission's lack of preparation and contacts for such recruitment. To help solve this problem the Commission had created an Advisory Committee on Administrative Personnel and a special Administrative Placement Unit within its own organi-

48 USCSC, *Sixty-sixth Report*, 1949, p. 13.

422

zation. These were continued. In addition, the Commission opened up some examinations on a continuous basis, developed new tests, and broadened the range of positions for which certain types of top level examinations, such as that for Administrative Officer, might provide entry.

In the recruitment of much needed professional, technical, and scientific personnel, an Advisory Committee on Scientific Personnel, an Advisory Committee on Personnel in the Social Sciences, and a number of special departmental advisory and examining committees aided not only in recruitment but also in the design and allocation of position descriptions. Junior Scientist and Engineer examinations were also devised.[49] The detailed classification system made it difficult for scientists and other technical personnel to move toward general administrative posts, though not nearly as difficult as, for instance, in Great Britain.

In accord with the intent of the Veterans' Preference Act of 1944, a special effort was made to attract qualified veterans into the service, as well as to see that veterans' rights were protected. A special Veterans Service Section was formed within the Commission. An extensive program, involving the cooperation of regional veterans federal employment representatives, the Federal Personnel Council, and the officials of veterans organizations was also undertaken. As a result of both the great number of returning veterans and the Commission's special efforts to place them, there was an increase in the percentage of the civil service with veteran status from 31 to 47 per cent between June 30, 1946, and June 30, 1949.[50] What the full effects of veteran preference have been or will be is a highly arguable question, capable of generating considerable heat in Washington and elsewhere. The fact that the veteran population is relatively young and represents a full-scale cross-section of potential employees with somewhat more than average health and ability means that the service should not suffer for some time to come. Moreover, preference does not apply to promotions. Still, it is clear that preference fosters procedural red tape and that it may hamper the employment or retention of the most qualified persons.

[49] For scientific recruitment in the Navy, for instance, see James A. Nielson, "Examining for Scientific Personnel," *Public Personnel Review*, X (October, 1949), 210.

[50] USCSC, *Sixty-sixth Report*, 1949, p. 13. By 1949 some 57 per cent of the men and 10 per cent of the women in the service were entitled to preference. Same, p. 42. The employment of veterans then leveled off and the proportion of veterans in the civil service remained at approximately 50 per cent during the period from 1949 to 1958. For a more complete analysis of veteran preference in the federal service, see USCSC, *History of Veteran Preference in Federal Employment* (Washington: Government Printing Office, 1955). For a critic's view of preference at this time, see Samuel H. Ordway, Jr., "The Veteran in the Civil Service," *The Annals*, CCXXXVIII (March, 1945), 133.

From the point of view of recruitment and placement, the greatest criticism has been levied against the so-called "absolute" 10 point preference, granted primarily to disabled veterans and resulting in their placement at the top of a register even though their passing score may only be 60. Legislation in 1953 modified these preference provisions by permitting the 5 and 10 point preference bonus to be added to a veteran's score only if he first made a passing grade of 70. In addition, persons receiving the 10 point preference bonus were no longer entitled to be placed at the top of the register unless they had been certified as having at least a 10 per cent disability. These amendments to the veteran preference legislation somewhat reduced the criticism against veteran preference, but did not fully resolve the problem. This was especially true for appointing officers who still frequently found the tops of appointment registers clogged with disabled veterans and other 10 point preference recipients, with the result that it was difficult to reach for appointment many of those really best qualified. There are various ways to circumvent this difficulty, but they are often time-consuming or politically dangerous, with the result that administrators are reluctant to use them. The matter of 10 point absolute preference has been a constant source of irritation contributing neither to the efficiency nor morale of the service, however beneficial to those receiving the preference. Several attempts were made during the Truman administration, particularly after the report of the First Hoover Commission, to modify the preference provisions, but none was successful.

Evaluation. Taken altogether, the Commission's postwar recruitment, examination, and placement program represented a gigantic task unique in the annals of testing.[51] Certainly the main objective of the Commission, the return of the service to a fully competitive basis, with proper concern for the competing rights of war-service appointees, the returning veterans, and the general public, was well on its way to accomplishment by 1950. Both the Commission and the line agencies may be criticized for not being sufficiently positive in their search for new talent, but they were growing increasingly so.

Decentralization, too, was reasonably successful. During the fiscal year of 1949, for example, 52.1 per cent of all placements were made from registers developed by local boards of examiners, especially the new galaxy of establishment boards and special committees of expert examiners which functioned within the line organizations.[52] Unques-

---

[51] The testing programs of the military services and the Educational Testing Service at Princeton, N.J., compare in terms of numbers of persons involved, but not in the scope and variety of abilities and occupational skills tested.

[52] USCSC, *Sixty-sixth Report*, 1949, p. 15.

tionably the Commission made a valiant attempt to bring the departments and agencies into decision-making with respect to the recruitment, examination, and placement process. The agencies, in turn, accepted much of the responsibility offered.

Position-Classification and Pay

By the end of the war the twin problems of position-classification and pay were greatly in need of attention. Neither had received much consideration for fifteen years, while the great expansion of the service during the thirties and forties together with the wartime inflation had played havoc with such policies as were in existence in 1945.

Position-classification. Until the passage of the Ramspeck Act of 1940 the Commission's responsibilities for position-classification were limited to the departmental service. The Ramspeck Act authorized the President to extend to the field service the Commission's jurisdiction over the classification and allocation of jobs to appropriate pay scales. But with the coming of World War II little was done. On January 16, 1945, pursuant to authority granted by the Ramspeck Act of 1940, the President directed the Commission to proceed with position-classification for the field service where position-descriptions and salary determinations had become increasingly chaotic both as a result of the war and the lack of any central review agency.

By this time the Commission's classification policies were being severely criticized on two major counts: (1) for a failure to produce satisfactory position allocation standards for agency guidance, especially in the field service where administrators were largely on their own; and (2) for a too rigidly centralized preaudit of position descriptions in the departmental service. In neither the field nor the departmental service was there any real balance between centralization and decentralization at the close of the war. For the lag in the standards program the Commission itself must be held largely accountable, as it clearly had the power to develop them under the terms of the original Classification Act of 1923. For the tight preaudit procedure, the Comptroller-General must receive most of the blame as a result of his restrictive interpretations of the finality of departmental action on position-classifications. The Commission could not decentralize much more than it had as far as the departmental service was concerned.[53]

---

[53] On the Commission's role, see Ralph S. Fjelstad, "Congress and Civil Service Legislation, 1933–1947" (unpublished Ph.D. dissertation, Department of Political Science, Northwestern University, 1948), pp. 332–40. For the Comptroller-General's position and the legal problems involved in the preaudit procedure, see L. DeWitt Hale, "Let's Rewrite the Classification Act," *Personnel Administration*, VIII (June, 1946), 13 and 19.

Under the stimulus of the presidential directive, the Commission made a concerted effort at the end of the war to develop adequate standards for both the field and departmental services, and to expand and refine a developing postaudit procedure,[54] especially for the field services. By this time, however, the tremendous growth of the federal service since 1940 greatly complicated the problem and made the Commission's task a major one. In September, 1939, the Commission's classification responsibilities had embraced only 83,000 positions, all within the District of Columbia; and the monthly average of classification actions during 1939 had totaled only 4,269. By 1945 the Commission governed not only the classification actions for 250,-000 departmental positions but also for 1,100,000 field service positions.[55] Altogether, these positions involved almost half of the estimated 1,500 occupations and 15,000 categories of positions represented in the postwar civil service.[56]

However, the Commission commenced to review such standards as it had previously published and to issue new standards rapidly on a regular schedule. By the time of the Korean crisis a total of 8,381 "class" standards, covering between 80 and 90 per cent of the positions under the Classification Act, had been published.[57] In developing these standards the Commission sought the active support and cooperation of the departments and agencies as well as of numerous committees of professional and scientific groups.

During the same period the Commission's preaudit controls for the departmental service were slightly relaxed. In April, 1947, when sufficient standards had been issued, the Commission commenced a systematic postaudit program of agency classification actions in the field

---

54 For wartime precedents for a postaudit, upon which the Commission built after the war, see USCSC, *Sixty-second Report*, 1945, pp. 47–51.

55 Same, pp. 47–48.

56 The estimate of 15,000 appears in Commission on Organization of the Executive Branch of the Government, hereafter cited as "First Hoover Commission," *Task Force Report on Federal Personnel*, hereafter cited as "*Task Force Report*," (Washington: Government Printing Office, 1949), p. xi, where the phrase used is "15,000 basic skills." This terminology is not warranted, for all this figure apparently represents is the number of different position titles in the federal service. All fields of employment, in comparison, according to Department of Labor data, embrace about 25,000 job titles. The remaining data are also estimates, based in part on information provided the writer by O. Glenn Stahl, Director of the Bureau of Programs and Standards, U.S. Civil Service Commission, and in part on Harold H. Leich, "Job Specialization in the Federal Service—Good or Bad?" *Personnel Administration*, XX (March–April, 1957), 31.

57 See USCSC, *Sixty-sixth Report*, 1949, p. 25; and *Sixty-seventh Report*, 1950, p. 37. A "class" is defined as "a group of positions sufficiently similar in respect to the essential character of their duties, responsibilities, and consequent qualification requirements that for each of them the same descriptive title can appropriately be used, the same qualifications for entrance can reasonably be required, the same tests of fitness can appropriately be used, and the same scale of compensation can be applied with equity." USCSC, *Training Course in the Basic Principles and Techniques of Position-Classification* (Washington: Civil Service Commission, 1946), p. 1.

service. During the next two years some 57,000 position allocations in several hundred field offices were reviewed, and the Commission reported the program a success.[58] There was, nevertheless, a continuing stream of criticism from the departmental service where, despite the great pressure for rapid reorganization after the war, few new positions could be created or old positions reoriented to new functions until after the Commission had placed its seal of approval upon the proposed position descriptions.[59]

With the passage of the Classification Act of 1949, sparked by the report of the First Hoover Commission, the Civil Service Commission was finally enabled to supervise position-classification by means of a postaudit in *both* the departmental and field services. In addition, the Commission received unprecedented authority to enforce its findings should such prove necessary. However, much criticism still continued, particularly of the standards being enforced. As one experienced personnel man put it:

. . . the Civil Service Commission . . . is sacrificing quality for mass production, and is forcing standards on the agencies that are technically invalid for many reasons, and that in style and content are so ambiguous and incomplete as to leave the classifier in the same state of uncertainty that existed before they were issued.[60]

These complaints were to some extent justified; and, with the increasing manpower problem always in the foreground, classification was to remain a touchy problem, especially because of its effect on the salaries which agencies might pay for personnel. Nevertheless, by the time of the Korean war much progress in standards development and in decentralization of the position-classification function itself had been made.

Pay. By the end of the war much of the pay structure of the federal service was badly in need of revision as a result of inflation.[61] Inflation had struck the service after World War I also, but the depression of 1921 had reversed the movement enough that wage and salary

[58] USCSC, *Sixty-fifth Report*, 1948, pp. 28–29; and *Sixty-sixth Report*, 1949, pp. 25–27.
[59] See, for example, Charles S. Hyneman, *Bureaucracy in a Democracy* (New York: Harper and Bros., 1950), pp. 396–415. See also Cahn, as cited in footnote 19, p. 233, for some conclusions resulting from a 1947 survey of middle-management opinion on the subject of classification.
[60] Donald McInnis, "Does Position Classification Work?" *Personnel Administration*, X (March, 1948), 33.
[61] The whole matter of salaries and other monetary arrangements in the federal service, including maintenance allowances, hazardous pay, geographic differentials, retirement, and the like, involves an extraordinarily complex web of legislation, procedures, and regulations. Only major problems and trends have been considered in this study. For further information see the references in the "supplementary notes" to this chapter.

427

increases had not been as urgently required as at the close of World War II.

Even during the war the rising cost of living, the requirement of frequent overtime, the increasing wages granted within private industry, and the necessity of recruiting within a highly competitive manpower market had forced some wage increases. The War Overtime Pay Act of 1943, supplementing and revising miscellaneous overtime pay legislation passed intermittently from 1940 through 1942, provided for overtime pay in most job categories and for a flat bonus to those not obtaining overtime. In effect, the War Overtime Pay Act provided a modest raise for nearly all federal employees paid straight salaries and represented the first general salary increase since 1930. Wage board employees paid the "going rate" needed no such legislation. These wartime provisions were superseded by the Federal Employees Pay Act of 1945, which increased the basic rates by a sliding scale varying from 20 per cent at the bottom to 8.9 per cent at the top. This was shortly followed by the Federal Employees Pay Act of 1946, increasing salaries generally by about 14 per cent, but with a range of from 20 to 2 per cent and with a ceiling limitation of $10,-000. The Postal Rate Revision and Federal Employees Salary Act of 1948 increased all salaries by a flat $330, with the effect of producing a sliding scale varying from 30.6 to 3.3 per cent.

The outstanding cumulative result of these pay raises was a narrowing of the gap between floor and ceiling pay rates, a result emphasized further by the progressive income tax levies. The workers at the bottom, for obvious political reasons, have received the most legislative attention, although all the studies of federal pay scales since World War I have shown federal employees in the lower pay brackets to be best off in comparison with their counterparts in private industry.[62] Until the passage of the Classification Act of 1949 ceiling salaries received little attention despite the fact that it was in the top levels that recruiting had for ten years been one of the most pressing governmental personnel problems.[63] During this period the Civil Service Commission consistently supported salary increases in top as well as bottom positions, usually on a straight percentage basis, but Congress did not.

[62] See, for example, U.S. Congress, House, *Closing Report of Wage and Personnel Survey*, prepared by the Personnel Classification Board, 71st Cong., 3d Sess., House Doc. 771 (Washington: Government Printing Office, 1931), pp. 114–30, for the single most extensive survey. See also Civil Service Commission Chairman Robert Ramspeck's testimony before the Senate on May 16, 1951, as contained in a Commission press release of that date, for a summary of this development.

[63] For the situation in 1937 see President's Committee on Administrative Management, *Report with Special Studies* (Washington: Government Printing Office, 1937), pp. 125–27. For that in 1949, see First Hoover Commission, as cited in footnote 56, pp. 31–33.

Federal wage policy. All this postwar activity in the realms of position-classification and pay only underlined the fact that the federal government has never actively implemented a systematic wage policy. Throughout most of our history, wages, as well as the position-classification structure underlying them, have received attention only when something had to be done if the service was not to suffer seriously. Even then only stop-gap measures have been adopted. In 1949 the First Hoover Commission pointed out that over 90 per cent of all federal positions were subject to the same employment procedures, but less than 50 per cent were subject to any one set of wage policies. For instance, by 1947 approximately 46 per cent of the federal service within the continental United States was paid under the terms of the Classification Act of 1923. An additional 25 per cent, consisting largely of skilled and semi-skilled craftsmen and laborers in governmental industrial-type establishments, was paid "prevailing rates" through the wage board system, largely controlled by the departments and agencies. A further 25 per cent was paid under the terms of a special postal classification act, administered almost exclusively by the Post Office Department; and the final 4 per cent was paid under "miscellaneous" systems, including those of the Foreign Service and the TVA.[64]

The First Hoover Commission recommended the development of a "comprehensive pay policy" for the federal service. This would have involved a thorough study of federal wages, the application of the "going rate" principle to a much wider range of federal jobs, a relinquishment by Congress of detailed control of wages, and the delegation of considerable authority to the Civil Service Commission and the line agencies.[65] But Congress was not receptive to such sweeping measures and little was done toward such ends during the Truman administration.

Employee Development and Utilization

Prior to the late thirties only the military services had been much concerned with the systematic training and development of public employees once they entered the service. Since long before 1883, the assumption had been that qualified employees were available some-

---

[64] From data supplied by the Employment Statistics Staff of the Civil Service Commission, quoted by Fjelstad, as cited in footnote 53, p. 319.

[65] First Hoover Commission, *Personnel Management* (Washington: Government Printing Office, 1949), pp. 24–28. For a general discussion of the variables involved in wage determination, see O. Glenn Stahl, *Public Personnel Administration* (4th ed.; New York: Harper and Bros., 1956), ch. x. There has been no thorough study of federal wages and wage practices since that conducted by the Personnel Classification Board in the late twenties.

where and that either the examination system or the normal functioning of partisan politics would find them and bring them into the service. After they arrived on duty, their future was largely their own affair. Official assistance or even encouragement of employee development while on the job was rare. Congress declined to support most such activities, usually on the grounds that they were a "frill."

In the thirties the unprecedented range of activities undertaken by the federal government underscored the need for new personnel with new skills and the reorientation of many of those already in the permanent service. The combined efforts of the Civil Service Commission, some of the line agencies, particularly the newer ones, the President's Committee on Administrative Management, and President Franklin D. Roosevelt finally broke the dyke of tradition. The increasing difficulty of recruiting competent technical and administrative personnel from outside the service during the forties and early fifties further emphasized that the federal service must utilize its own personnel to the utmost.

Training. Pre-entry training continued apace all through the thirties and forties with the rapid expansion and recognition of collegiate programs in public administration. Most of these programs remained integral parts of Political Science and Government Departments of colleges and universities. But a few schools such as Syracuse, the University of Southern California, New York University, American University, and Cornell developed largely self-contained programs. By the forties the Master of Public Administration (M.P.A.) degree was well recognized, and by the academic year of 1952-53 more than a hundred colleges and universities throughout the country were offering graduate work specifically oriented toward public administration and labeled as such.[66] A significant body of literature and experimentation was also emerging, much of which was summarized in 1948 by Dwight Waldo in *The Administrative State,* the first study of the political theory of American public administration.[67] There were in addition, of course, the more traditional programs oriented toward medicine, law, and the like from which the public service had drawn personnel for generations. Pre-entry training in public administration was not, however, as professionalized at either the graduate or undergraduate levels as similar training in business administration had been for thirty years. By the end of the war there were no undergraduate

---

66 Public Administration Clearing House, *Educational Preparation for Public Administration: A Catalog of Graduate Programs, 1952–53* (Chicago: Public Administration Service, 1952). Most of the 104 schools listed in this catalog also offered some undergraduate work, as did many other institutions not listed.

67 (New York: The Ronald Press.)

schools of public administration comparable to the many undergraduate business schools; and it was not until 1946 that Cornell's Graduate School of Business and Public Administration offered the first two-year M.P.A. program designed to be comparable to and offered in conjunction with the increasingly popular two-year Master of Business Administration curriculum. Training in personnel administration was also expanding, though the emphasis lay much more on personnel problems in private enterprise than in public agencies. Thus the nation's educational system was pouring out an increasing number of students better prepared for the public service than ever before.[68]

Interestingly, the traditional antipathy toward formal educational requirements for public office was reasserting itself at the same time through the Veterans' Preference Act of 1944. Section 5 of this act provided: "No minimum educational requirements will be prescribed in any civil service examination except for such scientific, technical, or professional positions the duties of which the Civil Service Commission decides cannot be performed by a person who does not have such education." This requirement, applying to both veterans and nonveterans, has had to be strictly interpreted. It is still in effect.

Post-entry training under governmental auspices was having more of a struggle. In 1939 the Civil Service Commission had added a Coordinator and Director of Training to its central staff, and a small training advisory staff performed valiantly during World War II. Interagency training conferences were held to assess needs, new training materials were produced, and a central reference service was maintained. An ambitious supervisory training program was also developed, and an internship program for promising lower and middle management talent launched. Personnel skills inventories and manpower utilization were increasingly emphasized during the conflict.

After the war the Commission requested appropriations to continue and to expand these activities, but, instead, had to curtail them because Congress declined to cooperate. A succession of appropriation cuts decimated the Commission's central training staff and by 1947 orderly activities in the fields of employee development and utilization were largely abandoned.[69] Only the administrative internship program, begun by the National Institute of Public Affairs in 1943 and taken over by the Commission in 1945, survived. This was expanded in 1949 and by the early fifties this type of training program was well established not only within the Commission but within a number of

---

[68] For further information see the "supplementary notes" to this chapter.
[69] For a summary of the Commission's wartime training activities and immediate postwar difficulties see McDiarmid, as cited in footnote 33, pp. 1087-95.

departments and agencies.[70] The First Hoover Commission noted the dearth of staff development planning. Under the joint stimulus of the Hoover Commission and a special report by the Bureau of the Budget on management improvement, the President assigned to the Civil Service Commission during 1950 the general responsibility for supervision of service-wide staff development programs. A Director of Executive Development was then appointed and agencies were encouraged to submit plans for in-service transfer and training of top-level employees to remove what Commissioner James M. Mitchell then called the "curse of excessive specialization." [71] The Korean crisis interrupted this movement and at best its accomplishments were modest under President Truman.

With the Commission largely out of training activities during the late forties, employee development was perforce decentralized, without much overall control. Certain special enactments and appropriations permitted some in-service training in job categories for which there were no private equivalents. The Department of Justice, for example, has for many years conducted extensive training programs for personnel of the Federal Bureau of Investigation; and the Treasury Department's Training Division has provided special courses for newly appointed revenue agents. But on the whole, even the line agencies, except for the military services, were handicapped by the lack of enabling legislation. Outside the military services, only a few governmental agencies, such as the State Department, the Weather Bureau, and the Central Intelligence Agency, were able to utilize private facilities for training civil servants at public expense. Thus, while there was an increasing interest in and need for training and systematic employee development programs during the postwar years, accomplishment was erratic and spotty. The First Hoover Commission recommended that "Congress should enact legislation which will clearly set forth the policy of the Federal Government on the conduct of training programs for civilian employees." [72] But the Hoover Commission did not attempt to outline the possible content of such a policy and Congress, during the Truman administration, was reluctant to act on its own.[73]

---

[70] On this type of training program see J. Henry Brown, Jr., "The Federal Administrative Intern Program," Public Personnel Review, XI (January, 1950), 10; and U.S. Civil Service Commission, Guide for Internship Training in the Federal Service, Pamphlet 46 (Washington: Government Printing Office, 1952).

[71] James M. Mitchell, "Recent Progress in Federal Personnel Administration," Public Personnel Review, XI (October, 1950), 181.

[72] First Hoover Commission, as cited in footnote 65, p. 23.

[73] For further background information see U.S. Congress, Senate, Committee on Post Office and Civil Service, Subcommittee on Federal Manpower Policies, Training and Education in the Federal Government, 83d Cong., 1st Sess., Sen. Doc. 31 (Washington: Govern-

Promotion and transfer. In the realms of promotion and transfer, integral aspects of any career system, the Civil Service Commission was only a bit more successful. At the root of the difficulty was the high degree of occupational specialization typical of the American as opposed to many foreign civil services.[74] A civil servant who originally qualified for a too narrow specialization has often had great difficulty in qualifying later for promotion or transfer to a post requiring more general or other specific qualifications. Lucius Wilmerding, Jr.'s criticism of 1935 was still valid a decade later:

> Classifications of such complexity are to be condemned because of the fetters which they place upon department heads in the management of their business. If a man cannot be advanced to work of slightly greater difficulty than that to which he was initially assigned, or if a man cannot be transferred from one kind of clerical work to another, without in the one case being formally promoted and in the other reexamined, departmental business may easily bog down in a welter of red tape.[75]

All through the twenties, thirties, and early forties, the tendency of the classification mechanism to impede lateral and upward movement by its failure to recognize employee potential was to some extent circumvented because the departments and agencies were usually left to their own devices in matters of promotion and transfer.[76] But this solution was at the expense of the classification system as a whole. Moreover, it made for numerous inequities in promotion and transfer policies as among the various agencies, and sometimes encouraged labor pirating.

In 1939 the Commission attempted to set up a central competitive promotion system which called for the filling of vacancies from departmental registers. Departmental resistance to a curtailing of prerogative and congressional failure to provide funds for the experiment

---

ment Printing Office, 1953); and U.S. Congress, House, Committee on Post Office and Civil Service, *Training of Federal Employees*, 83d Cong., 2d Sess., Committee print (Washington: Government Printing Office, 1954).

[74] However, Lewis Meriam has noted: "Some students of the British national system point out that the British do not use such narrow classes in their central control agency, the Treasury, and that is true. But it is also true that many of the operating departments of the British government have their own detailed sub-classifications within the broad classifications established by law and Treasury regulations. These departmental sub-classifications resemble ours and indeed appear to be a necessary part of efficient personnel administration. The difference between the two systems with respect to classes is perhaps not as great as it has been painted." *Public Personnel Problems from the Standpoint of the Operating Officer* (Washington: The Brookings Institution, 1938), p. 31.

[75] *Government by Merit* (New York: McGraw-Hill Book Co., 1935), p. 57.

[76] Writing about the period before 1939, Lewis Meriam states, "While the writer was in the classified civil service, dealing with personnel as an operating man, he had in several years only one case in which the Commission did not approve promotion papers as a matter of routine." As cited in footnote 74, p. 7.

kept the program from materializing. During World War II even the routine controls exercised earlier largely went by the boards. It was not until 1949 that the Commission reconsidered its promotion and transfer policies in any detail. At the urging of the First Hoover Commission, a new promotion policy was formulated in April, 1950, with the assistance of the Federal Personnel Council. The departments and agencies were directed to prepare programs conforming to general standards, but were permitted considerable latitude of operation.[77] The Commission relaxed its classification and appointment procedures to permit federal agencies participating in "executive development agreements" to rotate selected employees freely among a number of types of positions in order to broaden the background of these potential executives. In addition, the Commission reduced the number of restrictive qualifications required for promotion to some higher positions, such as personnel officer, for example.[78] The Korean conflict interrupted this attempt to systematize promotions. But by 1958 they were being handled with more planning combined with more flexibility than ever before in the history of the federal service.[79]

At the end of the war the controls to channel transfers into war agencies were abolished. Instead, the Civil Service Commission encouraged retransfers of permanent employees back to the older established agencies. Intradepartmental transfers were stimulated by the executive development agreements, mentioned above, but beyond this, little was done. Historically, the component parts of the federal administrative mechanism have tended to remain somewhat apart from each other. With respect to inter- and often intradepartmental employment opportunities, each employee has been on his own.

Efficiency ratings. There was general agreement after the war that the efficiency rating system needed overhauling. This perennial sentiment received special legislative attention in 1946. For the first time Congress provided that no public employees, except those in the T.V.A. and the field service of the Post Office Department, might be rated as to efficiency except through a system approved by the Civil Serv-

---

[77] The standards were (and still are as of the time of writing) as follows: "(1) Consult employees on appropriate aspects of the program; (2) State the policy in writing and make it available to all employees; (3) Provide for broad areas of selection and consider individuals outside the organization to assure selection of the best qualified; (4) Assist employees to develop themselves for promotion; (5) Use realistic qualifications requirements; (6) Apply the same standards for selection systematically and equitably to all interested employees who meet the minimum standards; and (7) Provide for release in all cases of employees selected for promotion." USCSC, Inspection Service, *Building Better Promotion Programs* (Washington: Government Printing Office, 1952), p. ii. See also USCSC, *Press Release,* April 11, 1950.

[78] See Leich, as cited in footnote 56, pp. 33–35.

[79] For a summary of the situation as of 1956, see O. Glenn Stahl, as cited in footnote 65, pp. 148–52.

ice Commission. At the same time employees were given the right to appeal their ratings to the Commission. As efficiency ratings were tied into the reduction-in-force formula, this right was increasingly exercised during the late forties. In those agencies which failed to develop new systems, the Commission maintained its uniform efficiency rating system, established during the thirties. Nevertheless, there was increasing dissatisfaction with all the systems in use after the war.[80] They tended to be static measures of performance, too little related to employee development and too closely tied in with reductions-in-force and removals. The First Hoover Commission concurred in these charges, and in 1950 the Civil Service Commission recommended that Congress authorize major modifications of the procedures then in effect. Specifically, the Commission wanted to abolish the uniform system, permit each department to develop an appropriate system, separate ratings from other personnel actions so that they might be used more for employee development, and eliminate the cumbersome appeals system. This was the typical trend toward decentralization.

The result was the Performance Rating Act of 1950, which went part way toward the ends outlined above, but which retained the appeal system and the close relationship to personnel actions. Adjectival ratings were, however, reduced from five to three—"Outstanding," "Satisfactory," and "Unsatisfactory"—and some flexibility was permitted the departments and agencies.[81] The principal net gain lay in the increasing use of performance ratings as a positive aid for supervisors in employee evaluation and development. On the other hand, since nearly all employees received the middle rating of "Satisfactory," performance was reduced to a negligible factor in, for example, reductions-in-force. Seniority and veteran status became predominant instead. All in all, it is questionable whether the legislation of 1950 left the problem of performance evaluation any better off than it had been before.

Separations and removals. The Civil Service Commission also encouraged administrative officers to utilize more fully their authority with respect to separations and removals. Little was accomplished, however, partly because certain postwar statutes relating to veterans made the process more difficult than ever before.

The original Veterans' Preference Act of 1944, like the Lloyd-La-Follette Act of 1912, specified that a removal could take place only for cause and in writing, with a chance for employee reply. In addition, the 1944 law required the Civil Service Commission to investi-

---

[80] See, for example, Cecil E. Goode, "Is There an Answer to the Service Rating Problem?" *Public Personnel Review* (October, 1947), p. 187.
[81] Over sixty agency plans of many types had been approved by the summer of 1951.

gate the sufficiency of the reasons outlined by the removing officer; and a 1947 amendment made it "mandatory" for an "administrative officer to take such corrective action as the Commission finally recommends." As nearly 50 per cent of the postwar federal service was composed of veterans, this must be considered a major amendment to the policy first set forth in the Lloyd-LaFollette Act. The result was that by 1947 the removal authority of most appointing officers was checked more than at any previous time in our history. The constitutionality of legislation by which Congress mandates the President in removals is open to question. But there has been an increasing tendency during recent years to limit, procedurally or otherwise, the removal power, particularly of subordinate officers.[82]

Employee Relations

Here again, the postwar program of the Civil Service Commission was designed to capitalize on wartime innovations.

Welfare. Employee health and welfare programs, which had been aptly described as the "dark continent" in our personnel system,[83] were in special need of attention. A Federal Interdepartmental Safety Council had been organized in 1937. Its goal had been a 40 per cent reduction in deaths and injuries to government workers by 1942. But in 1943 Secretary of Labor Frances Perkins reported that eleven out of twenty-one major federal employing agencies had experienced increases rather than decreases in accident frequency rates.[84] Many federal agencies had rates considerably higher than those of Dupont, U.S. Steel, and General Motors. By contrast, the Department of Agriculture had cut its frequency rate almost in half. It was clear that government agencies could, if they wished, do something about accident control and prevention.[85] Though some of them, especially the military industrial establishments, developed safety programs of some magnitude and reduced their accident rates consist-

---

[82] The Humphrey and Morgan cases of the thirties served principally to emphasize the shadowy line of demarcation between executive and legislative control of the personnel of the federal government. So has the more recent case of *Roth* v. *Brownell*, 215 F. 2d 500 (1954), 384 U.S. 863 (1954). On this point see Glendon A. Schubert, Jr., *The Presidency in the Courts* (Minneapolis: University of Minnesota Press, 1957), ch. ii, "Presidential Management of Public Personnel."

[83] "Our Dark Continent," *Personnel Administration*, V (October, 1942), 2.

[84] "The Safety Problem," *Personnel Administration*, V (March, 1943), 2.

[85] See R. R. Zimmerman, "Are Federal Employees Expendable Too?" *Personnel Administration*, VI (April, 1944), 2; USCSC, *Sixtieth Report*, 1943, p. 21; and the annual reports of the U.S. Employees' Compensation Commission, redesignated in 1946 as the Bureau of Employees' Compensation of the Federal Security Agency and transferred to the Department of Labor in 1950.

ently, the government, on the whole, lagged behind industry in this respect throughout the postwar years.[86]

On the public employee health front the military agencies, aided by their own medical staffs, have long been leaders.[87] Many civil agencies developed health programs during the war, if for no other reason than to cut down absenteeism. These and other non-military efforts were greatly aided by the Federal Employees' Health Act of 1946, passed in part through the efforts of the Civil Service Commission.[88] This law permitted agencies to develop health programs under the supervision of the Public Health Service, which in turn set up a Federal Employee Health Division (now Branch) to direct the effort and to operate some health programs on a contractual basis. During the postwar period at least one joint health service, serving many regional offices too small to run their own full-time programs, was set up in Denver. However, many federal agencies have never possessed adequate funds for more than cursory health precautions.

Counseling programs, occasionally assisted by trained psychiatrists, were well developed in only a few agencies by 1950.[89] But a Federal Recreation Committee was functioning under the auspices of the Federal Personnel Council. Many welfare associations of various types, primarily organized by the employees themselves, were operating sizable programs by the end of the war, especially in the departments of Agriculture, Interior, and the Treasury. Credit unions, group health and hospital insurance programs, and educational and recreational activities of all types existed to varying degrees in many agencies by 1950, despite few federal laws on such subjects.[90]

All told, however, the federal employee welfare program did not compare favorably to that of progressive private employers. Despite advances during the forties, the federal effort reflected a lack of administrative and legislative stimulation. The Civil Service Commission was occupied with many other affairs. Legislators tended to look upon such activities as frills, and administrators found the development of

---

[86] See Stahl, as cited in footnote 65, pp. 386–89. It has been suggested that, since employee compensation benefits, increased in 1949, are paid from a general compensation fund rather than deducted from agency budgets, administrators are less safety conscious than they might otherwise be.

[87] F. C. Smith, "War Department's Health Program in Washington," *Personnel Administration*, VI (March, 1944), 10.

[88] USCSC, *Sixty-second Report*, 1945, pp. 3–4; and McDiarmid, as cited in footnote 33, p. 1077.

[89] See, for instance, Verne K. Harvey and William C. Strang, "Personal Adjustment of Federal Employees," *Personnel Administration*, VI (December, 1943), 1.

[90] See a series of articles by Joseph D. Cooper in the late 1941 issues of *Personnel Administration*.

complicated programs for employee welfare a drain upon already taxed time, energy, and appropriations.

Fair employment. The touchy and complex matter of discrimination in public employment received more positive treatment. Before 1940 the civil service rules forbade discrimination only on the grounds of politics and religion. On November 7, 1940, the rules were amended to prohibit also discrimination because of race. Three weeks later the Ramspeck Act of 1940 prohibited discrimination in federal employment because of race, creed, or color.

During the war the Civil Service Commission and the President's Committee on Fair Employment Practice together policed discriminatory activities within the civil service under a series of executive orders, which added national origin to the list of prohibited bases for administrative action. However, enforcement procedures were weak, depending primarily upon the executive authority of the President, publicity, reports to other administrative officers, and the like. The lack of adequate indexes of discrimination was partially overcome in 1944 by Civil Service Commission and FEPC joint efforts.[91]

After the war, the Commission carried on alone in the fair employment field, until July 26, 1948, when the President directed the establishment of a Fair Employment Board within the Civil Service Commission and the appointment of a Fair Employment Officer within each agency. At the same time the notably successful program to end discrimination and segregation in the armed services got under way. A seven-member board was set up on October 21, 1948, and continued to function until replaced in 1955 by the President's Committee on Government Employment Policy. The agency personnel officers were usually designated the Fair Employment Officers. The Civil Service Commission received the authority to prescribe appropriate regulations in consultation with the Board; and in March, 1949, minimum standards were laid down for agency guidance.[92] From July, 1948, through December, 1951, a total of 488 complaints were filed, mostly by Negroes, against 27 agencies. The bulk of the cases were settled at agency level, with approximately one out of nine appealed to the Board.[93] Apparently the anti-discrimination policies were ef-

91 For the wartime experience see Gladys Kammerer, *Impact of War on Federal Personnel Administration, 1939–1945* (Lexington: University of Kentucky Press, 1951), pp. 50–55; and Louis Ruchames, *Race, Jobs, and Politics* (New York: Columbia University Press, 1953), pp. 150–51.

92 USCSC, *Sixty-sixth Report*, 1949, pp. 46–47 and 53–54.

93 See Morroe Berger, *Racial Equality and the Law* (Paris: UNESCO, 1954), pp. 39–44; U.S. Civil Service Commission, Fair Employment Board, *Fair Employment in the Federal Service* (Washington: Government Printing Office, 1952); and USCSC, *Sixty-sixth Report,* 1949, pp. 46–47, and *Sixty-seventh Report,* 1950, pp. 48–49.

438

fective. One member of the Fair Employment Board testified in 1952 that, since the establishment of the Board, one-third of the federal agencies had hired Negroes as supervisors of mixed white and Negro groups or employed them as executives and top-level scientific and professional workers for the first time in their history.[94]

Appeals and grievance procedures. Procedures for the handling of employee grievances via the combined management-union channels so typical of private industry have not been customary in federal personnel management. But there have been many other types of appellate procedures involving grievances in the federal service, and in 1930 a Board of Appeals and Review was created within the Civil Service Commission. The board's prewar jurisdiction had primarily been limited to cases involving the conduct and rating of examinations, civil service status, position-classification actions in the departmental service, and controversies over the application of veteran preference. Most of the appeals concerned actions by the Civil Servcie Commission rather than the departmental officials.[95]

But employee appeals against various types of departmental and agency administrative action were increasingly authorized during the postwar years, and the appellate jurisdiction of the Board of Appeals and Review was greatly broadened. The Board was empowered to hear classification appeals from the entire service. Veteran preference appeals now involved removals as well as other preference rights. In addition, the Commission began to process considerable quantities of appeals relating to loyalty and security, reductions-in-force, discrimination, and performance ratings. A great galaxy of subordinate appeals and review agencies proliferated at the lower levels of both the agencies and the Commission. Altogether, the number of appellate personnel actions throughout the federal service was reaching extraordinary proportions during the middle and late forties. Moreover, court cases involving such matters were also multiplying.

Yet there was little systematization of appellate machinery or standardization of appeal rights and procedures. In 1953 a congressional subcommittee found at least eight categories of appeals and grievance actions which could be identified "as receiving special and separate procedural handling through different hearing channels." The subcommittee concluded that "everyone interviewed . . . has agreed that

94 U.S. Congress, Senate, Committee on Labor and Public Welfare, Subcommittee on Labor and Labor Management Relations, *Discrimination and Full Utilization of Manpower Resources*, Hearings on S. 1732 and S. 551, 82d Cong., 2d Sess., April 8, 1952 (Washington: Government Printing Office, 1952), p. 75; testimony by Fred C. Croxton.

95 For a brief history of the Commission's appellate process before World War II, see USCSC, *Fifty-sixth Report*, 1939, pp. 29–31.

439

appeals and grievances policies and practices in the Federal Government as a whole are in a state of confusion." [96]

Although there was some increase in job security, especially for veterans, many employees and employee organizations were highly critical of the procedural confusion and of the time often taken to settle cases. Administrative officers, too, resented the red tape as well as the fact that they often found themselves, rather than their employees, on trial. In addition, the total expense of this vast array of appellate procedure, though not precisely calculable, must have been great. In one case the cost has been estimated at $500,000.[97] All in all, while the federal government was consciously attempting to provide more protection for public employees during the postwar period, the results were not entirely to anyone's full satisfaction.

Employee participation in management. After the war neither public nor congressional opinion supported any increase in employee participation in management through unions.[98] The Civil Service Commission gave up any attempt toward this end and, if anything, labor-management relations in the federal service deteriorated during the Truman administration in comparison to the wartime period. But Congress was prepared to encourage participation by individual employees, which posed no threat to management and could easily be justified on the grounds of economy and efficiency.

Interest in federal employee incentive mechanisms dates from just before World War I, with the Departments of the Army and Navy pioneering with cash awards to employees for management improvement suggestions.[99] World War II saw a considerable increase of interest in all types of employee participation in management. However, only the suggestion systems survived intact and were to some extent improved upon in the years immediately after World War II. In 1946 Congress even authorized each department and agency to spend up to $25,000 annually for cash awards for "meritorious suggestions" put into practice. Many federal agencies cooperated.

A full-scale system of "incentive awards" for civil employees was first authorized by the Classification Act of 1949, which provided for suggestion programs, salary increases for superior accomplishment,

---

96 U.S. Congress, Senate, Committee on Post Office and Civil Service, Subcommittee on Federal Manpower Policies, *Appeals and Grievance Procedures in the Federal Government,* 83d Cong., 1st Sess., Sen. Doc. 33 (Washington: Government Printing Office, 1953), pp. 3–4.

97 For details of the two appeals by Orton T. Campbell against actions of the Public Printer, involving five years of litigation and, eventually, a Supreme Court decision, see same, p. 6.

98 For an extended discussion of unionization of public employees for the period since 1930, see ch. xiv.

99 Apparently the first legislative enactment fostering such awards dates to 1912 and involved the Department of the Army.

and honor awards. Under the joint supervision of the Bureau of the Budget and the Civil Service Commission a comprehensive program was outlined in 1950. Incentive awards committees were established in most agencies and standards were published to govern their activities. However, there was a good deal of red tape in the procedures and the sums involved were hardly munificent. There was, for example, a ceiling of $1000 for individual awards.

A congressional subcommittee investigated this system in 1952 and concluded that the federal program had been "hindered by a variety of factors, most prominent of which has been a lack of forceful top staff promotion and legislative complexities which have made the program too complicated to be administered properly." [100] By comparison, the subcommittee noted that "in the last fiscal year, employees of just two industrial concerns—Eastman Kodak and General Electric —turned in almost as many suggestions as did the entire body of eligible Federal employees (which exactly outnumbered them, 10 to 1)." [101] Nevertheless much progress was made after 1949. The Incentive Awards Act of 1954 improved the procedural base for the system, placed responsibility for its development squarely with the Civil Service Commission, and upped the award limits for individual employees to $25,000 in exceptional cases.

Boundaries of the Merit System

By the early nineteen forties the proportion of the federal civil service under some form of merit system almost certainly exceeded 90 per cent. In 1947, the first postwar year for which full statistics are available, the percentage of the service under a merit system *within the continental United States* exceeded 92 per cent. All through the Truman administration this percentage remained relatively stable.[102]

For the federal service as a whole, the percentage declined to roughly 85 per cent between 1943 and 1946, remained reasonably stable thereafter until 1956, and then rose slightly. The postwar decline and later rise of the merit system percentage was due to the appoint-

---

[100] U.S. Congress, Senate, Committee on Post Office and Civil Service, Subcommittee on Federal Manpower Policies, *Incentive Awards Program in the Federal Government*, 82d Cong., 2d Sess., Sen. Report 2101 (Washington: Government Printing Office, 1952), p. 19. A brief history of incentive awards in the federal service is contained in pp. 3–5.

[101] Same, pp. 7–8. For tables summarizing federal experience with the incentive awards program during fiscal years 1951 and 1955 respectively, see same, pp. 32–33, and USCSC, *Seventy-second Report*, 1955, pp. 252–53.

[102] The 1947 figure is calculated from USCSC, *Sixty-fourth Report*, 1947, p. 75. As suggested by the word "a," this percentage includes personnel of the Foreign Service, the TVA, and the like. See also *Sixty-ninth Report*, 1952, p. 96.

ment of several hundred thousand persons to government positions outside the confines of the United States. Because of the emergency and temporary nature of much of this overseas employment, few of the positions involved were formally placed within the competitive service until 1956, when it became obvious that the long-run commitments of the nation would require a relatively permanent and stable overseas staff. The overseas positions conveniently divide into two categories, those located within American territories and possessions and those within foreign countries. Many of the former have for many years been under the merit system, but almost none of the latter were brought within the competitive service until 1956. Total employment abroad, of both categories, reached a high of more than 850,000 in 1945. This figure declined to a relatively stable 150,-000 to 185,000 between 1949 and 1957. During the latter period civil employees in foreign countries numbered around 100,000, with many of them aliens not eligible for permanent posts.[103]

The patronage. It should not be assumed, however, that these percentages marked a clear dividing line between the patronage and the merit system. For example, all through the postwar decade some 30,000 rural letter carriers and more than 20,000 first, second, and third class postmasters, nominally in the classified service, actually fell into a sort of twilight zone. Though filled through examination and carrying tenure, these positions were still subject to political clearance.[104] On the other hand, the overseas positions, especially those in foreign countries, while technically open to patronage influence, were largely filled through procedures typical of private employment. Few competitive or other examinations were held for overseas posts, but minimal standards were normally required. While political influence sometimes was relevant, most of these positions were not much sought after by the average political appointee, whose future was apt to be jeopardized by any prolonged absence abroad. Further, during most of the postwar period there were sizable numbers of temporary employees, appointed through all sorts of *ad hoc* procedures, who occupied positions formally under the merit system. This happened because the Civil Service Commission was unable to supply enough eligibles through the competitive mechanism right after World War II and during the Korean crisis. Most of these persons came into the service through procedures involving little or no patronage influ-

---

103 See USCSC, *Sixty-ninth Report*, 1952, p. 91, for the "Trend of Federal civil employment by area, 1942–52," and the annual reports of the Civil Service Commission for data concerning later years.

104 For a discussion of the problems involved, see First Hoover Commission, as cited in footnote 56, pp. 133–35. See also Harris, as cited in footnote 15, scattered.

ence; and most of them eventually either qualified for permanent posts through examination or were replaced by merit employees.

Nor during the postwar period were the 125,000 or so domestic positions which were formally excepted from competition always subject to patronage influence. Many of them consisted of high level professional posts for which examinations were not customary or practical, positions within the various intelligence services, and a large number of more or less temporary positions at low levels, involving, for example, student trainees in naval shipyards, temporary field employees of the International Boundary Commission such as foremen, cooks, and axmen, seasonal caretakers at closed camps of the Department of Agriculture, and the like.

Under President Truman the civil patronage proper—posts both of interest to politicians and subject to various types of political clearance—actually consisted of the 50,000 or so post office positions mentioned above, some 1,000 or so top "political executive" posts, nearly 10,000 moderately important positions such as those of attorneys, U.S. marshals, collectors of customs, and collectors of internal revenue, and perhaps another 5,000 to 25,000 miscellaneous positions—the precise figure is unknown—mostly at the lower levels. This represents a grand total of roughly 70,000 positions, nearly half of them within the middle and upper levels of the service. However, in estimating the full utility of these offices to a political party, one must remember that many of them were subject to tenure restrictions of one sort or another by this time. The number of civil offices easily available to the party in power at any one point in time had probably diminished to less than 15,000 by the end of 1952.[105]

Through this period the patronage remained of considerable interest to politicians. Just prior to the 1948 election, when the Re-

---

[105] See Malcolm Moos, *The Republicans* (New York: Random House, 1956), p. 495. Unfortunately, there is no careful study of the extent of federal patronage in recent decades, nor has it been possible, because of the exhaustive research required, to make a full analysis here. The above figures are in part derived from Commission on Organization of the Executive Branch of the Government (the Second Hoover Commission), *Task Force Report on Personnel and Civil Service* (Washington: Government Printing Office, 1955), pp. 133–35; "Federal Jobs as Political Plums," *U.S. News and World Report*, XXV (July 9, 1948), pp. 21–23; Harris, as cited in footnote 15, scattered; Martin Packman, "Government Jobs," *Editorial Research Reports*, 1955–I (May 18, 1955), 359; Buel W. Patch, "Federal Patronage," *Editorial Research Reports*, 1948–II (October 20, 1948), 728; Herbert Hollander, *Crisis in the Civil Service* (Washington: Current Issues Publishers, 1955), scattered; and Moos, as cited in this note. They are also in part derived simply from the writer's conclusions after consideration of a wide range of miscellaneous civil service literature. For a complete listing of individual positions excepted from the competitive service at the end of the Truman administration, see the "Plum book" of 1953, U.S. Congress, Senate, *Positions Not Under the Civil Service*, 83d Cong., 1st Sess., Senate Doc. 18, Parts I and II, prepared by the Civil Service Commission (Washington: Government Printing Office, 1953). This survey does not, however, distinguish between positions which were in fact subject to patronage influence and those which were not.

publicans expected to capture the Presidency, the Senate delayed action on more than 11,500 presidential nominations for office.[106] The Republican platform of 1948 called for a general overhauling of the federal establishment and the party unquestionably intended to use the recommendations of the First Hoover Commission, created by a Republican Congress, as a springboard to some political paring. One of the primary issues of the campaign turned on the size and cost of the federal establishment. Though a friend of the merit system in his own state of New York, Governor Thomas E. Dewey, the Republican candidate, was at one point quoted as promising the "finest house cleaning in Washington there ever was." [107] Unquestionably much of his party concurred in this view, one which was hardly calculated to soothe the nerves of the federal service. But the Republicans did not win and the public service remained undisturbed by any turnover of the party in power.

Extension of the merit system. In its reports, published just after the 1948 election, the First Hoover Commission recommended the elimination of senatorial confirmation for postmasters, collectors of customs, and collectors of internal revenue. President Truman followed up these proposals in 1952 with a plan for placing the field offices of the Bureau of Internal Revenue under the merit system. Prior scandals within the revenue service in part prompted the action, and, after considerable debate, Congress reluctantly concurred in the change. This was a major reform. The immediate effect, however, was to blanket most of the incumbents into permanent posts, despite the protests of the National Civil Service League and others concerned with the improvement of the permanent service.[108] The President then promptly submitted further reorganization plans designed to place first, second, and third class postmasters, collectors of customs, and U.S. marshals firmly within the competitive service. While the House approved the proposal by substantial majorities, the Senate

106 Harris, as cited in footnote 15, p. 196. Harris has estimated that the number of federal positions subject to the confirmation of the Senate, hence open to the possibility of political influence, totaled approximately 10,000 under President Taft. By 1937 the number had risen to 40,000 or so, and by 1949 to well over 100,000. These figures include first, second, and third class postmasters as well as thousands of commissioned officers in the various uniformed services. In 1949 military confirmations reached the staggering total of 49,-956. Same, p. 331. The inclusion of military posts among those confirmed by the Senate accounts for the apparent discrepancy between the writer's estimates of civil positions subject to political influence and the total number of positions subject to potential political influence through confirmation procedures. Since before World War I, military appointments have normally been approved as a matter of course. In 1951, for example, none were rejected. Same, p. 16.

107 "Federal Jobs as Political Plums," as cited in footnote 105, p. 21.

108 For the League's analysis and public protest, see NCSL (the word "Reform" was dropped from its title in 1945), "Has Tax Reorganization Worked?" *Good Government,* LXX (July–August, 1953), 31.

balked at giving up its time-honored privilege of confirmation, and the plans failed of adoption. It is significant that the reorganization plans of 1952 were also opposed by the National Letter Carriers' Association as well as by a spokesman for the American Federation of Labor.[109] This illustrates the frequently close tie between employees of the Post Office Department and members of Congress. Over the years this has resulted in a considerable quantity of special legislation for postal employees, which to some extent has left them in a privileged position. On the whole the attitude of the postal unions has been somewhat equivocal with respect to the merit system and modern personnel methods.

No other significant extensions of the merit system were made during the Truman administration. The President did, however, provide a measure of job protection to many employees who, during the wartime and postwar periods, had moved from protected career posts to positions exempted from the merit system rules and regulations. This was accomplished, mainly in 1947, by regulations authorizing persons with permanent status to carry such status with them wherever they went. Permanent status was thus conferred on many persons as a sort of personal rank. President Eisenhower was severely criticized in 1953 for the abolition of this personal status. Estimates vary, but by then perhaps 50,000 persons were involved in this status problem.

The career service received unprecedented recognition under President Truman through the appointment of permanent employees to the high posts of Secretary of Agriculture and Postmaster General. In the Department of State the number of career appointments to top ambassadorial and ministerial positions was greater than ever before. The President's actions stemmed in part from the difficulties he was facing in obtaining senatorial approval of more partisan appointments and in part from his general tendency to support a career service. Truman like Coolidge was, however, fortunate in the fact that during a period of relative prosperity he had inherited a party whose hunger for public office had been considerably satiated during previous years in power. Under such circumstances one can afford the luxury of political forbearance.

The Loyalty Program

The major unanticipated segment of the Civil Service Commission's postwar program involved the twin problems of loyalty and security

---

[109] Harris, as cited in footnote 15, p. 353. For an excellent analysis of the Senate's position in 1952 concerning the confirmation of postmasters, collectors, and marshals, see same, scattered.

within the federal government. As had been the case under President Wilson, these matters became the subject of bitter and widespread debate after, rather than during, the war. The early postwar discovery of "top secret" documents in the New York office of the magazine *Amerasia*, the stories by Elizabeth Bentley and Whittaker Chambers of Communist activity within the federal government, and the startling disclosures of Russian espionage in the Canadian government combined to heighten uneasiness. As relations with Soviet Russia deteriorated through 1945 and 1946, the nation became increasingly agitated over the issue of Communists in government. Even more important, as disillusionment spread over the possibility of any simple solution to the world-wide pressures of communism, the architects of American political policies during the previous decade came under a dark cloud of suspicion. We quickly entered into what historian Eric Goldman has aptly described as the period of "The Great Conspiracy." [110] New Dealers, Alger Hiss, labor unions, progressive education, humanitarianism, and social reform of almost any sort, as well as Franklin D. Roosevelt, President Truman, the Department of State, and much of the federal service, became associated in many minds with the spreading power of communism. Many Americans were genuinely concerned about the reality of subversion. But others either looked for revenge on the New Deal, or saw visions of a major political issue around which the election of 1948—and later, 1952— might turn and the Truman administration be discredited. Again, the civil service found itself in the middle.

This was an issue too great for the Civil Service Commission to handle and for the most part it confined its postwar loyalty and security efforts to ministerial actions, carrying out as well as possible whatever duties and responsibilities were placed on its shoulders. Most of the argument and action stemmed from the complicated political interrelationships among President Truman, a divided Congress, and the nation at large.

The Truman loyalty program. After a 1946 congressional committee had recommended a full study of loyalty and security procedures, President Truman appointed a Temporary Commission on Employee Loyalty to examine the matter and to come up with specific recommendations. Reporting in February, 1947, the Commission found little uniformity among federal agencies in their approaches to security and loyalty and recommended new procedures and new standards to be coordinated through a central review agency. The President accepted the Commission's suggestions and incorporated them almost intact

---

110 Goldman, as cited in footnote 13, ch. vi.

into his revised loyalty program outlined in Executive Order 9835 of March 21, 1947.[111]

The order directed the Civil Service Commission to investigate and evaluate prospective public employees, while the departments and agencies were to screen and evaluate incumbents. Investigators were to look for evidence of treason and espionage, the disclosure of confidential information, action in favor of a foreign country at the expense of our own, the personal advocacy of the overthrow of the government by force and violence, and membership in organizations listed as totalitarian or subversive by the Attorney General. The final assessment was to be in terms of a finding that, "on all evidence, reasonable grounds exist for the belief that the person involved is disloyal."

In an effort to protect employees an attempt was made to set up reasonable procedures and to standardize them. Persons accused of subversive activity were to be granted the right of a hearing before a loyalty board. Departmental boards were to handle the cases of incumbents, regional boards those of applicants. The accused were to be furnished with charges, all nonsecret information, and the right to bring counsel. The accused might confront an accuser or one who had brought charges, but only if the latter chose to appear. Here the government elected to protect its informants, partly on the grounds that to do otherwise might destroy the usefulness of many intelligence agents. Decisions and findings concerning incumbents were to go to the head of their agency, who might approve or reject the board's recommendations. The employee was also entitled to appeal to a loyalty review board set up within the Civil Service Commission. Prospective employees might appeal to the loyalty review board against an adverse decision by a regional loyalty board.

Though the program seemed reasonable enough, it was greeted with considerable outcry from the public and with mixed feelings by Congress. Many Americans criticized the program as not sufficiently protective of the civil rights of public employees, while Congress, which had just come under Republican domination, was often critical of the protection afforded the government. Unsuccessful in its efforts to write and pass its own loyalty statute, the Eightieth Congress finally acquiesced in the Truman plan and appropriated $11,000,000 for it, approximately two-thirds to the FBI and one-third to the Civil Service Commission. This ended serious efforts to handle loyalty through legislative rather than executive procedures. A distinguished Republican, Seth W. Richardson, was selected to head the new Loyalty Re-

[111] The principal study of the Truman loyalty program as it developed under this order is contained in Eleanor Bontecou, *The Federal Loyalty-Security Program* (Ithaca: Cornell University Press, 1953). Also see the "supplementary notes" at the end of chs. xiv and xvi.

447

view Board and the program was well under way by the fall of 1947.

The investigation of prospective appointees was undertaken primarily by the Civil Service Commission's staff, with referral to the FBI for a further check in special cases. The incumbent investigative program was largely conducted by the FBI with transfer of information to the operating agencies via the Civil Service Commission. The military and other agencies with their own investigative personnel continued to use them, though not without an extensive liaison with the Commission and the FBI. Between October 1, 1947, when the program officially commenced, and April 27, 1953, when President Eisenhower revoked Executive Order 9835, the loyalty of 4,756,705 persons was checked. Approximately two-fifths of these were incumbents and the rest applicants. Reports of investigation on 26,236 persons had been referred to the appropriate loyalty boards. Of these, 16,503 had been cleared, 6,828 had had their cases discontinued because of resignation or application withdrawal, 1,776 were persons whose cases were yet incomplete, 569 were persons considered by the Department of the Army solely under special security laws; and 560 had been "removed or denied Federal employment on grounds relating to loyalty"[112]—all in all, a staggering investigative effort.

This does not portray the entire picture, though. Several important departments and agencies such as the Department of the Army, the Department of State, and the Atomic Energy Commission took a number of additional actions under special summary dismissal statutes. Dating from the war period, these statutes had modified the removal provisions of the Lloyd-LaFollette Act in the name of security. Several agencies were thus in a position to proceed either in terms of Truman's loyalty program or of these special security laws. In some cases the two programs operated side by side. But not until the passage of Public Law 733 in August, 1950, requiring a hearing before summary dismissal on the grounds of security, did the Army fully agree to process loyalty cases under the President's loyalty order. Though precise statistics are not available, at least 216 employees had been removed or released on security rather than loyalty grounds by the summer of 1952.[113]

The political aftermath. But these bare numerals convey little of the superheated atmosphere surrounding the Truman loyalty program, especially in the months just prior to the election of 1948. August saw the Chambers-Hiss controversy brought out into the open. At the same time the President, standing on the doctrine of the separation of

112 USCSC, *Seventieth Report*, 1953, p. 32.
113 From data provided in Bontecou, as cited in footnote 111, pp. 145–46.

powers, refused to turn over loyalty files to a congressional committee and characterized its efforts to investigate communism in government as a "red herring." The Department of Justice openly flouted the rules of the Loyalty Review Board by threatening to prosecute a number of employees whose cases had not yet been passed upon by departmental loyalty boards. Several members of these boards were reported as fearing for their own jobs if they exercised their best judgment and cleared certain employees. After a brief post-election calm, Senator Joseph McCarthy of Wisconsin opened his guns against the State Department, followed by a counterattack from the Tydings committee, and still another attack against the work of the Tydings committee by the McCarran committee. By the time of the Korean crisis many persons both in and out of the service were wondering what it would all come to.

To reconsider the loyalty program, especially in terms of the protection of the rights and freedom of individuals, President Truman established the President's Commission on Internal Security and Individual Rights in January, 1951. Unfortunately, Congress refused to modify certain conflict-of-interest statutes so that prospective staff members could accept appointments without undue personal sacrifice; and the Commission never got off the ground. The President's modification of the loyalty standard in the spring of 1951 actually lessened individual job security even more. The new standard—"reasonable doubt as to the loyalty of the person involved"—was merely a return to the guide which had been used during the war. But this change necessitated the reevaluation of many loyalty and security cases and confronted many federal employees with the danger of reversal of a previous clearance.

The lack of any systematic or uniform procedures for distinguishing between loyalty and security questions prompted the President in July, 1951, to request the National Security Council to look into the problem. Its Interdepartmental Committee on Internal Security reported in April, 1952, that there was still a great deal of confusion among procedures utilized for the consideration of loyalty, security, and suitability.[114] In early August the President wrote Robert Ramspeck, Chairman of the Civil Service Commission, that "the most de-

---

[114] Suitability involves such matters as veracity, criminal record, and general reliability. A person who may be a suitability or security risk—a drunkard, for example—may not necessarily be disloyal. At best, however, the problem of differentiating among these types of grounds for dismissal is a difficult one.

In 1952 the loyalty and security investigative functions of the FBI were largely transferred to the Civil Service Commission, to enable the FBI to concentrate better on its traditional functions relating to sabotage, interstate crime, and the like. Since 1952 nearly one-third of the funds of the Commission have been spent on activities relating to loyalty and security. Since the Commission's total funds remained about the same for the decade after the war, many of its traditional activities had to be cut back. Training, for example, was one of the casualties.

sirable action at this time would be to merge the loyalty, security and suitability programs, thus eliminating the overlapping, duplication and confusion which apparently now exists." [115] In effect, this was what President Eisenhower attempted to accomplish a little more than six months later, when he revoked Executive Order 9835 and set up his own loyalty program.

Aftereffects. It is important to note three immediate aftereffects of the loyalty controversies and policies under the Truman administration. First of all, the number of persons dismissed or refused employment was exceedingly small. Eleanor Bontecou, the foremost analyst of the Truman loyalty effort, has described them as "very small fry indeed." [116] Charges to the effect that the federal service was "honeycombed with subversives" were patently false.

More significant were the subtle influences stemming from the tense and uncertain atmosphere enveloping the federal service as a result of the charges, countercharges, investigations, and reinvestigations involved in the loyalty program. As President Truman himself later observed:

Demagogic attacks on the loyalty of government employees greatly hamper the task of conducting the government efficiently. Many good people quit government rather than work in an atmosphere of harassment. And these reckless attacks have made it doubly difficult to attract good people to government service.

In such an atmosphere of fear, key government employees tend to become mentally paralyzed. They are afraid to express honest judgments, as it is their duty to do, because later, under a changed atmosphere and different circumstances, they may be charged with disloyalty by those who disagree with them. Our nation cannot afford or permit such a mental blackout. [117]

Still, there was something approaching such a blackout. The loyalty controversy unquestionably contributed both to it and to the steady decline in public employee morale during this period.

Little more encouraging from the point of view of civil servants were the implications of a series of court cases which were processed through the federal judicial system during the late forties and early fifties. The loyalty program was upheld as constitutional, and the judiciary adhered fairly closely to the traditional doctrine that public employees have no constitutional rights to or in public employment. The old graphic dictum of Justice Holmes, that a policeman "has no

[115] Harry S. Truman, *Memoirs: Years of Trial and Hope* (Garden City, N.Y.: Doubleday and Co., 1956), p. 289.
[116] Cited in footnote 111, p. 146.
[117] Truman, as cited in footnote 115, p. 285.

"It's Sure Hard To Get Help These Days"

From *The Herblock Book* (Beacon Press, 1952).

constitutional right to be a policeman," was merely reaffirmed.[118] The only solace came from the fact that the Supreme Court was evenly divided in the case of *Bailey* v. *Richardson* in 1951.[119] The division affirmed a lower court decision favorable to the government and, in effect, denied that Dorothy Bailey had been punished without due process by dismissal under the loyalty program. But the very fact of the Supreme Court's inability to agree on the issue suggested a possible reconsideration or revision of our historic constitutional position on the relationship of public employees to their employment.[120]

"The Triumph of Techniques Over Purpose" [121]

Obviously the Civil Service Commission had accomplished unprecedented tasks by 1950. Still, morale was down, top jobs were hard to fill, and turnover was relatively high. Something was definitely wrong with federal public personnel management in the late forties.

Causes and effects. Certain difficulties were obvious, such as the political milieu surrounding the federal service. The inability of the Truman administration to set and maintain meaningful goals for the service was frustrating. Nor was tension eased on the federal scene by the impact of the loyalty program and the constant struggle between the President and Congress over appointments to the higher political posts. There was continuous criticism of the federal bureaucracy—with the word used this time in its most derogatory sense—not only by the resurgent Republicans but by many others as well. Equally important were the unprecedented manpower shortages stemming from postwar prosperity. For a personnel system based on an assumption of an over-supply of qualified eligibles this required an about-face of considerable dimensions. Yet only in the field of recruitment and examination was there a significant effort after the war to improve the government's competitive position as opposed to private enterprise.

True, competition had been restored and the merit system preserved. But in many respects this was precisely the trouble. Comprehensive as was the Commission's 1945 program, it looked more back-

---

118 *McAuliffe* v. *The Mayor and Aldermen of New Bedford*, 155 Mass. 216 (1892). See also Bontecou, as cited in footnote 111, ch. vi; Schubert, as cited in footnote 82, ch. ii; and Edward S. Corwin, *The President: Office and Powers* (4th ed.; New York: New York University Press, 1957), ch. iii, for analyses of the position of the federal courts on loyalty and security matters.

119 341 U.S. 918 (1951).

120 For a trenchant analysis of this constitutional issue see Arch Dotson, "The Emerging Doctrine of Privilege in Public Employment," *Public Administration Review*, XV (Spring, 1955), 77; and "A General Theory of Public Employment," *Public Administration Review*, XVI (Summer, 1956), 197.

121 This is the title of an article on public personnel management by Wallace S. Sayre in *Public Administration Review*, VIII (Spring, 1948), 134.

ward than forward. It was designed to revitalize personnel procedures, yes, but the mechanism to be renovated was still essentially that of the nineteenth century. This in itself would not have been so important, if the old basic concepts of merit, tenure, and political neutrality had not also become encrusted in a vast morass of procedure which seemed to many to have sucked the vitality out of the system. Modern public personnel management symbolized "the triumph of techniques over purpose," wrote Wallace S. Sayre, former director of personnel in the Office of Price Administration, in 1948.[122]

The complicated reemployment and reconversion formulae imposed upon the departments and agencies, the interminable loyalty investigations and reinvestigations, the many appeals and grievance procedures, the rigidities of the classification system, the almost universal application of the "rule of three" required by the Veterans' Preference Act of 1944,[123] and the tightening up of removal procedures had by 1950 limited administrative discretion in a way that had never before been true. "Of course it isn't easy to remove an employee," admitted Commissioner Flemming. But his corresponding exhortation to "have backbone" was by no means persuasive as an answer to the problem.[124] One may have backbone and still be too busy—time is money, too—to fight through a maze of procedures. Transfers are so much simpler.

The immense load of "personnel transactions" and the paper work they involved added to the burden and tended to produce in the minds of many administrators, and often the general public as well, a desperate feeling that personnel administration consisted primarily of record keeping. It was at this time that the *Federal Personnel Manual*, with its mass of rules and regulations as decreed by Congress and the executive branch, commenced to symbolize the merit system of Curtis, Eaton, and Schurz. "The crusade has ended up in the filing cases," said presidential assistant Jonathan Daniels.[125]

Decentralization reviewed. These developments might not have seemed so frustrating if they had not been viewed against a backdrop

---

[122] Same. See also Floyd W. Reeves, "Civil Service as Usual," *Public Administration Review*, IV (Autumn, 1944), 332; and Louis Brownlow, "Successes and Failures," in Leonard D. White (ed.), *Civil Service in Wartime* (Chicago: University of Chicago Press, 1945), p. 243.
[123] Legislative establishment of the "rule of three" in a time of reconversion, when fluidity would seem to have been highly desirable, resulted in the most rigid certification procedure in our personnel history. The Civil Service Commission has been criticized for its role in the adoption of this rule. For both sides of the question, see Reeves, as cited in footnote 122; Kammerer, as cited in footnote 91, pp. 107-8; and McDiarmid, as cited in footnote 33, pp. 1076-77.
[124] From an address before the Society for the Advancement of Management, December 19, 1946, quoted in Cahn, as cited in footnote 19, p. 171.
[125] As cited in footnote 7, p. 111.

of wartime personnel practice. Let us look, for example, at the important area of recruitment and placement, first in wartime and then in the postwar period. Patterson H. French has described his fairly typical wartime experience in the Office of Price Administration and the Bureau of the Budget as follows:

As the war effort progressed, the center of emphasis in finding people to fill jobs shifted from the Civil Service Commission to the operating agencies. . . .

Coupled with changes in the methods of finding potential employees, a change occurred in the controls over the appointment of people when candidates had been found. At least from the point of view of the operating official, customary controls in the form of registers, certification, and the rule of three virtually disappeared during the war. The appointment papers might carry some technical language, generally unintelligible to the operating executive, referring to "selective certification" or something known as the "U-100" examination (a very broad, unassembled examination for general executive personnel), or some other specialized appointment device. Regardless of technique—a matter of policy to the Civil Service Commission but of semantics to the operating man—the idea of picking an employee from a list of eligibles furnished by the commission was foreign to the experience of most wartime executives.

While administrators could go very far in hiring people of their own choosing without regard to formal examinations or the position of the candidate on the eligible list, candidates were required to meet certain standards that were maintained by the Civil Service Commission and by the agency personnel offices. In general, these standards were tied to the nature of the job and to the grade-level for which the candidate might be eligible.

. . . An administrator could move flexibly in one of his most important functions, that of building a staff that could carry out his responsibility as he saw it. At the same time, machinery was provided for a certain amount of consistency and certain basic standards.[126]

This was considerable decentralization under almost any definition, coupled with modest controls which maintained standards yet permitted operating officials a good deal of latitude in personnel selection.

After the war, however, the Civil Service Commission again brought the recruitment and examination mechanism under centralized control, returned to ranked registers and the "rule of three," and forced the reappointment of many displaced career employees in the face of departmental resistance. In a sense Commissioner Frances Perkins was right when she declared in 1950 that "the Commission *is* decentralized." [127] But, judging from the Commission's postwar *actions* as

126 "Wartime Personnel Administration in Federal Agencies," in Joseph E. McLean, *The Public Service and University Education* (Princeton, N.J.: Princeton University Press, 1949), pp. 27–28.
127 From notes taken by the writer on a speech by Commissioner Perkins at Roosevelt College in Chicago on October 19, 1950.

opposed to its policy statements, all decentralization in recruitment and examination really meant was the granting of authority to the line departments and agencies for participation in a process, the detailed workings of which remained firmly under the Commission's control. This relieved the Commission of some of its own detailed responsibilities, but obviously did not return to the operating officials any of the wartime flexibility to which they had become accustomed. Nor did it make personnel work an adjunct to management as was increasingly the case in private business.

The same held true with several other important aspects of personnel management such as position-classification and the whole gamut of activities subject to grievance and appeals procedures. A vast mass of procedural detail was now left to the departments and agencies, but there was little discretion available either to departmental personnel officers or, more important, to individual administrators faced with major personnel problems. "The decentralization of work load under strict procedural instructions binding those who do the work is a dubious administrative economy" observed Wallace Sayre in 1948, "it certainly does not represent an important new trend in the development of an adequate philosophy and method of personnel administration." [128]

To give the Civil Service Commission its due, many of the personnel practices most condemned after the war had arisen in the departments and agencies themselves.[129] But both the Civil Service Commission and the departmental personnel offices found themselves operating at this time under a goodly number of rigid congressional mandates, of which the Veterans' Preference Act of 1944 was the most pervasive. Ranked registers, the "rule of three," additional limitations on removals, and many of the complications in reduction-in-force procedures must be laid at its door.

Moreover, it was clear that, contrary to the strictures of Curtis, Eaton, and Schurz in the heyday of civil service reform, the federal service of 1950 had had its front and back doors *both* largely closed. There was not only little administrative discretion in hiring procedures, something the fathers of civil service reform had considered

---

[128] As cited in footnote 121, p. 137.

[129] Shortly after the report of the First Hoover Commission, Charles S. Hyneman pointed out: "It is noteworthy that the procedures which are described in detail in the report of the Hoover Commission's task force, and presented by the task force as models of objectionable practice, are in every case procedures which are pursued within the administrative department or agency. There is no statement in the task force report that such procedures are forced upon the administrative establishment by CSC [Civil Service Commission], and what I have learned from other sources causes me to believe that CSC is not to any significant degree responsible for them." As cited in footnote 59, pp. 408-9.

eminently desirable in their fear of political patronage, but there was also an increasing tendency to restrict firing and other forms of disciplinary action as well, a type of restriction which Curtis, Eaton, and Schurz had uniformly deplored. What had been intended as a freeing of the administrator's patronage bonds was ending in a new type of procedural bondage in the name of employee rights and security, for which Congress, the Commission, veterans organizations, public employee unions, and even the general public shared responsibility.

It was in protest against this prison of civil service procedure, from which at mid-century there appeared to be no escape, that John Fischer rebelled in 1947 and pleaded "Let's Go Back to the Spoils System!" [130] Such a remedy, would, as even Fischer implied, have thrown the baby out with the bath water. Nevertheless, Fischer's point was well taken, and it fell to the First Hoover Commission to attempt to devise some less drastic solution to the modern problems of the federal service.

The First Hoover Commission

Impressed by the postwar administrative problems of the federal service as well as by the size and heterogeneity of the executive establishment, the Eightieth Congress directed the bipartisan First Hoover Commission in 1947 to undertake the most extensive investigation of the executive branch ever contemplated up to that time. In early 1949 the Commission issued two reports dealing directly with personnel management in the federal government, one of them a preliminary Task Force study, prepared by a special Personnel Policy Committee, and the other a final report made by the Commission as a whole.

Conclusions and recommendations. In many ways the two reports repeated the recommendations of the President's Committee on Administrative Management of a decade before. They stressed executive responsibility for personnel management as a staff function, and again suggested a unification of top-level authority within the central personnel agency.

The Task Force report emphasized the problem of developing a career service during and after the war, the considerable turnover in federal employment, and the difficulty of obtaining personnel for various types of essential positions. It found the prestige of the federal service among college graduates anything but impressive, and took notice of the congressional concern with the growing cost of per-

<hr>

130 This is the title of Fischer's article on federal personnel management in *Harper's Magazine*, CXCI (October, 1945), 362.

sonnel activities. The Personnel Policy Committee concluded that these difficulties were "inherent, to a large extent, in the Government's procedures for (1) procuring, (2) developing, (3) compensating, and (4) supervising personnel." [131] The Task Force report recognized, however, that the difficulties within the federal service by no means stemmed entirely from the activities of the Civil Service Commission alone. It held the operating agencies equally responsible for time-consuming and complicated procedures not always required by law. But, more than anything, the requirements of existing legislation were recognized as major bars to the decentralization and reorganization of personnel management which the Personnel Policy Committee felt was desirable. Equally noteworthy was the attention paid to the line and staff relationships involved in personnel work, from those of the Commission to Washington personnel offices and on down into the field. The Task Force report was the first official document to outline a full-scale personnel program for all levels of the federal government.

The Hoover Commission concurred in general with its Personnel Policy Committee. Agreeing that "centralization of personnel transactions in the Civil Service Commission and in the central personnel offices of the departments and agencies has resulted in unjustifiable delays and stands in the way of a satisfactory handling of the Government's personnel problem," [132] the Commission presented twenty-nine recommendations. These called for a much greater decentralization of personnel transactions, within both the Civil Service Commission and the line agencies, and an emphasis on the development of more systematic line and staff relationships among all levels of personnel management. Pay plans should be unified and salaries raised. Position-classification should be decentralized and revised to allow for much greater administrative discretion. Employee development programs, particularly at the entering and top levels, should be undertaken. Employee participation in the formulation of personnel policies should be encouraged. The dismissal and reduction-in-force systems should be overhauled, most of the examination function decentralized to the operating agencies, and a system devised to measure the overstaffing of personnel sections.

Departments and agencies as well as the Civil Service Commission were blamed for procedural and organizational bottlenecks resulting from existing examination, recruitment, classification, promotion, efficiency rating, reduction-in-force, and removal procedures. At the same time the report of the Hoover Commission, and particularly

[131] First Hoover Commission, as cited in footnote 56, p. 9.
[132] First Hoover Commission, as cited in footnote 65, p. 3.

that of its Task Force, implicitly recognized that the requirements of existing statutes lay at the bottom of much of the trouble. Most of the more basic recommendations on pay, classification, recruitment, and examinations, for instance, required new legislation. However, the Commission was careful not to criticize Congress directly at any point. Nor did it refer to any of the political pressure groups responsible, in part at least, for the existence of the legislation which it indirectly deplored. Nevertheless, in pointing up the need for a relaxation of legislative control over administrative minutiae, the First Hoover Commission's personnel reports show their greatest insight.

Apparently the Task Force and the Hoover Commission both felt that, if one unified the Civil Service Commission and provided proper staff relationships between it and the departmental personnel offices, and, if one simplified procedures and paid civil servants more, the personnel problems of the federal government would largely be solved. In a lone dissenting report, Hoover Commissioner James K. Pollock complained, with justification, that "the report reflects an unduly limited concept of personnel administration, viewing it as a procedural, mechanical process called 'personnel transactions.' "[133]

Omissions. Commissioner Pollock's criticism becomes even more meaningful when one considers the range of public personnel problems which the First Hoover Commission as well as its Task Force *failed* to consider.[134]

Even in the field of organization, in which the Commission did its most thorough work, there were some obvious gaps. Perhaps most important, relationships between personnel and budget agencies were ignored. To be sure, both the Commission and its Task Force recommended that the Civil Service Commission function as a direct staff agent of the President in the manner of the Bureau of the Budget. But other vertical and horizontal relationships were not analyzed. The whole problem of top-level staff coordination of the personnel function with other executive staff functions was left up in the air

---

[133] Same, p. 47. Compared to the Hoover Commission and the Task Force, Pollock criticized the Civil Service Commission more than the departments and the legislative branch. He recommended that "a complete decentralization of personnel management be made to the responsible heads of the Federal agencies." A civil service equivalent of the Bureau of the Budget, with a limited staff and general rather than detailed supervision of departmental personnel agencies, would do the actual personnel service job. This plan involved considerably more legislative action than that contemplated by the other commissioners. Whether a law outlawing political favoritism, as advocated by Pollock, would be sufficient to guard the merit principle under such an arrangement has been a matter of considerable argument.

[134] The writer wishes to acknowledge the assistance of Edward Novotny in preparing an item by item comparative analysis of the Task Force and final reports on personnel of the First Hoover Commission. See also Paul P. Van Riper, "The Hoover Commission and Omission," *Personnel Administration*, XIV (November, 1951), 7.

despite its increasing importance.[135] In the realm of administrative operating effectiveness, the problems of overstaffing and personnel utilization, while discussed to some extent in the Task Force report, were side-stepped by the Hoover Commission.[136]

The Hoover Commission emphasized the development of a career service and the Task Force recommended the extension of the classified service. But there was scant attention paid to training and executive development. The extension of the merit system also received little attention in the Commission's final report, despite the fact, briefly pointed out by the Task Force, that nearly 200,000 employees were then serving in overseas positions where any career service was almost nonexistent. The difficult matter of maintaining a competent civilian staff for our widespread foreign operations was thus scarcely touched upon, despite the obvious needs of the times. Omitted also from the final report was any mention of the Task Force's recommendation for the inauguration of an employment information program to enhance the drawing power of the federal government in the personnel market at home. Thus the growing problem of recruiting qualified personnel both at home and abroad was largely ignored.

The extremely complex problem of expansion and contraction of the federal service during and after emergencies received no attention, despite the fact that the United States had just gone through such a period, and was shortly to do so again. The Commission was equally blind to problems stemming from the increasing dominance of the military over the civil service, though many tensions were already clearly apparent.

While the reports encouraged improved employee-management relations, the controversial field of public employee unionization was not mentioned. Other aspects of employee relations such as health, safety, housing, counseling, recreation, and the like were also passed by. It was this failure to tackle the most fundamental problems of human relations, then receiving so much attention in the world of private industry, that Commissioner Pollock so heavily scored in his dissenting opinion.

Moving into the more obviously "political" realm, discussion of the relationship of the permanent civil service to the great body of citizens, so important in a democracy, seems to have been deliberately

135 See, for instance, Arnold Kotz, "Budgeting for Personnel Staff," *Personnel Administration*, XI (September, 1948), 16. Interestingly enough, both the study of the federal civil service by Herman Feldman in 1931 and that by the President's Committee on Administrative Management considered this problem, even though it was then less pressing.

136 Overstaffing in *personnel* offices was, however, discussed in the final report. The omission of any consideration of overall manpower management was apparently intentional, for in his dissent Commissioner Pollock referred to the oversight and objected to it.

459

avoided. It was implied that promotion from within is the proper solution to the development of competent top-level civil servants. Mobility and turnover were considered solely as waste. There was, therefore, no mention of the possible desirability of any systematic movement into and out of the civil establishment and back and forth between industry and government. The Hoover Commission was equally silent on one of the most persistent problems in our public service: how to bridge the gap between career and political service. There seems to have been a bland assumption that the inclusion of top jobs within the competitive service would have little effect on the political control of the federal establishment by the majority party. Neither the place of the political administrator nor the duty of the career administrator to the politician, and vice versa, was touched upon. Nor was the related problem of the ethics of administrative action treated with any more care. Finally, the Hoover Commission was silent about the problem of loyalty, even though the harassment incident to and the time consumed in personal loyalty investigations had been a major deterrent to a career service.

Reaction and action. Despite their shortcomings, and perhaps partly because of them, the joint reports on personnel of the Hoover Commission and its Task Force stirred up much-needed public concern with our great civil establishment. They also provided a mass of information as a basis for action.

The Civil Service Commission accepted most of the recommendations with few reservations and tried to implement them.[137] Indeed, there is good evidence that much of the information available to the Task Force, as well as a number of the ideas presented in both reports, came from sources in or close to the Commission.[138]

With the approval of all concerned, the president of the Civil Service Commission was quickly redesignated as "chairman" and vested with the responsibility for the administrative direction of the agency's work.[139] He was to be served in turn by an executive director, the top career official in the Commission. The full Commission still was collectively responsible for basic rules and regulations and for the supervision of appeals and reviews. The first chairman, Commissioner Harry B. Mitchell, reported to Congress a year later that "my col-

---

[137] For the Commission's official position concerning the recommendations of the Hoover Commission see USCSC, *Sixty-sixth Report*, 1949, pp. 2–14; and *Sixty-seventh Report*, 1950, pp. 2–9.

[138] From a statement by Civil Service Commissioner Frances Perkins in an address at Roosevelt College in Chicago on October 19, 1950. The contribution of the Civil Service Commission, and particularly of ex-Commissioner Arthur S. Flemming, also a member of the Hoover Commission, has been further confirmed to the writer in a personal interview with another high-level representative of the federal service who prefers to remain anonymous.

[139] Reorganization Plan No. 5 of 1949, effective in August of that year.

460

leagues and I believe that the reorganization has been an unqualified success." [140] A four-point program to speed operations had been inaugurated and had, among other things, halved the elapsed time between examination announcements and the publishing of lists of eligibles. Within its own organization the Civil Service Commission continued the gradual decentralization of operations to its regional and local establishments. To assist the development of agency personnel management, as called for by the Hoover reports, it prepared an outline of a complete agency personnel program. No action was taken on the recommendation that an Office of Personnel be established in the President's Executive Office. A Liaison Officer remained, though with varying functions, and the general line of communications between the President and the Commission was left unchanged.

The recommendations concerning pay and classification were the most thoroughly implemented of the Hoover proposals. The Executive Pay Act of October 15, 1949, substantially increased the salary of the top executive officials of the government and provided new maximums for departmental and agency heads varying from $14,000 to $22,500. But the most sweeping revisions in salaries and other personnel matters were accomplished by the Classification Act of October 28, 1949. Replacing the 1923 act, the new law created three new top grades in the civil service—the first of the so-called "super-grade" positions—consisting then of 400 new positions with a salary ceiling of $14,000, nearly $4,000 more than ever before. Designation of the positions entitled to be included within the new grades rested with the Civil Service Commission, with the approval of the President required for the top twenty-five positions. For the rest of the service paid through Classification Act procedures, the basic rates of compensation were increased by about 4 per cent over those established in 1948. All in all, pay revisions between 1939 and 1949 increased the average salary of employees subject to the Classification Act from slightly under $2,000 a year to about $3,700 a year, with a minor reversal of the tendency to narrow the spread between top and bottom federal salaries. But the overall pay problem was by no means more than temporarily settled, because basic pay rates still lagged behind advances in the consumers' price index for this period.[141]

---

140 From a letter by Commissioner Mitchell to the chairman of the Senate Committee on Expenditures in the Executive Departments, November 17, 1950, as reprinted in U.S. Congress, Senate, Committee on Expenditures in the Executive Departments, *Reorganizations in the Executive Branch of the Government*, 81st Cong., 2d Sess., Sen. Report 2680 (Washington: Government Printing Office, 1950), pp. 12–14.

141 See U.S. Congress, Senate, Committee on Post Office and Civil Service, *Study of the Relationship Between Government Salaries and the National Consumers' Price Index of the Bureau of Labor Statistics, 1939–1951*, 82d Cong., 1st Sess., Committee print (Washington: Government Printing Office, 1951), for a detailed analysis.

A few minor pieces of wage and fringe benefit legislation also passed at this time provided for such things as increased travel pay and for special pay increases and privileges for a limited number of scientific and professional positions. The Hoover Commission proposal to pay many of the lesser postal, clerical, and subprofessional jobs the "going rate," as opposed to the fixed Classification Act rates, was, however, tabled, partly as a result of the opposition of the Civil Service Commission. This was one of the few proposals of the Hoover report which the Civil Service Commission rejected, in this case primarily on the grounds of the difficulty of accomplishing the task. A modified plan, suggested by the Commission, failed of adoption by Congress at this time; and it was not until the Eisenhower administration that further action on this proposal was taken.[142]

In addition, the Classification Act of 1949 consolidated five separate occupational "services" into two. The Professional and Scientific Service; Subprofessional Service; Clerical, Administrative, and Fiscal Service; and Clerical-Mechanical Service were combined in the General Schedule, usually abbreviated to "GS." The Crafts, Protective, and Custodial Service remained, but with the word "Service" changed to "Schedule." It was hoped that this consolidation would ease the problems of promotion and transfer as well as simplify classification procedures. To some extent this was the case, though the change did not entirely please those in the former Professional and Scientific Service, many of whom felt that they would receive greater recognition of their skills and status under a separate schedule. A few years later, when shortages of engineers and scientists grew more acute, the professional societies blamed much of the difficulty on the lack of identification and recognition within the Classification Act. The new law also permitted the devolution of the great bulk of classification actions to the departments and agencies under general Civil Service Commission supervision. Other sections of the Classification Act supported the development of a management-improvement program already started by the Bureau of the Budget, and provided for a study of hazardous employment by the Civil Service Commission, for various types of within-step increases in pay for superior accomplishment, for longevity pay, and for a study of efficiency ratings by the Commission. The required report on efficiency ratings was made by the Civil Service Commission in the spring of 1950 and was followed by the Performance Rating Act of 1950. As mentioned earlier,[143] this simplified efficiency ratings, but still failed to meet many objections.

142 See USCSC, *Sixty-sixth Report*, 1949, p. 7.
143 See p. 435.

Management development, test research, recruitment, performance awards, and promotion policies received a new impetus from the discussions following the Hoover report. At the same time Congress, more concerned with personnel costs than personnel procedures, authorized the House Committee on Post Office and Civil Service to investigate overstaffing.[144] As a result, a provision was inserted in the Independent Offices Appropriations Act for 1950, which limited the employment of persons engaged in personnel work to an arbitrary ratio of one such employee to 115 other employees. Typical of the congressional meat-ax approach to personnel problems, such ratios operated to circumscribe the kinds of activities which specialized personnel staffs could undertake in the development of modern personnel programs for their agencies. After the Korean war, these ceilings were relaxed somewhat. But they have continued for many smaller independent agencies, where they are most onerous, and in a few larger agencies.

In most other matters, new procedures recommended by the Hoover Commission were stymied because Congress would not pass the necessary legislation. Further decentralization of the examination system, modification of the "rule of three," revision of reduction-in-force procedures, and reconsideration of appeals and review procedures—especially those relating to dismissals—depended primarily on changes of the Veterans' Preference Act of 1944. As a result of strong pressure from veterans' organizations, which for the most part opposed the Hoover Commission's recommendations on these subjects, Congress refused to act.

Nevertheless, even if the recommendations of the Hoover Commission were neither all-encompassing nor fully implemented, a good deal was accomplished to improve federal personnel management between 1948 and 1950.[145] Had not the Korean conflict intervened unexpectedly, more might have been done.

The Korean Conflict

The final fillip to the reorganization of federal personnel management under President Truman came with the sudden commencement of hostilities in Korea late in June, 1950. While the national reaction this time was much more swift and decisive than a decade before, the federal service was no better prepared for a wartime type expansion.

---

[144] See U.S. Congress, House, Committee on Post Office and Civil Service, *Investigation of Employee Utilization in the Executive Departments and Agencies*, 81st Cong., 2d Sess., House Report 2457, Part I, June 30, 1950; Parts II and III, December 5, 1950; Parts IV, V, and VI, January 1, 1951 (Washington: Government Printing Office, 1950–51).

[145] For the Commission's point of view see James M. Mitchell, as cited in footnote 71.

The emergency agencies of World War II had been completely demobilized by March, 1950, just three months before the new crisis; and the new mobilization planning mechanism created by the National Security Act of 1947 had already shown itself inadequate even for handling the cold war.[146] There was no civilian equivalent of a military reserve, nor any accepted blueprint for meeting a new civilian personnel emergency. There had been some advance planning for a new wartime emergency, but little for a partial mobilization of the type required for the Korean operation. The problem was further compounded by the fact that the manpower pool available for civil expansion was smaller than ever before. Only in one sense was the federal civil service better prepared to meet the new emergency than that of World War II: the experience gained in the latter conflict was still close at hand.

Emergency personnel policies. It was on this experience that the Civil Service Commission drew during the summer and fall of 1950. The Commission immediately appointed liaison representatives to major segments of the Department of Defense, with broad authority to act for the Commission. On July 14 an agreement was concluded with the defense agencies, giving them much of the same type of broad appointing authority which they had during World War II. This again permitted "emergency-indefinite" appointments "for the duration," for which normal hiring procedures were greatly relaxed. As in the previous conflict, the Civil Service Commission planned to prevent any sizable increase in the permanent service so that, in turn, the inevitable reductions-in-force could be managed more easily.

Ever since the early forties the legislative branch had been greatly concerned over the size of the civil establishment, and had investigated manpower utilization repeatedly. Shortly after the start of the Korean conflict the Senate directed its Committee on Armed Services to look into the preparedness program of the government, with again a special emphasis upon manpower utilization, both civil and military, in the defense agencies.[147] The net result of all this investigative effort was not only to stimulate more effective manpower utilization within the executive branch, but also to heighten the endemic congressional fear that the executive agencies were not entirely to be trusted when it came to economy in the employment of personnel. Therefore, in September, 1950, Congress sought to strengthen the hand of the Civil Service Commission in controlling the expansion of personnel during

---

146 See, for example, Edward H. Hobbs, *Behind the President* (Washington: Public Affairs Press, 1954), chs. vi, vii, and viii.

147 See the extensive series of pamphlet reports issued by this committee's Preparedness Investigating Subcommittee during 1951 and 1952.

the Korean conflict. This was done through the controversial Whitten Amendment, a rider to the Supplemental Appropriation Act for 1951. The amendment required at least one year's service in the next lower grade for promotion, and arbitrarily limited the size of the permanent service within each department and agency to that effective on September 1, 1950.[148] This meant that any sizable increase in personnel to meet the needs of the new emergency would have to be accomplished through temporary appointments. Theoretically the legislation still permitted permanent appointments to be made up to the levels of September 1, 1950. In practice this was found to be impractical as well as inequitable because not all agencies were equally affected by the emergency. Therefore the President issued Executive Order 10180 on November 13, 1950, "Establishing Special Personnel Procedures in the Interest of the National Defense." The effect of this order and the Civil Service Commission's implementing regulations were:

(1) To place new appointments to almost all types of positions on an indefinite basis.

(2) To suspend peacetime restrictions relating to (a) State apportionment of appointments to positions in the departmental service, (b) length of residence, and (c) the number of members of a family who may be employed in the Federal service at the same time.

(3) To place all transfers, promotions, and reinstatements on an indefinite basis.

(4) To authorize the Commission to set up a system of reemployment rights in order to encourage transfers to defense agencies.[149]

The President also directed the Commission to coordinate the civilian recruiting efforts of all agencies in the executive branch and to expand the operations of the boards of civil service examiners.

With the creation shortly thereafter of a new Office of Defense Mobilization to coordinate the government's emergency program, and with Arthur S. Flemming selected to direct this agency's overall Manpower Policy Committee, the reorganization of the federal service for the Korean conflict was substantially completed. By the end of 1950 the civil service was operating under a personnel control system closely paralleling that of World War II.[150]

The crisis continues. On January 5, 1951, the Department of Defense was given additional power to hire on its own authority whenever the

[148] See U.S. Congress, Senate, Committee on Post Office and Civil Service, *Analysis of the Whitten Amendment*, 83d Cong., 1st Sess., Senate Doc. 35 (Washington: Government Printing Office, 1953).

[149] USCSC, *Sixty-eighth Report*, 1951, pp. 2–3.

[150] For a more detailed summary of the Commission's emergency personnel program during 1950, see USCSC, *An Informal Progress Report from the Chairman*, as appended to a Commission press release of February 2, 1951.

Commission's registers were inadequate. The Commission had also relaxed many age limitations and physical requirements and was urging the fullest utilization of women and the physically handicapped. Beyond this, the Commission had been able to accelerate its pre-appointment loyalty and security checks for sensitive positions so that clearances were being made within ten working days. In many instances examination and placement procedures had been similarly streamlined.

To insure conformance to minimum standards and to legal requirements, the Commission began early in 1951 to strengthen its Inspection Service. It simplified and standardized the organizational pattern of its regional offices. It organized a new referral unit to interview business executives who came to Washington to make their services available. It codified qualifications standards for positions under the Classification Act, simplified the *Federal Personnel Manual* and other procedural handbooks, and published guides for the development of agency personnel programs. By the end of June, 1951, nearly 2,500,000 civil employees were on the rolls of the executive agencies, an increase of more than 520,000 during the fiscal year. To maintain this employment level, a total of more than 1,000,000 persons had been brought into the service. Most of the increase, 487,200, came in the military agencies, with an additional 15,300 employees hired to staff the new agencies concerned with defense production and economic controls, and with about 5,900 more occupied either with civilian defense or the control of subversive activities.[151]

As 1951 moved into 1952 the Civil Service Commission became more and more concerned over the decline in the percentage of federal civilian personnel occupying permanent posts, a phenomenon which this time stemmed largely from the Whitten Amendment. The rider had been modified in both 1951 and 1952, but the ceilings on permanent appointments still remained. To prevent inequities between defense and non-defense agencies, the Commission had maintained its indefinite appointment system. About 99 per cent of the appointments after November of 1950 were in this category. As a result, only 55 per cent of federal civil employees held permanent posts by June, 1952.[152] As the Commission noted, "continuance of this trend would ultimately result in the virtual elimination of career employment in Government and the lack of a stable work force." [153] The Commission further objected to the Whitten Amendment because the inability of the govern-

151 USCSC, *Sixty-eighth Report*, 1951, p. 9.
152 Same, p. 5; and USCSC, *Sixty-ninth Report*, 1952, p. 92. These figures apply to the continental United States only.
153 USCSC, *Sixty-eighth Report*, 1951, p. 5.

ment to offer any assurance of firm and lasting employment hampered recruitment. At the same time the reintroduction of large numbers of "indefinites" into the civil service, as well as the transfer of many career employees into emergency agencies, revived concern over the reduction-in-force (RIF) formulae. By 1952 the various RIF categories had mushroomed to twenty-three, with the result that even small reductions-in-force produced much "bumping" of one category by the next in a sort of chain reaction. A special study of the problem, undertaken during 1951 by a Senate subcommittee, revealed the following fairly typical case:

In another agency our staff investigators worked side by side with agency personnel people in conducting a reduction in force in which 164 employees were to be separated. . . . We found that the personnel office was required to take 1,553 personnel actions over a period of 4½ months. These 1,553 actions included such paper work as reduction-in-force notices, reassignments at the same grade, offers of lower grade, reduction-in-force extensions, cancellations of reassignments, reassignments extended, reduction-in-force notices rescinded, employees transferring out, and employees retiring because of reduction in force.

The end result of the 1,553 personnel actions, and the reshuffling and confusion they created, was not that 164 people were involuntarily separated as was planned. Instead only 25 people in the lower grades were involuntarily separated. The reason for this anomaly was that, during the 4½ months period in which reduction in force was taking place, 399 employees left the agency voluntarily. We cannot say that all of the 399 left because of the confusion and reshuffling of the reduction in force. But the agency itself says that 97 workers definitely left because of the reduction in force, and that 200 other employees left the agency because they had received or thought they were in danger of receiving reduction-in-force notices.

The ironical fact is that many of those who left would not have received separation notices. But their leaving, as a result of the hurly-burly of current reduction-in-force practices, forced the agency into the position of having to conduct an intensive recruiting campaign on top of a reduction in force. . . .

The direct administrative costs of conducting that particular reduction in force amounted to a total of 13,000 man-hours, or $33,500. When we consider that the objective of laying off 164 people was never reached, due to the fact that many employees left the agency voluntarily, and that the end result was the involuntary separation of only 25 employees, the direct cost of laying off those 25 workers amounted to more than $1,300 per employee. This does not include the cost of recruiting new employees. . . .

. . . the indirect costs . . . were even greater. These may be measured in terms of the estimated time that branch officials spent in solving the problems that arose, the loss in working effectiveness of its employees, and the time spent in training employees who were shifted into new jobs. Officials of that agency estimated the indirect costs . . . to be $125,000. When this is added to the direct costs of $33,500, the total cost . . . reaches $159,-000. . . .

Measured Government-wide, these costs mean that the Federal Government is wasting thousands of man-hours and spending millions of dollars every year laying off employees.[154]

As the subcommittee concluded, it was likely that in many cases the cost of implementing a reduction-in-force was equal to or greater than the economies anticipated by the action.

A House subcommittee blamed both the Civil Service Commission and the departments and agencies for the creation of a "series of regulations and orders which are so complex, confusing, and arbitrary as to make proper administration impossible." [155] There was justice in this complaint. Yet Congress was unwilling to concede that its own legislation, especially the Veterans' Preference Act of 1944 and the Whitten Amendment, also bore major responsibility for inefficiency, delay, and waste of time and money.

Late in 1952, the Civil Service Commission proposed new layoff procedures. RIF categories were to be reduced from twenty-three to six, bumping rights of indefinite employees eliminated, and the remaining bumping rights restricted as to geographical area and organizational unit. There were to be three major layoff groups composed of "career," "career-conditional," and "indefinite" employees. To comply with RIF requirements of the Veterans' Preference Act of 1944, each of these was divided into veteran and non-veteran groups. Final action on this proposal was not taken, however, until after the Eisenhower administration came into power.[156]

In the name of economy. To systematize the annual and sick leave regulations of the federal service Congress had passed the Annual and Sick Leave Act of 1951. This legislation permanently reduced annual leave for employees in a number of categories for the first time in the twentieth century. During a period of manpower shortages, it reduced fringe benefits which were already meager compared to private industry. But the most irritating action was taken through the Thomas Leave Rider of 1952, which required the forfeiture each June 30 of all unused annual leave earned in the preceding calendar year. As there had never been any unemployment compensation benefits for

154 U.S. Congress, Senate, Committee on Post Office and Civil Service, Subcommittee on Federal Manpower Policies, *Utilization of Manpower in the Federal Government*, 82d Cong., 2d Sess., Sen. Report 1342 (Washington: Government Printing Office, 1952), pp. 5–6. This subcommittee was better known as the Johnson Subcommittee. Its investigating staff was headed by Melvin Purvis, a former FBI agent.

155 U.S. Congress, House, Committee on Post Office and Civil Service, Subcommittee on Manpower Utilization, *Study of Civilian Manpower Utilization in the Federal Government: Preliminary Report*, 83d Cong., 1st Sess., Subcommittee print (Washington: Government Printing Office, 1953), p. 9.

156 For the Commission's proposal on this subject, see its press releases of September 11, 1952, and December 19, 1952.

federal employees, it had been customary for decades to accumulate a few months of annual leave as a financial cushion. Fortunately, the Thomas Leave Rider, which would have removed this cushion, was repealed the next year. But its passage had seriously hurt the morale of employees.[157] Other riders, passed at this time in the name of economy but deplored by the Commission on the grounds of administrative inflexibility, included the Jensen-Ferguson Amendment, which controlled the filling of vacancies by an arbitrary formula in order to reduce personnel ceilings, the Byrd Rider, which cut down the size of publicity staffs in the federal service for two years by a flat 25 per cent, and riders which set arbitrary ratios for the number of personnel workers within the departments and agencies. Considered as a whole, the formal legislative actions of Congress during the Korean conflict, while reflecting a legitimate concern with the size of the federal service, were mainly of a negative sort. They cut and pruned primarily from a "meat-ax" point of view, they were accompanied by widespread publicity critical of the ability and integrity of the service as a whole, and they lacked a positive approach to personnel management. Fundamentally, the continued growth of the service during the Korean conflict reflected the emergency needs of the times; and the service reached a total of slightly more than 2,600,000 employees by the end of fiscal year 1952, an increase of approximately 117,000 over the previous fiscal year.[158] After reaching a peak in July, 1952, federal employment began to decline during the late summer and fall of 1952, thus bringing reduction-in-force problems sharply into focus.

Other developments during the emergency. Not all of the activities of either the Congress or the Civil Service Commission during the years of 1950, 1951, and 1952 related to the Korean affair. The Performance Rating Act of 1950 went into effect during the emergency, executive development again came to the fore, and recruiting and examination policies continued to be overhauled, with special emphases placed on the recruitment of young people from college and of much-needed top-level executives. Chairman Robert Ramspeck, who succeeded Commissioner Harry B. Mitchell as head of the Commission in March, 1951, undertook with some success an extensive "facts versus myth" campaign to counteract public attitudes toward the federal service. And preliminary studies were commenced in 1952 looking toward the rationalization of federal employment overseas. Here Congress showed to its best advantage during the Korean emergency, for these needed

---

[157] For a brief summary of the new annual and sick leave provisions, see USCSC, *Sixty-ninth Report*, 1952, pp. 68–69; and *Seventieth Report*, 1953, p. 43. A brief history of modern federal leave provisions is found in Stahl, as cited in footnote 65, pp. 406–9.

[158] USCSC, *Sixty-ninth Report*, 1952, p. 11.

studies came largely at its request. Final action was not taken, however, until late in Eisenhower's first term.

Congress was also willing to consider, if somewhat reluctantly, the effects of the inflation accompanying the Korean action upon the pay scales of the service. Federal employees paid in accord with prevailing rates had already received consideration, and the need for increases for salaried employees was apparent. Public Law 201, approved on October 24, 1951, raised the entrance rate of each Classification Act grade by 10 per cent, but provided that no increase would be less than $300 or more than $800. The average overall increase was $358, with the range varying from 19.9 per cent in the lowest grade to 5.7 in the highest.[159] Unfortunately, this act again reflected the tendency of Congress towards compression of pay scales, a tendency which had been only modestly relieved two years before through the Classification Act of 1949. However, a series of supplementary enactments, commencing with the Defense Production Act of 1950, expanded to nearly 1,000 the number of positions included within the "supergrades" of GS 16, 17, and 18.[160] While these positions were originally designed primarily to encourage personnel from private enterprise to enter the service more or less temporarily, they also provided avenues of further promotion for career civil servants.

Even so, President Truman and his chief executive heads continued to encounter severe frustrations in the recruitment of top-level executives for both political and nonpolitical posts. Prominent figures in the worlds of commerce, industry, and finance were reluctant to associate themselves with any aspect of an administration frequently highly critical of business and to accept positions which almost always insured conflict with a cantankerous Congress. Low salary scales for top jobs and the conflict-of-interest statutes compounded the problem.[161] In a discussion of the Washington "executive famine," *Fortune* magazine noted in late 1950 that just before the Korean conflict the government was run "with over fifty of the 400-odd varsity positions vacant." [162] Despite the obvious problems, the Truman administration failed to search for a systematic solution.[163]

159 Same, pp. 44–45.

160 Same, pp. 46–48.

161 For references on the important conflict-of-interest problem, see the "supplementary notes" at the end of this chapter.

162 "Washington's Executive Famine," XLII (October, 1950), 73.

163 The Carnegie Foundation and the Public Administration Clearing House did, however, support John J. Corson's study of *Executives for the Federal Service* (New York: Columbia University Press, 1952). More recently, a good deal of attention has been given to the problem of top-level executives, both political and nonpolitical. See especially the reports of the Second Hoover Commission.

The military build-up after hostilities began only set off a more frenzied search for executive talent. Since there was no civilian reserve, the recruitment of top personnel to staff the new emergency agencies was again conducted through such miscellaneous procedures as appeals to patriotism and personal friendship.[164] Very few government agencies had even maintained a roster of potential emergency executives. The fortunate experience of one of those which did keep such a list has been related as follows:

> The usefulness of civilian rostering, where it did exist, was exemplified after Korea in the Field Service of the Department of Commerce. A constantly updated roster had been kept after termination of the War Production Board's activities, with ten to a dozen men listed in relation to each major type of key position. Because of the availability of this list, the number of field offices of the Department could be raised, after Korea, from 42 to 105 in 81 days, and the number of personnel from 396 to 1,802 with 69 per cent of the men recruited having seen service in WPB, and the others having been found through these key people.[165]

To some extent career civil servants gained from the difficulty of outside recruitment. Of a total of 253 positions classified at GS 15 and above in eight federal agencies, 74.7 per cent were filled between July 1, 1950, and April 1, 1951, by people already in federal employ.[166]

Moreover, there were the usual substantial supplements of "without compensation" (WOC) personnel and of temporary experts and consultants. WOC personnel had dropped to a low of about 24,000 during late 1947 and then gradually increased during the Korean emergency. During 1951, for example, an average of more than 90,000 WOC personnel were attached to the government. Since then this number has slowly increased until it reached more than 100,000 during 1956.[167] Most of these individuals have served part time only, frequently merely as members of advisory committees. Some, perhaps several hundred, have occupied important policy-making posts, particularly in connection with defense agencies during the Korean

164 For some illuminating testimony on appointment procedures within one of the new Korean emergency agencies, in this case the Office of Price Stabilization, see the remarks of Michael V. DiSalle, Director, before the Joint Committee on Defense Production, March 2, 1951. U.S. Congress, Joint Committee on Defense Production, *Hearing*, 82d Cong., 1st Sess., Defense Production Act Progress Report No. 4, March 2, 1951 (Washington: Government Printing Office, 1951).

165 National Planning Association, *Needed: A Civilian Reserve* (Washington: The Association, 1954), p. 29.

166 John J. Corson, as cited in footnote 163, p. 26.

167 From data supplied to the writer by the Employment Statistics Office of the Civil Service Commission.

conflict. The formerly popular category of "dollar-a-year man" was not revived.[168]

Neither WOC's nor consultants had to comply with civil service regulations in order to be employed. Hiring of consultants was specifically authorized by law after World War II and most governmental agencies have used them. The use of consultants has sometimes been criticized on the grounds that it permits excessive payment for work which should come under the purview of established positions. Criticism of WOC employment has stemmed more from the potential conflict of interest inherent in the relationship of a WOC's private capacity to his public duties.

Civilian supremacy over the military. No discussion of the Korean conflict would be complete without some reference to President Truman's spectacular dismissal on April 11, 1951, of General of the Army Douglas MacArthur from his positions of Commanding General of the U.S. Army Forces, Far East, U.S. Commander-in-Chief, Far East Command, Supreme Commander for the Allied Powers in Japan, and Commander-in-Chief, United Nations Command. Republicans and even many Democrats raged, but the President stuck to his decision, backed by the unanimous support of the Joint Chiefs of Staff. If the military services under President Truman seemed at times greatly to overshadow their civilian counterpart, this action, together with Truman's support of civilian control of atomic energy, to some extent redressed the balance.

The State of the Service in 1952

The merit system struggles of the twenties and thirties represented efforts to centralize the direction of public personnel management within the Civil Service Commission. From a legal point of view this was accomplished by the beginning of World War II. But wartime emergencies forced a decentralization in personnel management which approached abdication and frequently left many affairs of the public service in the hands of the departments and agencies under only nominal controls. This experience demonstrated clearly the limitations of directing public personnel management from the center.

With the return to peace, the Civil Service Commission, capitalizing upon World War II experience, tried to initiate a decentralization based upon standards and postaudit inspection. But Congress was on

---

[168] See U.S. Congress, House, Committee on the Judiciary, Antitrust Subcommittee, *Interim Report on WOC's and Government Advisory Groups*, 84th Cong., 2nd Sess., April 24, 1956 (Washington: Government Printing Office, 1956), for a more complete analysis of the problems involved in utilization of WOC's and dollar-a-year men since World War II.

the whole uncooperative and many of the detailed controls of the past returned. Decentralization often deteriorated into a type of workload decentralization which discouraged initiative and permitted little time for any imaginative contemplation of personnel management. This in turn produced its own cathartic, partly in the form of public and official criticism of a "civil service as usual" approach and finally in the reports of the First Hoover Commission and its Task Force on personnel management. The legislation immediately following these reports alleviated some of the difficulties. But the Veterans' Preference Act of 1944 remained almost unchanged; and the addition during the Korean conflict of the Whitten Amendment, the Thomas Leave Rider, and the riders arbitrarily placing a ceiling on personnel staffs, left matters, if anything, more confused than before. Despite the admonitions of Curtis, Eaton, and Schurz, by mid-twentieth century both the front and back doors to the service had been largely closed, resulting in considerable turmoil within the federal edifice.

Strong leadership within the Civil Service Commission had in a magnificent and unprecedented effort restored the competitive career system after World War II. But only the most sanguine observer could accept the Commission's description of the federal service of 1950 as "in better condition than at any other time in its history." [169] It is true that by 1950 the essential mission of civil service reform, that of delivering the federal government from the clutches of patronage, had been largely accomplished. But the postwar decline in employee morale and "the triumph of techniques over purpose" made it only too clear that all was not well in the civil establishment.

At mid-century, the federal service faced a frustrating dilemma. For seven decades civil service reform had aspired to *control* federal administrators and politicians in an effort to eliminate patronage, and the policing function of personnel management was still deeply embedded in the bias of many public personnel staff members. On the other hand, the trend in the world of private enterprise since the twenties had been distinctly to view personnel work as a *positive aid* to management. Many public personnel administrators and critics of the federal service, varying from the representatives of private business who dealt with the government to the President's Committee on Administrative Management of 1937 and the First Hoover Commission, deplored the negative policeman approach. Congress, however, resisted, not so much on patronage grounds as in the name of a less partisan mixture of democracy and employee security against allegedly arbitrary administrative action. It continued to emphasize con-

169 USCSC, *Sixty-eighth Report*, 1951, p. 1.

trol as the primary function of the Civil Service Commission and departmental personnel agencies. The postwar Civil Service Commission and departmental personnel staffs were in many ways forced to straddle a barbed wire type of personnel fence. To combine the personnel control functions, which in private enterprise lay largely apart from personnel management in the hands of employee unions and government agencies, with the service functions of a private industrial personnel staff, which was entirely devoted to the management point of view, was an almost impossible task.

Underneath it all lay, of course, the nature of American politics. Congress, under great pressure from millions of veterans and the increasing legions of public employees and resentful of a long-standing dominance by the executive branch, sought by fair means and foul to bring the federal service to heel during the late forties and early fifties. To some extent it was successful, but with severe damage both to the concept of positive personnel management and to the morale of public employees. Nor was President Truman able to reverse the trend and salvage much from the political wreckage. All this only pointed up another fundamental difficulty facing the postwar federal service: that is, the failure of American politics to provide its public service with any clear guidelines for action.

Those who have explained the postwar malaise of the federal service primarily in terms of an incomplete career system and of inadequate pay and perquisites have told only a small part of the story. The prestige and morale of the public service have always been functions of more than salaries, personnel procedures, and mechanical organization. They are functions of political values and conflict as well. When in a period of national and international tension the political forces in a federal government with a separation of powers are locked in bitter struggle, the public service is bound to reflect the conflict. When the quarrel revolves in part around differing views of the proper place and function of the public service, that institution must inevitably reflect a good deal of paralyzing apprehension.

Under Franklin D. Roosevelt the federal service had basked in the light of social reform and to a great extent had been both the object and agent of that reform. Despite wage cuts, great patronage inroads, and chaotic personnel management, the morale of the service was extraordinarily high and it went about its tasks with dispatch. After World War II, however, that sense of mission was lost. The civil service bore the burden of its New Deal allegiance, and became itself an object of often hysterical attack.

In mid-twentieth century the function of the civil service as an instrument of national purpose once again became a prime political issue, as it had in 1829 and 1883. Should the federal civil establishment be a positive force for the implementation of national policy? To this fundamental political question some said, "Yes," during the Truman administration. Others cried, "Socialism!"

This essentially political conflict lay at the root of the difficulties of the federal service during the postwar years, much more than any failure to provide adequate pay or to tighten up the career system. And the election of 1952, which placed General Dwight D. Eisenhower in the White House and the Republican Party in power after an enforced twenty-year political fast, only served to heighten the tension.

SUPPLEMENTARY NOTES

Position-classification and pay. For the period of the forties, see especially, Ismar Baruch, *History of Position-Classification and Salary Standardization in the Federal Service, 1941–1944* (Washington: U.S. Civil Service Commission, 1945); the series of articles by Baruch in the issues of November, 1944, September, 1945, January, 1946, and January, 1947, of *Personnel Administration;* and his discussions of wartime and other pay problems appearing in the April, 1944, and October, 1945, issues of *Public Personnel Review.* Pay trends since 1923 are analyzed briefly but well in a Civil Service Commission press release of May 16, 1951, summarizing Chairman Robert Ramspeck's congressional testimony on that date. See also R. Fjelstad, "Congress and Civil Service Legislation, 1933–1947," as cited in footnote 53, ch. vi; O. Glenn Stahl, *Public Personnel Administration,* as cited in footnote 65; the reports of the First and Second Hoover Commissions; and U.S. Congress, Senate, Committee on Post Office and Civil Service, *Study of the Relationship Between Government Salaries and the National Consumers' Price Index of the Bureau of Labor Statistics, 1939–1951,* as cited in footnote 141.

University training for the public service. On this subject see, for example, the report of the first postwar conference on the subject, held at Princeton in 1946: Joseph E. McLean (ed.), *The Public Service and University Education,* as cited in footnote 126. See also William Anderson and John M. Gaus, *Research in Public Administration* (Chicago: Public Administration Service, 1945); American Political Science Association, Committee for the Advancement of Teaching, *Goals for Political Science* (New York: William Sloane Associates, 1951), ch. iv; Roscoe C. Martin, "Education for Public Administration," in U.S. Department of Health, Education, and Welfare, Office of Education, *Education for the Professions* (Washington: Government Printing Office, 1955); and Dwight Waldo, *The Study of Public Administration* (Garden City, N.Y.: Doubleday and Co., 1955).

The conflict-of-interest statutes. There has been little systematic study and analysis of the conflict-of-interest problem, which has become of increasing importance in the recruitment of top executives, especially the so-called "political executives" occupying posts outside the competitive system, since World War II. For most of the information readily available at the time of writing, see Edwin McElwain and James Vorenberg, "The Federal Conflict of Interests Statutes," *Harvard Law Review,* LXV (April, 1952), 955; U.S. Congress, Senate, Committee on Armed Services, *Compilation of Certain*

475

Memoranda Prepared by the Office of the Senate Legislative Counsel on Conflict of Interest Statutes, 84th Cong., 1st Sess., Committee print (Washington: Government Printing Office, 1955) ; and the Douglas report on *Ethical Standards in Government,* as cited in footnote 14. On occasion Congress has modified these statutes to permit certain types of personnel to accept government posts, especially temporary ones, without too much personal sacrifice. But it was the refusal of Congress to enact such a modification which, for example, forced the resignation of the entire Nimitz Commission on Internal Security and Individual Rights in 1951. A more spectacular case in point was the dilemma presented by these statutes to Charles Wilson upon his nomination by President Eisenhower to the position of Secretary of Defense. Under considerable pressure, Wilson finally divested himself of his General Motors holdings, almost certainly at a considerable financial sacrifice.

CHAPTER 16

The Federal Service in Transition

1953–1958

The administration of Dwight D. Eisenhower, just as the administration of Theodore Roosevelt, marked a distinct watershed in American public affairs. Politically, the effect of events from 1952 to 1958 was, despite much protestation, to confirm the positive role of big government in the affairs of the nation, a role which T. R. had so vigorously outlined. Administratively, both regimes were to set the federal service off in new directions but dimly ·perceived at the time.

Moreover, both men espoused a new and more liberal Republicanism upon which they were able to base a high level of popularity. But here the parallel largely ends, for in personality, experience, and attitude—in the crucial matter of political style—T. R. and Eisenhower are miles apart. And it is in the personal approach of Dwight D. Eisenhower to the Presidency and American politics that one must seek the initial key to an understanding of the federal service in the first Republican administration in twenty years.

The Transference of Power

Perhaps most important in determining the character of the new administration was the fact of Eisenhower's political inexperience. It verged on naïveté, not in terms of politics defined as diplomacy, for this he understood consummately well, but in terms of politics as a partisan and overtly manipulative struggle for power. Such a background, while suggestive of troubles to come, was by no means a

477

political liability during the Republican nomination fight against the clearly partisan Senator Robert A. Taft in 1952. General Eisenhower, then and later, distinctly appealed to great numbers of Americans who were disenchanted with both the Left and the Right and more concerned with prosperity and a lessening of the national tension level than with continued personal and ideological in-fighting.

Eisenhower the candidate. Though possessing intelligence and great charm, candidate Eisenhower, with minor exceptions, steadfastly refused to exert these assets in a partisan fashion. Nor had he changed his approach by 1958. More than perhaps any president since Washington, he was to rise above politics as it is ordinarily pictured. Indeed, one of the great strengths of the Eisenhower administration has lain in an ability to sweep a good many potential problems under the rug, to emphasize unanimity rather than difference, and to bring a certain amount of good will back into political fashion.

From the beginning Eisenhower has represented a type of non-partisanship, an approach to politics peculiarly relevant to our mid-century political stalemate. The middle-of-the-road "dynamic-conservatism" of the New Republicanism's "new look" has signified an attempt to straddle the gap between Harry S. Truman and Senator Taft, between Senator Herbert H. Lehman of New York and Senator Joseph R. McCarthy of Wisconsin, through a return to an essentially pragmatic as opposed to ideological concept of political action. In this respect also, Eisenhower reminds one of Washington.

But such a pragmatic approach has its hazards, especially when combined with a certain lack of understanding and appreciation of the facts of American partisan political life. Within the frame of reference of this study, Eisenhower's initiation into the determinants of political power came with the curious Morningside Heights conference with his erstwhile rival, Senator Taft of Ohio, in New York City on September 12, 1952. Taft was not only permitted to draft a statement of Eisenhower's political philosophy, but Eisenhower also agreed to refrain from any political punishment of Taft's supporters in the event of a Republican victory. "General Eisenhower has stated without qualification," announced Taft, "that in the making of appointments at high levels or low levels there will be no discrimination against anyone because he or she has supported me. . . ." [1] While this was the only formal promise which Taft exacted in return for his support of Eisenhower's candidacy, the whole statement implied a much more sweeping accommodation to the senator than even

[1] As quoted in Robert J. Donovan, *Eisenhower: The Inside Story* (New York: Harper and Bros., 1956), p. 104.

many Republicans cared to admit; and it became a matter of considerable controversy. Whatever the wisdom of coming to terms with his major political rival within the Republican party, Eisenhower early put himself on record as willing to abstain from using one of a new president's prime political weapons for the forging of party unity—namely, the manipulation of the patronage. This was, and would continue to be, a marked departure from the political tactics of, say, both Roosevelts, who were quite capable of making such an agreement but who would have declined to put it in writing, much less in a draft prepared and released to the press by one of their political rivals. Combined with the tendency of leading Republican congressional leaders, accustomed to the tactics of opposition rather than positive action, to fly off in all political directions at once, any presidential reluctance to control the party mechanism through any and all means at command foretold a certain amount of disaster.

Eisenhower did clearly perceive, however, that major campaign ammunition lay in the issues of "corruption" and "loyalty." Here he and the rest of the party were at first in considerable agreement. While declining to be photographed with Senator McCarthy on the presidential campaign train as it rolled into Wisconsin, the General, in a speech immediately following one by the Senator at Green Bay on October 3, 1952, firmly stated:

> The differences between me and Senator McCarthy are well known to him and to me, and we have discussed them. . . .
> I want to make one thing very clear. The purposes that he and I have of ridding this Government of the incompetents, the dishonest, and above all the subversives and the disloyal are one and the same. Our differences, therefore, have nothing to do with the end result that we are seeking. The differences apply to method. . . .[2]

With Eisenhower supporting the control of subversives by executive rather than congressional action, the stage was set well before the election for some of the discord to come. Once again, the federal service was to become the bone of contention in a way which had not been the case since the days of Presidents Arthur and Jackson. "Clean up the mess in Washington!" became a prime political slogan of the Republican party of 1952 as it moved into power in both the executive and legislative branches of government.

Interregnum. In many repects the changeover from the Truman to the Eisenhower administration was one of the most orderly transfers of power from one political party to another in our history. This was

2 As quoted in Merlo J. Pusey, *Eisenhower the President* (New York: The Macmillan Co., 1956), pp. 29–30.

even more remarkable in light of the Twentieth Amendment, which had drastically curtailed the time available to a new administration for organization purposes. Like Hoover, President Truman offered assistance and, unlike F. D. R., Eisenhower accepted. Moreover, there was an unusual measure of prior planning on the part of the President-elect and his associates.

Presidential assistants-designate Joseph Dodge and Henry Cabot Lodge, Jr.,[3] quickly moved into the budgetary process and foreign relations, respectively, with the blessing of President Truman. The membership of the new cabinet was determined within barely a month after the election; and by December, 1952, there had already been considerable collaboration between incoming and outgoing officials at the departmental level, especially within the Treasury in light of the immediacy of budgetary decisions. When it came to further appointments, the President-elect and his advisers were able to draw upon a study of the duties and responsibilities of federal politically appointed executives prepared by the consulting firm of McKinsey and Co. and initiated at the request of Herbert Brownell in June, 1952.[4] Further anticipating administrative problems to come, Eisenhower brought together soon after the election a team composed of Milton S. Eisenhower, Arthur S. Flemming, and Nelson A. Rockefeller to consider reorganization proposals. This group, later designated as The President's Advisory Committee on Government Organization, produced more than twenty studies within a few months and many administrative developments were to stem from its efforts.[5]

On November 18, 1952, Eisenhower and President Truman met personally. This session was followed by a briefing attended by top aides of both men. Finally, in an unprecedented move, Eisenhower called his cabinet-to-be together at the Hotel Commodore in New York City for a two-day planning conference on January 11 and 12, 1953. This event inaugurated the novel fact, if not concept, of the cabinet as an integrated team, notable for an absence of the interpersonal and political fireworks traditionally associated with the activities of our politically appointed department heads. By this time the White House staff, captained by Governor Sherman Adams of New Hampshire, had been assembled and to some extent organized for action.

---

[3] These men shortly became respectively, Director of the Bureau of the Budget and head of the U.S. delegation to the United Nations.

[4] Efforts of a similar sort on behalf of Governor Thomas E. Dewey, prior to the election of 1948, had proved premature.

[5] Ex-Civil Service Commissioner Arthur S. Flemming, as a member of the White House official family under Eisenhower, continued to influence the development of public personnel management significantly. Later he became Director, Office of Defense Mobilization. He was also a member of both Hoover Commissions.

480

When one considers that President Wilson, for example, had not even met all his cabinet members before his inauguration, the Eisenhower preparations for the transference of power appear in startling contrast to the past. Here one senses not only the new president's thorough preparation in and understanding of administration as an organizational problem, but also the business orientation of the great bulk of his associates.[6] However, despite the key position of Sherman Adams and the appointment of both the Republican National Chairman, Arthur E. Summerfield, and his Finance Committee Chairman, Sinclair Weeks, to the Cabinet, there seems to have been a notable absence of *political* planning. There was no Farley, no organized clearance system for patronage problems, no clear decision such as had been made by Franklin D. Roosevelt, to use the patronage as a "steel-pointed pic,"[7] and no plan to take care of "the faithful."

In a new administration forthrightly dedicated to the pursuance of a major readjustment of the governmental mechanism—indeed, a sweeping reorientation of the moral and political climate of the nation—such reticence was unprecedented. One can only judge that, if the comparatively vast managerial experience of the new heads of office resulted in almost a textbook concern for the niceties of administrative transition, their relative innocence, especially that of Eisenhower himself, in the methods of rough and tumble partisan maneuver left their political rear almost completely unguarded. Important also was the new president's view of Congress as a partner rather than antagonist in the political process. Possessing what biographer Robert J. Donovan has described as a "traditionalist's conception of the separation of powers," Eisenhower then and frequently since has referred to himself as a "Constitutional President."[8] All this merely underlined the essentially conservative nature of the new administration from a constitutional point of view, as well as the difficulties inherent in a political position which, while avowing a desire for great changes, implicitly disavows many of the means by which they might be accomplished.

The men around the President. Though the Eisenhower regime was justly described from the beginning as a "business administration," the Democratic characterization of the Cabinet as "nine millionaires and a plumber" was overdrawn. Nevertheless, the political experience of Postmaster General Summerfield, Secretary of Commerce Weeks, and ex-Governor of Oregon and Secretary of the Interior Douglas McKay,

---

[6] For a most perceptive analysis of the changeover, emphasizing also its effects upon the civil service, see Herman M. Somers, "The Federal Bureaucracy and the Change of Administration," *American Political Science Review*, XLVIII (March, 1954), 131.

[7] See the introductory sections of ch. xiii.

[8] As cited in footnote 1, p. 83.

the legal backgrounds of Secretary of State John Foster Dulles and Attorney General Herbert Brownell, the professional experience in religious affairs of Secretary of Agriculture Ezra Taft Benson, and the newspaper holdings of the new Secretary of Health, Education, and Welfare, Oveta Culp Hobby, did not disguise the predominantly private enterprise orientation of the group. The appointment of George M. Humphrey and Charles E. Wilson, both distinguished business leaders, to the crucial posts of Secretary of the Treasury and Secretary of Defense only emphasized the point, which Wilson quickly underscored before a congressional committee with an unguarded remark that was easily twisted into "What is good for General Motors is good for the country." All in all, it was a traditional Republican cabinet, distinguished primarily for its forthrightness and teamwork. Though it espoused a crusade, its members, individually, could hardly be classed as crusaders. These were no Brain Trusters or New Dealers appealing to the educated youth of the nation in the manner of F. D. R. and his cohorts. True, a mildly successful effort had been made by Eisenhower, and especially by his controversial Vice-President, Richard M. Nixon, to capture the voters who had grown up since the Great Depression. But there was little attempt to bring them into the government. Instead, the Under Secretary of the Interior announced in late 1953, evidently with some pride, that he had got rid of "a group of Ph.D.'s from Harvard and Columbia." [9] The general complexion of the new Republican administration was middle-aged and often anti-intellectual.

While much the same could be said for President Truman's entourage, there was, nevertheless, a distinct difference in tone. The new White House staff, under the watchful eye of chief-of-staff Adams, was more serious, much more formal and anonymous, and certainly less salted with political characters of the type of Harry H. Vaughan.[10] Above all, the President was concerned that the new administration avoid the corruption and cronyism which had from time to time plagued the Truman administration. As early as January 12, at the

9 As quoted from the *Washington Post*, September 29, 1953, in Somers, as cited in footnote 6, p. 146. In the new administration, notes Somers, "These people—'egg heads' is now the accepted term—are not in good standing." Same. Here the contrast between the Eisenhower administration and that of the two Roosevelts is clear and sharp.

10 For analyses of White House personalities and the operations of the well-known Eisenhower executive staff system, see Donovan, as cited in footnote 1, chs. i, ii, and v; Pusey, as cited in footnote 2, chs. iii and iv; Jay Franklin (pseudonym of John Franklin Carter), *Republicans on the Potomac* (New York: The McBride Co., 1953); and Richard E. Neustadt, "The Presidency at Mid-Century," a paper presented before the annual meeting of the American Political Science Association, Washington, D.C., September 8, 1956, and "Presidency and Legislation: The Growth of Central Clearance," *American Political Science Review*, XLVIII (September, 1954), 664–71.

Hotel Commodore meeting with his cabinet-elect, Eisenhower firmly laid down the rule that anyone who claimed his friendship should be denied consideration for appointment.[11] Even before that he had caused a thorough check to be made of the personal and political backgrounds of his principal associates-to-be, for he insisted that his appointees' past records be beyond reproach.[12] On February 25, 1953, he instructed his department heads to guard against situations which might promote scandal and he directed the Department of Justice to be alert to questionable practices.[13] The Attorney General soon ordered U.S. Attorneys to cease private law practices, and put an end to secrecy in pardons and all civil cases in which the government took part. Moreover, the power to determine whether defendants were able to stand trial was taken from the Department of Justice and given to the courts. In the manner of Theodore Roosevelt and Coolidge this proscription of favoritism was almost immediately followed up with a series of prosecutions which included a number of prominent Republicans. While the Eisenhower administration has been accused of "giveaways" in its avowed support of private enterprise, there has apparently been little personal peculation of the sort endemic prior to 1953.

The administration was to be plagued, however, with a series of conflict-of-interest cases, commencing with the Senate's adamant position against the confirmation of Wilson as Secretary of Defense unless he divested himself of his General Motors holdings. Much more damaging were the events leading to the resignation of Secretary of the Air Force Harold E. Talbott in the summer of 1955. An even more spectacular case involved the role of Adolphe H. Wenzel, simultaneously a consultant to the Bureau of the Budget and a vice-president of the financial institution backing the controversial Dixon-Yates contract proposals for the support of the T.V.A. by private power. Inept White House management of this affair intensified public criticism, and for a complex of reasons the whole project was dropped. A different but related matter involved the administrator of the General Services Administration, Edmund F. Mansure, who resigned after testifying that "practical politics" had influenced his decision with respect to a large brokerage contract.

The numbers of businessmen associated with the administration as compared to its predecessors intensified this sort of problem and

---

[11] Donovan, as cited in footnote 1, p. 11.
[12] Same, p. 80.
[13] A more general directive went to all agency heads in June, 1954, after some housing scandals. For a brief catalog of the administration's actions in the prosecution and follow-up of various scandals, see Donovan, as cited in footnote 1, pp. 80–82.

483

the inadequacy of many of the relevant conflict-of-interest statutes, to which the Second Hoover Commission later called public attention, left a considerable margin for error. The administration has dealt reasonably firmly with such cases, though in comparison to Theodore Roosevelt, for example, Eisenhower has been slower in action and more reticent in public condemnation of particular individuals. To some extent this has reflected the President's disinclination to engage in personal controversy as well as his stated policy of leaving such matters to his subordinates whenever possible.[14]

On the whole, the political executives of the Eisenhower administration have been reasonably able men, often better known, however, for their administrative skill than their political sensitivity. Many of them, such as Secretary of Defense Wilson, accepted positions of great responsibility at considerable personal sacrifice. Yet, despite its business orientation and Eisenhower's avowed intent to seek the best available talent, the new Republican administration faced almost as many problems as its predecessor in the recruitment of first rate men for top political posts. This difficulty was highlighted by the report of the Second Hoover Commission. But even now, all one can say is that the problem has been well outlined and that considerable attention is being devoted to it by both academicians and administrators, public and private.[15]

Teamwork. The extreme loyalty and effective teamwork of the Eisenhower top executives deserves further emphasis. The President has been able to command as full a measure of devotion as any of his predecessors. The result has been superb staff work, unparalleled in American public administration. Nor has this cooperation been limited to the immediate White House associates of the President. It has been exhibited to a considerable degree on down the line. From time to time the planned insulation of the President from the multitudinous calls on his time has resulted in "Palace Guard" charges against the executive staff, especially by those used to the administrative short-circuiting and free-wheeling often encouraged by Franklin D. Roosevelt. On the other hand, it was the institutionalization of this staff work which did much during the President's illnesses to preserve the administration from the type of political paralysis which developed during the incapacity of President Wilson. But the crucial question in early 1953 was whether this staff system, combined with

---

14 For a more complete analysis of the conflict-of-interest cases during the first term of the Eisenhower administration, see same, ch. xxv.

15 See, for example, John Corson, *Executives for the Federal Service* (New York: Columbia University Press, 1952); and Paul T. David and Ross Pollock, *Executives for Government* (Washington: The Brookings Institution, 1957).

the President's known popularity and his policy of congressional conciliation, would be able to control the turbulent political milieu in which the new administration was quickly immersed.

"The Politics of Revenge" [16]

The answer to this question was only too quick in coming. Despite overwhelming election majorities for Eisenhower, the Republicans held but a bare majority in the House and the Senate. The legislative segment of the new administration was no more united on basic issues than the outgoing one and unaccustomed to the formulation of positive solutions to political problems. Moreover, the Korean conflict and the peccadillos of a number of Truman appointees had generated a considerable number of investigations which the new Congress showed no signs of desiring to drop. Indeed, the Republican campaign promises to "drive the rascals out" and to "clean up the mess in Washington" stimulated the legislative branch to new heights of charges and countercharges, oratory, and inquisitiveness. No sooner had Congress got under way than the Department of State, for example, found itself involved in no less than ten simultaneous investigations.[17] The anticipated honeymoon period, traditional in American politics, simply never arrived. With its political defenses down, the executive branch was quickly hard put to maintain any sort of status as opposed to Congress.

The federal service. The federal service became one of the main objects of contention and controversy. In June and July of 1952, during the Korean conflict, civil positions in the executive branch, both at home and abroad, reached a high point of a little over 2,570,000 persons. With the ebbing of hostilities the total gradually declined slowly until a figure of about 2,530,000 was reached in June, 1953. Thereafter, under the twin emphases of demobilization and economy, the decline was more precipitous, with approximately 150,000 more positions eliminated by June, 1954. Employment levels then remained fairly stable at a figure approximating 2,350,000 for the better part of two years. Finally, in the summer of 1956, after the approval of appropriations for the fiscal year of 1957, the number of positions commenced to rise again, reflecting a more or less normal peacetime increase in federal civil employment.[18]

16 This phrase has been taken from the title of ch. iii of Samuel Lubell's *Revolt of the Moderates* (New York: Harper and Bros., 1956).

17 Donovan, as cited in footnote 1, p. 37.

18 The annual totals in this paragraph were supplied to the writer by the Employment Statistics Office of the U.S. Civil Service Commission. These are revised figures which do

485

The pressure commences. Thus the new administration initially faced a declining job market in the federal service. To an administration dedicated to economy and a curtailment of governmental functions, this was welcome. On the other hand, while many politically undesirable incumbents (from a Republican viewpoint) might be released through reductions-in-force—and some were, though this is difficult to document precisely—such reductions provided little solace for those looking for patronage.

For the holdover bureaucracy, too, the decline in total positions meant uncertainty, a feeling which was greatly heightened by the anticipatory effects of Republican campaign oratory on a civil service, fewer than 6.6 per cent of which had lived through a previous change in party control.[19] The Republicans were challenging not only the size of the service, but also its loyalty and its neutrality.

Thus the federal service of 1953, contrary to that of the years immediately previous, was to come under *both* executive and legislative attack on the triple grounds of economy, partisanship, and loyalty. With its defenses modest at best, it is no wonder that the period commencing with November, 1952, has been termed "The Time of the Jitters" for the federal bureaucracy.[20]

Economy, Reorganization, and Reductions-in-Force

While the curtailment of federal functions proved disappointingly difficult for the Republicans, the gradual liquidation of Korean defense agencies made possible much of the steady decline in positions noted above. Commencing with the creation of the new Department of Health, Education, and Welfare in the spring of 1953, a series of

---

not entirely match those in the annual reports of the Commission. The totals of federal civil employment exclude the civil personnel employed in the judicial and legislative branches. During the period from 1950 through 1956 these approximated an annual average of 4,400 for the judicial branch and 22,000 for the legislative branch. See the Commission's *Monthly Report of Employment* for a few more precise estimates for particular dates and for monthly totals for the calendar year of 1956. Uncompensated employees, also omitted from civil employment totals, averaged about 80,000 during 1950 and 100,000 during 1956.

19 From a survey made by the Civil Service Commission in 1950, as reported by then-Chairman Robert Ramspeck. USCSC, *Press Release*, November 26, 1952. The same survey also indicated that the average length of service of federal civil employees was nine years.

20 Somers, as cited in footnote 6, p. 131. It should be noted, however, that the available evidence, though scanty, suggests that federal employees, despite Republican campaign promises, supported President Eisenhower at the polls in about the same proportion as the voting population as a whole. In Washington the popular hypothesis is that federal employees tend to vote against the incumbent administration, whatever its politics. In the 1956 election, for example, the President's majorities declined in the congressional districts immediately surrounding the District of Columbia from the figures of 1952, while they rose in most other places. The voting behavior and political attitudes of public employees need much further study and analysis.

executive reorganization proposals reoriented a number of federal agencies. No less than ten reorganization plans went into effect in the first half of 1953. Not long after, in early 1955, came the report of the Second Hoover Commission. The resultant shuffling about, which continued over a period of years, brought changes which were unquestionably needed. It also brought charges of manipulation for political purposes, which are hard to substantiate but which probably contain some truth.[21]

Manpower utilization. Important, too, for its impact on the service was the almost continuous series of investigations and reports on manpower utilization, especially those stemming from the activities of the House and Senate Committees on Post Office and Civil Service. The work of the committees was often well done and well received. But the tenor of the findings was not always calculated to put the service at ease. The following recommendations, for example, made in August, 1953, by the House Subcommittee on Manpower Utilization were typical:

The subcommittee recommends that the heads of the departments and agencies—
(1) Make an immediate review of the special units within their organization with a view toward their elimination. . . .
(5) Make every effort to instill a profound respect for efficiency and economy at every level of operations. . . .
(7) Make every effort to properly and efficiently administer their personnel programs within present laws, orders, and regulations so as to eliminate abuses, violations, and questionable treatment of the individual Federal employee. In order to accomplish this, it will be necessary to overcome a defeatist attitude on the part of some of the administrators and may require an injection of new blood in positions of administrative authority.[22]

Military and civil-military manpower management. Even the uniformed services came under careful scrutiny. The renascence of the military

---

[21] Joseph Young (ed.), *Federal Employees' News Digest,* VI (April 15, 1957), 2-3, reports, for example, that: "Chairman Johnson of the Senate Post Office and Civil Service Committee has charged that Federal agencies are engaged in inter-city mass transfers of employees in hopes that they would resign and could be replaced by political appointees." The article states that Senator Johnson's information was based on a recent Comptroller General's report indicating that nearly 50 per cent of the 3,500 employees in Grade 7 and above in the Immigration and Naturalization Service had been transferred to other cities during the previous three years. According to Young, James A. Campbell, president of the American Federation of Government Employees, had declared that these mass transfers were for the purpose of forcing older workers to retire so that they could be replaced. All this is suggestive of patronage, but not conclusive.

[22] U.S. Congress, House, Committee on Post Office and Civil Service, Subcommittee on Manpower Utilization, *Study of Civilian Manpower Utilization in the Federal Government: Preliminary Report,* 83d Cong., 1st Sess., Subcommittee print, August 9, 1953 (Washington: Government Printing Office, 1953), pp. 10-11. This is only one of a whole series of such documents put out at this time, many of which provide detailed information on the workings of departmental management, especially personnel management.

487

during Korea, the fact that approximately one-half of the federal civil service was employed in the Department of Defense, and the overwhelming proportion of the budget assigned to military expenditures all caused Congress, as well as the executive branch, to commence one of the most extensive arrays of examinations of military and civil-military organization, manpower utilization, and personnel practices in our history. To some extent, this activity was a carry-over from the last years of the Truman administration; but it received a new impetus with the receipt of the Rockefeller report on April 11, 1953, which was followed by a major reorganization of the armed services.[23] The massive and complex interrelationships of the great civil and military personnel systems, one based on rank-in-the-job and the other on rank-in-the-man, began for the first time to receive serious and long overdue attention, which culminated in a special report of the Second Hoover Commission on personnel problems in the Department of Defense.

Some results. Out of all these investigations a good deal of legislation was to come, involving both civilian and military personnel. Some of the reports were highly critical and reminded one of the rather narrow approach to economy and efficiency characterizing the twenties. But many others produced forward and positive results. While Congress may be heavily censured for many things during the first two years of the Eisenhower administration, it deserves praise for its attitude toward executive reorganization and its detailed and often searching consideration of many personnel and manpower problems. One can credit these reports with considerable stimulation of systematic manpower planning, something which had never really been done throughout most of the federal civil service. However, this constant hum of activity on the manpower and organization front gave the federal service little chance to rest and catch its breath. The implicit and explicit criticism involved in these endeavors unquestionably contributed something to the very evident drop in morale during the calendar years of 1953 and 1954.

The Patronage

As if it were not enough for many civil servants to face unemployment as a result of economy cuts and reorganizations, there was a

---

23 On this and related topics see Timothy W. Stanley, *American Defense and National Security* (Washington: Public Affairs Press, 1956). The Rockefeller report was preceded by a few weeks by Truman's Sarnoff Commission report on military manpower utilization. U.S. Congress, Senate, Committee on Armed Services, *Sarnoff Commission Report*, 83d Cong., 1st Sess., Committee print (Washington: Government Printing Office, 1953). The Sarnoff group had not met, however, until after the November, 1952, elections. This commission's main recommendation was a general 10 per cent cut in defense personnel and expenditures.

THREE VIEWS OF PATRONAGE

From *New York Times Magazine*, July 5, 1953.

**Chipping Off
the Barnacles**

Ralph Yoes in
San Diego Union.

**The Last Days
of Sitting Pat**

Bert Whitman in
Stockton Daily Record.

**Civil Service
or
Self-Service?**

Robert York in
Louisville Times.

renascence of spoils system tactics during the first two years of the new regime. From a Republican point of view, the whole civil service was suspect. The campaign of 1952 had been based upon an assumption of widespread corruption and disloyalty, and Republican leaders felt that a general housecleaning was imperative.

The situation in January, 1952. But housecleaning was difficult when approximately 85 per cent of a total of 2,500,000 civil servants were under the tenure protection of the merit system. Another 10 per cent, and perhaps more, consisted either of persons employed overseas (whose positions were not of much interest from a patronage point of view) or of persons in agencies such as the T.V.A., FBI, and the Department of State, with merit and tenure systems of their own. This meant that in many departments such as Labor, Agriculture, Defense, and Health, Education, and Welfare, there was only a handful of positions lending themselves to partisan appointment. By 1953 perhaps only 15,000 positions were immediately open to free and easy removal for political purposes, though another 50,000 or more offices could be anticipated as terms of office expired or incumbents died or resigned.[24] With total civil employment declining, the picture was depressing from a partisan point of view. From the point of view of the bureaucracy the only bright spots on the horizon in early 1953 were the fact of relatively full employment, which eased much of the pressure for patronage, and the hope that President Eisenhower himself might forestall a full scale spoils raid.

The patronage system under Eisenhower. In general, it is clear that Eisenhower upheld this hope, though by a devious route. His disclaimer of friendship as a qualification for office has already been noted, as well as his agreement with Senator Taft. Moreover, the need to consider problems of patronage often annoyed Eisenhower, and he usually refused to take a direct hand either in setting forthright limits to patronage or in managing it. This, together with a lack of coordination, especially noticeable for several months during 1953, between the White House and the Republican National Committee, combined to fragment the dispensation of patronage under the Eisenhower administration so that it has never had the central focus which was so obvious in the person of Jim Farley under F.D.R.

Certainly Eisenhower opposed any major overturn of the merit system, and on at least one recorded occasion firmly rejected a proposal by Deputy Secretary of Defense Roger M. Kyes that every department head be given authority to remove 10 per cent of his em-

---

24 For the calculations on which this figure is based, see the previous chapter, p. 443 and note 105.

ployees without regard to regulations then on the books.[25] On the other hand, Eisenhower had never up to 1958 taken a firm stand as to where the patronage should end and the merit system begin.

At the beginning, the center of political clearance for top posts lay with Sherman Adams, and for the most part it remained there. Summerfield, the Republican National Chairman during the election, went to the office of Postmaster General, but, unlike Farley, relinquished his party post. Not until Leonard W. Hall assumed the chairmanship in the spring of 1953 was there effective National Committee leadership. One of Hall's first actions was to propose not only that the National Committee be given a more active part in dispensing patronage, but also that patronage be used more tellingly to support the administration's program. To this the President, with reservations, agreed; but little was actually done to ease the plight of the new National Chairman during 1953. Adams maintained his grip on appointments, frequently acting as a buffer between department heads and Congress. Hall finally protested in July, 1953, that he could not find six members of Congress indebted to the new administration for appointments. Yet by 1955 it was reported that nearly 70,000 positions had been filled through the White House patronage mechanism.[26] Though some positions have probably been counted more than once as a result of being filled more than once, this figure accounts for nearly all the jobs available for partisan appointment. The pickings for the National Committee have thus been the leanest in history.[27] Congress, too, continually complained of a paucity of political posts and, while not often contesting Eisenhower's nominees as it had those of President Truman, was to remain disgruntled. Certainly the decline of Republican congressional representation in 1954 and the spectacular failure of the President to carry Congress with him in 1956 indicated a basic weakness in the Republican organizational machinery, caused in part by the administration's failure fully to consider political means as well as ends.

Political appointments in the departments. Actually, most top posts were filled through the efforts of major department heads, with congressmen, governors, National Committee members, and others bringing their problems directly to them and with Sherman Adams frequently serving as umpire. At a cabinet meeting on October 30, 1953,

25 Donovan, as cited in footnote 1, p. 170.

26 For the White House patronage mechanism, see same, pp. 96–101.

27 *Time* reported on June 7, 1954, for example, "To date the National Committee has placed only 2,500 of the faithful in good jobs (*i.e.*, jobs paying $5000 to $7000, and requiring no technical or professional skill), a paltry percentage of the payroll and a figure which one single California-sized state would have sniffed at in the good old days." "Politics Without Patronage," LXIII (June 7, 1954), 23.

the President noted that this was with his express approval.[28] As might be expected, this resulted in a most uneven personnel policy with respect to political appointments and removals.

Secretary of the Treasury Humphrey made it clear at the very beginning that he assumed that Treasury employees were loyal and would be cooperative. By contrast, Secretary of Commerce Weeks was distinctly suspicious and almost immediately found himself embroiled in the unfortunate Astin case, in which the head of the National Bureau of Standards was threatened with dismissal for not trimming his scientific judgments to the whims of the marketplace.[29] Secretary of State Dulles was ambivalent, stating in a widely quoted remark that his department consisted "as a whole" of loyal Americans.[30] Nor did he support Robert L. Johnson as new head of the International Information Administration in his "Voice of America fight" with Senator McCarthy and others.[31] At both the cabinet and sub-cabinet levels there was much frank distrust of the permanent service. However, as department heads and their chief assistants became acclimated to the facts of political life, reconciled to the idea that more business in government was not enough, and directly acquainted with the great competence and ability of many higher civil servants such as Dr. Astin, this distrust died down and was probably no more widespread than usual by, say, 1955.

From a patronage point of view, the Eisenhower department heads were as a group a distinct disappointment to many Republican politicians. Leonard Hall discovered to his dismay one day, for example, that, of five prospective appointees whom department heads had asked him to clear with local political leaders, all were Democrats.[32] Secretary of Agriculture Benson and Secretary of Defense Wilson were frequently criticized for not paying enough attention to political requirements. Considered altogether, the patronage and employment policy picture at the departmental level reflected a good deal of confusion, with department heads caught between their desire for competent men and the demands of practical politics. Herman Somers' 1953 conclusion seems justified that "there is little evidence to support

28 Donovan, as cited in footnote 1, p. 11.

29 For a brief summary of this case, involving an important scientific position, see Pusey, as cited in footnote 2, pp. 71–73. After heavy criticism Weeks retreated, Assistant Secretary Craig R. Sheaffer who had stirred up the imbroglio left for home, and Astin was left firmly in his position.

30 As quoted in John Osborne, "Is the State Department Manageable?" *Fortune*, LV (March, 1957), 267. This article is an excellent summary of the development of State Department personnel and managerial policies in recent years, a subject which is only touched on in this study.

31 Martin Merson, Johnson's executive officer, has documented this dismal story in *The Private Diary of a Public Servant* (New York: The Macmillan Co., 1955).

32 Donovan, as cited in footnote 1, p. 100.

the view that desire for patronage, in the raw sense, has motivated department heads, despite intense pressure from sections of Congress." [33]

The Willis Directive. Finally in May, 1954, the so-called "Willis Directive" was issued in an effort to coordinate the distribution of the patronage. It consisted of two mimeographed booklets, titled "Operation People's Mandate," which outlined a new plan for handling top appointments. Designed in the office of Charles F. Willis, Jr., an assistant to Sherman Adams, the new program provided for a special assistant in each department and agency to control vacancies in both the higher competitive and political posts by reporting them to the Republican National Committee. The Committee was to be given time to recommend candidates with satisfactory political clearances. The plan was put into effect but, remarkably, did not come to general public notice until Jerry Kluttz broke the story in October, 1954, in the *Washington Post and Times Herald*.[34]

A storm of criticism arose. In a press conference held shortly thereafter the President avowed his support of the new plan, but indicated that it was not intended to apply to any offices within the competitive system. There is no evidence, however, that the Willis Directive was thus amended, and the system had not been formally abolished by early 1958. This attempt to set up a triple personnel system in federal agencies was confusing to both the civil service and the general public. There were special assistants for patronage, security officers applying the loyalty and security statutes, and the regular agency personnel offices handling routine personnel matters. In addition, there was often a battery of manpower utilization analysts. As an administrative solution to the problem of distributing the patronage,

---

[33] As cited in footnote 6, p. 146. There is a vast literature, pro and con, concerning the patronage policies of the Eisenhower administration, varying from the profound concern of Herbert Hollander as expressed in his *Crisis in the Civil Service* (Washington: Current Issues Publishers, 1955) to Arthur S. Flemming's optimistic "The Civil Servant in a Period of Transition," *Public Administration Review*, XIII (Spring, 1953), 73. For one of the better summaries of the patronage problem by early 1955, see Martin Packman, "Government Jobs," *Editorial Research Reports*, 1955-I (May 18, 1955), 359. Packman documents fairly well some of the congressional opinion.

[34] Kluttz' regular civil service column in this newspaper and his *Federal Employee Newsletter* (first published in early 1949), together with Joseph Young's column in the *Washington Star*, Young's *Federal Employees' News Digest* (started in August, 1951) and his *Federal Employees Almanac* (issued yearly since 1954), and John Cramer's column in the *Washington Daily News*, provide major sources of current and detailed information concerning the federal civil service, particularly for the post–World War II period. The vast clipping file of the U.S. Civil Service Commission Library, which goes back to the time of William McKinley and which contains most of these columns, is unique as a documentary source for the public service. See also the Commission's mammoth cumulative bibliography, the most important and inclusive now available in the field of personnel management, public or private, entitled *A Bibliography of Public Personnel Administration Literature*, and first published by the Commission's Library in 1949, with annual supplements since that date. The writer is more indebted to these sources than his notes can possibly indicate.

the Willis proposal had some merit. Most of this was siphoned off, however, by inept handling. Despite the President's statement supporting the merit system, the secretiveness surrounding the plan and the uncertainty of its application gave the impression—probably a correct one—that this was a thinly veiled raid on the federal service. Moreover, it proved difficult for the Republican National Committee to supply many of the high level scientific, professional, and administrative officials which were most in demand.[35]

The patronage at lower levels. In a report to the Senate Committee on Post Office and Civil Service, James R. Watson, Executive Director of the nonpartisan National Civil Service League, analyzed the patronage situation at the lower levels in early 1957 as follows:

While the use of the Willis plan in some of the major departments was limited, this was apparently not so true in non-Cabinet organizations. Whether or not the exact Willis procedure is being followed, there is persuasive evidence that in several of the independent and regulatory agencies, political clearance is required for appointment and promotions even below grade 14 and that the special assistants dominate the management, with the personnel directors relegated to strictly routine duties.

This report is not intended as a list of suspicious political activity nor as a collection of rumors and tales of individual scandals. There is, however, sufficient material to cause concern about the managing of personnel of the Housing and Home Finance Agency. Among technically experienced individuals in this agency there has been a high turnover and politics has so affected the overall picture that the technical phases of administering personnel in HHFA are under suspicion and ridicule. There is also evidence that in some of the regulatory agencies there are serious problems of personnel and staffing concerning both regular career persons and nonstatus people in the legal and professional groups. For instance, regional directors in the National Labor Relations Board (which are career positions) have been subjected to some degree of political clearance in the geographic areas where the offices are located. One vacancy remained open many months, allegedly because the Republican Senator from the State where the office is located wanted leading industries to agree on a candidate. There are also reports indicating that some sort of political clearance of appointments was a regular feature of the general reorganizing of the NLRB.[36]

All this was nothing very new, however. With each change in party control since before World War I the personnel of the independent

35 For the most complete analysis of the content and history of the Willis Directive, see U.S. Congress, Senate, Committee on Post Office and Civil Service, *Administration of the Civil Service System*, 85th Cong., 1st Sess., Committee print No. 2, 1957 (Washington: Government Printing Office, 1957), pp. 27–36 and 83–144. The bulk of this report on the federal service, one of the more significant efforts of the Senate committee, was prepared by James R. Watson, Executive Director of the National Civil Service League, who was employed during the winter of 1956–57 as a special consultant to the committee.

36 Same, p. 34.

regulatory agencies have been selected with an eye to the economic and political orientation of the party in power. On this score the Eisenhower administration has been no worse, and perhaps even a little more self-denying, than some of its predecessors. When one considers that the evidence favors Postmaster General Summerfield's statement before the Senate Post Office and Civil Service Committee on February 7, 1955, that there had been less politics in the postal service than in any previous period, the "raw patronage" picture, to use Somers' term again, was much less damaging than many had feared it would be.[37]

The line between the political and permanent services. Most of the activity described above took place outside the confines of the merit system. What was happening meanwhile to the traditional distinction between the political and permanent services?

The new administration was prepared to sponsor and to implement a more positive personnel program, though whether it cleared up or blurred the distinction even more is a matter of argument. The membership of the Civil Service Commission was not fully reconstituted until the end of April, 1953. Once this was done the President quickly moved by executive order on May 1 to redesign the relationship of the Civil Service Commission to the chief executive. All vestiges of the Liaison Office for Personnel Management in the White House were abolished. Philip Young, former dean of the Graduate School of Business at Columbia University and the new Chairman of the Commission, received the new title of Presidential Adviser on Personnel Management. He was, in addition, invited to attend cabinet meetings and to serve as the President's right-hand man with respect to federal personnel matters. All this was in line with the intent of the First Hoover Commission and most similar study groups. But it did raise the question of whether, under such an arrangement, the Commission could adequately perform its traditional watchdog function.

This question assumed even greater importance when an executive order of March 31, 1953, inaugurated the new and highly controversial *Schedule C* of "Positions of a confidential or policy determining character." [38] Actually, this was a long overdue step toward a more

---

[37] Charges against Summerfield have not stood up well thus far. See, for example, an address by Civil Service Commissioner George M. Moore before the annual convention of the National Association of Postmasters, Kentucky chapter, Lexington, Kentucky, May 17, 1954. USCSC, *Press Release*, May 14, 1954.

[38] See USCSC, *Seventieth Report*, 1953, pp. 2–3; and Flemming, as cited in footnote 33, pp. 75–76. Essentially, *Schedule C* was carved out of the old *Schedule A*, which had consisted of policy-making and other positions, appointment to which did not require examination. The new *Schedule A* retained the "other positions," which consisted mainly of those for which examinations were considered impractical. *Schedule B*, consisting of positions subject to noncompetitive examination, remained the same.

precise identification of policy-making posts unsuitable for inclusion in the permanent service. It had the blessing of the Civil Service Commission and Arthur S. Flemming, and was approved in general outline by the Second Hoover Commission.[39]

Although the Civil Service Commission promised from the beginning that "only a relatively small number of Federal positions will be placed in this schedule," the uncertain patronage policy of the new administration made this proposal suspect, and it received a good deal of criticism of an anticipatory sort. Actually, by October 11, 1954, for example, no more than 1,127 positions had been placed within the new category, though agency heads had sought exemption for more than double that number.[40] Approximately 52 per cent of the positions in the new schedule consisted of transferrals from *Schedules A* and *B* (very few from the latter, however), 23 per cent were new positions, and 25 per cent were transferrals from the competitive service.[41] Most of the argument lay over these latter positions, and the Task Force on Personnel and Civil Service of the Second Hoover Commission was to term these exclusions from the merit system as "the most significant cut-back of the competitive service in its history." [42] As many relatively high posts were involved, this was in a sense true, though President McKinley's withdrawals from the competitive service far exceeded the total number of posts involved here. The schedule was also criticized—this time on more solid ground —for containing a number of lower level jobs, where the connection to policy seemed remote. Nevertheless, the new development was on the whole an advance in clarifying the relationship between political and nonpolitical executives. That the move was stimulated by the concern of a new administration to enable its top political executives quickly to bring around them a few persons of their own choosing, without going through the strict and often time-consuming merit system procedures, fanned controversy but did not make the step any less rational.

Considerably more spectacular was the President's decision, also on March 31, 1953, to cancel the removal protection of federal employees

---

[39] For an extensive discussion of the fact and theory of *Schedule C*, as well as the history of the problems involved, see Commission on Organization of the Executive Branch of the Government, *Task Force Report on Personnel and Civil Service* (Washington: Government Printing Office, 1955), pp. 35–38 and Appendix B. This study will henceforth be cited as the "*Task Force Report on Personnel*," and its authors as the "Second Hoover Commission."

[40] See same, p. 36; and, for example, USCSC, *Press Release*, January 5, 1954, which indicated that, as of that date, 868 positions had been placed in *Schedule C* as opposed to 810 rejections.

[41] USCSC, *Seventy-first Report*, 1954, p. 9.

[42] *Task Force Report on Personnel*, as cited in footnote 39, p. 192.

serving in *Schedule A* posts. This action involved 134,000 full-time positions and was widely advertised as opening the patronage floodgates.[43] But the case is not quite so clear. Approximately half of the personnel in the 134,000 posts still retained the removal protection of the Veterans' Preference Act of 1944. Moreover, 68,000 *Schedule A* positions were overseas and not much subject to patronage pressure. If one exempts a few other minor categories of employees also not affected, only some 30,000 persons occupying domestic posts never under the merit system in the first place were potentially affected.

What the President had done was to retract the removal protection given by President Truman in 1947 to persons with competitive status who had, for one reason or another, accepted positions outside the merit system. The executive order of March 31, 1953, merely "restored *Schedule A* to where it was prior to 1947." [44] The Civil Service Commission had recommended the order in part because it felt "that it was inequitable to afford protection against removal and thus tie the hands of an agency head in vacating *Schedule A* jobs when he had complete freedom of choice of appointment." [45] Here the Commission came perhaps as close as any time in its history at conniving at a patronage grab. The Commission further argued, with justification, that there should be some distinction with respect to removal protection as between persons in career posts and those, whatever their original type of appointment, in excepted positions.

From time to time there was criticism of specific Commission actions in assigning particular positions or groups of positions to the various *Schedules A, B,* and *C.* These actions were reminiscent of a few similar removals of full merit system protection made by Franklin D. Roosevelt in the middle thirties, though in the earlier cases the Civil Service Commission itself was not directly involved. The reasons, for instance, for placing state directors of the Farmers Home Administration of the Department of Agriculture in *Schedule A* in 1953 are obscure. There was more justice in moving the positions of field deputy marshals from the competitive service to *Schedule B* in late 1954, but the decision was heavily criticized.[46]

One cumulative effect of these changes was to dampen the ardor of

43 See James M. Burns, "Policy and Politics of Patronage," *The New York Times Magazine* (July 5, 1953), 8. "Now President Eisenhower is breaking the patronage log jam," he stated. "His recent Executive Order withdraws about 134,000 Federal positions from civil service."

44 See the Commission's *Press Release,* July 8, 1953, entitled "Questions and Answers Concerning Persons Serving in Schedule A Positions." At this time approximately 50 per cent of the civil service consisted of veterans.

45 Same.

46 See, for example, Hollander, as cited in footnote 33, p. 4. For the Commission's justification, see its *Press Release* on the subject, December 27, 1954.

those who had pressed for more direct presidential control of federal personnel management. The position of the Chairman of the Civil Service Commission as a close adviser to the President with near-cabinet status was to rebound to the benefit of the permanent service through the new administration's legislative program for that service. But the chairman's status between 1953 and 1958 made it difficult for him or the Commission as a whole to maintain, much less publicly exercise, a critical attitude toward patronage maneuvers which might involve the permanent service. The anomalous position of the chairman was emphasized in February, 1957, when Chairman Young, with the President's authorization, requested cabinet officers and agency heads again to list career jobs which they felt ought to be taken out of the competitive service and placed in the political categories. The propriety of issuing such a request under the signature of the Chairman of the Civil Service Commission was widely questioned.[47]

In addition, the chairman's overriding control of the administrative affairs of the Commission since 1949 has made it doubtful whether the type of informal but effective leadership typically exerted before 1949 by the minority party member of the Commission, usually an expert in personnel matters of the caliber of, say, Leonard D. White or Arthur S. Flemming, would again be possible. After Philip Young's resignation as chairman in the spring of 1957, for example, the Commission's chief residue of expertise again rested with the minority party member, Frederick J. Lawton, former Director of the Bureau of the Budget under President Truman and long-time career civil servant.[48] However, Lawton's position was now one from which it was most difficult to do any leading.

In early 1957 James R. Watson, writing both as Executive Director of the National Civil Service League and as a congressional consultant, argued for the return of the Civil Service Commission to something resembling its traditional semi-independent position and the creation of a new Office of Personnel Management in the White House, as a sort of personnel equivalent of the Bureau of the Budget.[49] Apparently influenced by this and similar arguments, the administration modified its top-level personnel mechanism in the fall of 1957.

---

[47] Young explained later that the intent of the letter was to carry out certain recommendations of the Second Hoover Commission concerning the separation of political and career executives. However, the fact that the letter did quote the Hoover Commission almost verbatim was not enough to stifle criticism. See the *Federal Employees' News Digest*, VI (March 11, 1957), 1–2; and the *New York Times*, March 1, 1957, sec. C-12, p. 1.

[48] Both Young and George M. Moore, the two Republican commissioners, were replaced at the same time in 1957 by new commissioners, neither one of which was known for his personnel experience.

[49] U.S. Congress, Senate, Committee on Post Office and Civil Service, as cited in footnote 35, pp. 41–53.

Then Rocco C. Siciliano, former civil servant, lawyer, and industrial relations expert, was appointed to the new post of presidential Special Assistant for Personnel Management. To all intents and purposes, the administration had returned by the end of 1957 to the type of tripartite top-level personnel management relationship which had characterized most of the period between 1939 and 1953. Sherman Adams and the National Committee controlled the patronage; Siciliano functioned as had the earlier Liaison Officer for Personnel Management; and the Chairman of the Civil Service Commission served both as a staff adviser to the President and as operating head of his agency. This arrangement has always been criticized for its failure to pinpoint responsibility for federal personnel management as a whole. The argument over the proper organization for top-level federal personnel management seemed likely to continue unabated as of early 1958.

Congress and the patronage. Congressional attitudes toward the patronage followed traditional lines after 1952. The Republican legislators, in control of Congress from 1953 to 1955, promptly requested the Civil Service Commission to publish the usual "Plum Book," which listed the positions potentially open to political appointment.[50] Democratic congressmen, playing the usual role of the minority party, became the upholders of merit. When the Democrats assumed control of the legislative branch in 1955 a steady stream of criticism of Republican patronage and personnel policies poured forth, as much from partisan sentiments as from any abiding love for merit.

Nevertheless, the legislative branch refrained from overt raids on the permanent service. There were no significant attempts to extend the principle of senatorial confirmation beyond traditional boundaries. Nor was there restrictive legislation, typical of the middle thirties, which barred the President from issuing orders to include newly created positions in the competitive service. In addition, the period from 1953 into 1957 was to inaugurate a good many legislative measures of benefit to the federal service.

At no time, however, did Republican congressmen become reconciled to the patronage distribution policy—or lack of it—pursued by the executive branch. This policy was a constant bone of contention with the White House. The Willis Directive was unquestionably in part conceived as a means to quiet the discord. Nevertheless, by early 1958, the Eisenhower administration still had not solved either the

---

50 U.S. Congress, Senate, Committee on Post Office and Civil Service, *Positions Not Under the Civil Service*, 83rd Cong., 1st Sess., Senate Doc. 18, Parts I and II (Washington: Government Printing Office, 1953). The Commission apparently refused, however, to accede to the Senate's request for a list of some 125,000 positions paying $4,200 or more and filled by indefinite employees.

political or administrative problems of patronage distribution. The Second Hoover Commission was soon to highlight the now endemic difficulties in recruiting political executives, but, interestingly enough, up into 1958 no one had seen fit to consider the problem of *administering* the patronage as worthy of a major research effort.[51] The tendency of academicians and reformers to concentrate a great deal of their efforts at political analysis and prescription on the ideas of political neutrality and non-partisanship is to be regretted. The President of the American Political Science Association for 1956-57, E. E. Schattschneider, wrote in 1948:

. . . It was the professors who invented and popularized the idea of non-partisanship, a Nirvana in which all good citizens act like college professors who are afraid of losing their jobs. . . . The assumption is that people who do not take sides are morally superior to people who do, . . .

. . . .

Political scientists have not produced a theory of political action, nor have they destroyed the wicked and stupid anti-political superstitions which confuse and inhibit the natural leaders of the community.[52]

These conclusions are still quite relevant a decade later.

Indeed, it is reasonable to suggest that the failure of the Eisenhower regime to face the problem of patronage in a forthright and determined manner was to some extent responsible for the bitter and often indiscriminate new waves of legislative attacks on the civil service which followed the 1952 election. Congress, too, was under a mandate to "clean up the mess in Washington."

Loyalty and Security

Congressional distrust of the bureaucracy was reflected in the economy and efficiency moves already recorded. But the most devastating blows came from a legislative concern, by no means limited to Republicans, over the twin issues of loyalty and security.

Executive Order 10450. From the beginning, Eisenhower, as had Truman, considered these matters as essentially the concern of the executive branch. Therefore, it was with no hesitation that he pro-

---

[51] The most recent study of the patronage as a political problem is contained in both editions of the American Assembly's *The Federal Government Service* (New York: Columbia University, 1954), pp. 81–112. This analysis by Harvey C. Mansfield, under the title of "Political Parties, Patronage, and the Federal Government Service," is by far the best on the subject now in print. Nevertheless, Mansfield did not attack the problem of the administration of patronage, nor did he propose solutions to the important issues he raised. Much more needs to be done.

[52] *The Struggle for Party Government* (College Park, Maryland: University of Maryland, 1948), pp. 6–7.

mulgated Executive Order 10450 on April 27, 1953, and set in motion the main reorganization of the loyalty and security program since 1947.

Under the terms of President Truman's loyalty program, there had been separate procedures for the determination of loyalty, security, and suitability. Early in 1952 the Interdepartmental Committee on Internal Security had pointed out that it was almost impossible to draw clear lines of demarcation among these procedures. The Republican administration accepted this point of view, and the new executive order provided for merging these programs, this time primarily under the authority of the Summary Dismissal Statute of 1950.[53] The Truman Loyalty Review Board and the regional boards were abolished, and a decentralized program was put into effect. Each agency head was given complete responsibility for the security of his own organization. The new effort was to be based around a more stringent standard; namely, whether the employment of an individual was "clearly consistent with the interests of the national security." [54]

At the departmental level procedures varied somewhat, but, in general, an employee undergoing investigation was to be informed of the charges against him and given the opportunity of requesting a hearing. Hearings were to be held before boards consisting of employees of agencies other than the one to which the person concerned belonged. Board decisions were to be advisory to a department head, with the latter's decision final. The investigative system set up under the Truman administration was largely continued. To provide some sort of overall control, the Civil Service Commission was required to make a continuing study of the program with periodic reports to the National Security Council. The Commission was also directed to maintain a security-investigations index covering all persons investigated by any department or agency. A year later the President required all agencies to report to the Commission the action taken in each individual case.[55]

By his new program the President sought to take the initiative from all too eager congressional hands, and simultaneously to strengthen the government's hand in protecting itself against subversion and to protect trustworthy employees through better screening and other procedures. This was an ambitious endeavor. It should

---

[53] This statute gave the heads of eleven major agencies the right to dismiss employees summarily in the interests of national security. It also authorized the President to extend its terms to other agencies as necessary, a power which he exercised in Executive Order 10450.

[54] Executive Order 10450.

[55] For literature on the Eisenhower loyalty and security program, see the "supplementary notes" to this chapter.

be noted, however, that the "Eisenhower Security Program," described above, was not the only component of our national security effort. Of unusual summary interest is the following paragraph from the 1956 loyalty-security report of the New York City Bar Association:

> There are now several personnel security programs. One is the program for Federal civilian employees under Executive Order 10450, which is applicable to 2,300,000 persons. A second is the Industrial Security Program of the Department of Defense. It covers the nearly 3,000,000 persons who, as employees of contractors with the military departments, have access to classified information. A third program is that of the Atomic Energy Commission, which extends to its own employees and to those of its contractors' employees who have access to classified information. They come to about 80,000 persons. Then there is the Port Security Program which applies to about 800,000 seamen and long-shoremen. Finally, there is the International Organizations Employees Program which extends to over 3,000 Americans in the employ of these organizations.[56]

In addition, there is the security program for 3,000,000 uniformed military personnel. However, given the orientation of this study, only the Executive Order 10450 program is considered in any detail.

Congressional attitudes. In one sense Executive Order 10450 was a success in forestalling Congress. The loyalty and security effort remained largely an executive program. In another sense, it was a capitulation, albeit one which reflected the 1952 election returns, as the new system implicitly recognized the congressional feeling that the Truman program had been too "soft." In addition, for the better part of two years, Congress was to wreak havoc on the executive branch in general, and on large numbers of individual civil and military employees in particular, through a trying series of legislative hearings and investigations in many of which Senator McCarthy, the new chairman of the powerful Senate Committee on Government Operations and head of its important Permanent Subcommittee on Investigations, played a spectacular part.[57]

It all started with a fight over the appointment of careerist Charles E. Bohlen as ambassador to the Soviet Union, a struggle which the administration won only with the vigorous support of Senator Taft. After this, however, the administration seemed to abandon any effort to checkmate McCarthy, and in succession he and his assistants and supporters plowed a deep furrow through the Department of State,

---

[56] *Report of the Special Committee on the Federal Loyalty-Security Program of the Association of the Bar of the City of New York* (New York: Dodd, Mead and Co., 1956), p. 4.
[57] In 1953 alone, he initiated 157 inquiries. *New York Herald Tribune*, May 3, 1956, sec. 2, p. 12.

the International Information Administration, the Central Intelligence Agency, and, especially, the Department of the Army.[58] The Senator from Wisconsin finally overreached himself in the depressing Army-McCarthy hearings during the summer of 1954, when he openly invited federal employees to feed him information, even in violation of law. While this in turn led to McCarthy's censure by the Senate on December 2, 1954, and to his rapid decline as a dominating figure in the Republican party, the damage had been done. For two years almost no influential member of the administration had effectively supported the federal service against constant and vitriolic attacks. All evidence indicates that by the fall of 1954, the morale of federal civil employees had hit a new low.[59] Typical is the following extract from President Luther Steward's address to the biennial convention of the National Federation of Federal Employees in the fall of 1954: "It is unquestionably a fact that relations between administrators and employees have deteriorated below any point within the past 40 years. . . . Defamation and suspicion had done their work too well. . . ." [60]

Executive policies. But Congress was not alone responsible for this sad state of affairs. The executive branch had almost been outdoing it in a parallel series of controversial actions. Here again, a brief selective catalog is enough. First of all, the new security program required everyone to be cleared all over again. Abraham Chasenow, for twenty-three years an employee in the Hydrographic Office of the Navy, was suspended, dismissed, and then, after public prodding by the *Washington Daily News,* rehired a year later with an apology. Secretary Dulles then dismissed career diplomat John Paton Davies, Jr., after he had been cleared several times previously. In the Ladejinsky case, Secretary of Agriculture Benson fired an employee whom Harold Stassen quickly re-employed. Through all this wound the strands of the complicated J. Robert Oppenheimer case, as a result of which the connection of one of the nation's foremost atomic scientists with the Atomic Energy Commission was severed. This was, as Robert J. Donovan put it, "one of those affairs that go to the root of human conflict." [61] The result

58 For a useful summary of these and related activities, see Donovan, as cited in footnote 1, chs. vi and xviii.

59 This is hard to "prove," but the literature of the period is almost unanimous in regarding 1954 as a twentieth century low point in federal employee morale. For a pair of well-reasoned if mildly opposing points of view, both of which, however, agree on diagnosing an unusually low state of public employee morale through 1953, see Joseph E. McLean, "The Government Climate," and John Gange, "Another View of the Government Climate," in Society for Personnel Administration, *The Federal Career Service,* Pamphlet 8 (Washington: The Society, 1954), pp. 19 and 29, respectively.

60 *The Federal Employee,* XXXIX (October, 1954), 1. Steward had then been head of the NFFE for nearly forty years.

61 As cited in footnote 1, p. 297; see ch. xxi, for the "Ups and Downs of the Security Program."

was as much or more dissatisfaction with the Eisenhower security procedures as had stemmed from Truman's prior efforts.

The President recognized that much of the criticism was justified, and in the summer of 1953 he initiated a series of procedural modifications designed to result in fairer and more consistent management of the security program.[62] Meanwhile, the so-called "numbers game," involving the question of how many persons had been fired for what kind of security reasons, raged through 1954 and 1955. This controversy spotlighted the lumping together of various types of security actions under the Eisenhower program, as well as the likelihood that the number of persons actually dismissed on any particular type of charge during the Eisenhower administration would probably never be known.

Re-examination. The decline of Senator McCarthy and a growing concern over the implications of the security program for the long haul finally resulted in 1955 in a joint resolution of Congress creating a bipartisan Commission on Government Security, known as the Wright Commission. To some extent this removed the controversy from the supercharged atmosphere surrounding the usual congressional investigating body. However, three Senate committees, one House committee, and several citizens groups were also studying various aspects of the security program. The most wide-ranging and searching of these latter inquiries was that instigated by the Bar Association of the City of New York and supported by the Fund for the Republic. The early 1956 report of this investigation called for a more coordinated and centrally directed security system, considerable procedural revision, an even more general standard, and the application of the system solely to sensitive positions.[63] In June, 1956, the U.S. Supreme Court ruled that the President's extension of the Summary Dismissal Statute of 1950 to *all* government posts had been improper since the law applied only to sensitive posts.[64] Immediately, the administration moved to reorganize the security program around a distinction between sensitive and non-sensitive posts, a reform which had often been advocated. Finally, the Wright Commission reported in June, 1957, with the most exhaustive analysis of the federal security program ever made up to that point.

The Wright Commission found that "since the beginning of the current security program established by Executive Order 10450, the

---

62 See especially the seven procedural changes outlined by Attorney General Brownell with Eisenhower's endorsement in early 1955. See the *New York Times*, March 6, 1955, p. 29, for the text of Brownell's directive.

63 As cited in footnote 56. See especially pp. 3–21.

64 *Cole* v. *Young*, 351 U.S. 536 (1956).

vast majority of so-called 'security removals' have in fact been suitability removals, handled under normal civil service or related procedures." [65] The Commission recommended a two-way division of the present security mechanism into (1) a suitability program based on traditional Lloyd-LaFollette Act procedures, and (2) a loyalty program designed with careful regard both for the national security and individual rights. The loyalty standard for refusal of employment or for removal "should be that, on all the information there is reasonable doubt as to the loyalty of the individual to the Government of the United States." [66] This would represent a return to the Truman standard of 1951. An elaborate code of rights and privileges for individuals under investigation was proposed, along with a list of criteria for establishing "reasonable doubt." These suggested criteria included most of those already in use, but added refusal to testify upon the ground of self-incrimination before an authorized inquiry. Finally, the Commission proposed that a new agency, a Central Security Office, be created directly subordinate to the President. This office would serve both as an advisory appeals board and as the administrative mechanism responsible for the uniformity and efficiency of the entire program. The Commission's proposals were received as well or better than most loyalty and security efforts. But to carry out the Commission's suggestions required considerable legislation, and Congress was ready to adjourn just as the report was issued. Moreover, at the same time the Supreme Court issued several decisions concerning various loyalty and security cases, at least one of which created considerable confusion as to the limits of the government's authority with respect to loyalty and security as opposed to an individual's civil rights.[67] At any rate, no action had been taken by early 1958.

While the events associated with the loyalty and security programs of the federal government have deeply disturbed many Americans during the past decade, from a historical point of view, there has

[65] Commission on Government Security, *Report* (Washington: Government Printing Office, 1957), p. 85. In addition to the federal civil personnel security program, the Wright Commission dealt with the programs affecting military personnel, industrial security, port security, employees of international organizations, the classification of documents, passport regulations, and the control of aliens. In addition, the Commission recommended an entirely new security program for the civil air transport system.

[66] Same, p. 41.

[67] In a special statement appended to the end of his Commission's report, Chairman Loyd Wright said: "As this is written to meet a publication deadline, confusion has been compounded by the decision of *Jencks* v. *United States*. When we are striving to survive the insidious attacks of the Kremlin seeking to destroy our government of law, it is disheartening that 'blind justice' is unnecessarily blinded to realism. I respectfully urge the Congress that if we are to keep pace with our enemies who seek to infiltrate our Nation to subvert us, immediate legislation must be passed to negative the grave consequences that will flow from this confusing decision." Same, p. 687. The case in question was decided on June 3, 1957.

been distinct progress. Certainly the Eisenhower security program, while perhaps no less controversial than that of President Truman, is a far cry from the Star Chamber proceedings of the Civil War and even World War I. By 1957 there was every evidence that Congress, the executive branch, and the general public were reconciled to the hard task of sitting down, thinking through, and implementing a security program which might better accomplish the infinitely difficult task of, at one and the same time, protecting individual employees as well as the nation at large.

The Fog Begins to Lift

If the decline of Senator McCarthy in late 1954 was to signal one watershed on the federal employee horizon, a series of events, also dating from 1954, was to suggest the approach of another. Unfortunately, the controversies outlined in the preceding sections were to obscure the new administration's very real accomplishments for the merit system and for civil employees as a whole.

Reorganization of the Civil Service Commission. The new position of the Chairman of the Civil Service Commission has already been noted. This was quickly supplemented by the most sweeping reorganization of the internal managerial mechanism of the Commission ever undertaken. It was a reorganization long overdue, and one which recognized that, if the Commission were to keep pace even with its own avowed program, it must redesign itself accordingly.

The initial move, a reduction in April, 1953, of the Commission's regional offices from fourteen to twelve, was relatively minor, reflecting primarily the agency's contribution to the economy and efficiency effort. The major action came in late August, 1953, involving the entire central office in Washington and to some extent the field service. It consolidated approximately twenty-five line and staff units into twelve, delegated clearcut authority to the Executive Director, greatly reduced the span of control, reemphasized the concept of decentralization with standards, and, for the first time, gave prime roles to research and planning as fundamental tools of Commission programming and management.

More specifically, most of the Commission's Washington divisions and staff units were brought together into five major bureaus: Bureau of Programs and Standards, Bureau of Departmental Operations, Bureau of Field Operations, Bureau of Inspection and Classification Audits, and Bureau of Management Services. Only three staff units continued to function separately, the Office of the General Counsel and the Security Appraisal and Public Information Offices. Brought directly into the office of the Executive Director was the old Federal Personnel Council, redesignated as the Interagency Advisory Group. Reporting directly to the Commission remained the Board of Appeals and Review, the International Organizations Employees Loyalty Board, and the Fair Employment Board. The latter was abolished in 1955 and replaced by the President's Committee on Government Employment Policy. This new committee continued, however, to maintain its headquarters in the Civil Service Commission building and one of its five members has represented the Commission.

As the Commission said in its brochure announcing these changes to its own nearly 5,000 employees, "The new structure more definitely separates (a) the planning, (b) the execution, (c) the control, and (d) the checkup or inspection functions and responsibilities." In turn, the Commission felt, "This will increase our emphasis on the leadership, the planning, and the personnel improvement aspects of the Commission's total responsibilities and give them the attention they deserve." [68] All this was accompanied by a considerable reshuffling of top personnel and the appointment of a new executive director from the career service outside the Commission, John W. Macy, Jr. Chairman Young and Macy were to work unusually effectively together and the combined changes in personnel and organization structure were to impart a new sense of vigor to an agency which had been under attack as a bit "stuffy" and obsessed with details. In November, 1953, the Commission reduced the more than 8,000 post office boards of examiners, many of which were dormant, to approximately 1,100 functioning boards and 2,000 information points.[69] At the same time the functions of the nearly 800 agency boards of examiners were reemphasized and somewhat strengthened as a means of maintaining adequate liaison among Commission staff, agency personnel officers, and operating officials.

This reorganization effort survived a considerable amount of investigation. By 1957 it seemed to be firmly rooted and, as far as a simple reorganization under existing statutes and policy would permit, to meet the needs of the times. The main criticisms were directed at the dual position of the chairman and the seeming inability of some of the staff to reorient themselves to the more positive

---

[68] Both these quotations are from USCSC, *The Reorganization of the Civil Service Commission* (Washington: Government Printing Office, 1953), p. 2. See also USCSC, *Press Release*, August 20, 1953, concerning the reorganization; and USCSC, *Organization and Activities of the United States Civil Service Commission* (Washington: Government Printing Office, 1955). See also the various editions of the *United States Government Organization Manual* for comparisons with earlier organizational systems.

[69] USCSC, *Press Release*, November 3, 1953.

role envisioned by, especially, Chairman Young and his new executive director.[70]

Affirmation of purpose. With the new security program, the creation of *Schedule C,* and its own reorganization well under way by the fall of 1953, the central personnel agency turned its energies toward the formulation of a new action program. The next three years were to see both a mass of forward-looking legislation and a distinct decline in the negative and restrictive approach which had characterized many prior congressional measures.

First of all, the Commission took formal notice of the uneasiness of civil employees throughout the first months of the Eisenhower administration and endeavored to reassure them of the intent of the new regime to respect the career service. At the same time the President increased his public utterances in support of the merit system. On August 20, 1954, he released a letter to Chairman Young expressing his gratification "that during the past eighteen months the career civil service system has met the tests brought about by a change of administration." [71] Emphasizing the 1952 Republican platform promise to bring to the federal service "the best practices of progressive private employers," Eisenhower also outlined in some detail his expectations for the future. He expressed himself as particularly interested in the "creation of a Federal career service dedicated to carrying out effectively the policies and programs of the administration in office regardless of political considerations." This meant in turn, he felt, a strengthened examining and selection program, an improved promotion program, and the stimulation of transfers among the various federal personnel systems. Finally, the President reemphasized his concern to keep politics out of the service, his desire for more clearly defined career opportunities, and his support of the Civil Service Commission's efforts to assist departments and agencies in improving their personnel operations.

This was a comprehensive program, the sincerity of which was hurt by the nearly simultaneous public airing of the Willis Directive. But the date of this letter does more or less coincide with the low point of federal employee morale during the Eisenhower administration. From this point on, the actions, as opposed to the words, of the new administration were to weigh as much in favor of the merit system as they had previously seemed to bear against it.

---

[70] See especially U.S. Congress, House, Committee on Post Office and Civil Service, *United States Civil Service Commission,* 84th Cong., 2d Sess., House Rept. 1844, March 1, 1956 (Washington: Government Printing Office, 1956); and U.S. Congress, Senate, Committee on Post Office and Civil Service, as cited in footnote 35, pp. 11–12 and 41–53.

[71] This and the two following quotations are from USCSC, *Press Release,* November 1, 1954.

The Commission's program for 1954. All through the summer and fall of 1953 legislative and other proposals were developed by the Commission staff and discussed with other governmental agencies and their personnel staffs as well as with employee and veteran organizations. A recommended program was then presented to a subcommittee of the Cabinet, specially designated by the President to consider personnel policies. Most of the program was approved and a few items added, such as a proposal for employee group life insurance. The final recommendations then became part of the President's legislative program, which was in turn cleared with congressional leaders. The result of this precedent shattering effort at coordination of personnel policies was an outstanding success, for most segments of the program were approved by Congress in the spring and summer of 1954.[72]

Of major significance in enabling the federal government to meet its private enterprise competition during a period of continued manpower shortages was a series of new fringe benefits. Group life insurance and unemployment insurance were made available for the first time and on a basis comparable to that in private industry. More equitable overtime and other premium pay rates, as well as an extension of longevity pay increases, some adjustment in minimum pay rates, and uniform allowances, were also provided. The incentive program was considerably broadened and the potential awards greatly increased. Especially welcome was a significant modification of the restrictive provisions of the Thomas Leave Rider on the accumulation of annual leave. The payment by the government of the return travel expenses of all overseas employees and their dependents was authorized. Temporary increases in the annuities of retired employees were made permanent and the survivorship benefit relating to accumulated leave was liberalized. Considered together, these actions comprised the most significant fringe benefits legislation in the history of the federal service. By the end of Eisenhower's first term, the civil service compared well to private industry in such matters.[73]

Nearly 120,000 civil employees were vitally affected by the abolition of the Crafts, Protective, and Custodial (CPC) Schedule of the position-classification system. Approximately 70,000 crafts, trades, and manual labor positions were placed under the wage board prevailing rate system, which meant substantial pay raises for many of the persons

---

[72] On the formation and execution of the Commission's 1954 legislative program see USCSC, *Seventy-first Report*, 1954, pp. 15–26.

[73] For some comparisons as of the winter of 1953–54, see Edith B. Kidney, *Fringe Benefits for Salaried Employees in Government and Industry*, Personnel Report 542 (Chicago: Civil Service Assembly, 1954).

concerned. The remaining 50,000 positions, involving guards, messengers, and firefighters, were placed in the General Schedule (GS), with small increases for many and guarantees against loss in salary for the rest. The action also eliminated some inequities between the blue- and white-collar pay systems, and improved the government's competitive position with industry at lower levels. The legal limit on the number of top super-grade positions was also increased by 150.

While the restrictive Whitten Amendment of 1952 was not repealed, as recommended by the Civil Service Commission, it was considerably modified. The statutory limit on the number of permanent civil servants in the executive branch was upped 10 per cent. This and a few other modifications permitted the Commission to inaugurate a new and badly needed appointment system, the basic ideas for which had been first conceived in the last months of the Truman administration. The Korean conflict, like World War II, had brought in its wake a mass of temporary and indefinite appointments, diluting the permanent service. Early in 1953 the Civil Service Commission had acted to limit the impact of reductions-in-force and to protect employees with permanent status much in the manner employed after World War II. Some twenty tenure groups, which had tended to "bump" each other with chain-reaction effects highly corrosive on employee morale and managerial efficiency, were merged into three. Each of these was subdivided into veterans and non-veterans. The right of veterans to replace non-veterans in the lowest group, consisting of employees without competitive status, was withdrawn; and the geographical limits of "bumping" were curtailed. While there was still considerable dissatisfaction on the part of many employees, the numbers involved were not nearly as great as after World War II; and the system worked reasonably well.[74]

With the modification of the Whitten Amendment in 1954, the Commission again reoriented its appointment and status system.[75] Through Executive Order 10577, effective January 23, 1955, the three categories were redefined as "indefinite," "career-conditional," and "career"; and the system was extended to include many more personnel actions than merely reductions-in-force. By this time more than 670,000 employees, 34 per cent of the permanent service, were still in the indefinite category. Those who had at some point qualified

---

[74] For a perceptive discussion of this problem as well as that of the patronage during early 1953, by the Washington correspondent of the London *Economist*, see Helen Hill Miller, "D.P.s in D.C.: The Riffed and the Miffed," *The Reporter*, IX (August 4, 1953), 27.

[75] "Status" has been defined by the Commission as "a standing in Federal employment that permits a qualified employee in the competitive civil service to be transferred to other competitive positions and permits a qualified former employee to be reemployed without again being required to take an open competitive examination. Possession of status also is an advantage to Federal employees in layoffs." USCSC, *Press Release*, July 29, 1954.

for their position through competitive examination, altogether about 400,000 persons, were immediately converted to career or career-conditional status. The latter category was designed to contain those persons who qualified for the career service but who had served for less than three years. Those who remained for the full three year period automatically attained full career standing. At the same time, the Commission stepped up its examining program, as it had after World War II, in order to give the remaining indefinites a chance to qualify for career-conditional appointments. By June 30, 1955, only 120,000 indefinite employees, comprising about six per cent of the permanent service, had not yet qualified. The continuation of an additional 110,000 temporary employees meant that, by the middle of 1955, approximately 88 per cent of the permanent posts were held by either career or career-conditional appointees. To put the matter another way, the permanent service was by then about back to the near-normal which had characterized it in 1950. At the same time the new system, in the words of the Commission, gave the federal personnel system "flexibility while assuring stability of the career service during expansions and contractions resulting from limited national emergencies." [76] From now on there would be a cushion of approximately 10 per cent of the service, which could be expected to come and go with some fluidity and with minimal repercussions on the great bulk of employees desiring a career with the federal government. This has represented a major change in the organization of the permanent service and was one of the most significant innovations to be undertaken in the period since World War II.

In many other matters considerable progress occurred during 1953 and 1954. A new roster of qualified personnel officers was established. Position-classification standards were improved, though they were to remain a major problem. A start was made in combining inspection and classification audit functions, and the agency appraisal and advisory systems were revised. The Commission was achieving more success than ever before in its deliberate policy to strengthen the position of agency personnel offices and line management. Agency boards of examiners were constantly being pushed to absorb more of the examining and related functions at the field level. In addition, a whole new series of publications aimed at line management was begun. [77] Recruitment, examination, and placement were strengthened

---

[76] USCSC, *Seventy-second Report*, 1955, p. 105. For further details of the plan, see the Commission's annual reports for 1953, 1954, and 1955. The writer has also had the benefit of information contained in a battery of Commission press releases on this subject.

[77] See especially USCSC, *Seventy-first Report*, 1954, ch. iv; and, for example, USCSC, *Evaluating Your Personnel Management*, Personnel Management Series, No. 6 (Washington: Government Printing Office, 1954).

through additional test research, and the stimulation of recruitment by departments and agencies. However, a proposal to up the "rule of three" to a "rule of five" was turned down by Congress, and a general pay increase of 5 per cent was vetoed by the President on the grounds that the bill in which it was contained merely continued many inequities and lacked a needed postal reclassification.

Finally, the Commission's emphasis on consultation with employees and employee organizations in the formulation of personnel policies deserves further mention. Such consultation was to play an important part in the development of the Commission's program, and was further supported at this time by a *Statement of Management-Employee Relations in the Federal Government*. While not departing much from traditional concepts, this statement was distinctly a landmark when judged in terms of previous Republican declarations on the same general subject. The Civil Service Commission was evidently prepared at this time to sponsor a union-recognition proposal, but it was turned down at cabinet level. Apparently the Truman administration had also turned down an effort to step up the formal consultative relations between organized employee groups and the government. A union-recognition bill was introduced under legislative auspices in 1956, but failed. Both Congress and the executive branch considered such a proposal again in 1957. While no service-wide directive had appeared by January, 1958, employee-management consultation along more or less formal lines was becoming increasingly prevalent and federal employee union recognition was in the offing.

The program for 1955. The new appointment and status system came into fruition in 1955, and the federal service again approached something resembling normalcy. Still, the Civil Service Commission continued to press for needed legislation, with a good deal of success.

Most important from the standpoint of the bulk of civil employees was the enactment of comprehensive pay legislation. In March, 1955, the salaries of federal judges, members of Congress, and U.S. Attorneys were increased, followed in the summer by general increases for civil employees in all three branches of government. The Federal Employees Salary Increase Act of 1955 provided for an across-the-board raise approximating 7.5 per cent for the more than 950,000 employees in positions under the Classification Act. The Postal Field Service Compensation Act of 1955, which included this time a provision for a new position-classification system, upped salaries immediately in the postal field service by 6 per cent, with the promise of about 2.1 per cent more after reclassification proceedings. A new quota for top positions in grades GS 16, 17, and 18 raised the potential number to 1,200 and gave the Commission authority to revise the list of such positions from time to time. However, the declining pay ratio between top and bottom permanent positions was relatively unchanged, with GS 15 employees receiving in 1955 only 4.88 times as much pay as the average unskilled laborer, as compared to 8.82 in July, 1928. Since the 1955 statutes did not increase pay at the GS 18 level, the pay ratio between the very top Classification Act positions and those of unskilled laborers declined slightly, from one to 6.12, to one to 5.69. [78] Further fringe benefits provided for substantial increases in retirement benefits, increased travel allowances, improved pay and benefits for Foreign Service personnel, the payment of bond premiums by the government instead of by employees, and the removal of some inequities from previous fringe benefit legislation.

On other fronts, too, there were important developments. Especially significant were the new efforts at career staffing, executive development, and training. A new college level recruitment and examining effort was undertaken, emphasizing careers rather than jobs, with the broader Federal Service Entrance Examination replacing the Junior Management Assistant examination. During the winter of 1955–56 this brought a record response of nearly 50,000 applications, and indicated what could be done under a positive recruiting program at the lower levels. The response also confounded critics who had predicted a great drop in federal college recruitment as a result of the McCarthy imbroglios. The program was accompanied by the formulation of a new training policy, which was considered by the Cabinet and approved by the President. Issued by direction of the President on January 11, 1955, the new Federal Training Policy statement, the first comprehensive outline on this subject in almost twenty years, directed the heads of departments and agencies to formulate more systematic training plans, to encourage employee development, and to see that maximum opportunities for development were provided and utilized.[79] The Civil Service Commission was to monitor the program, and it almost immediately commenced to issue a series of advisory publications for agency guidance.[80] The simultaneous efforts of the Society for Personnel Administration, including annual executive development conferences as well as another series of widely distributed pamphlets, did much to assist.[81] With the cooperation of The Brookings Institution, a two-year experi-

---

[78] See USCSC, *Seventy-second Report,* 1955, ch. viii, for a discussion of pay and related legislation.

[79] The directive is reproduced on p. 36 of USCSC, *Seventy-second Report,* 1955.

[80] See, for example, the Commission's 1955 pamphlets on *Improving Orientation Programs* and *Developing Management Potential Through Appraisal Panels,* Personnel Management Series, Nos. 7 and 8 (Washington: Government Printing Office).

[81] See, for example, Homer T. Rosenberger, *How to Organize and Administer an Employee Training Program,* Pamphlet 11 (Washington: Society for Personnel Administration, 1956). This is only one of more than a dozen such publications issued by the Society between 1953 and 1957.

ment in executive development for top federal career officials was launched; legislation to permit wider use of non-governmental training facilities was drawn up; and a survey to determine training needs among top levels of the federal service was conducted.[82] Several agencies, notably the Departments of the Army, Navy, and Air Force and the Veterans Administration, became engaged in extensive civilian executive development programs at this time. Lower level supervisory training programs, among which those of the Departments of the Army and Air Force were especially well developed, were budding in many agencies. A seven-point career staffing and manpower utilization program, endorsed by the Cabinet and approved by the President in the summer of 1955, rounded out the program. In summary, almost all aspects of civilian employee training received a greater impetus under the Eisenhower administration than ever before.

Other important accomplishments during 1955 included the extension of the competitive service to include 10,000 overseas positions in Alaska, and the completion of plans, since carried out, to bring about 25,000 Department of Defense overseas positions within the merit system and out of *Schedule A*.[83] These actions represent one of the major extensions of the merit system in history. Beyond this, the Commission undertook continued research on classification standards and tests, and moved to develop plans for the utilization of older workers. Maximum age limits were removed for most civil positions and dual compensation limits for retired military personnel in civil posts were upped from $3,000 to $10,000 in the summer of 1955. Activities in support of promotion programs were stepped up, the Commission's publications and issuances system was improved, its extensive program for the physically handicapped was extended, and a mobilization plan for the federal personnel system was begun. Within another year this plan was to be linked with the first coordinated civilian executive reserve system designed for the federal government. Organized under Arthur S. Flemming's Office of Defense Mobilization, the new reserve system authorized departments and

[82] USCSC, Bureau of Programs and Standards, *Study of Backgrounds and Reported Training Needs of a Sample of Federal Executives* (Washington: The Commission, 1955). This is at present one of the major sources of information concerning the social characteristics of the top levels of the permanent civil service.

[83] By the summer of 1955 there were approximately 215,000 overseas positions filled by employees hired directly by the United States, of which about 88,000 were filled by U.S. citizens. This figure does not include some 325,000 non-U.S. citizens working primarily for the Department of Defense under contracts or other arrangements where hiring was done by someone other than the U.S. Government. The above actions brought into the competitive service most of the overseas positions for which examinations were practicable except those in certain island dependencies and many in the Canal Zone. See USCSC, *Seventy-second Report*, 1955, ch. vi, for a résumé of the overseas employee situation. There is also a relevant battery of congressional reports and hearings.

agencies "to launch training programs for qualified men and women volunteering to fill executive Government posts in the event of mobilization." [84] How well this new system would work is not yet clear, but for the time being it filled a major gap in mobilization planning. [85]

Other major developments in process by 1955. A picture of federal personnel management from 1953 up into 1955 would not be complete without a brief consideration of two further programs of major importance—the reorganization of the Foreign Service of the Department of State, and the administration's unusually energetic efforts to end discrimination within the federal service and elsewhere. The Wriston Report of 1954 recommended that the State Department's functional staffs, largely procured through normal civil service procedures, be integrated with the separately recruited Foreign Service; and, in the first major reorganization of Foreign Service personnel policies since 1924, this was done during 1954–55. [86] Following, as it did, immediately on the heels of a reduction-in-force from 30,000 to 20,000 employees in 1953, the "Wristonization" of the Foreign Service shook the Department of State to its very foundations. Recent reports indicate that, while there is much yet to be done, the reorganization has been enough of a success that it is unlikely to be overturned in the near future. It is all the more significant as representing the first attempt in our history to rationalize and integrate the relationships of two types of personnel systems, one involving rank-in-the-man and the other rank-in-the-job.

Working on a much wider front, the administration was also making unusually effective efforts to follow through on a general program of antidiscrimination on the grounds of race or color. The entire federal service was involved, both civil and military. Segregation was completely eliminated on naval bases. With government encouragement great holes were driven into the segregation customs in private establishments in Washington, and segregation was ended in the city's government. For the first time a Negro secretary and a Negro administrative staff member were appointed in the White House; and J. Ernest Wilkins, as Assistant Secretary of Labor, became the first Negro to hold a sub-cabinet post and the first ever to attend a cabinet meeting. [87] To see that federal agencies conformed to the government's non-discrimination policies, a new Committee on Government Em-

---

[84] Office of Defense Mobilization, *Press Release*, February 23, 1956. The plan followed Executive Order 10660, February 15, 1956. For details of the system see ODM, *General Administrative Order* 1–7, March 1, 1956.

[85] See National Planning Association, *Needed: A Civilian Reserve*, Planning Pamphlet 86 (Washington: The Association, 1954).

[86] For references to Foreign Service personnel management, see the "supplementary notes" to this chapter.

[87] See Donovan, as cited in footnote 1, ch. xi.

ployment Policy was constituted under White House auspices. While the administration was in many respects only strengthening policies started under the Truman administration, new heights of accomplishment were reached both within the federal service and elsewhere. In this respect, the government was clearly a "model employer."

Through most of these developments one could perceive that the Civil Service Commission's reorganization and emphasis on program planning, research, and policy coordination with all interested agencies and organizations was clearly paying off. Altogether, during the two years from late 1953 through the summer of 1955, perhaps more seminal actions involving federal personnel management were taken than in any comparable period. Just as important, civil employee morale was on the upswing for the first time in almost a decade.

Three Study Groups

At this point the Civil Service Commission was also to have the benefit of three major studies of important aspects of the federal service. These were in addition to those by congressional committees, the Wriston Committee, the Rockefeller Committee, and many other similar groups constituted under private, public, or mixed auspices. Indeed, during the decade from 1946 through 1956, there were more studies and analyses of various aspects of the federal service, both civil and military, than in the previous century. Nor was the end in sight by 1958.

The Sixth American Assembly. To a considerable extent a brain child of Dwight D. Eisenhower while President of Columbia University, the American Assembly was formed in 1950 to provide a nonpartisan forum for the discussion of topics of national interest. In 1954 the sixth topic of Assembly concern became the subject of a special research report entitled *The Federal Government Service: Its Character, Prestige, and Problems.* This was followed with a "Final Report" by the participants, a group of fifty-two distinguished citizens from all walks of life.

The principal long-run contribution of the Assembly lay in its inclusive and penetrating research report, prepared in advance by well-known specialists in public administration under the direction of Wallace S. Sayre of Columbia University as the Assembly's Technical Director. Highlighted in these papers were a series of basic public personnel issues, such as the top-level organization for federal personnel management, the relationship of personnel management to line management, the relevance of traditional merit system concepts to modern conditions, the proper place and function of patronage and political appointments, the development of a coordinated career system throughout the government as a whole, the relationship of public to private personnel management and unions, loyalty and security organization and procedure, and the control and development of bureaucratic accountability and responsibility within a democratic framework based on a separation of powers. About the only major subjects left relatively untouched were those of ethics and conflicts-of-interest, the administration of the patronage, and civil-military personnel relationships.

These research studies, designed primarily to raise issues and questions, left most of the answering to the participants. Here the Assembly shone a little less brightly, reflecting the inevitable effects of compromise among such a large and diverse group of individuals. Nevertheless, the final report was significant, and shadows of Assembly recommendations were clearly cast over some of the civil service legislation previously outlined as well as the report of the Second Hoover Commission.

The Second Hoover Commission. The report of the Sixth American Assembly was but a prologue to another report, this one more specifically devoted to a definitive prescription for the federal service. Like its 1949 counterpart, the Second Hoover Commission was composed of a battery of task forces, all submitting reports to a commission of twelve members, five of whom, including the chairman, had been members of the earlier commission. Here we are concerned primarily with the efforts of two of these task forces, one which considered the civil service alone, and another which dealt with special personnel problems in the Department of Defense. Drawing upon these task force reports, the Hoover Commission proper prepared, in turn, its own final reports on these subjects. Let us consider first the two reports—task force and final—relating to the federal civil service.[88]

Like its predecessor, the Second Hoover Commission was high in praise of the quality of civil service personnel and bent its efforts to maintaining that quality. This the Commission and its personnel task force feared was being undermined by a combination of low pay, inequitable procedures, especially in the security field, and a failure to provide fully for long term attractive careers for permanent servants and for adequate short term recruitment of political executives.

---

[88] See Commission on Organization of the Executive Branch of the Government, *Personnel and Civil Service: A Report to the Congress* (Washington: Government Printing Office, 1955), hereafter cited as "Second Hoover Commission, *Report on Personnel and Civil Service*"; and *Task Force Report on Personnel*, as cited in footnote 39. The writer wishes to acknowledge the assistance of Dean F. Bock in preparing an item by item analysis of these two reports.

The Task Force and the Commission concentrated a great deal of their efforts on the last two problems. The reports emphasized the desirability of drawing a distinct line between policy posts and career posts. For the latter, a more rigid concept of political neutrality, involving even program neutrality, was recommended along with a proposal for a "Senior Civil Service." This was to consist of 1,500 to 3,000 top level career civil servants with at least five years of experience, who were to be granted extra pay and emoluments as well as rank-in-the-man so that they might form a pool of readily transferrable career executives. When asked which single one of his study group's proposals he especially favored, ex-President Hoover later declared, "I would pick the recommendation for the setting up of a senior civil service." [89] Careful consideration was also given to the possible methods for a more systematic recruitment of political executives, especially at the sub-cabinet level; and both reports supported revision of the conflict-of-interest laws. At the same time the Task Force stressed the need for removing all forms of patronage pressure from offices not properly in the confidential or political executive categories, a point of view in which the Commission itself only mildly concurred. In general, the reports accepted the trend of development represented by the creation of *Schedule C*, but indicated that the philosophy underlying this trend should be even more sharply delineated and implemented.

For the permanent service as a whole the reports emphasized the need for executive development and training on a more complete and systematic basis. Compression of position-classification levels, higher pay at upper levels, and a greater utilization of the prevailing-rate pay system at lower levels were advocated to remove rigidities and ceilings in the pay structure for Classification Act employees. These curbs tended to militate against effective recruitment in competition with private industry. It was felt that recruitment itself should be much more positive, with a renewed emphasis on college-level inputs and with the substitution of category examination ratings of, for example, "outstanding," "well-qualified," "qualified," and "not qualified," for many types of positions for which decimal numerical ratings were highly artificial.

In considering other "large-scale employment practices" the reports recommended a radical revision of the undiscriminating performance rating system under which approximately 98 per cent received "satisfactory" ratings. There was to be a new emphasis on performance ratings as a tool for employee development in the manner of much

---

[89] Neil MacNeil and Harold W. Metz, *The Hoover Report: 1953–1955* (New York: The Macmillan Co., 1956), p. 29. See especially ch. ii of this book, which summarizes the "Personnel and Civil Service" recommendations.

of private industry. Here and through the possibility of reducing employee turnover the Task Force felt the most effective economies could be made.[90] On the revision of dismissal practices, the Task Force was much more demanding in its suggested changes than the Commission itself, recommending extensive modifications in almost all aspects of veteran preference and a return to the Lloyd-LaFollette Act dismissal procedure which had been modified for veterans in 1944. Further veteran preference modifications were advocated in order to provide more equitable reduction-in-force procedures, especially for permanent non-veteran civil servants with considerable tenure. Decentralization as a continued personnel management concept was strongly stressed; a new codification of personnel rules and regulations was deemed most important; and the use of Supervisor-Employee Councils in the formulation of personnel policies was advocated by the Task Force.

In considering the various types of merit systems then in effect— T.V.A., Foreign Service, etc.—the reports indicated a desire for more interchange of personnel among them. Steps to bring as many overseas civil servants as possible into the merit system were proposed. The Task Force was quite critical of the dual position of the Chairman of the Civil Service Commission, but the Hoover Commission itself "found great improvements" as a result of the agency's 1953 reorganization and evidently decided to disagree with its Task Force's findings on this point. At the departmental level further decentralization of personnel functions was felt to be extremely important.

Altogether, the final report of the Second Hoover Commission on civil service spelled out some nineteen specific recommendations, generally concurring with its Task Force report except with respect to the dual position of the Chairman of the Civil Service Commission, the emphasis to be placed on revision of veteran preference, and the need to revise the loyalty and security program. Here again, the final report by default took issue with the Task Force Report; for the Hoover Commission itself completely ignored its Task Force's proposal for "clarification of the 'security problem' through a thorough official inquiry." [91] The Task Force Report was especially distinguished for its recognition of and prescriptions for the problem of the relationship between the political and permanent services, prescriptions with which the final report concurred in main outline.[92] As compared to the reports of the First Hoover Commission, those of

90 Task Force Report on Personnel, as cited in footnote 39, pp. xxii and 91.
91 Same, p. xvii.
92 From the point of view of this book, the Task Force study was notable for the research on both historical and current topics which it undertook. Most of this research has been presented in the appendices, charts, and tables following the Task Force report proper. See same, pp. viii–ix and 149–251.

the Second recognized to a much greater degree the crucial importance of political leadership in personnel management and contained refreshing and positive emphases on employee morale, motivation, and development. On the other hand, the 1955 reports were sadly deficient in their treatment of employee-management relations and unions, as well as in consideration of public personnel problems at the departmental and agency level. Moreover, while all the major studies of the federal service within the decade between 1946 and 1956 have strongly espoused decentralization, none of them, as one critic recently noted, has developed any "effective formulas for decentralization." [93] As of 1958, here lay a fertile field for exploration.

In its consideration of military and civil-military personnel matters, the Second Hoover Commission clearly charted new ground.[94] In main outline both the Commission and its special subcommittee Task Force concluded that the closer integration of military and civilian personnel practices was long overdue on the triple grounds of economy, effective administration, and improved employee morale. The Commission provided a forward looking though controversial blueprint for the greater specialization of personnel in support activities, the delineation of civilian and military roles in the defense effort, the development of comparable personnel standards for civilian and military managers in support activities, and the strengthening of career patterns for both civilian and military personnel.[95]

The Kaplan Committee. While the Hoover Commission was investigating the federal service in general, the Committee on Retirement Policy for Federal Personnel, created by law in July, 1952, was publishing the first comparative study of federal retirement systems ever made. The research report, issued in January, 1954, was followed by a series of exhaustive analyses and recommendations concerning, in sequence, retirement systems for the uniformed services, retire-

93 Harry L. Case, "Past, Present, and Future Studies of Federal Personnel Administration," *Public Administration Review*, XV (Spring, 1955), 99.

94 See Second Hoover Commission, *Subcommittee Report on Special Personnel Problems in the Department of Defense* (Washington: Government Printing Office, 1955); and Second Hoover Commission, *Business Organization of the Department of Defense: A Report to Congress* (Washington: Government Printing Office, 1955), Part III.

95 For a more detailed consideration of these recommendations and the complicated policy questions involved, see Lem. F. Thom, "Better Defense Through Better Personnel Management," *Personnel Administration*, XIX (November–December, 1956), 26. See also the two-volume "Cordiner Report" on military and civilian personnel practices in the Department of Defense, issued early in 1957 by the Defense Advisory Committee on Professional and Technical Compensation, Vol. I on *Military Personnel* and Vol. II on *Civilian Personnel* (Washington: Government Printing Office).

Attention should also be called to the Second Hoover Commission's reports on *Legal Services and Procedure*. These outlined for the first time extensive career proposals for federal attorneys, long excluded from the merit system, first by political tradition and more recently by congressional restriction.

ment systems for the civil service, the financial status and policies of federal retirement systems, and the special benefit provisions of federal retirement systems.

By 1954 over 5,312,000 civilian and military employees were covered under some twenty-two retirement systems. The old age and survivors insurance provisions of social security covered an additional 600,000 temporary employees.[96] In main outline, the committee, headed by H. Eliot Kaplan, longtime Executive Director of the National Civil Service League and former Comptroller of the State of New York, recommended some consolidation and integration of retirement systems, a revision of the structure of survivor benefits, and the integration of retirement systems with the Social Security Act, all with the object of strengthening the retirement systems, particularly from an employee standpoint. At the same time the committee rejected the pay-as-you-go method of financing retirement benefits, in favor of a middle-of-the-road funding policy which would prevent the accumulation of undue reserves. For the first time it was possible to consider as a whole the many federal retirement systems and policies, involving some $6 billion of assets and more than $30 billion of future unfinanced obligations.

Reactions and Action: 1955–58

That Congress, not to mention the general public, should have had some difficulty in digesting this outpouring of research data and recommendations in the face of an approaching presidential election is hardly surprising.

The election of 1956. The civil service felt the impact of the election first through a stepping up of legislative investigating efforts by the Democratic-controlled Congress during the winter of 1955–56. As of January 15, 1956, for example, the Department of Agriculture alone, then under heavy fire, had become the subject of more than eighty simultaneous inquiries.[97] As the campaign developed, Adlai Stevenson, again the Democratic candidate, frequently attacked the administration, as did the representatives of several public employee unions, for its vacillating policy with respect to the dividing line between the patronage and the permanent service. The so-called "numbers game," involving the accuracy of statistics on security cases, also continued

[96] These figures are taken from the Kaplan Committee report which is contained in U.S. Congress, Senate, Committee on Post Office and Civil Service, *Retirement Policy for Federal Personnel*, 83rd Cong., 2d Sess., Senate Doc. 89, Parts I, II, III, IV, and V (Washington: Government Printing Office, 1954), Part I, p. 31.

[97] From information recently supplied to the writer by former Assistant Secretary of Agriculture James A. McConnell.

to generate considerable political heat. However, by 1956 the Eisenhower administration could point to an impressive civil service improvement record, and the campaign turned on other issues deemed by the voters more important than federal personnel management.

While the election returned Eisenhower to office by a most impressive margin, the renewed Democratic control of both the House and the Senate clearly suggested that the power of the Republican party depended more than most Republicans cared to admit on the extraordinary personal appeal of Dwight D. Eisenhower. With the Twenty-second Amendment estopping the President from running again and the Democrats in control of both houses of Congress, it looked as if the federal service would continue to find itself uncertainly balanced between two fairly equal political forces.

New personnel measures. The additional fact that the Eisenhower administration and its Civil Service Commission had already proceeded to implement many of the Hoover Commission's and the American Assembly's recommendations also contributed to the relative paucity of legislative and administrative measures affecting the federal service during 1956 and 1957 as compared to 1954 and 1955. Still, a number of significant actions were taken.

The matter of executive pay was finally acted upon in July, 1956, with the top pay for cabinet members increased to $25,000 and with that for GS 18 positions upped to $16,000. Additional high level administrative and scientific positions were created in order to place the federal government in more effective competition with industry, and authority was granted to pay up to $19,000 in some of these positions. A considerable number of miscellaneous pay and fringe benefit increases were made for small groups of employees omitted from previous legislation. Military leave with pay was granted to the postal service; and civil service retirement benefits were significantly liberalized, though a bill to implement the Kaplan Report more fully died in committee.

Congress also approved in 1956 a proposal providing six year staggered terms of office for civil service commissioners, to take effect on March 1, 1957. On this date, Chairman Philip Young retired in favor of former Congressman Harris Ellsworth for a two year term; Commissioner George M. Moore was replaced by Christopher H. Phillips, former Deputy Assistant Secretary of State for International Affairs, for a four year term; and Commissioner Frederick Lawton, the Democratic member, was retained for a six year term. While this action provided for more continuity in top level Commission management, it also meant that the legislative program of the Commission was for the most part suspended during the spring and summer of

1957, pending confirmation and orientation of the new commissioners. What this reorganization would mean was not immediately clear. However, when Commissioner Phillips, who resigned in late 1957 to become a United States representative to the United Nations, was replaced on January 2, 1958, by Bernard L. Flanagan, there was considerable criticism. Flanagan, a former secretary to Senator Aiken of Vermont, had been special assistant handling patronage requests in the Veterans Administration and then the General Services Administration. There was speculation that the administration's efforts toward the formulation of a new and more liberal labor-management relations policy for federal employees, the aspect of federal personnel management with which Commissioner Phillips had most actively concerned himself, might be delayed.

Meanwhile, the Hoover Commission's civil service proposals, especially as they related to the definition of a precise line between political and permanent posts and the creation of a Senior Civil Service, set off considerable debate. It was thought by some that a more rigid concept of civil service neutrality was unrealistic both from a psychological point of view and also from the standpoint of the known predispositions of legislators, many of whom were deemed likely to ignore the Hoover Commission's proposals that they deal entirely with political executives. The Senior Civil Service concept ran into trouble, not only because many high level civil servants saw themselves either as "whirling dervishes" rotating from position to position at someone's whim, or as a selected group of "sitting ducks" all too clearly visible for congressional sniping, but also because of a long-standing American aversion to anything even suggesting a closed British-type administrative class.[98] Even so, it was generally agreed that more should be done for the top levels of the career service, and to this end the administration called a special conference in December, 1956. In August, 1957, a five-member bipartisan Career Executive Committee, chaired by Arthur S. Flemming, was set up by the President to recommend and draft a career executive program for the federal government. The committee recommended the establishment of a bipartisan Career Executive Board. This was done by executive order on March 4, 1958.

Certain of the Hoover Commission's position-classification and pay recommendations were attacked as mixing up the traditional concept of equal pay for equal work with one based on supply and demand.

---

[98] For a summary of various opinions for and against the concept of the Senior Civil Service, see the writer's paper entitled "The Dialectics of the Senior Civil Service," presented before a panel session at the annual meeting of the American Political Science Association, Washington, September 6, 1956.

523

This criticism was justified, but there were also many who supported the change, some going so far as to suggest that the overall position-classification plan governing white collar civil employees since 1923 be scrapped in favor of a much more decentralized and variable system of occupational groups and pay systems.[99] It was certainly true that by 1957 the great pressure to improve the government's recruiting position with respect to private industry was producing a good deal of legislation which tore considerable gaps in the concept of equal pay for equal work. This was especially true in the case of professional, scientific, and technical employees. The wage board pay system for blue collar workers was already geared to supply and demand. The proposals for improving the pay and recruitment system for political executives met more approval, with one result in the form of the 1956 executive pay increases and another in the form of a special conference on the problem held at Princeton University in March, 1956. A general pay raise was approved by Congress in the summer of 1957, but was vetoed by the President on the grounds of inequity and inflation. However, he promised action in 1958.

As for other matters of concern to the federal service, the Federal Service Entrance Examination was opened to college juniors for the first time in the fall of 1957. A more systematic and concerted effort to improve promotion programs was undertaken. The Civil Service Commission reached agreements with the T.V.A. and the Atomic Energy Commission to permit the relatively free transfer of permanent personnel between the separate personnel systems of these agencies and that supervised by the Commission. And the Commission had prepared a new agenda of legislation for submission to Congress early in 1958. This included requests for needed training authorizations, a health insurance and major medical expense program, travel expenses for interviews and for reporting to first duty station, the up-grading of positions calling for new college graduates from GS 5 to GS 7, and a number of minor provisions. The Commission was continuing its emphasis on research and careful prior planning in the formulation of new programs and objectives for federal personnel management. A greatly heightened public and congressional concern over many aspects of federal management, stemming from the disconcerting news in the late fall of 1957 of spectacular Russian successes in military weapons and scientific technology, made it almost certain that all reasoned proposals to strengthen the federal service would be received with careful attention.

99 See John Bamberg, "The Second Hoover Commission on Position Classification and Pay," *Public Personnel Review*, XVI (April, 1955), 98.

The Seventy-fifth Anniversary of the Pendleton Act

By the seventy-fifth anniversary of the Pendleton Act—1958—it was clear that the treatment of the federal service under the Eisenhower administration had undergone the "conventional cycle" Herman Somers had predicted in the fall of 1953.[100] At first under heavy attack and subject to patronage inroads, the service recovered with the aid of both executive and legislative assistance. By 1957 morale was up once again after nearly a decade of decline, more college students than ever were taking the Federal Service Entrance Examination, and even the Department of State seemed more relaxed. This is not to say that all was well with the service or to imply that morale was what it might be or what it had been during the late thirties. But a significant effort had been made to attack major personnel problems and considerable success had been achieved.

The 1956 presidential election had, above all, confirmed big government as a bipartisan fact, a matter which the executive budget submitted by President Eisenhower to Congress in early 1957 further emphasized. There would be more arguments over the size of the bureaucracy, but it was unlikely that in the years to come there would be any successful attempts drastically to prune it in the manner many Republicans had almost gleefully anticipated in the winter of 1952–53. The voting public was in no mood to terminate the services to which it had become accustomed, and there was every prospect that more would be sought. Moreover, the gigantic defense requirements of the cold war were dramatically underscored by the realization in late 1957 of the great advances of Soviet science.

At the same time a good deal had been accomplished toward rationalizing public personnel management at the federal level. The many proponents of presidential leadership in personnel matters via a managerially streamlined Civil Service Commission had seen their wishes fulfilled, though there were some qualms in retrospect. Much of the advance personnel planning and programming which, again, had long been advocated, had been produced. Under a reorganized and considerably revitalized Civil Service Commission, the concept of decentralization with standards was gradually being implemented about as fully as existing statutes would permit. The boundary lines between the political and permanent segments of the service were being clarified. Though much more remained to be done, some modest efforts were being made to attack the traditional departmentalism and highly specialized character of the federal service. Manpower planning, career staffing on a moderately long-run basis, and employee develop-

100 As cited in footnote 6, p. 146.

ment and training had become much more than catch words. While there was still not enough managerial and professional talent to go around, an improved political climate, increasing fringe benefits, and more active recruiting were combining to provide the government access to a larger proportion of a tight labor market. The subcontracting of governmental functions such as research and development was also widely utilized to better the government's competitive position.[101]

Mobilization planning, the initiation of a civilian reserve system, and the redesign of the service so as to provide a continuous cushion of indefinite and career-conditional employees between the permanent service and the hazards of emergency ups and downs of federal employment had for the first time substantially prepared that service for anything but an all-out war. The complex interrelationships of the civilian and military personnel systems were under systematic review, and the nation was even awaiting, reasonably dispassionately, action on the report of the Commission on Government Security. It was quite true that up to 1954, as R. N. Spann pungently put it in the most observant and detailed analysis of the federal service made by any foreigner since Lord Bryce, "The public service had had to run pretty hard even to stay in the same place." [102] But by the end of Eisenhower's first term the whole massive mechanism of the federal bureaucracy was stirring and change was in the air, most of it looking forward rather than backward.

On the other hand, fundamental matters were still pressing for diagnosis and remedy. Of these, three in particular presented unusually knotty problems and hardly a start had been made toward solving them. First, there was the historic problem of the patronage and the recruitment of competent political executives. Defined in its traditional, hit-or-miss terms, patronage *was* obsolete. It simply could no longer adequately supply the talent necessary to direct and control a modern, technically advanced society. But this fact had by no means removed the need for the overt manipulation of political power if political programs approved by the voting public were to be satisfactorily implemented. The disastrous failure of Dwight D. Eisen-

101 See U.S. Congress, Senate, Committee on Post Office and Civil Service, *Manpower Utilization by the Federal Government Through the Use of Private Contract Labor,* 83d Cong., 1st Sess., Senate Doc. 32 (Washington: Government Printing Office, 1953), p. 1. By such practices the government was, of course, to some extent competing with itself. At the time of this report perhaps 5,000,000 persons were employed directly or indirectly under contract.

102 "The Eisenhower Civil Service and the Reformers," *Public Administration,* XXXIV (Summer, 1956), 143. See also his series of two articles entitled, "Civil Servants in Washington: I—The Character of the Federal Service," *Political Studies,* I (June, 1953), 143; and "Civil Servants in Washington: II—The Higher Civil Service and Its Future," *Political Studies,* I (October, 1953), 228.

hower and his associates to push much of their legislative program through Congress during 1953 had only underscored this fact, and at the same time demonstrated that nonpartisanship was by no stretch of the imagination a satisfactory substitute for effective political control. The Sixth American Assembly and the Second Hoover Commission had emphasized the need for competent political executives. But no one had as yet seriously tackled the interrelated problems of patronage management, the control of political executives, and, through them, the control not only of the bureaucracy but also of the political party in power. In this latter and much more complex sense, patronage was by no means obsolete, but there was as yet little explicit recognition of this fact, and no forthright attempt to face it.

Just as pressing, but equally lacking a ready prescription, were the legal and moral issues surrounding the rights and duties of public employees. The 1951 report on ethics by the Douglas Committee had been largely ignored, and despite a recommendation by the Second Hoover Commission to the contrary, Congress appeared to be in no hurry in 1958 seriously to reconsider ethical matters or our antique conflict-of-interest statutes. But the rights as well as the duties of civil servants were unclear. The historic concept of public employment as a privilege rather than right still held as a legal doctrine. And the rigid application of the Hatch Act, the proscription of the right to strike, and an often arbitrary loyalty and security system seemed hardly in full accord with constitutional guarantees. Fortunately, the general public was more disposed than at any time in the previous decade to reconsider the problem of public employee rights, to the end that the second class citizenship of civil servants might at least be somewhat ameliorated. But little had been accomplished in this direction by the close of 1957.

What public employees had lost in civil rights, they had gained in job security. An intricate system of veteran preference, a web of appeals and review procedures, and an increasing number of restrictive dismissal orders and statutes had almost succeeded in reviving the ancient concept of a property right in public office. With the support of the federal judiciary, which has been intervening more and more frequently on behalf of federal employee job security since World War II,[103] these developing monetary and property rights of

[103] For summaries of recent cases in point, see the annual reports of the Civil Service Commission. Unfortunately, there has never been a careful study of federal civil service law as a whole. Oliver Field's *Civil Service Law* (Minneapolis: University of Minnesota Press, 1939) is primarily oriented to state and local problems. Edward S. Corwin's and Glendon A. Schubert, Jr.'s, studies of the Presidency in relationship to the courts, *The President: Office and Powers* (4th ed.; New York: New York University Press, 1957), and *The Presidency in the Courts* (Minneapolis: University of Minnesota Press, 1957), cover well

public employees clearly tended to negate effective administration. Nor were there any signs that the rigid net of procedural controls laid out in the *Federal Personnel Manual* and buttressed by a growing conglomeration of statutes was likely to be relaxed in the near future. Manipulating the controls, though with a reluctant hand, was the Civil Service Commission. By 1958 the Commission had significantly decentralized its examining and recruitment process, and was straining to move beyond a mere workload decentralization in the other aspects of personnel management. But the prospects were dim unless much greater discretion could be granted to all levels of line management within the departments and agencies.

Here we face the ultimate dilemma of the merit system of Curtis, Eaton, and Schurz, a dilemma implicit in the Pendleton Act of which they were the principal architects. This statute was specifically designed to control the front door to the service through its concept of competitive examination. But, once controls are instituted, it is tempting to use them in ways not originally contemplated; and the Pendleton Act for the first time made possible centralized direction of almost all aspects of public personnel management. For example, it made veteran preference administratively feasible; and already by 1900 the back door of removal was not swinging quite as freely as before. The Lloyd-LaFollette Act closed it some more, and a renewed and strengthened veteran preference shut it still further after both world wars. The rapidly developing public employee organizations, in their search for a rationale for their existence, helped bring the movement into its final and modern phase. By the nineteen thirties and the Great Depression the interests of these pressure groups were coinciding with a massive public concern over employment security, a security to be obtained, it was argued, through the planned intervention of government. And, just as governmental action was conceived as the solution to the insecurities of private employment, so was it increasingly thought of as providing an answer to the real and fancied insecurities of civil servants. In the nineteen twenties a powerful Senator Smoot had castigated public employees for desiring retirement legislation and interfering with a free hand for management. The reports of congressional committees on the mid-twentieth century federal service were entirely different in tenor and tone. While many of these reports indicated a desire to strengthen the managerial structure of the executive branch, they increasingly paid primary obeisance

---

the President's powers of appointment and removal and, to some extent, the legal issues involved in loyalty and security and political activity cases. But these matters comprise only a small portion of the issues and problems involved in civil service procedure and related administrative actions. Much more needs to be done.

to a vast array of actual and potential personnel inequities at the expense of general management. If, before the nineteen twenties, the burden of proof lay on the employee, by the nineteen fifties it lay on the administrator. The result was increasing red tape, greater procedural controls, more restrictive dismissal procedures, and more and more review and appeals boards—all in the name of justice, security, and fair play for civil employees, and all wreaking havoc with flexibility, administrative discretion, decentralization, and, ultimately, the individual employee again. The latter could retain his job "rights" if only he had the time and money to plow through the morass of administrative and legal minutiae to find out what they were. Moreover, the cost of administrative and judicial appeals was almost prohibitive. He now had to struggle against the very governmental mechanism he had helped create to preserve his rights. A vicious circle was clearly in operation.

Considered from a more fundamental viewpoint and in terms of the underlying interpretive thesis of this study, it was finally apparent by mid-century that the concept of governmental intervention, originated to compensate for the injustices perpetrated under the individualistic and acquisitive economics of the nineteenth and early twentieth century, had begun to erode the Protestant Ethic. A new Social Ethic, to use a term popularized by William H. Whyte, Jr., in his study of *The Organization Man,* had risen and was displacing it.[104] It has been the function of men such as Whyte, David Riesman, and Erich Fromm to point out the effects of this Social Ethic upon industrial organization and behavior. It is important to emphasize here that the effects were no less apparent within the federal service, and perhaps even more so.

First of all, further decentralization of public personnel management and any much greater return of the personnel staff function into the main stream of line management would have to await major modifications of a myriad of restrictive federal statutes. If we are to recognize the validity of much of the newer human relations and organizational research, we must, as Harry L. Case, Director of Personnel for the T.V.A., has cogently argued, "somehow be brought to an awareness that personnel administration today is something more than passing laws and writing regulations." [105] Up to now, with the Pendleton Act as a lever, the federal service has for most purposes been treated as a corporate whole as far as personnel management is concerned. But by 1958 the whole was too great and complex. The

---

104 (New York: Simon and Schuster, 1956), ch. ii.
105 As cited in footnote 93, p. 101.

continuation of this policy could only lead to more and more inequities and more and more administrative confusion. Centralization had outrun its optimum utility. The Second Hoover Commission questioned the inherent advantages of a neatly Weberian hierarchic administrative system bound together by precise and rigid procedures in the name of control. Controls and due process are crucial with respect to civil rights. But the civil rights of public employees have in fact been only moderately protected by administrative procedure, by legislation, or by the courts. And controls in the form of a web of procedure are appropriate to curb a management which is capricious and arbitrary. They become much less meaningful, and, indeed, downright obstructive for both employees and management alike, under two conditions: (a) when employees possess the civil rights which permit them to argue their own case with management on something like equal terms, and (b) when management is aware of both the deep human desire for individual expression and the utility of creativeness on the part of all employees, from the top to the bottom. This awareness is rapidly spreading through the federal service, just as it is in American private industry. This is the ultimate meaning of the whole movement for better human relations, about which so much has been written in recent years.

To move further in the direction of job security and to fail to review the meaning of the Bill of Rights for public employees is to ignore the new look which much of federal management has assumed during the last three decades. From an administrative point of view, it is to assure a slow bureaucratic death through strangulation by a morass of red tape, costly alike to management and to all employees. From a political point of view, the courts, in their lack of concern for the civil rights of public employees and their overconcern for job security rights in terms of tenure and the curb of managerial discretion, have put the cart before the horse and taken a position more appropriate to an avowedly socialist state than to a democracy based on individual freedom. The danger here is only too obvious. Perhaps some day a third Hoover Commission will seriously undertake to devise a new administrative mechanism more appropriate both to the diversities and complexities of modern big government and also to the concepts of individual dignity and creativeness. This is what Harry Case meant when he suggested not long ago that "the next report on federal personnel should be written on the subject of 'democracy in federal administration.' " [106]

It would seem, therefore, that the Pendleton Act has carried with

[106] Same.

it the seeds of its own potential destruction. As the vehicle for a useful and efficient administrative device it will soon be obsolete, even a barrier to progress, if action along the lines suggested above is not taken soon. Like the spoils system it replaced, the civil service law of 1883 has after seventy-five years, become a conservative institution. Now it is protective, not of business, property, and acquisitive economics, as the spoils system had been, but of outdated controls, restrictive and costly procedures, and another species of property right, this time relating to public office.

Coming full circle, political reform in the United States had by mid-century gone so far in the direction of economic reform in the name of security, with all its red tape and regulations, that there were movements once more toward the articulation of a New Individualism emphasizing flexibility and individual creativity. It was no whimsey that made John Fischer cry out in *Harper's* during 1945, "Let's Go Back to the Spoils System." [107] The year 1953 came entirely too close for comfort toward a realization of the approach to public personnel management implicit in Fischer's remark. Let us not in 1958, therefore, tarry overlong in devising a new theory of American public administration looking forward rather than backward, and a new concept of public personnel management to match it. Both are even now overdue.

SUPPLEMENTARY NOTES

The Eisenhower loyalty-security program. There is a wide range of literature relating to the loyalty and security problem both before and after 1953. For the Eisenhower period, the best sources for summary purposes are the *Report* of the Commission on Government Security, as cited in footnote 65; the 1956 *Report of the Special Committee on the Federal Loyalty-Security Program of the Association of the Bar of the City of New York,* as cited in footnote 56, which contains extensive bibliographical references; and Robert N. Johnson, "The Eisenhower Personnel Security Program," *The Journal of Politics,* XVIII (November, 1956), 625. For a summary of administrative procedures in effect just prior to the issuance of Executive Order 10450, see U.S. Congress, Senate, Committee on Post Office and Civil Service, *Personnel Investigations of Employees and Applicants for Employment in the Executive Branch of the Government for Loyalty, Suitability, and Security,* 83d Cong., 1st Sess., Senate Doc. 29 (Washington: Government Printing Office, 1953). This report (p. 20) concurred in the judgment that "the existence of the three separate programs of loyalty, suitability, and security is the primary factor which results in confusion, duplication, delay, and waste," but recommended that the Civil Service Commission be designated as the agency to coordinate these programs. For a reasoned and articulate analysis of the consequences of the American

---

[107] *Harper's Magazine,* CXCI (October, 1945), 362. This was the title of his article.

postwar preoccupation with loyalty, with some special references to the public service, see Morton Grodzins, *The Loyal and the Disloyal* (Chicago: University of Chicago Press, 1956), especially Part V, "Some Policy Considerations." For references to earlier periods, see the discussions of loyalty in the two previous chapters.

The Foreign Service. Only the high points of Foreign Service personnel development have been touched on in this study. For the organizational and personnel situation in the Department of State just prior to the Eisenhower administration, see James L. McCamy, *The Administration of American Foreign Affairs* (New York: Alfred A. Knopf, 1950); The Brookings Institution, *The Administration of Foreign Affairs and Overseas Operations* (Washington: Government Printing Office, 1951); and Arthur W. Macmahon, *Administration in Foreign Affairs* (University, Ala.: University of Alabama Press, 1953). The Wriston Report was released in June, 1954; see U.S. Department of State, Secretary of State's Public Committee on Personnel, *Toward a Stronger Foreign Service,* Department of State Publication 5458 (Washington: Government Printing Office, 1954). This was both preceded and followed by an extensive set of hearings in Congress; see, for example, U.S. Congress, House, Committee on Government Operations, International Operations Subcommittee, *Administration of Overseas Personnel,* 84th Cong., 1st Sess., Hearings before a Subcommittee of, etc., Parts I, II, III, and IV in 2 vols. (Washington: Government Printing Office, 1955 and 1956). See also The American Assembly, *The Representation of the United States Abroad* (New York: Columbia University, 1956); and John Osborne, "Is the State Department Manageable?" as cited in footnote 30, for recent evaluations.

CHAPTER 17

Personnel is Power—A Theory of Governmental Reform

Civil service reform and public personnel management normally lack glamor. We find it difficult to associate heroism with the merit system. Yet this is a topic which has moved men to considerable heights of oratory. It was civil service reform which Senator Roscoe Conkling was aiming at when he hurled his oft-quoted rejoinder to George William Curtis during the New York State Republican Convention of 1877: "When Dr. Johnson defined patriotism as the last refuge of a scoundrel, he was unconscious of the then undeveloped capabilities and uses of the word 'Reform.'" [1]

Our government is allegedly a government of laws and not of men, but the many and acrimonious quarrels over public office during the course of American history only underline the fact that he who administers the law is often more important than the law itself.

Out of the Past

Today it is difficult to conceive of the tremendous changes which have taken place in the American national public service since its reorganization under the Constitution of 1789. Through nearly seventeen decades the federal service has grown from an institution of a few hundred employees to one which, by January 1958, was able to command in peacetime the efforts of some 2,350,000 individuals through its civil branches alone.

[1] Alfred R. Conkling, *The Life and Letters of Roscoe Conkling* (New York: Charles L. Webster and Co., 1889), p. 541.

Institutional analysis. The analysis of the development of any modern social institution is, like the whole of which it is but a part, necessarily a complex thing. Often the interpretative path of least resistance lies in a simple recognition of the metamorphosis of the seeming unities of previous ages into the bewildering multiplicities of a technological civilization. This path has here been foresworn in favor of a more analytical approach. To put the matter another way: the development of the American public service has not been merely the product of a "wonder-working Providence" but rather the result of a developing American social purpose and structure both of which can be systematically outlined. Such an approach, briefly sketched in the opening chapter, has underlain the intermediate chapters and is summarized here both to make the analytical framework of this study more explicit and also to provide a suitable concluding overview of the genesis and growth of the American public service.

In broadest outline the evolution of our civil establishment, like that of most other elements in our social system, has involved a peculiar amalgam of largely European theory and practice, catalyzed by and compounded with the events and pressures associated with the dramatic conquering of a continental wilderness. The device of the nonpolitical civil service, which has provided one of the main subjects of study here, and which became embedded in our political system through the Pendleton Act of 1883, was fundamentally a European invention. But from the very beginning the American version of this administrative contrivance assumed a character all its own. We do have today a nonpolitical national service, but it is by no means the precise equivalent of that of England, France, Germany, or any other nation. Many forces have intervened to change the pattern. Unique political habits and institutions, differing views as to the ends to which social institutions ought to be directed, and an enviable and isolated economic position have reacted together to produce a public service which can only be labelled "American."

The first century and the first "reform." In the early days of the Republic the civil service was designed to serve the needs of a conservative and somewhat aristocratically inclined voting public. While General Washington and his successors in office were interested in competence and efficiency, they were careful to choose as public officials those persons who thought as they did and who represented the interests of what then might legitimately, and in an European sense, have been called the American upper classes. Despite a mild movement toward a broadened base of political action under the Jeffersonian Republicans, the federal civil service remained for forty years primarily the instrument of these classes.

However, as the effects of a rapidly expanding frontier, fostering in turn a more dynamic and free-wheeling economic system, commenced to permeate American society on a significant scale, the government and the politics it represented were reoriented to conform to the individualistic, equalitarian, and decentralizing tendencies of early nineteenth century democracy. A political system designed to assist the commercial and business interests of the Federalists evolved by 1829 into the more inclusive democracy of the agrarian Jacksonians; and the public service, then widely considered to be unrepresentative, was rudely adjusted accordingly. Thus the first reorientation of the American federal service, through the spoils system of Senator Marcy, was the product of an essentially grass roots movement aimed at controlling the government for the benefit of those who, under the stimulus of the Protestant Ethic, would freely exploit the undeveloped resources of a continent.

Andrew Jackson's theories of public office came both to symbolize and to support the individualistic and equalitarian spirit of his times as well as the social mobility characteristic of American society. His concept of the spoils system as "reform" also served to dignify and fortify the organizational system of the new democracy. Democratic politics is considerably more expensive initially than aristocratic politics. In the absence of corporate contributions, the offices furnished that margin of financial and personal incentive which permitted the political machinery of a Martin Van Buren to flourish. The equally important necessity to bridge the gaps within a governmental system based upon both a horizontal and a vertical division of political power, placed a further premium upon any and all devices available for the coordination of public policy now that the unifying forces of the Federalist period were largely gone. But beyond this, the growing size of the executive establishment forced, of necessity, an increasing subletting and delegating of administrative authority, including the appointing power. Thus, the spoils system—and it deserves to be called a system—furnished both a political and an administrative solution to many of the pressing problems of a developing nation.

Nor was the result always as inefficient as frequently charged. In one sense the spoils system as it evolved before the Civil War represented the kind of phenomenon which we now associate with the French cabinet. Every four years or so the "deck was shuffled" again. From 1830 to 1860 many of the same familiar figures glided in and out of public office, depending upon the fortunes of politics in that uncertain period of rapidly alternating political control. So, while there was often great turnover in office, there was, as Carl Russell Fish noted a half century ago, never a complete severance from the past. Even the most ardent advocates of rotation in office sometimes wondered if their doctrine was actually as effective as it had been intended to be. And, if efficiency is a function of the accomplishment of social purpose, the spoils system was unquestionably an effective instrument for the implementation of fundamental policy, however repugnant it may seem to fastidious critics.

But, if the spoils system was a radical institution in 1829, it had become a political bulwark of the established order by 1865. Soon, however, this order and all it represented came under attack. The Civil War had greatly accelerated industrialization, the effects of which were quickly felt, if not fully understood, by large portions of the voting public. A society of individualists and equalitarians was gradually conditioned through the sensational and traumatic events of the Gilded Age to an understanding that, in a civilization rapidly being technologically transformed, the Protestant Ethic could lead to some peculiar results not at all in accord with the theories of Jacksonianism. A bewildering rash of stubborn protests against the status quo quickly signified the depth of popular feeling and unrest within many segments of American society.

By the eighteen seventies the problem was not that the voting public failed to understand the nature and value of cooperative effort as a solution to social problems. An earlier age had taught the necessity of collective action through voluntary association in time of need, and corporate enterprise itself was a tribute to the thoroughness with which we had learned that lesson. The difficulty lay in the fact that our individualistic though cooperative society had seldom organized its collective efforts through the compulsory agency of government. In fact, agrarian democracy had fostered a compelling antipathy to the restrictive tendencies of government. Protestantism, here as elsewhere, had reinforced this belief, and there was nothing in a political system based on a separation of powers and federalism to encourage any augmentation of governmental authority.

Nevertheless, large sections of the voting public began to believe for various reasons that they were receiving less than their due of what there was to get. The grass roots pressures for reform steadily built up in strength. Competing for popular favor, there were on the one hand groups like the Populists, who would make fundamental changes in the political and economic structure, and on the other hand, the little eddy of civil service reformers, who desired to attack only the obvious surface symptoms of the underlying difficulties.

The Pendleton Act of 1883 and the second reform. The proposals of Curtis, Eaton, and Schurz, translated almost verbatim from prior British experience, rejected the approach to civil service reform advocated by Clay, Calhoun, and Webster and typified by the Tenure of Office Act of 1867. The new civil service reformers, aiming at the redirection and refinement of the appointing rather than the removal power, sought to control the distribution of public offices before rather than after the fact. More specifically, the reformers wished to encourage the development in the United States of what we know as the *merit system:* that is, a system of civil service recruitment and tenure based upon (1) competitive entrance examinations, (2) relative security from partisan removal, and (3) political neutrality and nonpartisanship in public office. Had they had their way, the reformers would have gone one step further and, by limiting recruitment to the bottom levels of the service and by emphasizing promotion from within, set the stage for the development of the same closed type of bureaucratic system that was solidifying then in Great Britain.

As has often been the case in this country, the British concept of a neat and orderly devolution of political authority under the parliamentary system appealed to the equally orderly and intellectual minds of American civil service reformers. Congress was, however, much less impressed and, in a series of amendments, modified the original proposals for American consumption. The end product, the historic Pendleton Act of 1883, recognized a growing demand for expertise in the management of public affairs, the need for continuing stability in many portions of the executive establishment, and the popular clamor for a reorientation of the underlying ethics of office-holding. But, it also presaged the evolutionary development of a public service just about as well suited as the spoils system had been to the relatively classless, highly mobile, equalitarian, and individualistic society of the post-Civil War period, and well attuned to the political problems inherent in a constitutional federalism and separation of powers. While we copied the English example in a general way, the civil service law of 1883 clearly indicated that we would take our time about it, that we would develop some characteristics in the organization of our public service which might rightly be considered as all our own, and that we would have extreme difficulty under our fundamental law in developing a service as nonpolitical as that of the British.

Even the reformers themselves, though enamoured of British experience, could not tear themselves entirely away from their American environment. First of all, with little or no dissent, they accepted the legislative decision as a proper decision and immediately took an active part in its administrative implementation. But, more important, the ends they sought by means of the reform of the American public service through the merit system were by no means synonymous with those of Northcote and Trevelyan in England. For the British, the renovation of their civil establishment had meant the type of class reorientation of politics which more nearly resembled the American experience in 1829. For the United States, the statute of 1883 was the vehicle for reform and purification of a political system long since democratically oriented. It was in this different guise that the merit system became politically effective in this country.

The American civil service reformers had no quarrel with the basic premises of American society—economic, political, or moral. They had themselves prospered within its framework and saw no reason to question its essential validity. But in the scandals of the era of General Grant, for example, they saw the perversion of the individualistic and equalitarian principles they had always supported. Most of these men had taken an active part in the events leading up to the Civil War, and for them the transference of allegiance from a defunct antislavery movement to civil service reform was simple. To men like Carl Schurz, political bondage to the partisans of the spoils system—whom he and his friends now castigated as the *new aristocracy* of "plunder and patronage"—seemed little more than another form of slavery, with equally vicious implications for the body politic. Curtis, Eaton, Schurz, and the rest merely proposed a sort of purified political man to rescue the economic man from bankruptcy. Through a new and more democratic procedure known as the merit system, they felt many such political men would enter the public service and turn it in new directions. For the second time, the civil bureaucracy was being attacked as unrepresentative of the ideals and aspirations of the nation at large. This time the free competition of the merit system would replace free-wheeling politics as the touchstone to a new democracy and new morality in public life, which, to the civil service reformers, seemed necessary if the nation was to survive.

In simplest terms, all the movement called for was a change in the type of personnel at the helm of the government. Such a program, cloaked in a garb of Victorian morality, was the limit to which the majority of the voting public would permit the legislative branch of the federal government to proceed by 1883. Civil service reform was the reform least objectionable to the immediate interests of the greatest number of voters in the post-Civil War era. It was passed in preference to the more substantive economic measures advocated by Henry George, the Populists, and others like them in their direct approach to reform.

Considered in broader outline, the approval of the Pendleton Act of 1883 represented a temporary resolution of the crucial ethical dilemma then confronting the average citizen, who felt a need for some sort of collective action against the problems then facing him, but who still was deeply and emotionally committed against taking that action through the instrument of coercive public authority. Somehow, if, God willing, *good men*, good more in a moral than efficiency sense, were brought in and left to manage the affairs of the nation, all would be well once again. From one point of view the logic was unassailable, for goodness is, by definition, desirable. What goodness was to consist of in terms of political action was, however, obscure. As Herbert Croly observed, while arguing for another round of reform in 1914:

. . . The early reformers were not sufficiently thorough. They failed to carry their analysis of the prevailing evils far or deep enough, and in their choice of remedies they never got beyond the illusions that moral exhortation, legal prohibitions and independent voting constituted a sufficient cure for American political abuses.[2]

Of course, no millenium even approached in the years immediately following the passage of the Pendleton Act. Grover Cleveland, the archetype of the "good political man," was little more successful in solving the problems of the day than his predecessors. As the distinguished reformer, Oswald Villard, later sadly concluded in his autobiography, he and the rest of the country had probably tended to "stress too much getting a 'good man' into high office rather than changing fundamental conditions . . . one always hopes for a short cut."[3]

In a sense, however, the reformers—and the voting public as well—were right in insisting on civil service reform as the "first" post-war reform. Simple honesty in public affairs and technical competence in administration were necessary before any more fundamental reforms could hope to succeed. The merit system struck a responsive chord in terms of the needs of the modern state, and the new reform, almost the only fundamental governmental reform to be undertaken between 1870 and 1900, was destined to survive and gradually to prosper.

Nevertheless, it began to be quite obvious by the end of the Cleveland era that the placing of good men in office was not sufficient to cure the ills of the body politic. To put it another way: Morality was not enough. Therefore, for the second time since the Civil War, a movement grew urging extensive reforms via the political mechanism.

Progressivism and the civil service. The Progressives, carrying on under new auspices much of the unfinished business of the Populists,

2 *Progressive Democracy* (New York: The Macmillan Co., 1914), p. 9.
3 *Fighting Years* (New York: Harcourt, Brace and Co., 1939), p. 183.

advocated extensive political and economic changes as well as further administrative and structural reforms. But, for a second time and for similar reasons, the voting public refused to move very far in accepting any stringent control over the distribution of goods and services. Instead, the nation implicitly concluded that, if good men were unable to bring about the changes desired, the trouble lay with the political and administrative *machinery* at their disposal.

Thus, through the late nineties and the early nineteen hundreds, such procedural and organizational reforms as the direct election of senators, the general staff, the Australian ballot, the initiative, referendum, and recall, and the reorganization of state and local government were legislatively implemented in rapid succession. Public administration became respectable as a field of political science; bureaus for administrative research mushroomed; scientific management influenced the industrial as well as the governmental world; and under President Taft the first comprehensive inquiry into the nature of the federal administrative and organizational mechanism was made under the new watchword of "economy and efficiency."

The ethical imperatives of the nineteenth century were still too strong and the reality to which they were related not sufficiently unattractive for most Americans to react to the requirements of social change through much more than another variation of the old morality. Again, the voting public took what seemed to be the easiest way out. Administrative reform immediately threatened the income or position of relatively few individuals and was, in addition, most attractive to a business world which was beginning to feel the press of increasing taxation. Economy and efficiency—in a dollars-and-cents, short term, business sense rather than in any long-term social sense— was extremely appealing to the large segment of the population which felt that, since it had prospered through such methods, government also could not help but benefit.

Under Theodore Roosevelt the public service began to be subjected to the influence of the drive for administrative and organizational reform. Itself a kind of mechanical procedure, the merit system easily floated along in the main stream of the larger movement, profiting this time from a secondary rather than primary role. Under energetic presidential auspices, the competitive segment of the civil service quickly expanded to a point beyond which it was not to proceed far for nearly thirty years. The rules governing the competitive service were recodified in a form to last just as long. The concept of a career service was formulated and actively promoted; and the boundary lines between the permanent service and the patronage were clarified. Civil service reform thus commenced a metamorphosis into public personnel management. On the outside, the National Civil Service Reform League began to discard the moral diatribes of its youth for calmer paragraphs on the dollars-and-cents value of the merit system; and superannuation, position-classification, and salary adjustments developed into secondary political issues. The prestige of the service was not yet very high and it possessed little sense of corporate unity, but under the stimulating guidance of Theodore Roosevelt, morale was clearly rising. It would not be long before the civil bureaucracy, nourished by the positive state, would be close to the center of political power.

However, great doses of economy and efficiency were unable to forestall the political debacle of William Howard Taft in 1912. The economic problems which had pressed for solution in the eighteen eighties and nineties still cried out for action. Grover Cleveland and Theodore Roosevelt had merely prepared the way for the great ground swell of public opinion which rose to a crest in the election of Woodrow Wilson to the Presidency and which demanded modification of the economic system through governmental intervention. By this date a large proportion of the voting population had implicitly or explicitly concluded that a good man with good organizational machinery could not cope with the times. Morality had not been enough. Nor was a simple renovation of the apparatus of American democracy sufficient, either.

The civil service and the positive state: the first phase. But bringing the New Freedom to legislative fruition was not accomplished without a struggle in which the heretofore steady growth of the merit system came to a grinding halt. Once again, as the exigencies of economic politics taxed the power of the chief executive to turn his election mandates into reality, the manipulation of the public offices provided a major means for more exalted ends. Despite his previous connections with the National Civil Service Reform League, Woodrow Wilson quickly learned, under the astute guidance of his Postmaster General, that in full-scale political warfare all weapons must be used.

The merit system was not completely eclipsed, but the great progress of the first decade of the twentieth century was rudely interrupted, first by the Democratic demands for patronage after decades of frustration, and later by the requirements of the First World War. Amid the more basic quarrels over fundamental national and international policies, the problems of the federal service tended to drop further and further from the political consciousness of both Congress and the general public. Simultaneously, the wartime inflation underscored the failure of the federal government to keep the pay and perquisites of the civil service abreast of those of private industry.

In 1916 the wage curves of government and business finally crossed, with that for the federal service dropping below that of private industry for the first time in American history. Employee turnover skyrocketed to heights hardly contemplated even under the spoils system, and within two years the first service-wide union of public employees was organized and in action. All this only highlighted the chaotic state of federal public administration by the end of World War I and the failure of Congress to pay much attention to the needs of the service as outlined in 1913 by the Commission on Economy and Efficiency of President Taft.

That the public service did not suffer more in the years before 1920 was in part due to the fact that, after all, the Wilsonian program was hardly a revolutionary one. Moreover, the impact of the spate of legislation between 1913 and 1915, as well as the demands of global warfare, brought the greatest expansion of the federal service up to that time. With the patronage system and other types of informal recruitment completely inadequate to meet the wartime personnel requirements, the Civil Service Commission served for the first time as a central recruiting agency for the great bulk of the federal mechanism. As a result of its wartime endeavors, the Commission significantly influenced—also for the first time—the personnel procedures of private industry. In the technical aspects of examination and recruitment the federal government was by 1920 considerably ahead of business and industry, and in the years to follow many private employers were quick to apply these aspects of the merit system to their own affairs.

Far more important, however, was the explosive suggestion, implicit in the wartime expansion of governmental authority, that there might be some merit in the radical idea that government could be a positive good. For the experience of the war years had clearly demonstrated that, when the nation so desired, almost any scale of collective endeavor was feasible. The positive potential of a coordinated supervision of the American productive machine was, to be sure, only briefly and imperfectly illustrated at this time. But the idea remained, and the slowly but surely increasing prestige of the federal public service in recent decades may best be dated from this point. So also may we date from this time the beginning of the effective decline of the nineteenth century version of the Protestant Ethic which had for so long tended to estop the growth of the positive state.

Even so, when the dangers of war were over and the twenties commenced to prosper, the American public, as if in penance for its brief aberration, turned to the past. The old voluntaristic ethic seemed valid once more. But it was not quite the same. There could be no return to unbridled competition. Rather, a version of the New Nationalism first asserted by Theodore Roosevelt came to the fore. Under this doctrine the new Progressive State which the Republicans had inherited was turned to the positive support of private enterprise as opposed to its limitation and control. The business of government was now explicitly business, and the great new granite structure housing Hoover's cherished Department of Commerce symbolized the new conception of government.

While the great growth of the public service under Woodrow Wilson was quickly arrested, the number of civil employees was never reduced to within 100,000 of its prewar total. The federal service was by no means placed on a pedestal during the twenties, but neither was it seriously challenged. Indeed, under the business orientation of the Republican party the economy and efficiency of President Taft flowered again, with considerable benefit to the service. The Budget and Accounting Act of 1921 provided a much-needed governmental control mechanism, with the President's hand in fiscal affairs greatly strengthened. By 1923 both a new retirement system and a new position-classification scheme had been put into effect, and shortly thereafter the first personnel director for a major federal department was appointed. Under Coolidge, the Harding scandals were quickly brought under control, and with President Hoover came the first of a long series of executive reorganizations. By 1932 the merit system encompassed 80 per cent of the offices and the Civil Service Commission was close to becoming the central public personnel agency which had been envisioned twenty years earlier.

Meanwhile, however, Calvin Coolidge had reportedly predicted to his Secret Service bodyguard, Colonel Edmund Starling, "They're going to elect that superman Hoover, and he's going to have some trouble. He's going to have to spend money. But he won't spend enough." [4] Those in political power during the early thirties could not reach past their ethical views of the proper function of government for the political invention necessary to meet the economic crisis. Their answer to depression was, as it had always been, economy and charity; and civil servants suffered with everyone else.

The civil service and the positive state: the second phase. In 1932 the Democrats also suggested economy. But when Franklin D. Roosevelt came into office the unprecedented necessities of immediate events swept the administration far past its campaign promises into the famous Hundred Days. It took no revolution to transfer almost over-

---

[4] Thomas Sugrue, *Starling of the White House* (New York: Simon and Schuster, 1946), p. 263.

night to the national government more power over persons and property than any government in this country had ever effectively possessed except during the First World War. The American social system had always been capable of cooperation when the need was great enough, and the collectivist effort under the auspices of the Blue Eagle was marked with a sort of religious fervor. Government assumed an importance it had never before enjoyed during peacetime. Stimulated both by a sincere desire to be of service during a crisis as well as by a lack of employment opportunities in private enterprise, an unusually large number of the more socially inventive graduates from the nation's educational system entered the public service during the years before the Second World War. The administration, somewhat fearful of the traditional practice of calling upon the business community for emergency assistance, encouraged this trend. For the first time the federal service ranked high as an occupational goal among the youth of the nation. In turn, under the aegis of the New Deal and its truly powerful concept of positive political action, the civil bureaucracy reached the apex of its prestige and power during the first half of the twentieth century.

This was by no means a neutral and nonpartisan civil bureaucracy recruited entirely through staid merit system procedures. Indeed, throughout the first term of Franklin D. Roosevelt, the merit system was hard put to maintain itself. The public service had always felt the impact of a change in party control; and under F. D. R. and the unprecedented problems of the thirties, all things, including the offices, were subordinated to the politics of profound social change. Fortunately for those in the competitive service in 1933, enough new offices were created to forestall a patronage raid of the McKinley variety, but civil service reform was shelved for nearly five years. Nor was it revived until the merit system and the administrative machinery of the government became so neglected and their state of disrepair so shocking that it was realized something would have to be done or the entire social program might be endangered. The President's Committee on Administrative Management pointed the way to reform in 1937. At the same time, the gradually improving economic conditions gave the American public a breathing spell in which to consider the possible dangers inherent in placing almost unlimited powers at the disposal of the executive branch. Only then did civil service reform again, for the first time since the eighteen eighties, become an important political issue on which even F. D. R. felt he was vulnerable.

From 1938 through 1940 social politics stood aside while a renewed concern over the state of the public service manifested itself. As the whole civil establishment was tightened and centralized, so also with public personnel management. The Civil Service Commission at long last found itself at the helm of a consolidated system of public employment. Meanwhile, the loose employment procedures of the thirties had brought into the service a multitude of persons from private enterprise, the universities, and elsewhere, with the result that both the service in general and personnel management in particular were fairly bubbling with new procedures and concepts, many of them imported from the non-governmental world. This meant the end of the traditional isolation of public and private personnel management into separate and almost watertight compartments. Cross-fertilization between the two was henceforth to become more and more the norm rather than the exception. This presaged another type of struggle, however, between those who saw the prime function of the merit system as control of the patronage and those who looked forward to the elimination of rigid controls in favor of the industrial concept of personnel work as a positive aid to line management.

Almost immediately, however, it was necessary rapidly to readjust the federal service to the requirements of another world war. Centralization of personnel management became of necessity an extremely loose decentralization. Examinations were reduced to interviews, and the old procedural controls of the merit system were greatly relaxed. With the tremendous demand for civil and military personnel and the virtual disappearance of unemployment, the problem of manpower allocation and control arose for the first time. The spirit of our second great wartime cooperative effort was still voluntaristic. But it was an intensely felt voluntarism, verging almost on submission and carrying with it an extraordinary concentration of governmental authority. By 1945 the nation seemed almost one vast public service, with the executive branch of the government at the helm and at the height of its power under F.D.R.'s astute political guidance.

But, with Roosevelt's death and the end of the war, both the spirit and the framework of the voluntaristic house of cards began to collapse. Yet it left behind it a vastly strengthened sense of the potentialities of collective effort and a heightened desire to fulfill more completely than after World War I some of the alleged goals of the war. A renewed fear of depression and the continuation of Cold War on the international scene somewhat bolstered the political forces in favor of maintaining a government of positive powers through a time of peace and relative prosperity. However, the sedative effects of continued prosperity, the evident power of communism, and a reaction against the overwhelming power of an executive branch which had often generated as much controversy as it had settled, combined to produce an almost schizophrenic attitude toward government during the late forties. The fact that, while we had won the war, almost nothing seemed settled, only built up the tension. Typically, a scapegoat was sought and for many it became the federal service, which for a decade had loomed so large on the political scene.

Underneath, two fundamental ethical imperatives were clashing. By 1945 the old Jacksonian combination of liberty and equality had split, with business enterprise emphasizing the former, labor the latter, and agriculture somewhere in between. Many saw in the New Deal a slow but sure drift to socialism and sought refuge again in the individualism of the old Protestant Ethic. Others, seeing the ameliorating effects of New Deal social legislation in terms of equality and security, sought to build even further on the newer Social Ethic. Further complicating the issue and effectively blocking any solution in fully traditional terms were the exasperating requirements of foreign policy. From 1945 through 1952 American politics was fought more along ideological lines than during any period since the late nineteenth century and, before that, just prior to the Civil War. Once again the struggle was to a great extent focused on the civil service as not only a prime symbol but also an effective center of political power.

Under the combined impact of the post-World War II reduction-in-force, the expansion and contraction stimulated by the Korean affair, the struggle of Congress to regain something of its former political status at the expense of the executive branch, a new and trying loyalty program, and a series of scandals, the service was hard put to maintain itself. Basically, three major forces were at play on the civil bureaucracy during the Truman administration. While the Civil Service Commission struggled valiantly to rebuild the merit system, others, with their power largely centered in Congress, were attempting to bring the civil service to heel. In addition, the new concepts of employment security which had been focused on private industry during the thirties were turned toward the federal service, with the encouragement of veterans organizations, the public employee unions, and the many others who simply sought to control the discretion of the executive branch through any means at command. This meant that, while the Civil Service Commission, the First Hoover Commission, and most administrators sought a new decentralization in personnel management, much postwar legislation, particularly that concerning veteran preference, more or less explicitly worked in favor of centralization.

Not only was the political system operating at cross purposes, but the merit system of the Pendleton Act was being used as a control mechanism in a manner which had never been intended by Curtis, Eaton, and Schurz in 1883. All this generated, in turn, still further inequities and insecurities, for the service was simply too great and complex to be efficiently governed through relatively rigid rules administered from the top of a hierarchy. If the Social Ethic was producing peculiar results within industry by the postwar decade, so it was also within the civil bureaucracy. Despite the warnings of the first civil service reformers, both the front and back doors to their merit system were largely closed by 1950. This resulted in considerable confusion within the federal establishment and contributed to the steady decline in public employee morale.

Meanwhile, a strengthened if somewhat discordant Republicanism approached the election of 1952 determined to make the pruning and cleansing of the federal service a major issue of the campaign. Thus President Eisenhower came into office with a popular mandate to do something about the "mess in Washington." Once again, for the third time, there was a widespread feeling that the federal service was unrepresentative. In a limited sense the charge was true. The temper of the service as a whole was unquestionably more in tune with a positive state than with a concept of a national government with strictly limited powers. The new administration's distrust of the civil bureaucracy became almost immediately apparent through a simultaneous stepping up of economy moves, security efforts, and patronage manipulations along with congressional investigations. Again employee morale plummeted, to reach in 1954 a new low for the last thirty years. That the Republicans moved more slowly in reorienting the civil establishment than many of its partisans had hoped, was a tribute both to the President's unwillingness to permit a full scale spoils raid and to the fact that most of the service was by this time sufficiently indoctrinated with the concept of political neutrality to be able to serve a new master effectively. Prosperity and full employment further relieved some of the pressure.

At the same time, however, the business orientation of the new administration supported a major attack, reminiscent in tenor of the twenties, upon many fundamental personnel problems. In this effort even Congress finally acquiesced with a good deal of grace, largely ceasing its negative and restrictive approach to personnel matters in favor of more positive legislation in support of the President's program. With almost textbook attention to the views of the President's Committee on Administrative Management of 1937 and the First Hoover Commission, the Civil Service Commission was reorganized and strengthened as an arm of the executive branch, the line between the patronage and the permanent service was sharpened, the service was for the first time cushioned against the impact of emergencies, pay and fringe benefits were increased to more competitive levels, training and employee development programs were promoted on an increasingly effective scale, some dents were made in the traditional departmentalization of the service, civil-military personnel relations were given long overdue attention, and decentralization in public personnel management was again greatly stressed. In sum total this was perhaps the most impressive set of accomplishments ever realized on the federal personnel scene during any equivalent period. Even the Second Hoover Commission found little fault with this program in main outline. As a result of these actions as well as a growing understanding of the requirements of governmental administration on the part of the new political executives, morale was clearly on the upturn in 1955 for the first time in a decade. If at the end of Eisenhower's first term the administration and the civil bureaucracy were hardly the bosom friends they had been under Roosevelt, they were at least mutually respectful of each other's position, a state of affairs which in the long run is probably more desirable.

The election of 1956 confirmed Eisenhower's popularity. It also confirmed the positive state and the civil bureaucracy which it implies. However, this was not a New Deal confirmation on ideological grounds. Rather, the election signified a relatively rational acceptance of the fact that most of what the federal government was doing needed doing in light of the times. In a sense, the Eisenhower administration's chief claim to fame will probably lie in its very considerable success in stimulating a return to a pragmatic conception of politics. Such a concept, which lies at the heart of the New Republicanism, means the assessment of the relative merits of individualism and equality, and the legislation relating to them, more in terms of every-day workability and practice than of theory. Compared to the New Deal, this is conservatism, but a conservatism more like that of Andrew Jackson and Abraham Lincoln than that of Mark Hanna and William McKinley.

What was happening underneath was, of course, that the Protestant Ethic had been generating its own purgative in the form of political rules controlling the distribution of goods, services, and income. The immediate success of these rules had somewhat undermined the surface validity of the old Protestant Ethic in favor of a new Social Ethic. But by mid-century the Social Ethic and the regulations it brought with it had produced so many unanticipated consequences that it, too, was being challenged. In effect, the Protestant and Social Ethics were to some extent cancelling each other out, with a new amalgam beginning to form. This synthesis, while modifying the

Social Ethic's Weberian concept of a hierarchic organization with rigid controls in favor of pluralism and decentralization, also sought to conserve much of the Protestant Ethic's individualism through a new human relations emphasis on the recognition of individual dignity and potential creativity.

Into the future. Barring some unexpected international conflict, all this means that the civil bureaucracy will in the next decade or so probably have something of a breathing spell in which to adjust itself to the traumatic events of the last twenty years. The times augur well also for a somewhat calmer political climate in which some of the still unsolved problems outlined at the end of the previous two chapters may receive the attention they require. And finally, there is the possibility of a new theory of public administration, including public personnel management, in which the emphasis may lie more on what is now being called "democracy in administration" and less on centralization and all-embracing control systems designed more to prevent than to produce.

Lest these conclusions seem too optimistic, we must recognize, of course, that politics can never be placid. The form and functions of the civil bureaucracy of the national government will never cease to be of great and legitimate concern to the body politic. This is likely to be especially true when the bureaucracy is so close to the center of political power. However, it seems clear that by the beginning of Eisenhower's second term in the White House another great watershed in American political development had been reached, this time signifying that at long last the need for an intelligent, flexible, and well organized civil service had been accepted by the great majority of the nation.

Representative Bureaucracy

If our great civil bureaucracy is to become, as Norton Long has argued it should,[5] a fourth branch of government, what does this do to our concepts of administrative responsibility? In simpler terms: If the civil service must be, how can it be kept under control?

Theories of responsibility. Our traditional tendency has been to deplore its existence. This we can continue to do. But such an approach is futile unless accompanied by a simultaneous willingness to abolish many of the functions now performed by the federal government. Even if a revised and strengthened federalism were to force the dele-

---

[5] Norton Long, "Bureaucracy and Constitutionalism," *American Political Science Review*, XLVI (September, 1952), 808.

gation of many such functions to state and local governments, the essential nature of the problem would change very little. Cities and states must have bureaucracies too.

Then there are those who would invoke on almost any occasion the "rule of law" and throw all quarrels with the federal government and its representatives into the courts. Others would rely upon codes of ethics and expanded conflict-of-interest statutes, or upon budgets and audits of various types, all buttressed with considerable penalties for any overstepping of bounds. Still others would bring the civil establishment completely within the grasp of a tight presidential fist and, through a greatly broadened concept of executive accountability, render the bureaucracy accountable too; while a fifth group would largely rely upon Congress, legislative investigations, and popular control through our congressional representatives.[6] All these approaches to administrative responsibility have some merit when applied with discretion and when we do not rely upon any one of them exclusively, as many of their proponents would have us do. They all have one concept in common—namely, that of restrictive control *by someone on the outside looking in*. This is the approach of the policeman and quite valid for situations in which civil servants have obviously transgressed political and social mores, but it inevitably invokes the time-honored question: Who polices the policeman? to which there is no satisfactory answer.

If we accept J. Donald Kingsley's basic proposition that "the essence of responsibility is psychological rather than mechanical," our dilemma with respect to bureaucratic responsibility is not what it is frequently made out to be. True responsibility, he argues, "is to be sought in an identity of aim and point of view, in a common background of social prejudice, which leads the agent to act as though he were the principal."[7] This suggests that we would do well to approach the problem of responsibility from *within* as well as without. To some extent we have done this in the United States. The concept of professionalism, through which professional standards and scientific objectivity become measures of administrative action, relies primarily on an internalized and voluntary pattern of behavior. Professionalism can often keep administrative discretion within bounds more severe than a legislature would dare to prescribe. Even military commanders seldom interfere with the considered decisions of lower-ranking officers of the Medical Corps. Of a similar character is the

6 For a more exhaustive summary and critical analysis of the various points of view described thus far, see Arch Dotson, "Fundamental Approaches to Administrative Responsibility," paper presented before a session of the annual meeting of the American Society for Public Administration, New York City, March 9, 1956.

7 J. Donald Kingsley, *Representative Bureaucracy* (Yellow Springs, Ohio: The Antioch Press, 1944), p. 282.

merit system's doctrine of political neutrality. Through the constant inculcation of this doctrine public employees can be conditioned to serve whatever party may be in power in the same sense that military personnel are trained from the beginning to respect civilian control. But neither neutrality nor professionalism carried to any extreme is much protection against the wide range of administrative decisions which lie largely outside the domains of science, the professions, and a narrow sort of administrative expertise concerned mainly with means. All the great issues of war and peace, and many of those relating to democracy and domestic tranquility, are of this greater order. Neutrality and professionalism are extremely useful types of internal as opposed to external controls, but they are frail reeds in times of crisis and only modestly helpful during the ordinary course of events.[8]

For its role in suggesting still another approach to administrative responsibility, a study of the historical development of the American civil bureaucracy derives one of its principal justifications. Considered as a whole and over a time span of nearly two centuries, our civil service stands out as both unusually responsive and responsible to the democracy which it supports. There have been no palace revolutions, extremely few traitors, and no sabotage of importance throughout the history of our federal service. While there has been some lining of individual pockets at public expense, this has never become an approved practice. Our civil servants have truly represented their nationwide constituency and have attempted to "serve" in the highest sense of the word. When we go further and compare the day-by-day administrative behavior of the American civil establishment with that of many other bureaucracies the world over, the contrast in terms of comparative responsiveness is often impressive.

All this has come about as much as a result of our civil bureaucracy's representative character as from anything else. Kingsley maintains that the representative character of the British civil service is the principal key to its success. But we have, in practice if not in formal theory, developed the idea of bureaucratic representation to a finer point than the British, with broad implications for bureaucratic control the world over. This suggests, then, that the concept of a *representative bureaucracy* may be a most useful major addition to our arsenal of weapons bearing on the problem of administrative re-

---

[8] If carried too far, neutrality can result in the passive acquiescence of a bureaucracy, either civil or military, to the overturn of the government. The demise of the Weimar Republic of Germany is an example. Though the point has not often been made, one of the principal justifications of the loyalty and security program lies in its setting of limits to the concept of neutrality. Of an essentially similar order is the type of civil service examination requirement which explores whether or not the prospective employee is in sympathy with the statutes which he may have to carry out. Especially in its early days, the T.V.A., for example, frequently applied such a yardstick.

sponsibility, control, and direction. Let us, therefore, define the idea now as well as we can and then, through consciously directed experience, refine it still further.

The concept of representative bureaucracy. Kingsley chose to define "representative bureaucracy" by a brief analogy to the selection theories which underly the membership of democratic legislative bodies.[9] Norton Long has gone one step further when, in describing the merits of our civil service, he argues that "the democratic character of the civil service stems from its origin, income level, and associations." [10] This implicitly brings us to the definition presented in this study's opening chapter, and which it is appropriate to state again here: *A representative bureaucracy is one in which there is a minimal distinction between the bureaucrats as a group and their administrative behavior and practices on the one hand, and the community or societal membership and its administrative behavior, practices, and expectations of government on the other.* Or, to put it another way, the term representative bureaucracy is meant to suggest a body of officials which is broadly representative of the society in which it functions, and which in social ideals is as close as possible to the grass roots of the nation.

This preliminary definition suggests that to be representative a bureaucracy must (1) consist of a reasonable cross-section of the body politic in terms of occupation, class, geography, and the like, and (2) must be in general tune with the ethos and attitudes of the society of which it is part. Both of these criteria the American federal service meets more completely than most civil bureaucracies. In the recent past the only major segment of the civil service somewhat out of step has been the Foreign Service of the Department of State, and this fact as much as any other lay behind the recommendations of the Wriston Committee in 1954 and the Service's subsequent reorganization.[11] Particularly since the passage of the Pendleton Act, which opened up the federal service more completely than ever before, all segments of American society—religious and nationality groups, blue

---

9 As cited in footnote 7, p. 282.

10 As cited in footnote 5, p. 813.

11 In a chapter entitled "The American Roots," the Wriston Committee concludes, "The examination system . . . has produced a corps of officers which is not geographically representative, nor adequately reflective of the wide and essential variety of American life. . . . The Committee is strongly of the opinion that the Service will never attain the full measure of public support it should and must have until its corps of officers becomes more broadly representative of American life. There is only one sure way of thus generating a sense of national participation. It is to set up a recruiting system able to draw upon young Americans in all the States and from all walks of life." Secretary of State's Public Committee on Personnel, *Toward a Stronger Foreign Service,* Department of State Publication 5458 (Washington: Government Printing Office, 1954), pp. 39 and 41. See also James McCamy and Alessandro Corradini, "The People of the State Department and Foreign Service," *American Political Science Review,* XLVIII (December, 1954), 1067.

collar and white collar workers, scientific and technical personnel, women, Negroes, and the rest—have received easy access to governmental employment opportunities. Indeed, for many of these groups, notably women, Negroes, and certain nationality minorities, the federal service has provided a major ladder for upward social and occupational mobility.[12]

Above all, throughout our history we have been wary of rigid and formalistic requirements for entrance into the federal service. Discrimination on the grounds of political affiliation, nationality, religion, and race are forbidden. Educational level, intellectual ability, and skills are measured more by examination than by diploma. Age and physical requirements have been held to a minimum. Though it has often been criticized, the apportionment provision of the Pendleton Act, which has required the Civil Service Commission to pay some attention to the geographical dispersion of applicants for posts in the city of Washington, has served a useful purpose. And even a modest veteran preference can be supported on the grounds that veterans, comprising a major segment of the skilled population, might not otherwise be able to come into the service in appropriate numbers, especially right after a war.

From a positive point of view, the American public service has been built upon our traditional values emphasizing individual capacity as well as freedom and equality of opportunity. It has been nourished by a mechanism which not only recognizes ability but which is willing to recognize ability wherever it is. As Herman Somers recently pointed out, "In a dynamic economy and in an open society there are other choices than a general 'spoils system' or a permanent and 'closed group' of civil servants."[13] We in the United States have found our "other choice" through an open door policy for the federal service combined with a recruitment, examination, and placement system which makes that policy a reality for the great mass of citizens. Indeed, it is not too much to say that the provision of another choice is the unique contribution of the Pendleton Act.

Developing a representative bureaucracy. To refine the concept of representative bureaucracy further, this suggests that it is possible to develop such a bureaucracy in at least three ways: through the spoils system, the closed system, and what is here termed *the opportunity system* of the Pendleton Act. In the United States we have tried all three of these avenues—the closed system under the Federalists, the spoils system under the Jacksonians and the early Republicans, and

12 For references to the available data on the social composition of the federal service, see the "supplementary notes" to this chapter.
13 "The Federal Bureaucracy and the Change of Administration," *American Political Science Review*, XLVIII (March, 1954), 151.

the opportunity system from 1883 to the present.[14] This experience supports reasonably well the additional general proposition that, within a democracy dedicated to the values of both liberty and equality, the opportunity system carries with it major advantages over the others. It is no bar to competence in the way that the spoils system may be, and it is less susceptible to corruption. It is not as likely to generate irritation and resentment in the way that a closed system has both in this country and elsewhere. And, of the three, it is the most likely to produce both a fully representative civil establishment and an intelligent one.

However, the opportunity system of building a representative bureaucracy has been subject to some criticism, mainly on two counts. It makes some kinds of professionalism more difficult. A relatively free recruitment of public service personnel based primarily upon federal examinations limits the ability of professional associations to raise occupational standards. Still, professionalism can be carried to extremes and may be unduly restrictive, especially when described in terms of college degrees, courses, and the like, among which there is wide variation in terms of the training they represent. The major criticism has come from those who emphasize a *career system*.[15] This type of system emphasizes recruitment from the bottom, promotion from within, and the planned movement of personnel both vertically and horizontally. The Senior Civil Service proposal of the Second Hoover Commission aimed in this direction.

Actually the career system verges on the closed system, and those who promote it have usually either implicitly or explicitly relied on the British example in their argument. Therefore, it is important to consider the current relevance of British experience.

We should bear in mind at least two things: (1) that the prestige of the British public service, as revealed by both a Gallup poll and recruitment statistics, is probably something less in the minds of the British than is the prestige of our own service in the minds of Americans; [16] and (2) that, if any emulating is being done these days,

---

[14] This three-category approach can be multiplied further. There can be, for example, closed systems such as that of the Federalists which was based on a mixture of patronage and merit; and there can be closed systems such as that of the British, based on competitive examinations. A spoils system may verge on the opportunity system during an early virtuous and restrained Jeffersonian stage. Nevertheless, the three approaches to representativeness outlined above cover the principal ones within much of the world's experience.

[15] See, for example, the approach of several of the papers reprinted in Society for Personnel Administration, *The Federal Career Service*, Pamphlet 8 (Washington: The Society, 1954).

[16] In 1947 the American Institute of Public Opinion asked this question in both the United States and England: "Assuming that the pay is the same, would you prefer to

it is primarily by the British of us—in permitting the lateral entry of new talent at nearly all levels during the past twenty years, in a less rigid treatment of specialists, and, by 1956, even in the controversial area of loyalty and security.[17] Insofar as our view of the civil service is colored by the antique rosy lens of the British example, we are reflecting what is at mid-century a largely irrelevant past, and someone else's at that. Our historic relationship with the British over the civil service forms a curious pattern. Though few Americans are aware of it, some of the inspiration for the British civil service reforms of 1850 and after came from our Federalist bureaucratic tradition.[18] We then turned around and reimported a version of the British reforms in 1883, modifying the basic concept for American consumption; and in the period since World War II the British appear once again to be moving in our direction. Unquestionably we can do a great deal more than we have in promoting careers, but we can do it without completely adopting the restrictive principle of entirely promoting from within and without sacrificing the type of lateral entry into the service which has saved the federal service on more than one occasion during emergencies. Of course, the argument can be turned around to suggest that lateral entry was necessary because there had been no career system. But, bearing in mind that the

---

work for the United States [the word "British" was substituted for this in Great Britain] government or for a private firm?" The final tabulation was as follows:

	Government	Private firm	No Opinion
United States	41%	40%	19%
Great Britain	37%	45%	18%

From "The Quarter's Polls," *The Public Opinion Quarterly*, XI (Winter, 1947–48), 651. In 1955 for the first time in the history of the British civil service, there were fewer successful candidates for the administrative class than vacancies. See "Civil Service Fights Losing Fight for Recruits," *Manchester Guardian*, September 22, 1955, p. 2. The year 1956 saw no improvement.

17 In 1947 a special committee introduced a report for the Fabian Society on *The Reform of the Higher Civil Service* (London: Fabian Publications and Victor Gollancz, 1947) with these remarks (p. 5): "It is possible to argue that the Civil Service has been saved from disaster by two wars, both of which brought in new blood in large quantities. At the present time, when new tasks are being laid upon the Civil Service and when new techniques must be evolved to deal with them, the temporary civil servants are leaving in large numbers. We think that there is little doubt that the time is ripe for another overhaul of the Civil Service." See also the British government's "Statement on the Findings of the Conference of Privy Councillors on Security" of March 8, 1956, as reprinted in connection with "Britain Turns to U.S. Ideas for Weeding Out Security Risks," *U.S. News and World Report*, XL (March 30, 1956), 108. For a more extended analysis reflecting much of the point of view expressed above, by a recent on-the-spot observer of the British civil service, see Herman M. Somers, "Some Reservations about the Senior Civil Service," *Personnel Administration*, XIX (January–February, 1956), 10. For a current argument by analogy to the British and French civil service systems, see Ellsworth Wolfsperger, "Careers and Competition," in Society for Personnel Administration, as cited in footnote 15, p. 110. This is more restrained and relevant than most such references, but still one with which the writer takes issue.

18 See ch. ii on this matter.

British service also found it necessary during recent years to permit lateral entry, it would appear that the sounder approach is to support such entry. Indeed, there is much to be said for David E. Lilienthal's 1948 proposal for Universal Public Service, "a fluid kind of citizen-service" in which most Americans would take part in public life at some point in their careers. "Here," he said, "I differ with some students of public affairs: it seems to me that the advantages of the permanent career public service are customarily overstated, in the light of our American needs, and that the disadvantages have not been sufficiently understood." [19]

This brings us to the two basic principles underlying the opportunity system, one positive and one negative and complementing each other. The first of these relates to *the wisdom of free occupational choice.* This freedom can be supported solely on ideological grounds as a logical corollary to freedom in general. However, it can be supported on equally cogent administrative grounds. The post-World War II attempt of the Army to develop rigidly precise career ladder systems for both enlisted men and officers provides a case in point. These systems were rapidly formulated in great detail and rigorously applied immediately after World War II and up into the Korean conflict. Pathological symptoms occurred almost immediately in the forms of widespread discontent among enlisted men and officers, torrents of criticism of too detailed personnel regulations from commanding officers at all levels, frequent failure of the career plans to provide personnel competent in new techniques, and the obvious inability of any such system to provide for the vagaries of human behavior with respect to occupational preference in a social milieu which emphasizes choice and mobility. As the systems broke down, a lesson was learned which the designers of the new executive development programs in the civil bureaucracy should by all means bear in mind. The Army's career program has now been considerably loosened up from the standpoint of the individual soldier. The point is not that we should do away with career plans and opportunities, but rather that we should make them vehicles of as much individual choice as humanly possible. We must design our promotion programs and our personnel development systems in terms of "opportunity for" as opposed to "management of" those most directly concerned. This is also one of the most fundamental propositions deriving from the vast new literature on the subject of "human relations."

The negative version of this first principle is *the danger of over-institutionalization.* This is intended to imply that the dysfunctional

19 "For U.P.S.—Universal Public Service," *New York Times Magazine* (June 27, 1948), 44.

effects of social institutions when carried to extremes are evident in political and administrative phenomena also. This should not prevent us from planning for administrative careers, but it should warn us that it must be done with considerable tolerance for flexibility and for choice. We must provide not only for the lessons of the past but also for the possibilities of a future which is certain to be highly complex and indefinite.

In this connection Warner and Abegglen's recent analysis of business leadership in the context of the American social system is peculiarly relevant:

There is no easy solution to the problem of maintaining the proper balance between the forces of movement and transition and the forces of persistence and inertia. The great division of labor made up of the important and the less important jobs which get the work done for the American collectivity is largely responsible for the continued advancement of our technology and economic enterprise, and the increased enrichment of our civilization. If this be true, the survival of our way of life in competition with other economic systems is greatly dependent on successfully filling these positions with competent, able men who have advanced and proved their ability in a freely competitive system.

The American credo that the best man should get the job is a sound one. This is the proper meaning of equality of opportunity. All qualified men and women of every social and racial background must be rewarded with promotions and pay to do the jobs necessary for the maintenance and advancement of this society and all its people. This must be true not only of powerful majorities dealing with members of minorities, but of powerful minorities dealing with members of the majority. Such is the proper secular meaning of the worth of the individual. He is valued and respected in his own right, but the respect and honor given him are expressions of his worth and his contributions to the collectivity. Occupational advancement and social achievement are the just rewards and expressions of competition, of successful functioning in jobs important to the firm and the industry and to the society and its people. There seems to be increasing evidence that most American business men recognize and are attempting to operate their businesses on these premises.[20]

This is also an answer to those who argue for a more closed civil bureaucracy by analogy to American business, for the true meaning of our business experience can only be expressed in terms of free occupational choice and the opportunity system.[21] The great institu-

---

[20] W. Lloyd Warner and James Abegglen, *Big Business Leaders in America* (New York: Harper and Bros., 1955), pp. 224–25.

[21] The available evidence suggests that social mobility, of nearly all types, is on the increase rather than the decrease in American business. See same, chs. ix, x, and xi; and William H. Whyte, Jr., *The Organization Man* (New York: Simon and Schuster, 1956), ch. xxi. Again, this is not to argue against better promotion plans, which the federal service badly needs, but to suggest that closing them off too much to lateral entry is not the solution.

tional curses of the federal service at the present time are over-centralization, over-proceduralization, over-departmentalization and a much too rigid position-classification system. Some dents have been made in these but much more can be done. Let us hope that they will not be compounded with too complex and too "managed" development systems which select personnel for the future in terms of what made for success in the past, and which offer mere assignment rather than opportunity.

Representative bureaucracy at home and abroad. Let us not forget that on the three major occasions when the federal service found itself in serious trouble—in 1829 and 1883 especially, and in 1952 to a lesser degree—the basic criticism stemmed from charges of unrepresentativeness. When this is the case, most of our present negative approaches to the control of bureaucratic action are useful but provide mainly the means for emergency measures decidedly uneven in their effects. If we can maintain the ideal of representativeness in our civil establishment and maintain it consciously, we are more likely to control bureaucratic behavior at its source by a sort of internal thermostat far more efficient and much less likely to set off a chain reaction of unexpected results.

Let us also remember that the principal legacy of civil service reform and the Pendleton Act of 1883 is the opportunity system approach to bureaucratic representation, which still is the one most appropriate for a nation with a social ethos based on liberty *and* equality. The meaning of 1952 and immediately afterwards is not yet quite so clear, but suggests that the opportunity system, while under attack, is holding up reasonably well. It will continue to do so, if we bear in mind its purpose and essential principles. We in America must outline and follow more precisely than ever before the middle path between a Weberian centralized and "punishment-centered" administrative mechanism and feudal anarchy.[22] We must examine searchingly the neatly hierarchical administrative theories outlined so well by the President's Committee on Administrative Management of 1937. And, we must launch a concerted attack on the great institutional barriers to a more flexible and creative civil service.

All this is meant to suggest that the concept of representative bureaucracy offers one of the few positive approaches toward a new theory of administrative responsibility and perhaps even of public administration in general. But to those at home and abroad who

---

[22] See ch. i, pp. 5–7. See also the "supplementary notes" to this chapter for a brief discussion of the term "punishment-centered bureaucracy" as used by Alvin Gouldner, and for some of the contributions of social science research to the problem dealt with here.

might desire to utilize the concept of a representative bureaucracy where it has never been in existence before—and there is a good deal of loose importing and exporting of social institutions these days—one must offer a warning. This concept carries with it some profound implications for any social system in which it is implanted, suggesting—as does any form of broad representation—at least a modest acceptance of pluralism, pragmatism, and compromise. These are explosive doctrines to nations and societies which are not used to them and not prepared to accept their practical implications, political, economic, and, above all, ethical. Therefore, it may well be that for some the old Federalist semi-aristocratic civil service system, with its personnel selected through patronage but on a basis of relative competence, may provide a better preliminary procedure. Or for others, some sort of relatively closed system based on an indigenous type of examination system may be more appropriate. Nations moving slowly toward full representation in legislative matters may find it equally appropriate to move slowly in "reapportioning" their civil establishment. In details an almost endless number of patterns is possible. However, for nations with or aspiring to social ideals similar to those of the long-established democracies, a movement in the direction of a representative bureaucracy may be desirable, precisely because of its implications.

The opportunity system for maintaining administrative representation is almost atomic in its suggestion of a classless society, great social mobility, and relatively free competition. This combination may generate revolution as well as administrative efficiency and must be handled with unusual care. But, again, for a society either deeply committed to or closely approaching democracy in the freest and most responsible sense of the term, and to whom pragmatism and pluralism are no strangers, the opportunity system offers much. For it carries with it not only a reenforcement of modern democratic ideals throughout the crucial administrative arm of the state but also has much to commend it in its explicit recognition of individual ability, the most precious asset of any nation, and especially of one which is yearning to take its proper place in the world.

The Constitution and the Patronage

Many ascribe the frequent disorderliness of American public administration, which they greatly deplore, to the conflict inherent in our constitutional division of powers. Arguing from analogy to business and the parliamentary system or merely from so-called "management principles," some of these critics have suggested that our troubles would cease if we could only bring the executive and legislative branches into a more tightly interlocked and coordinated system than is possible under the doctrine of the separation of powers. A few would go so far as to change our entire framework of government into a parliamentary system, with its neat and orderly devolution of power from the legislature to the executive, and from the political executives to the permanent civil service. If this is not possible, let us at least, others argue, bring all of the executive branch clearly under the direct power and authority of the President. Then to clarify functions further, let us carefully separate the political and permanent services, with politics of almost all types ascribed to the former and administration to the latter. These last two suggestions are, for example, explicit in the report of the President's Committee on Administrative Management of 1937 and many of the reports of the two Hoover Commissions.[23]

Unquestionably many useful and desirable renovations of our perennially proliferating executive establishment have been accomplished as a result of recommendations based more or less on the theories outlined above. But this approach has not only about reached the end of its greatest utility but has also served to obscure a number of most important considerations.

First of all, this approach, which is fundamentally that of centralization, either largely ignores the great need for decentralization or makes it more difficult even when it is considered desirable. But enough has been said on this subject earlier and it is appropriate here to suggest only that, as pluralism and indeterminacy seem to be prevailing in the scientific world of today, perhaps it is time to recognize the limitations of what may be termed the "Newtonian physics of public administration." We do not need more personnel *management* and centralized controls. We do need more stimulation and opportunity both for the managers and the managed alike in the federal service.

More important, in their attempt to bring back into vogue the old concept of a relatively impenetrable wall between politics and administration as first propounded by Woodrow Wilson and popularized by F. J. Goodnow, the critics of the separation of powers have tended to obscure the fundamentally political basis of government and of administration as well. It is assumed by both Hoover Commissions that the problems of the permanent and political services

---

[23] For other expressions of a desire for more "rationality" in American public administration and prescribing much more extreme remedies, see Dotson, as cited in footnote 6, pp. 8–23.

will be largely solved if the former is taken completely out of politics —a questionable possibility in any event—and the latter selected on a more systematic basis, and if patronage is declared obsolete and eliminated. Such an approach attempts to avoid politics rather than to cope with it. This, in turn, raises an even more fundamental problem, with which no one has as yet dealt in detail.

Throughout our history patronage has not only helped to fill the void between citizen and public official, but has also frequently been equally effective in easing the political friction inherent in the division of powers. As this study has occasionally emphasized, the value of astutely distributed patronage to a chief executive interested in obtaining the enactment of a legislative program on a national scale can be almost beyond calculation. Certainly no president, not even General Washington, has forsworn its manipulation for deliberate political purposes. Considered from the technical and narrow standard of administrative efficiency, patronage politics may lead to corruption and chaos. However, from a longer term and broader social and political efficiency standpoint, it has provided one of the few constitutional influences making for governmental decisions in terms of national rather than particularized pressures and interests. The difficulties of the Eisenhower administration in obtaining congressional sanction for its legislative program and the administration's reluctant and fumbling policy with respect to the patronage and politics in general are not unrelated.

The civil establishment can benefit from a more precisely defined concept of political neutrality. But if this is carried to extremes, it may well undermine the very unity and political efficiency which, presumably, the exponents of orderliness in American public administration wish above all to see develop. One of the greatest fields for political and administrative inventiveness now lies, not in much more nonpartisanship, but in providing for the closer integration of politics with administration so that the worst aspects of the spoils system are avoided and fundamental political policy-making is aided rather than blocked.

The integration of politics and administration in this fashion is a delicate and, some may feel, insoluble problem. But the alternative, fundamental constitutional change, is clearly out of the question.[24]

---

[24] This discussion has been limited to the impact of our horizontal division of national powers. For the impact of federalism, which, however, is declining and is almost certain to continue to do so, see the brief discussion in ch. xiii, pp. 333–34. For a more extended analysis of both federalism and the separation of powers and their impact upon public personnel administration, see Paul P. Van Riper, "The Constitution and the Patronage," *Personnel Administration*, XI (November, 1948), 1, and "Separation of Powers and the Civil Service," *Virginia Law Weekly*, VII (March 10, 1955), 1.

Conclusion and Caveat

In any evaluation of the American civil bureaucracy it is crucial first to understand that it is a *political* institution. The basic and bedrock function of providing the ultimate purpose and goals toward which the energies of civil servants may be directed is performed by our democratic political system. The morale, prestige, and effective power of any organization are mainly determined, as analysts of administration uniformly agree, by the intelligence, speed, and precision brought into the process of policy formulation and guidance. When fundamental policy is confused or vacillating, the institution through which that policy is to be implemented will reflect a similar and reciprocal uncertainty down through its various echelons. To a considerable extent this has been the situation in which the federal civil service has found itself in the last decade.

Since World War II American politics has been largely in stalemate, while the complex forces representing the Left and the Right, the domestic and the international, have been fighting out the direction in which the nation shall go. Only briefly through the Korean crisis did we have any widely accepted postwar national policy except that of hasty improvisation and more or less watchful waiting. Our indecision has stemmed not from any lack of ideas, but from a lack of organic agreement within the body politic. In turn, the federal service has been caught in not one middle but several, with either conflicting policies or no policies at all to guide it.

Sensing that all was not well with the service, we have subjected it since 1945 to more major inquiries and more detailed prescriptions than ever before in our history during even tenfold this length of time. But the problems of the service are still not solved to anyone's full satisfaction. In the absence of top policy guidance, we have endeavored to patch and prune, and to shore up and improvise, within a purely administrative frame of reference. This has been done with a great deal of skill, especially under the Eisenhower administration with its very real talent for organization and management in the restricted sense of these terms. By 1958 the service had to some extent recovered from the series of shocks it sustained after the war. But it seems quite clear at this time that we can do only so much for the service by upgrading its pay, providing for more systematic promotions, modifying the position-classification scheme, and similar actions, most of which involve a largely mechanical manipulation of either pay or procedures.

Even consolidating the personnel function within line management and placing both more firmly under White House control have distinct limits. The civil service may, like the Army of the Potomac under General George B. McClellan, be well-armed, well-trained, and ready to go. But if there is no one to lead it and nothing clearly outlined to be done, its potentialities can hardly be fully realized. From a more positive viewpoint, our current political stalemate will probably provide the service with a more or less lengthy period in which to absorb the administrative reforms of the past few years. It is likely that, before long, the morale and prestige of the service will reach a plateau, one much higher than that which characterized 1954 but still not approaching that of the decade from 1935 to 1945. Without any firm decision concerning what to do and what not to do, the corporate unity and sense of purpose that are essential for the full nourishment and stimulation of any social institution will still be missing from the federal service.

If we further analyze the American civil bureaucracy as a center of national power, again we find that the civil service of 1958 is not what it was two decades ago. Power, too, is a function of both purpose and organization. The fundamental purpose of the civil service, that of managing the civil affairs of the nation, has not only been weakened by indecision but undermined by the times. Under the impact of international tension and conflict another great bureaucratic system with another great purpose behind it, that of the military, has become the dominant instrument of effective political power at the national level.[25] To be sure, the Second Hoover Commission finally sought to provide some sort of approach to the reciprocal and often competitive relationships of what can now be described as not one but two great executive bureaucratic establishments. In our habitual concern for civil domestic affairs, we have neglected the military, and largely failed to realize, much less cope with satisfactorily, the potential ultimate meaning of the garrison state. Our American bureaucratic history has much to suggest for the management of civil matters, but offers few guidelines to follow in the direction of a great military establishment in peacetime, and none at all for the effective coordination of these two institutions. This is to suggest, then, by way of a final conclusion and caveat, that the largely unexplored area of civil-military relations within our great executive branch must not remain much longer untouched and uncharted. To do so is not only to court great damage to our traditional civilian federal service but also to imperil the even more fundamental constitutional doctrine of civilian control.

25 For relevant studies of civil-military relationships, see the "supplementary notes" to this chapter.

This underscores the fact that the ultimate problems of the federal service are political problems, capable only of political solution and guidance. In the days of Jefferson and Jackson and of Curtis, Eaton, and Schurz, the political forces at work on the molding and forming of our federal civil establishment in the United States lay primarily within our continental control. Today the prevailing influences are of international as well as national character. The issues are sharper, the pressures greater, and the potential penalties for failure far more proscriptive than ever before in our history. The impact may be expected to fall everywhere in proportion. That the American public service will soon again be permitted the long stretches of relatively undisturbed evolution so characteristic of the century and a half before 1940 seems unlikely.

In our democratic counter-revolution against the trends of the times in many parts of the world, we have been compelled to view and review many aspects of our traditional life. One of our areas of basic concern, even in times of relative tranquility, has been the place of the American civil bureaucracy in the development of national policy and national life. It is no wonder that the problems of public personnel management seem more complex than ever before. Convulsion and violence characterize the entire political world. As varies the political whole so does the use of public office, the instrument, and often the basis, of political power.

SUPPLEMENTARY NOTES

The social composition of the federal service. For a brief study of the social composition of the federal service at the turn of the century, see ch. vii. Since then, the service has, appropriately, reflected the general trend in the labor force towards increasing proportions of scientific and technical personnel, women, Negroes, blue-collar workers, veterans, and certain nationality groups. Though badly needed, there is no modern equivalent of the studies of the federal service made in 1904 and 1907 at the instigation of Theodore Roosevelt. However, for a considerable amount of data concerning the social composition of the post-World War II civil service see the sources in footnote 11; the various sections of this book relating to women, veterans, scientific and professional personnel, and Negroes; and the following selected list of sources: The reports of the First and Second Hoover Commissions on civil and military personnel, especially that of the Second Commission; C. Wright Mills, *The Power Elite* (New York: Oxford University Press, 1956), Donald R. Matthews, *The Social Background of Political Decision-Makers* (Garden City, N.Y.: Doubleday and Co., 1954); Reinhard Bendix, *Higher Civil Servants in American Society* (Boulder: University of Colorado Press, 1949); Frances T. Cahn, *Federal Employees in War and Peace* (Washington: The Brookings Institution, 1949); Jerome M. Rosow (ed.), *American Men in Government* (Washington: Public Affairs Press, 1949); Solomon Fabricant,

The Trend of Government Activity in the United States Since 1900 (New York: National Bureau of Economic Research, 1952); Dwaine Marvick, *Career Perspectives in a Bureaucratic Setting* (Ann Arbor: University of Michigan Press, 1954); The President's Committee on Government Employment Policy, *A Five-City Survey of Negro-American Employees of the Federal Government* (Washington: Government Printing Office, 1957); USCSC, Bureau of Programs and Standards, *Study of Backgrounds and Reported Training Needs of a Sample of Federal Executives* (Washington: The Commission, 1955); U.S. Department of Labor, Bureau of Labor Statistics, *Federal White-Collar Workers,* Bulletin 1117, published in cooperation with the USCSC (Washington: Government Printing Office, 1951); USCSC, Employment Statistics Office, *Occupations of Federal White-Collar Workers,* Pamphlet 56 (Washington: Government Printing Office, 1955); U.S. Department of Health, Education, and Welfare, U.S. Public Health Service, National Institute of Mental Health, *Federal Management Intern Career Patterns,* prepared by E. Grant Youmans (Bethesda, Md.: The Institute, 1955); Earl Strong, "Executives in the Federal Service," *Personnel Administration,* XVI (March, 1953), 3; and the annual reports and other regular statistical publications of the Civil Service Commission.

Bureaucratic theory and social science. In an analysis of a particular industrial concern, Alvin Gouldner uses the phrase "punishment-centered" to describe the pattern of bureaucracy most explicitly outlined by Max Weber, the first modern analyst of the subject. This pattern is defined as one "based on the imposition of rules, and on obedience for its own sake." *Patterns of Industrial Bureaucracy* (Glencoe, Ill.: The Free Press, 1954), p. 24. Gouldner also discovered another pattern of bureaucracy, perhaps implicit in Weber's early analysis, but never brought out in any systematic form. This other pattern of bureaucracy, he says, "may be termed the 'representative' form of bureaucracy, based on rules established by agreement, rules which are technically justified and administered by specially qualified personnel, and to which consent is given voluntarily. In examining factory patterns which exemplify this type, closer attention deserves to be paid to the role of 'consent' and to the diversity of sources from which it springs." Same. Gouldner's analysis closely supports the interpretation developed here, even in terminology.

Actually, a number of social science movements are at mid-century converging on this central problem of how to maintain organizational and societal unity without sacrificing individual dignity and creativeness. The T.V.A. has suggested the "grass roots" approach as has Baker Brownell in his Montana project, as well as the southern agrarians concerned with county and other local unit regeneration. The bureaucratic school has brought forth the patterns suggested by Gouldner and Peter Blau. Ordway Tead, Dwight Waldo, John R. P. French, Jr., Arthur Kornhauser, Alfred Marrow and others have helped to bring into focus the concept of "democracy in administration." From the standpoint of industrial management the new exponents of decentralization, represented institutionally by DuPont and General Motors and academically by, for example, some of the writings of William H. Newman, have been complemented on the public administration side by Jane Perry Clark and others who have followed in the path of a cooperative "new federalism." Finally, one of the more explicit aims of the growing human relations movement has been to emphasize consent, individual and group participation, and the relaxation of rigid controls. Altogether there is by 1958 a most impressive body of literature and thought which seems to be groping in the same "middle" direction which is emphasized in this study. However, no one has as yet brought all these points of view together in any systematic way to form a new theory of administration. This is an immense and challenging task which badly needs to be undertaken, and soon.

Civil-military relations and personnel management. For the studies of military affairs most relevant to this analysis, see C. Wright Mills, *The Power Elite,* cited above; and Samuel P. Huntington, *The Soldier and the State* (Cambridge, Mass.: Harvard University Press, 1957). Huntington (p. 354) notes, for example, that "military officers wielded far greater power in the United States during this period [1946–1955] than they did in any other major country." Mills documents this further with an analysis of the growing and complex interrelationships among the elites of business, politics, and the military, and comes to similar conclusions. This writer does not, however, accept all of Mills' analysis of current American politics, feeling that Lubell's, cited several times in the previous two chapters, is more complete and realistic. While the writer concurs with Mills' conclusion with respect to the federal civil establishment, that (p. 241) "neither professional party politicians, nor professional bureaucrats are now at the executive centers of decision," he does not feel that Mills' prescription recommending a much tighter and more closed career system for the civil service supplies an adequate answer to the problem of providing a civil bureaucracy which can balance that of the military. This is like accepting totalitarian methods to fight totalitarianism within a democracy. On elite theory in general, see Harold D. Lasswell, Daniel Lerner, and C. Easton Rothwell, *The Comparative Study of Elites* (Stanford, Calif.: Stanford University Press, 1952).

INDEX

INDEX

INDEX

INDEX

INDEX

79
81
8?
85
88